THE ECONOMIES OF ASIA
1950–1998

THE ECONOMIES OF ASIA 1950–1998

Critical perspectives on the world economy

Edited and with a new introduction by Robert Ash and Anne Booth

VOLUME III

The Four Tigers

London and New York

First published 2000
by Routledge
11 New Fetter Lane, London EC4P 4EE

Simultaneously published in the USA and Canada
by Routledge
29 West 35th Street, New York, NY 10001

Routledge is an imprint of the Taylor & Francis Group

Typeset in Times by RefineCatch Limited, Bungay, Suffolk
Printed and bound in Great Britain by Clays Ltd, St Ives plc

British Library Cataloguing in Publication Data
A catalogue record for this book is available from the British Library

Library of Congress Cataloguing in Publication Data
A catalogue record for this book has been requested

ISBN 0–415–14051–X (set)
ISBN 0–415–17949–1 (volume 3)

CONTENTS

VOLUME III THE FOUR TIGERS: KOREA, TAIWAN, HONG KONG AND SINGAPORE

PART III: GOVERNMENT INTERVENTION AND INDUSTRIAL POLICY

PART IV: FOREIGN TRADE, FOREIGN INVESTMENT AND TECHNOLOGY TRANSFER

PART V: HUMAN RESOURCE DEVELOPMENT AND CHANGING LABOUR MARKETS

INTRODUCTION

Robert Ash and Anne Booth

RAPID AND EGALITARIAN GROWTH?

The vast literature which has accumulated on these four economies over the last two decades testifies to their importance to all students of the development process in the latter part of the twentieth century. Each of the four is in some sense 'odd' or even unique; two are in fact city states with little or no rural hinterland while the other two are 'torsos', split off by the violent forces of twentieth century Asian history from the larger states with which they might naturally belong if historical, cultural and linguistic affiliations determined national boundaries. It is probable that South Korea will be unified with the communist north at some future date, but the conditions under which such unification will take place and the costs to the southern economy are far from clear. Taiwan, or the Republic of China, is in an even more anomalous position; the great majority of its population no longer appear to want unification with China under any terms, but China itself shows no sign of relinquishing its claims over what it views as an errant province.

Even the two city states are hardly similar and they face very different futures. Hong Kong was until June 1997 a British colony with an overwhelmingly ethnic Chinese population; it is now a special administrative region of China with guarantees that its own systems of governance will be maintained for at least 50 years. Few doubt that in the longer term it will be fully absorbed in China but the terms and conditions of complete integration are still uncertain. Singapore, which achieved independence from Britain in 1963 as a state within the Malaysian federation, broke away from that federation in 1965 and has since been an independent republic. Its large Chinese majority (around seventy per cent of the total population) means that it is ethnically very different from its Malay neighbours, and although it has played a full role in the ASEAN organisation since its inception, it is still viewed with some suspicion by these neighbours. At the same time its close economic links with Malaysia and Indonesia in particular mean that its economic and indeed its political future is still very tied to theirs.

Why does the rest of the world continue to be so fascinated by these four oddities? The answer of course lies in their spectacular economic achievements which have catapulted them into the ranks of the developed (or 'high income' to use the World Bank's terminology) countries in the space of around four decades. Certainly in the early 1950s, neither Singapore nor Hong Kong would have been counted among the 'poorest of the poor' in Asia, and their per capita GDP may well have been rather higher than that of most other large connurbations in the region. But few can deny that they have grown very fast since the late 1950s, not just compared with other economies in Asia, Africa or Latin America, but also compared with most other large cities. Certainly they have had the advantage of being able to control population inflows, but even so by the end of the twentieth century their per capita GDP was on a par with the richer states of Western Europe. Adjusted for differences in purchasing power, per capita GDP in both city states was by 1995 around $23,000, or almost 20 per cent higher than that of their former colonial overlord, the United Kingdom (World Bank 1997: 215).

The achievements of Taiwan and South Korea are more directly comparable to those of other parts of the developing world, as both were quite poor, predominantly agrarian economies in the early 1950s. After the partition of the country, South Korea had to cope with a large influx of migrants from the north, as well as the destruction of much vital infrastructure. Taiwan began its phase of accelerated growth from a more favourable base; per capita GDP was certainly higher than in mainland China in the 1950s and indeed higher than in South Korea or Japan (Table 1).

A remarkable feature of the economic performance of South Korea, Taiwan, Hong kong and Singapore was the sustained per capita GDP growth, which they maintained over more than three decades. Between 1960 and 1990, growth in real per capita terms, adjusted for the terms of trade, was between six and seven per cent per annum (Table 1). This led to at least a seven-fold increase in per capita GDP during this period. Between 1985 and 1995, annual average growth in per capita GDP was still maintained at between six and seven per cent, with the exception of Hong Kong where it was slightly below five per cent (Table 2).

Table 1 Rates of growth of GDP, 1960–1990

	Per capita GDP (1985 dollars adjusted for changes in the terms of trade)		*Annual rate*	*Average growth*
	1955	*1960*	*1990*	*1960–90*
Singapore	n.a.	1,649	11,964	7.0
Hong Kong	n.a.	2,115	14,649	6.3
Taiwan	1,120	1,258	8,211	6.3
South Korea	815	899	6,866	6.9

Source: Penn World Tables, version 5.6.

Table 2 Annual average growth rates of GDP and components

	Taiwan	*Hong Kong*	*South Korea*	*Singapore*
Per capita GDP growth				
1965–85	6.4	6.1	6.6	7.6
1985–95	6.2	4.8	7.7	6.2
Aggregate GDP growth				
1969–70				
Agriculture	3.4	−3.4	4.4	5.0
Industry	16.4	8.2	17.2	12.5
Services	7.1	12.4	8.9	7.7
GDP	9.2	10.0	8.6	8.8
1970–80				
Agriculture	2.0	−4.6	3.2	1.8
Industry	11.5	9.3	15.4	8.8
Services	8.5	n.a.	8.5	8.5
GDP	9.1	9.3	9.5	8.5
1980–1990				
Agriculture	1.8	n.a.	2.8	−6.2
Industry	7.6	n.a.	13.1	5.4
Services	9.3	n.a.	8.2	7.2
GDP	8.1	6.9	9.4	6.4
1990–95				
Agriculture	0.3	n.a	1.3	0.5
Industry	5.0	n.a.	7.3	9.2
Services	7.8	n.a.	7.9	8.4
GDP	6.4	5.6	7.2	8.7
Percentage share of the service sector in total GDP				
1960	43	62	41	78
1980	47	67	45	61
1995	58	83	50	64

Source: *World Development Report, 1978*, Table 2; *World Development Report, 1982*, pp. 112–13; *World Development Report, 1987*, pp. 203; *World Development Report, 1997*, pp. 214–15, pp. 234–35. Supplementary data on Taiwan since 1970 from *Taiwan Statistical Data Book*, various issues.

As would be expected, sustained growth over a period of three decades led to substantial structural change. In 1960 the agricultural sector still accounted for around 40 per cent of total GDP in South Korea and 28 per cent in Taiwan; by 1976 these shares had dropped to 27 per cent and 12 per cent respectively. In 1976, the share of the industrial sector in GDP was 34 per cent in South Korea, 45 per cent in Taiwan, 34 per cent in Hong Kong and 35 per cent in Singapore (World Bank 1978: Table 3). The lower shares in Hong Kong and Singapore are noteworthy because agriculture accounted for only a tiny share of total GDP in both city states. In other words, by the mid-1970s the service sector already accounted for over 60 per cent of total

Table 3 Gross enrollment ratios[a]: 1960–1995

	Taiwan	*South Korea*	*Hong Kong*	*Singapore*
Primary				
1960	67	94	91	112
1980	99	110	107	108
1995	101 (1994)	95	99 (1994)	107 (1994)
Secondary				
1960	37	27	24	32
1980	90	78	64	58
1995	96 (1994)	99	85 (1994)	68 (1991)
Tertiary				
1960	n.a.	n.a.	4	6
1980	23	15	10	8
1995	45	55	n.a.	35 (1994)

Note:
[a] Gross enrollment ratios refer to numbers enrolled at the level indicated as a percentage of the numbers in the relevant age cohort. A ratio in excess of 100 means that some pupils are outside the normal age limit for that level of education.

Sources: World Bank (1978), Table 18; Unesco (1997), Table 3.2.

GDP in both economies; while in Singapore that share did not change greatly over the next two decades in Hong Kong the service sector's contribution was over eighty per cent by 1995 (Table 2; see also Howe, this volume, Chapter 5, Table 5.2).

Social indicators relating to health and education also showed an upward trend although there were some striking differences between the four economies. Taiwan, Hong Kong and Singapore all had low infant mortality rates and high life expectancies in 1960 compared with countries in Latin America and Southern Europe at similar levels of income (World Bank 1978: Table 17). By 1976 life expectancy in all three economies was 70 years, which was only slightly lower than the average for the industrialised countries. By contrast, South Korea had a relatively low life expectancy in 1960 of only 53 years, and this had increased to 61 years by 1976. Educational indicators show that South Korea, Hong Kong and Singapore had already reached close to universal primary enrollments by 1960, although secondary enrollments were lower, and in the case of Singapore only amounted to slightly over half the relevant age cohort in 1976 (Table 3).

The record of sustained growth in both Taiwan and South Korea was especially remarkable in that it appeared to be quite egalitarian. In Taiwan, the early phase of accelerated growth was accompanied by a decline in inequality (Ranis, 1974; 287–8; Ho 1978: 141). In 1974 the bottom 20 per cent of the household income distribution received almost nine per cent of total income and the top 20 per cent 39 per cent; the ratio of these two shares was 4.4, and dropped to 4.2 by 1981 (Table 4). These ratios suggest a very

Table 4 Indicators of income distribution and per capita GDP

Country/Year	*Bottom quintile*	*Top quintile*	*Ratio*	*Income per capita*
Taiwan				
1974	8.8	38.6	4.4	3,149
1981	8.8	37.0	4.2	4,528
1985	8.4	37.6	4.5	5,449
1990	7.5	38.6	5.2	8,211
1996	7.2	38.9	5.4	n.a.
Hong Kong				
1966	4.7	58.0	12.3	3,535
1971	5.9	49.1	8.3	4,748
1980	5.4	47.0	8.7	8,565
Singapore				
1982–83	5.1	48.9	9.6	8.565
South Korea				
1970	7.0	44.0	6.3	1,694
1988	7.4	42.2	5.7	5,742

Source: *Taiwan Statistical Data Book, 1988*, pp. 76–77; Chau and Hsia (1975), Table III-2; World Bank (1994), pp. 220–21.

even distribution of income, and although they increased somewhat between 1981 and 1996, it is obvious that rapid income growth in Taiwan has been unusually egalitarian in its consequences.

South Korea is also considered to have been very successful in combining growth with equity. Adelman (1974: 280–5) points out that very substantial redistribution of wealth was the 'unintended yet almost inevitable result of the end of Japanese rule' and the subsequent civil war which led to the country's partition. In 1945 Korea was primarily an agricultural economy, dominated by tenant farming. The land reforms 1947 and 1950 had a major impact on land distribution, but by setting a ceiling of three hectares on the size of paddy holdings, they generated a structure of small-scale, owner-operated farms. Rampant inflation and the huge refugee problem resulting from partition ensured that the country began its period of accelerated economic growth from a situation in which the great majority of the population was very poor. In addition You (this volume, Chapter 20) suggests that the rapid expansion of employment in the modern sectors of the economies of both Taiwan and South Korea allowed many poor people to increase their incomes and prevented the distribution of income from becoming very skewed in the early phases of industrialisation.

Certainly the available evidence indicates that the process of rapid growth in South Korea was not accompanied by any sharp increase in inequalities. Adelman (1974: 284) acknowledged the fragmentary nature of the data on the size distribution of income, but argued that by 1964 the distribution was 'among the best in the developing world' and remained so in 1970. She quoted data which suggested that in 1970 the top quintile of the income distribution controlled 44 per cent of income, and the bottom quintile seen per cent. By 1988 these shares had changed only slightly (Table 4). In that year, the distribution of income, as summarised by the ratio of the shares of the top and bottom quintiles, was rather more skewed than in Taiwan in 1985 when per capita GDP was roughly similar. You (this volume, Chapter 20) presents data which shows that the Gini coefficent in both South Korea and Taiwan increased somewhat during the phase of accelerated growth (after 1970 in South Korea and after 1980 in Taiwan) but still remained low in both economies compared with other parts of Asia.

The two city states show a rather different relationship between growth and equity. In the case of Singapore, the evidence suggests that in the 1960s, when accelerated economic growth began, the distribution of income was quite skewed, and in the next three decades, up to the mid-1990s, there was little change (Rao this volume, Chapter 21). By 1982/83 when per capita GDP in Singapore was about what would be achieved in Taiwan by 1990, the share of household income accruing to the poorest quintile of the population was only 5.1 per cent while the richest quintile accounted for 49 per cent of income. The resulting ratio of 9.6 indicates a very skewed distribution of income, at least in comparison with either Taiwan or South Korea (Table 4). In Hong Kong, Chau and Hsia (1975: Table III-2) argued that there was a decline in household income inequality between 1966 and 1971, although between 1971 and 1980 the quintile shares showed little change (Table 4). Again compared with both Taiwan and South Korea, the distribution of income in Hong Kong in 1980 could hardly be considered egalitarian, as Howe (this volume, Chapter 5) points out.

The skewed distribution in the early 1960s in both Singapore and Hong Kong was in part the result of the colonial legacy; colonial civil servants and expatriate managers in the private sector were paid generous salaries and allowances and remuneration in senior management positions in both the civil service and the private sector thereafter remained geared to international trends. At the same time wages of unskilled and semi-skilled workers were determined largely by demand and supply in the local labour market, and were well below levels prevailing in the OECD economies, at least until the mid-1980s. It can, however, be argued that the provision of low cost housing at subsidised rentals, especially in Singapore, has boosted the real incomes of the poorer sections of the population to an extent that is not fully taken into account in household income surveys. Howe (this volume, Chapter 5) argues that in Hong Kong, where the provision of public housing has not kept up with demand, and where wages at the bottom end of the distribution have stagnated or fallen, life is still very hard for a substantial minority. Indeed an underclass of homeless unemployed is emerging as a result of the recent economic downturn.

In addition to the less egalitarian distribution of household incomes, it should be noted that both Singapore and Hong Kong (and indeed Taiwan and South Korea) have enjoyed consistently higher savings and investment rates than the average for the OECD countries. The proportion of total GDP devoted to household consumption expenditure is, for example, much lower than in the USA or the European Union. Given the more skewed distribution of income in the city states, this would suggest that the bottom one or two quintiles of the income distribution in Singapore, for example, are likely to have been worse off than the lower quintiles in, for example, Germany, even though per capita GDP in 1995 (corrected for differences in purchasing power) was actually higher in Singapore. In all four economies, the absence of social welfare provision on the generous scale available in Western Europe leaves little room for doubt that higher unemployment will lead to an even more skewed distribution of income. In addition, as these populations age, and as increasing numbers move into the over 65 age groups, there is likely to be a growing problem of poverty among the elderly, who have not been able to make sufficient provision for their old age while still in work.

THE DEBATE OVER SOURCES OF GROWTH

Given the rapid growth that has occurred in all four economies since1960, it is not surprising that numerous scholars have tried to identify and explain the sources of such growth. One influential body of literature has addressed the issue through the use of the 'growth accounting' methodology pioneered by Abramovitz and others in the mid-1950s. Others have sought to explain rapid growth in terms of unusual 'initial conditions', thought to have prevailed in the 1950s, which created an unusually supportive environment for accelerated economic growth. Some influential contributions to the growth accounting literature (including that of Alwyn Young, this volume, Chapter 6) were used by Krugman (1994) to support his claim that the much-vaunted Asian miracle was in fact a 'myth', in the sense that growth derived not from spectacular improvements in factor productivity but from rapid accumulation of capital. As Chen (this volume, Chapter 7) points out, Krugman's analysis can be challenged on several grounds. One is that he relied on only a very small selection of all the growth accounting studies that have been carried out in East Asia during the past two decades and largely ignored both the empirical and conceptual problems inherent in interpreting their results. Chen's paper makes clear just how diverse the results of the various East Asian studies have been, and how sensitive results are to the particular methodology used. While not denying that the concept of total factor productivity growth is a useful one, Chen stresses its limitations and the dangers inherent in using TFP estimates as a basis on which to make predictions about the future course of economic growth, either in East Asia or indeed elsewhere.

Whatever conclusions are drawn from the growth accounting debate, there can be little doubt that both the labour force and capital stock did grow rapidly in these four economies from the 1950s until the 1990s. The rapid growth of labour supply reflected rapid population growth in the period up to 1970, as well as a jump in female participation rates. As Bauer points out (this volume, Chapter 19), labour force growth rates were bound to slow sharply in all four economies in the 1990s and will continue to do so in the first decade of the next century. By 2020 15 per cent of the population of Singapore will be over 65, compared with 13 per cent in South Korea and 12.7 per cent in Taiwan. All four economies saw a rapid increase in investment expenditures as a share of GDP in the years from 1955 to 1980, although only South Korea has seen a consistent rise since then (Table 5). Collins and Bosworth (1996, Table 6) argue that total factor productivity growth (increases in output per unit of factor input) in all these economies account for a considerable share of GDP growth per worker in the decade from 1984 to 1994.

Another school of thought has sought to explain the rapid growth in these economies by stressing the unusual 'initial conditions' prevailing in all four economies, but especially Taiwan and South Korea. From the late nineteenth century (Taiwan) or the early twentieth century (Korea) until 1945, both were colonies of *Japan*. The emphasis on the Japanese colonial heritage is deliberate, for there were important differences, as well as similarities, between Japanese and Western colonialism in various parts of Asia. One difference lay in education policies. At least partly because of a wish to inculcate Japanese cultural values into their subject populations, the Japanese colonial authorities did expand access to primary, and even to some extent post-primary, education. Tsurumi (1977) points out that the Japanese developed a more

Table 5 Investment expenditures as a percentage of GDP, 1955–1990[a] (five-year averages centered on the years shown)

Year	*Taiwan*	*South Korea*	*Hong Kong*	*Singapore*
1955	10.5	9.2	n.a.	n.a.
1960[b]	12.6	7.9	21.7	11.0
1965	16.3	14.1	22.2	20.9
1970	21.6	22.0	17.2	34.8
1975	26.8	24.3	19.5	34.9
1980	27.3	29.4	22.3	36.5
1985	21.6	28.9	18.4	37.5
1990[c]	23.1	36.9	18.2	33.0

Note:
[a] The ratios are estimated from data in 1985 international prices.
[b] For Singapore and Hong Kong, the data refer to 1960 only.
[c] For Taiwan the data refer to 1990 only. For South Korea the data refer to averages for 1989–91.

Source: As for Table 1.

Table 6 Government expenditures as a percentage of GDP, 1955–1990[a] (five-year averages centered on the years shown)

Year	*Taiwan*	*South Korea*	*Hong Kong*	*Singapore*
1955	22.1	17.4	n.a.	n.a.
1960[b]	23.2	16.0	1.6	7.0
1965	20.3	13.4	6.9	8.7
1970	19.0	12.5	6.8	10.5
1975	15.4	11.3	6.5	9.3
1980	14.9	10.8	6.4	8.5
1985	14.4	9.2	6.3	9.8
1990[c]	14.8	8.5	5.8	8.2

Note:
[a] The ratios are estimated from data in 1985 international prices.
[b] For Singapore and Hong Kong, the data refer to 1960 only.
[c] For Taiwan the data refer to 1990 only. For South Korea the data refer to averages for 1989–91.

Source: As for Table 1.

extensive education system in Taiwan than any other colonial power with the exception of the Americans in the Philippines.

Wade (1990: 108) goes further and argues that Taiwan was not a typical underdeveloped country in the 1950s; he points to

> a long experience of fast manufacturing growth, going back to the 1930s; an unusually productive smallholder agriculture; a more than averagely literate population; large amounts of U.S. aid and advice; unusual political stability; unusual leadership commitment to economic growth and military strength; fluid social stratification; and several other presumably progrowth conditions.

Other authors such as Rodrik (this volume, Chapter 10) also emphasise the fact that in 1960 both South Korea and Taiwan had social indicators which 'placed them among the ranks of countries at several times their income levels', although we have already argued that this was more true of educational indicators than of demographic ones, especially in the case of South Korea. Amsden (1979) stressed the importance of scientific advances in agriculture in Taiwan under the Japanese. She also drew attention to the positive impact of land reform (1949–53) and the government's key role in distributing agricultural inputs to cultivators. Recognition of such benefits is not, as Amsden acknowledges, to ignore that the Kuomintang (KMT) government meanwhile extracted a substantial surplus out of agriculture in the 1950s and 1960s. But the more important strand in her argument is that the KMT regime's move from the mainland, and its close association with the American aid agency, led to indigenous power structures being pushed aside in a manner that would have been impossible elsewhere in Asia, or elsewhere in the developing world.

In the two city states, the politicians and officials, both expatriate and local, who controlled key economic decisions after 1960 proved remarkably astute in adapting the institutions of British colonial rule to developmental purposes. Singapore faced a grim economic future in 1965 after the PAP government pulled out of the Malaysian federation, and the British government announced its intention to close the large naval base. Key economic ministers such as Goh Keng Swee made no secret of the fact that the government would have to play an important role in planning Singapore's economic future; the result was a pragmatic mix of *dirigisme*, and market-friendly policies which were highly successful in attracting foreign investors to use Singapore as a platform for producing a range of manufactured goods from electronics, textiles and garments to refined petroleum products. In the late 1960s, the average educational attainment of the labour force was still low, and there was little attempt to attract even medium technology enterprises to Singapore. Rather the aim was to create enough unskilled and low wage employment to mop up the large numbers of people who were still either jobless or eking out a precarious existence in insecure service sector employment.

Some critics argue that the Singapore strategy led to 'excessive' capital accumulation, some of it in sectors of the economy, such as housing development, where productivity of capital was bound to be low. Young (1992) in his comparison of Singapore with Hong Kong tries to find a possible explanation of his finding that in some years between 1970 and 1990 the contribution of total factor productivity growth to output growth was actually negative. He suggests that

> Singapore is a victim of its own targeting policies. In individual sectors, Singapore probably has experienced total factor productivity growth. This improvement in productivity, however, is masked by the further and further movement beyond the society's level of industrial maturity; that is, a growing output-reducing distortion (Young 1992: 43).

In other words, Young's argument is that the Singapore government constantly pushed the manufacturing sector into new technologies which were really beyond the capacity of the labour force, so that there was insufficient opportunity for learning by doing. He concedes the difficulty of proving the argument, although it is certainly plausible that the relatively poor educational attainment of the Singapore labour force in the 1960s and 1970s should have affected the manufacturing sector's capacity to absorb new technology. In their analysis of the sources of economic growth in East Asia, Collins and Bosworth (1996) explicitly allow for improvements in education per worker. They find that in the Singapore case such improvements accounted for around ten per cent of observed growth in output per worker over the decade from 1984 to 1994. As growth in capital stock per worker only accounted for around 40 per cent of growth in output per worker, they argued that the remaining 50 per cent should be ascribed to TFP growth, a very different finding from that of Young (Collins and Bosworth 1996: Table 6).

In Hong Kong, the expansion of educational opportunities in both public and private sectors played a key role in upgrading labour skills and accommodating the rapid growth and associated structural changes in the local economy. In the 1960s and 1970s, total employment in Hong Kong was growing by about 3 per cent annually, and by the early 1980s, participation rates were above 80 per cent for males, and almost 50 per cent for females (Howe, 1983). Even more interesting than such figures is the finding that already only about a third of the workforce were employed in manufacturing activities. This was of course a reflection of the rapid growth of tertiary sector employment – in commerce, finance, government and other services. These kinds of structural changes could not have occurred if educational and training programmes capable of providing the workforce with appropriate skills had not been available. Indeed, in Hong Kong development of public education was one of the ways in which, in a basically *laissez faire* context, public policy was able to influence and facilitate not only economic growth, but also social development.

In a more general investigation of Hong Kong, Krause (1988: S50) argues that favourable initial conditions included the access to the UK market provided by the system of imperial preference, and subsequently GSP and other market access privileges. But of course the crucial question remains; given that many other UK colonies, and indeed other former colonies in Asia and Africa, also enjoyed such privileges, why was Hong Kong so much more successful in exploiting them? Krause, like many others, thinks that the government was important, both in what it did and in what it did not do. It is time to look in more detail at the literature on the role of government in the success of the 'miraculous four'.

THE ROLE OF GOVERNMENT

While few economists familiar with the evolution of these four economies over the past three decades are likely to deny the importance of government policies in promoting rapid economic growth and structural change, a lively debate has emerged since the late 1980s about the nature of government intervention, and especially about the extent to which it supported or supplanted market mechanisms in the allocation of resources. In her survey of the literature on industrial policy in East Asia, Smith (1995: 20) points out that a stream of writings emerged in the 1980s and 1990s, beginning with Johnson's influential study of MITI in Japan (Johnson 1982). These writings can be seen as a reaction to the 'canonical tradition' regarding rapid economic development in East Asia which developed in the 1970s, and was especially associated with international organisations such as the OECD, the IMF and the World Bank. According to this tradition, the so-called four tigers exemplified an alternative set of policies from those practised by either the centrally planned economies, or countries such as India that had favoured a combination of indicative planning, heavy regulation of the private sector, and support of state enterprises. Broadly speaking the governments in Hong Kong, Singapore, Taiwan and South Korea were praised for adopting 'outward- oriented' policies which did not discriminate against, or which actively encouraged, exports, kept public sectors reasonably small, and facilitated high levels of domestic savings and domestic capital formation (See Kuznets, this volume, Chapter 1).

The revisionists argued that this view was at best partial and downplayed, or entirely ignored important aspects of the East Asian story. At one extreme, Amsden (1989: 13–14) in her influential study of South Korea, claimed that the role of the state in late industrialising economies was to promote rapid technological catch-up by, if necessary, 'getting prices wrong' in order to create profitable investment opportunities. Wade's analysis of Taiwan conceded that in many respects government policy did conform to a number of neo-classical policy prescriptions including a stable and undistorted real exchange rate, low effective rates of protection, market-clearing wage policies, high bank interest rates and budget surpluses. But he also argued that many analyses of the Taiwanese experience by economists such as Ranis, Little and others downplayed the role of government planning and paid insufficient attention to the instruments through which the Taiwanese government had achieved its policy goals (Wade 1990: 71–2). Wade's own study provided an extensive analysis of the role of the economic bureaucracy and the way in which it 'governed the market' in the Taiwanese context.

The considerable literature stemming from Johnson's work had less to say about the two city states than about either Taiwan or South Korea, although, as Krause (1988: S64) argued, 'in terms of the government's role in the economy, they are almost polar extremes'. In Singapore, a debate about the role of government in promoting rapid economic development would hardly have seemed necessary since key government ministers, in particular Dr Goh Keng Swee, never made much secret of the fact that they saw their function very much in terms of intervening in the market in order to fulfil clearly defined policy goals. In a defence of PAP policy originally published in the mid-1970s, he wrote:

> Taking an overall view of Singapore's economic policy, we can see how radically it differed from the laissez-faire policies of the colonial era. These had led Singapore to a dead end, with little economic growth, massive unemployment, wretched housing, and inadequate education. We had to try a more activist and interventionist approach. Democratic socialist economic policies ranged from direct participation in industry to the supply of infrastructure facilities by statutory authorities, and to

> laying down clear guidelines to the private sector as to what they could and should do (Goh 1977: 104).

While critics of the PAP might have challenged the use of the adjective 'democratic' few have ever questioned the applicability of the term 'socialist'. Huff (this volume, Chapter 3) outlines the key areas in which government supplanted the price mechanism; one was the labour market, another was savings and a third was in the use of state enterprises to supply a variety of services ranging from housing and banking to utilities and transportation. By the mid-1980s there was indeed some dissatisfaction with this dirigiste approach; after Dr Goh left the cabinet younger ministers appeared to feel that a degree of deregulation and privatsation was in order. But at the same time, the response to the perceived shortage of skilled labour was a massive increase in government investment in secondary and tertiary education. The report of the committee established in 1985 to identify new directions for Singapore's economic growth pointed out that the Singaporean labour force in 1984 was still relatively unskilled in comparison with that of Taiwan, Japan or the USA (Republic of Singapore 1986: 114ff). The solution was to implement a manpower development plan whose aim would be to increase numbers of both university graduates and technicians. Accordingly, the two universities together with the polytechnics and vocational institutes were given enhanced government funding in the latter part of the 1980s and early 1990s, and numbers of graduates accelerated sharply.

In Hong Kong, the colonial authorities were more cautious about 'governing the market' than in Singapore, although the perception of the former British Crown Colony as the epitome of *laissez faire* government is now recognised to have been too simple. Youngson (1982: 84–9) and Howe (this volume, Chapter 5) both refer to a change in the Hong Kong government's approach to regulating the activities of the private sector in the 1970s. Whereas in the 1960s, market regulation was equated with central planning, by the end of the 1970s, much more emphasis was being placed on the potentially positive contribution of government policies. As Howe pointed out (1983: 522), by the early 1980s, the Hong Kong government's view of its role in economic management was captured in the philosophy of 'positive non-intervention':

> This emphasizes, on the one hand, the efficiency of market forces as an allocating mechanism, yet, on the other, the crucial role of government in providing a stable framework of law and regulation, and of fiscal and public expenditure practices. Government, in this view, must also provide certain elements of economic and social infrastructure . . .

The Hong Kong government was, however, not unaware of the attraction that an impression of a *laissez faire* system might have for foreign investors, especially those who were repelled by the open *dirigisme* of its arch-rival,

Singapore. It sought to emphasize the essentially conservative nature of its policies, while continuing to implement the principle of 'positive non-intervention'. Unlike Singapore, there was never any suggestion of espousing 'socialist' principles, although the orthodoxy that set itself against deliberately redistributive measures could not conceal the *de facto* redistributive impact of government spending policies (Howe, 1983; see also Howe, Chapter 5, this volume).

Youngson (1982: 35–47) discusses in some detail what the supposedly *laissez faire* government achieved between 1950 and 1980 in sectors such as housing, health and education. The results were in some respects even more impressive than in Singapore especially when it is recalled that Hong Kong had a larger population than Singapore in 1960 (three million in Hong Kong compared with 1.63 million in Singapore) and the growth rate was somewhat higher. In addition, as Youngson (1982: 84–9) argued, the government's approach to regulating the activities of the private sector also changed; whereas in the 1960s any suggestion of market regulation was equated with central planning, by the end of the 1970s there was a greater emphasis on the positive contribution which government policies could have.

Kuznets (Chapter 1, this volume) stresses the paradox that a high degree of interventionism, in economies such as those of Singapore, South Korea and Taiwan was not accompanied by high or rising levels of government expenditures relative to GDP. Indeed, he considers 'small public sectors' to be one of the distinguishing features of the 'East Asian Model'. He explains this in terms of the reluctance of the governments (including Japan's) that are the focus of his study to fund comprehensive social welfare programmes. Certainly there is little doubt that government expenditures did not grow as rapidly as GDP in either Taiwan or South Korea in the years from 1955 to 1980, with the result that the ratio of government expenditure to GDP (measured in 1985 international prices) declined continuously (Table 6). In Hong Kong and Singapore government expenditure ratios in the 1960s and 1970s were lower than in either Taiwan or South Korea, in part at least because of lower defence expenditures. But by the 1980s the ratio in Singapore was roughly similar to South Korea, although lower than Taiwan. Meanwhile, although the data in Table 6 suggest that Hong Kong's reputation for minimalist government is well-deserved, the evidence does also indicate that after the mid-1960s, government expenditures kept pace with rapidly growing GDP. Indeed, an analysis of trends in the main components of expenditure reveals that average growth of private consumption during the 1970s (9.8 per cent p.a.) was less than a percentage point higher than the corresponding figure for government consumption (8.9 per cent) (Howe, 1983: 514).

From 1984 (the date of the Sino-British Declaration on the future of Hong Kong) until June 1997, continuing economic development in Hong Kong took place in the shadow of its pending translation from the status of a British

Colony to that of a 'Special Administrative Region' (SAR) of China. During these years, liberalisation in the region manifested itself less in economic, and more in political terms – above all, in controversial efforts to introduce and extend democratic methods of governance. By contrast, in Taiwan and South Korea evidence of genuine and significant *economic* liberalisation was apparent alongside political initiatives.

In Taiwan, the government responded to emerging macroeconomic imbalances during the 1980s by instituting a major programme of economic liberalisation (Howe, this volume, Chapter 4; Li, 1995; Schive, 1995). This embraced a series of important initiatives, aimed at lifting interest rate restrictions, freeing the exchange rate, liberalising capital movements and deregulating the domestic banking system. Complementary measures meanwhile sought to find an enhanced economic role for Taiwan through a process of internationalisation, based on outward investment and an expansion of intraregional trade (especially *vis-à-vis* mainland China). All these initiatives were facilitated by the beginnings of what was to become an on-going process of democratisation. The inevitable outcome of such developments was a retreat by the Taiwanese government from its previous interventionist policies towards the espousal of a guidance role designed to ensure the efficient functioning of price and market mechanisms.

In South Korea, the dangers of a development strategy based on a high level of government intervention were already apparent in the 1970s. Not least, the growing size and complexity of the economy under the impact of high growth constrained the government's economic role and made it more difficult for it to direct economic growth through recourse to rigid controls (Cho and Kim, 1991: 52). For the time being, however, the adoption of the 'Heavy and Chemical Industries [HCI] Promotion Plan' under the Third Five-Year Plan (1972–76) made economic liberalisation and deregulation impossible. Indeed, in order to ensure that adequate investment and other material resources were made available for the new industries, the government felt compelled to *strengthen* its financial control of the economy (Cho and Kim, 1991: 52). Only in the wake of the assassination of President Park Chung Hee were the long-delayed economic reforms finally implemented. Thus, the 1980s saw an unprecedented degree of economic liberalisation take place in South Korea, as measures sought to dismantle regulatory controls.

CONSEQUENCES OF STRUCTURAL CHANGE

Reference has already been made to the inter-sectoral structural changes attendant on rapid economic growth in these four economies. Such changes were accompanied by important inter-industry shifts, especially in Taiwan and South Korea. Both these economies faced the challenge of having to adjust from specialisation in labour-intensive manufacturing activities to developing more capital-intensive industries – and finally more skill, knowledge and technology-intensive industries. Meanwhile, in Hong Kong, size constraints as well as the physical resiting of manufacturing enterprises across the border in China's Guangdong province highlighted opportunities available from growth based on tertiary sector expansion.

The role of small and medium-scale enterprises (*SME*), which still account for an overwhelming majority of all Taiwanese economic enterprises, has attracted economists' attention for their key role in facilitating Taiwan's industrial development and economic modernisation. Howe (this volume, Chapter 4) places particular emphasis on the responsiveness of Taiwan's SMEs, arguing that their ability to react not only to changes in demand, but also to new technical opportunities (especially in the electronics and information technology equipment industries – the sector in which Taiwan has come to assume a global significance) has been critically important to the maintenance of their international competitiveness and market share.

To place sole emphasis on the role of Taiwanese SMEs is, however, to neglect the importance of the inter-firm networks (including trade associations) within which they have operated so successfully. Such networks have made a huge contribution in overcoming raw and intermediate material, and investment constraints that otherwise might have proved insurmountable. To emphasise the contribution of SMEs is also not to deny the parallel role of their larger-scale counterparts. In this respect, it is instructive that by the end of the 1980s, large-scale units contributed almost 40 per cent of Taiwan's GNP, compared with 44 per cent for SMEs. The top 100 large-scale units, representing a mere 0.1 per cent of all enterprises, generated 23 per cent of GNP (Myers, 1998: 41).

Industrial change and modernisation are inseparable from technological advances. The technological challenge for economies, like those of Taiwan and South Korea, that are moving towards increasingly knowledge-intensive industrial structures is formidable. Raising R&D expenditure in order to strengthen indigenous science and technology resources is an obvious and essential response to this challenge. Ranis (this volume, Chapter 9) discusses the considerable achievements of both Taiwan and South Korea in increasing research and development expenditures as a percentage of GDP since 1980, and emphasises the important role which government played in this. In Taiwan, the use of fiscal and other incentives facilitated significant increases in R&D spending from a mere 0.48 per cent of GDP (1978) to 1.82 per cent (1994) – close to the 2 per cent target for 1995 (Simon, this volume, Chapter 16). Given the prevalence of SMEs in Taiwan's firm structure, it is not surprising that the government should have made a major contribution to the rise in R&D spending. Simon pointed out that this pattern contrasts with that of South Korea, where the *private* sector played by far the most important role as a source of funds for R&D expenditure.

No assessment of recent industrial and technological changes in Taiwan would be complete without mention of the role of the Hsinchu Science and

Industry Park. Its defining characteristic was the emphasis on the development of high-technology industries, as revealed by an average ratio between firms' R&D expenditure and value-output of 5.4 per cent (and in some individual cases, more than 10 per cent) (Simon, this volume, Chapter 16). Although the original aim of the park was to attract high technology firms from overseas, it rapidly became home to 'spin-offs of government research institutes for the micro-electronics industry'. Several such firms expanded very rapidly in the 1980s and 1990s (Baum and Sherry 1999: 13).

Much has been made of the technological benefits of FDI inflows. Simon (this volume, Chapter 16) draws attention to Taiwan's ties with the United States and Japan as an important mechanism for technology transfer. Meanwhile, Taiwan's own foreign investment sorties overseas have also come to generate useful technological spillover effects. In taking issue with those who would propose a common pattern of causality underlying the growth experience of all four economies, Howe (this volume, Chapter 4) cites differences in their approaches to FDI as evidence of widely divergent policy stances. In contrast to South Korean hostility to FDI, the dubious gains from Hong Kong's *laissez-faire* attitude to foreign investment and the predominance of FDI-related export-oriented manufacturing in Singapore,

> Taiwan alone . . . has been successful in both attracting FDI and then achieving the strong spillover effects that provided the technological and commercial basis for development of exporting in the 1980s and 1990s.

INTERNATIONAL TRADE AND ECONOMIC GROWTH

Almost all studies of the rapid growth of these four economies since the 1950s have stressed the importance of export growth. Certainly there can be little doubt that exports grew rapidly relative to GDP in both South Korea and Taiwan in the 1960s and 1970s. By 1980, exports and imports were 100 per cent of GDP in Taiwan and seventy per cent in South Korea (Table 7). In the South Korean context Amsden (1989: 72) has argued that

> Korea's high trade ratio cannot be understood as merely a response to its small market. By world standards, Korea is not a small country . . . Rather, Korea's high trade dependence is a matter of history and politics.

Amsden goes on to point out that a major reason for the emphasis placed by the Park regime on export growth was that such growth was seen as the only way of freeing the economy from reliance on American aid. But once under way the benefits of the export boom were soon obvious to the wider community, especially in creating employment in export-oriented manufacturing industry. The various devices employed by both the Korean and Taiwanese

Table 7 Exports and imports as a percentage of GDP, 1955–1990[a] (five-year averages centered on the years shown)

Year	*Taiwan*	*South Korea*	*Hong Kong*	*Singapore*
1955	22.8	12.0	n.a.	n.a.
1960[b]	31.5	16.8	190.0	360.9
1965	40.6	25.9	161.5	259.2
1970	62.3	40.2	176.4	228.7
1975	87.3	64.7	165.8	300.3
1980	101.4	70.1	178.6	390.2
1985	97.5	71.5	213.6	328.0
1990[c]	89.9	63.0	268.8	363.7

Note:
[a] The ratios are estimated from data in current international prices.
[b] For Singapore and Hong Kong, the data refer to 1960 only.
[c] For Taiwan the data refer to 1990 only. For South Korea the data refer to averages for 1989–91.

Source: As for Table 1.

governments employed to encourage export growth have been much discussed. Amsden (1989: 66–9) stresses the importance of export subsidies, especially in the textile sector. In Taiwan, Wade (1990: 139–48) discusses a range of devices used by the government to promote exports, including the establishment of export processing zones, the provision of tariff rebates and preferential tax treatment for exporters, provision of short-term credit, the formation of export cartels and government assistance for export quality control and export marketing.

That such government assistance was an important factor in promoting exports can hardly be denied. A more controversial issue relates to the relationship between export growth, investment growth and GDP growth. Rodrik (Chapter 10, this volume) argues that it was the growth in investment which was the real driving force behind GDP growth in Taiwan and South Korea, with causality running from investment to imports, and from imports to exports. A rather different view of the relationship between investment growth, export growth and GDP growth in Taiwan is provided by Sundrum (1990: 226–30). His examination of the time series data on both investment growth and export growth indicated that the correlation between lagged export growth and investment growth was rather small, while that between lagged investment growth and export growth was much stronger. This might suggest that it was increases in exports which triggered more investment, but in fact Sundrum argues that both forces were probably at work.

> To begin with, the devaluation of the currency and the liberalisation of trade in the late 1950s led to a growth of exports, initially of primary products and labour intensive manufactures. The growth of exports in turn induced a growth of investment and technological progress.

> Hence, Taiwan's competitive position improved steadily, as her export prices fell relative to other countries, and led to further expansion of exports, increasingly of capital intensive and high technology manufactures (Sundrum 1990: 230).

This 'virtuous cycle of export-led growth' also occurred in the two city states, although the historic entrepot role of both these economies ensured that the ratio of exports and imports (including re-exports) was already very high in 1960 (Table 7), the openness ratio increased over the 1960s and 1970s, although in Singapore the ratio appears to have fallen again since the early 1980s. In Hong Kong exports continued to grow in volume terms at over 15 per cent per annum in the early 1990s, in spite of the fact that many labour-intensive manufacturing enterprises relocated to southern China (World Bank 1997: 243). In Singapore the government has been anxious to prevent a rapid decline in the manufacturing sector, and there the emphasis has been on developing new more capital and skill-intensive export industries (Pang, this volume, Chapter 15). Between 1990 and 1995, export volume growth accelerated to over 16 per cent (World Bank 1997: 243).

An important recent feature of the foreign economic relations of all four countries has been their increasing involvement with the economy of the Chinese People's Republic. Initially, the clearest expression of such involvement was the rapid expansion of merchandise trade within what became known as 'Greater China' (a triangular relationship embracing two southern Chinese provinces – Guangdong and Fujian – Hong Kong, and Taiwan), and the accelerated expansion of cross-border capital flows (especially FDI) from Hong Kong and Taiwan (Ash and Kueh, this volume, Chapter 13).

Such developments had a profound effect on growth and structural change in all three regions. In the early 1990s, however, the parameters of the transnational Chinese economy encapsulated in the concept of Greater China began to change. Hong Kong's economic relations with the mainland encountered new challenges, as when (in 1994) attempts by Beijing to exclude simple assembly processes from preferential foreign investment incentives and to limit foreign investment in real estate – activities which had hitherto attracted a major share of Hong Kong capital flowing into southern China – had a deterrent effect on Hong Kong entrepreneurial investment across the Chinese border. Meanwhile, the establishment of formal diplomatic relations between China and South Korea signalled an enhancement of trade and investment relations, which rapidly took the economic relationship between the two countries to a new level. Economic relations with ASEAN member countries – most notably, Singapore – also grew stronger. Taiwan's economic relations with the mainland continued to maintain the previous momentum of growth, subject though such relations were to the uncertainty and vagaries of the two countries' political relationship.

The looming presence of the PRC is a dimension that cannot be ignored.

By 1997, the four economies together were the collective destination of 33 per cent of all Chinese exports and the source of 30 per cent of its imports (China, State Statistical Bureau, 1998: 626–8). They also accounted for 57 per cent of total FDI inflows into China (ibid., 639). Stated differently, the four economies included China's second-largest (Hong Kong), and fourth-, fifth- and sixth-largest (Korea, Taiwan and Singapore) trading partners. Hong Kong remains China's single most important source of foreign capital, while the ranking of the other three economies exactly mirrors their importance as trading partners.

Implied in such figures are differing degrees of economic dependence on the mainland, although the problems – actual and potential – of increased reliance have been most marked for Hong Kong and Taiwan. In the case of Hong Kong, 'dependence' is better described as symbiosis, the SAR's economy having become closely integrated with that of the Pearl River Delta in Guangdong province. Not all are agreed that the net economic impact of such integration has been unqualifiedly beneficial. In particular, Cheng and Tsang (1997: 71) have argued that in the wake of cross-border industrial relocation, the gains accruing to Hong Kong were of a mainly static nature. As such, they merely substituted for genuine technological upgrading (a more secure basis for productivity growth), meanwhile leaving the Hong Kong economy to follow the less secure path of 'Manhattanisation'.

For obvious political reasons, the government in Taipei has consistently pursued a cautious attitude towards the development of trade and investment relations with mainland China. Here, we would make just two points. The first is that Taiwan is by no means an unequal partner *vis-à-vis* the mainland. After all, in 1997 its per capita GDP (calculated according to PPP) was at least four times higher than that of the PRC and, small as it is, its aggregate GDP is a not insignificant fraction of that of its huge neighbour. But it is also true that the retreat of the state from its previous close involvement in managing the Taiwanese economy has reduced the effectiveness of the government's efforts to control and limit Taiwanese entrepreneurs' investments in mainland China. Any assessment of Taiwan's economic vulnerability should reflect the tension between such considerations.

THE IMPACT OF THE CRASH OF 1997

By 1997, the World Bank classified South Korea, Hong Kong and Singapore as high income economies; Taiwan was not included in the World Bank's league table, but as its per capita GDP was above that of South Korea, it too would have been included in the high income group. This classification carried with it the implication that these four economies had graduated into the ranks of the developed world, and that while their growth rates may well slow down, they were unlikely to be subjected to violent shocks. Certainly all were small, open economies and to that extent vulnerable to sudden fluctuations in the world economy but their economic institutions were considered by most observers to be robust enough to cope with such fluctuations without too much domestic damage. The events of 1997/98 were to put these assumptions to the test, to an extent which could never have been predicted even a year earlier.

The problems in the South Korean economy had in fact already become apparent well before the decision of the Thai government to float the baht in early July 1997 precipitated what is now widely termed the 'Asian crisis'. Although growth rates had been robust up to 1996, the current account deficit had widened sharply in both 1995 and 1996 to almost five per cent of GDP, the highest level in recent Korean experience. Financial deregulation had encouraged Korean banks and large companies (chaebol) to borrow abroad to finance their expansion into new products and export markets. Unfortunately as in Thailand, merchandise export growth slowed sharply in 1996, in part at least because of the declining competitiveness of key export sectors such as steel, semi-conductors and automobiles. As Smith (1998: 70) argued, there was an assumption among many Korean companies that their cost advantage *vis-à-vis* Japan because of the strong yen would last indefinitely and they were caught unawares by the yen depreciation.

The combination of high foreign indebtedness and the export slowdown led to severe problems for several chaebol and in January 1997 Hanbo Steel went bankrupt. According to Chang (1998: 224–5), after the bankruptcy it was revealed that Hanbo's entry into the steel industry had come about as the result of corrupt favours granted by highly placed individuals, including the second son of then President Kim Young Sam. What this episode demonstrated was the demise of the system of 'generalistic' government-business relationships which emphasised rational criteria for intervention rather than particular favours to specific conglomerates. What had emerged by the early 1990s was a far more 'particularistic' or 'cronyist' system which spread throughout the manufacturing sector.

Chang (1998: 228–9) also argued that other factors triggering the crisis in the Korean economy was the rapid liberalisation of the capital account which permitted large companies to borrow in international capital markets to finance production expansion. By the mid-1990s debt-equity ratios in a number of large Korean companies were very high, and rising. The Korean situation can be contrasted with that in Taiwan where there were fewer large conglomerates and many more medium-scale enterprises. Not only did this discourage the kind of corporate cronyism which became rife in Korea, Thailand and Indonesia in the early 1990s, but it also meant that firms usually financed expansion from retained profits or from the so-called kerb market whose high interest rates deterred large-scale borrowings. In addition the Taiwanese government made greater use of capital controls to prevent foreign borrowing for speculative purposes. As a result, corporate debt-equity ratios in Taiwan were among the lowest in Asia.

Taiwan is one of very few economies in East or South East Asia which is predicted to enjoy positive economic growth in 1998; forecasts made by the OECD in the latter part of 1998 indicated a GDP growth rate of around 4.5 per cent in 1998 and four per cent in 1999. South Korean GDP by contrast is expected to contract by around six per cent in 1998. Neither Hong Kong nor Singapore have escaped contagion; the Hong Kong GDP is expected to contract by five per cent in 1998, and that of Singapore to stay flat, or at best grow very slowly. Neither economy suffers from the same problems as South Korea or Thailand, Indonesia and Malaysia; the banking sectors are reasonably healthy and corporate foreign indebtedness is much lower. But Singapore is inevitably affected by the slowdown in the rest of ASEAN, especially Indonesia and Malayia, while Hong Kong faces a formidable list of policy challenges which Howe (this volume, Chapter 5) discusses in detail. But the prospects for the miraculous four as the twenty-first century dawns are not entirely bleak, for reasons which we will address in the last part of this introduction.

FUTURE PROSPECTS

By early 1999, Taiwan's economic prospects appeared to most observers to be among the best in Asia. But in spite of the fact that it had emerged relatively unscathed from the crisis, its financial sector was showing signs of strain, and business confidence was reported as declining. Taiwan's future is, according to some analysts, likely to be closely linked with the degree of success it achieves in establishing itself as an Asia-Pacific 'Regional Operations Centre' (APROC). The logic of this policy is grounded in Taiwan's central and strategic position in the Asia-Pacific region and the consequent promises this holds for it to become an 'international services and communications/ transshipment node' (Howe, Chapter 4, this volume). Fulfilment of the APROC goal would have the additional benefit of facilitating the globalisation of Taiwanese companies and obviating problems associated with the alternative policies based on enterprise relocation.

But for the time being, Taiwan's ability to transform itself into a comprehensive regional operations centre, embracing communications and financial services, as well as transportation facilities, will be constrained by the inadequacies of its existing infrastructure. Indeed, it is difficult to foresee Taiwan being able to compete with Hong Kong (or for that matter, Singapore too) in these areas for some time to come. It has even been argued that security factors arising out of uncertain cross-Strait relations *vis-à-vis* mainland China might permanently debar Taiwan from fulfilling the role of a financial centre in the Asia-Pacific region (Cabestan: 1998: 235). If this is true, then Taiwan's economic future must still rest with medium, and high technology manufacturing. Here its assets are indeed formidable: a well-educated labour force, a dynamic and resilient SME sector combined with large enterprises which have not been nurtured on a diet of government subsidies, low levels of corporate debt, a high degree of export orientation and a tradition of government support of industrial research and development.

In South Korea the inevitable restructuring of the *chaebol* in the wake of the financial crisis will take time, and will bring in its wake considerable unemployment. It is predicted that as many as two million South Korean workers will be unemployed in 1999, around eight per cent of the labour force. In an economy where involuntary unemployment has been largely unknown for over a decade, this must affect both business confidence and social stability. But on the plus side, the process of democratisation has produced a government which has credibility and legitimacy both at home and abroad. In addition there is, as in Taiwan, a well-educated labour force and a competent and reasonably clean public service.

The two city states may appear to face a more uncertain future. Singapore wants to emulate Taiwan and develop a robust, technologically dynamic industrial sector, while at the same time strengthening its role as a regional finance and service sector. In doing this, it has the advantage of strong economic institutions and a political system dominated by a party which, in spite of four decades in power, seems still to be untainted by corruption. But the Singapore economy has close trading and financial ties to both Malaysia and Indonesia and is inevitably affected by the severity of the contraction in both these economies. Its growth prospects in the medium term are thus linked quite closely to a broader regional recovery.

Hong Kong may be facing the least secure future of all. Growth may recover in 1999, but is likely to be slow over the next few years, and business and consumer confidence will stay subdued. Out-migration of young professionals and managers will accelerate. Certainly the government can take pride in the fact that it has weathered both the Asian crisis and the political transition from British colony to special administrative region of China with the currency peg intact. But its future is now linked irrevocably to that of China itself, a 'Manhattan' appended to a large, poor and potentially unstable mainland. It is hardly a comfortable position, and Hong Kong's political leadership will need all the managerial and diplomatic skills it can muster to ensure both economic dynamism and social stability in the years ahead.

REFERENCES

Adelman, Irma (1974), 'South Korea' in Hollis Chenery et al., *Redistribution with Growth*, London: Oxford University Press.

Amsden, Alice (1979), 'Taiwan's Economic History: A Case of Etatisme and a Challenge to Dependency Theory', *Modern China*, Vol. 5(3), July 1979, 241–80, as reprinted in Robert H. Bates (Editor), *Towards a Political Economy of Development*, Berkeley: University of California Press, 1988.

—— (1989), *Asia's Next Giant: South Korea and Late Industrialization*, New York: Oxford University Press.

Baum, Julian and Andrew Sherry (1999), 'The Taiwan Difference', *Far Eastern Economic Review*, February 11, pp. 10–14.

Cabestan, Jean-Pierre (1998), 'Taiwan's Mainland Policy: Normalization, Yes; Reunification, Later' in David Shambaugh (Editor), *Contemporary Taiwan*, Oxford: Clarendon Press.

Chang, Ha-Joon (1998), 'South Korea: The Misunderstood Crisis', in Jomo K. S. (Editor), *Tigers in Trouble: Financial Governance, Liberalization and Crises in East Asia*, London: Zed Press.

Chau, L. and R. Hsia (1975), 'An Anatomy of Income Distribution in Hong Kong', in *Income Distribution, Employment and Economic Development in Southeast and East Asia*, Tokyo: Japan Economic Research Centre and Manila: Council for Asian Manpower Studies, July.

Cheng Yuk-shing and Tsang Shu-ki (1997), 'The Economic Link-up of Hong Kong and Guangdong: Structural and Developmental Problems' in Joseph C. H. Chai, Y. Y. Kueh and Clement A. Tisdell (Editors), *China and the Asian Pacific Economy*, Economics Conference Monograph No. 3, Department of Economics, The University of Queensland, Australia.

China, State Statistical Bureau, *Zhongguo tongji nianjian* (*China Statistical Yearbook*), Beijing: State Statistical Publishing House, various issues.

Cho, Lee-Jay and Kim, Yoon Hyung, (1991), *Economic Development in the Republic of Korea: A Policy Perspective*, *Honolulu*, University of Hawaii Press.

Collins, Susan M. and Barry B. Bosworth (1996), 'Economic Growth in East Asia: Accumulation versus Assimilation', *Brookings Papers on Economic Activity*, No. 2, pp. 135–203.

Goh Keng Swee (1977), *The Practice of Economic Growth*, Singapore: Federal Press.

Ho, S. P. S. (1978), *Economic Development of Taiwan, 1860–1970*, New Haven: Yale University Press.

Howe, Christopher (1983), 'Hong Kong's Economic Relationship with China', *The China Quarterly*, No. 95.

Johnson, Chalmers (1982), *Miti and the Japanese Miracle: The Growth of Industrial Policy, 1925–75*, Stanford: Stanford University Press.

Krause, Lawrence B. (1988), 'Hong Kong and Singapore: Twins or Kissing Cousins?', *Economic Development and Cultural Change*, Vol. 36(3), Supplement, April, pp. S45–S66.

Krugman, Paul (1994), 'The Myth of Asia's Miracle', *Foreign Affairs*, Vol. 73, November/December 1994, 62–78.

Li, Kuo-Ting, (1995), *The Revolution of Policy Behind Taiwan's Development Success*, Singapore, World Scientific Publishing Company.

Myers, R. H. (1998), 'A New Chinese Civilization: The Evolution of the Republic of China on Taiwan' in David Shambaugh (Editor), *Contemporary Taiwan*, Oxford: Clarendon Press.

Ranis, Gustav (1974), 'Taiwan' in Hollis Chenery et al., *Redistribution with Growth*, London: Oxford University Press.

Republic of Singapore (1986), *The Singapore Economy: New Directions*, Singapore: Ministry of Trade and Industry.

Schive, Chi (1995),*Taiwan's Economic Role in East Asia*, Washington D.C., The Center for Strategic and International Studies.

Smith, Heather (1995), 'Industry Policy in East Asia', *Asian-Pacific Economic Literature*, Vol. 9(1), May, pp. 17–39.

—— (1998), 'Korea' in Ross H. McLeod and Ross Garnaut (Editors), *East Asia in Crisis: From Being a Miracle to Needing One?*, London: Routledge.

Sundrum, R. M. (1990), *Economic Growth in Theory and Practice*, London: Macmillan.

Tsurumi, E. Patricia (1977), *Japanese Colonial Education in Taiwan*, Cambridge: Harvard University Press.

Unesco (1997), *Statistical Yearbook 1996*, Paris: Unesco Publishing and Lanham: Bernan Press.

Wade, Robert (1990), *Governing the Market: Economic Theory and the Role of Government in East Asian Industrialization*, Princeton: Princeton University Press.

World Bank (1978), *World Development Report, 1978*, Washington: World Bank.

—— (1994), *World Development Report, 1994*, New York: Oxford University Press for the World Bank.

—— (1997), *World Development Report, 1997*, New York: Oxford University Press for the World Bank.

Young, Alwyn (1992), 'A Tale of Two Cities: Factor Accumulation and Technical Change in Hong Kong and Singapore', in O. Blanchard and S. Fischer (Editors), *NBER Macroeconomics Annual*, Cambridge: MIT Press.

Youngson, A. J. (1982), *Hong Kong: Economic Growth and Policy*, Hong Kong: Oxford University Press.

Part I

THE EAST ASIAN MODEL OF RAPID GROWTH

1

AN EAST ASIAN MODEL OF ECONOMIC DEVELOPMENT

Japan, Taiwan, and South Korea

Paul W. Kuznets

Any economic development model must have particular attributes if it is to be a convincing and operational model. The first of these is a significantly above average GNP growth rate that is neither offset by rapid population expansion nor tarnished by substantial income inequality. The record, in short, should be a successful one that is worth emulating. A second attribute is realism or, in this context, the existence of a country or set of countries whose performance conforms to the model. Balanced growth or big-push models of development may have theoretical appeal, for example, but the absence of specific country examples raises doubts of their feasibility and therefore lessens their appeal as models. Furthermore, theoretical or nonspecific models do not meet a major challenge in model building, which is to show that there is a set of economic characteristics that distinguishes a group of countries from other countries and therefore justifies classifying them as members of a distinct "model."

The model should also set forth the major economic relationships or the proximate reasons for rapid growth. Critics can then determine whether hypothesized relations prevail or not even if such relations do not establish ultimate causes. We can show that high investment ratios are necessary for rapid growth, for example, but we cannot demonstrate that the high savings ratios needed to finance the investment follow from the Confucian tradition. While one might prefer ultimate to proximate explanations, an economic development model should be acceptable if it provides a set of proximate or economic reasons for rapid growth.

Finally, the model should be reasonably replicable. While many countries might be able to adopt a successful policy or program, they cannot be expected to duplicate natural resource endowments or past world-market conditions. Rapid growth of oil exporters in the 1970s, for instance, provides little basis for emulation among the vast majority of developing countries with no oil. Similarly, Korea's phenomenal export expansion from

Source: *Economic Development and Cultural Change*, Vol. 3(3), 1988, Supplement, pp. S11–S44.

the mid-1960s to the late 1970s occured before worldwide recession and rising protectionism dimmed prospects for replication by latecomers who might want to adopt the Korean model. In addition, the distinction between ultimate and proximate suggests another, more general reason why a model may not be wholly replicable. Other countries may duplicate successful economic policies, but we cannot expect them to duplicate the social, cultural, or even the institutional arrangements that underlie the policies.

The East Asian model presented here possesses the successful record, specific country examples, acceptability, and replicability to a degree that should make it a convincing and operational model. Japan, South Korea (hereafter simply "Korea"), and Taiwan, the three East Asian countries that constitute the model, differ substantially in important ways. In particular, Japan is much more economically advanced than Taiwan and Korea and, as an independent nation-state, has had over a century to develop, compared with less than 40 years for the other two. Still, Japan is included because all three countries have had to overcome the economic problems faced by relatively large, densely populated, and resource-poor countries and because the three have overcome these problems in similar ways. Two other candidates for inclusion in any East Asian model, Hong Kong and Singapore, have been excluded. These two, members of the "Gang of Four" like Taiwan and Korea, have outstanding development records. Though their performance meets the success criterion, they are excluded because they have faced different, and in some ways lesser, problems as small city-states without agricultural sectors.

The difference in development levels between Japan and Taiwan and Korea was noted because it is likely to influence economic structure, composition of demand, productivity levels, and the other economic characteristics that affect performance and, hence, conformity to the model. Other such differences among the three should also be mentioned. One is the difference in market size. Japan's population is three times as large as Korea's, and Korea's is more than twice as large as Taiwan's (see Table 1.1). This inequality, combined with differences in per capita GDP on the order of five to one (Japan/Korea) and four to one (Japan/Taiwan), means that output (GDP) and expenditure in Japan are many times larger than in Taiwan or Korea. Where scale economies are significant, as in producing automobiles, it is hardly surprising that Japan's automobile industry is large, efficient, and internationally competitive, Korea's is just beginning to export, and Taiwan has yet to do so.

Another difference associated with developemnt level is a difference in economic structure. Agriculture accounted for only 4% of GDP originating in Japan in 1982, for example, whereas the figure for Korea in 1983 was 16% (Table 1.1). The GDP figures suggest that Japan has already become a serivce-oriented or "postindustrial" economy and that Taiwan and Korea are now in their industrial phases, with the shift from agriculture to industry likely to

Table 1.1 Country characteristics, 1983

	Japan	*South Korea*	*Taiwan*
Population (millions)	119.5	40.0	18.7
Average annual growth rate, 1953–83 (%)	1.1	2.2	2.7
GDP (in $U.S. billions)	1,157.5	76.6	49.8
GDP/capita ($U.S.)	10,120	1,740	2,010
GDP origination (%):			
Agriculture	4*	16	7
Industry	42*	37	45
Services	54*	47	48
Average annual GDP growth (%):			
1973–83	3.7	7.4	7.4
1963–73	10.3	10.7	11.1
1953–63	8.9	4.4	7.8
Exports ($U.S. billions)†	146.8	24.4	25.1
Imports ($U.S. billions)†	125.0	26.2	20.3
Trade ratios (%):‡			
1983	30	85	101
1973	22	62	88
1963	20	20	37
1953	25	12	22

Sources: IMF, *International Financial Statistics* (Washington, D.C.); World Bank, *World Development Reports* (Washington, D.C.); Statistics Bureau, *Japan Statistical Yearbooks* (Tokyo); Economic Planning Board, *Korea Statistical Yearbooks* (Seoul); Directorate-General of Budget, Accounting and Statistics (DGBAS), *Statistical Yearbooks of the Republic of China* (Taipei).

* 1982.

† Merchandise only.

‡ Exports + imports (of goods and services) ÷ GNP.

continue in Korea. A third difference, more a matter of size than of development level, is the difference in dependence on trade. Japan's trade ratios (exports + imports/GNP) have ranged from 20% to 30% from 1953 to 1983. Taiwan's trade ratios have risen from 22% to 101% during the same period, Korea's from 12% to 85% (Table 1.1). These figures show the greater importance of trade in Korea and Taiwan, where smaller markets limit the range of economic specialization. They also reflect the possibility of large increases from small bases and, possibly, greater emphasis on policies that serve to expand exports.

The Record

Despite differences among the three countries that should make for dissimilar performances, each has an outstanding record of development. Whether a record is "outstanding" in this context is a relative matter that depends on how performance relates to that of comparable countries. Countries comparable with Japan might be the 19 countries in the World Bank's industrial-market economy category (which includes Japan), while for Taiwan and Korea, the 22 countries in the World Bank's upper middle-income group should be suitable referents. Annual growth in per capita GNP during 1965–83 averaged 3.8% for upper middle-income countries, 2.5% for industrial market economies. The same figures for Japan, Taiwan, and Korea were 4.8%, 6.5%, and 6.7%, respectively (Table 1.2). Though the long period conceals wide variation in performance (see the decadal GDP growth rates in Table 1.1, for instance), overall growth of "The Three" is clearly well above the average for comparable countries.

The increase in per capita GNP reveals little about the increase in GNP itself or the extent to which the individual benefits of economic growth have been eroded by population increase. Average annual population growth rates in Taiwan and Korea have been somewhat below the upper middle-income group average, while Japan's growth rate is a little above the industrial-market economy average (Table 1.2). In fact, population growth has been decelerating in all three countries in recent years. The slowdown is a product of decline in already low (crude) death rates that is more than offset by larger declines in (crude) birth rates. These declines, in turn, have been associated with better sanitation, public health services, and medical care in the case of death rates, and, for birth rates, with successful population planning programs and, with development, the increasing advantages of small family size.[1] While population deceleration is not an unmixed blessing, since lower population growth limits market-scale economies and labor-supply expansion, deceleration not only favors growth of per capita incomes but should also provide benefits from slower urbanization, lesser demands on infrastructure, and rising labor productivity, which are likely to more than offset the costs of slowdown.

Even where growth of GNP per capita has been satisfactory, employment

Table 1.2 Comparison of per capita GNP and population growth of Taiwan, South Korea, and Japan with reference groups (%)

	Average annual GNP/ capita growth rate, 1965–83	*Average annual population growth rate*	
		1965–73	*1973–83*
Upper-middle income group	3.8	2.4	2.3
Taiwan	6.5	2.1	1.9
South Korea	6.7	2.2	1.6
Industrial market economies	2.5	1.0	.7
Japan	4.8	1.2	.9

Sources: World Bank, *World Development Report, 1985* (New York), Tables 1, 5, 19, 25; Statistic Bureau, Management and Coordination Agency, *Japan Statistical Yearbook, 1984* (Tokyo); Directorate-General of Budget, Acccounting and Statistics (DGBAS), *Statistical Yearbooks of the Republic of China* (Taipei).

has often lagged and income inequality has risen. "The recent tendency, therefore, has been to downgrade GNP increase as a success indicator and to erect instead a trinity of objectives: full employment, a high growth rate of GNP per capita, and more equitable distribution of income."[2] The employment component of the trinity is ignored here on grounds that the status of workers and employment arrangements in countries like Japan, Taiwan, and Korea are sufficiently different from those that underlie traditional (Western) labor-force concepts as to make published statistics misleading indicators of labor-market conditions in general and of unemployment and underemployment in particular.[3]

The distribution component, however, is of particular interest because rapid growth is usually uneven, so that some sectors and regions do not participate fully in the benefits of development. Rapid growth that benefits all is preferable to that which does not, particularly if some population groups are left in poverty. Though poverty still exists among The Three, and distribution estimates are subject to major statistical problems that make comparison particularly treacherous, the available evidence indicates that incomes in Japan, Taiwan, and Korea are distributed more equally than in most countries and that rapid growth has generally not led to increasing income inequality.

Gini coefficients calculated for the 1967–72 period in OECD member countries average .366 before taxes, .350 after. The corresponding estimates for Japan (1969) were .335 and .316, respectively.[4] Distribution in Japan is not only somewhat less unequal than in other industrial economies, but the Gini coefficients also hide the unusually large income share of households at the low end of the income scale. Japan's lowest quintile received 8.7% of all household income in 1979, for example. The same group received only 5.3%–5.4% in the United States, France, and Australia.[5]

Low levels of inequality in Japan have been attributed to exclusion of income in kind (expense accounts, e.g., are more important than elsewhere and are concentrated at the top end of the income scale), relative absence of underprivileged minority groups, *zaibatsu* dissolution, postwar land reform and inflation, and a combination of high savings propensities in most income brackets and low rates of return on most savings. Such a low level of inequality is surprising because functional distribution is highly skewed toward income from assets and away from "participation" income (entrepreneurial income and employee compensation). This does not increase household income inequality, as might be expected, partly because the postwar reforms and high across-the-board household savings have reduced the concentration of private wealth and partly because Japanese firms have tended to invest rather than to distribute profits.[6] Distribution over time, finally, reflects the so-called Kuznets curve, or an inverted **U**-shaped pattern. Gini coefficients rose from 1953 to around 1960, when Japan reached the turning point from labor surplus to labor scarcity, and then declined to 1975 as the income gap between agricultural and nonagricultural households diminished and income differences within employee households narrowed.[7]

Income inequality in Taiwan has probably been among the world's lowest, given Gini coefficients (1978) of only .289 before taxes and .285 afterward.[8] These unusually low figures evidently resulted from a rising wage share even before the turning point (i.e., functional distribution did not deteriorate) and only a slight Kuznets effect for urban households. The rising wage share was promoted by land reform, as in Japan, by early adoption of measures to raise agricultural productivity, and by an unusually dispersed pattern of industry that benefited the rural poor. Among urban households, the decline in wage share was limited by the labor-using bias of technological change. After the turning point, which occurred around 1978, urban as well as rural wage shares rose and overall inequality dropped as Gini coefficients declined from .32–.33 in the late 1960s to .29 in the early 1970s.[9]

A recent article by H. Koo cites Gini coefficients for household income in Korea of .332 in 1970 and .389 in 1980.[10] Though inequality has been greater than in Taiwan, these coefficients are still low by international standards and have placed Korea in the low-inequality group of countries.[11] Postwar inflation, asset destruction during the Korean War, and property confiscation after the military coup in 1961 should have all contributed to equality. As in Japan and Taiwan, equality had been promoted by land reform in the immediate postwar years. Korea differs from the other two, however, in the behavior of inequality over time.

B. Renaud found little evidence that the size distribution of income was worsening during the first decade of rapid growth (1963–72) and also found "all major indicators *within* sectors . . . moving in the direction of more equality."[12] In subsequent years, though a turning point was reached around 1975, income inequality has evidently increased.[13] The increase, according to Koo, follows from the transfer of labor from agriculture to industry, where inequality is greater; the disappearance of the equity-promoting effects of labor-intensive, export-led industrialization by the early 1970s; and the Park regime's economic program. This last included policies that favor the *chaebol* (large conglomerate enterprises) at the expense of small businesses and the state's "corporatist" control of labor, which resulted in below-average wage increases for workers in manufacturing. Inflationary financing through monetary policy also hit low-income groups (wage earners and renters) hardest, as did rising tax regressivity after 1965, when the share of indirect taxes in total taxes increased.[14]

Though distribution patterns in each country have not always been the same, as seen in Korea's recent increase in income inequality, common elements would appear to dominate. The main one of these is the low level of income inequality. Also, the small differences between before-tax and after-tax Gini coefficients and evidence of relatively limited public expenditure for social and welfare purposes (see Table 1.3) indicate that redistributive fiscal policy has not been important in curbing inequality. Turning points constitute another common element. Each of the three reached a turning point in the 1960s or 1970s, when labor surplus gave way to scarcity and the real wage increases that followed most benefited those at the bottom end of the income scale. Finally, land reforms took place in each country early in the post-World War II period. Reform was initiated by outside forces; American military governments in Japan and Korea, Chiang Kai-shek's mainland followers in Taiwan. Order may be significant with land reform for, as I. Adelman has argued, radical asset redistribution (i.e., land reform) is more likely to precede than follow rapid growth.[15]

ECONOMIC CHARACTERISTICS

The economic record in Japan, Taiwan, and Korea can be traced to a set of common economic characteristics or factors that might be expected to cause rapid growth. These characteristics, which constitute the model, should be pronounced in each of the three countries, should play major rather than minor roles in their development, and should be connected in discernible ways to the growth process. The characteristics discussed below are clearly open to objection on any of these criteria, especially since they are present in differing degrees among the three and because it is difficult or impossible to establish significance for institutional and policy characteristics. The choice of characteristics might also be faulted for omitting important common aspects of growth. This is especially likely since the "model" is not a formal one that incorporates all inputs, outputs, and sources of increase in output per unit of input. Nevertheless, the three countries share basic characteristics that should meet most of the criteria listed above.

The East Asian model presented here is characterized by high investment ratios, small public sectors, export orientation, labor-market competition, and government intervention in economic matters. Heavy investment may be necessary to expand economic capacity and output, but it is not sufficient for rapid growth if allocated inefficiently or to activities that do not increase output. Patterns of investment by sector, by type, and according to relative factor intensity in each of The Three have, for the most part, been efficient and output promoting. Public-sector size is not directly related to growth but indirectly through allocation of government consumption and investment. Public sectors are likely to be relatively large where state-owned enterprise output is important (as in Sub-Saharan Africa) or where the share of welfare and social outlay is large (Sweden). Since government production is often subsidized and public social expenditure may supplement rather than replace private outlays, fewer resources remain for private or for "productive" (i.e., output-expanding) outlays.[16] The contrast with Japan, Taiwan, and Korea

Table 1.3 Comparison of central government expenditure patterns of Taiwan, South Korea, and Japan with reference groups, 1982 distribution (%)

	Defence	*Education*	*Health*	*Housing amenities, Social Security Welfare*	*Economic services*	*Other**
Upper-middle income group	11.5	10.9	5.1	21.0	20.8	30.7
Taiwan (1983)	48.0	5.6	1.3	12.6	14.3	18.2
South Korea	31.3	19.5	1.4	10.5	13.3	24.0
Industrial market economies	13.9	4.8	11.7	40.4	9.7	19.5
Japan †	7.9	14.8	1.3	32.5	29.3	14.2

Note:
* Covers general administration, unallocable.
† Author's estimate.

Sources: See Table 1.2.

could not be greater. Public sectors are small, shares of state-owned enterprises in GDP are low, and little of what is spent goes for social or welfare purposes.

A major interest in recent development literature has been the role of export expansion in economic growth. Output for export is assumed to generate scale economies not available when producing only for domestic markets. It should also do more to foster competition and the introduction of new technology than import substitution.[17] Of particular interest here are the reasons for exceptional export performance by The Three, and its effects on their development. One reason for such performance and, possibly, for rapid growth of aggregate output and low income inequality as well has undoubtedly been labor-market competition or open labor markets in which labor unions play little or no role. This competition, following Lewis's argument, allows continual transfer of labor from the subsistence to the capitalist sectors that might otherwise be blocked before the turning point by supply restrictions.[18] Absence of the sort of work rules associated with strong unions and limited time lost to labor disputes have also contributed to productivity and to output growth.

The role of government intervention in economic matters and the significance of industrial policy in the East Asian model is certain to be controversial. First, there are pronounced differences in policy-making style among The Three, though perhaps lesser differences in control instruments. Second, there is disagreement on whether public policy has played a principal part in development or only a supporting role. If government policy has been important, it has been most important in Korea, then in Japan, and least important in Taiwan. The public-policy issue and some of the other issues that arise in establishing the model's economic characteristics are considered below in the remainder of this section.

High investment ratios

Comparison of gross domestic investment in each of The Three with their reference-group averages shows that investment ratios (gross domestic investment ÷ GDP) in Taiwan were about average for a middle-income country, those for Korea have risen from below average in 1965 to a little above average in 1983, while investment in Japan has been considerably above the industrial market-economy average (Table 1.4). These estimates are misleading as indicators of investment effort in several ways. First, single-year figures do not always represent the years around them. The 1983 ratios for Taiwan (23%) and Korea (27%), for example, are well below their 1974–83 averages (29.5% and 29.6%, respectively).[19] Second, the estimates include investment in physical capital but not in human capital. Investment in human capital (i.e., education) should improve labor quality and thus raise productivity just as investment in physical capital does.[20]

Table 1.4 Comparison of investment, savings, and public consumption shares of GDP or Taiwan, South Korea, and Japan with reference groups (%)

	Gross domestic investment			*Gross domestic savings*			*Public consumption*		
	1965	*1983*	*1990*	*1965*	*1983*	*1990*	*1965*	*1983*	*1990*
Upper-middle income group	23	22	24	24	23	23	11	13	16
Taiwan	23	23		20	32		17	17	
South Korea	15	27	37	8	26	37	9	11	
Industrial market economies	23	20	22	23	20	22	15	18	17
Japan	32	28	33	33	30	34	8	10	9

Source: See Table 1.2.

While such investment is excluded from investment ratios in other countries, the evidence available indicates that educational expenditure of The Three has been above average, hence its exclusion downward biases their investment ratios as indicators of investment effort. Greater effort is reflected in enrollment data that show, for example, that secondary school and higher education enrollments as proportions of people in the relevant age groups are considerably higher in Taiwan and Korea than enrollments in comparable countries and are about the same in Japan (Table 1.5). What we want to know here is input (i.e., investment), not output, but this is difficult to ascertain because much of the investment is private rather than public. Data on total expenditure (public, private, in school, out of school) are available for Korea, however, which show that outlays have been large. In 1966–75, for instance, they averaged 9% of GNP, equivalent at the time to a third of investment in physical capital.[21]

The investment-growth relation, where investment may be narrowly or broadly defined, should depend on allocation, productivity, factor-input

Table 1.5 Comparison of educational efforts of Taiwan, South Korea, and Japan with reference groups, (as % of age groups)

	Primary school enrollment	*Secondary school enrollment*	*Higher education (20–24 years old)*
Upper-middle income group	102	51	14
Taiwan	100	85	19
South Korea	100	89	24
Industrial market economies	102	87	37
Japan	100	92	30

Source: See Table 1.2.

proportions, and efficiency in general, as well as on level of effort. "Allocation" here refers to investment by type of capital, and it should affect output according to the shares of investment in capital that contribute directly to output (machinery and other equipment), indirectly (social overhead capital), or not at all (residential construction). Only fragmentary estimates of capital stock are available that show (on a net basis), for example, that residential buildings make up a quarter of Japan's stock of reproducible fixed assets while producers' durables make up 22%. Estimates for the United States show a similar share for producers' durables (23%), but a much larger share for residential buildings (35%). While an increasing portion of investment in Taiwan and Korea has gone for housing in recent years, the share of residential building is still somewhat below Japanese and well below U.S. levels. The allocation estimates suggest, therefore, that investment allocation in The Three has favored output growth and has probably favored output growth more than allocation in comparable countries.[22]

Sources of growth are usually divided between increases in factor inputs and increases in output per unit of input (productivity). High investment ratios of The Three should therefore have greater impact on growth where capital intensity is low and productivity increase is high. (That is, where K = capital, L = labor, and Y = output,

$$\Delta K/\Delta Y = \Delta K/\Delta L \div \Delta Y/\Delta L,$$

$\Delta K/\Delta Y$ will be low and investment impact high if $\Delta K/\Delta L$ is low, $\Delta Y/\Delta L$ is high.) Capital coefficients have in fact been relatively low in Japan and even lower in Taiwan and Korea. (In 1965–70, e.g., $\Delta K/\Delta Y$ was 2.9 in Japan, 4.4 and more in the United States, United Kingdom, France, and West Germany; comparable figures for Taiwan and Korea were 1.5 and 2.1, respectively.)[23] One reason is that productivity increases have been large (output per worker rose 31% in Taiwan, 42% in Korea, and 59% in Japan during the same period) and have offset increases in capital intensity as capital accumulation outpaced employment expansion. Capital intensity, in turn, differs greatly among The Three, reflecting Japan's higher level of development. The estimates of capital intensity (here, K/L) suffer from problems of deriving capital stock estimates and, in this case, from exchange-rate conversion biases, but differences are too large to result simply from error or bias. In 1970, for example, K/L was $4,564 in Japan, $507 in Korea, and $510 in Taiwan (1965 U.S. dollars).[24] With the subsequent increases in capital intensity and the slowdown in growth rates after the first oil shock (see Table 1.1), capital coefficients have risen, too. Incremental capital-output ratios ($\Delta K/\Delta Y$) during the 1973–83 period averaged 8.2 for Japan, 5.5 in Taiwan, and 3.2 in Korea.

Investment allocated in ways that maximize output growth and productivity increase and is consistent with relative factor supplies should be efficient in economic terms. However, other considerations—national security, social welfare, retention of office—may constrain economic efficiency, and, furthermore, the time dimension makes assessments of efficiency much more complex. For example, though high levels of protection against agricultural imports have raised food prices, and consequently wage costs in countries like Japan and Korea, protection is maintained to satisfy political or security interests. Similarly, Taiwan's unusually large defense establishment has undoubtedly been supported by sacrificing some unknown amount of economic growth.

Also, rapid growth today may be inconsistent with rapid growth tomorrow. The rapidity of Japan's growth in the 1960s, for instance, should have speeded industrial pollution and environmentalist reaction and contributed to the postwar generation's opposition to their elders' emphasis on economic growth.[25] In addition, the time dimension may upset the factor-proportions criterion. That is, it may not be efficient to adopt technology that suits existing factor proportions. Efficiency may require, as T. Blumenthal says of Japan, adoption of capital-intensive techniques from the start "to prepare the way for future factor proportions."[26] The efficiency question, in sum, is too complex to answer by referring only to some economic indicator (e.g., low capital coefficients) without weighing noneconomic and temporal considerations. Perhaps we should be satisfied, with D. Perkins, that investment is efficient in the "absence of numerous white elephants."[27]

High rates of investment have been supported by high levels of domestic saving, particularly in Taiwan and Japan (Table 1.4). In fact, the two countries have become capital exporters in recent years as their current account surpluses have grown. Korea, in contrast, has been a major international borrower, with foreign saving (measured according to the current-account deficit) in 1974–83 accounting for 15% of total saving. Savings ratios (domestic saving ÷ GNP) in Korea rose from 15% in 1965 to 29% in 1979, before falling somewhat in the early 1980s, and averaged 22% for the 1965–83 period. While these ratios are close to upper-middle income group averages, they are significantly below those of the other two, which raises the issue of why saving has been high in Japan and Taiwan and less high in Korea.

Distributions of domestic saving by source for Japan (1978–84) and Taiwan and Korea (1974–83) show that corporate saving is minor in all countries, though somewhat higher in Korea (10% of the total) than in the other two (4%–5%). The share of government saving is high in Taiwan (30%), intermediate in Korea (22%), and low in Japan (8%). This leaves depreciation—which accounts for a quarter of the total in Taiwan, a third in Korea, over 40% in Japan—and household or personal saving. This last accounts for a smaller share of a smaller total in Korea, so it is the main source of the difference in saving performance.

Japan's unusually high levels of personal saving have been attributed to the occupational composition of households (a large proportion of nonfarm, self-employed with high savings propensities), high workers' savings ratios, the "bonus" effect (large bonuses provide transient income that is likely to be saved rather than consumed, according to Milton Friedman's permanent-income hypothesis), an unusual life-cycle pattern that features high saving by older households (possibly because social security benefits are low), limited consumer credit, shortage of liquid assets, and a high growth rate of real income.[28] Personal saving has remained high even after growth slowed in the early 1970s, however, so new explanations have been advanced for this phenomenon. One of these, proposed by Y. Kosai and Y. Ogino, stresses the very strong social and psychological motivation to save for the unexpected, for education, housing, and old age, or what the authors call "the growth of middle-class consciousness."[29]

Some of the factors thought responsible for high personal saving in Japan can also be found in Taiwan and Korea: the "bonus" effect (though bonuses are smaller), limited consumer credit, absence of social security, high rates of real income growth. While these may be responsible for Japan's and Taiwan's unusually high level of personal saving, they do not account for Korea's lower level. T. Scitovsky, who tried to explain the difference between Taiwan and Korea, found several reasons for Korea's lower household savings. Among these are the high outlays by Korean parents for their childrens' education. Data needed to show that Koreans spend more on education than Taiwanese are not available, but the idea seems to be that outlays for education are a substitute for saving. Another reason may be Taiwan's higher real rates of return on saving. While higher returns would ordinarily inspire less, not more saving, Scitovsky notes that the higher rates provide an alternative to reliance on family support in old age in the absence of social security. Also, personal saving in Taiwan may offer more opportunity for economic independence by starting one's own business. Growth there has occurred mainly through expansion in the numbers of (small) firms rather than, as in Korea, by expansion of existing (large) ones.[30] Other possible reasons for lower personal saving in Korea might include absence of "a cultural proclivity to save" that is found in Taiwan, or the effect of taxes that create a "differential wedge" between social and private returns.[31] Whatever the reason, lower personal saving has had to be offset by foreign borrowing to finance investment, and so Korea, unlike Japan and Taiwan, has become a major debtor nation.

Small public sectors

The share of government in economic activity, measured in expenditure terms, appears to be relatively low among The Three. Uncertainty about the relative size of public sectors follows from the incompleteness of measures, inconsistent definitions of "government," and possible intercountry differences in the relative prices of publicly and privately produced goods and services. Public consumption, the indicator shown in Table 1.4, is incomplete because it excludes public investment and public investment may vary significantly among countries. In 1977–79, for example, the proportion of GDP allocated by the Japanese government to capital formation (6.1%) was almost double that of other OECD countries.[32] In Korea, accounts of public and quasi-public enterprises (such as the tobacco monopoly and KEPCO, the Korea Electric Power Company) are included with the private sector and not—as is the practice elsewhere—with the public sector. Also, American military assistance is omitted from government budgets, national accounts, and balance-of-payments statements. Finally, prices of government services are likely to be relatively low in low-wage countries like Korea, thus understating real public output when such output is compared with that of other, higher-wage countries like Japan. Despite such measurement problems, it is still possible to say something about the economic size of governments, the ways in which public expenditures are allocated, and the possible relation between public-sector size and economic performance.

Public consumption as a proportion of GDP in Japan has been well below the average for all industrial market economies (see Tables 1.2–1.5). Even when government expenditure is expanded to include consolidated central and local capital expenditures and transfers as well as current expenditure, the expenditure ratio (government expenditure divided by GNP) in 1977–79 for Japan, 29.8%, was well below the OECD average of 44.6%.[33] One reason for Japan's relatively small public outlays, seen in Table 1.3, has been low expenditure on defense, health, social security, and welfare. This table includes only central government outlays and therefore excludes local government expenditures (45% of total government outlays in recent years), but shares of these categories in total outlays are also low.[34] Other reasons for Japan's low outlays have been relatively rapid GDP growth, which raises the denominator of the expenditure ratios, and slow growth of expenditure during the 1960s, when tax rates were reduced before the first oil shock began to raise expenditures from the mid-1970s.

Public consumption in Korea has been a little below the upper-middle income group average, and in Taiwan it has been somewhat above. Again, public investment should be added before calculating expenditure ratios, which would yield 1983 ratios of 17% for Korea and 24% for Taiwan. The functional breakdown of central government expenditures (Table 1.3), where central governments account for about two-thirds of general government outlays in each country, shows unusually high outlays on defense, low outlays on health, housing, social security, and welfare and, in Taiwan, on education. (This last is explained by local financing of education as education's share rises to 21% when local is added to central expenditure.) The share of defense in Taiwan is so large, in fact, that if it were reduced to the upper-middle income group average, Taiwan's public consumption (Table 1.4) would drop to 11%, the group average. Clearly, the geopolitical situation and recent histories of conflict with neighboring countries have created atypical defense needs in

Taiwan and Korea. These, in turn, skew the pattern of public expenditure and, evidently, increase public-sector size as well.

Other factors than defense considerations ought to influence the size and pattern of public expenditure. Since demand for government services is highly income elastic, the expenditure ratio should rise with per capita income so that high-income countries have relatively larger public sectors than low-income ones. There are also supply-side reasons for rising expenditure ratios. Government output is relatively labor intensive, and productivity increase has therefore lagged because capital could not be easily substituted for labor. Any expansion of real government output therefore requires that government expenditure ratios grow, too. Institutional factors should also play a role in public expenditure. It has been found, for instance, that federal systems have higher expenditure ratios than unitary systems. Local governments in federal systems can shift revenue-raising burdens to the central government and so spend more than would be possible under a unitary system with no higher level of government to finance their deficits. Similarly, coalition governments evidently "buy" coalition by funding members' expenditure requests and so have higher expenditure ratios than single-party governments. Finally, the size of the dependent population (young and old) might be expected to affect government outlays for education and social security.[35]

Cultural and social values that emphasize family responsibility for individual welfare are often invoked to explain small public-sector size in countries like Japan, Taiwan, and Korea ("small" if Taiwan's above-average defense outlays are excluded from expenditure totals). Also invoked is the widespread belief in these countries that the state's primary role is to promote economic development and take care of "production first." Some of the institutional factors mentioned above should also explain why public sectors are relatively small. For example, none of The Three have federal systems or coalition governments (except for a coalition of factions within Japan's Liberal Democratic Party [LDP]), so that there is less pressure than would otherwise prevail to seek voter support by promoting public programs. Though there are reasons for expecting public sectors to be small among The Three, there is still the question of why small public sectors should be associated with rapid economic growth.

The impact of an increase in government expenditure on economic growth is not clearly or unequivocally specified by ad hoc economic theorizing. To the extent that public is less efficient than private spending, expenditure ratios and economic growth should be inversely related. Similarly, if government consumption is competitive with private investment, an increase in government consumption might be expected to slow growth. However, government "consumption" includes outlays for health care and education, which in the broad sense are investment, not consumption. While theory may not clearly predict the impact of rising government spending on output growth, recent empirical work reveals something of the relation between the two. D. Landau tested this relation and various hypotheses relating growth to economic structure, scale economies, population increase, and other variables using data from the UN International Comparison Project for 96 countries during the 1961–76 period.[36] He found, for different sub-periods and sets of countries grouped by per capita income level, that there was a significant negative relation between expenditure shares and growth rates. He also found a positive relation between growth and the share of public consumption allocated to education, which is consistent with the high shares of education (after Taiwan's share is adjusted to include noncentral outlays) shown for The Three.

Landau did not, however, relate growth rates to defense expenditures. Defense expenditure has been unusually important in Taiwan and Korea, if not Japan, and might be expected to reduce growth by absorbing resources (particularly industrial types of resources) that might otherwise have gone into investment. However, E. Benoit has found a significant, positive correlation (for 44 developing countries in 1950–65) between the share of GDP devoted to defense and the growth rate of nonmilitary output.[37] The relation may be spurious because high defense burdens were associated with high levels of foreign assistance and high investment rates that were more likely to be responsible for the rapid growth of civilian output than the military expenditure itself. However, Benoit has argued that, in addition to the indirect effects of defense expenditure (e.g., attracting foreign aid, encouraging investment), there are direct positive effects such as the boosting of aggregate demand, utilization of otherwise idle capacity, provisions of inputs into the civilian economy (roads, etc.), and creation of modern, economically useful skills. Though such direct effects are difficult to measure, Benoit's results suggest that the positive effects of defense spending have outweighed the negative, resource-withdrawal effects in countries like Taiwan and Korea.

Competitive labor markets

One characteristic shared by The Three that should have contributed to rapid growth but that has received surprisingly little attention has been labor-market competition. That is, unions, governments, or other market institutions have played little or no role in restricting supply or raising wage costs. Output could therefore be rapidly expanded by increasing labor inputs since even in Japan—where an aging population and declining participation might have limited labor-force expansion after the early 1970s—there have been large numbers of persons without jobs but willing to work or employed in low-wage, low-productivity work.[38] Labor inputs have been higher—and wage costs lower—than might have otherwise been the case because few hours have been lost through strikes, workers have been increasingly well educated, and there has been little decline in unusually long working hours.[39] In addition, other, less measurable characteristics attributed to Japanese,

Taiwanese, and Korean workers, such as adaptability, hard work, and strong motivation, have undoubtedly played an important part in The Three's economic successes.

Labor-market characteristics are probably ignored or neglected in explaining economic development because the influence of institutional arrangements or worker attributes on productivity and output growth cannot be measured. Therefore we cannot assess their relative importance or even determine whether a particular institutional change has the same effect in different countries. Still, wage costs are a product of wages and productivity, while productivity is influenced by skill and effort as well as by capital inputs and technology. The export record shows that low wage costs gave Japan and later Taiwan and Korea considerable comparative advantage in labor-intensive manufactures. Similarly, recent emphasis on "knowledge-intensive" (for Japan) or "skill-intensive" (for Korea) production and increasing comparative advantage in more technologically sophisticated products follows from the heavy investment in human capital (Table 1.5) that has increased labor quality in each country. Labor-market characteristics are too important, in short, to be ignored in explaining the economic record of The Three.

Japanese labor markets have been distinguished by a seniority wage system (*nenko chingin seido*), rather than by one based mainly on job classification and skills; a lifetime employment commitment (*shushin koyo*) that covers perhaps a third of all employees; weak enterprise-level unions; and spring labor offensives (*shunto*).[40] Market organization is too complex and exception ridden to characterize properly here, and, furthermore, distinctly Japanese organizational characteristics may have less to do with labor performance than universal variables such as employee status and job satisfaction.[41] Nevertheless, these characteristics have functional consequences that are worth examining.

Under the *nenko* system, for example, wages are set according to length of service and occupational status rather than according to job skills, which might suggest that the system rewards seniority rather than productivity. The system, however, was designed to promote cooperation and subordination to authority and has been used in conjunction with lifetime employment mainly to help firms retain human capital in industries where rapidly changing technology requires substantial outlays for on-the-job training.[42] Lifetime employment, in turn, might appear to cause wage-cost inflexibility in that low-wage could not be substituted for high-wage workers, nor could wage bills be reduced in time of recession by laying off workers. Labor costs have in fact been flexible, though, because management can always choose between producing within the firm or subcontracting and can hire or release irregular employees and reduce bonuses and working hours.[43] Enterprise unions are weak because employee-group interests differ, union leadership changes frequently, and union officials typically retain their enterprise jobs with consequent conflict of interests.[44] Finally, the nation-wide spring strike ritual is an anomaly in a system that stresses harmony of interests, but any impact on wages has probably been less a result of the *shunto* than of tightness or slackness of supply.[45] We may conclude that the system provides more flexibility than might be expected, reduces job turnover rates, increases retention of firm-specific capital, and limits time lost to strikes as well.

Labor markets in Taiwan and Korea are little influenced by union activity since "in Taiwan employees are not allowed to strike," while in Korea labor laws were amended to ban strikes in 1971 and later modified to further restrict union activity.[46] Governments have intervened in labor markets, particularly in Korea, where the Chun regime established wage-price guidelines, required advance notice of layoffs, and stipulated various allowances under the Labor Standards Law. Such intervention has had only a limited impact on market behavior, however.[47] Market performance has also been criticized on grounds that recruiting has been misguided, training is inadequate, separation rates are too high, or that manpower supplies are imbalanced. Still, labor markets have been efficient enough for prevailing wages to clear the markets. If there have been factor-market distortions, they have occurred in capital markets where—as in Korea—bank lending rates have been set (too low) by the government and excess demand for loans has been curbed by credit rationing.[48]

Though labor markets may be relatively free of government regulation or union intervention and, therefore, perform well as markets, market solutions do not necessarily conform to generally accepted social or economic standards. Factory workers in Taiwan and Korea suffer from long hours, low pay, poor working conditions, sex discrimination, and consequent low job satisfaction and high frustration.[49] Unions are too weak to protect workers from such ills, nor have governments shown much interest in protecting them. However, unfettered labor markets have undoubtedly been necessary if not sufficient for rapid labor absorption and spectacular increases in real wages and high-quality employment in The Three.[50] These increases have probably done more to improve the economic welfare of workers than any feasible combination of government regulation and union intervention.

Export expansion

Unusually rapid export growth, one of the hallmarks of The Three, has increased the importance of exports in each country's output structure. In 1983 the export share of GDP rose from 11% in 1965 to 14% in Japan, from 9% to 37% in Korea, and from 19% to 55% in Taiwan. Export growth rates responsible for increasing export orientation have been well above reference-group averages even after the first oil shock. Annual growth of exports in middle-income countries averaged .5% in 1973–83; the figures for Taiwan and Korea were 11.8% and 14.8%, respectively. Exports of industrial market economies rose at an annual average rate of 4.2% during the same period; in Japan, the figure was 7.4%. Such unusual behavior is of particular interest in evaluating development. In this case, it raises questions of why exports expanded so rapidly and of how export expansion contributed to above-average growth rates.

The foundation of Japan's subsequent export acceleration was established in the 1950s with the aid of plans formulated by MITI (Ministry of International Trade and Industry) to modernize and rationalize the heavy manufacturing and chemical industries. Various forms of export promotion were adopted, quotas were used to provide protection from import competition, and local firms were encouraged to buy or license foreign technology.[51] Marketing, financing, absorption of exchange risk, materials acquisition, and transport-insurance-storage functions were largely handled by the *sogo shosha*, or general trading companies. During the 1960s, when GNP grew even faster than envisaged under Premier Ikeda's income-doubling plan, growth was export led in that the fastest growing sector was manufacturing and, within manufacturing, output for export grew faster than output for the domestic market. Export growth from 1961 to 1971 has been attributed to four factors: growth of world income and trade, increased Japanese price competitiveness, structural changes that expanded manufacturing output capacity, and liberalization of foreign commercial policy. Of these, the first and third were particularly important and accounted for four-fifths of the growth.[52] The same factors, operating in reverse, can be cited as reasons for the halving of Japan's export growth after the first oil shock.

Taiwan and Korea used the usual policy array of tariffs, quotas, and multiple exchange rates to promote import substitution after independence. With the end of easy import substitution and the consequent slowing of economic development, Taiwan and Korea undertook a "second postwar restructuring" in which currencies were unified and devalued and import restrictions eased.[53] These changes only evened the field in which import substitutes and exports were competing; credit preference, tax exemptions, and other more direct measures were also adopted to promote exports so that "the domestic rewards for exporting . . . [were] at least equal to, and possibly greater than, the rewards that would exist under free trade."[54] Restructuring or liberalization generated a manyfold increase in exports as the new policies unleashed each country's considerable comparative advantage in producing labor-intensive manufactures. Though balance-of-payments effects of the two oil shocks were particularly severe in Taiwan and Korea, the two countries recovered well because—unlike some other developing countries—they maintained their "outward-oriented" strategies and have continued to expand exports and export-market shares.[55]

Common elements in the export record of The Three provide reasons why exports grew so fast in each country. One was the combination of exchange-rate depreciation (or failure to appreciate in Japan) and promotion measures that tilted incentives in favor of exports rather than import substitutes. Another was the rapid growth of world income during the 1960s and the beginning of the 1970s that increased demand for any country's exports. If one asks why The Three were able to increase their shares of an increasing export total, the answer goes beyond enabling policies to their considerable comparative advantage in labor-intensive manufactures and, later, in increasingly capital-intensive or skill-intensive products.[56] An important element in this advantage was undoubtedly their competitive labor markets that served to hold down wage costs. Finally, exports continued to expand even after the oil shocks of the 1970s slowed the growth of world income. Continued expansion under such unfavorable circumstances can be traced to active promotion measures and to industrial policies that have favored new industries with export potential.[57]

While a relation has been established between export expansion and superior growth performance, we do not fully understand why performance should be much better in export-promotion than in import-substitution regimes. Export expansion contributes directly to GNP growth, of course, but this cannot explain much of GNP growth in countries like Japan where exports have accounted for only 10%–15% of GNP. Also, because The Three are poor in natural resources, the import content of exports is high so that the effect of export expansion on GNP growth is offset to some extent by a coincident increase in imports.[58] In addition, other, indirect effects of export expansion may play a role in GNP growth. Export markets are much larger than domestic markets so that the benefits of scale economies, specialization, and division of labor are more available to exporters than to producers for the domestic market. Also, export industries should affect growth through their influence on other, nonexport industries. Blumenthal has shown that in Japan, for example, export industries buy more from other industries per unit of output, or are more highly integrated into the economy, than nonexport industries. He also cites Mitsuo Saito's estimates of technological change that show the rate of technological change to be higher in export than in other industries.[59] In addition, increase in export earnings permits import expansion and, in the case of Korea, an increase in foreign borrowing that has been used to raise investment levels and, hence, output growth.[60]

Other possible effects on overall growth of an export-oriented trade regime stem from policy and economic behavior. Economic behavior is better in export-oriented than in import-substitution regimes because firms must compete with others in international markets rather than rely on the protection of sheltered domestic markets. Growth also occurs through the expansion of the more efficient producers rather than the more protected ones. Export-promotion strategies were initiated in Taiwan and Korea by devaluation, liberalizing imports, and reducing the web of controls needed to protect domestic producers. In each case there were benefits from avoiding the restrictions required by import-substitution policies that had distorted relative prices and from avoiding the foreign-exchange crises (associated with import substitution) that had led to stop-go macroeconomic policies. Finally, though the success of the export-promotion strategies was not assured at first and the new policies faced opposition from import-substitution interests, "success breeds success." When the new trade regimes eventually succeeded, they received the public support that has preserved them to this day.[61]

Government intervention

The standard instruments of monetary, fiscal, or commercial policy should influence economic behavior and economic variables such as income distribution, factor shares, and economic structure even in the most market-oriented economy, especially where public sectors are large. Since public sectors are small in The Three, yet governments have been more than usually influential in economic matters, influence must come from using standard macroeconomic instruments in new ways or from developing different means to reach policy goals. Any review of economic policies in The Three shows that both routes to influence have been taken, and that each government employs some form of industrial policy to influence the course of development. The extent as well as the effect of intervention is open to different interpretations. Opposite policies have been used at different stages of development and it is not easy to accept that actions to encourage as well as to reduce competition, for instance, both involve intervention. Still, review of public policy suggests that intervention has been pervasive in The Three, and has probably been greatest in Korea, least in Taiwan.

Government intervention in Taiwan stems from a "strong tradition of state interference in the management of economic activity."[62] Perhaps the best-known example was the *kuan-tu-shang-pan* ("official supervision, merchant management") system during the T'ung-chih Restoration of the 1860s.[63] The tradition was reinforced by Sun Yatsen's belief that planning was needed even in a market-oriented economy, by his goal of high growth rates and stability, and by his view that all groups should share the benefits of development. These views are reflected in Taiwan's land reform of 1949–55 and the reduction of trade controls and unification of exchange rates that began in 1958. Subsequently, resources have been directed toward construction of modern factories, export processing zones, and, recently, to a park for high-technology firms at Hsinchu. There have also been periodic drives to expand infrastructure in order to keep up with private-sector growth (the Ten Major Development Projects of 1974, the Twelve of 1979). Coordination of these policies was provided from the mid-1960s by the CIECD (Council for International Economic Cooperation and Development), later by the EPC (Economic Planning Council) and more recently by the FEC (Financial and Economic Committee) and the EPDC (Economic Planning and Development Council). Characteristic of intervention has been the attempt to balance public needs (mainly defense) with a desire to encourage private enterprise.

In Japan, the first phase of postwar intervention was marked by MITI's efforts to revive and expand basic industries from 1949 to the mid-1960s. Then accession to GATT, the IMF, and the OECD required liberalization of commercial policy, while industrial-policy emphasis shifted from heavy to "knowledge-intensive" industries. Since the first oil shock, emphasis shifted once more to cost reduction with economic deceleration, restructuring and assistance for declining (mainly energy-intensive) industries, and expanding public investment to offset the deflationary effects of slower GNP growth on private investment.[64] Intervention has taken many forms, including administrative guidance, MITI's "visions" of desirable future trends, government-business consensus building, tax incentives, credit allocation through the Bank of Japan's "window guidance," financial intermediation (postal savings have been allocated by the Ministry of Finance's Fiscal Investment and Loan Program, or FILP, to policy-implementation organizations such as the Japan Development Bank and the Export-Import Bank), import and foreign-investment controls, licensing of foreign-technology imports, and direct subsidies to research and development projects. The government has also encouraged a form of competition—Eleanor Hadley's "cut-throat oligopoly"—and indirectly subsidized loans to priority sectors.[65] Of these policy instruments, administrative guidance is particularly important. It is much stronger than elsewhere, possibly for cultural or historical reasons, but mainly because high-level civil servants often assume important business positions on retirement.[66] Administrative guidance also illustrates another Japanese characteristic, which is the discrepancy between form and content that may conceal the actual strength or significance of policy instruments and policy institutions.

Government intervention in the Korean economy since the early 1960s has operated within a framework of 5-year plans, annual budgets and, from 1980, medium-term fiscal plans. Planning, budgeting, and performance evaluation have been combined under the EPB (Economic Planning Board), while the president monitors large-scale projects.[67] With only occasional exceptions, the means used to implement plans have not been specified in the plans but have included the usual array of tax incentives, import protection, export-promotion devices, credit preference, and industry targeting. Credit allocation and foreign-loan guarantees have been particularly potent instruments in Korea because large firms have had no financial affiliates (as have the postwar Japanese conglomerates, or the *keiretsu*) and have been even more highly leveraged than their Japanese counterparts. Evidence of intervention was particularly apparent during the late 1970s, in the expansion of heavy and chemical industries, but has also been seen in the drive to adopt the new *Tongil* high-yield rice variety after 1974, the recent emphasis on development of "skill-intensive" manufactures, and export targeting in which monthly meetings of the president, top bureaucrats, export-association executives, and large firm heads became the focus of a national drive to expand exports.[68]

One distinctive feature of government intervention has been the unequal roles of government and business, so that "Korea, Inc." is much more apt in describing the local scene than "Japan, Inc." was in describing government-business relations in Japan.[69] Also, the strength of the system is less in the planning than in effective implementation, which distinguishes Korea from most other developing countries.[70] A statement by President Chun in 1982 calling for "institutional reforms to strengthen the functioning of the market mechanism" might appear to mark the end of "Korea, Inc." and government intervention. The slow pace of subsequent reforms indicates, however, that the imminent demise of intervention is unlikely.[71]

The effect of government policies on the pace of development is difficult to determine. One reason is that there are no clear relations between means and objectives as is true of traditional fiscal and monetary policies. Another reason is that the means employed have been largely indirect rather than direct so that credit subsidies, tax incentives, and the more visible policy instruments may not be as significant as administrative guidance and other less visible means. In addition, timing, political, and implementation variables intervene between policy and development. The Three, even Korea, have had unusually stable governments so that they could adopt long-run policies that anticipate rather than simply react to changing circumstances. Implementation has been effective not only because it has been uninterrupted by short-term political changes but also because political developments removed or reduced competition from business and labor. In addition, bureaucracies have been responsive to policy directives so that, when policy decisions are made, they can be implemented.

Though local conditions may have favored effective government intervention, policies can be misguided and, more important, intervention may play a secondary role in The Three's economic performance. Recent controversy over Japan's industrial policy has focused on this issue, with a revisionist view holding that free-market forces rather than industrial policy have been responsible for Japan's economic success.[72] The difficulties of establishing the effects of policy on growth and the exogenous role of government in economists' paradigms are responsible for the controversy. It is not likely to be resolved until more is known of the intervening institutional variables or, as P. Trezise has put it, until we know how MITI's administrative guidance "translates into decision making at the level of the firm."[73]

CONCLUSION

The East Asian model of economic development set forth here has focused on five shared characteristics that seem significant in the contemporary economic development of Japan, Taiwan, and Korea. They are economic characteristics and include high investment ratios, small public sectors, competitive labor markets, export expansion, and government intervention in the economy. These economic characteristics are not found only in The Three, though, taken together, they may be; nor are they the only economic characteristics that account for economic success. Large and efficient investments in human capital and well-developed capacities to absorb new technology are two other economic features shared by The Three that immediately come to mind in constructing an East Asian model. One could add overcrowding (high man/land ratios) and scarcity of natural resources, though, taken at face value, these are handicaps rather than sources of economic strength. It is possible, however, that virtue springs from necessity and that ample arable land or abundant natural resources mainly permit governments to postpone the difficult decisions needed to promote development rather than provide the wherewithal needed to finance development. Though the list of economic characteristics examined is not exhaustive, it should include most of those that have been significant in explaining the economic performance of The Three.

Other, noneconomic characteristics of The Three, such as ethnic and linguistic homogeneity, relatively compact geography, manageable population size, and the Confucian tradition have not been considered in the model even though they have undoubtedly influenced labor productivity, savings behavior, and other aspects of economic performance. They are excluded because, like land area and natural resources, they are given and therefore not subject to policy action or are social, cultural, and political characteristics that are only slightly less amenable to intervention. If a model is to serve any useful purpose, it should, as noted earlier, be replicable and therefore deal in variables that can be influenced by policy. The economic characteristics examined here are all subject to policy manipulation, so the issue is not so much whether they can be reproduced but whether they ought to be reproduced.

The idea that replication is feasible needs to be qualified because history does not repeat itself. For example, when P. T. Bauer argued that Nurkse's vicious-circle thesis was invalid as "it is inconsistent with the very existence of developed countries" all of which "started by being underdeveloped," he failed to consider that today's developed countries were developing in an era when there were no other more economically advanced countries, whereas today's less developed countries not only face competition from already more developed countries but can take advantage of being latecomers.[74] As A. Gerschenkron has noted, "the industrial history of Europe appears not as a series of mere repetitions of the 'first' industrialization but as an orderly system of graduated deviations from that industrialization" and that "the more delayed the industrial development of a country, the more explosive was the great spurt of its industrialization."[75] Latecomers, in short, do not have to reinvent the wheel or the spinning jenny. Their growth is likely to be more rapid and to take forms different from those of their predecessors.

Whether the East Asian model ought to be followed depends on whether current and foreseeable circumstances are sufficiently like those faced by The Three to justify using the same policies that they used. The slowdown of international trade that followed the oil shocks of the 1970s and the deflation in the early 1980s, which have both contributed to current protectionism, provide a case in point. Since circumstances are now less favorable for export expansion, neo-trade pessimists have argued that other countries cannot expect to repeat The Three's earlier success. It has also been argued that if others try to emulate the successful exporters, rising import penetration would be met with increased protection.[76] These arguments are mistaken. They are inconsistent with the facts because a dozen new exporting countries (NECs) had already expanded their manufactured exports more rapidly than did the newly industrialized countries (NICs) during the 1970s.[77] Also, the penetration argument ignores product cycles and shifting comparative advantage. New exports displace as well as add to existing exports when comparative advantage shifts and other countries begin to export later in the product cycle. In addition, export performance is mainly a function of domestic supply conditions, not external demand. How else can we explain the increasing share of The Three's exports in world markets even after the slowdown in world trade that followed the first oil shock?[78]

Applicability of the East Asian model should also depend on whether the strategy employed by The Three has been responsible for their economic success. This issue is unlikely to be settled soon, but similar strategies have been associated with similar results, and there are enough plausible connections between the two to indicate that the policy set used by The Three was at least partly responsible for their economic success. The strategy, to recapitulate briefly, emphasized rapid growth based on high rates of investment. This has been mainly private investment as public sectors were kept small. In addition, labor market competition has been preserved and output for export encouraged. Government intervention, though restricted by the need to keep exports competitive, has been pervasive. Intervention, by providing information and reducing risk, has been indirect as well as direct and has been primarily aimed at altering the structure of production to anticipate changes in demand and in comparative advantage.

Two aspects of the East Asian model's policy features are noteworthy. One is that policy typically works by influencing rather than replacing private market decisions. This reduces conflict between public-policy and competitive-market solutions for economic problems. Another is the heavy emphasis on economic growth and the public's expectation that the government will intervene in the economy to promote growth. This emphasis on growth means that dynamic rather than static considerations are paramount, and dynamic efficiency is a topic about which the traditional neoclassical market paradigm has surprisingly little to say. Though the growth imperative has not prevented major mistakes, it has focused priorities so that policies are reasonably consistent and efficient. This is very different from the sort of stop-go, ad hoc, contradictory policies found elsewhere. The contrast suggests that policymakers in many countries, not only developing ones, need to know more about the economic characteristics of the East Asian model.

ACKNOWLEDGMENTS

This article was prepared for a conference, "Why Does Overcrowded, Resource-poor East Asia Succeed—Lessons for the LDCs?" to celebrate the thirtieth anniversary of Vanderbilt University's graduate program in economic development, Nashville, October 17–19, 1986.

NOTES

1 Population per physician, e.g., dropped 20% on average from 1965 to 1980 in upper-middle income countries. The decline was 30% in Taiwan, 47% in Korea. Also, each country has instituted an official family planning program: Korea in 1963, Taiwan in 1974. The evidence suggests that program acceptance has acted to decrease fertility. See Albert I. Hermalin. "Taiwan: Appraising the Effect of a Family Planning Program through a Real Analysis," in *Essays on the Population of Taiwan* (Taipei: Institute of Economics, Academia Sinica, 1973), pp. 73–113; and Peter J. Donaldson, "Evolution of the Korean Family-Planning System," in *Economic Development, Population Policy, and Demographic Transition in the Republic of Korea*, by Robert Repetto et al. (Cambridge, Mass.: Harvard University Press, 1981), pp. 222–58.

2 Lloyd Reynolds, "China as a Less Developed Economy," *American Economic Review* 65 (June 1975): 418.

3 In Korea, e.g., more than half of all employed persons in 1982 were self-employed or family workers who do not risk unemployment. The utility of conventional labor-force classifications is examined in Henry Bruton's "Unemployment Problems and Policies in Less Developed Countries," *American Economic Review* 66 (May 1978): 51–5.

4 Malcolm Sawyer, *Income Distribution in OECD Countries.* OECD Occasional Study (Paris: OECD, 1976). pp. 16–17

5 World Bank, *World Development Report, 1985* (New York: World Bank), table 28.

6 Andrea Boltho, *Japan: An Economic Survey, 1953–73* (London: Oxford University Press, 1975), pp. 168, 182.

7 Toshiyuki Mizoguchi and Noriyuki Takayama, *Equity and Poverty under Rapid Economic Growth: The Japanese Experience* (Tokyo: Kinokuniya; Hitotsubashi University, Institute of Economic Research, 1984), pp. 46–7. The turning point has been dated by Ryoshin Minami, "The Turning Point in the Japanese Economy," *Quarterly Journal of Economics* 82 (August 1968): 380–402, and "Further Considerations on the Turning Point in the Japanese Economy," pts. 1 and 2 *Hitotsubashi Journal of Economics* 10 (February 1970): 18–60 and 11 (June 1970): 58–112.

8 Shirley W. Y. Kuo, Gustav Ranis, and John C. H. Fei, *The Taiwan Success Story* (Boulder, Colo.: Westview Press, 1981), p. 140.

9 John C. H. Fei, Gustav Ranis, and Shirley W. Y. Kuo, *Growth with Equity: The Taiwan Case* (New York and London: Oxford University Press; Washington, D.C.: World Bank, 1979), pp. 83–4, 126–9. The turning point was dated by Fei and Ranis in "A Model of Growth and Employment in the Open Dualistic Economy: The Cases of Korea and Taiwan," *Journal of Developmental Studies* 11 (January 1975): 32–63.

10 Hagen Koo, "The Political Economy of Income Distribution in South Korea: The Impact of the State's Industrialization Policies," *World Development* 12 (October 1984): 1030. Though not identified, these are probably after-tax estimates.

11 Hollis Chenery et al., *Redistribution with Growth* (London: Oxford University Press; Washington, D.C.: World Bank; and University of Sussex, Sussex: Institute of Development Studies, 1974), table 1.1

12 Bertrand Renaud, "Economic Growth and Income Inequality," in *Korea: A Decade of Development*, ed. Yunshik Chang (Seoul: Seoul National University Press, 1980), pp. 111–41. Possible widening of between-sector income differentials has been questioned by Choo (Choo Hakchung, *Widening Urban-Rural Income Differentials in Korea: A Re-examination*, KDI Working Paper no. 82-05 [Seoul: Korea Development Institute, 1982]).

13 Bai Moo-ki, "The Turning Point in the Korean Economy," *Developing Economies* 20 (June 1982): 130–8.

14 Koo, pp. 1031–5.

15 Irma Adelman, "Development Economics—A Reassessment of Goals," *American Economic Review* 66 (May 1975): 302–9.

16 State-enterprise output is frequently priced below cost when the output is a wage good, such as bus fares, that affects wage costs and hence export competitiveness. Below-cost pricing increases budget deficits and, to the extent that deficits are financed by inflationary means, also contributes to the distortions (such as exchange-rate overvaluation) that inhibit growth.

17 See Donald B. Keesing, "Outward-looking Policies and Economic Development," *Economic Journal* 77 (June 1967): 303–20. The case for export has been strengthened recently by econometric analysis of marginal factor productivities for export and nonexport sectors (Gershon Feder, *On Exports and Economic Growth*, World Bank Staff Working Paper no. 508 [Washington, D.C.: World Bank, February 1982]).

18 W. Arthur Lewis, "Economic Development with Unlimited Supplies of Labour," *Manchester School of Economic and Social Studies* 22 (May 1954): 139–91.

19 These last are simple (unweighted) averages of annual ratios calculated in current prices.

20 This is recognized in growth accounting studies where, e.g., almost a quarter of GNP growth in the United States from 1929 to 1957 was traced to additional education (Edward F. Denison, *The Sources of Economic Growth in the United States and the Alternatives before Us* [New York: Committee for Economic Development, 1962], p. 73).

21 The government covered about half of in-school expenditure during this period. Out-of-school expenditure (for books, transport, extracurricular activities, and room and board) is privately financed, and accounted for 40%–50% of the total (Noel F. McGinn et al., *Education and Development in Korea* [Cambridge, Mass.: Harvard University Press, 1980], pp. 15–28).

22 Evidence in point, besides Japan's relatively small housing stock, has been Korea's high ratios of urban households to urban housing units (Bertrand Renaud et al., "The Demand for Housing in Developing Countries: The Case of Korea," *Journal of Urban Economics* 7 [1980]: 317). Power shortages, transport bottlenecks, and other signs of inadequate investment in infrastructure in Korea during the late 1960s, and in Taiwan during the early 1970s, are also evidence of allocation that has favored output growth rather than demand for public amenities or social capital.

23 Yutaka Kosai and Yoshitaro Ogino, *The Contemporary Japanese Economy* (Armonk, N.Y.: M. E. Sharpe, 1984), p. 4. Estimates for Taiwan and Korea are mine.

24 The estimate for Japan is from Kosai and Ogino, p. 5; for Taiwan, from Shirley W. Kuo, "The Economic Development of Taiwan," in *Economic Development in Taiwan*, ed. Kowie Chang (Taipei: Cheng Chung Books, 1968), pp. 88–90; for Korea,

from Wontack Hong, "Capital Accumulation, Factor Substitution, and the Changing Factor Intensity of Trade: The Case of Korea (1966–1972)," in *Trade and Development in Korea*, eds. Wontack Hong and Anne O. Krueger (Seoul: Korea Development Institute, 1975), p. 68.

25 On reaction to the priority accorded economic growth, see Takafusa Nakamura, *The Postwar Japanese Economy* (Tokyo: University of Tokyo Press, 1981), pp. 209–11. On environmental damage and the reaction to it, see John W. Bennett and Solomon B. Levine, "Industrialization and Social Deprivation: Welfare, Environment, and the Postindustrial Society in Japan," in *Japanese Industrialization and its Social Consequences*, ed. Hugh Patrick (Berkeley and Los Angeles: University of California Press, 1976), pp. 439–92.

26 Tuvia Blumenthal, "Factor Proportions and the Choice of Technology: The Japanese Experience," *Economic Development and Cultural Change* 28 (April 1980): 559.

27 Dwight H. Perkins, "Plans and Their Implementation in the People's Republic of China," *American Economic Review* 63 (May 1973): 229.

28 Toshiyuki Mizoguchi, *Personal Savings and Consumption in Postwar Japan* (Tokyo: Kinokuniya, 1970), chaps. 1–3. See also Milton Friedman, *A Theory of the Consumption Function* (Princeton, N.J.: National Bureau of Economic Research, 1957).

29 Kosai and Ogino, pp. 113–17.

30 Tibor Scitovsky, "Economic Development in Taiwan and South Korea, 1965–1982," in *Models of Development: A Comparative Study of Economic Growth in South Korea and Taiwan*, ed. Lawrence J. Lau (San Francisco: Institute for Contemporary Studies, 1986), pp. 170–8.

31 Ramon H. Myers, "The Economic Development of the Republic of China on Taiwan, 1965–1981," in Lau, ed., p. 19. The concept of "differential wedge" is Williamson's (Jeffrey G. Williamson, "Why Do Koreans Save 'So Little'?" *Journal of Development Economics* 6 [September 1979]: 343–62).

32 Frank Gould, "Public Expenditure in Japan: A Comparative View," *Hitotsubashi Journal of Economics* 23 (February 1983): 62 (Table 5).

33 Ibid., p. 58 (table 1).

34 Composition of expenditure by economic (functional) category is shown here for central governments only, though total outlays by all levels of government would be preferable. The latter could not be used, however, without sacrificing comparison with the World Bank's country groupings that are limited to central-government consumption.

35 Paul L. Solano, "Institutional Explanation of Public Expenditure among High-Income Democracies," *Public Finance* 38 (1983): 440–58.

36 David Landau, "Government Expenditure and Economic Growth: A Cross-Country Study," *Southern Economic Journal* 38 (1983): 738–92.

37 Emile Benoit, *Defense and Economic Growth in Developing Countries* (Lexington, Mass.: Lexington Books, 1973).

38 Boltho (n. 6 above), pp. 111–15.

39 This has been particularly true of Taiwan and Korea. In manufacturing, e.g., from 1973–83 Taiwan's average work week dropped less than 1% a year to 48.2 hours in 1983. In Korea, from 1972–82 the average work week rose from 56.0 to 58.7 hours!

40 Job turnover is much lower in Japan than in the United States; e.g., earnings profiles are steeper (particularly with respect to firm-specific tenure), and these differences hold for small as well as for large firms (Masanori Hashimoto and John Raisian, "Employment Tenure and Earnings Profiles in Japan and the United States," *American Economic Review* 75 [September 1985]: 721–35).

41 Robert M. Marsh and Hiroshi Mannari, *Modernization and the Japanese Factory* (Princeton, N.J.: Princeton University Press, 1976), p. 337.

42 Yasukichi Yasuba, "The Evolution of Dualistic Wage Structure," in Patrick, ed. (n. 25 above), pp. 249–99.

43 After the first oil shock, with the aid of a new employment insurance law that offset costs of firms in depressed industries that furloughed workers with pay, large (500 or more workers) manufacturing firms reduced employment through "management slimming" (*genryo keiei*) by more than 800,000 workers from 1974 to 1978, or 19% of the 1974 level (Nakamura [n. 25 above], pp. 250–2).

44 "Becoming a union officer does not mean giving up promotions in the enterprise. On the contrary, it often leads to promising careers within management" (Hisashi Kawada, "Workers and Their Organizations," in *Workers and Employers in Japan: The Japanese Employment Relations System*, ed. Kazuo Okochi, Bernard Karsh, and Solomon B. Levine [Tokyo: Tokyo University Press; Princeton, N.J.: Princeton University Press, 1973], p. 235).

45 Real wage increases average 15.8% a year in manufacturing from 1965 to 1973, e.g., but only 1.4% a year from 1973 to 1983.

46 Joseph S. Lee, "An Empirical Study of the Functioning of the Labor Market in Taiwan," *Academia Economic Papers* 8 (March 1980): 181. The strike ban was repealed in Korea in 1981, but union power was reduced by restricting union shop contracts (negotiable only with management's consent), limiting collective bargaining to the enterprise level, and prohibiting union locals from accepting outside help. Union membership, already low (only 23% of organizable workers in 1979), declined subsequently (Bai Moo-ki, "Structural Transformation of the Korean Labor Economy," *Korean Economic Journal* 21 [December 1982]: 606 [in Korean]).

47 Kim Sookun, *Employment, Wages, and Manpower Policies in Korea: The Issues*, Korea Development Institute Working Paper Series 82-04 (Seoul: Korea Development Institute, August 1982), pp. 57–8, 65–8.

48 "Although . . . capital was implicitly subsidized through a variety of credit-rationing devices, the Korean labor market seems to have been fairly distortion free by the late 1960s" (Wontack Hong, "Export Promotion and Employment Growth in South Korea," in *Trade and Employment in Developing Countries*, ed. Anne O. Krueger, Hal B. Lary, Terry Monson, and Narongchai Akrasanee [Chicago: National Bureau of Economic Research; University of Chicago Press, 1981], 1:353).

49 Lee, pp. 17–79; Oh Sun-joo, "The Living Conditions of Female Workers in Korea," *Korea Observer* 16 (Summer 1983): 185–200.

50 Industrial wages tend to be higher than service-sector wages, employment for wages is more desirable than unpaid family work, and most industrial jobs are located in urban areas where living conditions are evidently more appealing than in rural areas. In manufacturing, the major industrial category, employment rose from 1965 to 1973 at an average annual rate of 3% in Japan, 10% in Korea, and 11% in Taiwan. Annual increases in real manufacturing wages average 9% in Taiwan and Korea and 16% in Japan. Even after the first oil shock, manufacturing employment continued to rise significantly in Taiwan and Korea (5% and 6% a year, respectively, from 1972 to 1983), as did real wages (6% and 8% respectively).

51 Though technology acquisition in Japan could be explained by the desire to close a technology gap caused by prewar and wartime isolation, Blumenthal was arguing in the mid-1970s that this explanation no longer held (Tuvia Blumenthal, "Japan's Technological Strategy," *Journal of Developing Areas* 10 [July 1976]: 245–55).

52 Lawrence B. Krause and Sueo Sekiguchi, "Japan and the World Economy," in *Asia's New Giant*, ed. Hugh Patrick and Henry Rosovsky (Washington, D.C.: Brookings Institution, 1976), pp. 418–23.

53 Analyses of Taiwan's trade policies are given in Samuel P. S. Ho, *Economic Development in Taiwan: 1860–1970* (New Haven, Conn.: Yale University Press, 1978), pp. 190–8; and Maurice Scott, "Foreign Trade," in *Economic Growth and Structural Change in Taiwan*, ed. Walter Galenson (Ithaca, N.Y.: Cornell University Press, 1979), pp. 314–45. Also T. S. Lee, K. S. Liang, et al., "The Structure of Effective Protection and Subsidy in Taiwan," *Economic Essays* (National Taiwan University) (November 1975), 6: 55–175. For Korea, see S. Kanesa-Thasan, "Stabilizing an Economy: The Korean Experience," in *Practical Approaches to Development Planning: Korea's Second Five-Year Plan*, ed. Irma Adelman (Baltimore: Johns Hopkins University Press, 1969), pp. 257–76; Paul W. Kuznets, *Economic Growth and Structure in the Republic of Korea* (New Haven, Conn.: Yale University Press, 1977), pp. 151–60; and Charles R. Frank et al., *Foreign Trade Regimes and Economic Development: South Korea* (New York: National Bureau of Economic Research; Columbia University Press, 1975), pp. 49–76. The "second postwar restructuring" is a term coined to describe the sort of trade liberalization policies adopted by Taiwan, Korea, and other developing countries in the late 1950s and early 1960s (Benjamin I. Cohen and Gustav Ranis, "The Second Postwar Restructuring," in *Government and Economic Development*, ed. Gustav Ranis [New Haven, Conn.: Yale University Press, 1971], pp. 431–69).

54 Anne O. Krueger, "The Experiences and Lessons of Asia's Super Exporters," in *Export-Oriented Development Strategies*, ed. Vittorio Corbo et al. (Boulder, Colo.: Westview Press, 1985), p. 197, n. 14.

55 Bela Balassa, *The Newly-Industrializing Developing Countries after the Oil Crisis*, World Bank Staff Working Paper no. 508 (Washington, D.C.: World Bank, October 1980); Paul W. Kuznets, "Response to External Shocks: The Experience of Four Countries," *Economic Notes* (1982), pp. 123–40.

56 Youngil Lim, "Review Article: What is Pushing Korean Industrialization?" *Korean Studies* (University of Hawaii, Center for Korean Studies) 2 (1978): 186–8; and Paul W. Kuznets, "Economic Development, Export Structure, and Shifting Comparative Advantage in the Pacific Basin Region," in *The Industrial Future of the Pacific Basin*, ed. Roger Benjamin and Robert T. Kudrle (Boulder, Colo.: Westview Press, 1984), pp. 35–58.

57 Active promotion, including arm twisting, has occurred in Korea. See Yung Whee Rhee et al., *Korea's Competitive Edge: Managing the Entry into World Markets* (Baltimore: World Bank; Johns Hopkins University Press, 1984), chap. 3. Industry targeting includes choice of import-substitution industries as well as industries with immediate export potential since the import-import substitute-export sequence (Akamatsu's "Wild-Geese-Flying" pattern of growth) has been found in Japan and, later, in Taiwan and Korea. See Kaname Akamatsu, "A Historic Pattern of Economic Growth in Developing Countries," *Developing Economies*, preliminary issue no. 1 (1962), pp. 3–25; and Jaime de Melo, "Sources of Growth and Structural Change in the Republic of Korea and Taiwan: Some Comparisons," in Corbo et al., eds. p. 229.

58 Comparison of nine countries for which either Denison-Solow or Christensen-Jorgenson sources-of-growth studies are available reveals "that Japan, South Korea, and Taiwan were the only countries . . . for which the import content of exports was higher than that of domestic demand" (de Melo, p. 235).

59 Tuvia Blumenthal, "Exports and Economic Growth: The Case of Postwar Japan," *Quarterly Journal of Economics* 86 (November 1972): 620–2.

60 The importance of increasing imports for growth, even in resource-poor countries like The Three, cannot be demonstrated except by counterfactual argument. Korea's "growth-through-borrowing" strategy is discussed in my "Government and Economic Strategy in Contemporary South Korea," *Pacific Affairs* 58 (Spring 1985): 62–3.

61 This and some of the preceding points can be found in Anne O. Krueger, "Export-Led Industrial Growth Reconsidered," in *Trade and Growth of the Advanced Developing Countries in the Pacific Basin*, ed. Wontack Hong and Lawrence B. Krause (Seoul: Korea Development Institute, 1981), pp. 16–22, and in her "The Experience and Lessons of Asia's Super Exporters," pp. 197–201.

62 Myers (n. 31 above), p. 42. The text here owes much to Myers's discussion of "The State and the Private Sector," also in Lau, ed., pp. 42–54.

63 Albert Feuerwerker, *China's Early Industrialization* (Cambridge, Mass.: Harvard University Press, 1958), chap. 1.

64 Thomas A. Pugel, "Japan's Industrial Policy: Instruments, Trends, Effects," *Journal of Comparative Economics* 8 (December 1984): 421–2; and Sueo Sekiguchi and Toshihiro Horiuchi, "Foreign Trade and Industrial Policies: A Review of Japanese Experience," in Benjamin and Kudrle, eds. (n. 56 above), pp. 81–101.

65 Competition may have been encouraged to promote efficiency in protected, oligopolistic markets, while the "indirect subsidy" derives from the view that government priority eliminates risk so that lending to firms in priority sectors is "virtually risk free" (see Andrea Boltho, "Was Japan's Industrial Policy Successful?" *Cambridge Journal of Economics* 9 [June 1985]: 191–2).

66 The practice, termed "*amakudari*," or "descent from heaven," is described in Chalmers Johnson, *Japan's Public Policy Companies* (Washington, D.C.: American Enterprise Institute; Stanford, Calif.: Hoover Institution, 1978), chap. 5.

67 For a description of implementation mechanisms, see Miyohei Shinohara, Toru Yanagihara, and Kwang Suk Kim, *The Japanese and Korean Experience in Managing Development*, World Bank Staff Working Paper no. 574 (Washington, D.C.: World Bank, 1983).

68 Rhee et al. (n. 57 above), pp. 15–18. Also U.S. Agency for International Development, *Korean Agricultural Research: The Integration of Research and Extension*, AID Project Impact Evaluation no. 27 (Washington, D.C.: AID, January 1982), p. iv; and Taewon Kwack, *Industrial Restructuring Experience and Policy in Korea in the 1970s*, KDI Working Paper 84-08 (Seoul: Korea Development Institute, August 1984).

69 Patrick and Rosovsky, eds. (n. 52 above), pp. 48–52; and Leroy P. Jones and Il Sakong, *Government, Business, and Entrepreneurship in Economic Development: The Korean Case* (Cambridge, Mass.: Harvard University Press, 1980), pp. 66–9.

70 Edward S. Mason et al., *The Economic and Social Modernization of the Republic of Korea* (Cambridge, Mass.: Harvard University Press, 1980), pp. 263–69, 293.

71 Kuznets, "Government and Economic Strategy" (n. 60 above), pp. 55, 64–5.

72 The policy-market controversy is examined from the policy point of view by Boltho. See his "Was Japan's Industrial Policy Successful?"

73 Philip H. Trezise, "Industrial Policy Is Not the Major Reason for Japan's Success," *Brookings Review* 1 (Spring 1983): 18.

74 P. T. Bauer, "The New Orthodoxy of Economic Development," *Rivista internazionale di scienze economiche e commerciali* 12 (September 1965): 833.

75 Alexander Gerschenkron, *Economic Backwardness in Historical Perspective* (Cambridge, Mass.: Harvard University Press, 1962), p. 44. For example, the industrialization (growth in share of industrial product in GDP) that took 40–45

years in Sweden and Japan took only 20 years in Korea (Kuznets, *Economic Growth and Structure* [n. 53 above], p. 50).

76 The neopessimists of the 1980s follow in the tradition of the pessimists of the 1950s and early 1960s, such as Ragnar Nurkse and Raul Prebisch. For example, see W. Arthur Lewis, "The Slowing Down of the Engine of Growth," *American Economic Review* 70 (September 1980): 555–64; and William R. Cline, "Can the East Asian Model of Development be Generalized?" *World Development* 10 (February 1982): 81–90. Cline's East Asian model actually refers to the Gang of Four, all less developed countries, but might as well refer to The Three.

77 Oli Havrylyshyn and Iradj Alikhani, "Is There Cause for Export Optimism? An Inquiry into the Existence of a Second Generation of Successful Exporters," *Weltwirtschaftliches Archiv* 118 (1982): 651–62.

78 On these points, see also Gustav Ranis, "Can the East Asian Model of Development be Generalized? A Comment," *World Development* 13 (April 1985): 91–104; and Gerald M. Meier, "The New Export Pessimism," in *Economic Policy and Development: New Perspectives*, ed. Toshio Shishido and Ryuzo Sato (Dover, Mass.: Auburn House; London: Croom Helm, 1985), pp. 19–32.

2

WHERE DO HIGH GROWTH POLITICAL ECONOMIES COME FROM?

The Japanese Lineage of Korea's "Developmental State"

Atul Kohli

Questions about the wide range of (economic) performance of underdeveloped countries today . . . belong as much to history as (they) do to economic analysis.

Sir Arthur Lewis

[We] turn to history and only to history if what we are seeking are the actual causes, sources, and conditions of overt changes of patterns and structures in society.

Robert Nisbet

2.1 INTRODUCTION

Three decades of sustained, high economic growth has made South Korea a "model of development." Performance of other developing countries is now often judged against that of "East Asian newly industrializing countries (NICs)," including South Korea. Scholars and policy makers around the world have become curious: "How did South Korea do it?; "Can others learn from the experience?" A large body of literature has developed—some of it of rather high quality—attempting to interpret the Korean political economy.[1] A central debate in this literature concerns the relative roles of the state and of the market in explaining South Korea's economic success. While hardly any sensible observer continues to deny the state's extensive role in Korean economic development, the current debate bogs down over the interpretation of this role, i.e. over the extent to which state intervention was "market conforming" versus "market distorting," or to use a related set of concepts, the extent to which the state "led" rather than "followed" the market.[2]

Source: World Development, Vol. 22(9), pp. 1269–93.

Interesting and significant as this debate is, it is also incomplete. Much of it revolves around unraveling the economic role of the South Korean state and, in turn, tracing the impact of this role on economic outcomes. The prior question of why the South Korean state was able to do what it did, and the related genetic issue of the historical roots of the Korean political economy thus tend to be underemphasized. Since there is much to be learned about the Korean "model of development" by adopting a longer historical perspective, especially tracing its origins back to its Japanese colonial lineage, this neglect is unfortunate.

For example, few "developmentalists," if any, ascribe much significance to the continuities that link colonial and postcolonial Korea. This is certainly so among the more strictly economic analysts of South Korean growth experience;[3] however, somewhat surprisingly and unfortunately, this problem also characterizes the works of several institutionally sensitive scholars of South Korea. Among the latter, some discuss the colonial period but quickly conclude that the impact was not of lasting significance (e.g., Jones and Sakong, 1980, pp. 22–37), others deny the contributions of this past altogether,[4] and yet others virtually ignore it, presumably because of a view that significant changes in South Korean economy began only after the adoption of an "export-led model of development" in the early 1960s.[5] Korean scholarship on Korea has its own, albeit understandable, blind spots; the nationalist impulse often leads to a denial of any continuity between colonial and postcolonial periods, lest the contemporary achievements be viewed as a product of a much disliked colonial rule.[6] Only a handful of Korean specialists, especially those with a strong historical bent, have understood and emphasized the Japanese colonial roots of the more recent, high-growth Korean political economy.[7] Building on the insights of this last group of Korean specialists, I attempt in this essay to reinterpret some specific historical materials with the hope of deriving general lessons of interest to scholars of comparative and international development.

The argument below is that Japanese colonial influence on Korea, in 1905–45, was decisive in shaping a political economy that later evolved into the high-growth South Korean path to development. Japanese colonialism differed in important respects from the colonialism of European powers. As late developers, the Japanese made extensive use of state power for their own economic development, and they used the same state power to pry open and transform Korea in a relatively short period. Japanese colonial impact was thus more intense, more brutal and deeply architectonic; it also left Korea with three and a half decades of economic growth (the average, annual growth rate in production was more than 3%) and a relatively advanced level of industrialization (nearly 35% of Korea's "national production" in 1940 originated in mining and manufacturing).[8] While there were important discontinuities in the postcolonial period, the grooves that Japanese colonialism carved on the Korean social soil cut deep. The decade and a half following the departure of the Japanese was at least chaotic, and often tragic. When the dust settled, however, South Korea under Park Chung-Hee fell back into the grooves of an earlier origin and traversed along them, well into the 1980s. Of course, this was not inevitable; historical continuities seldom are. Korea had competing historical legacies: e.g., there was the distant legacy of Chosŏn (i.e. of Korea under the rule of Yi dynasty) of corrupt court politics at the apex; then there were indigenous revolutionary tendencies that found expression in North Korea; and there was the possibility of considerable American influence. Moreover, completely new paths could have been charted. Subsequent decisions were thus critical in putting South Korea on a path that reestablished historical continuities. Nevertheless, it is difficult to imagine South Korea adopting a growth path that it did without a deeply influential Japanese colonial past.

More specifically, I trace below the colonial origins of three patterns that we now readily associate as elements of the South Korean "model." First, I discuss how the Korean state under the Japanese influence was transformed from a relatively corrupt and ineffective social institution into a highly authoritarian, penetrating organization, capable of simultaneously controlling and transforming the Korean society. This is followed by an analysis of a second pattern, namely, the new state's production-oriented alliances with the dominant classes, an alliance that buttressed the state's capacity to both control and transform. Relatedly, it is also important to take note of the structural changes in the economy; not only did the colonial economy experience steady growth and industrialization, but it also became rather heavily export-oriented, including exports of manufactured products. Finally, there was the third pattern of brutal repression and systematic control of the lower classes in both the cities and the countryside. The cumulative impact of these state–class configurations was to help create a framework for the evolution of a high-growth political economy. I also, toward the end of this discussion, briefly suggest—though not develop, leaving that for another essay—how these patterns continued into subsequent periods.

It is important to reiterate that the main task of this paper is not to set the historical record straight. That is for historians of Korea; they are already busy doing so and I am only building on some of their work. Given the importance of the South Korean case in the contemporary discourse on development, it is important that developmentalists understand what country specialists already know; I thus hope to reinterpret and synthesize some specific materials with general implications. Three sets of general ideas will be debated via the historical materials. First, there are Korea-related comparative questions. For example, how much choice does a developing country really have when adopting a specific development strategy; i.e. to what extent was South Korea a beneficiary of its historical inheritance, as distinct from creating anew a high-growth, export-oriented "model of development?" Closely related is the issue of transferability of the Korean "model" across national boundaries: if the roots of contemporary South Korean political economy are indeed as deep as a relatively unique colonial experience, can others really emulate the experience? Second, at a higher level of generality, there are theoretical issues revolving around the concept of "developmental states": what characterizes them and where do they come from? Finally, at the most general level, there is at least an implication in this essay that some of the variations we notice today among the more or less dynamic Third World political economies may have some of their roots in a variable colonial past. If so, a further investigation of this analytical claim would require reopening the issue of the colonial roots of the contemporary Third World that has unfortunately been lost in the postdependency scholarship on development.

2.2 THE CONSTRUCTION OF A COLONIAL STATE

(a) The old, "predatory" state

By the time the Japanese gained decisive influence over Korea—say around 1905, after the Japanese victory in Russo–Japanese war of 1904—the old state within Chosòn was already in an advanced state of disintegration. While it is not necessary to recall historical details, a brief understanding of the state–society links in late Chosòn are essential to appreciate changes wrought by Japanese colonial power.[9] The Yi dynasty had provided continuous and, for the most part, stable rule to Korea for nearly 500 years. The same intricate state and class alliances that were responsible for this stability, however, also became major constraints on successful adaptation to changing external pressures, especially in the second half of the nineteenth century. For example, the clearest manifestation of the powerlessness of a centralized monarchial state was the continued inability to collect taxes owed to the state on agrarian incomes, especially from the powerful Yangban elite, the landowning-official class of Korea (Palais, 1975). This recurring inability, in turn, came to be associated with several problematic political trends: First, the state resorted to squeezing the peasantry via "taxation" (e.g., corvee labor and military service), contributing to brigandage and a restive peasant population. Second, the state's limited resources exacerbated the competition and tensions in what was already a personalized and factionalized elite at the apex of the political pyramid. Finally, financial limitations made it difficult to mobilize any serious military response to growing external pressures.

How does one explain powerlessness in a centralized polity? The leading historian of late Yi Korea, James Palais, traces the roots of this conundrum back to the manner in which the monarchy and the Korean officials-*cum*-aristocrats, the Yangban, mutually checked each others powers. The power of the Yangban class rested in part on access to hereditary land wealth but also on a close identification with the centralized bureaucracy, which helped both secure socioeconomic privileges and was a further source of wealth and power.

Royal authority, in turn, was seldom all that great. Being under Chinese suzerainty, Korean emperors did not enjoy the "mandate of heaven" that the Chinese emperors possessed. In addition, the recruitment of the aristocracy to the bureaucracy via the examination system enabled landed power to be deeply embedded all through the Korean state, checking the scope of Royal authority *vis-à-vis* the Yangban.[10] While this balance of power was a source of stability for several centuries, as external pressures grew, and along with it the state's need for taxes and other socioeconomic resources, it also became a major constraint on monarchial power to initiate reforms: The monarchial state, according to Palais, "could not solve the problem of creating adequate political authority for the achievement of national goals." Yi state was thus simultaneously "centralized and weak."[11]

In addition to the limiting balance of power between the monarchy and the Yangban, there were other factors at work that contributed to the Yi state's ineffectiveness. First, it was not merely the presence of a powerful land-controlling strata in society that limited the state's capacity. As I discuss below, the colonial state in Korea carved out a different type of ruling alliance with the same landowning class, but with a vastly more effective state. The key factor at work in Yi Korea was thus the direct control that landed groups exercised on state offices (Fairbank, Reischauer and Craig, 1978, p. 307). Second, the Korean monarchy remained to the end a highly personalistic, patrimonial institution. In the words of Cumings (1981), the Korean monarchs were incapable of acting along "the modern distinction between public and private realms" and thus incapable of designing state-led national goals of economic development (p. 10). Third, the ruling strata below the monarch was highly factionalized.[12] Such strife in the ruling strata made it difficult to design cohesive responses to growing challenges. Finally, it is important to note that the reach of the Yi state from the center to the periphery was rather limited. While provincial and county officials were directly appointed from Seoul, each county magistrate was responsible for governing nearly 40,000 people (there being some 330 magistrates for about 12 million Koreans).[13] Since these magistrates were rotated frequently, they often depended on the well-entrenched Yangban elite for local governance. Moreover, the lower level officials—below the magistrate—were not salaried employees. They were rather a hereditary group who were allowed to collect and keep some local taxes as compensation for their services. These petty functionaries operated virtually as local czars, not easily influenced from above and responsible for the "venality and exploitation of the peasant population" (Lee in Eckert *et al.*, 1990, p. 111).

In sum, the ineffectiveness of the Yi state was rooted in part in the pattern of state–class linkages and in part in the design of the state itself. Regarding the latter, a personalistic apex, a factionalized ruling strata, and a limited downward reach of central authorities, were all significant characteristics contributing to the state's powerlessness. This state—weak from the inside and hemmed in by powerful social actors from the outside—contributed little, if any, to sustained economic progress.[14] Worse, when faced with growing security challenges and related fiscal crises, the Yi state turned on its own society, becoming rapacious and predatory. The views of several historians and observers of the day converge on such a perspective on the precolonial Korean state: programs of the Yi government became "embezzlement facilities for a rapacious officialdom" (Lee in Eckert *et al.*, 1990, p. 179); "maladministration . . . of the native Yi dynasty had affected adversely the whole of Korean public service" (Ireland, 1926, p. 92); "one of the strongest and most fixed impressions made (during my travels to Korea) was that of the well-nigh hopeless corruption of Korean court;"[15] and the Korean government "takes from the people directly and indirectly, everything that they earn over and above a bare subsistence, and gives them in return practically nothing."[16]

Since corrupt and ineffective states are indeed a common feature in parts of the contemporary Third World, one may genuinely wonder: how was Korea's "predatory" state historically transformed into what some may describe as a "developmental" state?[17] The impact of Japanese colonial power was decisive in altering both the nature of the Korean state and the relationship of this state to various social classes. The transformation of the state is discussed immediately below and the changing relationship of the state to social classes in subsequent sections.

(b) Toward a "developmental" state

The Japanese military victory over the Russians in 1904 marked the emergence of Japan as the major regional power, a power that had been rising steadily since the Meiji restoration in the 1860s. Subsequently, Japan, with the acquiescence of Western powers, had a relatively free hand in dominating and molding Korea. Japanese motives in Korea, like the motives of all imperial powers, were mixed; they sought to control it politically and to transform it economically for their own advantage. Security concerns were probably dominant insofar as Korea had been an object of regional power competition for quite some time (Conroy, 1960). Given the mercantilist nature of Japanese political economy, however, it does not make much sense to raise the old question on imperialism of whether security was more important than economic interests. More than in the case of most imperial powers, the Meiji oligarchs of Japan readily associated national power with national wealth and national wealth with overseas economic opportunities (Duus, 1984, pp. 132–3).

Certain unique aspects of Japanese imperialism are essential to note for a full understanding of the colonial impact on Korea (Peattie, 1984, pp. 3–60). First, the Japanese had themselves barely escaped being imperialized. As both late developers and late imperialists, Japan colonized neighboring states with whom they shared racial and cultural traits; it was as if England had colonized a few, across-the-channel continental states. Proximity meant that many more Japanese ended up playing a direct role in colonial rule, including a much larger role of military and police, than was ever the case in European overseas colonies. The near geographical contiguity and shared cultural and racial traits also implied that the Japanese could realistically consider their rule to be permanent, leading eventually to a full integration of colonies into an expanded Japan. As will be discussed below, this possibility, in turn, influenced both the economic and political strategies of Japan in Korea, especially the Japanese-initiated industrialization of Korea.

Furthermore, Japanese colonial strategy was deeply informed by their own successful domestic reform efforts following the Meiji restoration. Of all the colonizing nations, Japan stands out as nearly the only one with a successful record of deliberate, state-led political and economic transformation. By trial and error the Meiji oligarchs had designed a political economy that was well suited for the task of "catching up" with advanced Western powers. The essential elements of this political economy are well known and can be briefly reiterated: the creation of an effective centralized state capable of both controlling and transforming Japanese society; deliberate state intervention aimed, first at agricultural development, and second at rapid industrial growth; and production of a disciplined, obedient and educated work force. It was this model of deliberate development, with its emphasis on state building and on the use of state power to facilitate socioeconomic change—in contrast say, to the British, who having created a private property regime, waited in vain for Bengali *zamindars* in India to turn into a sheep farming gentry—that moved the Japanese colonizers.[18] In Peattie's words, much of what Japan undertook in its colonies "was based upon Meiji experience in domestic reform" (Peattie, 1984, p. 29).

It is not surprising that the earliest Japanese efforts in Korea were focused on reforming the disintegrating Chosòn state; both political control and economic transformation depended on it. A fair number of political reforms had thus in fact been put into place during 1905–10, especially 1907–09, even prior to the formal annexation of Korea in 1910. Subsequently, the decade of 1910–20 was again critical, when, under very harsh authoritarian circumstances, a highly bureaucratized and a deeply penetrating state was constructed.

A key architect of the early reforms in 1907–09, whose role helps us trace the origins of the design of the new Korean state, was the Meiji oligarch and the former Meiji era premier of Japan, Ito Hirubumi. Ito as a young man had been one of the handful of leaders who had led the Meiji "revolution" and who had subsequently participated in the reform efforts that followed the destruction of Tokugawa Shogunate. Ito had travelled extensively in Europe and had been fascinated with Prussian bureaucracy as a model for Japan: the Prussian "model" offered to him a route to Western rationality and modernity without "succumbing" to Anglo-American liberalism (Halliday, 1975, p. 37). Within Japan, Ito in 1878 had "led the campaign to make the bureaucracy the absolutely unassailable base and center of political power in the state system." Subsequently, Ito helped reorganize Tokyo University in 1881 as a "school for government bureaucrats" and by 1887, "a basic civil service and entrance apprenticeship based on the Prussian model was installed."[19] With this experience behind him, when Ito was appointed in the early 1900s to run the Korean protectorate, and where his powers as Resident-General were near absolute—"The uncrowned King of Korea"—he was quite self-conscious of his task: "Korea can hardly be called an organized state in the modern sense; I am trying to make it such" (Ladd, 1908, pp. 435 and 174).

Ito and his successors set out to deliberately construct a new Japanese-controlled Korean state. The first task was to gain central control. With superior military power behind them, the Japanese in 1907 dismantled the Korean army, repressed those who "mutinied," incorporated other army officers into a Japanese-controlled gendarmery, and forced the Korean monarch to abdicate. Having captured the heart of the state, the colonial rulers sought to systematically create a depersonalized "public arena," to spread their power both wide and deep, and to coopt and/or repress native Korean political forces. For example, the patrimonial elements of the monarchial state were destroyed rather early, and replaced by a cabinet-style government run by Japanese bureaucrats.[20] Since the appointments of these and other lower level bureaucrats were governed by "elaborate rules and regulations which, in the main followed(ed) the lines of the Imperial Japanese services," the new Korean state quickly acquired a "rational" character (Ireland, 1926, p. 104; and H.I.J.M.'s Residency General, 1909, p. 45); scholarly observers have in retrospect characterized the Japanese colonial civil service as "outstanding," composed of "hard working and trusted cadres," who deserve "high marks as a group" (Peattie, 1984, p. 26). Elements of the highly developed, Japanese style of bureaucratic government were thus transferred directly to Korea.

(i) The new civil service

While other colonial powers in other parts of the world also created a competent civil service (e.g., the British in India), the Japanese colonial project was qualitatively distinct; both the extent and the intensity of bureaucratic penetration was unique. There were some 10,000 officials in the Japanese–Korean government in 1910; by 1937, this number was up to 87,552. More than half of these government officials in 1937, 52,270 to be exact, were Japanese. Contrast this with the French in Vietnam (where, by the way, the presence of the French was already more significant than, say, that of the British in Africa), who ruled a nearly similar sized colony with some 3,000 French; in other words, there were nearly 15 Japanese officials in Korea for every French administrator in Vietnam (Robinson, in Eckert *et al.*, 1990, p. 257). The presence of Korean bureaucrats, trained and employed by the Japanese, was also sizable: nearly 40,000 Koreans qualified as government officials just before WWII. While most of the Koreans did not occupy senior positions in the colonial government, there can be little doubt that, over the four decades of colonial rule, they became an integral part of a highly bureaucratic form of government. Moreover, during WWII, as the demand for Japanese officials grew elsewhere, many Koreans moved higher up in the bureaucratic hierarchy. I will return below to the issue of continuity: this sizable cadre of Japanese-trained Korean bureaucrats virtually took over the day-to-day running of a truncated South Korea, first under US military government and eventually when a sovereign state was formed.

One further characteristic of the colonial government that needs to be underlined is the successful links that the Japanese created between a highly concentrated power center in Seoul, and a densely bureaucratized periphery. All bureaucracies face the problem of how to ensure that central commands are faithfully implemented by the officials at the bottom rung. This, in turn, requires ensuring that lower level officials respond mainly to those above them in the bureaucratic hierarchy, rather than to personal interests, or to the interests of societal actors with whom they interact. The Japanese in Korea were quite self-conscious of this problem and repeatedly experimented till they arrived at arrangements deemed satisfactory.

Of course, certain circumstances were helpful in establishing authority links between the center and the periphery: ruling arrangements in Seoul were highly authoritarian—the power of the Japanese Governor Generals in both policy making and implementation was absolute and nearly all of them were senior military men—and Korea was not a very large country (again, for example, note the contrast with the role of the British in India). The Japanese, however, took additional actions.[21] For example, when confronted with corrupt regional or local officials, the central authorities experimented—in line with "new" institutional economics—with paying these officials higher salaries, especially "entertainment-allowance," with the hope that, if more satisfied, they may perform public tasks better. When this did not work, or at least not fully, the colonial authorities further centralized, leading up to even less discretion, and more rule-governed behavior for lower level officials. These officials in the early colonial period were even required to wear crisp uniforms, replete with swords, so as to distinguish them sharply from an average citizen—thus creating a state–society, or a public–private, distinction through the use of symbolic politics—as well as to convey the will of the state in the far reaches of the society. When such efforts also failed to secure full compliance, Korean officials would be replaced by the more socialized and complying Japanese officials, at least until more suitable Koreans, who were likely to comply, could be found for the job.

(ii) The police force

In addition to the civil bureaucracy, the other essential arm of the new Korean state that the Japanese helped develop was a well-organized police force. Once again, there is nothing unique about colonial powers developing a police force; what is noteworthy here are both the extensive and the intensive nature of police supervision in colonial Korea. The colonial police force was designed on the lines of the Meiji police force insofar as it was highly centralized, well disciplined and played an extensive role in social and economic reforms.[22] The police force in colonial Korea grew rapidly: from some 6,222 gendarmes and police in 1910 to 20,777 in 1922 and again to over 60,000 in 1941 (Robinson in Eckert *et al.*, 1990, p. 259). One scholar suggests that at the height of the colonial rule, there were enough police so that the lowest level policeman knew "every man in the village" (Chen, 1984, p. 225). While senior police officers were normally Japanese, over half the police force was made up of Koreans, often lower class Koreans. These Koreans were trained by the Japanese in police academies, especially established within Korea for the purpose. Records indicate that for every Korean police position there were 10–20 applicants (Chen, 1984, p. 236), suggesting a level of cooperation between Koreans and Japanese that probably pains the modern Korean nationalist sentiments. Beyond formal training, the Japanese maintained very close supervision over their police force, for example, during 1915–20, about 2,000 policemen—or nearly one out of every 10 available policemen—were sternly disciplined every year for transgression of police rules (Chen, 1984, pp. 236–9).

This extensive and closely supervised police force, that penetrated every Korean village, performed numerous functions other than "normal" police duties of law and order maintenance. Powers granted to police included control over "politics, education, religion, morals, health and public welfare, and tax collection" (Robinson in Eckert *et al.*, 1990, p. 259). The police, who presented themselves in military uniforms, again replete with swords, also had summary powers to judge and punish minor offenders, including the punishment of whipping. Even in production, local police were known to have "compelled villages to switch from existing food crops" to cash crops and to adopt "new techniques" in rice production so as to facilitate exports to Japan. Moreover, during land surveys (conducted during 1910–18; more on this below), as a result of which tenancy and conflicts over land increased, local police "always intervened in favor of landlords."[23] It is thus not surprising that even a Japanese observer was led to conclude that Terauchi (the first Japanese Governor General of Korea, following Ito and formal annexation) and his successors had transformed the "entire Korean peninsula into a military camp."[24]

One final aspect of the police role concerns the links between the police and local society via local elites. The police successfully utilized the proverbial carrot and stick to incorporate "village elders" and others into a ruling "alliance." The police thus buttressed their already extensive powers by working with, rather than against, indigenous authority structures. So armed, the police used the knowledge and influence of the local elites to mold the behavior of average citizens in such diverse matters as, "birth control, types of crops grown, count and movement of people, prevention of spread of diseases, mobilization of forced labor and to report on transgressions" (Chen, 1984, p. 226). The police and many local elites thus came to be viewed and despised by Koreans at large as "collaborationists"; unfortunately for Koreans, while many of the landed elite were indeed eventually eliminated as a political force (i.e. via land reforms following the Korean War), much of the colonial police force was incorporated directly into the new state structure of South Korea.

In sum, the personalized and factionalized Yi state with a limited reach in society came to be replaced by a colonial state with considerable capacity to penetrate and control the society; this state was simultaneously oppressive and efficacious. A highly centralised apex with near absolute powers of legislation and execution—and thus of setting and implementing "national" goals—and a pervasive, disciplined civil and police bureaucracies constituted the cores of the new state.

(iii) The politics of the new state

The politics practiced by the new rulers added to the state's capacity to convey its will to the society. Except for a somewhat liberal interlude in the 1920s, for the most part, the political practices of the Japanese colonial state in Korea were brutally authoritarian. For example, Korean newspapers were either suspended or heavily censored, political protest was met with swift retribution, and political organizations and public gatherings were generally banned. Those professing Korean nationalist sentiments were thus either exiled or remained fragmented; while there was latent and scattered sympathy for nationalists and for communists all through the colonial period, a coherent nationalist movement was never allowed to develop.[25] The Japanese used "thought police" to detect and eliminate political dissidence, and also developed a "spy system" to buttress the civil and police bureaucracy that was "probably better developed in Korea than anywhere in the world" (Grajdanzev, 1944, p. 55).

The colonial authorities were quite self-conscious about their use of repression as a means to instill fear in the minds of Koreans and thus to minimize dissidence and reinforce bureaucratic control: in order to avoid "restlessness" in the "popular mind," note government reports of the period, it was "essential" to "maintain unshakable the dignity of the government" and "to impress the people with the weight of the new regime" (Government-General of Chosen, 1914, pp. 2–3). When Koreans still resisted, Governor-General Terauchi Masatake supposedly responded, "I will whip you with scorpions" (quoted in Peattie, 1984, p. 18), and when eventually the Koreans succumbed, the gloating satisfaction is also obvious in official documents: "they have gradually yielded their obstinate prejudices and their disdainful attitude" (Government-General of Chosen, 1935, p. 81).

In spite of the awesome state that the Japanese created, it would be a mistake to believe that a thorough bureaucratic penetration and politics of fear were the only ruling instruments in the hands of the colonialists. There is no doubt that bureaucratic growth enabled the new state to undertake many more economic activities that contributed to economic growth (more on this below), and that repression enabled the establishment of order, freeing the state elite to focus on other "developmental" matters. Nevertheless, bureaucratic and repressive power are seldom enough to elicit a measure of cooperation—from, at least, some groups in society—that is essential for generating economic dynamism. We must thus also take note of some other, nonrepressive ruling instruments that the new colonial state put to use.

First, a segment of the Korean political elite in the precolonial period was quite favourably inclined toward Japan.[26] These Koreans from the political class were both officially and unofficially incorporated into the new system of colonial rule. Second, and relatedly, the colonial state forged numerous implicit and explicit "alliances" with Korean propertied classes. The nature of these turned out to be of critical long-term significance. While I return to a detailed discussion of this issue below, it should be noted here that, on the whole, Korean monied groups—in both the city and the countryside—did not oppose colonial rule. Most of them benefited from this rule and generally went along—some even with enthusiasm—with the colonial project. Third, the Japanese undertook considerable expansion of education, facilitating propaganda and political resocialization. Whereas in 1910 nearly 10,000 students attended some sort of school, by 1941 this number was up to 1.7 million and the rate of literacy by 1945 was nearly 50%. The focus was on primary education and the curricula was designed with the "object" of raising "practical men able to meet the requirements of the state."[27]

To conclude this subsection, the Japanese colonialists in Korea replaced the decrepit Yi state with a centralized and powerful state. This was no liberal state; it was more statist *vis-à-vis* the Korean society, and considerably more repressive, than even the statist and illiberal Japanese political economy of the period. Central decision making was highly concentrated in the office of the Governor General. The Governor General's will, reflecting the imperial design and goals, was translated into implemented policies via the use of an extensive, well-designed and disciplined bureaucracy. The new state also achieved considerable downward penetration; both the civil and police bureaucracies reached into the nooks and crannies of the society, while continuing to respond to central directives: Korean elites in the localities were incorporated into the ruling "alliance"; and, when all else failed in the

Japanese efforts to control and transform Korea, there existed a well-functioning intelligence service to buttress the state's supervisory role. While a fuller understanding of how power was generated in this system, and the uses to which it was put, will emerge in due course, it should already be evident as to how the precolonial, ineffective state was transformed into a state that—for better or for worse—could get things done.

2.3 THE COLONIAL STATE, PROPERTIED CLASSES AND ECONOMIC CHANGE

The colonial state in Korea was a busy state. While pursuing the imperial interests of Japan, it evolved a full policy agenda, including the goal of economic transformation of Korea. The broad strategy of transformation was two pronged the state utilized its bureaucratic capacities to directly undertake quite a few economic tasks; and, more important, the state involved propertied groups—both in the countryside and in the cities, and both Japanese and Koreans—in production-oriented alliances leading up to sustained economic change. The results measured by the criteria of growth and industrialization (though not by such other criteria as human rights, national self-determination and fair economic distribution) were a considerable success. Since successes generally begets emulation and continuity, it is important to analyze the colonial economic strategy.

Two general observations ought to be noted at the outset. First, while the Governor-General in Korea possessed near absolute powers, he was nevertheless an agent of the Japanese imperial government. The colonial state in Korea thus pursued, not Korean, but Japanese needs and interests that changed over time.[28] In broad brush strokes, during the early phase, say, the first decade of the colonial rule, Japan treated Korea mainly as a strategic gain that could also be exploited in a fairly classic fashion: exchange of agricultural products for manufactured goods. Subsequently, as Japanese demand for food outpaced its own supply, the colonial state aggressively undertook measures to increase food production in Korea. Manufacturing was discouraged in this early phase, again in a fairly classic fashion, to protect Japanese exports to Korea. Following WWI, however, with swollen company profits, Japan sought opportunities for export of capital and thus relaxed restrictions against production of manufactured products in Korea. At the same time, following the need to coopt nationalistic pressures within Korea, the colonial state also involved selected and prominent Korean businessmen in the growth of manufacturing. Aggressive industrialization of Korea occurred only in the 1930s. This was in part a result of Japan's strategy to cope with the depression—i.e. to create a protected, high-growth economy on an empire-wide scale—and in part a result of Japan's aggressive industrialization, again on an empire-wide scale, that reflected national power considerations.[29] Japan was able to switch its imperial policies in Korea frequently and decisively; this, in turn, underlined the highly centralized nature of authority within the Japanese controlled Korean state.

The second related observation concerns the pressures on the Governor-General in Korea to simultaneously pursue imperial interests and run a cost-effective government. Reading through historical documents of the time, especially the annual reports of the Governor-General in Korea, it becomes clear that, among their various achievements, the colonial authorities in Korea wanted to emphasize their repeated efforts to enhance revenues and to minimize expenditures, especially by rationalizing the bureaucracy.[30] Since any shortfall between revenues and expenditures within Korea had to be financed by the Japanese Imperial government—and typically, there was a net revenue inflow from Japan to Korea—one presumes that constant and firm pressure was maintained on respective Governor-Generals to boost the cost-efficiency of public services. Unlike many other governments, the colonial state in Korea did not operate with a "soft budget constraint." On the contrary, there was consistent pressure to economize, "hardening" the budget constraint, with significant, positive "trickle-down" effect on the efficiency of the bureaucracy, including the economic bureaucracy.

(a) Increased state capacity

The increased capacity of the new colonial state in Korea to directly undertake economic tasks is evident fairly early in the historical record. For example, there was the issue of state capacity to collect taxes. The old Yi state, one may recollect, proved quite incapable of extracting taxes from society, especially revenues from landowners. The contrasting performance of the colonial state is notable. Land revenue in 1905, the year the Japanese influence in Korea started to grow, was some 4.9 million yen; by 1908, this had jumped to 6.5 million yen, or a real increase of some 30% in three years.[31] Subsequently, numerous other sources of revenue were added to that obtained from land—e.g., railways, post office and customs; and receipts from the ginseng monopoly and from such public undertakings as salt manufacture, coal mines, timber work and printing bureaus—and the jump in revenue intake was phenomenal. Whereas the total revenue in 1905 (land and other revenues) was 7.3 million yen, by 1911 one year after formal annexation, the total revenue intake was 24 million yen, or an increase of more than 300%.[32] The factors that help explain this increased state capacity were two-fold. First, the colonial state, backed by superior coercive power, snapped the stranglehold landowning groups had on the Yi state, pensioning off the Yangban elite, and replacing them by Japanese career bureaucrats; I will return to this issue below. Second, the colonial elite utilized the newly created civil and police bureaucracy to collect taxes. More specifically, as early as 1906, 36 revenue collection officers, again replete with uniforms and swords, were posted all over Korea to identify cultivated land, owners of the land, and the revenue due from the land (H.I.J.M.'s Residency General, 1908, Chapter V). While the rate of taxation on land was not increased, it was regularized. In addition, uniformed revenue officers worked in conjunction with local police officers in the process of tax collection, lest any one forget this newly established separation of state and society, or the willful presence of the new state in society.

The successful land survey that the Japanese conducted in Korea during 1910–18 similarly highlighted the efficacy of the new state. The Yi state had repeatedly discussed such a comprehensive land survey but never carried it out; the bureaucratic capacity was absent, as was the power to confront land controlling groups who wanted to hide the extent of their taxable lands. By contrast, the colonial state made an exhaustive land survey a priority. Over a period of eight years the Japanese invested some 30 million yen in the project (compared, say, to the total revenue intake of the Government-General in 1911 of 24 million yen). The survey "mapped all plots of land, classified it according to type, graded its productivity and established ownership."[33] While Japanese civil servants supervised the entire project, Korean landowners cooperated and eventually benefited; local land investigation committees, for example, who were responsible for investigating the "ownership, location, boundaries and class of land" were composed of "land-owners themselves" (Government-General of Chosen, 1912, p. 13). As a result of the survey, the colonial state secured a revenue base and, less obviously, enhanced its control over the Korean agrarian sector by involving the landowning classes as ruling partners. What the Korean landlords lost in terms of autonomy from, and influence over, the traditional Yi state, they made up by, first, securing new, Western-style, legal private property rights and later (as discussed below), by enhanced profits from land (Robinson in Eckert *et al.*, 1990, pp. 266–7).

Over time, the colonial state in Korea undertook numerous other projects of economic value. This is no place for a comprehensive discussion; I simply wish to flag some of the main areas.[34] First, the Government-General invested heavily in infrastructure, so much so that Korea's roads and railways were among the finest that a developing country inherited from their colonial past. Second, as mentioned above, the Japanese made significant investments in Korea in primary education. Given the long gestation period, however, the returns on this investment were probably reaped, less by colonial Korea, but more by the two sovereign Koreas who inherited a relatively literate labor force. Third, the colonial government ran a number of economic enterprises directly: e.g., railways, communications, opium, salt and tobacco. Judged by the regular financial contribution that these public undertakings made to public revenues, they were run relatively efficiently. Finally, the Government-General played an important role in the overall process of capital accumulation. While I will return to this issue again below, and the direct role of the new colonial state in extracting taxes has already been noted, a few other points also deserve attention. The currency and banking reforms that the new colonial state undertook rather early led to a significant jump in private, institutional savings: e.g., deposits in the Bank of Chosen (Korea) doubled from some 18 million yen in 1911 to 37 million yen in 1913 and the number of depositors in the postal savings bank went up from about 20,000 in 1909 to 420,000 in 1913 (the corresponding sums of deposits being 120,000 yen in 1909 and 981,000 yen in 1913) (Government-General of Chosen, 1914, p. 19). Later during the colonial rule, the Government-General required Koreans to buy government bonds that helped finance the industrialization drive of the 1930s. While capital inflows from Japan remained the dominant source, local capital accumulation also increased considerably. The colonial state in Korea, even more than the Japanese Meiji state on which it was modeled, became heavily and directly involved in economic tasks, and judged strictly by economic criteria, performed these tasks rather effectively.

More significant than the state's direct economic role was the indirect role that led up to the involvement of wealthy groups in productive activities. The mechanics of how these state–private sector alliances were created are important because similar arrangements were later central to South Korea's phenomenal economic success. The dynamics of change in both the agrarian and industrial sectors thus deserve our attention.

(b) The state and the agrarian sector

The colonial state restructured its relationship with the Korean landed classes. The highest Yangban elite who held offices in the Yi state were pensioned off (Government-General of Chosen, 1911, pp. 18–19). As career bureaucrats took over official functions, the direct control of landed classes on the state weakened. The successful land survey further confirmed the supremacy of the new state because, as a result of it, the capacity of the landed classes to evade the reach of the state had shrunk. In return, however, the state offered the landowners plenty, so as to not only not alienate them, but to make them active partners in executing the state's goals. For example, the Japanese introduced a new legal code—based on the Meiji legal code—that created Western-style legal private property, thus securing the control of Korean landed groups over land in perpetuity. While the Japanese in the process ended up owning significant amount of agricultural land in Korea, most Koreans who controlled land prior to the arrival of the Japanese maintained, nay, even expanded their land ownership.[35] Moreover, as mentioned above, many among the landed elite were incorporated into local governance, cooperating with and helping local agents of the state maintain control over villages. While students of colonialism often distinguish direct and indirect colonial rule, the Japanese political arrangement in Korea utilized both forms: direct bureaucratic penetration was buttressed by the authority of local influentials. This arrangement also suggests that, contrary to some recent arguments, the presence of a landowning class does not necessarily inhibit the formation of a powerful "developmental" state; much depends on the specific relationship of the state and landowners.[36]

The Japanese colonial government periodically made significant efforts to boost agricultural production, especially Korea's main product, rice. The underlying motivation was changing Japanese economic needs: e.g., prior to 1919, the efforts to boost production were minimal. Following a rice shortage and related riots in Japan in 1918, a major plan to expand rice production in Korea was implemented. The success on this front contributed to "over production" and following a glut and pressures from Japanese rice producers, all plans to increase rice production were cancelled in 1933. Again, however, the war with China in 1938–39 created food shortages in Japan and Korea was "resuscitated as a granary of the Empire."[37]

During the early phase the Japanese focused their efforts on land improvement, especially on irrigation, drainage and reclamation of arable land. The resulting increase in production was not huge and resulted both from extensive and intensive efforts; e.g., increase in rice production during 1910–24 averaged around 1.5% per annum and land productivity in the same period improved at about 0.8% per annum (Suh, 1978, p. 73, Table 33). Subsequently, when rapid increase in rice production became a goal, Korea's Japanese rulers utilized the knowledge acquired during the Meiji transformation and concentrated their efforts on spreading the use of improved seeds, fertilizer and irrigation. The gains were significant: the percentage of paddy land using improved seed doubled during 1915–40, reaching 85%; fertilizer input expanded 10 times during the same period (Suh, 1978, p. 77, Table 34; and during 1919–38 land under irrigation increased annually by nearly 10% (Suh, 1978, p. 73, Table 33; and Ishikawa, 1967, pp. 84–109). As a result, rice production during 1920–35 grew at nearly 3% per annum and nearly two-thirds of this growth resulted from improvements in land productivity.[38] The overall rate of increase in rice production per unit of land for the colonial period (1910–40) averaged a respectable 2% per annum (compare this, for example, with India's post-Green Revolution—say, 1970 to present—rates of productivity increase in cereal production; they have been only a little higher than 2% per annum). While some of these improvements may have been a "spontaneous" response to food shortages and higher prices in Japan, it is nevertheless difficult to imagine a relatively quick increase in supply without significant public efforts, especially in providing new seeds and in facilitating the spread of fertilizer.

It is a sad fact that increases in production in Korea did not lead to improvement in food consumption. Bulk of the increased production ended up in the export market and imported goods did not become consumption items for the vast majority. As a well documented study concludes, "per capita use of food grains as a whole declined substantially after the early years of the colonial period." The same author points out that this disjuncture between production and consumption was a result of several causes, but mainly due to a combination of population growth and few nonagricultural opportunities that increased the burden on tenants and on small farmers (Suh, 1978, pp. 86–7). If there was steady growth in production but the consumption for the majority of the population declined, given the considerable inequality in land ownership, it is likely that the incomes of landowning groups mushroomed. Other available evidence is consistent with this proposition: the rates of return on agricultural investment were very high for most of the period; income inequalities widened; and, as noted above, there was rapid growth of small depositors in saving institutions. The general point is that Korean landowning groups did rather well under colonial government; they became part of an implicit but comfortable ruling alliance.

Three other characteristics of the changing agrarian sector are noteworthy. First, Japanese corporations and entrepreneurs ended up owning large tracts of Korean agricultural land—anywhere from one-quarter to one-third of all the arable land. This was a result of a conscious government policy that began with the hope of attracting Japanese immigrants to Korea, but when that goal met with only limited success, Japanese corporations became heavily involved. Especially significant as a landowner was the infamous Oriental Development Company (e.g., see Moskowitz, 1974), which, like most other Japanese landowners, leased lands to tenants, collected rents in kind, most often rice, and sold the rice in the export market back to Japan. The rate of return on such activities was high, higher than in Japan, and many a fortunes were made (Suh, 1978, p. 85, Table 39). From our standpoint, the direct involvement of the Japanese in Korean agriculture helps explicate two points: the mechanics of how the more advanced techniques of agricultural production may have been transferred from Japan to Korea; and the mechanics underlying "forced exports," whereby Japanese landowners sold rice grown in Korea back to Japan directly.

A second characteristic of the changing agrarian sector was its heavy export orientation. For example, while total Korean rice production during the colonial period nearly doubled, rice exports to Japan during the same period increased six times (Suh, 1978, p. 92, Table 43). In addition, while the overall economy of the Japanese empire was protected, trading within the empire was relatively free of tariffs and other restrictions. Rapid growth of exports to the metropole with a more advanced agricultural sector thus points to an additional source—the quintessential source of competition—that must have also contributed to sustained improvements in agricultural productivity. Finally, the geography of the changing agrarian scene is worthy of attention. Rice production and Japanese ownership of Korean land were both more concentrated in the southern half of Korea. Bulk of rice exports also originated in the South. The southern half of Korea thus developed a relatively productive agriculture during the colonial period.

To conclude this discussion on the changes in the agrarian sector, two developments of long-term consequence need to be underlined. The nearly obvious point is that a productive agriculture was a necessary component of rapid economic growth, first during colonial Korea, and later, even more prominently, in sovereign South Korea. While many developing countries, such as in Africa, are still attempting their agricultural revolution, and others, such as India and the Philippines, hailed the Green Revolution from the mid-1960s onward, Korea was already undergoing a biological revolution in agriculture in the first half of this century. Just before WWII, rice yields in Korea were approaching Japanese yields, which were then among the highest in the world (e.g., if the US yields in 1938 were 100, Japan's were 154 and Korea's 111) (Grajdanzev, 1944, p. 87; and Ishikawa, 1967, p. 95, Charts 2–5). Rapid increase in agriculture production, in turn, provided both food and inputs to sustain an industrial drive on the one hand, and on the other hand, yielded high incomes and savings that found their way back into a growing economy. A decade hence, after land reforms were implemented in South Korea, the productive agricultural base and related incomes also contributed to the emergence of a domestic market for manufactured goods.

The other less obvious legacy concerns the "model of development" that undergirded the agrarian transformation. As in Meiji Japan, but even more so, the colonial state in Korea established its superiority as the key actor that would direct economic change. The state then employed various carrots and sticks to incorporate the propertied groups in a production-oriented alliance. A key focus of the state's efforts was improving the technology of production, namely, better seeds, fertilizer and irrigation. Even after decolonization, these efforts left behind a bureaucratic infrastructure that was adept at facilitating technology-intensive agricultural development. Moreover, public subsidies from the colonial state helped improve the profitability of private producers, as well as productivity and production. This pattern of state and propertied class alliance for production, centered around technology and other public subsidies, would of course repeat itself in subsequent periods, and in numerous other economic activities, especially in industry, to which I now turn.

(c) The state and industrialization

The extent of Korea's industrialization during the colonial phase was both considerable and nearly unique in the comparative history of colonialism: the average, annual rate of growth in industry (including mining and manufacturing) during 1910–40 was nearly 10%; and by 1940, nearly 35% of the total commodity production originated in the industrial sector (Suh, 1978, p. 48, Table 11; and p. 46, Tables 17 and 18). While analyzing the why and how of this experience below, as well as its long-term significance, the main point is not that South Korea somehow inherited a relatively industrialized economy. It did not! A fair amount of the heavy industry was located in the north and significant industrial concentrations were destroyed during the Korean war. Nevertheless, a war-destroyed economy, with an experience of rapid industrialization behind it, is quite different than a tradition-bound, nearly stagnant, agrarian economy.[39] I will return below to the issue of the creation of a trained and disciplined working class. At the apex of the social pyramid, and from the standpoint of the colonial legacy, several issues of long-term significance deserve our attention here: the style of development, especially a state-dominated, state–private sector alliance for production and profit that emerged under Japanese rule; the emergence of a significant entrepreneurial strata among Koreans; and a growing economy whose structure was already heavily export oriented.

The Japanese approach to Korea's industrialization went through three more or less distinct phases. During the first decade of the colonial rule, Japan sought to protect Korean market as an outlet for Japanese manufactured goods. Rules and regulations were thus created to inhibit the start up of new factories in Korea by both Japanese and Korean entrepreneurs. The fact that annual growth rates in the manufacturing sector during this decade still averaged a respectable 7%, reflected the very low starting base. This growth had several components. First, there were the new public sector investments in power, railways and other infrastructure. The private sector growth originated mainly in food processing industries—especially rice mills—that were initiated by Japanese migrants with the hope of selling rice back to Japan. Exchanging Japanese manufactured goods for Korean rice and other primary products was, of course, the initial colonial policy. The Government-General thus helped Japanese entrepreneurs start up these mills by providing both financial and infrastructural support. Finally, some of this early growth also involved the participation of Koreans. Small-scale manufacturing did not require the permission of the Government-General. Moreover, incomes of landowning Koreans had started to rise and not all of their demand could be met by Japanese imports. Emulating the Japanese migrants, Koreans set up small industries (often called household industries in Japanese colonial documents; they employed 10–20 workers) in such areas as metals, dyeing, paper making, ceramics, rubber shoes, knitted cotton socks and sake and soy sauce. The number of small factories thus increased from 151 in 1910 to 1,900 in 1919; 971 of these 1,900 factories were owned by Koreans (Park, 1985, pp. 16–18).

WWI transformed Japan from a debtor to a creditor country. With swollen company profits, the Japanese imperial government sought opportunities for Japanese capital overseas, including in Korea. Restrictions on manufacturing in Korea were abolished and thus began a second phase in Korean industrialization. Japanese investors did not rush in. The competitive pressure from Japanese manufactured goods was considerable and the Government-General wanted to encourage complementarities rather than competition between Japanese exporters to and Japanese investors in Korea. The colonial state supported a select few Japanese investors by helping them choose areas of investment, providing cheap land, raising capital for investment, guaranteeing initial profits via subsidies and by moving workers to out-of-the-way locations. As a result, major business groups such as Mitsui and Mitsubishi moved into Korea; others followed. The average, annual rate of growth in industry during the 1920s was over 8%. A significant component of this was Japanese private investment in textiles, some in processing of raw materials and some rather large scale investments in mining, iron, steel, hydroelectric power, and even shipbuilding. The number of factories employing more than 50 workers went up from 89 in 1922 to 230 in 1930 (Park, 1985, p. 42).

Korean participation in this second phase, while a distant second to the role of Japanese capital was not insignificant. Relatively small-scale, Korean "household industries" continued to mushroom. Their growth reflected several underlying trends: rising demand resulting from growing incomes of wealthy Koreans and Japanese in Korea, as well as economic growth in Japan; the role of Japanese factories as "Schumpeterian innovators" that were followed by a "cluster" of Korean imitators; and forward and backward linkages created by Japanese investments (Chung, 1973, p. 93). Moreover, after the Korean nationalist outburst in 1919, the colonial government liberalized its ruling strategy for several years and sought to coopt some wealthy Korean businessmen. Enterprising Koreans with initial capital—often with roots in land wealth—were thus allowed to enter medium to large-scale trade and manufacturing. Those willing to cooperate with the Government-General were also provided credit, subsidies, and other public supports. Of the 230 factories that employed more than 50 workers in 1930, 49 thus came to be Korean owned (Park, 1985, p. 42). South Korean nationalist historiography often underestimates the level of cooperation between Japanese colonial state and native Korean capital. Revisionist historians, however, have now documented the extensive nature of such cooperation (Eckert, 1991, and McNamara, 1990). In the words of Eckert, "Korean capitalism . . . came to enjoy its first flowering under Japanese rule and with official Japanese blessing" (Eckert, 1991, p. 6). Major Korean *chaebols*, such as Kyungbang—the most prominent Korean group during the colonial period, that began in textiles—Kongsin Hosiery, Paeksan Trading Company, Hwasin Department Store and Mokpo Rubber Company thus got started during this period.[40]

During the 1930s and well into WWII, Korea underwent very rapid industrialization. The rate of industrialization hastened and the process acquired considerable depth during this phase. The annual, average rate of growth of industry was nearly 15% and a significant component of new growth originated in heavy industries, especially chemical industry. The moving force behind these developments was, once again, government policies. As the Western world went into a depression, and protected economies sprouted, Japan aggressively sought growth by creating an import-substituting economy of sorts on an empire-wide scale (Schumpeter, 1940,

Chs. XXI. 3 and XXII. 8). After annexing Manchuria in 1931, moreover, Korea became an advanced military supply base for the Japanese war efforts in China. The Korean economy was thus developed by the colonial government as part and parcel of an empire-wide strategy to promote rapid growth, with a potential war always in mind.

The development of hydroelectric power in northern Korea during the 1920s and early 1930s had brought down costs of electricity and thus barriers to starting new factories. Raw materials such as coal and iron ore were also concentrated in the same part of Korea, reducing transportation costs. With wages for workers nearly half of that in Japan, and absolutely no labor protection laws (more on this below), "market conditions" for investment in Korea, especially in northern Korea, were far from adverse during the 1930s. There was also a "push" factor at work: the Japanese imperial government had tightened control on Japanese industry within Japan, while giving business a freer hand elsewhere in the Empire. Nevertheless, direct role of the Government-General in encouraging business into Korea was essential. The colonial state periodically laid out its industrial policy, indicating the preferred direction of economic change, especially given war planning, where the government expected demand to grow. Moreover, government and business cooperated to an extent that contours of corporate policy were "indirectly fixed" by the government's economic plans (Eckert, 1991, p. 73). Another analyst notes that "adaptability to state economic priorities was a prerequisite for successful large-scale enterprise" in colonial Korea (McNamara, 1990, p. 9).

The Government-General utilized several economic and noneconomic instruments to ensure compliance with its preferred economic direction. First, the colonial state kept a "tight control on the colony's financial structure" (Eckert, 1991, p. 73). The Chosen Industrial Bank, which helped finance new investments, and which had controlling interests in a number of diverse industries, was controlled by the Government-General. This was a critical issue for Korean investors who had no other independent source of credit. Even for Japanese *zaibatsu*, who could raise some of their finances from corporate sources in Japan, cooperation with the state was important; for example, the Government-General floated compulsory savings bonds within Korea as a way of helping Japanese companies finance some of the gigantic investment projects (hydroelectric power and fertilizer plants) in northern Korea. Second, there were the perennial subsidies; one analyst estimates that these were of the order of 1% of "GNP" per year (Chung, 1973, p. 91). These were used selectively to promote government's priorities. For example, the highest subsidy for a time was provided to Mitsubishi to encourage gold mining; the Japanese imperial government needed the gold to pay for such strategic imports from the United States as scrap iron, copper and zinc.[41] The next largest subsidy was provided to producers of zinc and magnesium, products necessary for manufacturing aeroplanes. And so on (Grajdanzev, 1944, pp. 138–40). Tax exemptions were similarly used discriminately to both encourage and direct economic activity.

While it is difficult to assess the significance of noneconomic factors in this state-directed, state–business alliance, they are nevertheless worth noting. The Governor-General would periodically exhort businessmen to eschew narrow "capitalistic profits and commercial self-interest" and to consider the economic "mission" of Korea from the standpoint of the "national economy." The direction of influence between the state and business is also nicely captured by the fact that both Japanese and Korean businessmen referred to the Governor-General as *jifu* (a loving father), highlighting the benevolent upper hand of the state. Again, in the words of Eckert, businessmen were intricately incorporated into the policy making process and what they lost in "autonomy," they made up for "magnificently" by way of "corporate profits."[42]

A few specific examples of government–business cooperation will further help flush out the nature of this mutually convenient alliance. The example of government subsidies for Mitsubishi to encourage gold mining has already been noted. Mitsu was similarly granted the ginseng monopoly by the Government-General in exchange for a healthy share of the sprawling profits as taxes on the monopoly. The case of the smaller Onoda cement factory has been studied in detail and is interesting (Park, 1985, pp. 83–99). The Government-General discovered large limestone deposits in Korea during its surveys. This information was provided to cement manufacturers in Japan. The Government-General also indicated its needs for cement within Korea, thus encouraging Onoda to invest in Korea. Most important, the Government-General laid the ground work for Onoda's expansion by ordering provincial governors to buy cement from Onoda factories for all government construction projects during the agricultural expansion phase in the 1920s, and regularly set aside nearly 10% of the annual budget intended for agricultural production projects for purchase of this cement.

The level of cooperation between the Government-General and colonial Korea's largest Japanese business group, Nihon Chissō, was so intricate that it is difficult to tell where the public efforts ended and private efforts began. For example, the preliminary work for the construction of hydroelectric power plants—such as the necessary surveys, choice of location, soil tests—was conducted by the Government General. Private energies of Nihon Chissō were then tapped but, again, the Government-General played a critical role in capital accumulation by putting at the company's disposal the service of government controlled Industrial Bank, and by floating savings bonds. The government further helped move workers from the south to the labor-scarce northern region, where power generators were to be located, and subsequently remained deeply involved in the pricing and distribution of electrical power. What the government got out of all this collaboration was a ready supply of cheap electricity in Korea which, in turn, became the basis for rapid industrialization. From Nihon Chissō's point of view, hydroelectric power was only one of numerous projects that the company undertook in Korea. What it did buy in the process was enormous goodwill of the Government-General that subsequently was translated into opportunities for expansion in a number of other lucrative fields, such as nitrogen and fertilizer production.

Several of the larger Korean Business groups also benefited from a close cooperation with the Government-General. For example, new research has documented how the largest Korean business group, Kyongbang, financed its investments with the help of the Government-General (Eckert, 1991). The subsidies provided by the government during 1924–35 added up to nearly "one fourth of the company's paid-up capital in 1935" (p. 84). Furthermore, the main source of finance was loans from the government-controlled Chosen Industrial Bank. Personal relationships of key actors helped secure the bonds between Kyongbang, the Industrial Bank and the Government-General. The terms of the loans were very favorable, indicating a comfortable and close relationship between the colonial state and a Korean business group. Another research similarly documents the close cooperation between the colonial state and the Min brothers in the field of banking and Pak Hung-sik in commerce; these ventures eventually matured into such major Korean *chaebols* as the Hwasin Department Store (McNamara, 1990).

Within the framework of a war economy, the planned government–business cooperation became the basis of very rapid industrialization of Korea during 1930–45. During some years the rates of growth were especially breathtaking: for example, during 1936–39, industrial production more than doubled. By the early 1940s, agricultural and industrial production were nearly at par (both providing some 40% of the national production); and by 1943, heavy industry provided nearly half of the total industrial production (Park, 1985, p. 51, Tables 11 and 12). Some specific patterns within this overall economic transformation also deserve our attention, especially because they proved to be of long-term significance.

First, the colonial state preferred to work with large business groups. Following the Meiji model, but with a vengeance in Korea, the Government-General utilized various means to encourage the formation of large-scale business enterprises: larger groups enjoyed preferred interest rates on credit, lower charges on electricity, direct price supports, and indirect subsidies such as lower transportation costs on government-controlled railways. Nearly two-thirds of the total production in the late 1930s was thus produced by only a handful of Japanese *zaibatsu* in Korea. Since the Korean, family-centered, but gigantic enterprises also came into their own under this regime, herein may lie the origin of *chaebols*.[43]

It is important to underline a second pattern, namely, that a significant strata of Korean entrepreneurs emerged under the colonial auspices. Many of these would go on to establish such major *chaebols* of modern South Korea as Samsung, Hyundai and Lucky. If judged mainly by the proportion of total private capital or of large enterprises that Koreans owned, the Korean presence in comparison to that of the Japanese appears minuscule.[44] As has been pointed out by others, however, this approach is misleading. A significant minority of firms (nearly 30%) were owned jointly by Koreans and Japanese. More important from the standpoint of the emergence of an entrepreneurial class was the scale of Korean participation by 1937: "there were 2,300 Korean run factories throughout the industrial spectrum, and about 160 of these establishments employed over 50 workers" (Eckert, 1991, p. 55). Since these figures are for all of Korea, and since it is fair to assume that most of these must have concentrated in the South after the communists took over the northern half, one may observe with some confidence that colonialism left behind a considerable density of entrepreneurship in South Korea.

A third pattern concerns the geographical distribution of industry. Those wishing to deny continuities with the colonial period again point to the fact that much of the industry was located in the north and was thus not inherited by South Korea. This is partly true, insofar as the largest chemical and other heavy industries were indeed located in the northern provinces. A number of qualifications, however, are also needed. The chemical, metal and electricity-generating industries, that were concentrated in the North, constituted 30, 8 and 2.2% respectively of the total industrial production in 1938.[45] That adds up to some 40%, leaving a good chunk for the South. More than half of the total industry was probably located in the South. The nature of southern industries was also distinct; they tended to be in such fields as food processing, textiles, machine and tools and tobacco related industries. By contrast, the industries in the north were highly capital intensive, high-cost production units that were not well integrated with the local economy. Northern industries were much more likely to evolve into "white elephants," requiring continuous protection, rather than into nimble, labor-intensive exporters of consumer products.

The last pattern that needs to be noted concerns the deep ties that came to link colonial Korean and Japanese economies. This pattern is, of course, not unique to Japan and Korea; it tends to characterize many metropoles and their colonies. What is unique, however, is the degree to which Korea was already an exporting economy, and the degree to which it was already exporting manufactured products to Japan during the colonial phase. If the average "foreign trade ratio" for a country of the size of Korea in 1938–39 was 0.24, Suh (1978) estimates that Korea's foreign trade ratio in those years was around 0.54, suggesting that Korea was exporting twice as much as any other comparable economy. Moreover, 43% of these exports were manufactured goods (Suh, 1978, pp. 120–21, Table 58). How many other developing countries in the world emerged from colonialism with this type of an economic profile? Critical to note here is not only the structure of the economy that was inherited by South Korea, but also the psychological legacy: whereas most developing countries emerged from WWII with a distrust of open economies—because they either associated openness with stagnation (as in India), or import substitution with successful industrial growth (as in Brazil)—many South Korean elites came to associate, rather early, an export orientation with a high-growth economy.

To sum up this section, the highly authoritarian and bureaucratic state that the Japanese helped construct in colonial Korea turned out to be a rather efficacious economic actor. The state utilized its bureaucratic capacities to directly undertake numerous economic tasks: anywhere from collecting more taxes, to building infrastructure, to undertaking production directly. More important, the state incorporated property-owning classes in-production-oriented alliances. The colonial state was highly purposive: it put increasing production near the top of its priorities. Propertied classes were offered various rewards—especially, handsome profits—for cooperating with the state in fulfilling this economic agenda. The state, in turn, utilized numerous means—including promotion of technology, control over credit, subsidies, capital accumulation, and even noneconomic exhortations—to ensure compliance from both Korean and Japanese landlords and businessmen. As a result of this state–business alliance, the economy was successful in exporting manufactured goods. Moreover, as documented by revisionist historians, a substantial strata of Korean entrepreneurs developed, who either flourished while cooperating with the state, or who wished for larger government support so they could also flourish. In either case, a "model" of development—inspired by Meiji Japan, but also transformed in a colonial setting—was in the making that would situate a state-directed economy with state–business alliance at the heart of the strategy of transformation.

2.4 THE COLONIAL STATE AND THE LOWER CLASSES

The colonial authorities sought to transform Korea in accordance with Japanese imperial needs. Controlled involvement of the lower classes—peasants and workers—was essential for the success of this project; and both the colonial state and the propertied classes collaborated to ensure their compliance. While historical studies of lower classes in colonial Korea are meager—and as they become available, we may well be led to change our minds—the scattered evidence that is available suggests that both peasants and workers lived highly constrained lives, deriving few benefits from Korea's rapid economic transformation. These outcomes, moreover, were part of a deliberate plan that served important political and economic interests. From a political standpoint, the highly repressive and penetrating colonial state succeeded in imposing order on Korean society; this freed the state to focus its political energies in the pursuit of a narrow, production-oriented agenda. On the economic front, incomes and wages generally lagged behind productivity gains, facilitating higher profitability, savings and investments. Moreover, since much of the growth was export oriented, lagging incomes and the limited mass demand did not become a constraint on growth.

Since repression and exclusion of the lower classes was integral to the colonial political economy, and since critical components of this "model," especially the harsh political control of the working class, continued well into the future, it is important to analyze the structure and the dynamics of the labor-repressive strategy. As far as trends in the colonial countryside were concerned, recall that precolonial, Yi Korea was hardly a haven for the lowly tenants, peasants or others at the bottom of the social hierarchy. Yi Korea was a slave society, at least until 1800, and even though the practice of slavery declined sharply through the 19th century, it was the Japanese who abolished slavery in Korea. The recurring fiscal crises of the Yi state had also led Korean rulers to squeeze the peasantry, especially via indirect taxation, thus contributing to misery, rebellion and brigandage. What the Japanese did in this situation was rationalize the strategies of both extraction and control.

While well-organized gendarmes subdued pockets of openly rebellious peasants, and continued to do so for quite some time, bulk of the peasantry was systematically brought under state's domination. First, the legalization of private property in the hands of landlords, and a regularization of land rents, created a legitimate basis for tenancy as the modal relationship adjoining the tiller and the landowner. While tenancy had existed in Korea for a long time, given steady population growth, tenancy increased throughout the colonial period; toward the end of the period, nearly 70% of farming households worked under tenancy arrangement of one type or another (Robinson in Eckert *et al.*, 1990, p. 307). And as most students of agrarian societies understand, tenancy as the main mode of production makes tenants dependent on landowners, and dependencies tend to be especially severe where tenants are not legally protected, where attempts to forge tenant organizations are met with swift retribution, and where the weight of the state is mainly behind the landowners.

The Japanese strategy for controlling the peasant population was twofold: direct and effective downward penetration of the state; and incorporation of landowning or other influential local groups as ruling allies. Both of these themes have been discussed above. To the best of my knowledge, there are no detailed studies available (at least not in English language) as to how this system worked in practice, especially from the viewpoint of the peasant. As far as one can make out, while sporadic peasant rebellion never died out, the ruling strategy was effective at establishing a repressive order.[46] In addition to severe economic dependencies, which sap the rebellious energy of any social group, the effectiveness of control rested on a combination of direct and indirect rule. The traditional system of influence within villages, as well as of information flows, was buttressed by a well-organized bureaucracy: local police with uniforms and telephones; tax collectors, also replete with uniforms; and an intelligence service that periodically prepared reports for the provincial and central governments on a wide variety of issues.

The Korean working class originated under Japanese rule. While Korea was still largely an agrarian country in the 1940s (more than 70% of the population still derived its livelihood from agriculture), a considerable working class had also come into being by then. For example, if there were less than 10,000 industrial workers in 1910, the population of industrial workers had reached 1.3 million in 1943 (Park, 1985, Part I). Assuming a minimum family size of four, a good 20% of the population must have thus depended on industrial work for their livelihood. Moreover, another 15% of Koreans lived outside of Korea in the Japanese empire, a significant minority working as unskilled urban labor in Japan and some in Manchuria. Since many of the workers within Korea had been moved from the populated south to factories in the north, and since most of the Koreans working in the Empire returned to Korea when the Empire disintegrated, a significant minority of the population in colonial Korea found itself moved around and uprooted from its traditional society niche.[47]

The colonial state collaborated with both Japanese and Korean capitalists to devise the structures of control for this working class. The state provided the broad framework, which, in its essence, was brutally simple: attempts to create labor union were prohibited; trespasses were met with severe retribution; and few, if any, laws existed to regulate and protect workers (Grajdanzev, 1944, p. 182). While these restrictions did not fully succeed in eliminating unionization attempts and even strikes (Park, 1985, pp. 60–8; Asagiri, 1929; and Chen, 1930)—especially in the somewhat more liberal 1920s, and again in the late 1930s, when with a war economy, labor demand and thus labor's bargaining power increased—they do help underline the highly anti-labor stance of the colonial state.

Within this broad framework, individual companies had a fairly free hand in setting down labor management practices (at least until the war years, when the state actively got involved in the control and mobilization of labor). Not surprisingly, Japanese companies, such as the Onoda cement factory—which, as already noted, has been studied in detail—adopted a Japanese labor management style.[48] Japanese managers sought to create a skilled, disciplined, and hierarchically organized work force in exchange for decent wages—that were often higher than earnings in both Korean-owned factories and in agriculture, but lagged way behind the steady productivity gains—and job security. Young Koreans of peasant origins, with only little education, were hired at a rather early age (say 18–22), provided on-the-job training, occasionally sent to Japan for more specialized experience, punished severely for lack of punctuality or diligence, rewarded for loyalty and steady performance, and for those who survived the various tests and hurdles, given assurances of continuous service pension and retirement fund benefits. The carrots and sticks appear to have been quite successful: in this one specific case, at least, over a few decades, young Korean peasants were transformed into "Onoda men," who, in spite of such social problems as being treated as inferior to Japanese workers, took pride in their skilled industrial work in a Japanese company.

Since there is very little research available that does not depend on company documents, one has to be wary of how "satisfied" and "loyal" Korean workers really were. There was very little real increase in wages throughout this period of high growth. Moreover, when economic opportunities increased during the hypergrowth of the 1930s, workers voted with their feet: e.g., the rate of turnover in the Onoda cement factory during the 1930s rose sharply as skilled workers took their skills elsewhere for higher wages (Park, 1985, p. 142). Most important, workers were totally prohibited from forming any organizations of their own. Any efforts were met with dismissal, arrest and a permanent police record. Industrial relations in colonial Korea were thus "absolutely one sided," favoring the management (Park, 1985, p. 142). Workers were closely supervised. The factories themselves were "very closed, isolated, and protected place(s)." The work place was "closed to outsiders by a wire fence, the constant patrol of its guards and the availability of police protection in case of an incident." Finally, closing the state and company cooperation loop, the Japanese management "kept radical elements out by tight inspection and in doing this they were fully supported by government policy and a strong police posture" (Park, 1985, p. 184).

Worker's conditions in Korean-owned factories were certainly no better, and may have been worse. One case study of the largest Korean business house that is readily available would certainly support this view.[49] For example, 80% of the workers at Kyongbong's textile mill were unmarried peasant girls in their late teens, some even recruited from tenant families who worked the lands owned by the mill owners. The factories operated round-the-clock, each girl working a grueling 12-hour shift, with one 40-minute rest time. Since labor control was deemed essential, work was under "intense labor supervision." Discipline inside the factory was "severe" and extended to personal lives. All the girls lived in dormitories within a factory compound and needed permission to both leave the compound and to receive visitors. The system resembled "a low-security prison." Whenever labor conditions in this and other plants became turbulent, "strikes were repressed with the same energy as was used to repress communism." State "intimidation and force" were thus central to this relatively simple and "crude approach to social control."

During the war years social controls on workers tightened as the state got directly involved in labor management. A *sampo* system was established, whereby, "industrial patriotism clubs," involving employers and employees, were created, aimed at increasing production. Workers' representatives—paid full-time salaries by employers—and employers formed associations that designed programs of "educating the workers, making the production process more efficient and preventing disputes among workers."[50]

In sum, a bureaucratic and penetrating authoritarian state collaborated with property-owning groups in colonial Korea to carve out a rather repressive and exclusionary strategy to control the laboring classes. This strategy of control, moreover, was necessary for rapid economic transformation. With majority of the lower classes subdued, the colonial state was free to concentrate its architectonic energies on devising and pursuing a strategy of economic transformation. Moreover, the political capacity to hold wages behind productivity gains facilitated high rates of profitability and thus continued investment and growth.

2.5 GENERAL INFERENCES

If Korea at the turn of the 20th century was a mini-China, by mid-century, Japanese colonialism had transformed it into a mini-Japan. While this statement both oversimplifies and distorts, the grain of truth in it is essential for understanding the subsequent high growth political economy of South Korea. Moreover, if this claim is acceptable, a number of general inferences follow. In order to draw these out, I address three themes below: the implications of the historical materials discussed above for a comparative understanding in Korea; the insights that can be derived from these historical materials for the study of the nature and origins of "developmental states"; and finally, some general thoughts on the importance of reopening the issue of the variable colonial pasts of developing countries, so as to fully appreciate the roots of the divergent paths that these countries are now traversing.

(a) Korea in a comparative perspective

It is clear that Japanese colonialism in Korea helped establish some basic state–society patterns that many now readily associate as integral to the later South Korean "model" of a high-growth political economy. These patterns include a highly bureaucratized, penetrating and architectonic state, a state-dominated alliance of state and property owners for production and profits, and repressive social control of the working classes. Demonstrating parallels between historical and contemporary situations, however, is clearly not enough to sustain an argument for historical continuity; one also needs to point out the mechanisms whereby continuity was maintained.

It would take a separate essay to fully demonstrate exactly how and why there was a fair amount of institutional continuity between colonial Korea and subsequent South Korea, especially under Park Chung-Hee.[51] In any case, elements of such an argument already exist in the literature (Cumings, 1984b; Eckert, 1991; and McNamara, 1990) and, for our present purposes, a brief outline will suffice. There was more than a 15-year interlude, a traumatic interlude one may add, between the Japanese leaving Korea and when a truncated South Korea settled on a high-growth path under Park Chung-

Hee. This interlude was marked by a US occupation, a civil war, a division of the country into communist and anti-communist halves, establishment of a government with some nationalist and democratic credentials in the South, and then a degeneration of this government under diverse pressures, leading up to a military coup. In spite of all of this social drama, when diverse historical legacies were simultaneously unleashed and when the future was anything but certain, how did South Korea under Park Chung-Hee end up resembling colonial Korea in its basic state–society outlines?

The answer resolves in part around the structures that were simply never altered in any fundamental way, and in part around conscious choices made by leaders of South Korea. For example, Cumings has demonstrated with great care how and why the US occupying forces in Korea left the colonial state more or less intact; the alternative would have been to unleash a popular revolution of nationalist and radical forces. As a result, the bureaucracy, the police and the military that sovereign South Korea inherited were essentially colonial creations. In Cumings's words, in spite of a prolonged American involvement in Korean affairs, "it was Japan's impact that lasted," and "whether it was in the military, the bureaucracy or the polity, Americans during the occupation found themselves playing midwife to a Japanese gestation, rather than bringing forth their own Korean progeny."[52]

Not only were state structures kept intact but the state's capacity and willingness to direct economic change, as well as the economic instruments used by the state—e.g., control over credit—continued from colonial to post-colonial periods.[53] There is little evidence, moreover, that Korean businessmen in South Korea objected much to these arrangements. On the contrary, there was also a fair amount of continuity in the state-dependent nature of Korean capitalism. For example, Eckert (1991, p. 254) has found that "60 percent of the founders of South Korea's top fifty chaebol" had participated directly in business under colonial auspices. Since these businessmen had either flourished with the help of the colonial state, or complained and periodically petitioned the colonial state for more support, it is likely that their political preferences strengthened the state-directed, state–business alliance for production and profit. Finally, the corporatist patterns of worker control were also colonial in origin: the employer–employee "clubs" for promoting "patriotism" and production, in the words of a labor analyst, became "one of Japan's permanent contributions to Korea's industrial relations system" (Ogle, 1990, p. 6).

None of these continuities were inevitable. North Korea, a product of the same historical legacy, clearly went on a very different path. In South Korea, the chaos of the Rhee period could have continued indefinitely; or, alternatively, a new leadership could have undertaken basic changes and put South Korea on a totally different path. The postcoup leadership, however, chose continuity with colonial patterns. While complex motivations of national security and of protecting sectional social interests were at work, it was the nature of the leadership which finally undergirded the choice of continuity. Park Chung-Hee was a product of Japanese colonial Korean army, trained in Japanese military academy in Manchuria. Chong-Sik Lee, one of the leading Korea scholars in the United States, describes him as a "Japanophile," fascinated by the "Meiji model," and bent on steering Korea along the Japanese path to modernity (Lee, 1985, pp. 62–3). South Korean leaders often covered such proclivities with an anti-Japanese rhetoric here and a nationalist flourish there. Desirous mainly of high economic growth, however, leaders such as Park Chung-Hee knew well that the key elements of the "model" left behind by the Japanese were still intact in the early 1960s: a highly pervasive and penetrating state that could be turned authoritarian, purged of corruption and made to refocus attention on matters economic; a state-dependent business strata that understood the benefits of cooperating with a purposive state; and a highly controlled working class. Since this "model" had worked in the past, until proven to the contrary, or unless it had to be abandoned, there was no reason why it ought not also work for sovereign South Korea. Moreover, the extent to which postwar Japan remained a "reference society" for South Korea was itself, in part, a production of considerable colonial contacts that had created links of language, economic structures and a shared understanding of how to construct high growth political economies.

If the case for considerable continuity is thus persuasive—and this does not necessitate denying either some important changes in the subsequent political economy, or the credit due to Koreans for their economic achievements, for they could have easily derailed the whole process—it follows that the roots of the high growth Korean political economy lie deep in a unique colonial experience. Two further implications follow. First, quite a few development scholars compare South Korea's economic performance to that of other slower growing developing countries. The underlying assumption often is that, all of these countries began from more or less the same starting point of very low per capita incomes in the 1950s, but somehow South Korea, and a few other newly industrializing countries (NICs) rushed ahead. The question then becomes, "Why South Korea?" In light of the discussion above, this manner of posing the question appears inappropriate. The starting point for comparison has to be deeper in history, especially in the formative colonial phase. Even if South Korea's low per capita income in the 1950s was similar to that of an India, Brazil or a Nigeria, South Korea's starting point was very different: it had a much more dynamic economy in the half a century preceding the 1950s and, by the 1950s, its deeper state–society configurations were relatively unique.

Second, some development scholars pose the puzzle of South Korea's phenomenal economic success in the following terms: Why was South Korea able to switch to an "export-oriented policy" in the early 1960s, whereas many other developing countries continued on the "import substitution" path (e.g., Haggard, 1991). Again, this manner of framing the comparative question is somewhat misconceived. South Korea indeed made some important policy changes under Park Chung-Hee, but their significance can easily be exaggerated; moreover, the state–society configuration that enabled these policies to succeed had deeper historical roots. In this sense, South Korea under Park Chung-Hee did not so much "switch," as it fell back into the grooves of colonial origins, or, more precisely, chose one of the two or three main alternatives that were available to it from its complex historical legacy. Revolutionary communism, a corrupt and wasteful autocracy of the Rhee type and a more US-style open democracy were all realistic possible paths along which South Korea could have traveled. The key elements, however, of the eventual path it adopted—a Japanese-style, state-driven export economy—were deeply etched into the social fabric. More specifically, Korean economy, especially southern Korean economy, was already export-oriented, its entrepreneurs had considerable experience in selling abroad, and the state within this economy had learned from its own history that strong support for business and exports, and tight control over labor, was a route to high economic growth.

(b) Nature of "developmental states"

Among scholars who share the view that states have played both a positive and a negative role in economic development, a pressing subsequent question concerns the comparative analysis of "developmental" and "predatory" states.[54] More specifically, what distinguishes patterns of state intervention in the economy, and why do some developing country states end up successfully transforming their economies, whereas others end up as "rent seekers," preying on their own society's scarce resources? While detailed comparative analyses are the best route to develop answers to this complex but important question, the single country materials presented above also speak to the issue, especially because the Korean case is central to any such analysis and because the Korean state was itself, at the turn of the century, transformed from a "predatory" to a "developmental" state.

Evans (1989) has described "developmental states" as exhibiting the characteristic of "embedded autonomy"; "autonomy" of bureaucratized states from social entanglements gives them a capacity to direct social change, and social "embeddedness," in turn, especially the links these states forge with business and industrial classes, enable state elites to incorporate these powerful groups in the state's economic project. The historical materials analyzed above are not inconsistent with this account of "developmental states." Nevertheless, the Korean historical materials also suggest some qualifications and further specifications.

The first important qualification concerns the issue of where the policy goals of any state directed economy come from. Arguments about "developmental states," whether in Evans's or in other versions, often focus more on explaining a state's capacity to implement goals and less on where these goals come from in the first place. The latter issue requires an explicit focus on the political process of a society. Policy goals of any society reflect complex processes involving how the highest authorities balance their own preferences against national and international pressures. In the colonial Korean case discussed here, it was clear that the major shifts in policy goals—trade of raw materials for manufactured goods, followed by encouragement of food production in the early phase; encouragement of Japanese investments in manufacturing, along with some Korean participation during the middle phase; and finally, in the last phase, a war economy with rapid industrialization—mainly reflected Japanese priorities, with an occasional concession to Korean pressures. In sovereign polities, this process of policy prioritization is often highly complex and would require a more detailed study than the colonial type of case discussed here. Nevertheless, the general point ought to be clear: since efficacious states can be used by their leaders to accomplish various goals, including nondevelopmental goals, the politics of how developmental goals emerge as a priority must be an important component of any study of "developmental states."

The juxtaposition of the late Chosòn or Yi state against the colonial state also yields some further insights about "predatory" and "developmental" states. The late Chosòn state was personalistic and factionalized at the apex, and it had very little downward reach in the society, it was also deeply penetrated by landowning classes. These characteristics bequeathed political incapacity. The result was that the Yi state was quite incapable of laying out and pursuing an agenda of socioeconomic change. By contrast, the colonial state turned out to be highly efficacious. While this was no developmental state in the sense that it helped develop the whole society—on the contrary, it was a rather brutal, exclusionary state, not to mention that it was a colonial state—it nevertheless could establish order and facilitate economic growth. How did it achieve this capacity? The changes introduced by the Japanese that helped increase state capacity can be best thought of as changes along three dimensions: changes in the state structures; creation of new economic instruments in the hands of the state; and new patterns of state–class relations. Since all of these have been discussed in some detail above, now they only require a brief reiteration.

First, the significant changes in the state structure were three: creation of centralized authority with a clear agenda of change; depersonalization of authority structures, so that public and private interests were first separated and only then reintegrated on a new basis, with public goals mainly in command; and downward penetration of the state's authority in society via the creation of a disciplined bureaucracy.[55] These changes enabled the new political authorities to formulate specific public goals and to implement them in the far reaches of the society.

Second, the state also created a number of economic instruments that did not exist before and that enhanced the state's capacity to direct the economy:

a rationalized currency system, banks and other credit institutions that the state controlled, long and short-term economic plans, production-oriented new technology, and a variety of direct and indirect subsidies. Finally, the state and social classes established a new relationship. In both the countryside and the city, the state and property-owning classes entered an alliance that was set mainly on the state's terms, but that was nevertheless mutually beneficial: the state desired and succeeded in securing steady increases in production, whereas the property-owning groups received enough political support to ensure healthy profits. The state and property owning classes also collaborated to control peasants and workers in what amounted to a successful labor-repressive strategy.

This last point directs attention to another important modification in Evans's type of formulation of "developmental states," namely, the significance of downward penetration of systematic political control. Far too much analytical attention is being devoted in contemporary attempts to understand "developmental states" to the apex of the political economy. This is unfortunate because the relationship of the state to laboring classes, especially the modalities of participation and control in the process of production, is a central part of the "story" of how and why some states succeed in industrializing their economies. For example, it is clear in the account above that the colonial state and Japanese and Korean businessmen collaborated, not only to strictly control any demand-making or dissident actions of workers, but also to train them at work, pay a living wage, transmit some pride in their endeavors and provide job security. This combination of "carrots and sticks" generated considerable control over the lives and behavior of workers. While hardly conducive to the creation of a free and desirable society, this control, in turn, contributed to both productivity gains and, more importantly, enabled the state to single-mindedly pursue economic growth.

A bureaucratized and penetrating authoritarian state with clear growth-oriented goals, armed with a panoply of economic instruments, and allied with propertied but against laboring social classes, this is the stuff of which transformative power in the hands of the state is made of. Or so, at least, emerges from the study of this one specific case. Neither the brutal, controlling nature, nor the colonial origins of this specific "developmental state" can be recommended to others on normative grounds. Yet, for those who believe that states have an important role to play in facilitating economic development, the question remains: how can power to develop be generated without outside forces remolding state structures, or without states that repress and control large majorities of their own citizens? The study of other cases and imaginative rethinking may yield insights into how to approximate "developmental states," without acquiring some of their worst features.

(c) Rethinking comparative colonialism

Finally, I wish to conclude with some speculative thoughts concerning future research directions. Developmental success has always ignited intellectual inquiry: why did "they" succeed? Why not the "others"? Marx and Weber struggled over these questions, trying to understand the early rise of capitalism in north-western Europe. Ever since, successful industrializers have attracted scholarly attention. It is hardly surprising that in our own times the successful NICs should attract similar attention. The puzzle is especially appealing when, in a group assumed to be more or less similar, some move ahead, while others are left behind. Scholarly imagination then wants an explanation for both the speedy growers and the laggards.

A variety of answers have been proposed in recent years as to why some developing countries have better performing economies than others; these vary from sharply market-oriented answers, through more state-focused analyses, all the way to religion and culture as the real variables. What many of these efforts in the hands of "developmentalists" lack, unfortunately, is historical depth. Large-scale processes of historical transformation often tend to display long historical continuities; when they do not, ruptures, new beginnings and shifts in path are dramatic. Establishment of sovereignty or, at least, the post-WWII beginning, is often assumed by development scholars as the "new beginning" from where comparative analyses of developing countries must begin. This trend is unfortunate, because it is likely that a significant component of the explanation for why countries traverse different developmental paths lie in their colonial heritage.

An earlier generation of "dependency" scholars were well aware of historical continuities. However, that body of scholarship lost its intellectual sway for a variety of reasons, including the tendency to homogenize the anti-developmental nature of all colonialism. A central question in the minds of a new generation of scholars became, "why are developing countries traversing such different paths." Any framework that mainly drew attention to a universal constraint (e.g., "world capitalism" or "neocolonialism") was thus likely to loose appeal; satisfactory answers would rather have to explain why countries dealt differently with the same set of constraints. Unfortunately, however, scholars in rightly discarding dependency propositions, also threw out the proverbial baby with the bathwater; they threw out the colonial pasts of the developing world. Instead of asking, could the roots of varying performances be located in a variety of colonial pasts, most developmentalists now focus on the nature of post-WWII states, social structures, and policy choices as the primary explanations of divergent performances.

If the historical discussion in this essay is persuasive, it suggests that the roots of economic dynamism in the critical case of South Korea are located, at least in part, in the state–society relations created under the auspices of Japanese colonialism: as a late developer, who had perfected a state-led model for catching-up in the world economy. Japan in its colonies constructed a political economy which also turned out to be well suited at catching-up. In other historical cases, different colonial powers, in different time periods, pursued a variety of colonial ruling strategies. They thus left behind a variety of political economies: distributive politics and a slow-growing economy in India; incomplete states that readily turned into predatory states in much of Africa; semi-sovereign political economies that came to be dominated by foreign investors and agrarian oligarchies prior to the onset of deliberate, state-led developmental experiments in large parts of Latin America. Is it not possible that the legacy of colonialism, though varying from case to case, especially region to region, was of long lasting significance in much of the developing world? If so, it behooves scholars interested in understanding divergent paths of contemporary developing countries to once again pay attention in their comparative analyses to the colonial pasts of these countries.

ACKNOWLEDGMENTS

I would like to acknowledge the helpful comments of the anonymous reviewers and the following: Bruce Cumings, Anthony D'Costa, Frank Dobbin, Cary Fraser, Stephan Haggard, Koichi Hamada, Chung-in Moon, James Palais, Gustav Ranis, Benjamin Schneider, Robert Wade and John Waterbury. This paper was written during 1992–93, while I was on sabbatical and, thanks to T. N. Srinivasan, a visitor at the Economic Growth Center, Yale University. Financial support from Ford Foundation is also acknowledged. Final revision accepted: March 15, 1994.

NOTES

1 The literature here is rather large; the bibliographies in any of the following sources (especially Amsden and Woo) offer a complete list of references. An incomplete list (listed alphabetically) of some of the major works with a political economy focus would include: Amsden (1989); Cumings (1984a); Deyo (1987); Haggard (1991), especially the chapter on South Korea and some of his other work cited therein; Jones and Sakong (1980); Mason *et al.* (1980); Westphal (1990); and Woo (1991).

2 The conceptual distinction between government's leading or following the market is made in Wade (1990), especially p. 28 and chapter 10. The scholar who has probably gone the farthest in suggesting that Korean government "distorted" prices to get growth up is Alice Amsden. See, Amsden (1989), especially chapter 6. For the argument that South Korean and other East Asian economic successes resulted from "free market" conditions, see Balassa's essays in his own edited volume (1981); and Krueger (1980).

3 See, for example, Frank, Kwang and Westphal (1975); Hasan (1976); and Krueger (1979). For an early exception, see Kuznets (1977).

4 See, for example, Amsden (1989), when in five pages (pp. 31–5) the author quickly concludes that the "inheritance" left by the Japanese colonialists to Koreans was "useless" for their future developmental struggles.

5 Haggard, for example, has made valuable contributions to unraveling the "why" and "how" of South Korean industrialization. Bulk of his analytical energy, however, is devoted to the onset of export-led model under Park Chung-Hee. See, for example, Haggard (1991), the chapter on South Korea, where only about two paragraphs are devoted to the colonial period.

6 I am afraid I have only examined the English language publications of Korean scholars. One good example of the nationalist bias in what is otherwise an excellent study is, Suh (1978). My confidence in extrapolating the broader assertion from limited materials was enhanced when another scholar, who had examined many of the Korean language sources, reached the same conclusion. See, Woo (1991), pp. 19–20.

7 Most significant here are the contributions of Cumings. He states his basic thesis in a summary form in Cumings (1984a). Scattered but brilliant insights on this topic can also be gleaned from his other writings: Cumings (1981); Cumings (1990); and Cumings (1984b). Another very important book that helps trace historical continuities is Eckert (1991). Also see, Woo (1991); and McNamara (1990).

8 While these issues will be discussed in greater detail below, the economic data here is taken from Suh (1978, Tables 11 and 17). Note that the "national production" data do not include construction, trade, services and public utilities that are generally included in the more conventional "national income" data; the latter for pre-WWII Korea are not readily available.

9 The best book on the late Chosòn continues to be Palais (1975). For a differing account, see, Choe (1972). A good "overview" account is provided by Ki-baik Lee in Eckert, *et al.* (1990). For another useful but abbreviated account that helps put traditional Korea in a comparative perspective *vis-à-vis* China and Japan, see Fairbank, Reischauer and Craig (1978), chapters 12 and 20.

10 For a discussion of how "open" or "closed" Korea's examination system may have been to non-Seoul based landed elite, see, Wagner (1974). Prolonged study of Chinese classics that was necessary to succeed in the exams appears to have been a major impediment for those without an independent source of wealth. Nevertheless, below the highest levels, there is evidence to indicate that some merit-based recruitment did occur.

11 Palais (1975), especially chapter 1–4 and 14. The direct quotes are from p. 5. Palais has informed me in a personal communication that he has modified some of these views. While these are not readily available to me, they are apparently developed in Palais (forthcoming).

12 As I read the historical evidence, Palais is probably correct in denying intraelite factionalism the central place in his analysis of the political problems of Yi Korea. See Palais (1975), especially the "Introduction." Nevertheless, most historical treatments document a deeply factionalized elite in Yi Korea. See, for example, Ki-baik Lee in Eckert *et al.* (1990), where he concludes that "intra-bureaucratic strife" rendered "the decision making process dilatory and ineffective," p. 110. Fairbank, Reischauer and Craig (1978), also note that factional struggles were "hereditary" and "endemic" in Yi Korea (p. 313). I see no analytical conflict, therefore, in suggesting factionalism as an additional debilitating trait.

13 See Palais (1975) chapter 2. Palais cites the figure of 10 million for Korean population in the mid-19th century. Later research has revised this estimate upwards. See Mitchell (1979–80). Lowe this reference to James Palais.

14 This is not to suggest, as Palais rightly corrected me on his comments on this paper, that the state did not on occasion aid economic activity. There is also some evidence from revisionist historians that late Yi Korea experienced a degree of

economic dynamism, but none to suggest that this was state induced. Cumings cites the work of Korean historian Kim Yông-Sôp to suggest that pre-Japanese Korean agriculture was probably not stagnant. See Cumings (1984b), p. 491. Also see Shin (1975).

15 See Ladd (1908). While this is a highly pro-Japanese, even a prejudiced, account, there is no reason to not make use of some of its more descriptive observations.

16 The quote is from George Kennan, a friend of Theodore Roosevelt, who influenced Roosevelt's attitudes toward Korea. It was cited—though not approvingly—in Grajdanzev (1944), p. 35.

17 I use quotations around the evocative concepts of predatory and developmental states to indicate my considerable discomfort in describing these states as such. Predatory is misleading because it creates a state versus society image; in reality, where "predation" prevails, political and economic elite often collude to squeeze and misuse a society's resources. Developmental is also misleading because the states so described are often not strictly developmental. For example, both the Japanese colonial state and the subsequent South Korean state under Park Chung-Hee, while successful agents of economic transformation, were also, to varying degrees, rather brutal states. The normative calculus, in turn, of evaluating a state that is simultaneously brutal and helps promote economic growth is clearly complex. In any case, two recent and useful essays that discuss the concept of developmental states are, Johnson (1987); and Evans (1989).

18 Kublin (1959) has argued that Japanese "colonial doctrine" evolved in Formosa (later Taiwan) and was subsequently implemented in Korea. This is true insofar as Formosa was colonized in 1895 and Korea in 1910. It is important to note, however, that Kabo reforms in Korea (tried around 1895) and early experimentation in Formosa were simultaneous efforts, both probably a product of a single "colonial official mindset" in Japan—a product of Meiji Japan—with simultaneous political learning going on in both Korea and Formosa.

19 Halliday (1975), pp. 35–6. For a discussion of the development of the Prussian bureaucracy, especially concerning how some such traits as an *esprit de corps*, an ethos of public service, a degree of insulation from aristocratic interests, tight internal authority structure and a relative absence of corruption, developed, see Rosenberg (1958); and for evolution of this bureaucracy in 19th century Germany, see Bonham (1991), especially chapters 2, 7 and 8.

20 For details see, H.I.J.M.'s Residency General (1908).

21 The following examples are taken from various reports on "administration" that the Japanese colonial government published regularly. See, for example, H.I.J.M.'s Residency General (1908); and Government-General of Chosen (1921, chapter on "local administration").

22 One scholar of Meiji Japan thus notes: "The police . . . had operational responsibility for a bewildering variety of government programs and policies in addition to public safety, traffic control, and criminal investigation and apprehension. They enforced economic controls, discouraged unionism, inspected factories, censored publications, licensed commercial enterprises, arranged for public welfare aid, supervised druggists and publications, controlled public gatherings, managed flood control and fire prevention, maintained surveillance of people suspected of "dangerous thoughts," and did countless other things that brought government close to the daily life of every Japanese." See Spaulding (1971), pp. 36–7.

23 Chen (1984), pp. 228–31. It is important to note that the extensive role of the police remained intact throughout the colonial period. For example, when Americans finally arrived in Korea after the Japanese surrender, they found (e.g., in

South Cholla province) that police departments were the biggest within the local bureaucracy, and within the police departments, "economic sections" of the police were important. See Meade (1951), p. 31.

24 The quote is from Shakuo Shunjo and is cited in Chen (1984), p. 222.

25 See Lee (1963). For a discussion of the brief, more liberal interlude, see Robinson (1989).

26 For example, when confronted with the fact of being left behind in the race to modernity, many Koreans had looked to Meiji Japan as a model for their own advancement; for better or for worse, therefore, "modernity" to many Koreans came to be represented by Japan. See Henderson (1968, p. 67). Moreover, some Korean elites, enamored with Japan, had participated in Japanese-supported Kabo reforms of 1895. Later, the pro-Japanese Korean organization, *Ilchin-hoe* (Advancement Society) enjoyed considerable support in 1905–10; for example, as its least popular phase in 1910, the *Ilchin-hoe* still enjoyed a membership of nearly 140,000 and had some one hundred subsidiary organizations. See, for example, Chandra (1974, p. 52).

27 The quote is from official documents of the Government-General and taken from Ireland (1926, p. 190).

28 For one review of Japanese colonial economic policies, see Ho (1984, pp. 347–86).

29 See, for example, Schumpeter (1940), especially chapters IX–XI, XXI and XXII, and the conclusion.

30 The reference is to Government-General of Chosen, *Annual Report on Reforms and Progress in Chosen (Korea)*, Keijo, (Seoul), published regularly—for the most part, annually—during 1910–39. See, for example, the 1914 report, where in the opening chapter, repeated references are made to "financial efficiency" and to the "economy of administration."

31 The figures are from H.I.J.M.'s Residency General (1908 and 1909). The real increase was probably somewhat less because this simple calculation does not take account of increase in production, which, in any case, we know to have been relatively small in those years.

32 The 1905 figure is from H.I.J.M.'s Residency General (1907), and the 1911 figure is from Government-General of Chosen (1910–11). While reliable data on inflation for these years is not readily available, there is no indication in government documents of huge price increases.

33 See Robinson in Eckert (1990), p. 265. There is apparently also a good doctoral thesis on the subject of this land survey by Edward Gragert at Columbia University. Unfortunately, I was unable to locate this unpublished manuscript.

34 For a full discussion, see Ho (1984).

35 The colonial government's own assessment is interesting. While lamenting the political opposition from educated Koreans, government documents of the period note: "People of the upper class having personally experienced imperial favor and being in a position to feel directly or indirectly the benefit of the new regime, seem to be contented with it." See Government General of Chosen (1914), p. 64. Also see Robinson in Eckert, *et al.* (1990), pp. 266–7.

36 Migdal (1988), for example, tends to view state capacity in agrarian societies as inversely related to the power of landowning and other traditional elites. Evans (1987), makes a similar argument.

37 For these policy swings and for the direct quote, see Grajdnazev (1944), pp. 92–4.

38 Suh (1978), p. 73, Table 33. Also see, Ishikawa, (1967), pp. 84–109.

39 This distinction can be sharpened by using the concepts of "idea gaps" and "object gaps" proposed in the "new" economic growth theory. Whereas the

"object gap" refers to lack of concrete objects as factories, that direct attention to savings and investment bottlenecks in development, the "idea gap" refers to the knowledge base on which development rests. The "new" growth theory emphasizes (as did several old growth theories) the role of knowledge and technology in economic growth: See, for example, Romer (1993). One may thus argue that in Korean colonial economic history, even if "objects" were destroyed during decolonization, the legacy of "ideas" was substantial.

40 The point here is not that these same groups subsequently facilitated Korea's export-led growth. Some contributed to this process, others failed and yet other new ones also emerged. The point here is instead that a "system" was being created. I am indebted to Chung-in Moon's criticisms that forced me to clarify this point.

41 There is a great self-congratulatory discussion of how Governor-General Ugaki thought of this scheme to provide subsidies for gold mining. See his speech in, Government-General of Chosen (1935), pp. 85–7.

42 All the materials in quotations in this paragraph are from Eckert (1991), pp. 73–4. Note that the exhortations to businessmen began rather early with colonial rule. A government report of 1914 notes that the Governor-General called business leaders to a party, explained government's policies, and urged them to be concerned not only with profits but "to bear in mind the promotion of the interest of the state." See Government-General of Chosen (1914), p. 13.

43 This theme is well developed in McNamara (1990), pp. 127–30.

44 This, for example, is the approach adopted in Suh (1978).

45 These and the subsequent facts concerning geographical distribution of industry are from Grajdanzev (1944), Appendix III.

46 For evidence on the nature and extent of lower class restiveness, especially as expressed through the communist movement. See Scalpino and Lee (1972), chapter III.

47 See, Cumings (1981), chapter 2 for a moving discussion of the human toll exacted by the large scale movement of Koreans under Japanese rule.

48 The following account is based on the case study of Onoda cement factory in Park (1985), Part II, B, sections 1, 4, 5, and 9.

49 See, Eckert (1991), chapter 7, from where the account in this paragraph is drawn.

50 This quote and the materials in this paragraph are drawn from Ogle (1990), p. 6.

51 I am currently involved in writing such an essay, but in the context of a larger study from which the present essay is drawn. The larger study is a comparative analysis of the "state and economic development" in four countries, namely, Korea, Brazil, India and Nigeria.

52 See Cumings (1984b), pp. 479–80. For his detailed analysis of why and how Americans left the colonial state more or less intact in Korea, see Cumings (1981), chapter 5.

53 See Woo (1991) for the specific issue of state control over credit.

54 For one insightful analysis of this question, see Evans (1989).

55 Note that Evans's "autonomy" component of the "embedded autonomy" formulation (1989) mainly directs attention to the second of these three structural components.

REFERENCES

Amsden, Alice, *Asia's Next Giant: South Korea and Late Industrialization* (New York: Oxford University Press, 1989).

Asagiri, "Korea: Labour movement," *The Labour Monthly*, Vol. 11, No. 9 (September 1929), pp. 568–70.

Balassa, Bela, *The Newly Industrializing Countries in the World Economy* (New York: Pergamon, 1981).

Bonham, Gary, *Ideology and Interests in the German State* (New York: Garland Publishers, 1991).

Chandra, Vipin, "An outline study of the *Ilchin hoe* (Advancement Society) of Korea," Occasional Papers on Korea, No. 2 (Seattle: University of Washington, March 1974), pp. 43–72.

Chen, Ching-Chih, "Police and community control systems in the empire," in Ramon Myers and Mark Peattie (Eds.), *The Japanese Colonial Empire* (Princeton: Princeton University Press, 1984), pp. 213–39.

Chen, Ta, "The labor situation in Korea," *Monthly Labor Review*, Vol. 31 (November 1930), pp. 26–36.

Choe, Ching Young, *The Rule of the Taewongun, 1864–1873: Restoration in Yi Korea*, East Asian Research Center (Cambridge, MA: Harvard University, 1972).

Chung, Young-Iob, "Japanese investment in Korea, 1904–45," in Andrew Nahm (Ed.), *Korea under Japanese Colonial Rule* (Center for Korean Studies, Western Michigan University, 1973).

Conroy, Hilary, *The Japanese Seizure of Korea, 1868–1910* (Philadelphia: University of Pennsylvania Press, 1960).

Cumings, Bruce, *The Origins of the Korean War: The Roaring of the Cataract* (Princeton: Princeton University Press, 1990).

——, "The origins and development of the Northeast Asian political economy: Industrial sectors, product cycles and political consequences," *International Organization*, Vol. 38, No. 1 (Winter 1984a) pp. 1–40.

——, "The legacy of Japanese colonialism in Korea," in Ramon H. Myers and Mark R. Peattie (Eds.), *The Japanese Colonial Empire* (Princeton: Princeton University Press, 1984b), pp. 478–96.

——, *The Origins of the Korean War: Liberation and the Emergence of Separate Regimes 1945–1947* (Princeton: Princeton University Press, 1981).

Deyo, Fredric C. (Ed.), *The Political Economy of New Asian Industrialism* (Ithaca, NY: Cornell University Press, 1987).

Duus, Peter, "Economic dimensions of Meiji imperialism: The case of Korea, 1895–1910," in Ramon H. Myers and Mark R. Peattie (Eds.), *The Japanese Colonial Empire* (Princeton: Princeton University Press, 1984), pp. 128–63.

Eckert, Carter, J., *Offspring of Empire: The Koch'ang Kims and the Colonial Origins of Korean Capitalism, 1876–1945* (Seattle: University of Washington Press, 1991).

Eckert, Carter, J., Ki-baik Lee, Young Ick Lew, Michael Robinson, Edward W. Wagner, *Korea Old and New: A History* (Korea Institute, Harvard University, 1990).

Evans, Peter, "Predatory, developmental and other apparatuses: A comparative political economy perspective on the third world state," *Sociological Forum*, Vol. 4, No. 4 (Fall 1989), pp. 561–87.

——, "Class, state and dependence in East Asia: Lessons for Latin Americanists," in Fredric D. Deyo (Ed.), *The Political Economy of the New Asian Industrialism* (Ithaca, NY: Cornell University Press, 1987), pp. 203–26.

Fairbank, John K., Edwin O. Reischauer and Albert M. Craig, *East Asia: Tradition and Transformation* (Boston: Houghton Mifflin Company, 1978).

Frank, Charles R. Jr., Kwang Suk Kim and Larry E. Westphal, *Foreign Trade Regimes and Economic Development: South Korea* (New York: Columbia University Press, 1975).

Government-General of Chosen, *Thriving Chosen: A Survey of Twenty Five Years' Administration* (1935) (no place of publication listed).
——, *Annual Report on Reforms and Progress in Chosen (Korea) (1918–21)* (Seoul: 1921).
——, *Results of Three Years' Administration of Chosen Since Annexation* (Seoul: 1914).
——, *Annual Report on Reforms and Progress in Chosen (Korea) (1908–09)* (Seoul: 1909).
——, *Annual Report on Reforms and Progress in Chosen (Korea) (1911–12)* (Seoul: 1912).
——, *Annual Report on Reforms and Progress in Chosen (Korea) (1910–11)* (Seoul: 1911).
——, *The Third Annual Report on Reforms and Progress in Korea (1909–10)* (Seoul: 1910).
Grajdanzev, Andrew J., *Modern Korea* (New York: The John Day Company, 1944).
H.I.J.M.'s Residency General, *The Second Annual Report on Reforms and Progress in Korea (1908–9)* (Seoul: 1909).
——, *Annual Report for 1907 on Reforms and Progress in Korea* (Seoul: 1908).
Haggard, Stephan, *Pathways From the Periphery: The Newly Industrializing Countries in the International System* (Ithaca: Cornell University Press, 1991).
Halliday, Jon, *A Political History of Japanese Capitalism* (New York: Pantheon Books, 1975).
Hasan, Parvez, *Korea: Problems and Issues in a Rapidly Growing Economy* (Baltimore: Johns Hopkins University Press, 1976).
Henderson, Gregory, *Korea: The Politics of Vortex* (Cambridge, Mass.: Harvard University Press, 1968).
Ho, Samuel Pao-San, "Colonialism and development: Korea, Taiwan, and Kwantung," in Ramon Myers and Mark Peattie (Eds.), *The Japanese Colonial Empire* (Princeton: Princeton University Press, 1984), pp. 347–86.
Ireland, Alleyne, *The New Korea* (New York: E. P. Dutton and Company, 1926).
Ishikawa, Shigeru, *Economic Development in Asian Perspective* (Tokyo: Kinokuniya Bookstore Co., 1967).
Jones, Leroy P., and H. Sakong, *Government, Business and Entrepreneurship in Economic Development: The Korean Case* (Cambridge: Harvard University Press, 1980).
Johnson, Chalmers, "Political institutions and economic performance: The government business relationship in Japan, South Korea and Taiwan," in Fredric C. Oeyo, (Ed.), *The Political Economy of the New Asian Industrialism* (Ithaca: Cornell University Press, 1987), pp. 136–64.
Krueger, Anne, "Trade policy as an input to development," *American Economic Review*, Vol. 70, No. 2 (May 1980), pp. 228–92.
——, *Studies in the Modernization of Korea: The Developmental Role of the Foreign Sector and Aid* (Cambridge, MA: Harvard University Press, 1979).
Kublin, Hyman, "The evolution of Japanese colonialism," *Comparative Studies in Society and History*, Vol. II, No. 1 (October 1959), pp. 67–84.
Kuznets, Paul, *Economic Growth and Structure in the Republic of Korea* (New Haven: Yale University Press, 1977).
Ladd, George Trumball, *In Korea with Marquis Ito* (New York, Charles Scribner & Sons, 1908).
Lee, Chong-Sik, *Japan and Korea: The Political Dimension* (Stanford, CA: Hoover Institution Press, 1985).
——, *The Politics of Korean Nationalism* (Berkeley, CA: University of California Press, 1963).
Mason, Edward, *et al.*, *The Economic and Social Modernization of the Republic of Korea* (Cambridge: Harvard University Press, 1980).
Meade, Grant E., *American Military Government in Korea* (New York: Columbia University King's Crown Press, 1951).

Migdal, Joel, *Strong Societies and Weak States: State–Society Relations and State Capabilities in the Third World* (Princeton: Princeton University Press, 1988).
Mitchell, Tony, "Fact and hypothesis in Yi Dynasty economic history: The demographic dimension," *Korean Studies Forum*, No. 6 (Winter–Spring, 1979–80), pp. 65–93.
Moskowitz, Karl, "The creation of the Oriental Development Company: Japanese illusions meet Korean reality," Occasional Papers on Korea, No. 2 (Seattle: University of Washington, March 1984).
McNamara, Dennis L., *The Colonial Origins of Korean Enterprise 1910–45* (New York: Cambridge University Press, 1990).
Ogle, George E., *South Korea: Dissent Within the Economic Miracle* (London: Zed Books Ltd., 1990).
Palais, James B., *Confucian Statecraft and Korean Institutions* (Seattle: University of Washington Press, forthcoming).
—— *Politics and Policy in Traditional Korea* (Cambridge, MA: Harvard University Press, 1975).
Park, Soon Won, "The emergence of a factory labor force in colonial Korea: A case study of the Onoda Cement Factory," Ph.D. Dissertation (Cambridge, MA: Harvard University Press, 1985).
Peattie, Mark, "Introduction," in Ramon Myers and Mark Peattie (Eds.), *The Japanese Colonial Empire* (Princeton: Princeton University Press, 1984).
Robinson, Michael E., *Cultural Nationalism in Colonial Korea, 1920–1925* (Seattle: University of Washington Press, 1989).
Romer, Paul, "Idea gaps and object gaps in economic development," Paper presented at the World Bank Conference on "How do National Policies Affect Long Run Growth" (Washington, DC: February 7–8, 1993).
Rosenberg, Hans, *Bureaucracy, Aristocracy and Autocracy: the Prussian Experience, 1660–1815* (Cambridge, MA: Harvard University Press, 1958).
Scalpino, Robert, and Chong-Sik Lee, *Communism in Korea, Part 1: The Movement* (Berkeley: University of California Press, 1972).
Schumpeter, E. B., *The Industrialization of Japan and Manchukuo 1930–1940* (New York: The Macmillan Company, 1940).
Shin, Susan J. S., "Some aspects of landlord–tenant relations in Yi Dynasty Korea," Occasional Papers on Korea, No. 3 (Seattle: University of Washington, June 1975), pp. 49–88.
Spaulding, Robert M. Jr., "The bureaucracy as a political force, 1920–45," in James William Morley (Ed.), *Dilemmas of Growth in Prewar Japan* (Princeton: Princeton University Press, 1971).
Suh, Sang-Chyul, *Growth and Structural Changes in the Korean Economy, 1910–1940* (Cambridge, MA: Harvard University Press, 1978).
Wade, Robert, *Governing the Market: Economic Theory and the Role of Government in East Asia Industrialization* (Princeton: Princeton University Press, 1990).
Wagner, Edward, "The ladder of success in Yi Dynasty Korea," Occasional Papers on Korea, No. 1 (Seattle: University of Washington, April 1974).
Westphal, Larry E., "Industrial policy in an export-propelled economy: Lessons from South Korea's experience," *Journal of Economic Perspectives*, Vol. 4, No. 3 (Summer 1990), pp. 412–59.
Woo, Jung-en, *Race to the Swift: State and Finance in Korean Industrialization* (New York: Columbia University Press, 1991).

3

WHAT IS THE SINGAPORE MODEL OF ECONOMIC DEVELOPMENT?

W. G. Huff

3.1 INTRODUCTION

With a population one-quarter of 1% of China's, Singapore's GDP is 10.8%. Its manufactured exports are twice the value of Brazil's (World Bank, 1993A, and 1991, p. 59). Facts like this have had a considerable impact on thinking about economic development. As one of the four East Asian NICs, Singapore has pushed development economics towards a new 'empirical' phase which draws on country experiences—especially the East Asian NICs of South Korea, Taiwan, Hong Kong and Singapore—to develop theory (Stern, 1989, p. 621; Riedel, 1988; Hughes, 1988). Yet if the international demonstration effect of the Asian four is strong and the development policy advice distilled from their experience is to do as they have done, there still remains significant disagreement on what they actually did (World Bank, 1993B, p. 81; Amsden, 1989; Nolan, 1990; Wade, 1990; Taylor, 1993; Summers and Pritchett, 1993; Summers and Thomas, 1993).

The present article therefore has two main purposes. Although few could doubt the importance of outward orientation for Singapore, an island of just 3.1 million people in 1992, with trade (imports + exports) normally about 350% of GDP, one purpose of the article is to analyse in the context of Singapore an aspect of the Asian NIC experience still subject to disagreement: the mix between active government policies and market forces. I argue that the Singapore model featured a strongly interventionist government and planning, which went well beyond the World Bank's 'market-friendly' approach to include 'market replacement'. In Singapore, decisive departures from the price mechanism and a domestically managed regime allowed capitalism to work. As Singapore's recent *Strategic Economic Plan* observed, 'Economic planning has played a very significant role in the development of Singapore for more than thirty years' (Singapore, Economic Planning Committee, 1991, p. 14). If anything, Singapore, often cited as the 'most successful of the four "Asian dragons"' (Giordano and Kato, 1993, p. 1) is in harmony with Keynes's (1980, p. 386) conclusion that planned development

Source: Cambridge Journal of Economics, 19, pp. 735–59.

is the 'more efficient' alternative. Singapore exemplified a rational *dirigisme* 'which combines plan and market in a creative partnership' (Nolan, 1990, p. 59).

Second, the article attempts to unravel Singapore's development model since political independence in 1959 and the election of the People's Action Party (PAP), the only party to have held power in independent Singapore. A distinctive feature of the Singapore model was government control over wages and labour. This allowed three further features of the model to emerge. First, a small economy like Singapore's can usefully be thought of as able to tap a perfectly elastic supply of capital at a given world rate of profitability. Wage control was basic to the required rate of profit. Second, it was fundamental to the Singapore model that capital came in the form of direct foreign investment and gave rise to almost complete multinational enterprise (MNE) dominance in the manufactured export sector. Third, labour-intensive jobs created by MNEs allowed Singapore to utilise surplus labour and rapidly ended unemployment. Full employment, combined with Singapore's rising labour productivity, enabled the government to force a high level of domestic saving. These were, in turn, mobilised to build a superb infrastructure. Infrastructural facilities, fiscal incentives and Singapore's location on the world's main East–West communications route combined with low wages as the independent variables explaining MNE investment. In Singapore, multinationals contributed substantially more than in the other three Asian NICs to the high investment ratios and rapid capital accumulation characteristic of all four countries.

The Singapore model resembled South Korea's and Taiwan's, although not Hong Kong's, in the strong government control exercised over the price mechanism in key economic sectors. Industrialisation in Singapore, however, occurred under more restricted labour supply conditions than in the other Asian NICs, including Hong Kong, where between 1945 and 1955 massive labour inflows caused a population increase of about 400%, with continued rapid growth into the mid-1960s (Szezepanik, 1958; Chow and Papanek, 1981). Its split with Malaysia in August 1965 allowed Singapore, constituted as an independent republic, effectively to close its borders and regulate labour flows. Like Hong Kong, but in contrast to South Korea and Taiwan, by the 1980s Singapore had turned to internationally traded services as the most dynamic component of the economy. Singapore's unusually strong locational advantage was vital to its becoming a major world exporter of services, which by 1992 were almost equivalent in value to Switzerland's (GATT, 1993). The Republic's 'natural resource' of location and uniqueness as a city state have particular relevance to the Singapore model's likely replicability.

The paper is structured in seven further sections. The next reviews Singapore's macroeconomic performance. Sections 3.3 and 3.4 focus respectively on the manufacturing sector and economic planning. Section 3.5 looks at the issues of 'oversaving' and 'overinvestment' which have arisen as a consequence of government direction of the economy. In Section 3.6, the Singapore model is further disaggregated by examining financial and business services. Section 3.7 analyses the relationship between macroeconomic policy, planning and economic development. The concluding section considers the Singapore model's relevance to development theory.

3.2 MACROECONOMIC PERFORMANCE

Between 1960 and 1992, Singapore's real gross national product increased thirteenfold. Singapore advanced from the world's 33rd highest per capita income in 1965 to rank 17th by 1992, ahead of Spain, New Zealand and Ireland (World Bank, 1994). Infant mortality and life expectancy are, respectively, among the lowest and highest in the world. There has been full employment since 1973 and absolute poverty is virtually non-existent. Gini coefficients for individuals were around 0.46 in the mid-1980s (Lim, 1988, pp. 401–2; Islam and Kirkpatrick, 1986). Yet even with income per head of US$15,730 in 1992, Singapore has not fully achieved developed country status. The reasons for this, explored below, are part of a wider strategy of heavy reliance on foreign companies and workers; in 1992, 32.8% of GDP accrued to non-Singaporeans, i.e. neither citizens nor permanent residents (Singapore, Department of Statistics, 1994).

Five characteristics of Singapore's economy immediately attract attention: sustained rapid growth; sharply increasing export orientation; exceptionally high saving and investment; low inflation; and fundamental structural transformation. These are indicated here, and discussed at length in subsequent sections.

At the end of the 1950s, Singapore's per capita income was already higher than almost anywhere in Asia and over one-third of the United Kingdom's (Benham, 1957, 1959; Silcock, 1959). Furthermore, from 1960 to 1966, real GDP increased at an annual average rate of 5.7% (Table 3.1), largely due to

Table 3.1 Singapore macroeconomic indicators, 1960–1992 (%)

	1960–66	*1966–69*	*1960–69*	*1970–79*	*1980–92*
Annual real GDP growth rate	5.7	13.6	8.0	8.3	6.7
Annual inflation rate[a]	1.1	1.0	1.1	5.8	2.4
Savings ratio[b]	6.7	18.2	11.5	28.8	42.9
Investment ratio[b]	17.5	24.8	20.7	40.5	41.3

Note:
[a] GDP deflator.
[b] The savings ratio and investment ratio are defined respectively as Gross National Savings and Gross Capital Formation divided by Gross Domestic Product. All variables are in real terms deflated by the GDP deflator.

Sources: Singapore, Department of Statistics, 1988, 1993B, 1994; Singapore, Ministry of Trade and Industry, 1994.

government expenditure on infrastructure and protected, import-substituting industrialisation in the context of Singapore's union with Malaya to form Malaysia. In 1959, the Economic Development Board was set up as 'the spearhead for industrialisation by direct participation in industry' and building necessary infrastructure (Singapore, Economic Planning Unit, 1964, p. 37; see also Singapore, 1961; O'Connor, 1966). Heavy government developmental expenditure, which included the Board's new industrial estate at Jurong, created a base for future export-oriented industrialisation, although it yielded little in either industrial production or exports until at least the mid 1960s (Goh, 1970; Singapore, Economic Planning Unit, 1964). In the latter half of the 1960s a resurgence of Singapore's historic role as a trade and service centre for the surrounding region provided the main impetus to growth (Goh, 1970, pp. 10–11; Singapore, Ministry of Finance, 1969, p. 3), while by 1967 manufactured exports also began to contribute significantly to GDP. A doubling of growth during the 1960s, together with infrastructure and institutions established in that decade—the Economic Development Board and its offshoots, the government-owned Development Bank of Singapore and Jurong Town Corporation—provided a foundation for Singapore's continued expansion. During the 1970s, and again from 1980 to 1990, real GDP more than doubled, with further rapid increase in the 1990s.

From 1970 to 1979, manufactured exports became the engine of Singapore's growth. The proportion of direct manufactured exports to GDP rose from 12.7% in 1966 to almost half in 1979 and nearly three-fifths in 1992.[1] Indicative of the export-led nature of growth in manufacturing is that after 1967 direct exports of manufactures grew considerably faster than manufactured output (Table 3.2).

High saving and investment characterised Singapore's economic development. In the 1950s 'one of the great open questions [was] whether the new

Table 3.2 Singapore real annual average growth rates in manufacturing, 1960–1992 (%)

	1960–92	*1960–67*	*1967–73*	*1973–92*
Direct exports	15.5	10.4	31.8	10.4
Output	11.9	12.0	22.7	8.7
Value added	12.3	12.2	26.7	8.5

Notes:
(1) Data are deflated by the GDP deflator for manufacturing.
(2) Statistics refer to firms with 10 or more workers, and exclude petroleum, rubber processing and granite quarrying.
(3) For 1960 only, output and value added figures include petroleum.

Sources: Singapore, Department of Statistics or Economic Development Board. Annual series 1960–61–1992. *Report on the Census of Industrial Production*, Singapore; Singapore, Department of Statistics, 1988; Singapore, Ministry of Trade and Industry. Annual series, 1988–1993. *Economic Survey of Singapore*, Singapore.

democracy of Singapore can exercise the self-restraint necessary to emulate the capital creation of Victorian England, based on voluntary abstinence, or of Communist Russia, based on compulsory abstinence' (Caine, 1956, p. 5). The PAP government enforced state-directed abstinence, and the savings ratio (Table 3.1), under 10% for most of the 1960s, averaged 29% in the 1970s and over 40% from 1980—the world's highest. From the start, the government decided on a high investment ratio as 'the paramount need . . . in an economy which wants to expand its basic wealth at a fast rate, a target like 20% or more should be aimed at' (Singapore, 1963). In fact, the investment ratio was sustained at over 40% during the 1970s and 1980s (Table 3.1). However, domestic saving explained only a part of Singapore's high investment, which relied heavily on direct foreign investment by MNEs. Indeed, between 1980 and 1990, Singapore was the largest single less-developed country recipient of direct foreign investment, and received almost 13% of all such investment in developing countries (United Nations, 1992).

Development in Singapore occurred with low inflation, remarkable for an economy already chronically short of labour by the late 1970s. From 1961 to 1992, the GDP deflator rose at an annual average rate of 3.9%. Its increase was 2.6% or less during 19 of 32 years, and exceeded 5% in only 7 years, despite high world inflation and Singapore's very open economy.

One aspect of structural transformation in Singapore was the shift towards manufacturing (Table 3.3). Its share in total output grew from 16.6% in 1960 to 29.4% by 1979. In 1992, manufacturing contributed 27.6% of GDP and accounted for 27.5% of employment. The other structural change was the increasing importance of services, which in Singapore traditionally include the three categories of transport and communications; financial and business services; and public administration, community, social and personal services. After 1978, financial and business services, reflecting Singapore's development as an international financial centre, emerged as an engine of growth, and were the economy's fastest-growing sector. In 1992, they provided 26.1% of GDP, or almost as much as manufacturing, but, reflecting their often capital-intensive nature, made up under 11% of employment, about one-third of that in manufacturing.

3.3 GOVERNMENT CONTROL AND EXPORT-ORIENTED MANUFACTURING

The basic distinction between a market system and economic planning is reliance on the price mechanism or its replacement by government intervention involving some combination of incentives, disincentives, commands and controls aimed at a consistent means-end hierarchy. The present section shows how Singapore attained international competitiveness and industrialised through government control and directives which replaced the price mechanism in three crucial areas. One involved government direction of

Table 3.3 Singapore GDP and employment by industrial sector, 1960–1992 ($m at 1985 market prices, persons and %)

	1960	*1969*	*1979*	*1992*
(a) GDP				
Total ($m)	5058.5	10,730.0	26,284.7	64,771.0
Agriculture & quarrying	3.8	2.7	1.5	0.4
Manufacturing	16.6	23.2	29.4	27.6
Construction & utilities	7.0	10.7	9.1	6.8
Commerce	24.6	22.9	19.4	18.2
Transport & communications	8.8	7.2	11.6	14.7
Financial & business services	14.0	16.5	18.9	26.1
Other services	19.6	15.7	12.2	10.2
(b) Employment				
Persons (000s)	471.9	650.9	1021.0	1576.2
Agriculture & quarrying	7.3	3.8	1.6	0.3
Manufacturing	15.7	22.0	28.9	27.5
Construction & utilities	6.1	7.8	6.3	7.1
Commerce	24.2	23.5	23.3	22.6
Transport & communications	10.7	12.1	11.6	10.1
Financial & business services	4.6	3.5	7.1	10.9
Other services	31.4	27.3	21.2	21.5

Notes:
(1) For GDP, the percentage shares may not add to 100%, since imputed bank service charges are deducted and import duties added to arrive at total GDP, but account is not taken of these for individual industries.
(2) Employment figures for 1960 are from the 1957 Census and for 1969 from the 1970 Census.

Sources: Singapore, 1964; Department of Statistics, 1981, 1983A, 1988, 1994.

the labour market. Second, state-owned enterprises (SOEs) constituted a fundamental departure towards planning. Third, government instituted a programme of forced saving. Each aspect will be discussed in turn, and then related to infrastructure provision and private sector capital accumulation.

3.3.1 Labour market direction and multinationals as entrepreneurial substitutes

Appropriate wage levels were fundamental to the internal supply response, enabling Singapore to take advantage of export-oriented industrialisation which, after 1965, was made possible by an international search for cheap labour in developing countries. An inter-war wage differential substantially above the rest of Asia had persisted into the 1960s, leaving Singapore with wage costs '20–30% too high for world markets' (United Nations, 1961, p. 115). Although Singapore's wages might eventually have come down through market forces, the government decisively effected adjustment to market clearing levels. Two measures, the Employment Act and the

Industrial Relations (Amendment) Act of 1968, 'de-politicised the labour movement, established *de facto* government control over unions [and] transferred bargaining power from workers to employers' (Lim and Pang, 1986, p. 11). Few work stoppages occurred after 1967; by 1977 they were virtually eliminated. Singapore's total of two work stoppages involving 159 workers in the 16 years 1978–1993 cannot have reflected a free labour market (Singapore, Department of Statistics, 1991; Singapore, Ministry of Labour, 1994).

By 1969, for comparable job classifications in the key semiconductor and office machine assembly industries, hourly compensation costs in Singapore were less than one-eleventh of the United States' level, and below those in South Korea, Taiwan and Hong Kong. Productivity in Singapore was equal to the three latter, and at least as high as in the United States (United States Tariff Commission, 1970, pp. 166–73; Leong, 1971). Government direction of wages mobilised labour in Singapore by allowing it to realise a latent comparative advantage based on a relative abundance of unskilled workers. As was observed, 'The electronic components we make in Singapore probably require less skill than that required by barbers or cooks, consisting mostly of repetitive manual operations' (Goh, 1970, p. 27). Unemployment dropped from 8.9% in 1966 to 4.5% in 1973—effectively, full employment (Singapore, Department of Statistics, 1983A). Moreover, the proportion of own account (i.e. self-employed) and unpaid family workers in Singapore's labour force fell from 20.7% in 1970 to 7.8% by 1990 (Saw, 1984, p. 40; Singapore, Department of Statistics, 1993A).

Full employment would almost certainly have set up strong inflationary wage pressure and internationally uncompetitive pay rises had not the government in 1972 inaugurated the National Wages Council, a tripartite body comprising government, employers and trade unions, which published guidelines for pay increases. Although not mandatory, these were closely observed. The government controlled unions; more than this, a measure of its power was that, in the absence of any overt enforcement mechanism, foreign MNEs did not bid up wages, despite incentives to do so as a result of labour scarcity and Singapore's attractiveness as a production location due to its excellent infrastructure and cluster of complementary firms already there. Real wage rises averaged just 1.7% from 1973 to 1978 (Singapore, Ministry of Trade and Industry, 1985, p. 20), but then, boosted initially by a three-year wage correction policy decreed by Singapore planners, doubled by 1990 (Table 3.4). Between 1975 and 1993, however, Singapore manufacturing labour costs grew more slowly than in the Asian NICs, and continuously moved towards the average in these countries (Table 3.5)—a yardstick used by the government to measure success in containing labour costs.

Foreign multinationals were more dominant in Singapore than in any other less developed country export success story. The electronics industry quickly became, in terms of both job creation and output, the mainstay of this MNE presence and of Singapore's manufacturing industry. In 1975,

Table 3.4 Singapore real average monthly earnings for all workers, 1978–1993 (1988 = 100)

1978	57.9	1986	91.4
1979	60.5	1987	93.8
1980	63.3	1988	100.0
1981	63.5	1989	107.3
1982	70.8	1990	113.3
1983	77.1	1991	119.6
1984	83.2	1992	126.5
1985	89.4	1993	131.3

Sources: Singapore, Ministry of Labour. Annual series 1988–1993. *Yearbook of Labour Statistics*, Singapore.

Table 3.5 Singapore, United States, Japan and Asian countries hourly compensation costs for production workers in manufacturing, 1975–1993 (current US$ and index, United States = 100)

	1975		*1980*		*1993*	
	$	*Index*	*$*	*Index*	*$*	*Index*
United States	6.36	100	9.87	100	16.79	100
Japan	3.05	48	5.61	57	19.20	114
Singapore	0.84	13	1.49	15	5.38	32
South Korea	0.33	5	0.97	10	5.37	32
Taiwan	0.40	6	1.00	10	5.23	31
Hong Kong	0.76	12	1.51	15	4.31	26
Asian NICs	0.50	8	1.15	12	5.15	31

Note: Asian NICs refers to a United States trade-weighted average level for Singapore, South Korea, Taiwan and Hong Kong.

Source: US Department of Labor, 1994.

wholly and majority foreign-owned firms already dominated the manufacturing sector, and in 1992 accounted for nearly three-quarters of manufacturing output and value added and 85% of direct exports (Table 3.6). Thus, within manufacturing, whatever linkages existed were largely to other foreign-owned firms (Lim and Pang, 1986, p. 92).

The reliance on foreigners, together with Singapore's lack of an indigenous technological contribution to manufacturing, marks the Republic as not being a developed country. Singapore, even in 1986, was industrially 'still predominantly a manufacturing production base. Products are designed overseas, and then only produced in Singapore factories on our production lines' (Lee, H. L., 1986, p. 7; see also *Straits Times Weekly*, 1990; Hu, 1994). Although after 1981, as MNEs poured into Singapore to make computer components and peripherals, manufacturing took on an increasingly high-tech look, the Republic's chief attraction remained reliable and adaptable

Table 3.6 Singapore manufacturing statistics by capital ownership, 1968–1992

	Output *$m and %*	*Value-added* *$m and %*	*Direct exports* *$m and %*
1968			
Total	2175.7	611.8	n.a.
Wholly local	41.1	40.8	
Majority local	12.8	15.2	
Wholly or majority foreign	46.1	44.0	
1975			
Total	12,610.1	3411.1	7200.7
Wholly local	18.0	24.3	8.9
Majestic local	10.7	13.0	7.0
Wholly or majority foreign	71.3	62.7	84.1
1992			
Total	77,275.9	24,911.1	46,906.8
Wholly local	16.2	17.6	8.4
Majestic local	9.6	12.2	7.1
Wholly or majority foreign	74.2	70.2	84.5

Note: Figures include petroleum but exclude rubber processing and granite quarrying.

Source: Singapore, Department of Statistics or Economic Development Board. Annual Series, 1968–1992. *Report on the Census of Industrial Production*, Singapore.

unskilled, especially female, labour at a fraction of the wages paid in developed countries. The speed of technical change emanating from developed country electronics industries meant that this labour could be retrained and redeployed more cheaply than a new machine could be designed, and afforded MNEs flexibility for short and varying production runs (Lim and Pang, 1984). In 1990, 72% of those in electronics production were female, compared to 43% in the rest of manufacturing (Singapore, Economic Development Board, 1992); wages in the electronics industry were below the manufacturing average, itself less than wages in most other industrial groupings (Singapore, Ministry of Labour, 1993). The value-added share of gross output measures technical development in manufacturing; Table 3.7 shows that between 1978 and 1992 this ratio rose somewhat for manufacturing as a whole, but in the electronics industry actually fell.

Growth accounting has failed to discover technical change in Singapore, measured as total factor productivity. It has been argued that total factor productivity growth was next to nil because the speed of technical change in Singapore did not give adequate time for 'learning by doing' gains to be realised (Young, 1992, 1994). This fails to understand the quickly-exhausted nature of the learning curve, and so the limited gains available in the particular international division of labour on which Singapore's spectacular manufacturing growth depended. Singapore has in fact benefited from higher value-added activities (even in some parts of the electronics sector), and

Table 3.7 Singapore manufacturing value added as a percentage of output, 1973–1992

	1973	*1978*	*1984*	*1992*	*% of total 1992 manufacturing value added*
All industries	32.0	26.3	27.0	34.6	100.0
Electronic products and components		32.2	29.9	27.9	38.5
Electrical machinery and apparatus	39.0[a]	33.7	37.6	38.7	4.4
Transport equipment	46.8	47.4	51.7	45.2	8.6
Machinery except electrical and electronic	39.9	49.1	45.7	38.5	6.4
Fabricated metal products	36.8	34.5	38.7	37.8	7.1

Note: Figures include petroleum refineries and products.
[a] Includes electronic products.

Source: As for Table 6.

Singaporeans were increasingly employed as technicians and in supervisory positions. But for electronics, the bulk of technological progress and learning gains were found in developed countries where research and development and process and product design concentrated.

By the late 1980s it appeared doubtful whether Singapore's legislation and policy instruments like the National Wages Council, which successfully regulated wage costs in a full-employment economy, were also able to effect industrial restructuring towards higher value-added activities and the increased productivity which is the heart of the economic development process (Disney and Ho, 1990; Lim, 1988, pp. 35–6). That the Republic's leaders recognised the need for more indigenous development of technology as well as training programmes and education to effect restructuring was indicated by a planning departure in the 1990s to achieve productivity gains through technical progress: the state was to spearhead research and development (Singapore, National Science and Technology Board, 1991; Straits Times Weekly, 1992A).

3.3.2 State-owned enterprise

After the PAP's early 1960s abandonment of a (colonial-inherited) ideology which confined government to the provision of infrastructure, the state moved aggressively into direct participation in industrial, commercial and financial activities (Lee, 1974). Thus, although private enterprise, strategically supported by the state, was regarded as the main force for growth, Singapore's government, like South Korea's (Song, 1990, pp. 118–19), recognised the potential for public enterprise as a lead factor in the development process and showed no hesitation in moving into any area of the economy essential to expanding technological and export capacity, notably iron and steel and ship-repair and ship-building. By 1974, public enterprises were thought to account for 14–16% of all manufacturing output (Lee, S. Y., 1974, p. 64). More important, many traded services came through public enterprises. These included Neptune Orient Lines (shipping), Intraco (trading), the Development Bank of Singapore and Singapore Airlines—this last by the 1990s making Singapore as a country the world's fifth largest international air carrier behind the US, UK, Japan and Germany (*Straits Times Weekly*, 1992C).

The Singapore development model carries the lesson that public enterprise organised through a sort of political entrepreneurship can be run efficiently and at a profit. In achieving this, Singapore's government had the advantage that public ownership began afresh rather than through the nationalisation of already loss-making enterprises; subsequently, unsuccessful ventures were shaken up and, if unable to be turned around, eventually liquidated. By the mid-1980s, prior to privatisation beginning in late 1985, the government wholly or partially owned some 490 companies, including 30 statutory boards through which the government organised infrastructure provision. However, these often had 'substantial commercial operations' and their monopoly power, either legislated or natural, enabled the government to realise large profits, so long as reasonable commercial efficiency was maintained (Singapore, Ministry of Finance, 1987). In 1984/85, seven statutory boards with commercial operations (i.e. excluding the Monetary Authority of Singapore, Central Provident Fund and Board of Commissioners of Currency with large investment income earnings) made substantially higher profits than the ten most profitable companies listed on Singapore's stock exchange (Seah, 1986).

Management of state-owned enterprise was highly centralised. Control was effected through three holding companies run by three government ministries. Interlocking companies and interlocking directorships gave a few top civil servants, each with more than ten directorships, considerable leverage over government holdings. Overall, the government 'monopolised a fair share of entrepreneurial and business brains in its enterprise [and] tapped the private sector by seconding business elites into its enterprises' (Low, 1984, p. 274).

The still-cautious course of privatisation after almost a decade (government retains large stakes in major undertakings like Singapore Airlines) reflects the absence of any real argument in Singapore for the superior economic efficiency of private ownership, combined with the PAP's reluctance to surrender direction of strategic sectors of Singapore Inc. In part, however, privatisation which makes available on advantageous terms equity in enterprises built up with public funds allays complaints that state-owned enterprise 'crowds out' local private enterprises. More important for the government, partial privatisation of state-owned enterprise, including statutory boards for telecommunications and post (as Singapore Telecom), introduces a depth otherwise lacking in the Stock Exchange of Singapore. Increased stock market capitalisation is necessary to attract a critical mass of foreign fund managers and institutions to pre-empt competition from rapidly-growing countries like Thailand and Malaysia and establish Singapore as the central stock market within the Association of South East Asian Nations, complementing its other international financial functions (Singapore, Ministry of Finance, 1987, p. 43; *Financial Times*, 1990).

3.3.3 Government-forced saving

The driving force in Singapore's saving process was public sector saving, which increased from less than one-quarter of national saving in 1974 to three-fifths by 1984 (Table 3.8). Public sector saving consisted of the government's budget surplus and surpluses realised by statutory boards. Within the public sector, profits from natural monopolies in effect subsidised deficits in government priority areas like housing. Seven main boards—the Housing and Development Board, Jurong Town Corporation, Public Utilities Board, Port of Singapore Authority, Urban Redevelopment Authority, Telecommunication Authority of Singapore and Sentosa Development Corporation—were central in determining public sector saving.

The private sector's contribution to Singapore's high saving rate (Table 3.8) was substantially due to saving forced by the government through a social security scheme—the Central Provident Fund. One estimate was that between 1967 and 1989 it raised Singapore's overall saving rate by 3.8% (Monetary Authority of Singapore, 1991A). The Central Provident Fund could increase the domestic saving rate because (unusually among developing countries) it operated on the provident fund principle: on retirement, individuals were paid benefits determined by total past contributions from themselves and their employers plus interest, rather than payments being made to retirees from the contributions of those still working. Contribution rates, divided about equally between employee and employer, rose from 10% in 1967 to 38.5% in 1980 and a peak of 50% in 1984 before declining somewhat.

In addition to the Central Provident Fund, the government had no hesitation in rigging the market to obtain control over remaining voluntary private savings. A large indirect transfer of savings from the private sector to the government resulted from voluntary deposits with the Post Office Savings Bank. The Bank was required to lend mainly to statutory boards or government corporations, or to lodge the deposits it took with the Monetary Authority of Singapore. Deposits with the Bank were tax-exempt, and two years after becoming a statutory board in 1972, it began to offer a higher interest rate than commercial banks. By the mid-1980s, purely savings deposits with the Post Office Savings Bank exceeded those of all Singapore's

Table 3.8 Singapore sources of gross national savings, 1974–1985

	Gross national savings	Public sector savings		Private sector savings: Central provident fund		Private sector savings: Other (corporate + personal)	
	$m	*$m*	*% GNS*	*$m*	*% GNS*	*$m*	*% GNS*
1974	3220	736	22.8	643	20.0	1841	57.2
1975	3985	1362	34.2	821	20.6	1802	45.2
1976	4580	1470	32.1	831	18.1	2279	49.8
1977	5079	2021	39.8	888	17.5	2170	42.7
1978	5928	2230	37.6	1027	17.3	2671	45.1
1979	7300	2801	38.4	1534	21.0	2965	40.6
1980	8282	3407	41.1	2036	24.6	2839	34.3
1981	10,483	4261	40.6	2599	24.8	3623	34.6
1982	12,885	5936	46.1	3506	27.2	3443	26.7
1983	16,306	8649	53.0	3849	23.6	3808	23.4
1984	18,596	11,291	60.7	3166	17.0	4139	22.3
1985	16,543	11,052	66.8	4159	25.1	1332	8.1

Notes:
(1) Gross national savings equal public sector savings plus private sector savings. Public sector savings are the current surplus in the consolidated accounts of the public sector, which consists of government plus seven major statutory boards, namely the Housing and Development Board, Jurong Town Corporation, Public Utilities Board, Port of Singapore Authority, Telecommunication Authority of Singapore, Urban Redevelopment Authority and Sentosa Development Corporation. Central Provident Fund savings are the net addition that year to the accumulated fund due to members. Because of members' withdrawals of funds, this figure was normally less than members' contributions. Other private sector savings are gross national savings minus public sector and Central Provident Fund savings. Figures which divide other private sector savings into corporate and personal savings are not available.
(2) The 1985 figure for public sector savings is provisional. Comparable figures for public sector savings are not available after 1985, owing to changes in the official statistics.

Sources: Singapore, Department of Statistics, 1988, pp. 56–58; Singapore, *Parliamentary Debates*, vol. 36, no. 10 (28 February 1977), cols, 607–8, vol. 37, no. 7 (27 February 1978), cols. 485–86, vol. 38, no. 7 (5 March 1979), cols. 417–18; Singapore, Ministry of Trade and Industry, *Economic Survey of Singapore 1979*, p. 30, *1980*, p. 36, *1981*, p. 40, *1982*, p. 45, *1983*, p. 49, *1984*, p. 43, *1985*, p. 34, *1986*, p. 38, *1987*, p. 46; Singapore, Department of Statistics, *Yearbook of Statistics 1982/83*, p. 194, *1985/86*, p. 216.

commercial banks put together (Wong, 1986; Lim, 1988; Monetary Authority of Singapore, 1993).

3.3.4 Infrastructure and housing provision

Few countries exemplify as well as Singapore Keynes's (1972, p. 113) observation that building a 'well-equipped, up-to-date, go-ahead and efficient national plant depends on the mood and policy of the government'. Borrowing from the Central Provident Fund gave the government a cheap, typically below-market interest rates, non-inflationary source of finance which could be used to provide infrastructure and public goods. And in its public sector mobilisation of finance by the extraction of savings through monopoly power, Singapore operated a state-directed capitalism which, in Gurley and Shaw's (1967) terminology, is a technology of finance resembling socialist central planning more than private free market capitalism. Domestic capital resources were mobilised for economic development when the government used its control over savings to invest in infrastructure and housing (Sandilands, 1992).

Infrastructure provided under government auspices was the most modern and efficient possible, including port, airport, telecommunications, roads and a mass rapid transit system. The effect was to provide a subsidy for business in Singapore, which reduced expenses both in operating within the Republic and in reaching world markets, so-called 'distance costs' (Helleiner, 1973). Ready-to-move-into factory sites were provided at Jurong and other industrial estates. Planning which emphasised technical education and industrial training further subsidised industry, while government promotion of education in English reduced distance costs by facilitating communication between expatriate MNE personnel and Singaporeans.

3.3.5 Private sector investment and capital accumulation

The rapid accumulation of physical capital which characterised the Singapore model came principally from the private sector (Table 3.9). Even from 1960 to 1966, when planning in Singapore stressed government provision of infrastructure, the public sector accounted for no more than 38% of all gross fixed capital formation in Singapore. During the 1970s, and from 1980 to 1992, nearly three-quarters of this capital formation came from the private sector.

Singapore's high investment could increasingly have been domestically financed (Table 3.1), and by the late 1980s gross national savings were greater

Table 3.9 Singapore gross fixed capital formation by public and private sectors, 1960–1992 (1985 market prices, annual averages)

	Gross fixed capital formation	*Public sector*		*Private sector*	
	$m	*$m*	*%*	*$m*	*%*
1960–66	1093.0	423.3	38.2	684.3	61.8
1967–69	2382.2	716.4	30.2	1652.2	69.8
1960–69	1479.8	511.2	34.4	974.7	65.6
1970–79	6648.6	1800.3	27.4	4782.1	72.6
1980–92	17,498.2	4715.7	26.8	12,906.2	73.2

Note: Variables are deflated by the GDP deflator.

Sources: Singapore, Department of Statistis, 1988; Singapore, Ministry of Trade and Industry, Annual series, 1988–1993. *Economic Survey of Singapore*, Singapore.

than gross capital formation. However, well before this occurred, the government had begun to invest a high proportion of Singapore's public savings abroad in equities and bonds, real estate and short-term assets, with a consequent accumulation of large foreign reserves, in early 1994 conservatively estimated at US$51 billion, and among the world's highest. In effect, through this government investment abroad, Singapore exchanged an outflow of national savings for an inflow into the domestic economy of private foreign capital, which brought with it technology and assured access to markets. The exchange explains a part of what might otherwise seem a paradox: that high saving largely relied on the public sector but high investment came chiefly from the private sector. Direct foreign investment made a growing contribution to Singapore's capital formation, and rose from perhaps one-tenth of the total in 1967–1969 to as much as one-quarter by 1980–1992 (Table 3.10).

Government injections in the form of infrastructure, investment incentives and an increasingly educated workforce were fundamental in explaining Singapore's large private sector investment. Every $1 increase over the preceding decade in public sector capital formation was associated with an increase in private sector capital formation of $3 during the 1970s and $2.8 for 1980–1992 (Table 3.9). The relationship does not indicate causation, but is at least suggestive of the possibility of long-term 'crowding in', rather than 'crowding out', due to government expenditure. A crowding in effect might also be expected because government injections were strongly complementary to the private sector and increased both the economy's absorptive capacity and investors' confidence (Aschauer, 1989; Taylor, 1991). Crowding in would help to explain the paradox of high public sector saving and yet reliance on

Table 3.10 Singapore measures of the contribution of direct foreign investment to capital accumulation, 1967–1992 (1985 market prices, annual averages)

	Gross fixed capital formation (GFCF)	*Foreign investment in manufacturing sector gross fixed assets*		*IMF figures for direct foreign investment in Singapore*	
	$m	*$m*	*% of GFCF*	*$m*	*% of GFCF*
1967–69	2382.2	261.4	11.0	219.0	9.2
1970–79	6648.6	896.7	13.5	1471.3	22.1
1980–92	17,498.2	2112.3	12.1	4609.3	26.3

Note: For 1980–92, the figures for 'Foreign investment in manufacturing sector gross fixed assets' refer to 1980–91.

Sources: As for Table 9; Singapore, Economic Development Board, Annual series, 1967–1992/93; *Annual Report* or *Yearbook*, Singapore; International Monetary Fund, *Balance of Payments Statistics Yearbook*, vol. 27, *1967–74*, p. 1 of Singapore section, vol. 29, *1978*, p. 532 and part 1 of the following years: *1985*, p. 559, *1986*, p. 581, *1987*, p. 597, *1992*, p. 617, *1993*, p. 613; International Monetary Fund, *International Financial Statistics Yearbook 1990*, 634–35, *April 1994*, p. 480.

private sector capital formation: public sector savings which financed infrastructure brought even higher private sector investment. But a possible drawback was that the private industry crowded in was largely foreign.

3.4 PLANNING FOR MANUFACTURING DEVELOPMENT

The leaders of independent Singapore began with a general belief in the effectiveness of planning, but no definite idea of the course it should follow. Singapore's leadership was, however, strong, largely independent of local interest groups and dedicated to the goal of economic development—also characteristics of successful planning in South Korea and Taiwan. In Singapore, a coherent, clearly defined development strategy, essential to any shade of planning (Chakravarty, 1991), emerged from the later 1960s as the political leadership/planners increasingly perceived the strength of the world economy's new flows of trade and foreign investment. As part of that strategy, Singapore's leaders found control over key domestic markets and institutions the most effective way to respond to these opportunities in the world economy in order to meet the main planning objectives of providing jobs, absorbing surplus labour and rapid economic growth (Goh, 1989). There was no ideological commitment to free enterprise as such: 'The government has to be the planner and the mobiliser of the economic effort' but 'the free enterprise system, correctly nurtured and adroitly handled, can serve as a powerful and versatile instrument of economic growth' (Goh, 1972).

Interventionism in Singapore was organised around government directives, and so had considerably more force than indicative planning. Evaluation of development plans and planning objectives is complicated by the fact that, like most government matters in Singapore, described even now as a 'corporate state that is mainly run by PAP technocrats' (Kim, 1992, p. 119), principal documents were kept secret.[1] Only 'highlights' of the *Economic Development Plan for the Eighties* were published, although subsequent plans were discussed more fully, and plan review procedures have now been given a public fascia (Singapore, SEP Working Group, 1993). It is clear, however, that planning for manufacturing development in Singapore never involved detailed blueprints, because of the priority accorded to reaction to the international market, the impossibility of predicting its course and the need for flexibility to ensure a quick and competitive response. Instead, requirements common to all industries—good infrastructure and a cheap, disciplined and trained labour force—were made prime objectives and systematically met.

More than this, Singapore planners took a view of the future and, helped by intelligence from Economic Development Board overseas offices, closely monitored the world market. Initiatives were undertaken to attract industries regarded as desirable for long-term development. For example, the potential of electronics was spotted on a 1966 ministerial visit to Taiwan (Wee, 1966;

Goh, 1992). The Economic Development Board targeted manufacturing activities, in that the Board looked for industries beneficial to Singapore—on criteria like value added, skill content and capital intensity—which were likely to be attracted to the Republic, enquired as to the necessary incentives and then provided them (Singapore, Economic Development Board, 1993B, pp. 26–27). This incentive structure, including tax concessions associated with pioneer status for new industries and worker-training programmes, was continually revised in light of planning objectives. The government also took significant equity shares in foreign, private-sector projects—petrochemicals, and in 1991 production of dynamic random access memory chips—to promote strategic industrial clusters (Low *et al.*, 1993, p. 99; Hu, 1994).

But in manufacturing, the aims remained general; Singapore planners' approach to the international economy contrasted with the targeted protectionism and idea of 'picking winners' practised in Japan, South Korea and Taiwan, and perhaps possible for a large developing country. Rather, in keeping with a tiny domestic economy, Singapore adhered to free trade and tried to be attractive to a range of activities through supply oriented policies, an approach later likened to backing all the horses in a race (Goh, 1992; Singapore, Economic Planning Committee, 1991, p. 68). In the public sector, largely responsible for infrastructural development, rolling 5-year plans operated.

Singapore planning featured the concentration of decision-making in a few hands, also observed elsewhere in East Asia (Jones and SaKong, 1980; Wade, 1990). In Singapore's 'top-down' approach, at the summit the planning system was described as 'a high degree of good and eclectic steersmanship' (Low, 1988, p. 259). Typically, the same men, for example Goh Keng Swee, Hon Sui Sen and Joseph Pillay, served as directors for a host of SOEs and PAP government development initiatives, which economised on entrepreneurial talent (Singapore Trade and Industry, 1969A and 1969B; Lee, 1984; Bryant, 1985, p. 13). Moreover, the policy helped to ensure loyalty to the government and to further its tight control. The PAP leadership achieved effective implementation of plans and policies through the lower levels of bureaucracy by a willingness to pay government officials as much or more than the private sector and an emphasis on individual accountability (Chew, 1988, pp. 222–3).

Singapore planning was, as elsewhere in East Asia, strongly market oriented, but government-business cooperation, which in South Korea featured government as the senior partner controlling domestic entrepreneurs (Mason, 1980, p. 294), found, in Singapore, government as a junior partner to the needs of foreign enterprise. The planning strategy of Singapore, like that of any country, is not directly applicable elsewhere, and the high foreign presence promoted may be its least transferable aspect.

3.5 OVERSAVING OR OPTIMAL SAVING UNDER STATE DIRECTION?

The Singapore government's control over saving and promotion of a high rate of investment owed much to state socialism. Under this system, the determination of an optimal share of savings in national income is a policy choice and, equally, the possibility of wasteful overinvestment is a danger (Kalecki, 1972). Although in Singapore reliance on foreign investment limited the state's scope to determine the investment share, whether or not the government enforced 'oversaving' was an important macroeconomic issue by the mid-1980s. Singaporean critics of the government maintained that the saving level decreed led to a misallocation of resources: high saving did not maximise the nation's utility owing to the unnecessary sacrifice of current consumption. This critique, increasingly heard by the late 1980s as the savings ratio began to exceed the investment ratio, was emphatically disputed by the government (Koh, 1987, pp. 85–6; Lim, 1988, pp. 37, 234–5; Lee, H. L., 1992; *Straits Times Weekly*, 1992B).

A number of influential Singaporeans and non-Singaporeans also argued that Singapore planners were guilty of promoting overinvestment. Young (1992) found that as a result of overinvestment, the Singapore before-subsidy rate of return on capital had been pushed to one of the lowest in the world, and suggested that government policy of targeting to attract industries was a mistake. Young's calculations showed a real rate of return on capital which averaged 10.3% for 1980–1989; this compared to an average real prime lending rate of 5% (the latter calculated using the GDP deflator and Singapore, Department of Statistics, 1991, p. 236).

There is no entirely satisfactory answer to the questions of oversaving and overinvestment in Singapore. The high level of saving may be justified in part on the positive grounds of making at least some contribution to low inflation, discussed below, and partly on the normative grounds of promoting both the spread of home ownership and external security through foreign reserve accumulation. Whether or not the saving rate was optimal in the sense of maximising the present value of Singaporeans' total expected utility over some given time cannot be known because of the practical impossibility of discovering and aggregating individual utilities to arrive at any meaningful social utility function (Sen, 1961; Eckstein, 1961). Clearly, however, there was a revealed state preference function built around the priorities of infrastructure, housing and foreign reserve accumulation (Drewnowski, 1961; Domar, 1957, pp. 253–4).

Because Singapore in effect exchanged through investment abroad part of its domestic savings for foreign capital inflows in the form of direct foreign investment, high investment in Singapore could have been achieved without such high saving. Saving and investment levels were separate issues insofar as Singapore could have saved less and still avoided an unacceptably high balance of payments current account deficit. However, investment levels can be judged on a criterion other than utility maximisation (Ellman, 1989, pp. 132–9). In Singapore, they appear consistent with the approach developed to apply to socialist economies that optimal investment is that which maximises economic growth. Horvat (1965) argued that the optimal investment ratio, determined by an economy's absorptive capacity or ability to make productive use of new investment, was around 35%. Given the undoubtedly high absorptive capacity in Singapore, and since an urban economy requires considerably more capital than one with a rural sector (Lewis, 1966), investment ratios in the Republic seem unlikely to have been excessive, judged on the criterion of growth maximisation. Evidence which indicates that Singapore had among the world's lowest before-subsidy real rates of return on capital suggests that additions to output from further investment (the marginal efficiency of investment) may have been close to zero. If so, Singapore's share of investment in national income approached growth maximisation. Almost certainly the Singapore government, in keeping with the stress which historically it placed on investment (Singapore, 1963), has had growth, not utility, as its maximand—a policy decision confirmed by recent statements (*Straits Times Weekly*, 1994, 1995).

3.6. FINANCIAL AND BUSINESS SERVICES: NATURAL COMPARATIVE ADVANTAGE AND ITS AUGMENTATION

In the development of financial and business services, a more precise planning strategy prevailed than for manufacturing. It was set out in a plan for the 1970s (Hon, 1972), strengthened in the *Economic Development Plan for the Eighties* (Singapore, Ministry of Trade and Industry, 1981) and further elaborated later that decade (Singapore, Ministry of Trade and Industry, 1986A). Significantly, this more targeted approach to planning reflected Singapore's greater market power in attracting financial services based on 'natural' comparative advantage—i.e., when a free, competitive market prevails. Location on the world's main East–West communications network and the existing presence in the Republic of a critical mass of international financial institutions, ancillary services and infrastructure gave Singapore more freedom to 'pick winners' in financial services than in manufacturing. Starting in the later 1960s, the rapid expansion of international financial intermediation emphasised and widened Singapore's locational advantages. The island linked the Atlantic, Middle East and Pacific regions, which in the 1970s enabled Singapore to become a funding centre, acting as an entrepôt between deposit centres like Bahrain in a region of surplus funds and arranging centres like Hong Kong near ultimate borrowers. Because Singapore bridged the time zone gap between the New York/London and Hong Kong/Tokyo markets, it could emerge as a leading foreign exchange dealing centre with the initiation of 24-hour international trading. By the 1990s, Singapore was the fourth-largest foreign exchange market after London, New York and Tokyo (Singapore, Ministry of Trade and Industry, 1993, p. 66).

Financial services would not have become an engine of growth in Singapore's economy in the absence of an activist government. In 1968, the Singapore government, in consultation with international banks, spotted the possibility of an Asian dollar market similar to that for Eurodollars. The government immediately reacted by abolishing for deposits made by Asian Currency Units (ACUs)—any banking unit operating in the Singapore Asian Dollar Market—a withholding tax of 45% on interest paid to non-residents, quickly followed by a variety of other measures aimed at establishing the market (Hodjera, 1978). This activist government policy 'stole the march on Hong Kong', where the authorities lacked a similar development commitment (Jao, 1985, p. 44 and 1979). Although Hong Kong subsequently moved to establish a dollar market, by then the advantage lay decisively with Singapore, and a successful challenge to the Republic proved impossible.

In the 1970s, the government moved aggressively to develop the economy's comparative advantage in financial and business services through the introduction of financial innovations. The Monetary Authority of Singapore, established in 1971 as a quasi-central bank, became a strong and responsive institution which, together with the Development Bank of Singapore, the government could use in its strategy to turn Singapore into the 'Zurich of the East' (*Financial Times*, 1973). When the market proved unresponsive, the government was willing to take the lead: the Development Bank of Singapore, and then the Singapore government itself, started the Asian Dollar Bond Market by floating US dollar-denominated bonds. As the private sector, after initial hesitation, embarked on similar initiatives, the Asian Dollar and Bond Markets—with their respectively short- and longer-term maturities—introduced significant market specialisation and complementarity in Singapore's offshore banking system (Singapore, 1973; Lee, S. Y., 1986). The Asian Dollar Market remained the more important of the two, and after reaching US$54.4 billion by 1980, grew to US$386.1 billion in 1993, annual average growth of 16.3% (Monetary Authority of Singapore, 1994).

Government policy which aimed at attracting international financial institutions to Singapore was also demonstrably successful. From 1981 to 1994, the number of foreign banks rose from 86 to 119, and merchant banks from 39 to 76. There were 198 ACUs, since virtually all banks and merchant banks dealt in Asian dollars (Monetary Authority of Singapore, 1994).

Singapore's ever-growing cluster of financial institutions created opportunities for specialisation and scale economies for these institutions, and so reinforced government efforts towards broadening and deepening financial services in the Republic. In association with the Monetary Authority of Singapore, the government targeted specific financial instruments and institutions and strongly encouraged them with fiscal incentives. The establishment of Singapore as a '"financial supermarket", offering the widest range of financial services' (Singapore, Ministry of Trade and Industry, 1981, pp. 10–11) was central to the *Economic Development Plan for the Eighties*; during that decade, every budget statement contained new measures aimed at financial innovation. By the later 1980s, as the government had planned, Singapore had a successful futures and options market, organised through the Singapore International Monetary Exchange (SIMEX) and linked to the Chicago Mercantile Exchange on a 24-hour, mutual-offset basis; merchant banking appeared to have taken off, and the Republic was increasingly a centre for fund management (Singapore, Ministry of Trade and Industry, 1991, pp. 8, 69–70; Monetary Authority of Singapore, 1991, pp. 29, 33, 1992, p.40, 1993, pp. 59–60).

3.7 MACROECONOMIC POLICY

Although macroeconomic policy is often regarded as only a short-term, even minor adjunct of structural and institutional planning, temporary macroeconomic instability can destroy attempts at longer-term planning, as it did in Britain in the wake of the 1966 exchange crisis and 1967 devaluation (Hare, 1985). Macro policy instruments evolved in Singapore were therefore essential to the overall planning effort and, like it, made effective through a high degree of government control in selected areas.

Singapore's exceptionally low inflation was a principal achievement of macroeconomic policy, and became a cornerstone of it. Macroeconomic management was unconventional, in that a government's ability to secure international competitiveness through limiting wage rises to productivity gains is not typically among the range of policy instruments available. In Singapore, the substitution of an institution—the National Wages Council—for a conventional macro policy instrument—the exchange rate—freed the latter to become a weapon targeted specifically on inflation. Because, in a heavily re-export economy like Singapore's, with a large, internationally traded goods sector, import and export prices tended to rise about equally, domestic inflation was kept low by allowing the exchange rate to appreciate in line with foreign inflation. The expectation of a rise in value of the Singapore dollar consequent on increased world inflation would have led to a rush of foreign funds into the Singapore currency, unduly pushing up its value, and making impossible control by the Monetary Authority of Singapore, had not the Singapore authorities prevented the 'internationalisation' of the Singapore dollar. The Monetary Authority of Singapore achieved this by imposing a withholding tax on interest earned by non-residents on Singapore dollar holdings, and issuing directives to the banking system not to make Singapore dollar loans to non-residents or residents for use outside the Republic, except to finance Singapore's external trade. Banks had to submit in writing any proposals for such loans exceeding S$5 million (Corden, 1984; Bryant, 1985, pp. 98–101; Lim, 1988).

To some extent, there was truth in the argument that Singapore's high, government-forced savings contributed to dampening inflationary pressures by mopping up private-sector purchasing power which would otherwise have gone into non-internationally traded goods—personal services, food distribution and, above all, building and construction—and pushed up their prices. Changes in Central Provident Fund employee contributions were used to control private-sector purchasing power, and, in conjunction with National Wages Council 'recommendations', to fine tune Singapore's international wage competitiveness (Wong, 1981; Hewson, 1981; Lim, 1982). High savings also helped to neutralise the expansionary effect of large inflows of foreign capital (Wong, 1986; Sandilands, 1992). However, the more important role of the high level of savings in macroeconomic management was to provide a non-inflationary way to finance the three government-defined priorities of infrastructure, housing and the accumulation of foreign reserves.

Insofar as the government 'released' Central Provident Fund savings back into the domestic economy, purchasing power was directed towards the first two of these objectives. Workers' savings, and implicit taxation of them, enabled the government to avoid financing infrastructure development through high income taxes or, more important, through money creation. The refusal of the Singapore government to incur government deficits financed by borrowing from a central bank made possible continued adherence to a currency board system which itself promoted low inflation.

The government channelled part of forced saving into a programme to increase home ownership. Beginning in 1968, individuals were allowed to make withdrawals at any time in their working life from compulsory Central Provident Fund savings to purchase homes, almost all of which the government built and sold at below-market prices. By 1990, 88% of households owned the houses they occupied compared to less than one-third in 1970 (Singapore, Department of Statistics, 1983B; Singapore, Department of Statistics, 1992). Home ownership was a government priority because of the social stability thereby promoted. The public housing programme also allowed the PAP to manipulate electoral constituencies and disperse political opposition (Lim, Pang and Findlay, 1993, p. 125). In addition to housing, subsequent further liberalisations of restrictions on the use of Central Provident Fund funds allowed withdrawals against spending on medical care, approved shares and some educational expenses. Most of these expenditures are, in a broad sense, investment, not consumption.

The rapid gains in real wages (Table 3.4) and home ownership for Singaporeans induced acceptance of government wage control, which completed a 'virtuous circle' of macroeconomic policy: low inflation, with consequent real exchange rate competitiveness, helped to ensure continued foreign capital inflows giving access to MNE technology and marketing which made real wage gains possible. Furthermore, these gains were largely guaranteed, since Singapore citizens were almost assured of a job. The job security of Singapore nationals was, in part, underwritten through hosting up to 200,000 guest workers by the mid 1970s who could be sent home, and so bore much of the risk of unemployment in an economic downturn. In 1985, there was a net reduction of 96,000 jobs, but over three-fifths of those affected were foreign workers (Singapore, Ministry of Trade and Industry, 1986B, p. 4).

3.8 CONCLUSION AND IMPLICATIONS FOR DEVELOPING COUNTRIES

The Singapore model is unlikely to be replicated elsewhere, not only because the Republic is a city state, but also because few others can develop services exports reliant on location, because of the unacceptability in many other polities of a heavy foreign economic presence, and because of difficulties in effecting the same degree of government control as in Singapore. When Milton Friedman (1990, pp. 12–13) looked at Singapore, he remarked that Lee Kuan Yew was a 'benevolent dictator' and drew the lesson that 'It is possible to combine a free private market economic system with a dictatorial political system'. But Singapore's experience was more subtle: its government used 'dictatorial' means to make the 'free market' work. Four main lessons may be adduced from Singapore's experience.

One is the positive role in economic development which extensive government intervention in selected sectors of the economy can play. Unable to influence the international economy, Singapore instead responded to international forces through manipulating the domestic economy. There, the PAP's control was total and, although replacing the price mechanism in fundamental respects, effective, because Singapore planners bore uppermost in mind international prices and costs. Wages were adjusted and kept to internationally competitive levels. As an institution, the National Wages Council compares with the national wage-fixing bodies championed for developed countries by J. Meade (1982) and D. Vines (1986). likewise, the government replaced the market to force a high saving rate. Through taxation via the Central Provident Fund, the high MNE presence in Singapore was made to create an important fiscal linkage and conduce to continued economic development. Here, Singapore's experience is worthy of wider attention from developing countries.

Second, Singapore illustrates the importance of investment in infrastructure and education. Both were paid for, in conjunction with government control of savings, by real resource transfers, not money creation, and so were not inflationary. Under these conditions, and owing to concentration on sectors complementary to private investment, Singapore's public investment and infrastructural creation was consistent with 'crowding in' not 'crowding out'. Singapore supports the case for planning and infrastructural investment to further the development process which is now being re-discovered by sources as diverse as the new growth economists (Boltho and Holtham, 1992) and the London *Economist* (1992).

Third, in an era of development theory whose practitioners are, even now, often wary if not dismissive of planning, Singapore is prominent as a country where economic planning, involving control over key macroeconomic variables and a systematic effort to co-ordinate public sector investment decisions and attract private investment, succeeded. Singapore's planning, as Chakravarty (1991) noted of Japan and South Korea, accorded an important role to the market and to achieving growth through it. And, just as he observed that a discussion of 'the market versus the Plan' offers too crude a dichotomy to explain what happened in Japan, South Korea or Taiwan (Chakravarty, 1987, p. 137), so Singapore, within a continuum between these two extremes, had a distinct planning experience: it differed from the targeting and 'governed markets' familiar in these other Asian countries (Boltho, 1985; Wade, 1990). Only internally could Singapore have the features of a governed market. Singapore planners recognised the limitations of small size and extreme openness in departing from free trade to govern the market. Perhaps in this regard Singapore's brand of interventionism offers a more realistic pattern for developing countries—often tiny economically—which aim to become late industrialisers.

Fourth, Singapore's experience suggests the weaknesses and limits of the kind of government control it exercised. Neither control over wages and subsidies to MNEs nor direction of savings delivered major technological gains in manufacturing which, despite the importance of services in post-1979 growth and their likely future dominance, remains fundamental to the island's economy. The need to restructure the manufacturing sector, and the danger that too-strong internal economic direction risks the loss of the substantial measure of consent from Singapore's population necessary for the long-term survival of any economic system, are the two biggest problems faced by the Republic in the late 1990s.

This article began by drawing attention to the present empirical phase in development economics. Investigation of Singapore's economic development consistent with such empiricism suggests a conclusion which might broadly be termed 'neo-structuralist', pointing to the scope for state intervention and the importance of specific country circumstances. Principal themes in the Singapore model of economic development—government intervention and planning, industrialisation, labour mobilisation and rapid capital accumulation—are what A. K. Sen (1983) identified as the core of development economics prior to a 1970s and 1980s neoclassical ascendence. If one prefers to think of this neoclassicism as a counter-revolution, then Singapore's experience accords with the argument for a counter-counter-revolution in development theory (Krugman, 1992). Whichever description is chosen, examination of Singapore's actual development strategy contradicts fundamentally neoclassical, including recent 'market-friendly', views. Since these have drawn considerable strength from interpretations of East Asia's four dragons, the Singapore model lends significant weight to the growing reassertion of a structuralist approach to development economics.

ACKNOWLEDGMENTS

University of Glasgow and Australian National University. I owe thanks to R. B. DuBoff, J. F. Ermisch, J. B. K. Hunter, J. M. Gullick, F. Scott, seminar participants at the Australian National University and its ECHOSEA Research Group led by A. J. S. Reid, and three anonymous referees of this journal for extensive and helpful comments on earlier drafts of this article. Research was supported by a grant from the Nuffield Foundation, and data collection by a grant from the Scottish Economic Society, which are gratefully acknowledged.

NOTES

1 Direct manufactured exports refer to goods not simply re-exported, and exclude petroleum. Statistics for direct manufactured exports can be calculated from the sources for Table 3.2.

2 The main published planning documents in Singapore were Singapore, Ministry of Finance, 1961; United Nations, 1961; Singapore Economic Planning Unit, 1964; Hon, 1972; Singapore, Ministry of Trade and Industry, 1981; Singapore, Ministry of Trade and Industry, 1986A; Singapore, Economic Planning Committee, 1991; Singapore, National Science and Technology Board, 1991; Singapore, SEP Working Group, 1993.

REFERENCES

Amsden, A. 1989. *Asia's Next Giant: South Korea and Late Industrialization*, New York, Oxford University Press

Aschauer, D. A. 1989. Does public capital crowd out private capital? *Journal of Monetary Economics*, vol. 24, September

Benham, F. C. 1957. *Economic Survey Singapore 1957*, Singapore, Government Printing Office

—— 1959. *The National Income of Singapore 1956*, London, Royal Institute of International Affairs

Boltho, A. 1985. Was Japan's industrial policy successful? *Cambridge Journal of Economics*, vol. 9, no. 1

—— and Holtham G. 1992. The assessment: new approaches to economic growth, *Oxford Review of Economic Policy*, vol. 8, no. 4

Bryant, R. C. 1985. *Financial Structure and International Banking in Singapore.* Brookings Discussion Papers, no. 29, Washington, D.C., Brookings Institution

Caine, S. 1956. The importance of capital, *Malayan Economic Review*, vol. 1, no. 1

Chakravarty, S. 1987A. The state of development economics, *Manchester School of Economic and Social Studies*, vol. 55, no. 2

—— 1987B. *Development Planning: The Indian Experience*, Oxford, Clarendon Press

—— 1991. Development planning: a reappraisal, *Cambridge Journal of Economics*, vol. 15, no. 1
Chew, S. B. 1988. *Small Firms in Singapore*, Singapore, Oxford University Press
Chow, S. C. and Papanek, G. F. 1981. Laissez-faire, growth and equity—Hong Kong, *Economic Journal*, vol. 91
Corden, W. M. 1984. Macroeconomic targets and instruments for a small open economy, *Singapore Economic Review*, vol. 29, no. 2
Disney, R. and Ho, S. K. 1990. Do real wages matter in an open economy? The case of Singapore, 1966–1987, *Oxford Economic Papers*, vol. 42
Domar, E. D. 1957. *Essays in the Theory of Economic Growth*, New York, Oxford University Press
Drewnowski, J. 1961. The economic theory of socialism: a suggestion for reconsideration, *Journal of Political Economy*, vol. 69, no. 4
Eckstein, O. 1961. Capital theory and some theoretical problems in development planning, *American Economic Review*, vol. 51, no. 2
Economist 1992. The case for central planning, 12 September
Ellman, M. 1989. *Socialist Planning*, 2nd edn., Cambridge, Cambridge University Press
Financial Times 1973. Growing sophistication in the financial community (Singapore Survey), 1 October
—— 1990. Pressing ahead with privatisation (Singapore Survey), 9 August
Friedman, M. 1990. A welfare state syllogism (speech to the Commonwealth Club, San Francisco), June
GATT 1993. *International Trade 1993 Statistics*, Geneva, GATT
Giordano, R. and Kato, S. 1993. Singapore: the most successful 'Asian dragon', *The International Economics Analyst*, vol. 8, no. 2
Goh, K. S. 1970. *Decade of Achievement* (budget speech, 1970), Singapore, Ministry of Culture
—— 1972. *The Asian*, 20 August
—— 1989. Interview with the author, 17 August
—— 1992. MNCs brought jobs and sparked change, *Straits Times Weekly*, 29 August
Gurley, J. G. and Shaw, E. S. 1967. Financial structure and economic development, *Economic Development and Cultural Change*, vol. 15, no. 3
Hare, P. 1985. Planning in a market economy: problems and lessons, *Royal Bank of Scotland Review*, no. 147, September
Helleiner, G. K. 1973. Manufactured exports from less-developed countries and multinational firms, *Economic Journal*, vol. 83
Hodjera, Z. 1978. The Asian currency market: Singapore as a regional financial centre, *IMF Staff Papers*, vol. 25, no. 2
Hon, S. S. 1972. *Economic Pattern in the Seventies* (budget speech), Singapore, Ministry of Culture
Hu, R. T. T. 1986. *Budget Statement 1986*, Singapore, Ministry of Communications and Information
—— 1987. *Budget Statement 1987*, Singapore, Ministry of Communications and Information
—— 1990. *Budget Statement 1990*, Singapore, Ministry of Communications and Information
—— 1991. *Budget Statement 1991*, Singapore, Ministry of Information and the Arts
—— 1994. *Budget Statement 1994*, Singapore, Ministry of Information and the Arts
Horvat, B. 1965. The optimum rate of investment reconsidered, *Economic Journal*, vol. 75
Hughes, H. 1988. Comments on John Fei's Evolution of development policy, in

Ranis, G. and Schultz, T. P. (eds.), *The State of Development Economics*, Oxford, Basil Blackwell

Islam, I. and Kirkpatrick, C. 1986. Export-led development, labour market conditions and the distribution of income: the case of Singapore, *Cambridge Journal of Economics*, vol. 10, no. 2

Jao, Y. C. 1979. The rise of Hong Kong as a financial centre, *Asian Survey*, vol. 19, no. 7

—— 1985. Hong Kong's future as a financial centre, *Three Banks Review*, no. 145, March

Jones, L. P. and SaKong, I. 1980. *Government, Business, and Entrepreneurship in Economic Development: the Korean Case*, Cambridge, Harvard University Press

Kalecki, M. 1972. Outline of a method of constructing a prospective plan, in Nove, A. and Nuti, D. M. (eds.), *Socialist Economics*, London, Penguin

Keynes, J. M. 1972. Essays in Persuasion, vol. IX, in Moggridge, D. (ed.), *The Collected Writings of John Maynard Keynes*, London, Macmillan

—— 1980. Activities 1940–1946 Shaping the Post-War World: Employment and Commodities, vol. XXXVII, in Moggridge, D. (ed.), *The Collected Writings of John Maynard Keynes*, London, Macmillan

Kim, S. P. 1992. Singapore in 1991, *Asian Survey*, vol. 32, no. 2

Kirkpatrick, C. 1986. Singapore at the crossroads: the economic challenges ahead, *National Westminster Bank Quarterly Review*, May

Koh, A. T. 1987. Savings, investment and entrepreneurship, in Krause, L. B., Koh, A. T. and Lee (Tsao), Y. (eds), *The Singapore Economy Reconsidered*, Singapore, Institute of Southeast Asian Studies

Krugman, P. 1992. Toward a counter-counterrevolution in development theory, *Proceedings of the World Bank Annual Conference on Development Economies 1992*

Lee, H. L. 1986. Singapore's economic policy: vision for the 1990s (speech by B. G. (Res) Lee Hsien Loong at the Commonwealth Institute, London), January

—— 1992. Keynote address at the Enterprise '92 Conference (speech by B. G. (Res) Lee Hsien Loong), 25 August

Lee, J. 1984. How MAS directs Singapore Inc., *Euromoney*, September

Lee, S. Y. 1974. Public enterprise and economic development in Singapore, *Malayan Economic Review*, vol. 21, no. 2

—— 1986. Developing Asian financial centres, in Tan, A. H. H. and Kapur, B. (eds.), *Pacific Growth and Financial Interdependence*, Sydney, Allen & Unwin

Leong, M. K. 1971. *Wage Levels of Selected Countries*, Singapore, Ministry of Finance

Lewis, W. A. 1966. *Development Planning*, London, Allen & Unwin

Lim, C. Y. 1982. The N[ational] W[ages] C[ouncil] as I see it, in Jayakumar, S. (ed.), *Our Heritage and Beyond: A Collection of Essays on Singapore, its Past, Present and Future*, Singapore, National Trades Union Congress

—— and Associates. 1988. *Policy Options for the Singapore Economy*, Singapore, McGraw-Hill

—— and Pang, E. F. 1984. Labour strategies and the high-tech challenge: the case of Singapore, *Euro-Asia Business Review*, vol. 3, no. 2

—— 1986. *Trade Employment and Industrialisation in Singapore*, Geneva, ILO

—— 1991. *Foreign Investment and Industrialisation in Malaysia, Singapore, Taiwan and Thailand*, Paris, OECD

—— and Findlay, R. 1993. Singapore, in Findlay, R. and Wellisz, S. (eds.), *Five Small Open Economies*, Oxford, Oxford University Press

Low, L. 1984. Public enterprises in Singapore, in You, P. S. and Lim, C. Y. (eds.), *Singapore: Twenty-five Year of Development*, Singapore, Nan Yang Xing Zhou Lianhe Zaobao

—— 1985. The financing process in the public sector in Singapore, *Bulletin for International Fiscal Documentation*, vol. 39, no. 4
—— 1988. The Singapore economy in 1987, *Southeast Asian Affairs*, vol. 15
—— *et al.* 1993. *Challenge and Response: Thirty Years of the Economic Development Board*, Singapore, Times Academic Press
Lyle, F. J. 1959. An industrial development programme, *Singapore Legislative Assembly*, Sessional Paper no. Cmd 5, Singapore, Government Printing Office
Mason, E. S. *et al.* 1980. *The Economic and Social Modernization of the Republic of Korea*, Cambridge, Harvard University Press
Meade, J. E. 1982. *Stagflation, Volume I: Wage Fixing*, London, George Allen & Unwin
Monetary Authority of Singapore 1972. *Annual Report 1971*, Singapore
—— 1989. *Annual Report 1988/89*, Singapore
—— 1990. *Annual Report 1989/90*, Singapore
—— 1991. *Annual Report 1990/91*, Singapore
—— 1991A. *Savings-Investment Balances in Singapore: Determinants and Medium-Term Outlook*, Singapore: Economics Department, Monetary Authority of Singapore
—— 1992. *Annual Report 1991/92*, Singapore
—— 1993. *Annual Report 1992/93*, Singapore
—— 1994. *Annual Report 1993/94*, Singapore
Nolan, P. 1990. Assessing economic growth in the Asian NICs, *Journal of Contemporary Asia*, no. 1
O'Connor, M. 1966. E[conomic] D[evelopment] B[oard] plays a vital role in industrial finance, *Singapore Trade*, July
Riedel, J. 1988. Economic development in East Asia: doing what comes naturally? in Hughes, H. (ed.), *Achieving Industrialization in East Asia*, New York, Cambridge University Press
Sandilands, R. J. 1992. Savings, investment and housing in Singapore's growth, 1965–90, *Savings and Development*, vol. 16, no. 2
Saw Swee-Hock. 1984. *The Labour Force of Singapore* (census monograph no. 3), Singapore, Singapore National Printers
Seah, R 1986. Statutory boards: tight grip on a hoard of treasure, *Singapore Business*, February
Sen, A. K. 1961. On optimising the rate of savings, *Economic Journal*, vol. 71
—— 1983. Development economics: which way now? *Economic Journal*, vol. 93
Silcock, T. H. 1959. *The Commonwealth Economy in Southeast Asia*, Durham, NC, Duke University Press
Singapore 1961. *Legislative Assembly Debates*, part 2 of second session, first Legislative Assembly, 24 May, cols. 1516–1545
—— 1963. *Legislative Assembly Debates*, vol. 22, no. 2, 28 November, col. 103
—— 1964. *Census of Population 1957*, Singapore, Government Printer
—— 1973. *Parliamentary Debates*, vol. 32, no. 10, February, col. 460
—— 1980. *Parliamentary Debates;* vol. 39, no. 10, March, cols. 628–631
Singapore, Department of Statistics 1981. *Yearbook of Statistics Singapore 1979/80*, Singapore, Singapore National Printers
—— 1983A. *Economic and Social Statistics, 1960–1982*, Singapore, Singapore National Printers
—— 1983B. *Census of Population 1980: Administrative Report*, Singapore, Singapore National Printers
—— 1988. *Singapore National Accounts 1987*, Singapore, Singapore National Printers
—— 1991. *Yearbook of Statistics 1990*, Singapore, Singapore National Printers
—— 1992. *Singapore Census of Population 1990: Release 2. Households and Housing*, Singapore, Singapore National Printers

—— 1993A. *Singapore Census of Population 1990: Release 4. Economic Characteristics*, Singapore, Singapore National Printers
—— 1993B. *Yearbook of Statistics 1992*, Singapore, Singapore National Printers
—— 1994. *Yearbook of Statistics 1993*, Singapore, Singapore National Printers
Singapore, Economic Development Board 1992. *Report on the Census of Industrial Production 1990*, Singapore, Singapore National Printers
—— 1993A. *Report on the Census of Industrial Production 1991*, Singapore, Singapore National Printers
—— 1993B. *Yearbook 1992/93*, Singapore, Economic Development Board
Singapore, Economic Planning Committee 1991. *Strategic Economic Plan*, Singapore, Singapore National Printers
Singapore, Economic Planning Unit 1964. *First Development Plan, 1961–1964: Review of Progress*, Singapore, Government Printing Office
Singapore, Ministry of Finance 1961. *Development Plan 1961–1964*, Singapore, Government Printing Office
——, Trade Division 1970. *Annual Report 1969*, Singapore, Government Printing Office
—— 1987. *Report of the Public Sector Divestment Committee*, Singapore, Singapore National Printers
Singapore, Ministry of Labour 1993. *Report on Wages in Singapore 1992*, Singapore, Singapore National Printers
—— 1994. *Yearbook of Labour Statistics 1993*, Singapore, Singapore National Printers
Singapore, Ministry of Trade and Industry 1981. *Highlights of Singapore's Economic Development Plan for the Eighties*, Singapore, Curriculum Development Institute and Ministry of Trade and Industry
—— 1985. *Economic Survey of Singapore 1985* (second quarter), Singapore, Singapore National Printers
—— 1986A. *The Singapore Economy: New Directions* (Report of the Economic Committee), Singapore, Singapore National Printers
—— 1986B. *Economic Survey of Singapore 1985*, Singapore, Singapore National Printers
—— 1991. *Economic Survey of Singapore 1990*, Singapore, Singapore National Printers
—— 1993. *Economic Survey of Singapore 1992*, Singapore, Singapore National Printers
—— 1994. *Economic Survey of Singapore 1993*, Singapore, Singapore National Printers
Singapore, National Science and Technology Board 1991. *Window of Opportunities: National Technology Plan 1991*, Singapore, Singapore National Printers
Singapore, SEP Working Group (Ministry of Trade and Industry) 1993. *Implementation of the Strategic Economic Plan*, Singapore, Ministry of Trade and Industry
Singapore Trade and Industry 1969A. Hon Sui Sen: key man for new era of industrial development, January
—— 1969B. Public servant with a talent for the bold plan, wide sweep, April
Song, B. N. 1990. *The Rise of the Korean Economy*, Hong Kong, Oxford University Press
Stern, N. 1989. The economics of development: a survey, *Economic Journal*, vol. 99
Stiglitz, J. E. *et al.* 1989. *The Economic Role of the State*, Oxford, Basil Blackwell
Straits Times Weekly 1990. Interview with Lee Kuan Yew, 'Singapore needs 10 more years to become a more mature society', 5 May
—— 1992A. PM: get ready for the super league contest, 22 August
—— 1992B. Too much savings? Not true—BG Lee, 29 August
—— 1992C. SIA makes it to tanks of world's top five airlines, 24 October
—— 1994. PM [Goh Chok Tong]: maximise growth while the going is good, 12 November

—— 1995. Singapore cannot slow down pace of economic growth, says BG Lee, 21 January
Summers, L. H. and Pritchett, L. H. 1993. The structural adjustment debate, *American Economic Review*, vol. 83, no. 2
—— and Thomas, V. 1993. Recent lessons of development, *World Bank Research Observer*, vol. 8, no. 2
Szezepanik, E. 1957. *The Economic Growth of Hong Kong*, London, Oxford University Press
Taylor, L. 1991. *Income Distribution, Inflation and Growth: Lectures on Structuralist Macroeconomic Theory*, Cambridge, MIT Press
Taylor, L. 1993. Review of World Bank, World Development Report 1991, *Economic Development and Cultural Change*, vol. 41, no. 2
United Nations 1961. *A Proposed Industrialization Programme for the State of Singapore*, New York, U.N. Commission for Technical Assistance
—— 1992. *World Investment Report 1992*, New York, United Nations Centre on Transnational Corporations
United States, Department of Labor 1994. *International Comparisons of Hourly Compensation Costs for Production Workers in Manufacturing 1993* (report 873), Washington DC, US Department of Labor, Bureau of Labor Statistics
United States Tariff Commission 1970. *Economic Factors Affecting the Use of Items 807.00 and 806.30 of the Tariff Schedule of the United States*, Washington DC, US Tariff Commission
Vines, D. 1986. Macroeconomic policy after monetarism, *Royal Bank of Scotland Review*, no. 152, December
Wade, R. 1990. *Governing the Market*, Princeton, Princeton University Press
Wee, C. C. 1966. Export—Singapore's new road to prosperity, *Singapore Trade and Industry*, August
Wong, K. P. 1981. The financing of trade and development in the ADCs: the experience of Singapore, in Hong, W. and Krause, L. B. (eds.), *Trade and Growth of the Advanced Developing Countries*, Seoul, Korea Development Institute
—— 1986. Saving, capital inflow and capital formation, in Lim, C. Y. and Lloyd, P. J. (eds.), *Singapore: Resources and Growth*, Singapore, Oxford University Press
World Bank 1984. *World Development Report 1983*, Washington DC, World Bank
—— 1991. *World Development Report 1991*, Oxford, Oxford University Press
—— 1992. *World Development Report 1992*, Oxford, Oxford University Press
—— 1993A. *World Development Report 1993*, Oxford, Oxford University Press
—— 1993B. *The East Asian Miracle: Economic Growth and Public Policy* (World Bank Policy Research Reports), Oxford, Oxford University Press
—— 1994. *World Development Report 1994*, Oxford, Oxford University Press
Young, A. 1992. A tale of two cities: factor accumulation and technical change in Hong Kong and Singapore, *NBER Macroeconomics Annual*, vol. 7
—— 1994. Lessons from the East Asian NICs: a contrarian view, *European Economic Review*, vol. 38, no. 3/4

4

THE TAIWAN ECONOMY

The Transition to Maturity of the Political Economy of its Changing International Status

Christopher Howe

Taiwan's economic performance from the mid-1950s to the mid-1980s is regarded as that of an archetypal Asian Newly Industrializing Economy (ANIE). It achieved rapid growth, marked structural change and an exceptional export performance. During the 1980s, however, important changes in the pattern of growth and associated policy challenges became evident. These changes partly reflected the internal evolution of the economy as it began to exhaust both its labour intensive comparative advantage and also, arguably, some of the benefits of the regulated and protective institutional structure that underlay early economic successes.[1]

This internal evolution coincided with two important external changes. One was the unfolding development of the PRC under the policies of economic reform and the open door. For Taiwan, these changes represented both a serious competitive threat and a potentially beneficial economic opportunity. They were a threat because China's rapid expansion of exports took place in the labour intensive, technologically unsophisticated sectors (especially textiles, clothing and shoes) that were still very important to Taiwan. The potential benefits arose because the complementarities between the two economies held out promise of gains from mutual specialization and restructuring, supported by Taiwanese foreign direct investment (FDI). Taiwan's ability to gain from changes in the PRC was obviously enhanced by ties of culture, language, former political unification and a history of cross-Strait economic relations stretching back to the early Ming dynasty.

At the same time as these momentous events were occurring in the PRC, the Asia-Pacific network as a whole was also changing. In 1985–86, under pressures generated by Japanese trade imbalances, the Plaza Accord led to a major re-alignment of the yen-dollar exchange rate. Although a relatively modest actor in the Asia-Pacific as a whole, this event was of major significance to Taiwan as it triggered not only a further wave of Japanese FDI, but also a wave of FDI from the ANIEs (including Taiwan) that led to a major

Source: *The China Quarterly*, No. 148 (December 1996), pp. 1171–95.

restructuring of the Asian economies. As Japanese companies globalized and the ANIEs relocated their labour intensive industries, the economies of Thailand and Malaysia, hitherto specializing in primary commodities and their processing, developed export profiles that were predominantly industrial in a space of only four to five years. Further, because of its unofficial dollar link, Taiwan was for a short but useful period a beneficiary of yen revaluation: its competitiveness (*vis-à-vis* Japan) increased in the United States, and its exports also gained some help from exchange rate factors and market opening initiatives in Japan.

These developments, dramatic as they were, need to be seen in the context of a much longer process of intra-Asian specialization–a process that stretches back to the early part of the century, but whose pace has been intensified since the 1980s by the particular accidents of the Japan–United States relationship and the upward volatility of the yen.

THE LONG RUN PATTERN OF DEVELOPMENT

Table 4.1 displays four indicators of Taiwan's economic development during 1967–95. This Table reveals that between 1967 and 1990, national product grew within a range of 8 to 10 per cent per annum, but fell to 6.4 per cent in 1991–95. Per capita growth was somewhat slower, but still very high by world standards. The exceptionally fast growth of 1967–80 was supported by high investment and very high rates of growth of exports. During the 1980s, however, these both fell. In the 1990s investment picked up, but the rate of growth of exports continued to fall. Throughout, investment has been supported by high domestic savings rates reflecting, in part at least, official policies to maintain a real interest return for household savers. Not shown in this Table, but of great importance, has been the growing contribution of

Table 4.1 Trends in select economic indicators for Taiwan, 1966/67–1995 (rates of growth, per cent per annum)

	National product	*Investment (GFCF)*	*Exports*	*Per capita income*
1967–80	9.8	13.8	18.6	6.8
1981–86	8	1.9	12.5	6.2
1987–90	8.5	13.8	7.2	7.5
1991–95	6.4	8.7	6.1	5.4

Note:
Data for 1995 are provisional estimates.

Sources: *Quarterly National Economic Trends. Taiwan Area The Republic of China* (Taipei: Executive Yuan, November 1994); *Zhonghua minguo tongji nianjian 1994* (*The Republic of China Statistical Yearbook 1994*) (Taipei: Executive Yuan, 1994); *The Monthly Bulletin of Statistics of the Republic of China* (Taipei: Executive Yuan, February 1996).

productivity increases. For the 1970s and 1980s this has been estimated to account for 41.4 and 56.8 per cent of growth respectively.[2]

Taiwan's economic growth has been accompanied by major changes of structure (Table 4.2). Agriculture's share of output has declined from 28.5 per cent in the 1950s to 3.6 per cent in 1994–95, while the share of industry peaked in 1980–87. The service share of the economy is now the largest sector and rising rapidly.

Broad inter-sectoral change has been accompanied by inter-industry shifts (Table 4.3), with a relative decline in food and food processing, textiles, and wood and paper, and corresponding rises of machinery and electrical goods. Particularly striking in recent years has been the rise of Taiwan's status as a manufacturer of electronic and information technology equipment of all kinds. In 1995, Taiwan was the third largest producer of these goods in the world, ahead even of Germany and behind only Japan and the United States (see below). Taiwan is also an important world producer of specialized plastics, aluminium and other metal products.

Turning now to the evolution of foreign trade, Table 4.4 shows the changing structure of exports and imports since 1953. The export data show how the economy's internal structure has been driven by changes in trade – especially in the early decades. The import data give a preliminary indication of the rise and fall of dependence in capital goods. The partners engaged in Taiwan's export trade are shown in Table 4.5. Of particular interest in this Table is the long-term fluctuation in the relative importance of Asian and North American partners. For while between 1957 and 1970 Asia fell and North America rose, more recently the Asian share has gained appreciably at the expense of the American. This reflects growing intra-Asian trading and divisions of labour and, in particular, the rise of cross-Strait economic links largely effected through Hong Kong.

Taiwan's economic growth and transformation since the Second World

Table 4.2 Changes in the relative importance of agriculture, industry and services in the economy, 1953–95 (percentage shares, current prices)

	Agriculture	*Industry*	*Services*
1953–60	28.5	24.4	47.1
1961–72	20.2	33.1	46.7
1973–79	11	43.2	45.8
1980–87	6.6	46	47.4
1988–93	4.1	42.7	53.2
1994–95	3.6	36.8	59.7

Sources: *Zhonghua minguo bashininian jingji nianbao* (*Republic of China Economic Report 1993*) (Taipei: Executive Yuan, 1994); *The Monthly Bulletin of Statistics of the Republic of China* (Taipei: Executive Yuan, February 1996).

Table 4.3 The manufacturing structure of Taiwan, 1953–92 (percentage shares of main sectors, current prices)

	Food	*Textiles and clothing*	*Wood and paper*	*Chemical products*	*Machinery*	*Electrical*	*Transport equipment*
1953–60	41.2	26	15.8	9.9	1.8	2.4	3.1
1961–72	28.9	22	14.2	15.4	4.1	9.3	6.2
1973–79	13.2	24.3	12.2	18.8	5	18	8.5
1980–87	10.9	25.8	11.6	15.1	5.2	20.8	10.6
1988–92	9.7	19.2	11.8	15.5	7	24.3	12.5

Source: As Table 4.2.

Table 4.4 The changing structure of Taiwan's export and import structures, 1953–95

	Exports			*Imports*		
	Agricultural	*Agricultural processed*	*Industrial*	*Capital goods*	*Raw materials*	*Consumer goods*
1953–60	18.6	65.3	16.1	20.2	70.5	9.4
1961–72	13.1	26.6	60.2	28.9	65.2	5.9
1973–79	5.4	7.8	86.8	27.7	65.6	6.6
1980–87	2	4.8	93.1	16.1	75.8	8.1
1988–93	.8	3.8	95.4	16.7	71.4	11.9
1994–95	1	3.5	95.6	16.1	71.4	12.5

Source: As Table 4.2.

Table 4.5 The country structure of Taiwan's export markets, selected years, 1957–95

	All Asia	*Japan*	*Hong Kong (PRC)*	*Europe*	*North America*	*Other*
1957	69	35	9	3	4	24
1970	38	15	9	10	42	10
1980	29	11	8	16	36	19
1990	38	12	13	18	35	9
1995	53	12	23	14	25	8

Sources: *Economic Statistics Annual. Taiwan Area People's Republic of China* (Taipei: Ministry of Economic Affairs, 1994); *The Monthly Bulletin of Statistics of the Republic of China*, February 1996; 'Record year for foreign trade,' *The Free China Journal*, 12 January 1996.

War have been accompanied by a demographic revolution and by rising standards of health and other forms of economic welfare. In the 1950s, the demographic problem was regarded with some alarm. Japanese health administration had halved death rates between 1906 and 1942, and were so effective that controlled comparison revealed Taiwan's health conditions to be superior to those in Japan itself. Mortality continued to decline after 1945 and, combined with rising fertility, appeared to place Taiwan in a classic underdevelopment/demographic trap, with a net growth of population in excess of 4 per cent. However the combination of economic development and falling fertility enabled Taiwan to escape from the problem. By 1984, the Net Reproduction Rate had fallen below one, and by the 1990s Taiwan was adjusting to the problems of labour shortage and looking with some apprehension at the prospect of serious population ageing.[3]

EXPLANATIONS OF TAIWAN'S POST-WAR ECONOMIC GROWTH PERFORMANCE

The domestic factors underlying Taiwan's economic performance in its early ANIE stage (1950s to mid-1980s) may be divided into two groups. The first comprises Taiwan's initial conditions. These included a rich endowment of agricultural and water resources and a central geographical location in the East Asian trading region – defined for this purpose as extending laterally from Thailand to Japan and horizontally from the Yangzi valley to Indonesia. In addition there was the Japanese colonial legacy. The overall impact of this is still argued about, but most scholars agree that it laid the foundations of Taiwanese agricultural modernization, created a market-oriented culture, improved the quality of Taiwan's human resource endowment and established the most foreign trade intensive economy in pre-war East Asia.[4]

A direct link between this colonial legacy and post-war trade performance has been Japanese continuity in the form of trading companies and FDI. The trading companies are still informally estimated to account for half of

Taiwan's trade flows, while Japan's share of inward FDI between 1976 and 1994 has typically been above 20 per cent. Together with American FDI, this has been instrumental in both the early stages of Taiwan's achievement of industrial competitiveness and, as shown below, the current processes of upgrading.[5]

The contributions of the second group of factors – policy, institutional and organizational – are more controversial. On the one side are those who emphasize the role of market development, domestic macro policies favourable to investment and savings, external orientation and progressive institutional liberalization. This group includes The World Bank and a number of distinguished Taiwanese economists. On the other side are those who, while not denying the importance of the former, place special emphasis on the role of state-private sector relations and other elements in the political economy of Taiwanese development. This group includes Alice Amsden, Chalmers Johnson, Robert Wade and Edwin Winckler. The functions of the state as outlined by the latter school include not only a framework of protection, foreign exchange manipulation and the promotion of Export Processing Zones, but also discriminatory inter-industry and inter-firm subsidization in support of private sector investment, learning and technology transfer, and an active role for public sector financial and productive enterprises.

The interventionists have a strong case, but the issues are not simple and refinement of our understanding of the mechanisms at work still has far to go. This is important not only for purposes of historical clarification but also for assessing the nature of the challenges now faced by Taiwan, both in relation to its transition to higher levels of maturity and to managing its relationships with the PRC. One problem here is that while state ideology tends to be reflected in official and prominent forms of public information and this reinforces awareness of the state's contribution, the microeconomic behaviour of individuals and units in the private sector is too easily undetected and unappreciated.[6]

One strand of important recent work on Taiwan has re-emphasized the special character of the small-scale sector which still, after all, accounts for 97 per cent of all Taiwanese economic enterprises.[7] This research is beginning to reveal more precisely why it is that networks of often rural-based, family-managed firms have evolved, through shifting sub-contracting relationships, degrees of specialization and flexibility that make them extraordinary instruments of efficiency. Efficient not only in the conventional sense of achieving low unit costs, but in combining this with a high degree of responsiveness to market fluctuations. The latter is particularly important, since it is the capacity to respond to changing fashions in textiles and clothing, and to the wave-like fluctuations in both demand and technical opportunity in electronics, that is crucial to achieving footholds of international competitiveness and market share in these sectors.[8]

New light has also been thrown on the private sector by Chen-tian Kuo, who has focused on the role of Taiwanese trade associations. He argues that these (with government support) are not obsessed by the protectionist and distributionist goals conventionally attributed to them, but develop their own agendas for productive efficiency and competitiveness.[9] The case of the Taiwan Electrical Appliances Manufacturers Association (TEAMA) is particularly persuasive in this respect, and is reminiscent in many ways of the positive functions of Japanese trade associations in Japan's development (functions at first not understood by foreign competitors, but later seen as a key to Japanese world-wide textile domination).[10]

One factor common to both sub-contracting and trade association approaches has been suggested by Charles Sabel, who has analysed the significance for economic development of the problems of co-operation, learning and monitoring under conditions of rapid change and uncertainty. On this view, achievement of economic efficiency depends crucially not only on macroeconomic environments and internal firm behaviour, but on a quality of inter-firm relationships that enables resources to be configured in newly productive and market responsive ways. Sabel argues that neither some commonality of "trusting" cultures nor "game play" approaches are persuasive explanations of the apparent success of some economies in creating stable, effective networks. These ultimately depend on the actors identifying the problem and developing specific, complex institutional devices that unite the learning and monitoring functions. They find ways, in other words, of unlocking the potential gains of specialization through flexible collaboration in a world intrinsically uncertain and unpredictable. These devices may eventually emerge as the Japanese "alliance capitalism" or the small firm networks and "state corporatism" of Taiwanese industrial associations (in all of which the state has an important but not dominating role)[11]

This research relates also to a third point, which is the contribution to Taiwanese performance of foreign investment. Many analysts have grouped the four ANIEs in ways that imply that not only their performance but also their growth mechanisms have similar patterns. I disagree strongly with this and the FDI issue is a good illustration of how widely these mechanisms in fact diverge. South Korea, for example, has been cautious, even hostile, to FDI, preferring licensing and other mechanisms to achieve technology transfer and international market access. Hong Kong has been *laissez-faire* in acceptance of FDI, but has failed to gain major benefits in the manufacturing sector from it. Singapore has been exceptionally pro-active in seeking FDI, but has remained an economy where foreign invested enterprises retained over 80 per cent of manufacturing output and exports from the 1970s to the 1990s.[12]

Taiwan alone has been successful in both attracting FDI and then achieving the strong spillover effects that provided the technological and commercial basis for development of exporting in the 1980s and 1990s. One reason for the achievement of spillover effects was precisely the policies of trade associations such as TEAMA, which effectively incorporated FDI into local manufacturing networks by a combination of carrot and sticks. The sticks included local content rules and other conditions agreed in collaboration with government. The carrot was the promise that networking with local producers would lower component and assembly costs, and thereby increase the international competitiveness of Taiwan-based MNCs. In practice, the spillover process was also associated with violations of intellectual property rights, which may have had short-run benefits for Taiwan but which have become a serious obstacle to the continuing MNC investment needed for the higher level upgrading process that was to follow.[13] Other factors contributing to the effectiveness of the spillover include educational and manpower policies; successful government selection of sectoral, industrial and technological (product and process) targets; provision of technology support institutions; and, almost above all in recent years, the growing contribution of returning Taiwanese, familiar with both the technology and market know-how necessary to build a competitive high technology sector in Taiwan.[14]

THE TURNING POINT OF THE 1980s

The confluence of three developments posed major challenges to both public policy and the private sector in the 1980s. First, the success of Taiwan as an exporter of labour intensive exports (many produced by foreign-invested enterprises in Export Processing Zones) began to exhaust itself. The labour supply tightened, unemployment fell below 2 per cent, wages (and rents) began to rise sharply and rates of growth of some exports began to slow.[15] By the mid-1980s, the economy had entered a phase of internal/external imbalance that is summarized in Table 4.6. When these data are examined the parallel course of the two imbalances is obvious; and 1986 stands out as the year in which both peaked, leading to an accumulation of foreign exchange, upward pressure on the Taiwan dollar, high liquidity, low interest rates and a "bubble" boom of land and stock market speculation. This configuration of

Table 4.6 External and internal imbalances in the economy, 1975–95

	Exports as % of GDP	*Imports as % of GDP*	*External imbalance as % of GDP*	*Saving as % of GDP*	*Investment as % of GDP*	*Internal imbalance as % of GDP*
1975	39.6	42.9	−3.3	27.1	30.7	−3.6
1980	57.5	53.7	−1.2	32.6	33.8	−1.2
1986	58.1	38.3	+19.8	37.3	17.5	+19.8
1990	46.7	41.8	4.9	28.1	23.1	+5
1994	44.1	42.2	+1.9	25.8	23.9	+1.9
1995	48.9	46.6	+2.3	26.1	23.8	+2.3

Source: Calculated from data estimated by the Directorate-General of Budget, Accounting and Statistics (DGBAS), *Industry of Free China*, March 1996.

events was caused by the continuation of incentives to export and save, combined with a serious weakening of the inducement to invest.[16]

The investment weakness was noticeable in the public sector, but more worrying was the weakness of private investment. This was partly a result of the ineffectiveness of the Taiwanese capital market as a means to direct savings into productive investment (rather than speculation); partly a reflection of the intrinsic difficulties of Taiwan's transition from a labour to a more capital and skill-intensive form of industrialization; and partly a result of political and economic uncertainties engendered by the reform and expansion of the PRC economy. Thus a phase which on a superficial view (booming trade surpluses, foreign exchange holdings and stock prices) seemed to indicate Taiwan's economic strengths, was in fact one calling for skilful management and a major shift of direction.[17]

ADJUSTMENT AND RESPONSE 1980s–90s

The response to this crisis can be observed at many levels. At the national level, in 1984 Premier Yu Kuo-hua initiated a policy of liberalization and internationalization. As a result, between 1983/84 and 1991/92 average tariffs were reduced from 31 to 9 per cent, and the number of commodities subject to non-tariff barriers fell from 26,768 to 9,053.[18] These measures were accompanied by a drive for the internationalization and regionalization of Taiwan's trading relationships at an institutional level. Taiwan joined APEC in 1991, achieved observer status at the GATT in 1992, and thereafter has continued to work actively for full membership of the World Trade Organization. This strategy had three distinct objectives. One was to force the internal pace of domestic restructuring. Another was to reduce trade frictions arising from bilateral trade imbalances. And a third was to integrate Taiwan into the *political* structure of global trade in ways that would strengthen its position in cross-Strait relationships. This interplay of the economic and political has been an essential feature of Taiwan's policies during the last decade. Neither the political nor the economic dimension can be understood independently.

At the firm level, two forms of adjustment and restructuring have been particularly important: foreign direct investment and a systematic upgrading of the industrial and trade structure undertaken in private-public sector partnership. Overseas foreign investment has been a central strategy of adjustment by Taiwanese firms during the past decade. The problem is that the statistical basis for understanding this is slight. Official data are highly misleading since they are based on approvals only. In most country cases, because of lags, approvals are higher than actual flows. In Taiwan's case, because so much investment is unrecorded, through third parties (and often of questionable legality), actual flows are far higher than official data. Thus the grand total of approved FDI for 1952–94 for all destinations, including the PRC, is just over US$13 billion.[19] However, commonly used figures for the PRC are in the region of US$25 billion; and recent work on South-East Asian investment puts the total for the main economies at about US$15 billion.[20] This suggests a grand cumulative total of at least US$50 billion, to include investments in the United States, Europe and other countries. Discrepancies between host country estimates of Taiwan inflows and Taiwanese official estimates of outflows are often considerably larger than this overall difference (up to 100-fold).

The motives for this investment and the character of the investors varies. But of immediate concern, the most interesting (and probably financially dominant) form of investment is that by smaller Taiwanese firms in Asia. This is distinct in character from, for example, typical Japanese investment in Asia. The latter is usually part of a concerted globalization of production, in which planning, R&D, marketing and often the supply of key components are retained in Japan, while local production bases are developed to take advantage of low wages, land and sometimes environmental protection costs. Japanese foreign investment often also involves *keiretsu* group co-ordination, including manufacturing, banking, trading company and other networked elements. The complexity of the whole operation (especially in the car industry) is often extraordinary. The net effect of this type of foreign investment is to leave substantial co-ordination, service and even production activities in Japan. The Taiwanese overseas investor, on the other hand, is typically engaged in a rescue operation from a home base that is administratively fairly unsophisticated. In building up a foreign presence, therefore, to maintain competitiveness the firm either has to continue to use local Taiwanese networks for supplies of raw materials, capital goods and components, in which case geographical proximity is vital, or it has to build or integrate into new local network – thereby effectively "hollowing out" most of its domestic activity. Much investment in Fujian has been of the former kind, with Taiwan supplying most of the capital equipment and recurrent inputs required; while the Malaysian personal computer network orchestrated by Taiwanese producers is a variant of the latter.[21]

As a solution to the Taiwanese restructuring and upgrading problem, overseas FDI by smaller firms remains an uncertain answer. It does not represent a stable form of globalization, is limited in geographical range, may have excessive hollowing out effects, and unless it becomes part of the upgrading process, must be vulnerable to rising competition from other Asian economies. In some ways the new, official upgrading policy of creating a regional communications and transportation node in Taiwan (APROC) may be seen as an attempt not only to attract international business but to assist Taiwanese companies to globalize rather than merely relocate their operations.

The domestic process of upgrading Taiwan industry, in contrast, is part of a much longer history of government intervention and support. This began with diversification away from the early dependence on textiles and simple labour intensive manufacturing in the 1970s but accelerated after the second oil shock in the early 1980s. In 1982, an Executive Committee to Develop Strategic Industries was established under the Industrial Development Board of the Ministry of Economic Affairs (MOEA). In 1984, the MOEA initiated a programme for the Development of New Industrial Products (DNIP). In 1991, these were transformed into a further, more targeted effort: the programme for the Development of Targeting Leading Products (DTLP). This was much more specific, designed to relieve serious technological bottlenecks, much of it focused on the electronics industry. By the time the DTLP programme was under way, the Hsinchu Science Park had also been running for more than a decade, and all these efforts were supported by the Statute for Upgrading Industries of December 1990.[22]

Again, in judging these efforts and their progress, it is possible to overstate the contribution of the public at the expense of the private sector. It is precisely the learning through ever-changing experiments to get the mix and form right that is so interesting, with a growing emphasis on the capacities of private sector alliances. The formulae adopted were not, of course, always appropriate. The early DNIP programme, for example, was judged not very successful and was later translated into the product-targeted DTLP arrangement. Similarly, there was the recent case of the Notebook PC Strategic Alliance. This involved official bodies and the TEAMA bringing together 46 firms in an alliance which sought to lower R&D and design costs in the creation of an internationally competitive Notebook PC in 1990. Although the PC was successfully designed in seven months, the Alliance broke up because the group was too heterogeneous, and the final product too standardized to form a basis for subsequent inter-firm competition based on product variation. In contrast, the Taiwan New Power PC Consortium, established in November 1993 and supported internationally by both IBM and Motorola, had, by mid-1995, successfully demonstrated that Taiwanese firms possessed the technological and commercial basis to compete in production of a whole new generation of products based on IBM's Power PC microprocessor.[23]

The speed with which the Power PC Consortium established its role and the total commitment of IBM and Motorola demonstrate the progress made by Taiwan's information technology (IT) industry in upgrading and achieving international competitiveness. In terms of global figures, this is confirmed by Taiwan's new status as the world's third largest producer of IT products in 1995, ahead of Germany and behind only Japan and the United States. This has been achieved by developing three levels of firms in the industry: those engaged in OEM (manufacture to specifications by purchasers); those in ODM (manufacture with a Taiwanese design contribution); and fully independent companies, responsible for the complete chain of activity from R&D to selling (Acer, followed by Tatung, Mitac, Umax and so on). Even with these large companies, however, the current trend is towards international alliances and divisions of labour, with partners specializing in R&D, production/subcontracting, or marketing and sales. What is impressive about the larger Taiwanese companies is that they are now equal and in some cases leading partners in these alliances; and that these alliances are now supported by two-way and multilateral flows of Taiwanese/American/Japanese FDI.[24] On the basis of their activities, moreover, Taiwan is moving on from carefully selected niche products and mass production of basic IT equipment to innovative products for networking, internet and multi-media applications, and even to the establishment of a series of semi-conductor foundries, whose viability will depend on orders from American chip-makers without such facilities. Since the capital expenditure involved in these foundries is of the order of US$1 billion each, this represents a strategic departure for the industry, but one which already shows signs of success. The political significance of these developments is discussed below.

In more general terms, Taiwan's upgrading has raised its share of R&D in National Income from 0.98 per cent in 1986 to 1.7 per cent in 1991. And in terms of the share of R&D personnel in the total workforce, in 1991 Taiwan was at 60 per cent of the Japanese level, ahead of France, and six times as intensive as the PRC – which itself, in relation to income, has quite high levels of technical manpower.[25]

The impact of upgrading on industrial and foreign trade structures, however, is complex. Between the mid-1980s and 1992–93, the share of technology intensive products in Taiwanese exports rose from the mid-30s level to above 40 per cent, but at the same time the share of technology intensive imports also remained high.[26] While this situation has spurred further targeted import substitution drives in high technology products and processes, it is not a surprising one. The evidence from other countries confirms that the most innovative economies tend to conduct a large *two-way* trade in technology intensive goods and services.[27] Nevertheless, the upgrading process is leading to some serious imbalances in Taiwanese trade, with the deficit against Japan being a particular problem. This deficit reflects high dependence on Japanese components and capital goods and has led to a further refinement of Taiwan's technology import substitution goals. In the case of car components, the Taiwanese are concerned that their self-sufficiency rate is actually declining.[28] This said, analysis of the changing pattern of Taiwan's industry and trade and, as shown in Table 4.7, the changing fortunes of individual product categories and products in Taiwan's industrial structure, shows that the results of the combined process of upgrading and relocation through FDI since 1986 are spectacular.[29]

When examining the role of the PRC in Taiwan's trade and structural transformation the problem of statistics again causes some, but not too serious difficulties. Basically there are two sets of data in use, those based closely on Hong Kong re-exports and alternative estimates by the Mainland Affairs Council and the Trade Bureau of the MOEA. The overall picture based on the latter estimates is that between 1985 and 1995 total trade grew by 35 per

Table 4.7 The changing structure of output in Taiwan: output gowth by broad product groups and individual commodities (1986 = 100)

	All manufacturing	*Textiles*	*Wood products*	*Chemicals*	*Electrical and electronic products*
1986	100	100	100	100	100
1990	118	95	85	141	145
1994	143	103	5	194	210
	Knitwear	*Shoes*	*Miniature motors*	*(Computer) monitors*	*Computer mice*
1986	100	100	100	100	100
1990	64	78	77	190	832
1994	59	33	47	313	2,785

Source: *Industry of New China*, December 1995.

cent per annum to account for approximately 10 per cent of Taiwan's total trade and 17 per cent of its export trade. The balance of trade is heavily in Taiwan's favour, being approximately US$13 billion in 1994.[30]

In terms of commodities, cross-Strait trade is mainly an inter-industry (FDI related) exchange, with Taiwan exporting machinery, raw materials and semi-processed goods, and importing finished goods, semi-processed goods and components. Given the close interplay between trade and investment, and the role of both in Taiwan's restructuring, it is unfortunate that knowledge of these flows is so poor. By 1995, official Taiwan data reported cumulative investment of US$5.6 billion, PRC data reported US$10.8 billion and unofficial data suggest up to US$25 billion. Wherever the precise truth on the total, three trends in these flows seem agreed by most analysts. First, the scale of flows accelerated very rapidly in the early 1990s. Secondly, whereas in the early stages "survival" investment in labour intensive activities by small and medium enterprises dominated, more recently larger companies have been investing in somewhat more skill intensive sectors. Thirdly, whereas the early investment focused on Fujian and Xiamen city, recent flows have been much more diversified. In 1995, for example, official (Taiwan) data showed that Shanghai and Jiangsu province alone accounted for more than 36 per cent of the investment flow.[31]

The net effect of cross-Strait economic links has thus been to assist Taiwanese restructuring. It has done this, first, by providing a destination for relocational forms of investment and, secondly, by providing a major new export market. Insofar as PRC imports have been Taiwanese capital goods linked to FDI, then the PRC has played a particularly important role in the sense that Taiwan was given the opportunity to expand exports from upgrading sectors in a sheltered market. Thus the PRC market formed a useful transitional step for Taiwanese exporters seeking to upgrade to full international competitiveness in the capital goods and skill intensive sectors.

Noted above was the competitive strength of Taiwanese firms that took the form of exceptional flexibility of output – a flexibility that allowed them on the one hand to respond and seize market share when demand jumped and, more prosaically, to survive if markets deteriorated suddenly. The high technology markets for upgrading firms are equally unpredictable. To take a small but, for Taiwan, very important example, percentage year-to-year variations in sales of modems since 1990 have been +52, +91, +88 and +152 respectively.[32] China has played an important role in creating the flexibility called for under these conditions, and it does this by providing huge back-up capacity at very low cost. To maintain unemployed IT production facilities in Taiwan (or in any developed economy) is now very expensive, but this is not apparently the case in China, particularly in the less developed locations. Taiwanese firms can therefore use their Chinese facilities to build capacity far ahead of demand, providing reserve capacity in the meantime.[33]

OBSTACLES TO TRANSITION

As an ANIE, Taiwan's development had a distinct and, in my view, unique combination of development characteristics. It was focused on labour intensive activities, developed the productive rather than modern service sectors, was highly dependent on networks of small and medium-sized firms and on a considerable role for government in terms not only of regulation and collaborative intervention, but even of ownership. Although its productive sector was oriented towards exports, it was not an open economy in the sense of Hong Kong, especially in the financial sector. Taiwan's economic development also bears the marks of its special, historically determined relationships with mainland China, Japan and the United States.

In order to maintain its growth and development, Taiwan has had to re-orientate in almost every respect. It now seeks to establish a skill and capital intensive industrial structure and to liberalize and open up its services sector. The latter is not simply an alternative to the manufacturing sector but a necessary complement to it. These processes involve changing the character of Taiwanese enterprises in important ways and reducing or changing the role of government. In this re-orientation, economics and politics move together. As Taiwan moves from being an anonymous producer of cheap, undifferentiated goods to a sophisticated producer of own-name brands and, in alliance with multinationals, creates new divisions of labour through FDI, it must increasingly conform to the international norms of economies that are advanced, open and liberalized. This trend is consistent with, and reinforced by, Taiwan's efforts to achieve *political* status through formal membership of international trade organizations; and this political evolution has to keep pace with changing political realities discussed elsewhere in this volume. Clearly, cross-Strait issues are becoming prominent and central here, but before turning to these, there are other purely economic difficulties in Taiwan's transition that must be mentioned if the total situation is to be understood.

First, the upgrading of the productive structure has proceeded impressively. Nevertheless, progress in transforming output with new and better goods is not the whole story. Because of the high proportion of employment in the labour intensive sector, even a striking transformation of the output structure of the economy is quite compatible with rising dualism in the economy, with a prosperous and successful high technology sector on the one side, but with the overall growth rate being brought down by a relatively depressed older sector where incomes are still low and unemployment a growing problem.[34] Between 1982 and 1993, for example, the export share of the small-scale sector declined from 74 to 58 per cent.[35] The crisis in the small-scale sector is widely discussed in Taiwan and upgrading legislation and other forms of government support are being developed.[36] Although some scholars have emphasized the feedback benefits of Taiwanese FDI – especially in the PRC – there is some evidence that hollowing out is occurring and Taiwan is currently maintaining a list of over 3,000 items that may not be imported into Taiwan from China; this list appears to be for employment rather than any broader, economic security consideration.[37]

A related issue is that of agriculture. The performance of agriculture for two decades was exceptionally good. This was based on foundations of technical modernization constructed by the Japanese, on the post-war land reform, and on the subsequent successful marriage of household-based farming and co-operative structures developed by government. As a result of industrialization, however, comparative advantage has moved strongly against the sector and some negative long-run effects of land reform are visible, not only in land use problems but in income inequalities arising from the microeconomic characteristics of part-time farming.[35] Under existing arrangements, as rice consumption quite predictably declines, the budgetary costs of protection are rising and the arrangements are, in addition, not acceptable under World Trade Organization rules. Agriculture has also become a serious source of friction with the United States and other Asia-Pacific economies with comparative advantage in agriculture.[39] However, change is very difficult, partly because of the role of vested interests, not only among producers but also in the agricultural bureaucracy and in agriculture-related monopolies such as tobacco and alcohol.[40] Moreover, the problems of budgetary cost and these other factors have to be reconciled with the fact that there is a real case for some level of protection of rice, on both security and environmental grounds.

The difficulties faced by the reform of the service sector and the liberalization of the economy generally are also numerous. In the most general terms, the Taiwanese economy has been plagued by financial scandals, over-regulation and, most recently, by revelations of the role of organized crime in public sector contracts.[41] This last is important, given the scale of current public infrastructure projects and the interest of Japanese and American companies in obtaining a share of them.[42]

More specific is the state of the government's APROC programme. Many of the objectives of this scheme are highly persuasive. Doubts about the future of Hong Kong and Japan's difficulties in developing into an international financial centre make it natural that Taiwan should seek to establish itself as an international services and communications/trans-shipment node. This *service* role, moreover, as noted above, is becoming an essential adjunct to playing an effective role in *production* networks.[43] One reason for this is the "alliance" character of industrial and trade development discussed above. Thus the ideal Asian country partner for Japanese and American multinationals needs to offer both an effective agglomeration of high technology suppliers, manpower and institutions *and* the infrastructure for efficient inter-firm communications. Another argument for APROC and service sector development is that whereas in the past Taiwan's small-scale sector benefited from the penetration of the Japanese trading companies, who handled much of the marketing and other service dimensions of their business, these are less likely to do so now, partly because for traditional exports they can find even lower cost sources in Asia, and partly because those Taiwanese firms that upgrade successfully will increasingly compete directly with Japanese firms, who are the trading companies' preferred customers.

At this stage, the main APROC developments are physical infrastructure projects and changes in administrative regulation designed to facilitate the APROC idea promptly. But compared to Hong Kong and Singapore, Taiwan's competitiveness is still weak and it is far from establishing the full institutional and informational framework required.[44] These shortcomings have been shown to be severe in the case of telecommunications. Official concerns about progress have been voiced and the decision of Acer, Taiwan's flagship multinational, to move its own headquarters out of Taiwan precisely because the island does not provide the communications services it requires, is an indication of the problems remaining.

The process of economic reform that Taiwan is seeking to accomplish is related to not only its external but also its internal politics. In this respect the legislative elections of December 1995 and their preamble are probably of more significance than the subsequent presidential election in 1996. The issues in the latter were predominantly external, but the issues in the former included many of a purely domestic kind. It has been argued that a factor in the early success of the Taiwanese development process was precisely that the Kuomintang government was remote from society, and hence could stand above the claims of clientalism and the distortions of the rent-seeking polity. How accurate such analyses are remains for further study. But it is already clear that the democratization of Taiwan is going to change the future of economic debate fundamentally.

Taiwan faces many controversial issues of economic policy. These include those of dualism, income distribution, corruption, and the future of small scale industry and agriculture already touched upon. Equally important are going to be the challenges of welfare provision under conditions of population ageing and the strains placed on traditional caring structures by industrialization and urbanization.[45] The future economic role of women and a range of matters relating to land and housing are also going to be important. Most of these problems were aired in the December election, and although the minority parties remain far from dominance (individually), the problems will have to be addressed by the government and will remain as vital elements in the political debate.[46] The precise impact of this new process is impossible to predict and raises issues beyond the scope of this article. But I have no doubt myself that these changes are for the better. While not a panacea or substitute for other elements in development, no serious intellectual case for the systemic superiority of an Asian, authoritarian form of development has yet been made, and there are powerful historical and theoretical arguments against it.[47]

CONCLUSION: THE CROSS-STRAIT CRISIS AND SOME ECONOMIC IMPLICATIONS

This conclusion briefly considers the impact of the February military confrontation and some of its longer-term effects. To measure the short-run impact in Taiwan three sets of indicators may be used. These are: actual trends in output; trends in the composite index of "monitoring indicators" (such as orders, exports, stock market indicators); and trends in businessmen's expectations.[48] If actual output is taken first, it would appear that a relatively stable growth rate for 1992–94 turned weaker during 1995, with the last quarter's growth of that year (4.9 per cent) being the lowest for six years. However, the behaviour of the monitoring index shows the downturn to have begun in the last quarter of 1994. This suggests that the economy was in a downturn *before* the political crisis of mid-1995, but that the crisis may have accentuated its impact.[49] The psychological indicator of business expectations, in contrast, follows the political story much more closely. This turned down in March 1995 and continued to decline throughout the year, with a slight recovery in January 1996. This pattern is very similar to that of the Taiwan stock market index (Taiex). This started 1995 at above 7,000, fell throughout 1995, reaching 4,800 in the crisis. The index then rebounded to the 6,000 level after the presidential election, supported by a strong inflow of foreign funds.[50] The immediate impact of the crisis on China is less clear. Apart from the substantial costs of the military action itself, however, the Chinese Minister for Trade and Economic Co-operation is on record as reporting and regretting a decline in trade and in direct investment from Taiwan.[51]

What of the longer term? The first point is that the crisis has drawn attention to the potential vulnerability of the Taiwanese economy to offensive naval quarantine action. In this sense, it is faced with a threat similar to the one that worried Japanese strategists in relation to the Soviet Union in the 1960s and 1970s. Secondly, the crisis has revealed the high potential political risks in the East Asia region generally, and more dramatically, for example, than have tensions over North Korea. As the South Korean Deputy Premier pointed out: "Asia is not as stable as Europe and North America. In fact, it's one of the most unstable regions in the world."[52] This judgment from within the region certainly has parallels outside it and these may affect long-term judgments about the region's economic potential.

On the positive side, however, Rha Woong-bae's comment also confirms that economic interdependence has created a network of countries in Asia, all of which could be immediately and very seriously economically affected by military activity in the Taiwan Strait. South Korea, Japan, Singapore and other ASEAN states all appealed openly for cessation of the confrontation. A major factor here is the dependence of these economies on inflows of capital from outside the region. Such flows are intrinsically far more unstable than trade exchanges and can disappear almost overnight on a change of Western or Japanese business sentiment (as both the PRC and Latin America have found during the past decade). Thus the PRC would have to weigh any future military action with Taiwan against very serious economic consequences in the region.

Within Taiwan, the longer-term economic reaction is lil:ely to be revealed in significant geographical diversification of both trade and investment. This process was already under way before the February confrontation. In 1995, for example, Taiwan's most rapidly growing export market was Brazil. In the case of FDI, the growing significance of non-Asian destinations for investment has already been shown. However, diversification within as well as away from China is likely to be particularly important, as Taiwan entrepreneurs assess the personal and business risks of investment in Fujian and Xiamen city. Appreciation of this no doubt lies behind reports that the Fujian province First Party Secretary, Jia Qinglin, lobbied hard in Beijing to have the confrontation averted. The future character as well as trends in the location of FDI must also have been affected by the cross-Strait crisis. At one level, there is an obvious range of economic complementarity between Taiwan and the PRC. The two economies have complementary resource endowment and the PRC is a natural point of relocation investment. Taiwan also has many types of expertise (notably in agriculture and food processing) that can form the basis for beneficial contacts.

As China itself develops, however, there is a potential for raising the level of division of labour to something that goes far beyond the "screwdriver" type of investment typical of the Xiamen experience, where the only mainland Chinese resources being used are often land and relatively unskilled labour. Some Taiwan analysts are very optimistic, for example, that a complex division of labour can be achieved in industries such as machinery. But practitioner businessmen with experience of the realities of mainland contract-making have reservations.[53] This returns the argument once again to the Sabel proposition: successful development has to reconcile monitoring and learning under conditions of uncertainty; and this calls for lengthy joint working experiences, leading to trust and the formulation of common and mutually acceptable objectives. Within Taiwan, and increasingly in an international context, the Taiwanese are mastering these arts. Transferring them to the sphere of business relations in the PRC is the problem. In thinking about this, it must be borne in mind that even between PRC partners there are serious systemic obstacles in this respect; and while a commonality of language and region are helpful in developing cross-Strait relationships, it has been far from a sufficient condition for success in the past. The net effect of the confrontation must be to make complex collaboration more difficult.[54] Even if a stable political framework for business were to be created in the near future, this would mark only a beginning of the upgrading process, not its imminent accomplishment.

Finally, and most important of all, is the political significance of the overall themes of this article: the growing interplay between trade and investment and the role of alliances in skill intensive industries. To take one last example, the GVC Corporation of Taiwan has recently joined forces with Packard Bell and the NEC Corporation to establish a major facility to manufacture computer monitors. This is a classic alliance that brings together American marketing, Japanese technology and Taiwanese versatility in sourcing components and assembly. The plant is to be located in Guangzhou. Damage to this company would therefore not only affect Taiwan, it would undermine economic development in South China and affect the strategic economic interests of both Japan and the United States. While a good example, this cannot be an isolated case for an economy that holds world market shares above 25 per cent in nine major IT products, and above 50 per cent in four of them.[55] Because of these trends, and because of the underlying social strengths achievable in societies that combine mixed economies and open polities, I believe Taiwan's long-term geopolitical position may be stronger than it is often estimated to be, and that the route to unification is more likely to be found on economic than military maps. Stalin once asked how many divisions the Pope had. His successors discovered that he had asked the wrong question. Analysts of the Taiwan problem who now assess national strength by counting aeroplanes (whether in Beijing or Washington) could be making a similar mistake.

NOTES

1 A valuable survey of some of the key issues is Ci Schive, *Taiwan's Economic Role in Asia* (Washington D C.: The Center for Strategic and International Studies,

1995). I am grateful to Professor Schive for this and for other materials. I should also like to express my appreciation for help to Joanna Bostel, Dr Peng Xiao-min of the Mainland Affairs Council and Dr Tsiang Yien-si of the Council for Agriculture. My discussants at the conference, Jeremy Mark and Professor Chen Po-chin, also provided me with helpful corrections and invaluable clues to thinking about these problems. None of the above has any responsibility for the views expressed in this article.

2 "Cong chuchang shengge tan Taiwan jingji texshuxing" ("A discussion of the specific characteristics of the Taiwan economy from the rise in output productivity"), *Tou shi liang'an sandi jingmao jiaoliu* (*Perspectives on Cross-Straits/Three Regions Economic Exchange*) (Taipei: Baolian wenhua, 1994), p. 26. This issue is controversial, see Jong-Il Kim and Lawrence J. Lau, *The Sources of Economic Growth of the East Asian Newly Industrialized Countries* (mimeo, Department of Economics, Stanford University, 1993). However, even Kim and Lau's data show that the *combined share* of capital and technical progress in Taiwan (1950s–90s) was the largest of the four ANIEs.

3 George W. Barclay, *Colonial Development and Population in Taiwan* (Princeton: Princeton University Press, 1954), ch. 6. Minami Ryosaburo (ed.), *Taiwan no jinko to keizai* (*Taiwan's Population and Economy*) (Tokyo: Ajia Keizai Kenkyujo, 1971).

4 Alice H. Amsden "Taiwan's economic history: A case of *étatism* and a challenge to dependency theory," reprinted in Robert H. Bates (ed.). *Towards a Political Economy of Development. A Rational Choice Perspective* (Berkeley: University of California Press, 1988), pp. 142–175; Christopher Howe, *The Origins of Japanese Trade Supremacy: Development and Technology in Asia, 1540 to the Pacific War* (Chicago: University of Chicago Press, 1995), ch. 12. For negative views see Taiwanese works cited in Howe above and, more recently, remarks in Cheng-tian Kuo, *Global Competitiveness and Industrial Growth in Taiwan and the Philippines* (Pittsburgh: University of Pittsburgh Press, 1995).

5 Chi Schive, *The Foreign Factor: The Multinational's Contribution to the Economic Modernization of the Republic of China* (Stanford: The Hoover Institution, 1990), and Schive, "Foreign firms and structural change in Taiwan," in Eric D. Ramstetter (ed.), *Direct Foreign Investment in Asia's Developing Economies and Structural Change in the Asia-Pacific Region* (Boulder: Westview Press, 1991), pp. 142–171.

6 This problem is also very important in evaluating the character of Japanese economic development, especially in the Meiji era. State activity is easily identified in the modern sector, but the evidence needed to understand agriculture and small-scale production (accounting for most of the workforce) remains much harder to identify.

7 For recent data on this sector see *Zhonghua minguo bashisannian zhong-xiao qiye baibishu* (*The 1994 White Paper on Small and Medium Enterprises*) (Taipei: Ministry of Economic Affairs, 1994).There are, however, serious definitional problems in figures quoted on this topic, since the definition of this sector has changed several times.

8 Susan Greenhalgh, "Family networks in Taiwan's economic development," in Edwin A. Winckler and Susan Greenhalgh (eds.), *Contending Approaches to the Political Economy of Taiwan* (Armonk, NY: M. E. Sharpe, 1990), pp. 224–45; G. S. Hsieh, *"Boss Island": The Subcontracting Network and Micro-Entrepreneurship in Taiwan's Development* (New York: Peter Lang, 1992). On the problem of fluctuations, Hsieh quotes year-to-year percentage variations in the demand for male outer garments 1973–78 as: –31, –8.8, +15.5, +36.7, –5.6 and +93.4 respectively. The more general economic significance of flexible, networked

industrialization is discussed in Michael J. Piore and Charles F. Sabel, *The Second Industrial Divide: Possibilities for Prosperity* (New York: Basic Books, 1984).

9 Chen-tian Kuo, *Global Competitiveness*, ch. 6. The weakness of Kuo's case is that he places too much emphasis on organizational factors. The significance of these needs to be related to underlying comparative advantage determined by resource endowment. However skilfully devised, organization can only have limited influence on the history of an industry where conventional forms of comparative resource advantage are being lost. But organizational factors will be crucial in the early stages of technology transfer and in reinforcing the capacity to exploit conventional competitive advantage. Orthodox analysis since Adam Smith has predicted that trade associations will be more concerned with distribution than production. An important modern version of this view is to be found in Mancur Olsen, *The Rise and Decline of Nations: Economic Growth, Inflation, and Social Rigidities* (New Haven: Yale University Press, 1982).

10 Howe, *The Origins of Japanese Trade Supremacy*, chs. 7–8.

11 Charles F. Sabel, "Learning by monitoring. The institutions of economic development," in Lloyd Rodwin and Donald A. Schon (eds.), *Rethinking the Development Experience. Essays Provoked by the Work of Albert O. Hirschman* (Washington, D.C.: The Brookings Institution, 1994), pp. 231–274; Michael L. Gerlach, *Alliance Capitalism. The Social Organization of Japanese Business* (Berkeley: University of California Press, 1992); Chen-tian Kuo, *Global Competitiveness*. On the Japanese system, many others have written on the same or closely allied themes including Mark Fruin, Ronald Dore and Mari Sako.

12 This is discussed in the comprehensive analysis by W. G. Huff, *The Economic Growth of Singapore. Trade and Development in the Twentieth Century* (Cambridge: Cambridge University Press, 1994).

13 By 1996, Taiwan had graduated off the United States "watch" list for intellectual property right violations.

14 The Hsinchu Science Park was established in 1980 primarily to facilitate the return of entrepreneurially-minded technologists to Taiwan. It has been extraordinarily successful, and almost half the firms in it are currently owned and managed by returnees (briefing by H. Steve Hsieh, Park Director-General).

15 Male unemployment reached its lowest level of 1.11% as early as 1980. It then rose above 2%, falling below that figure again in 1987. *Monthly Bulletin of Manpower Statistics Taiwan Area* (Taipei: DGBAS, January 1996), pp. 5–6.

16 There is nothing intrinsically amiss in a situation where savings exceeds investment, domestic consumption is less than production and the difference is reflected in the trade balance. The problem arises if there are no satisfactory ways of exporting the surplus, in which case the effects tend to be inflationary and may lead to a rise in the value of the domestic currency that "hollows out" productive activity and feeds speculative internal investment. If the surplus is recycled productively (in FDI, aid or other flows) then the capital exporting economy is performing a valuable international function, such as that performed by Britain in the 19th century, America for some of the 20th and Japan now.

17 These issues are discussed in Schive, *Taiwan's Economic Role in Asia*, ch. 3 and in Tzong-shian Yu, *Economic Development in Transition – The Case of Taiwan*, Discussion Paper Series No.9303 (Taipei: Chung-Hua Institution for Economic Research, 1993).

18 *Tou shi liang'an sandi jingmao jiaoliu*, pp. 40–41; Rong-I Wu, "New vigour in trade activity," *Free China Review*, Vol. 38, No. 10 (October 1987), pp. 27– 9.

19 Schive, *Taiwan's Economic Role in East Asia*, p.79.

20 *Taiwan's Small and Medium Sized Firms Direct Investment in Southeast Asia* (Taipei:

Chung-Hua Institution for Economic Research, 1995); "Duiwai touzi" (foreign investment) in *Jingji qianzhan* (*Economic Outlook*), No. 40 (July 1995), pp. 26–49.

21 On the heavy dependence on Taiwan for both machinery and other inputs see materials cited in Chin Chung, "Taiwan's DFI in mainland China: impact on the domestic and host economies," in Thomas P. Lyons and Victor Nee (eds.), *The Economic Transformation of South China. Reform and Development in the Post-Mao Era* (Ithaca, NY: Cornell University East Asia Program, 1994), pp.215–242, and in Chen Po-chih, "Taiwan's trade and investment in China" (mimeo, Taipei, 1995). In Malaysia, Taiwanese computer assemblers and cathode ray manufacturers are networked to Japanese and American semi-conductor manufacturers and to Malaysian suppliers of plastics, cables and simple metal components. See, Chung-Hua Institution for Economic Research, *Taiwan's Small and Medium Sized Firms Direct Investment in Southeast Asia*, p.415.

22 These comments and further details below are drawn mainly from *Technology Support Institutions and Policy Priorities for Industrial Development in Taiwan, ROC* (Taipei: Chung-Hua Institution for Economic Research, 1995); *Bashininiandu chanye jishu fazhan gaiyao* (*The Outline Development Plan for Technology, 1993*) (Taipei: Ministry of Economic Affairs, Office for Technology, 1994); *National Science Council Review* (Taipei: National Science Council, various years).

23 The history of the Notebook Alliance is described in *Technology Support Institutions and Policy Priorities for Industrial Development in Taiwan, ROC*, pp. 173–188. The Power PC case is analysed in John Mathews and Teresa Shuk-ching Poon, "Technological up-grading through alliance formation: the case of Taiwan's new PC consortium," *Industry of Free China*, December 1995, pp. 43–57.

24 "High-tech firms lead charge. Taiwanese pour cash into US," *Hong Kong Standard*, 14 February 1996. According to this article, there are 2,700 Taiwanese firms invested in the United States, over half of them in California, where they can get access to technology and skilled manpower not available in Taiwan. On the rationale for foreign investment in Taiwan see "Philips shows confidence in local branch," *The China Post*, 27 April 1996.

25 *Technology Support Institutions and Policy Priorities for Industrial Development in Taiwan, ROC*, p. 39.

26 *Ibid.* p. 47.

27 Japan, for example, is only just in balance on its technology trade (defined here as the balance of payments for technology, not the balance of technology intensive goods). It has large net imports from the United States, and net exports to Asian and other middle ranking economies. *Kagaku gijutsu hakusho: sengo gojunen kagaku gijitsu 1995* (*The 1995 Science and Technology White Paper: 50 Years of Post War Science and Technology*) (Tokyo: Okurasho, 1995), appendix tables.

28 In 1995, the deficit was $17.1 billion, up 17.4% on 1994. "Record year for foreign trade", *The Free China Journal*, 12 January 1996. In 1993, 84% of Japanese exports to Japan were classified as "heavy industry" with IT and vehicles being the most prominent items. *1994 Tsusho hakusho-kakuron* (*White Paper on Foreign Trade, Country Annex 1994*), pp. 290–6.

29 Data on the changing trade pattern and its skill and factor contents are provided in an important article by Wang Ming-hui, "Taiwan maoyi wanglao de qushi yanjiu" ("Research in the trends of Taiwan's trade network"), *Taiwan yinhang jikan* (*Bank of Taiwan Quarterly*), Vol. 46, No. 2, pp. 154–182.

30 See discussion in Shao Pei-jun, "Liang'an jingmao guanxi zhi xiankuang ji zhanwang" ("The situation and prospects for cross-Strait trade and economic relations"), *Taiwan jingji jinrong yuekan* (*Taiwan Economic and Financial Monthly*), Vol. 31, No. 3 (March 1995), pp. 54–63; Lin Li-jun, "Dui dalu jingmao wenti

zhi yanjiu" ("Research on mainland trade problems"), *Zhongguo dalu yanjiu (China Mainland Research)*, Vol.39, No.2 (February 1996), pp. 24–35; *Liang 'an jingji tongji yuebao (Cross-Strait Economic Statistics Monthly)* (Taipei: Mainland Affairs Council, No. 41, January 1996).

31 *Liang 'an jingji tongji yuebao*, No. 41 (January 1996), p. 29. The likely accuracy of these data is supported by the point that Jiangsu and the Shanghai region would be a natural location for the more skill intensive forms of investment. For evidence of the growing interest and informational infrastructure for Taiwanese investment in this region see *Taiwan daobao*, April 1996.

32 Data as Table 4.7.

33 Briefing from an OED/ODM computer manufacturer at the Hsinchu Park. At the time of the briefing, this firm was operating its PRC plant at only 45% of capacity, effectively holding the rest in reserve. The overall level of capital utilization in Taiwan manufacturing is normally about 80%. *Taiwan jingqi zhibiao (Business Indicators)* (Taipei: Executive Yuan, January 1996), pp. 3–12.

34 "Economy officially slips into recession territory," *The Free China Journal*, 29 December 1995. This is based on trends in leading indicators published in *Taiwan jingqi zhibiao.*

35 *Zhonghua minguo bashisannian zhong-xiao qiye baibishu*, p. 418.

36 Data on long-run employment trends are in *Monthly Bulletin of Manpower Statistics Taiwan Area*. According to this source the unemployment rate was as low as 1.4% in 1995 but had risen to 2.37% by March 1996. "Jobless rate highest in nine years. Shutdowns, layoffs on the rise," *The China Post*, 24 April 1996.

37 This problem has its parallel in Hong Kong where the combination of successful growth of the financial and services sector and industrial relocation is leaving a transitional problem of declining economic growth, rising unemployment and worsening distribution of income.

38 The share of agriculture in Taiwan's total exports declined from 62.4% in 1961 to 4.8% in 1993. The Council for Agriculture, *Nongye zhengce baibishu (White Paper on Agriculture)* (Taipei: The Council for Agriculture, 1995), p. 20; Tru-gin Liu, *Income Inequality in the Rural Areas of Taiwan during the Transitional Period of 1978–1987*, unpublished D.Phil. thesis, University of Oxford, 1992.

39 This experience has close parallels in U.S.-Japanese relations.

40 Sung Ming-hsien, "Agricultural development and challenges" and Osman Tseng, "Tobacco and wine monopoly faces pressure from GATT," *Business Taiwan*, 20–26 June 1994.

41 The Ministry of Finance and Central Bank introduced a new package of regulatory measures in December 1995, but this was described by one local critic as "basicaily a short term measure. . . and offers neither a long term perspective or a fundamental solution." *South China Morning Post*, 29 December 1995.

42 "Airport bidding scandal widens. Top gangster, businessman arrested," *The China Post*, 24 April 1996.

43 It is remarkable that because of its relatively advanced level of development and its central geographical location, the Japanese planned just such a central service role for Taiwan in their strategy for the Asia-Pacific 60 years ago. See Japanese sources cited in Howe, *The Origins of Japanese Trade Supremacy*, p. 360.

44 Taiwanese sources suggest that Hong Kong will soon have controlled media and, since the Singaporean media are already a government instrument, Taiwan could develop one of the freest media environments in Asia to support its service sector development. But while there are anxieties that parts of the Hong Kong media may become more self-censuring after 1997, on present performance, it would still take change of major proportions to enable the domestic English language

Taiwanese press to catch up with Hong Kong in coverage, liveliness and independence.

45 Under the traditional three-generation household system, the old, especially women, were cared for by daughters-in-law. As the daughters-in-law typically now have careers and heavy pressures of their own, this no longer works. Current Taiwanese policies for the old have not yet reflected this change. See, Chou Yah-jong and Hu Yow-hwey, "Social change and inter-generational relationships in Taiwan," in William Liu (ed.), *The Family and Human Values in the 21st Century* (forthcoming).

46 The DPP plays upon all the sensitive economic notes in its campaign literature. Particularly impressive is its study of the small and medium firm problem. Zhong-xiao qiye. *Taiwan jingji de mingmai* (*Medium and Small Enterprises. The Lifeblood of the Taiwan Economy*) (Taipei, October 1995). The fact that a woman stood as a vice-presidential candidate in the election gave notice of an important social and economic trend for the future.

47 Amartya Sen, *Economic Development and Social Change: India and China in Comparative Perspectives* (London: London School of Economics, STICERD Discussion Paper Series No. 67, 1995). Although mainly concerned with this debate as it affects countries at much lower levels of development than Taiwan, much of the argument in this paper is still relevant.

48 Businessmen's expectations may be measured by asking appropriate samples whether they think conditions in various respects are improving, deteriorating or stable. The answers are then summed to give a balance of optimism or pessimism. The theory of this methodology was developed by the Dutch econometrician Henri Theil, and although simple in method, *konjunkturtest* results can be used to make accurate predictions of actual trends and the method is, of course, far faster than waiting for the collection and processing of actual statistics. Indeed, in Britain, it was found that a *konjunkturtest* could predict investment trends in three weeks at a time when official data were nearly two years out of date.

49 Based on data in *Taiwan jingqi zhibiao*, January 1996; "Taiwan lowers GDP forecasts. Cross-Strait row squeezes growth," *South China Morning Post*, 16 February 1996.

50 "Words and weapons batter index," *South China Morning Post*, 16 February 1996; "Taiwan kabushiki shijo ni gaikoka money modoru" ("Foreign money returns to the Taiwan stock market"), *Nihon keizai shimbun*, 24 April 1996. During the crisis, both the stock and property markets were stabilized with special government funds.

51 "Tensions with Taipei 'have affected trade'," *Sunday Hong Kong Standard*, 10 March 1996.

52 "China-Taiwan crisis exposes 'Asia's core instability'," *Sunday Hong Kong Standard*, 10 March 1996.

53 This difference was apparent in discussion at a conference at the Chung-hua Institute in April 1996. MOEA, *Dalu jingji fazhan yantaohui* (*Conference on Mainland Economic Development*) (Taipei, 1996).

54 According to official PRC data, the success rate of technology contracts is only 25%, because parties cannot agree on prices. Li Baoshan and Su Weiwen, "Jishu shichangzhong jishu jiaoyi tedian ji qi jiage queding" ("The characteristics of exchange and price determination in technology markets"), *Zhongguo gongye jingji* (*China Industrial Economy*), No. 7 (1995), pp. 41–45.

55 The nine are: monitors, handheld and desktop scanners, PCs, network cards, motherboards, power suppliers, graphic cards, and keyboards.

5

HONG KONG'S REVERSION TO CHINA

The Political, Administrative and Economic Dimensions

Christopher Howe

Few watersheds in modern history have been as explicit and aroused as much interest as Hong Kong's reversion to China in July 1997. Before the event, British stewardship of the territory was variously praised, criticised and then subject to strongly contradictory messages during the final five year Governorship of Chris Patten.

But as the handover approached in the summer of 1997, Hong Kong had a per capita income of more than US$24,000, a high growth rate track record, declining inflation, low official unemployment, and an international economic status secure enough for it to act as host to the World Bank/IMF annual meeting. All attention in the run up was focussed on human rights and on political issues arising out of the imposition a Provisional Legislature to replace the Legislature elected in 1995 under an electoral system that China would not accept. A golden economic future was generally taken for granted.

By August 1998, however, Hong Kong's wealth measured by equity and property prices had fallen by approximately half; the output of the economy had been in absolute decline for two quarters; unemployment was a serious cause for concern; and the currency was under siege. At the end of that month the Government made the bold and controversial decision to intervene directly in securities markets. This produced a good reaction in terms of the Hang Seng Index and helped in the bottoming out process in property markets, nonetheless the real economy was still in decline as it entered 1999.

In these conditions, despite some concerns about legal and political events during the year, not much attention was being paid to political and administrative issues. The basic line of the Hong Kong Government has been that the structures of the Special Administrative Region are fine, but the economy is being affected by an Asian turmoil which is itself a product forces in the international financial system outside of regional control.[1]

Source: Japan Policy Research Institute Working Paper 52 (revised and expanded version), December 1998).

In my view, the mainstream perspectives of both a year ago and the present time are incorrect. There are two reasons for these misgivings. First, the SAR Government inherited an economy and policies with serious question marks over them. These included: (a) over-dependence by policymakers on the growth and public revenue creating effects of companies in the service; and property sectors; (b) a framework of financial regulation inadequate to its tasks; (c) a currency system that was vulnerable and whose workings under stress were not fully understood; (d) neglect of the employment and social dimensions of the accelerated economic restructuring of Hong Kong as a service economy; and (e) failure to deal decisively with long run trends in the degradation of Hong Kong's physical environment. On top of these fundamental problems, both the British and Chinese sides acquiesced in an asset inflation based boom that stimulated activity during 1996–97. In short, the Hong Kong economy has been a problem waiting to be recognised.

The second reservation about mainstream perspectives is the tendency to separate political and economic issues. This cannot be done because Hong Kong's capability for managing its economic and environmental future depends very much on the nature of its representational system and on the effectiveness of its policy making and bureaucratic arrangements. While not denigrating in any way those concerned with human rights, the issues go beyond these in a narrow sense. Thus to think coherently about Hong Kong we need both the insights of economics and knowledge of the institutional and political legacies of a century and a half of British colonialism. Thus while overall I remain firmly optimistic about Hong Kong, I think there is some way to go in reaching an adequate appreciation of its contemporary predicaments.

In this article I shall review the political and economic transitions, and then go on to discuss the relationship between them.[2]

THE POLITICAL TRANSITION

The colonial system of government in Hong Kong was at its most stable and productive during the 1970s and early 1980s. The core of the system was the Governor, who as the Monarch's representative and Commander in Chief had wide and detailed direct powers in every sphere of activity. In practice these powers were largely exercised under advisement and through the Executive Council (a form of cabinet). Exco was composed of the most senior government officials and a small group of important local citizens. Below Exco was the Legislative Council, on which served a wider and somewhat more representative group of local members (Chinese and expatriate). The highlights of Legco's year were to debate and pass the annual Budget legislation in Spring, and to hear and debate the Governor's annual policy address in Autumn. Key Exco members also served on Legco where they acted as intermediaries between Exco and those not privy to the meetings and papers of the higher body. In the 1960s both bodies were made up of officials and groups of nominated " Unofficials". By the 1980s Legco had evolved significantly, with the addition of new group of "unofficials" members representing and broader range of functional constituencies and electoral colleges.[3]

Within the administration, top bureaucratic positions (Colonial/Chief Secretary, Financial Secretary, Secretary for Security etc.) were invariably held by expatriates, while a growing number of other departments were headed by local officials.

The acceptability of this system rested on acquiescence in Britain's role in Hong Kong and on the pragmatic balance of benefits and disadvantages experienced by the population as a whole. In the 1950s and 1960s these benefits consisted primarily of the public order and legal framework needed to make a living. The system was rocked by the Kowloon Riots (1966) and then by the backwash of the Cultural Revolution, but in 1972 there appeared in Hong Kong the key modern Governor, Sir Murray (later Lord) Maclehose.

Maclehose's first task was to steer Hong Kong through the economic impact of the Oil Shocks back onto a path of High Speed Growth. Then, by using land sales and related revenues, he financed an expansion of housing, education and other social welfare expenditure. He also took decisive action against corruption in the police and established the Independent Commission Against Corruption. Politically, he introduced new "unofficials" to the Legislature Council, thereby making it a body more representative of the population as a whole. All of these policies did much to re-establish local acceptability of the colonial system in its final phases.

By the late 1970s Hong Kong was within twenty years of the expiry of the New Territories Leases. At this point, public sector planning required confirmation of the long term status of both property rights and of government decisions on infrastructure and other issues with implications beyond 1997. The private sector, too, which by then included some very substantial and internationally ambitious companies, was finding that corporate ambitions were being stymied by uncertainty about 1997.

Against this background Maclehose went to Beijing in 1979. Prior to this visit it had been widely believed in Hong Kong that a fifty year extension of the Leases was feasible, even likely. After it, the realisation that this was not the case began to sink in. Almost immediately, Maclehose initiated a democratisation process through reform of local government. In October 1980 he told Legco members: "Hong Kong is now too large, too complex, and geographically too spread out for the old system of centralised government to continue to be the complete answer; it must be supplemented with more strength at the District level".[4] This was a subtle manoeuvre, since it used functional arguments of administrative efficiency rather than any abstract considerations to make the inescapable case for change in the traditional political system.

By 1985 the District Board electoral rolls had 1.4 million registered voters and the turn out in the election of that year was a healthy 35.5%. The long term issue then became how far this democratic principle would be extended, particularly when it began to be applied in Legco. Beijing ultimately rejected the Patten version of this process (which was narrowly supported by Legco itself) and the planned "Through Train" for the 1995 Legislature was supplanted by a one year arrangement for a Provisional Legislature, with an election under a new system held in 1998.

To oversee this political transition, in December 1995 Beijing established a Preparatory Committee. This was a successor to the Preliminary Working Committee, a group which had been intensely unpopular in Hong Kong, with members jostled at the airport on their way to its first meeting in Beijing.[5] A Selection Committee succeeded the Preparatory Committee in November 1996. This was entrusted with three important tasks: choosing the first Chief Executive of the SAR, choosing membership of the first Provisional Legislature and, finally, of devising alternative electoral systems for the post 1997 Legislature.

In contrast to the Preparatory Committee, membership of the Selection Committee clearly became an important status symbol among the Hong Kong elite.[6] All told, 5800 nominees competed for its 400 seats. These came from almost all walks of life and most political parties. Civil servants, in spite of a legal appeal on the matter, were excluded.

Although Beijing had let it be known in 1996 that it wanted the Chief Executive to emerge by "consensus" rather than election, and that factionalism and politicking on the Selection Committee were to be strenuously avoided, the race for the job actually started long before these formal arrangements were put in place.[7] Some local figures emerged from obscurity to compete and others, more prominent, disengaged from positions in the colonial framework.

Early names to emerge in 1996 included Tung Chee-hwa, Chief Secretary Anson Chan and other names, some credible contenders, others not. As the year unfolded, contenders became increasingly active and their ambitions for this historic position ensured that at least in the ring of public opinion, a real contest would take place.

A particular surprise in this process was the vigorous and effective performance of Chief Justice T. L. Yang. Yang resigned his position and the luxurious accoutrements of office to participate. He appeared in the bookshops as the translator of a classic of Chinese patriotic history and published a policy platform that included support for social policies to assist the aged and a more interventionist approach to industrial policy. Opinion polls suggested quite clearly, however, that what took him to the top of the ratings was the fact that he was *not* a businessman. He was in fact a very plausible modern equivalent of the scholarly Confucian statesman. This is a personality still immensely appealing to Chinese people, as witnessed by Lee Tung-hui's political successes in Taiwan.[8]

Yang's early success prompted other candidates into a vigorous round of policy pronouncements and glad-handing around the community.[9] Two revealing events occurred during this process. First, several candidates offered photo opportunities of journeys on public transport – a system used by almost all citizens of Hong Kong every day of their lives, but quite foreign to those for whom air conditioned limousines are the normal mode of transport.[10] Even more significant was the meeting between Tung and Trade Unionists, after which it was reported that Tung had difficulty in believing that *any* households in Hong Kong were living on $HK4, 000 per month. (Surveys by voluntary agencies have suggested that up to 20% of households were in that position – even before the crash of 1997). Although Tung subsequently showed himself to be a very quick learner, the immediate reaction of the Trade Unions was that further dialogue with a candidate so remote from the realities of the world of their members would be fruitless.

In the final weeks of the selection process, Beijing's main problem was not in fact to stop factionalism on the Selection Committee, but to stop Tung, who was clearly Beijing's choice, from becoming a landslide victor, humiliating other candidates approved by Beijing. Despite appeals to the Committee members this could not be done. One approved candidate was eliminated in the first round ballot, and the final vote was a landslide with 320 out of 398 votes for Tung.

The Selection Committee then moved to the task of choosing the Provisional Legislature. This was a much trickier procedure. The selection of the Chief Executive, however short on modern democratic standards, was clearly a more open contest than the London based appointment of any British Governor had ever been. The Provisional Legislature, however, was to replace a Legislature that had been elected and had wide domestic and international approval. But with the transition imminent, demand for positions in the new order was becoming ferocious; with many would be legislators able to promote themselves among fellow members of the Selection Committee.[11]

These ambitions were contrary to Beijing's objective, which was to secure legitimacy by maximum continuity with the incumbent legislature, eliminating only a small number of "unpatriotic" members of the old chamber. This time the appeals of Vice-Premier Qian Qichen succeeded in their basic objective, with many formerly elected members continuing onto the new body. But local critics were not to be deflected. Meetings of the Selection Committee were ringed by protesters whose barracking on loudhailers was so effective that it led to an early change in the law banning such devices. After the process was complete Governor Patten observed that one chosen by 400 Beijing appointees had replaced a Legislature elected by an electorate of 1.38 million? For the Democrats, Martin Lee described the selection process as ". . . the darkest hour for democracy in Hong Kong since the June 4 massacre at Tiananmen".

When the Provisional Legislature took office a legal challenge was made to it. This was not upheld, but the terms of the judgement restricted the scope of its activities – essentially to that necessary for the continuation of effective government. A new election was then held on May 23rd 1998.

Under the new electoral system approved by Beijing, the number of members directly from geographical constituencies (on the so called "list basis") was restricted to 20. A further 30 were elected by 28 functional constituencies and 10 more were named by an Election Committee. This system gave 2.8 million people a vote, but the weight of functional members and those selected by the Election Committee ensured that overall control of the Chamber would not be a reflection of the popular vote. The largest functional constituency (education) had 61,000 voters, but the smallest two had only 50 each.

Historically, turnouts in Hong Kong had been in the 30%–40% range and much attention was focussed on this figure as an indicator of popular commitment to democratic politics. Election day itself had catastrophic weather, with rainfall in one area (Sha Tau Kok) being recorded as 300mm. In spite of this, the turnout was 53% (1.49 millions).[12] This is a remarkable figure, 4 percentage points higher, for example, than the turnout in the 1996 American Presidential election. Of the geographical seats, 18 went to the Democrat, Frontier and DAB party groups and two to independents. Democrats also had some success in the functional constituencies, notably that for IT, where the victor claimed that his success was the result of an attempted intervention in the poll by the Xinhua News Agency. Of the 20 legislators ousted from the old (1995) legislature, 18 found their way back to the new one.

I shall return to the implications of this background for economic issues later. But what can be affirmed immediately is that the genie of representative politics appears to be alive and well. It is true that in the final selection of the Provisional Legco and the Chief Executive, a small elite approved by Beijing exercised direct power, but in the selection of Chief Executive at least, the public played a significant indirect role in that aspirants to the office felt obliged to appeal for popular approval in ways that would be conventional in a democratic election. We might call this election behaviour an embryonic "as if" democracy, i.e. politicians acts as if they were responding to a democratically empowered population. The political awareness and activism demonstrated by the population during the transition is not surprising. The genie first released by Maclehose twenty years ago developed further in the 1980s as prosperity rose and growing numbers of Hong Kong citizens were educated and worked in western democracies, all of which laid the foundation for the turbulent, full blooded and controversial dash to popular democracy in the Patten years.

CHRISTOPHER HOWE

THE ECONOMIC TRANSITION

Hong Kong's present economic situation is the result of three related processes. One is the Thai currency crisis of summer 1997 and its ensuing impact in other parts of Asia. Second is the downturn of the domestic transition boom. And third are the fruits of longer-term problems, which were ignored in the transition years. I will discuss the last of these first and then turn to the handling of the other two.

Over the long run, Hong Kong has one of the highest growth rate records of any economy in the Second World War era. Academic debate about NIC growth has been vigorous in recent years. There is, however, little serious question about the major ingredients of Hong Kong's post-war performance. First, nature supplied a harbour that is one of the five best in the world. It is up to six fathoms deep, has narrow entrances with sheltering hills, and no silt bearing river entering into it. Its only drawbacks are typhoons and mists, and these it shares with Macao, which lacks its other advantages and might otherwise have been the natural base for western trade in South China.[13] Second, the Colonial government provided effective and relatively uncorrupt administration, an education system that retained a reasonable balance between provision for different aged groups and between vocational and academic forms of training. It also established a legal system based on English law, and a low tax regime based on the practices of successful entrepot operation and London's demand for colonial fiscal self-sufficiency. Within this framework, the local community provided savings, investment, manual skills, entrepreneurial spirit, and a stock of managerial and market experience, much of it first learned in pre-war Shanghai.[14] It also supplied world-wide commercial connections based on *both* the Chinese mercantile community, with its hundred year experience of international trade, *and* the expatriate businesses with their analogous western based networks.[15]

An important ingredient of Hong Kong's economic success not much commented on, has been the comparative harmony with which the Chinese and expatriate businessmen worked together and the smoothness with which the once mainly British expatriate community diversified its international origins and later (in the 1980s) adjusted to the rising power of Chinese competitors. This all contrasts markedly with the racial and nationalistic antagonisms that have plagued South East Asian economic development. It also contrasts with the continuing monolithic exclusionism of Japan. The weaknesses of the latter models have been fully revealed in the Asian crisis of 1997–99.

In recent years, however, the indicators show a deceleration in Hong Kong's growth rate, the relocation of industrial activity to China (and elsewhere), and the continued rise of the service and property sectors. Some key data that summarise these trends are shown below.

First, in Tables 5.1 and 5.2, we have data for GDP growth rates and

Table 5.1 Growth rates of real GDP (per cent per annum) 1961–1998

1961–73	9	1992	6.3
1973–75	1.3	1993	6.1
1975–80	11.6	1994	5.4
1980–92	6.4	1995	3.9
1992–97	5.1	1996	5
1998 (new official prelim.)	[–5]	1997	5.2
1998–2000 (official forecast in Feb. 1998)	5	1998	[–5]

Sources: Government of the Hong Kong Special Administrative Region, *Estimates of Gross Domestic Product 1961–1997*, February 1998; issues of *Hong Kong The Servicing Economy*, 1998–99.

Table 5.2 Structure of GDP (percentage shares of output, current prices) 1970–1996

Year	*Manufacturing*	*Services*	*Other*
1970	30.9	6.1	9
1980	23.7	67.5	8.8
1990	17.6	74.5	8.9
1996	7.2	84.4	8.4

Sources: as Table 5.1.

structural change. The growth rates date back to 1961, but acceptable estimates for structural change date only from 1970.[16]

The changing structure of GDP reflects the reversion of Hong Kong from being a labour intensive manufacturing exporter to its traditional role as an entrepot – but an entrepot that has augmented its traditional advantages with specialised experience gained in textiles and other light manufacturing activities during the intensive manufacturing phase of the 1950s–1980s.

The foreign trade dimension of this transformation is revealed in data for domestic exports and re-exports as shown in Table 5.3.

We see from Table 5.3 that while re-exports were less than half of domestic exports in 1980, they are currently more than six times as large. We also see the *absolute* decline in domestic exports since 1992 and a sharply declining rate of growth of re-exports.

Table 5.4 indicates the role of China in this transformation.

These transformations in output and trade have had major implications for employment and also for similar shifts in employment structure. These are shown in Table 5.5.

There are two schools of thought about the patterns of development these data reflect. One is that extreme specialisation in services is the expected outcome of Hong Kong's reversion to its role as a metropolitan provider for

Table 5.3 Domestic exports and re-exports * (growth rates and absolute amounts) 1980–1997

Rates of growth (per cent per annum)	*Domestic exports*	*Re-exports*
1980–85	13.8	28.5
1985–92	8.8	30.8
1992–97	–2	12.5
Total values, (current prices, billion HK$)		
1980		
1997	68.1	30
	211.4	1244.5

Note: There is some controversy as to the 'mark up' on Hong Kong exports to China, this is important to calculate the value added by such exports to Hong Kong and to understand the underlying trilateral trade relationships between Hong Kong, China and countries such as the United States. Government statisticians have suggested figures in the range of 14% to 25%. See, K. C. Fung, *Trade and Investment, Mainland China, Hong Kong and Taiwan,* City University of Hong Kong Press, 1997, pp. 54–55.

Sources: as Table 5.1.

Table 5.4 Hong Kong trade with Mainland China 1979–1996

	Hong Kong's domestic exports to the Mainland		*Hong Kong's re-exports to the Mainland*		*Hong Kong's total exports to the Mainland*		*Hong Kong's total imports from the Mainland*	
	HK$ billions	*% share*	*HK$ billions*	*% share*	*HK$ billions*	*% share*	*HK$ billions*	*% share*
1979	.603	1.1	1.315	6.6	1.918	2.5	15.130	17.6
1992	61.959	26.5	212.105	30.7	274.064	29.6	354.348	37.1
1993	63.367	28.4	274.561	33.4	337.928	32.3	402.161	37.5
1994	61.009	27.5	322.835	34.1	383.844	32.8	470.876	37.6
1995	63.555	27.4	384.043	34.5	447.598	33.3	539.480	36.2
1996	61.62	29	417.752	35.2	479.372	34.3	570.442	37.1

Source: Hong Kong Government, *Monthly Digest of Statistics*.

China and the East Asian region as a whole. On this view, not only is specialisation to be expected, but statistical information may distort the extent of de-industrialisation. Since many firms now classified as service providers are in fact still deeply engaged in the manufacturing chain, but have relocated the manufacturing element of their activity out of Hong Kong.[17]

Analysis of the evolution of Hong Kong's role in the world textile trade provides interesting support for this approach. Hong Kong is the world centre of the softgoods industry in the sense that while as a direct exporter it

Table 5.5 Changes in the distribution of the labour force, 1991 and 1997 (thousands)

	1991 (Sept.)	*1997 (Sept.)*	*Absolute changer*	*% change*
Total employment	2751	3122	+371	+13
of which:				
Manufacturing	655	309	−346	−53
Building/construction	64	78	+14	+22
Finance and banking	289	416	+129	+44
Retail/trade services	657	806	+149	+23
Restaurants and hotels	224	221	−3	−1
Other services	453	498	+45	+10

Source: Government of the Hong Kong Special Administrative Region, *1998 Economic Prospects*, 1998.

Table 5.6 Exports and re-exports of softgoods in 1994 (billions US$)

	Exports	*Re-exports*	*Totals*
Clothing	9.37	11.83	21.2
Footwear	.03	6.83	6.86
Textiles	1.92	10.52	12.44
Totals	11.32	29.18	40.5
Total including Hong Kong managed overseas production			50

Source: Hong Kong Government Industry Department, *1995 Techno-Economic and Market Research Study on Hong Kong's Textiles and Clothing Industries* (2 vols.), 1996. Vol. 1, Chapter 1.

is now small, as a centre for procurement, OEM, and textile related services of various kinds, it is unrivalled. The structure of trading activity in this sector is indicated below.

We see here that the total value of exports, re-exports, and of production managed overseas by Hong Kong firms was estimated at more than US$50 billion in 1994. The bundle of skills used in these businesses overlaps and undoubtedly the classification of the firms engaged in them is somewhat arbitrary at the margins.

Those happy with these trends have been the dominant orthodoxy in recent years and they see reunification with the mainland as an unqualified economic gain that lowers transaction costs for still further specialisation within the broad China region. This "golden" scenario has been supported by top officials, by bankers such as Sir William Purves (Hong Kong Bank) and Dr David Li (Bank of East Asia)[18]. It has also been espoused in *The Times* of London by the influential columnist William Rees-Mogg.

But there is an alternative view. This is that industrial relocation has been in the main a defensive strategy by firms unwilling and unable to invest in the long-term process of technological up grading. One reason for this problem is seen to be Hong Kong businessmen's preference for short term, "pirate" strategies which, in recent years, have focussed particularly on the attractions of property development on industrial sites. These entrepreneurial preferences, it is argued, have been reinforced by the failure of the financial sector to develop venture capital markets and its unwillingness to get involved in industrial finance unless supported by secured assets. A further problem is thought to have been failures of government policy in education and industrial support. Interestingly, systematic criticism of the golden service economy scenario come from very different backgrounds; including both the authors of the Massachusetts Institute of Technology study, *Made by Hong Kong*, and an official, pro-Beijing critique of Hong Kong's recent development history.[19]

According to the more sophisticated proponents of the new heterodoxy, in the long run, successful competitive strategies call for the closest integration of Research and Development, manufacturing, marketing and all other allied service activities. Hence, on this interpretation, the danger for Hong Kong is that if firms split the R and D and "service" from the manufacturing elements in the production chain too sharply, they will remain stuck in their present trajectory where sophisticated services are predominantly harnessed with low technology manufacturing activities. In this pessimistic scenario, Hong Kong will only remain competitive by locating output in ever cheaper and more distant labour cost regions. Further, even in the service sector, it is feared that Hong Kong may become vulnerable to competition as Chinese mainland cities accumulate new skills and as changing technology undermines Hong Kong advantages based on the harbour and container infrastructure.[20]

Another cause for anxiety created by current trends has been their impact on employment and income distribution. Comprehensive data on income (or indeed wealth) are not available, but the reality of extreme differentiation in Hong Kong is not in doubt. In 1996–97, shop assistants in large stores could earn as little as HK$3000 per month, and HK$8000–HK$10000 was the normal range for most semi-skilled manual occupations such as truck and bus driving. Meanwhile in the public services and professional sectors, significant numbers were on salaries of HK$50,000–100,000 and upwards. In the business sector, monthly incomes of HK$1 million were commonplace, with top rewards two to three times that level and supplemented by other benefits in shares and kind. These differentials are hardly touched by direct taxation.[21]

Data at the bottom end of the picture are hard to establish, but according to NGO estimates, real wages have been falling in the 1990s, up to 20% of the population has monthly incomes of HK$4000 (US$512) and less, and official data confirm that in a period when average real incomes per head were rising at 2.7% p.a., the real wages of workers in manufacturing recorded virtually no growth at all. Given the inflow of labour during this period and the unfavourable changing structure of demand for lower skilled work, these trends are exactly as one predicts.[22] At the very bottom, in 1994–95 it was estimated that 15.5% of all households and 11% of the population were living in "absolute poverty". This included 200,000 people who were in receipt of welfare payments estimated to provide support below the minimum subsistence level, and a further 450,000 who were not even in receipt of payments. As a proportion of the population in dire straits, these figures are well above current estimates for the comparable group on the mainland.[23]

Employment trends are equally disturbing. Trade Unionists have long disputed the 2%–3% range of the official unemployment figures, suggesting that a more accurate figure might be as high as 8%–10% (and higher still today). The drastic employment restructuring illustrated in Table 5.5 must have had a major impact on labour markets and the smooth re-absorption into employment of those displaced by industrial relocation is improbable, particularly in the absence of large scale re-training schemes. The problem is that in Hong Kong as elsewhere, official figures hinge on intrinsically elusive definitions of both "employment" and the active labour force. Given the absence of social welfare provisions in Hong Kong, inflation and other factors, pressures to work are high and hence it is likely that the actual participation rate (the proportion of the population of working age in or seeking work) is higher than the official rate of 61%. If so, then structural unemployment is higher than officially estimated. Further, in recent years many recorded as entering the "service" sector are family members who have been absorbed in family firms in what is essentially an income sharing device, where their net contribution to the economy is often negligible.

THE PROBLEMS OF 1997–99. ASSET DEFLATION, FINANCIAL REGULATION, AND THE ENVIRONMENT

Asset deflation and recent output trends

Let us now turn to shorter-term problems encountered during the political transition. The first of these is the asset-based rise and fall of economic activity.

The rise and fall of Hong Kong asset prices during the transition are indicated below. Table 5.7 shows key turning points in the Hang Seng Index. Property prices are rather more elusive, but in Table 5.8 I have summarised average transaction prices in well-known apartment blocks as reported in the weekly property supplement of the *South China Morning Post.* For commercial rents which reflect commercial property prices, I have quotations in Table 5.9 for Exchange Square at the top of the range, and for the rather more down market Bank of China Tower.

The pace of the property rise in the run up to July 1997 can be compared with the average rise for 1992–96. The figures for different blocks show a

Table 5.7 Representative values for the Hang Seng Index, 1995–99

January 1995	8,000
January 1996	10,000
January 1997	14,000
August 7 1997 (peak)	16,673
September 1997	9,000
August 1998	6,600–8,000
February (first week) 1999	9,500

remarkably common pattern and in this we find that by May 1998, most prices had already fallen back to the pre-boom levels. Prices went on falling during the summer of 1998. There are some signs of bottoming out in autumn 1998, although the market is reported to be nervous and patchy. Currently (early 1999) developers are selling new blocks at prices below development costs. No one is quite prepared to go on record as saying that prices have definitely bottomed at this point and it is recognised that a further fall would have implications for the banking system. Hong Kong banks' exposure to property is high, although the authorities remain confident that capital adequacy ratios can cope with any likely contingencies.[24]

As prices rose in the boom months of 1996–97, so did the number of transactions. By 1996 competition to buy new flats was so intense that a coupon giving the right to stand first in line to place a deposit was worth HK$1.5 million (even the 104th in line cost HK$.400,000)[25]. By autumn 1988, transactions had fallen to 25% of the peak level and a significant number of purchasers have been left with negative equity. In extreme cases, purchasers made commitments that could not be honoured because mortgage lenders would not provide the required loans on properties whose values had fallen sharply since contract.

What fuelled these extraordinary asset price movements? First, in the case of property, they were an exaggeration of a fairly regular cycle. In the normal case, developers seek to buy land at Government auction as near the bottom of the cycles as possible and then sell developed properties close to the top. The timing of the cycle is structured by the five-year grace period allowed by Government for developers to undertake construction. For developers who time transactions well, mark-ups on development costs are reported to be as high as 70%.

During 1996–97 additional factors fuelled both the property cycle and the share market. In the case of shares, domestic and international sentiment improved as uncertainties surrounding the transition were removed, dissipating the negative "Hong Kong" discount. These uncertainties included confirmation of the top leadership positions in the civil service and judiciary and even the arrangements for the Provisional Legislature. The share market also reflected the strength of Wall Street and relatively low interest rates in 1996.

Table 5.8 Index of transaction prices for apartment blocks in various locations, 1996–1999 (HK$ per square foot, May 1996 = 100)

	Happy valley	*Ap Lei Chau*	*Quarry Bay*	*Shatin (New Territories)*
May 1996	100	100	100	100
June 1997	158	142	153	148
May 1998	100	101	106	134
August 1998	78	72	90	84
January 1999	95	78	87	78

Compare: Official index of flat price increases, 1992–96, 15.6% p.a.

Note: These data will not always be entirely comparable, since the flats marketed may vary in position in the block, but the uniformity of the trends suggest that they give a reasonable view of what has been happening. Trends in luxury flats seem to have been even sharper, see "Millions lost as luxury flat prices plunge", *SCMP*, May 24, 1998.

Source: *South China Morning Post, Property Supplements.*

These factors also helped property, which was further exceptionally supported by a large inflow of funds from both overseas and Mainland Chinese. In the latter case, even quite small local government entities were reported to be on Hong Kong flat buying sprees, aided by loose foreign exchange controls. So strong were these trends that some large luxury blocks became almost entirely investor, rather than occupier owned.

The post-transition decline was prompted by changing sentiment and by interest rate rises required for the defence of the Hong Kong dollar. The latter were reinforced by the arrival of a region-wide "Asian" interest rate premium, imposed by international investors as they reassessed Asian prospects. The net result was that three-month inter-bank rates rose from approximately 6% at the handover, to 12% by the end of the year. Domestically, sentiment in the property market was further depressed by the Government announcement of a target of 85,000 new residential units per annum. These units were to be built by public and private sectors and supported by appropriate land policies. Demand for property was further undermined by weaknesses in the real economy, particularly those originating in the tourism and retail sectors.

Interest rate factors are particularly crucial in Hong Kong. This is because developers without land banks can only participate in the business through auction purchases that are highly leveraged with bank loans. Final private purchasers also require large bank provided mortgages. According to research by Goldman Sachs, up to 73% of average household incomes are spent to repay the US$450,000 mortgage needed for a typical (small) flat costing US$650,000.[26] On standard variable rate terms, therefore, the "Asian" premium alone could potentially put serious strain on household finance. Finally, falling inflation in Hong Kong had ended several years of negative real interest rates *before* the final boom in 1997, and this structural weakness

Table 5.9 Office rentals, 1996–98
(HK$ per sq. foot per month)

	Exchange Square	*Bank of China Tower*
May 1996	90	59
June 1997	80	56
May 1998	80	50
August 1998	70	46
January 1999	58	40

Source: as Table 5.8.

Table 5.10 Indicators of economic performance, 1997–98

	1997 3rd quarter	*1997 4th quarter*	*1998 1st quarter*	*1998 2nd quarter*	*1998 3rd quarter*	*1998 4th quarter*
	+6	+2.7	−2.8	−5.5	−7.1	−4.4
Unemployment rate (official series)	2.2	2.5	3.5	4*	5*	5*+

Note:
* Preliminary estimates.

Source: *SCMP*, Dec. 30, 1998.

in property demand was a negative factor waiting to reassert itself as the boom subsided.

The most recent performance of the economy is indicated by data for output and employment in Table 5.10.

The rise and fall of asset prices has been one factor in the deceleration and decline in the economy's growth rate. The tourist decline and the airport problems were additional factors. The role of the relative appreciation of the Hong Kong dollar in Asia is not yet clear. Surprisingly, businessmen in Hong Kong have found that their large loss of price competitiveness has not yet fed through as strongly as might be expected. This is because general dislocation and the credit shortage in South East Asian economies have made it difficult for them to respond to demand at any price. Hong Kong is expensive, but still functioning. However, this advantage can only be temporary. In the longer run Hong Kong has to reduce costs either through exchange rate adjustment or through the process of real wage and other cost reduction. It made such an adjustment in 1974/74 in response to the Oil Shock while on the Sterling link, but the process is likely to be much more difficult and socially difficult under present circumstances.

The environment

The environmental problems of Hong Kong have become acute in recent years. The clear blue skies of winter and the warm, swimmable seas of summer are now largely memories. The Government has a variety of programmes for monitoring, controlling and remedying problems and the current annual environmental spend is about HK$8 billions. Nonetheless, the existing situation is probably the most discreditable legacy left by the former colonial administration. Time and again strong words were spoken, monitoring begun, and legislation enacted, but either the political will to make these effective and to over ride the business community was not present, or, advice from officials on what was needed failed to match the gravity of the problems, or there was a mixture of both.[27] Even when workable legislation was available, some of Hong Kong's most prominent lawyers could be hired in defence of flagrant breaches of it. The severe implications of this failure, both for public health and the economy, were never adequately grasped.

During 1996–98 a series of environmental disasters and developments have at last brought these issues to the forefront. In the case of air pollution, monitoring is relatively recent, but since 1995 alone, 10 major alerts have had to be issued requiring children, old people and anyone susceptible to respiratory problems to remain indoors. The levels of suspended particles in the air (especially PM10) are dangerously high in the dry season and the Government has started publishing a synthetic measure of six pollutants. Recent readings at street have revealed pollution levels up to 170% worse than those taken from the 17–20 metre high monitoring points normally used to establish the danger points.[28] An estimated 2000 people die prematurely each year due to these problems and the incidence of child asthma, emphysema and related complaints are rising. These problems are often worst in the New Territories. In Tuen Mun, for example, it was estimated that air pollution would double between 1996 and the year 2000.

In January 1998 the Chicken flu virus hit Hong Kong. Eighteen people were seriously ill of who six died. This led to the slaughter of the chicken stock; a horrifying and economically damaging event. Subsequent analyses showed that far from being an isolated accident, 20% of the chicken population were carriers of the virus at the time of the outbreak.

Finally there is the sea, a continuing environmental anxiety. The Government has been active in clean ups of the harbour and has undertaken standard setting and systematic monitoring of the coastal environment since 1986. The problems are nonetheless daunting. Faecal pollution and E.coli readings and trends remain extremely bad in several areas, and there is a growing problem of "Red Tides" of marine algae. These tides can be directly harmful to humans and kill and contaminate fish by poisoning and sunlight deprivation. They are a complex and still unpredictable phenomenon which, since the 1980s, have been occurring in Hong Kong " . . . more frequently and the affected areas have become more widespread".[29] In April 1998 Hong Kong was affected by a major tide which killed most of the fish stock, leaving one to two thousand tons of dead fish floating in the sea. So confused was the handling of this disaster, that the public was not told whether the dead fish could even be eaten or even how long the clean-up process would take.

In the same month the *Guan Hang*, a small vessel carrying ammonium chloride, sunk in the sea off Tuen Mun, causing the precautionary closing of some of Hong Kong's "safe" beaches.[30] Of the 400,000–500,000 ship passages through Hong Kong waters, a high proportion are by similar craft, often carrying waste products of unknown type and origin, and many visibly scarcely able to float in the choppy waters of the inner harbour.

The problem is that none of these incidents were one off disasters of a kind now easily preventable by recognition of the problem and firm regulation. On the contrary, they are manifestations of cumulative trends, which have become intrinsically difficult to control: trends that threaten the health and quality of life of the Hong Kong people. The economic price narrowly measured is also likely to be high, particularly in relation to tourism. The chicken flu was disastrous for the 1998 New Year tourist season (normally a peak for Japanese and other visitors) and it damaged an attempt by Cathay Pacific airline to revive its fortunes with special offers over this period. Tourism is estimated to be Hong Kong's second largest industry, accounting for around 8% of output and a higher share of employment. Unlike Macao, property developers have already been allowed to undermine its attractiveness by the destruction of colonial period buildings. A reputation for environmental accidents and a rising trend in food-related sicknesses will be serious additional burdens in the quest for tourism competitiveness.

Financial regulation

The final challenge of the transition period that must be mentioned is financial regulation. Prior to the mid-1980s, financial regulation of any kind was rare in Hong Kong. This was true of the Stock Exchanges, brokerage houses, banks and deposit taking institutions of all kinds. A series of incidents led to major changes in this. Most spectaculars were the collapse of George Tan's Carrian Group. Tan was an illegal immigrant who, starting from a few minor deals in the 1970s built up a property conglomerate that eventually employed 33,000 people. Tan established a string of off the shelf companies (with names including "Smart Money" and "Eager Earnings") through which he borrowed large and ultimately unrecoverable sums. To the end, which came in October 1983, Tan was highly regarded by blue chip banks, investment advisors and accountancy firms in Hong Kong and London.[31] The legal case against him lasted thirteen years and was only closed in 1996, at immense cost to the local taxpayer

In the downturn of the early 1980s a number of smaller banks also got into trouble, usually from combinations of incompetence and fraud. Between June 1985 and March 1986 the Government was obliged to take no less than such four banks into some form of public custody.[32] As a result, a major programme of financial regulation was initiated. This was partly to avoid recurrence and partly, by then, to provide a system capable of withstanding shocks in the reversion process and insulation from the kinds of commercial malpractice rampant across the border.

Unfortunately this process has not been followed up with the vigour required. In April 1998, after an extensive examination of the financial and currency markets, the Financial Secretary issued his *Report on Financial Market Review*. This reported that "fine tuning" was all that was needed to improve Hong Kong's market and working of the peg. At the press conference introducing the *Report* he added to these findings his personal expectation that Hong Kong markets would be less affected in any future currency turmoil, an expectation that was wholly falsified by events within four months.[33]

In fact, as in previous slumps, the downturn of 1997–98 revealed new problems in both regulation and in the working of the link. Three brokerages have gone into default as has Peregrine Investment Holdings; one of the SAR's a most prestigious investment house. The turning point for Peregrine was discovery of its US$200–$300 million exposure to an Indonesian Taxi Company called "Steady Safe". The total deficit for Peregrine was reported to be in excess of US$ 2 billions.

Although triggered by the Asian crisis, early warnings of these problems were available. Peregrine itself had recently been nominated by the Hong Kong Securities and Futures Commission as one of two companies to participate in a survey of futures market practices undertaken by the Bank of International Settlements. The BIS subsequently reported that both Hong Kong companies fell "far short of key guidelines" and were only making satisfactory disclosures under 2 of 85 possible heads.[34] Further, in May 1998 the Chairman of the Securities and Futures Commission, Anthony Neoh, described the HK Stock Exchange as "a private club" that was failing "to adequately supervise its broker members". Commenting on the Exchange's refusal to establish a compensation fund, Mr Neoh compared it unfavourably with the much publicised Maria's bakery which, while going bankrupt, still went to great lengths to honour its free cookie tokens.[35] In thinking about this problem one must bear in mind that the Hong Kong business community has only emerged relatively recently from the world of Chinese money shops – a world where loans are made by informal word of mouth and where family and business money cannot be meaningfully distinguished. The modernisation of this commercial culture is well underway, but the impression given by Hong Kong's glassy skyscrapers and intensive computerisation can be a misleading indicator of how near to completion the process really is.[36]

THE FIRST YEAR OF THE NEW SYSTEM

I have now briefly surveyed some of the issues of the transition period. In conclusion I shall summarise government reaction to these and consider further the problem of Hong Kong's governmental capabilities in relation to the tasks ahead.

Let us start with individuals. Within the constraints of current arrangements both the Chief Executive and the Chief Secretary have displayed considerable strengths. The Chief Secretary has played a crucial role in post-colonial continuity. This has been buttressed not only by great experience and ability, but by the stature gained in resisting Beijing's attempt to undermine the colonial administration with a premature "loyalty oath" to the Provisional Legislature. In the event, Mrs Chan remained true to the old order until it was appropriate to transfer her allegiance to the new. Meanwhile Mr Tung, battered by the politician's worst enemy – the unexpected – and to some extent hampered by colonial and other legacies, has shown real strengths. Although quite inexperienced in any form of popular politics, he has represented Hong Kong effectively abroad and begun some important policy initiatives at home, notably in housing and technology policy.[37]

Performance by officials in the economic sphere has been more problematic. Response to the Asian crisis and its domestic economic repercussions was slow and failed for nearly a year to take account of the speculator double play on HSI futures and the currency. There also appears to have been misplaced confidence in the soundness of arrangements governing the currency system and financial regulation generally. There have also been moments of political insensitivity in relation to the seriousness of employment and social implications of the Hong Kong downturn.

In the run up budgets of 1996 and 1997, the Financial Secretary was confident and optimistic. In mid 1996, although worried about overheating, he did not act to control the boom and he dismissed as "ridiculous" mainland (Zhou Nan's) anxieties about Hong Kong's social spending commitments.[38] In his first SAR budget (February 1998) Sir Donald estimated growth at 3.5% for the year and he projected future growth for several years at 5%.

Some analysts were immediately concerned, noting the likely impact of the down turn in tourism, the completion of the airport, and poor trends in exports and re-exports. In March 1998 Mr Joseph Yam, Head of the Hong Kong Monetary Authority, gave remarkably optimistic addresses to meeting of bankers and analysts in Tokyo and London. Echoing the Chairman of the Federal Reserve Bank, he blamed Hong Kong asset deflation on previous "irrational exuberance", said that markets were working well, and he concluded: ". . . that is why the Hong Kong economy is not expected to be seriously affected by the [Asian] turmoil". Mr Yam affirmed the 3.5% target and added: ". . . the over-employment situation may ease; but, however one sees it, I hope unemployment would not become a serious problem".[39] As late as May 24th 1998, the Financial Secretary was affirming that it would be "premature and unnecessary" to revise his Budget forecast, but four days later the downturn was admitted.[40] The July data confirmed what was already all too visible to everyone else, unemployment was recognised as a serious issue, and asset and currency markets were continued to weaken through to August.

On August 14th the Hong Kong Government entered the share market to frustrate speculators making the double play with August futures, and on September 5th, new measures were announced in an effort to control and make more transparent any speculative activity.[41] Among hedge funds with interests in the Hong Kong market were those associated with George Soros which was reported to have a US$20 billion investment against the currency.

These moves proved controversial, with some members of the business community in strong support but others (including the Democrat politicians) highly critical. Mr Yam entered a vigorous defence of the Government's action. What was remarkable about at least one version of this, was that most of it was concerned to show that what had been done fell within the definition of acceptable intervention laid down by the former Financial Secretary, Sir Philip Haddon-Cave.[42] Sir Philip was certainly one of the three seminal Financial Secretaries in Hong Kong's post war history, responsible for several important innovations in financial policy and, as a former lecturer, willing to theorise. But to find Hong Kong policy in the world of the late 1990s being justified by administrative precedents a quarter of a century old was extraordinary. It is hardly surprising that politicians in dialogue with the bureaucracy during the summer of 1998 over serious unemployment issues described officials as ". . . too old fashioned and inflexible in their thinking".[43]

CAN HONG KONG COPE WITH ITS FUTURE?

So how do Hong Kong's capabilities match up to the tasks ahead?

First, it is important to emphasise how difficult any transition of this kind is bound to be. No post colonial transition has been easy, and precisely because this one was planned so far ahead and by parties of relative sophistication, the intrinsic problems to be addressed in creating a form of government that is both effective and socially acceptable have simply not been appreciated, particularly by those not involved.

Second, this was a unique transition in the sense that the outgoing power was given assurances that the incoming sovereign would allow, for fifty years, a continuance of the old "system", not only in the sense of many technical arrangements governing the currency, the use of established legal systems, governmental conventions and precedents of all kinds etc. but also in the broader sense of preservation of a "way of life". At a time when confidence was the issue, the more detail that was given on the maintenance of the old system, the better people felt about it. But these commitments were always of a more uncomplicated value to London than to either Hong Kong or Beijing.

For London, they reassured the Hong Kong population, investors, and foreign critics of British policy. But in Hong Kong what is sought by most is protection of their basic human rights, not shelter from the organisational consequences of the modern world. Systems and the way of life have been evolving rapidly in recent decades in Hong Kong and the notion of a fifty-year freeze is impossible to reconcile with the realities of changing opportunities and dangers.

The longer term problem with the two systems theory is that it leaves endless scope for argument as to what is or is not the unchangeable essence of Hong Kong that must be preserved, at the barricades if necessary. The shorter-term problem for economic policy is the persistence of some anachronistic government structures and ideologies of questionable relevance, of which Mr Yam's article referred to above is a good example.

For Beijing, too, Hong Kong and the two systems theory have been a serious political conundrum. First, after the agreements had been made persuaders had to be sent to local Party meetings all over China where the policy of tolerance of the Hong Kong system was hotly debated. More recently, however, the question seems to have been: "If the Hong Kong system is indeed the key to Hong Kong prosperity, why not adopt it in China?" This must surely have been pressed, since in 1996 President Jiang Zemin was obliged to make a statement to the effect that elements of the Hong Kong system such as the rule of law and political freedoms were *not* in fact the keys to Hong Kong. Jiang attributed Hong Kong's success to Chinese creativity and "open door" economic policies. The implication was that since with reforms these were both now available on the mainland too, Hong Kong no longer has any systemic advantage over the mainland. Given that people in Hong Kong do not generally accept this view, beneath rhetorical agreement over the two systems principle, lies a profound and potentially disruptive disagreement.[44]

The policy challenges

Let us now return to some of the main policy issues ahead and assess the working of the Hong Kong system in relation to them. There are three main arenas to highlight here: first are problems of the link, property and the role of government in asset markets; second is the role of government in guiding the structure of the economy; and third are the environment and other issues involving relations with Beijing.

The Hong Kong dollar link was introduced in September 1983 to stabilise a fairly desperate situation. As the Sino-British negotiations got difficult, leaks destabilised local financial markets and in particular the value of the Hong Kong dollar, which had been floating since the break from the pound during the first oil shocks. Under the link system, local currency is fully covered by reserves of US dollars and the link guarantee is given through the relationship between the note issuing banks and the monetary authority. In theory, divergence between market rates and the link will be closed by cash arbitrage, but in practice this is done by interest rate arbitrage. Ultimately, the system is vulnerable to a widespread panic in which local holders seek to convert their bank balances (rather than their cash) into foreign currencies.[45] This was what threatened in 1983, but was averted. In primitive economies where cash is a much larger percentage of the money supply than is the case in Hong Kong, the system is obviously that much more secure. In spite of early claims that the link system was sound, the authorities have subsequently acted in ways that do enable them to modify the "automatic adjustment" mechanism and its impact on interest rates.[46]

Under the link, Hong Kong's monetary conditions follow US trends and the price of any loss of confidence in the currency is high interest rates. At the time of its introduction, the link of $7.8 to the US dollar was expected to be subject to variation.[47] Such variation would have been justified, for example, by the strong appreciation of the yen and other Asian currencies against the US dollar after the Plaza agreement in the late 1980s. But the American accepted that adjustment was impossible for political reasons. The result was domestic over-heating. Because the confidence problem has remained, particularly in the run up to 1997, there seems to have been no further talk of a more flexible link, although the concept of "dollarisation" (i.e. adoption of the US$ as the local currency) was raised by commentators only to be firmly rejected by the authorities.

In the past decade it appears that the Hong Kong dollar may have been undervalued, since the strong rise in the price of "non-tradables" (including property) must have constituted the adjustment required for the real rate to respond to capital inflows and the performance of the tradable goods and services sector. This non-tradable inflation has had a serious knock-on effect in tourism.

In the aftermath of the Asian devaluations, Hong Kong's competitiveness in key areas has clearly become a problem. Indeed, in some manufacturing activities it was a serious issue before the crisis, with competitiveness only holding up in the mid-1990s on the basis of exceptional flexibility and quality factors. In price terms, exporters were reported to be in serious trouble.[48] The recent loss of competitiveness worsens the problem in manufacturing and is also serious for services and, especially, for tourism, which has been additionally affected by events in Japan. With good planning, you can have at least a week in a fine Thai resort for the cost of night in Hong Kong.[49]

How can real costs be brought down without devaluation? No magic productivity formulae are going to solve this and with a fixed link and declining inflation, the process is now under way in the only form possible – attempted and imposed direct wage cuts in the private sector.[50] This has already been shown to be immensely unpopular and divisive, partly because public sector sacrifices have been relatively very modest and inequalities were in many cases high to start with. On the other hand, to lose the link would have serious costs for confidence in Hong Kong financial markets, for the banking system, and for the real incomes of those in the public sector. The latter is an old colonial problem. British civil servants kept India on the Gold Standard to preserve the value of their pensions, thereby denying the Indian industry cotton industry a chance to compete against the silver standard economies in the late nineteenth century. In Hong Kong today, the link issue pits the interests of the employed against the unemployed, the public against the private sectors, and to some extent the financial against the manufacturing and tourism sectors.

The link, through the interest rate mechanism, is a major factor in the property market, although the latter is a problem that has been maturing for twenty years. High property prices in Hong Kong are no accident. They are the mechanism by which a regional metropolitan city asserts its specialisation, forcing out lower productivity activities, including all but the highest value added manufacturing. The growth of the property development industry and rising government dependence on property related revenues are natural consequences of this. In Hong Kong, two unusual features of the territory have reinforced this link. One is Crown, now SAR, and ownership of all freehold. The other is the large potential for land reclamation from the sea. These factors together are almost a licence to print money and explain the government's dependence on property transactions during the past twenty years.[51]

Under the colonial system, market forces were softened by the provision of public housing subsidy and active land policies for industry. But these policies have their problems too, as the crisis in public sector housing arrangements clearly shows. Escaping from the current situation and balancing the demands of developers, government's revenue and, in the private sector, owners, near owners and the housing destitute, is going to be extraordinarily difficult. The destitute include the 10,000 people living in cages, single people waiting 13 years for public housing, and recent immigrants. The grim and paradoxical nature of the property market in Hong Kong is illustrated by the fact that while luxury rents have approximately halved in the past eighteen months, rents for one man cages and family cubicles have risen by a third, as the newly unemployed have been added to the demand for these inhuman forms of accommodation.

The issue of government intervention in the economy includes intervention in markets for shares and property, but goes beyond. In the late 1970s and early 1980s the Government consciously rejected calls for any form of industrial policy to up-grade the technological capabilities of domestic industries. For a decade, the opportunities created by the accelerating reform movement in China provided an economic alternative to such processes. Now, however, as the limitations of low technology based regional specialisation become clearer, and as Hong Kong falls ever further behind Taiwan, Singapore and other Asian economies in technological capabilities, voices in favour of upgrading on the basis of the SAR's research and development potential in terms of the arguments mentioned earlier in this article are to be heard again. The new constituency for this includes Dr. S. Y. Chung, some Democrat and Liberal politicians; and in academia, Professor Charles Kao and local heads of tertiary institutions.[52]

From the outset of his administration, Mr Tung did indeed move decisively in this direction, bringing in new specialists and establishing a Commission on Innovation and Technology. The Commission issued its first report in autumn 1999, including proposals for a HK$5 billion fund.[53] The Commission identified a number of problems and possible solutions along lines previously indicated by Professor Charles Kao, the MIT authors of *Made by Hong* and others.[54] These included the notion that Hong King should focus on design-related activities (especially in relation to textiles), the application of information technology, the commercialisation of Chinese medicines, and the supply of professional and technological services generally. However, given the small size and managerial limitations of firms in Hong Kong domestic industry, the crux of the issue is clearly going to be the success that Hong Kong has in allying with mainland enterprises and institutions. Mainland exporters are largely stuck in low level, OEM based roles and the economy has excessive dependence on exporting through foreign invested firms. (Estimates suggest 50%–60% of exports now come through such firms). In addition, in spite of repeated high-level policy thrusts to change matters, mainland research and development capabilities are reported by Chinese specialists to be still too remote from commercial application.[55] The theory, therefore, is that a synergy needs to be struck between a more developed Hong Kong Research and Development potential, Hong Kong financial and commercial services, and mainland industrial enterprises. This could simultaneously provide a new role for Hong Kong and alleviate economic backwardness and foreign dependence on the mainland.

However, there is a long way to go. Hong Kong's current R and D spend has only recently risen from an estimated 0.01% of GDP in the early 1990s to, perhaps, 0.3% now. Even the latter is not firm and only a fraction of the 2%+ figures in Taiwan or Korea, or the 3%+ norm found in the United States and Japan. Further, Hong Kong corporate capabilities and culture remain unhelpful. Average firm size is small and falling and the practices of OEM based, sub-contracting business are in many cases merely a new form of the short term, minimum investment business strategies traditionally preferred by Hong Kong firms.[56] Major changes would also be impossible without new bureaucratic attitudes and capabilities too. None of this can be achieved overnight.

Discussion of industrial and technology policies leads us into the wider area of Hong Kong-mainland relations. Here we'll draw attention to only two of the issues that are likely to be serious problems in Hong Kong-Beijing relations. The first is the management of mainland access to Hong Kong capital markets. This is a central function for Hong Kong in its new role, and it will be expected both to provide capital and, even more important, handle flows on behalf of clients and investors outside of Hong Kong. The scale of this activity is now very large, partly because of the arrival of mainland corporations in Hong Kong and also because of the listing on the Stock Exchange of both mainland enterprise and enterprises with strong mainland connections – the "Red Chips" or "China Plays". Even where connections are not so large, mainland vehicles have taken useful stakes in all the key sectors of Hong Kong, including airlines, utilities, telecommunications and infrastructure.[57]

The dangers and difficulties of this role have been illustrated by two important cases in late 1998. The first involves the failure of the Guangdong International Trust and Investment Corporation. At one time there were over 800 of these free wheeling enterprises in China, although the number has now been reduced to about 240. The total liabilities of GITIC have been reported at US$2–3 billion, with more than 100 major Hong Kong and foreign creditors facing losses

Equally instructive, on a small scale, has been the case of a Guangdong official who was recently imprisoned for converting state funds to finance a speculative property transaction in Hong Kong, using family members and friends to set the deal up. Had the transaction not turned sour in the downturn, it seems unlikely that the matter would ever have come to light. In a sense, there is little difference between this kind of case and the problem of mainland local government officials losing local government funds gambling in Macao. Again the scale of the problems is suggested by the fact that only the losers seem to be found out.

Both cases indicate that Hong Kong financial institutions, although so close to the Guangdong financial scene, appear unable to make sound judgements about major Chinese companies or even, apparently, to understand the legal status of their client's liabilities and ensure redress. They also reveal just how easy it is for mainlanders based in a bureaucratic and politicised economy to behaviour fraudulently in Hong Kong. In other words, twenty years after the Deng reform and the opening of China, there is still no proper institutional basis for the "two systems" to relate for their mutual benefit through capital flows. Moreover, since China is currently deeply concerned about the impact of any slowing of capital inflows, these scandals, with their likely negative implications, could hardly have come at a worse time.

Finally we turn again to the environment. Recent trends and longer-term prospects for environmental quality are poor. The official view was summed up in a 1996 Government *Review* on its long-run thinking for planning and land use. This stated:

> The potential environmental impacts [of scenarios for the future] cast doubt on the long-term sustainability of continued demand-led development within the limits of current policies and proven technology. On the basis of currently predicted trends, *air quality* will continue to deteriorate. . . *traffic noise* is expected to exceed the parameters set out in the Hong Kong Planning Standards and Guidelines in many areas for both scenarios A and B. . . *sewerage and water quality* issues are of considerable concern as well . . . [and] a substantial concern arises in connection with the *disposal of solid waste*, as waste generation rates are forecast to exceed current estimates.[58]

The *Review* proposed no solutions to these problems, partly no doubt because they are the responsibility of another department, but also possibly because so many of the problems have their origins in the mainland. The Environmental Protection Department chief recently cited diesel engines (many of which are from the mainland) and pollution drift from Guangdong as the main causes of air quality decline.[59] We also know that mainland sources are a crucial contributor to the water pollution problem. Red Tides, for example, are by no means yet fully understood by scientists, but there is little doubt that the interaction of untreated sewage with particular sunlight and temperature conditions is one highly probable source. In Shenzhen, the local authorities report that only 10% of household effluent is treated, and this will also be the case for cities further up the China coast whose waters may come down to Hong. Thus, as *The South China Morning Post* summed it up three years ago: the mainland border is "The Frontier of Filth".[60] Solutions to Hong Kong problems must involve mainland relationships.

The policy challenges ahead of Hong Kong are therefore likely to be socially explosive, divisive as between different sectors of the economy, involve new relationships between Government and the private sector, and call for firm and successful relationships with Beijing and local Chinese authorities in South China. Can this be accomplished?

The evolving machinery of government

At this point it is worth returning for a moment to reconsider the elements that enabled Hong Kong to combine economic growth with tolerable social harmony for most of the post-1949 years. I would summarise this as follows. In the 1950s and early 1960s a highly centralised form of colonial government provided the security, basic housing and economic space required by most inhabitants. During the second half of the 1960s and the Chinese Great Cultural Revolution (1965–1976), both British rule and the inegalitarian form of economic development characteristic of Hong Kong came under stress.

The Maclehose reforms, the strengths of the civil service, and the continuing viability and dynamism of the economic system (even under the trying circumstances of the Oil Shocks) provided the basis for consolidation and further progress into the early 1980s.

The economic success of this period was based on continuing exploitation of Hong Kong's competitiveness in labour intensive and simple technology industries. Also important was the exceptional flexibility provided by a labour market which, largely for political reasons, was without unionisation or proper regulation and worker protection.[61]

Politically, power began to be to be decentralised at this time. Legco became more representative and the Government more sensitive to public opinion. However, at the Exco level, where Government and the economic elite fused, the ideology and interests of traders, bankers and those for whom manufacturing was a relatively peripheral source of profit, prevailed. For most of this group, whatever the previous focus of their businesses, property development was becoming the central activity. Few in the early 1980s had any serious awareness of the significance of either the rapid industrial progress in economies such as Taiwan and Korea or, more generally, of the revolutionary economic potential of contemporary developments in electronics.[62] It was this power structure that rejected calls for assisted industrial upgrading and a new chapter in technology policy, even on the smallest scale.[63] As a result Hong Kong's expenditure on R and D remained effectively at 0% of GDP for most of the 1980s, while in Taiwan and Korea, between 1983 and 1989 it rose from .91% to 1.38% and from 1.8% to 2.12% respectively.[64]

The 1990s are crucial to understanding current issues and the key to these years is the way in which the political economy became contentiously and almost totally enmeshed in the reversion process.

Economically, in its reborn entrepot role, Hong Kong benefited from the foreign investment based boom in China's economy during 1991–94. It then entered the transition cycle powered by the asset boom and airport construction outlined earlier in the paper.

In politics and administration, however, the foundations were laid for major new problems.

First, was the Patten drive to extend representative democracy through developments in the voting system for Legco. This greatly increased political awareness and transformed the answerability of Government to legislators and hence the role of senior civil servants. The latter now became public quasi-ministers, where previously they had exercised a similar function but in a much lower key. Because Beijing rejected this political path to the future, it accelerated the build up of its own political base in Hong Kong. The core of this group were members of the business elite, some of whom were in the old Legco/Exco structures, but many of whom were quite outside of them.[65] Beijing relied on this core in the various organs used to appoint the Chief Executive and the Provisional Legco and some members of it later became key participants in the post 1997 establishment. The very virulence of the controversies in these years enabled Beijing to play the patriotic card with much success, particularly with some who, owing everything themselves to the benefits of a free society and possession of foreign domicile rights, might in other circumstances been less willing to enter into the Mephistopholean pact.

Second, were new pressures on the Civil Service. Whatever its shortcomings, the virtues of the old system had included the spacious time horizons and sense of social responsibility shown by the expatriate career civil servants who led it. During the 1990s the service was affected by localisation, by political pressures from Patten and later Beijing, and by a general shortness of time horizons engendered both by the atmosphere of the time and by the changing (and legally disputed) contractual arrangements affecting careers.

As a result of this turmoil in the Civil Service some major policy issues were not addressed. One example of this is the management of the public housing sector and the overall housing issue. Another is the financial implications of current trends in public health. Housing and health have in common the fact that traditional relationships between public and private provision are now, for various reasons, no longer working. Both subjects are on the agenda of the new government, but both are in far more trouble than they would have been if effort had been spent in the 1990s building up civil service capability for long term policy formation and applying this to the issues. The problems in the third major social policy sector – education – are perhaps somewhat less urgent, since government has at least had the benefit of the ongoing machinery of the University Grants Committee and the Education Commission. These advisory bodies have provided inputs for strategic thinking; even government was arguably short on the administrative resources needed to take advice forward to proper maturity within the civil service machine.[66]

Mr Patten spent much time remarking on the strength of Hong Kong's public finances. This was understandable in view of his previous experience of government. But easy finance does not in fact make for good long term policy making and administration. Future historians may see the 1990s as a new variant of "Dutch Disease" i.e. "Hong Kong disease", where easy money produces not inflation, but policy neglect and a tendency to go for quick, consultant led, but ultimately expensive solutions.

Finally, one other development of the 1990s was the social and political consequences of the expansion of technology-oriented tertiary education initiated after the Tienanmen massacre under Governor Wilson.[67] The creation of new and up-graded institutions required recruitment of more than 3000 (net) additional tertiary teachers and researchers. This effectively created a new class of professionals; a class concerned with technology and critical of Hong Kong's failure to exploit it. Many of this new class came from American rather than the traditional British and Commonwealth sources and this group was more sensitive to the explosion of commercial applications based on electronics, biotechnology, the materials sciences, and other key technological frontiers. Professional development within the civil service did not, however, keep pace with this transformation and its demands.[68]

To proceed from here, Hong Kong needs a structure that will provide focussed new thinking, a bureaucracy capable of turning advice and new ideas into policies, and a legislature and executive that work together and can lead and educate, as well as represent the population by virtue of democratic authority. The present system is arguably insufficiently coherent and the democratic element too weak. As a result, divisive policy decisions may not be socially acceptable. The public and investors will have rising anxieties about the role of vested interests and corruption. And relations with China will be handled without the authority of tangible public support. Environmental reform is a policy area where democratic representation against vested interests both in Hong Kong and China is likely to be particularly important as a prerequisitie to effective action. For one striking lesson underlined by all that we have learned since the fall of the Berlin Wall (as well as by careful study of mainland China's record) is that while electorates may allow democracies to neglect environmental matters from time to time, authoritarian governments are consistently unable to handle them.[69]

Starting at the top, in the current system the Chief Executive is chosen by a process that allows Beijing a paramount say. The Chief Executive and Legco appoint Exco by a process in which the direct popular vote accounts for one third of the seats. There are several problems with this structure. First, Exco composition carries the danger that it may lean, consciously or otherwise, too closely to the business interest. This was a recognised danger under the colonial system, but at least the Governor was always distinct from the Exco group and in any case ultimately answerable to a Parliamentary backstop in London concerned with the wider social interest.[70] There is no comparable backstop in contemporary Hong Kong, since under the two systems principle Beijing is not supposed to intervene in domestic affairs.[71]

Second, although giving the appearance of being a cabinet, Exco has only an advisory role, with members serving part time, having no departmental responsibilities, and hence excluded from direct administrative power. Thus, for example, Hong Kong's historic decision to enter the share market was reportedly neither discussed nor even immediately reported to Exco. The Financial Secretary, an appointed civil servant, took the decision.[72]

Third, the old (pre-Patten) link between Exco and Legco has virtually disappeared. Since Legco remains the legislative power, but lacks powers to initiate most classes of bills and has no cross membership with Exco, a worrying lack of co-ordination seems in prospect. Legco could conceivably resort to seriously embarrassing blocking tactics if its members found sufficient common cause to wish to do this.[73]

Some inherited difficulties in the civil service have already been commented on. On the economic front, one obstacle to rethinking is the fact that the top Hong Kong official responsible for economic policy is very much defined by his job title: Financial Secretary. In the colonial system this was appropriate, as the priority of the home government was to ensure that colonies were financially self-sufficient. This was primarily a budget-making job, at which Hong Kong Financial Secretaries are highly skilled. The narrow conception of economic management implied by this title may have been reinforced by the fact that Chinese society in Hong Kong has many social devices that facilitate co-operation and self -help in the provision of medical, educational and other forms of welfare. These structures have been reinforced by the activities of Churches and other expatriate-led non-governmental organisations. Only later was this whole situation rationalised in terms of a *laissez faire* ideology of economic development. Fashionable as it became in the 1980s, this ideology was not actually observed in several major spheres of policy, including housing and education, where government money and control have always been strong. Thus traditional structures and ideologies carried forward into the SAR are not very helpful in reassessing economic policy traditions, and may even retain power to frustrate those trying to do so.

A further support for policy re-thinking would be a policy community that was outside of Government, but capable of providing research, critical thinking and debate of use to it. Here Hong Kong has peculiar difficulties. One is that because of the territory's size, the pool of talent is absolutely rather small. Another implication of size is that government, private sector and intellectual elites have interests that interlock closely. This is accentuated by the dominance of Government expenditure in education and research and by the recent trend towards careers that start in the public and end in the private sectors. As a result, there are relatively few people with the ability and freedom to make up the kind of critical community that is commonplace in most democracies. Hong Kong is also deficient in well funded, professional think tanks. This again reflects weaknesses inherited from the British system, where public funding dominates education and the governing elite is not really convinced that research into public policy is necessary or desirable.

A good illustration of these problems was the interest generated by the report Made *By Hong Kong* (1997), prepared by a team from the Massachusetts Institute of Technology. This report was an excellent job that did eventually receive Government support and some public funds. Nonetheless, the fact that detailed research on an issue so central to Hong Kong's future was undertaken on what was basically a private initiative, and by researchers from thousands of miles away and mostly unfamiliar with region, speaks for itself of Hong Kong's weak capabilities for policy related research.

To sum up, surveying the post-war colony from 1949 to the late 1980s, I would emphasise that the system of government was never static for long and that in spite of detours and failings, it was evolving in ways that increased its responsiveness to problems and the public interest, mostly for the better.

The 1990s were inevitably a complex period in which many left Hong Kong and those that stayed were understandably concerned to consolidate their positions and life chances. This weakened the core machinery of government. Even more serious, the bifurcation of politics in these years left a situation that was unbalanced in the sense that the popular power base of the incoming administration was much narrower than it might have been, and hence the administration was less well equipped to meet the immediate stresses of the post 1997 economy. In the longer run it is also potentially unstable, since the mechanisms of feedback through growing accountability to the electorate were suddenly derailed. The government says that it has now moved to the full "as if elected" form of democracy, but the authority and effect are not the same and the health of the system is sapped by the pointlessness of much opposition activity. The interests of different groups in Hong Kong are bound to conflict and, as far as possible, it is better that these conflicts are resolved through elections and the machinery of government than on the streets or in the courts.[74]

Finally, we can observe in retrospect that like the other Asian "tiger" economies, Hong Kong has benefited from two favourable post-war circumstances. One was the generally open world economic situation. The other was a *de facto* degree of political independence from great powers that was historically unusual and very helpful for so small an economy. This era may be coming to an end. In Hong Kong's case the SAR will have to find its future inside a completely new configuration of dependence on China. It is true that in some respects the Chinese system is flexible and that Hong Kong will be able to grow in a "borderless" economic region. But politically, as seen from the outside, China remains brittle and unpredictable and Hong Kong's dependence in this dimension constrains sensible change. But unless Hong Kong finds ways to rebalance its mechanisms and improve the coherence of its governmental processes, it will have difficulty in achieving the future its citizens deserve.

NOTES

1 Tung Chee-hwa, "Asian Sins alone don't explain this crisis", *International Herald Tribune*, June 17 1998.

2 For reasons of space and lack of expertise I have deliberately not undertaken any consideration of the legal aspects of the transition, although these are proving to be of growing importance, particularly since the Court of Final Appeal's recent judgements on the Right of Abode and the ensuing controversies.

3 In 1987, for example, Legco consisted of 10 Government officials, 22 appointed members and 24 members elected by other bodies and functional groups. Throughout this article, I have made use of the annual Hong Kong government *Reports*, which contain much basic information on personnel and statistics.

4 Hong Kong Government Information Services, *Address by H.E. the Governor Sir Murray Maclehose, GBE,KCMG,KCVO, at the opening session of the Legislative Council, 1st October, 1980*, para. 144. The same address for 1979 gave some preliminary thoughts and proposals on decentralisation, including the remark: "But over the last ten years your Government has paid increasing attention to the

views of the man in the street. . .The very urgency with which we press forward our policies and programmes for the betterment of Hong Kong imposes upon us an obligation to ensure that the impact of these upon individual people is considered, and dealt with in a way that has broad public consent", *Address by H.E. the Governor Sir Murray Maclehose, GBE,KCMG,KCVO, at the opening session of the Legislative Council, 10th October, 1979*, para. 46.

5 I was in Beijing during one of the Committee's sessions in 1994, staying at the hotel where meetings were taking place. A Hong Kong friend declined to meet me at the hotel because, although strongly pro-Beijing, he was anxious not to be observed by journalists and hence presumed to be in some way associated with the Committee's activities.

6 "Selection Committee contenders revealed", *The South China Morning Post (SCMP)*, Sept. 26 1996.

7 "China opposes ballot for Chief Executive", *Hong Kong Standard*, August 24 1996.

8 "Sir T.Liang rises in public opinion", *SCMP*. Oct. 6 1996. Lee, of course, is a former professor, an occupation unknown in high political places in most western democracies.

9 The programmes of the three candidates in the final ballot were published in "Tung pins hope on 'dream team'", *SCMP*, Nov. 28 1996.

10 "A new man on the Yau Ma Tei omnibus", *SCMP*, Nov. 3 1996.

11 "Legislators scramble for '97 role", *SCMP*, Dec. 1996.

12 "Actions that spoke louder than official words", *SCMP*, May 26 1998.

13 D. Tang and D. J. Dwyer, "The Port of Hong King" in S. G. Davis, *Land Use Problems in Hong Kong*, Hong Kong University Press, 1964.

14 Wong Siu-lun, *Emigant Entrepreneurs: Shanghai Industrialists in Hong Kong*, Oxford University Press, 1988. Judith Mary Nishida, *The Japanese influence on the Shanghaiese textile industry and implications for Hong Kong*, M.Phil. Thesis, University of Hong Kong, 1990. Many people feel that the Shanghai group now basically runs the SAR.

15 Gary Hamilton ed., *Business Networks and Economic Development in East and South East Asia*, Centre for Asian Studies, University of Hong Kong, 1991.

16 Much of the credit for the great improvement of Hong Kong statistics since the 1970s belongs to the Financial Secretary of the time, Sir Philip Haddon-Cave. In earlier days there may have been feelings among officials that economists and statistics were potentially subversive. However, even today there are serious lacunae, including an absence of full balance of payments figures and information on the distribution of wealth and income. Given the social implications of the latter, it is unlikely that anything will be done to remedy this. Indeed, this seems to be a "Greater China" problem, since in Mainland China meaningful data on income differentiation have been unavailable since 1957.

17 This problem is discussed in Cynthia Wong, "Statistics on trading firms with manufacturing-related functions", *Hong Kong The Servicing Economy*, August 1998, p. 6. Ms Wong points out that although the number of manufacturing firms declined by 38% between 1992 and 1996. If we add back firms in the service sector with manufacturing functions, i.e. they engage in cross border, subcontracting processing arrangements, the number of firms is only 5.3% less and the aggregate value-added of the combined group is 18.9% higher. Employment, however, is 29.2% lower.

18 David Li, "Pearl City Here We Come", *SCMP* , July 6 1996. The most persuasive and technically informed expression of this future is that given by Sir William Purves at conferences such as *Hong Kong Works*, designed to encourage British investment and commercial activity in Hong Kong.

19 Suzanne Berger and Richard K. Lester eds. *Made by Hong Kong*, Oxford University Press, 1997. In chapter 5, the authors remark that after an exhaustive analysis of firm level performance they have concluded that: "We do not think that the present [low technology] system can be sustained on its current trajectory". For the mainland view see, Zhou Yizhi ed., *Xiang Gang huigui congshu – Xiang Gang de wenhua* (Collection of books on the return of Hong Kong. Hong Kong's culture) New China Publishing House, Hong Kong, 1996, pp. 116–21. This is one of a series of five books, which represent an official Beijing view of Hong Kong. The series was prepared by the Chinese Academy of Social Sciences and the Xinhua News Agency in Hong Kong. Both Zhou Nan and Lu Ping personally endorsed it. In this volume, the British/Hong Kong government is criticised for its policy of economic non-interventionism and for ignoring Hong Kong's need for technological upgrading through investment in education and research.

20 "Slower HK cargo growth seen", *Freight and Shipping Post*, June 5 1996. This report noted Hong Kong's cost and congestion problems and the likelihood that future growth of intra-Asian trade would benefit lower cost transhipment providers such as Kaohsiung (Taiwan). Comparative data show that in 1994, Hong Kong container charges were higher than those in Los Angeles, New York, Hamburg and Seattle, and substantially above Pusan, Singapore and Kaohsiung. See the detailed study of Asian containerisation growth by Tadao Kawamoto, " [The] Revolution of distribution in East Asia and the development of capitalism", *Shimonoseki City University Review*, vol. 373, 1994.

21 During 1996 the relationship between pay and company profitability was very variable. Hong Kong Bank and Hutchison kept the two approximately in line but at the Bank of East Asia, Directors' remuneration grew at three times the rate of profits increase. "Director's pay surges past performance", *SCMP*, Oct. 6 1996. See also data in "The wheel of fortune rolls on", which reports that according to the latest accounts, four Directors in Hutchison collected more than HK$40 millions each. *SCMP*, Nov.1 1998.

22 Acceptance of extreme differentials of earned income was supported by Governor Patten as an entirely market determined matter, although his administration certainly did more than any previous one to provide welfare cushions for the elderly and needy. Arguing for latter, he once told his critics that a community with more Rolls Royce cars per head of the population than any in the world could easily afford the modest cost of his proposals. It was this willingness to call a spade a spade that made him so popular with the many, but intensely disliked by a few. See comments reported in, "In adversity lower salaries; overcome unemployment", *Pingguo ribao* (Apple Daily), Nov. 3 1998.

23 Hong Kong data in Raymond N. H. Ngan, "Social Welfare", in Joseph Y. S. Cheng ed., *The Other Hong Kong Report 1997*, The Chinese University Press, 1997, chap. 21.

24 According to Deutsche Morgan Grenfell, Hong Kong banks' exposure to property (more than 50%) is among the highest in the Asia region. "Chilled by an Ill Wind", *The Financial Times*, Oct. 23 1997. See also," HKMA fears bank losses ", *Hong Kong Standard*, Dec. 31 1998.

25 "7.2 billion [$] battle to snap up luxury flats", *SCMP* Dec. 8 1996.

26 Laura, O'Shea, "No shelter from the storm", *Asian Business*, January 1998.

27 Governor Wilson's statements to Legco in 1990 are an example of what, in retrospect, was misplaced official optimism: "I believe that major improvements to the environment are well within our reach. By the end of the decade, Hong Kong's hospitals will have fewer patients with lung disease. The air we breathe

will be cleaner. With the widespread use of unleaded petrol and the reduction in the number of diesel engines, there will be fewer complaints about noise and air pollution. More people will enjoy a good night's sleep, uninterrupted by noise from pile drivers, machinery or aircraft landing and taking off. Cleaner beaches will attract more visitors. Our Country Parks will remain intact, including those in Sai Kung, Pat Sin and south and west Lantau, as well as the interationally famous bird sanctuary at Mai Po. Even our massive infrastructure developments should have the capacity to improve rather than damage the environment". *Address by the Governor, Sir David Wilson KCMG, at the opening of the 1990/91 Session of the Legislative Council on 10 October 1990*, para. 83. Of the eight predictions made here, only that relating to the Country Parks proved correct. (Indeed, Sir David added his own Country Park trail to the fine one established by Sir Murray). Sadly, the biggest infrastructure project of – the entire airport – was rushed to completion for political reasons with completely inadequate care for environmental impact. The precious Mai Po marshes also remain under constant threat both from developers and from pollution carried from China by the Shenzhen River.

28 "Pedestrians caught in toxic trap". *SCMP*, June 21 1998. The pollution trap is worst at the multi-junction opposite Sogo Store in Causeway Bay. Public alerts are given when the pollution index exceeds 100. The original height of the monitoring units seems hard to justify. The normal recommended level is 3 metres, i.e. close to the level at which people experience direct effects. See chapters on measurement and monitoring in, Richard W. Boubel, et.al., *Fundamentals of Air Pollution*, Academic Press [Third Edition], 1994.

29 Hong Kong Government, Environmental Protection Department, *Marine Water Quality in Hong Kong in 1997*. This publication contains a detailed technical analysis of the ten zones of the water environment. The chapter on Red Tides is particularly helpful.

30 "Creeping pollution", *SCMP*, April 24 1998. Some beaches in Hong Kong are officially designated as safe. But senior doctors advise that all sea bathing is potentially hazardous, particularly because of risks of ear and eye infection. The proximity of "safe beaches" to areas of obvious severe industrial pollution suggests that this not an alarmist view. These issues are particularly important in relation to Hong Kong's competitiveness in tourism.

31 A detailed account of Tan's entry into respectable high finance was later supplied by a company insider, Thomas Heysek, "Inside George Tan's empire", *SCMP*, Sept. 20 1987. See also, "End of the road for Carrian", *The Financial Times*, October 10 1983.

32 "Catalogue of errors with a public interest", *Far Eastern Economic Review*, May 8 1986.

33 "Tough controls sought in landmark markets review", *SCMP*, April 24 1998.

34 "BIS report faults top HK dealers", *SCMP*, Nov. 10 1996.

35 "Neoh slams 'brokers club' ", *SCMP*, May 29 1998.

36 Chinese style banking was not restricted to Chinese banks. Reminiscing about his early career at the Hong Kong Bank at his retirement party, Sir William Purves pointed out that: "In those early days [the 1950s] banks lent money on the basis of trust and relationships not pledged assets. A previous chief manager of the bank put it in this way: 'Look them in the eyes and see if they are worth lending $5 million to. ' "Sir William's $5 million lesson", *SCMP*, May 29 1998.

37 Mr Tung did not, however, give the environmental problem the attention it deserved. In his first major policy address the subject rated 44 lines and although he spoke of a trial scheme to switch taxis to LPG, no dates were given for

even this modest proposal. *Building Hong Kong for a New Era* (Legco Address) October 8 1997.

38 "Tsang sees post-handover surge", *SCMP*, June 30 1996.

39 Joseph Yam, "Eye of the Storm" March 11 1998; Hong Kong Monetary Authority, The *Hong Kong Dollar Link* (March 3 1998).

40 "Tsang rules out need for revised growth forecast", *SCMP*, May 25 1998; "Hong Kong slides into negative growth", *SCMP*, May 27 1998.

41 Hong Kong Government, *Measures to Tighten up Securities and Futures Markets*, September 5 1998.

42 "Intervention true to guiding policy", *SCMP* August 24 1998.

43 "Unionists decry 'lack of vision' ", *SCMP*, June 16 1998.

44 A comprehensive official analysis of the Hong Kong economy's growth factors from the Communist viewpoint was published on the Hong Kong, Macao, Taiwan news page of *Renmin Jibao* (People's Daily) March 31, 1997. This argued that before China's open door policy (1978) the main growth factor was Hong Kong people – "most of whom are Chinese". After 1978, development was attributed to relocation and trade opportunties created by the "Open Door". The article estimated that Hong Kong firms employed 5 million workers in China, and that cumulative capital investment in manufacturing by Hong Kong firms was US$ 40 billions.

45 A valuable account of the linked system are papers by Professor Tsang Shu-ki, "Two Essays on Hong Kong's Currency Board System", Hong Kong Baptist University, May 1998.

46 Given the government's budget deficit and the use of reserves to cover some of this, the precise motives for HKMA transactions are often not clear. Perhaps this is what they want, to unsettle the speculators.

47 In an assessment of the system a few weeks after the link was established, a Hong Kong Bank publication commented: "The rate chosen fully discounts any reasonable assessment of the nebulous clouds which overhang Hong Kong's future and *should there be a breakthrough in the negotiations there is every prospect of a hefty upward revaluation of the HK$*" (my italics), Hong Kong Bank, *Hong Kong Economic Report*, November 1983. A contemporary academic analyst also supported the view that the link had been made at a level that undervalued the Hong Kong currency, and saw this as one of the factors enabling the link to work. Tzong Biao Lin, "The linked system of the dollar: it works, but how", mimeo November 1983.

48 The 1995 textile study found that American purchasers reported that Hong Kong did not feature at all as a direct future source of clothing and footwear, while it was top of their list of "declining" source locations; costs being even then described as 10%–20% too high. Hong Kong Government Industry Department, *1995 Techno-Economic and Market Research Study on Hong Kong's Textiles and Clothing Industries*, vol.2 p.62.

49 "Beating the tourism downturn – the outlook for Asia", *Hong Kong The Servicing Economy*, February 1998. Also, "Why the Japanese will skip Hong Kong", *Hong Kong Business*, August 1998.

50 These cuts are taking the form of straight money cuts, or of sacking some staff and forcing others to work longer hours for the same money. The effect is the same.

51 Estimates vary from 40%–70% of government revenue. See, "Hong Kong's finances: detour or dead end", Far *Eastern Economic Review*, November 26, 1982; Anthony Walker, ed., *Property and Construction in Asia Pacific: Hong Kong, Japan, Singapore*, Blackwell Scientific Publication, 1991.

52 Dr Chung, an Exco member in 1997–98, was a leader of Hong Kong's drive for

expansion of technologically oriented education. Although a former "unofficial" leader in the colonial system, his views on the value of industrial policies seem to be shifting, see, "Reflections on Manufacturing in Hong Kong", *Transactions of the Hong Kong Institution of Engineers*, December 1997.

53 *Building Hong Kong for a New Era* [Legco Address] October 8 1997 and, *Chief Executive's Commission on Innovation and Technology. First Report*, September 1998.

54 Charles Kao and Kenneth Young Eds., *Technology Road Maps for Hong Kong. An In-Depth Study of Four Technology Areas*, The Chinese University Press, Hong Kong, 1991; Kai-sun Kwong, *Technology and Industry*, City University Press of Hong Kong Press, 1997.

55 Charles Feinstein and Christopher Howe, eds., *Chinese Technology Transfer in the 1990s; Current Experience, Historical Problems and International Perspectives*, Edward Elgar, 1997.

56 There are of course a number of medium size and technologically impressive companies in Hong Kong, but they are the exceptions.

57 Listing was first allowed in 1993, since then 28 mainland corporations have raised HK$38 billion by posting their H shares. A further 54 firms have mainland ownership of 35% or more. Hong Kong Bank, *Economic Report*, June 1997.

58 Hong Kong Government, Planning, Environment and Lands Branch, *A Consultative Digest on the Territorial Development Strategy Review 1996*, pp. 48–50.

59 "Bid to fine drivers idling engines", *SCMP*, Sept. 24 1998.

60 "The Frontier of Filth", *SCMP*, July 27 1996.

61 Real wages dipped quickly after the shocks, and then recovered with the recovery of the economy. In contrast, more bureaucratic and regulated labour markets in the economies took much longer to make the required adjustments.

62 I recall one well known industrialist who told me with pride at this time (the early 1980s) that he took advantage of Hong Kong's *laissez faire* policies to locate there the low technology investments that he was not be allowed to make in Singapore.

63 The longer-term perspective on this issue is discussed in, Stephen Chiu, *The Politics of Laissez Faire. Hong Kong's Strategy of Industrialization in Historical Perspective*, Chinese University of Hong Kong, Hong Kong Institute of Asia-Pacific Studies, Occasional Paper No. 40, November 1994. The comments on the debate from 1978 onwards are also based on my own observations at the time and subsequent discussions with participants. The totality of the lack of interest by Government in technology in the early 1980s was symbolised by the outright rejection of a modest proposal to increase research spending in the universities by HK$40 millions over three years (i.e. by a little over one million pounds sterling per annum). This is a truly minuscule amount compared to the sums represented by the percentages quoted in the text.

64 Data from Anis Chowdhury and Iyanatul Islam, *The Newly Industrialising Economies of East Asia*, Routledge, 1995, p. 122.

65 Very important organisations in this respect were the Chinese Manufacturers Association and Chamber of Commerce, whose members were assiduously cultivated and who provided many key figures in the pro-Beijing lobby.

66 A good account of the health sector is Peter P. Yuen , "Medical and health issues" in, Joseph Y. S. Cheng, *The Other Hong Kong Report 1997*, chap. 20. At present the government is characteristically relying on a consultancy report on health financing, whose conclusions it has not decided how to address. In education, where the permanent advisory machinery does its job, the tendency is to accept this advice too easily, when it really needs thorough processing by those more familiar the full administrative and financial implications of proposals. In Britain, for

example, civil servants are thoroughly familiar with all the issues on which they receive external forms of advice.

67 A good short account of this expansion is, Nigel J. French, "The reform of Higher Education in Hong Kong", in David C. B. Tether ed., *Higher Education in a Post-Binary Era* , Jessica Kingsley, 1999, chap. 8.

68 Of particular importance was the up grading and expansion of the two Polytechnics, the opening of the Hong Kong University of Science and Technology in 1991, and the establishment of the HK Research Grants Council in 1990. Professor Charles Kao former Vice Chancellor of the Chinese University of Hong Kong and the President of HKUST, Professor Woo Chia-wei, have been notably vocal and important presences in this respect.

69 For exhaustive analyses of the current Chinese environmental situation see papers in, *The China Quarterly, Special Issue: the environment*, No. 156, December 1998.

70 In the 1970s, for example, the Labour government sent Professor H. A. Turner to Hong Kong to investigate the labour situation, reflecting anxieties in Britain about the poor state of labour market regulation in Hong Kong. See H. A. Turner, *The Last Colony: But Whose? A study of the labour movement, labour market and labour relations in Hong Kong*, Cambridge University Press, 1980.

71 Officials have stated firmly that during the currency crisis no words of advice were received from Beijing. However, in January 1999 it was reported that Beijing was so concerned about the state of the Hong Kong economy that a group was sent down to Shenzhen to consult with "old friends" from Hong Kong on the development of new strategies.

72 Kuan Hsin-chi, "Institution building in the New Special Administrative Region", *China Perspectives*, November/December, 1998.

73 At the end of 1998 Legco members complained of "lack of respect" from the Government who, when trouble was in the wind , reportedly resorted to arbitrarily withdrawing bills.

74 The "as if" principle was enunciated recently by the Secretary for Constitutional Affairs. "Yes we are not elected", he said, "but we should and can do our job . . . as if we are elected". See "Conflicting signposts on SAR's political path", *SCMP*, January 27, 1999. The property boom collapse has led both to violence in the streets and threatened disputes in the courts, as those left with unmanageable problems struggled with the support of legislators against the developers.

Part II

THE DEBATE OVER SOURCES OF GROWTH

6

THE TYRANNY OF NUMBERS

Confronting the Statistical Realities of the East Asian Growth Experience

Alwyn Young

6.1 INTRODUCTION

This is a fairly boring and tedious paper, and is intentionally so. This paper provides no new interpretations of the East Asian experience to interest the historian, derives no new theoretical implications of the forces behind the East Asian growth process to motivate the theorist, and draws no new policy implications from the subtleties of East Asian government intervention to excite the policy activist. Instead, this paper concentrates its energies on providing a careful analysis of the historical patterns of output growth, factor accumulation, and productivity growth in the newly industrializing countries (NICs) of East Asia, i.e., Hong Kong, Singapore, South Korea, and Taiwan.

Tables 6.1 and 6.2 and Figure 6.1 present some basic information on growth in the NICs, drawn from national accounts and census sources.[1] As seen in Table 6.1, the extraordinarily rapid and sustained growth of output per capita in all four economies, averaging some 6 to 7 percent per annum for two and a half decades, is truly remarkable. It is this record of growth, along with its apparent association with the rapid growth of manufactured exports, that has led most economists to believe that productivity growth in these economies must be extraordinarily high, particularly in their manufacturing sectors. This view, however, ignores an equally remarkable record of factor accumulation.

As Table 6.1 shows, one important area of factor accumulation has been labor input. The rapid postwar decline in birth rates (changing dependency ratios) and rising rates of female labor force participation have led to a substantial rise in the aggregate participation rate in each of the NICs.[2] In moving to measures of output per worker, rising participation rates remove an average of 1 percent per annum from the per capita growth rate of Hong Kong, 1.2 and 1.3 percent per annum from Korea and Taiwan, respectively, and a stunning 2.6 percent per annum (for 24 years!) from the growth rate of

Source: *Quarterly Journal of Economics*, August 1995, pp. 641–80.

Table 6.1 Growth rates (percent)

	Hong Kong (1966–1991)			*Singapore (1966–1990)*		
	N	*D*	*N – D*	*N*	*D*	*N – D*
GDP per capita	7.3	1.6	5.7	8.7	1.9	6.8
GDP per worker	7.3	2.6	4.7	8.7	4.5	4.2
Excluding agriculture	n.a.	2.8	n.a.	8.8	4.6	4.2
Manufacturing	n.a.	1.3	n.a.	10.2	6.2	4.0
Δ Participation rate		0.38 → 0.49			0.27 → 0.51	
	South Korea (1966–1990)			*Taiwan (1966–1990)*		
	N	*D*	*N – D*	*N*	*D*	*N – D*
GDP per capita	8.5	1.7	6.8	8.5	1.8	6.7
GDP per worker	8.5	2.8	5.6	8.5	3.1	5.4
Excluding agriculture	10.3	5.4	4.9	9.4	4.6	4.8
Manufacturing	14.1	6.3	7.8	10.8	5.9	4.9
Δ Participation rate		0.27 → 0.36			0.28 → 0.37	

Notes:
N = Numerator.
D = Denominator.
NA = Not available, the Hong Kong government has yet to develop constant price estimates of GDP by sector. GDP measures are at market prices, excluding import duties, however. Columns may not add up due to rounding.

Table 6.2 Educational attainment of the working population (percent)

	Hong Kong		*Singapore*		*South Korea*		*Taiwan*	
	1966	*1991*	*1966*	*1990*	*1966*	*1990*	*1966*	*1990*
None	19.2	5.6	55.1	⇓	31.1	6.4	17.0	4.5
Primary	53.6	22.9	28.2	33.7	42.4	18.5	57.2	28.0
Secondary +	27.2	71.4	15.8	66.3	26.5	75.0	25.8	67.6

Notes: Self-taught are included under primary. Hong Kong, Korean, and Taiwanese data refer to highest level of eduction 'attended' rather than completed. All percentages are calculated net of those reported as 'unknown.'

Singapore. Intersectoral transfers of labor have also been important. Thus, removing agriculture from the analysis lowers the growth rate of output per worker in Taiwan and South Korea by 0.6 and 0.7 percent per annum, respectively, reflecting the rapid decline in the share of agricultural employment in total employment in both economies.[3] Although the growth of manufacturing output has been unusually rapid in these economies, so has the growth of manufacturing employment. Once one accounts for the transfer of labor into manufacturing, one finds, surprisingly, that, with regard to labor

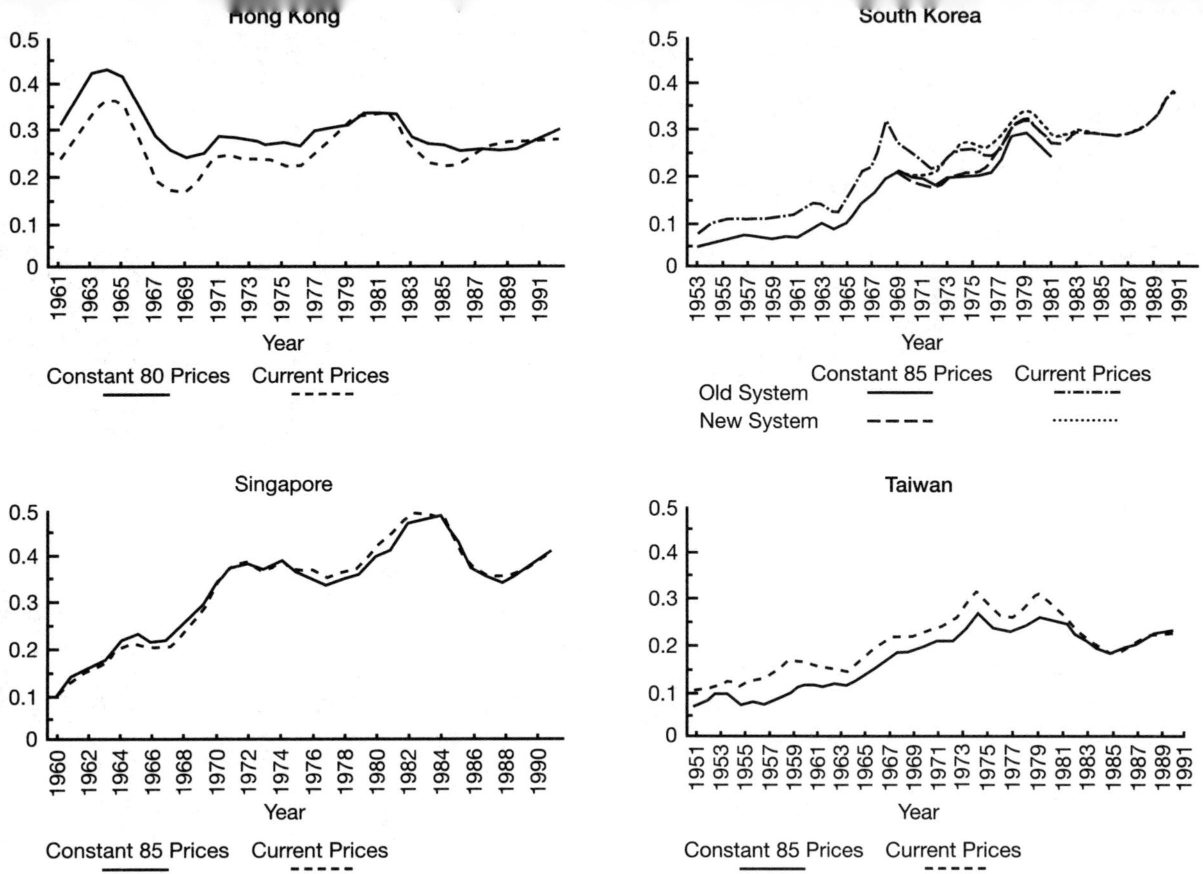

Figure 6.1 I/GDP Ratios

productivity growth, manufacturing in both Singapore and Taiwan actually underperformed the aggregate economy.

Capital input has also grown rapidly in the NICs. As shown in Figure 6.1, although the investment to GDP ratio has remained roughly constant in Hong Kong, in the other NICs it has risen substantially over time. In Singapore the constant price investment to GDP ratio, at 10 percent in 1960 had reached 39 percent by 1980 and an extraordinary 47 percent by 1984, after which it declined substantially, only to begin another rise in the late 1980s. In South Korea, investment rates, which were around 5 percent (in constant prices) in the early 1950s, exploded up to 20 percent in the late 1960s, reached 30 percent by the late 1970s, and were approaching 40 percent by 1991. Finally, in Taiwan the constant price investment to GDP ratio, at around 10 percent in the early 1950s, grew steadily to a high of 27 percent in 1975, after which it fluctuated around a value of about 22 percent.

Human capital accumulation in the East Asian NICs has also been quite rapid. As shown in Table 6.2 above, over the past two and a half decades the proportion of the working population in each economy with a secondary education or more has almost tripled or, in the case of Singapore, even quadrupled. By 1990/1991, some 18 to 20 percent of the working population in each NIC had some tertiary education.[4] In weighting labor input by sex, age, and educational characteristics (discussed further below), I have found that the improving educational attainment of the workforce contributes to about 1 percent per annum additional growth in labor input in each of these economies.

All of the influences noted above—rising participation rates, intersectoral transfers of labor, improving levels of education, and expanding investment rates—serve to chip away at the productivity performance of the East Asian NICs, drawing them from the top of Mount Olympus down to the plains of Thessaly. In a companion paper [Young 1994], I use simple back-of-the-envelope calculations and large international data sets to show that, with regard to productivity growth in the aggregate economy and in manufacturing in particular, the NICs cannot be considered to be strong outliers in the postwar world economy. This paper concentrates on a more careful analysis of these four economies, making use of the extensive statistical record embodied in their national accounts, population censuses, and sectoral, wage, and labor force surveys.

The remainder of this paper is organized as follows. Section 6.II presents a short review of methodology. Sections 6.III–6.VI then provide a country-by-country analysis of aggregate and sectoral total factor productivity growth. Section 6.VII contrasts this research with earlier work on productivity growth in the NICs, while Section 6.VIII summarizes and concludes. An Appendix provides a description of sources and some of the problems encountered in linking different data series.

6.II METHODOLOGY

A The translog index of total factor productivity growth

Consider the translogarithmic value added production function:[5]

$$Q = \exp [\alpha_0 + \alpha_k \ln K + \alpha_L \ln L + \alpha_t t + \tfrac{1}{2} B_{KK} (\ln K)^2 + B_{KL} (\ln K)(\ln L) + B_{kt} \ln K \cdot t + \tfrac{1}{2} B_{LL}(\ln L)^2 + B_{Lt} \ln L \cdot t + \tfrac{1}{2} B_{tt} t^2], \quad (1)$$

where K, L, and t denote capital input, labor input, and time, and where, under the assumption of constant returns to scale, the parameters α_i and B_{jk} satisfy the restriction:

$$\alpha_K + \alpha_L = 1, \qquad B_{KK} +, B_{KL} = B_{LL} + B_{KL} = B_{Kt} + B_{Lt} = 0. \quad (2)$$

First differencing the logarithm of the production function provides a measure of the causes of growth across discrete time periods:

$$\ln \left(\frac{Q(T)}{Q(T-1)}\right) = \bar{\Theta}_K \ln \left(\frac{K(T)}{K(T-1)}\right) + \bar{\Theta}_L \ln \left(\frac{L(T)}{\mathrm{L}(T-1)}\right) + TFP_{T-1,T,} \quad (3)$$

where

$$\bar{\Theta}_i = [\Theta_i(T) + \Theta_i(T-1)]/2$$

and where the Θ_i's denote the elasticity of output with respect to each input or, equivalently, assuming perfect competition, the share of each input in total factor payments. The translog index of TFP growth ($TFP_{T-1,T}$) provides a measure of the increase in output attributable to the time-related shift in the production function. In essence, the translog production function provides a theoretical justification for the use of average factor shares and log differences as a means of extending the continuous time Divisia analysis of productivity growth to data based upon discrete time periods.

To allow consideration of more finely differentiated inputs, one can assume that aggregate capital and labor input are, in turn, constant returns to scale translog indices of subinputs:[6]

$$K = \exp [\alpha_1^K \ln K_1 + \alpha_2^K \ln K_2 + \cdots + \alpha_n^K \ln K_n + \tfrac{1}{2}B_{11}^K(\ln K_1)^2 + B_{12}^K(\ln K_1)(\ln K_2) + \cdots + \tfrac{1}{2}B_{nn}^K(\ln K_n)^2], \quad (4)$$

$$L = \exp [\alpha_1^L \ln L_1 + \alpha_2^L \ln L_2 + \cdots + \alpha_m^L \ln L_m + \tfrac{1}{2}B_{11}^L (\ln L_1)^2 + B_{12}^L(\ln L_1)(\ln L_2) + \cdots + \tfrac{1}{2}B_{mm}^L(\ln L_m)^2].$$

First differencing the logarithms of these translog indices provides a measure of the growth of aggregate capital and labor input as weighted averages of the growth rates of their subinputs:

$$\ln\left(\frac{K(T)}{K(T-1)}\right) = \sum_i \bar{\theta}_{K_i} \ln\left(\frac{K_i(T)}{K_i(T-1)}\right) \tag{5}$$

$$\ln\left(\frac{L(T)}{L(T-1)}\right) = \sum_j \bar{\theta}_{L_j} \ln\left(\frac{L_j(T)}{L_j(T-1)}\right),$$

where

$$\bar{\theta}_i = [\, \theta_i(T) + \theta_i(T-1)]/2$$

and where the θ_i's denote the elasticity of each aggregate input with respect to each of its component subinputs or, again assuming perfect competition, the share of each subinput in total payments to its aggregate factor. In a manner analogous to the continuous time Divisia analysis, these indices adjust for improvements in the "quality" of aggregate capital and labor input by, to a first-order approximation, weighting the growth of each subinput by its average marginal product.

The appropriate measure of capital and labor input is the flow of services emanating from those inputs. For labor, one can reasonably assume that the flow of services is proportional to total hours of work; i.e., $L_j(T) = \lambda_{L_j} H_j(T)$, with

$$\ln\left(\frac{L(T)}{L(T-1)}\right) = \sum_j \bar{\theta}_{L_j} \ln\left(\frac{H_j(T)}{H_j(T-1)}\right). \tag{6}$$

Since data on capital utilization are rare, it is customary to assume that the flow of capital services is proportional to the measured capital stock (denoted by $C_i(T)$), with $K_i(T) = \lambda_{K_i} C_i(T)$ and

$$\ln\left(\frac{K(T)}{K(T-1)}\right) = \sum_i \bar{\theta}_{K_i} \ln\left(\frac{C_i(T)}{C_i(T-1)}\right). \tag{7}$$

Before proceeding further, it is worth considering whether deviations from the restrictive assumptions of the model outlined above might not lead to a downward bias in estimates of total factor productivity growth, and hence explain the low estimates reported in this paper. The absence of perfect competition, in the context of a constant returns to scale production function, could lead to mismeasurement of the elasticity of output with respect to each input, as factor shares need no longer reflect output elasticities. In particular, to the degree that monopoly profits are reflected in capital income, capital's income share will tend to overstate the elasticity of output with respect to capital. The reader can make an easy correction for this factor by adjusting the aggregate shares of capital and labor in the tables presented further below. However, since physical capital accumulation is only a small part of the NIC story, with increases in labor participation and educational attainment and the intersectoral transfer of labor all playing an equally important role,[7] within reasonable bounds adjustments along these lines are not likely to produce spectacular productivity estimates for the NICs.[8]

Relaxation of the assumption of constant returns to scale could either increase or decrease the productivity estimates. If the true aggregate production function is characterized by increasing returns to scale, perhaps due to externalities among factors, then the growth accounting residual actually overstates the true degree of productivity growth, since it captures the increase in production externalities brought about by the increase in factors of production. Conversely, if the true production is characterized by decreasing returns to scale, the growth accounting residual understates the degree of productivity growth.

Finally, it is worth addressing a common misconception concerning growth accounting adjustments for the "quality" of labor and capital input; i.e., that these adjustments implicitly incorporate any embodiment of technological change in those inputs. Fundamentally, the growth accounting procedure assumes that input i today is the same as it was yesterday; i.e., that a secondary educated 25-year-old female worker today is identical to a secondary educated 25-year-old female worker yesterday. In so doing, the procedure places any increase in the productivity of that input (whether or not embodied) into the residual. The weighting of capital and labor input in equation (5) above is no more than an extension of the standard two-factor (capital/labor) analysis, in which each factor is weighted by its income share, to the consideration of more numerous inputs which, for analytical convenience, are differentiated into lists of "capital" and "labor" inputs.[9]

B Measuring factor supplies

My analysis focuses on two aggregate inputs, capital and labor, subdivided into finer subinput categories. In general, I divide capital input into five categories: residential buildings, nonresidential buildings, other durable structures, transport equipment, and machinery. With the exception of my analysis of Singaporean manufacturing, I do not include land input, which is difficult to measure. To minimize any error, I focus my analysis of Taiwan and Korea on the nonagricultural economy, where land input accounts for only a small percentage of total payments to factors of production.[10] Labor is distinguished on the basis of sex (two categories), age (nine to eleven categories, depending upon the country and time period under consideration), and education (two to seven categories).

I estimate the capital stock using the standard perpetual inventory approach with geometric depreciation.[11] In following this approach, it is customary to initialize the capital stock series using a benchmark survey, such as a national wealth survey. In the case of the NICs, this approach is not productive. Neither Hong Kong nor Singapore has ever conducted such a survey, while, in the case of South Korea and Taiwan, the survey results are greatly at odds with the annual investment flows recorded in the national accounts. Table 6.3 reports the ratio of historical cumulative (undepreciated) investment to the value of gross (undepreciated) assets reported in the 1988 National Wealth Survey of Taiwan.[12] As the table shows, the aggregate numbers reported in the survey vastly exceed the *total* cumulative investment in the period 1951–1988.[13] Lest the reader believe that this discrepancy reflects pre-1951 purchases of capital, the survey also reported the date the assets were acquired, indicating that only a small fraction (e.g., 1 percent of machinery and transport equipment) was acquired prior to 1956. As Table 6.3 shows, at the sectoral level the discrepancies between the national accounts and the survey values are even greater, with the ratio of cumulative investment to reported gross assets reaching highs of 25.74 and lows of 0.10 for public enterprises in mining and utilities, respectively. In the case of South Korea, three wealth surveys have been taken, which allows for a time series comparison. Table 6.4 compares the gross assets recorded in each survey with an adjustment for cumulative investment in the intervening years.[14] As the table shows, the total nonresidential capital reported in the 1968 wealth survey, plus the ensuing nine years of investment flows, accounted for only two-thirds of the nonresidential capital reported in the 1977 wealth survey, implying that these assets "grew" by 50 percent in the intervening years. In the case of transport equipment, however, fully 76 percent of the gross assets reported in the 1968 survey, plus the ensuing investment, were unaccounted for in the 1977 survey. The incongruity between the stock values recorded in

Table 6.3 Ratio of cumulative investment to wealth survey gross assets: Taiwan, 1988

	Residential	*Non-residential*	*Other construction*	*Transport equipment*	*Machinery*
Economy	0.33	0.60	0.76	0.75	0.86
Mining *	n.a.	1.37	1.85	25.74	6.23
Utilities *	n.a.	0.47	0.10	1.23	1.48

Notes:
n.a. = Not applicable.
* Public enterprises only.

Table 6.4 Ratio of gross assets from survey to survey: South Korea (allowing for cumulative investment)

	Residential	*Non-residential*	*Other construction*	*Transport equipment*	*Machinery*
1968/1977	0.95	0.65	1.27	1.76	0.89
1977/1987	0.77	0.67	1.00	1.07	0.81

the national wealth surveys and the flow values of the national accounts calls into question any attempt to use the wealth surveys as a means of initializing one's estimates of the capital stock.[15]

As an alternative procedure, I initialize my capital stock series by assuming that the growth rate of investment in the first five years of the national accounts investment series is representative of the growth of investment prior to the beginning of the series.[16] Given positive rates of depreciation and a sufficiently long investment series prior to the first date of the analysis, the perpetual inventory approach is fairly insensitive to the level of capital used to initialize the series. For Hong Kong the published investment series begins in 1961. I use my own estimates of capital formation, which mimic the methodology of the Hong Kong government, to extend the series on all asset types back to 1947. For Singapore the published investment series begins in 1960. I use data on the construction of one-family equivalent residential units and retained imports of cement[17] to extend the residential and nonresidential durable structures investment series back to 1947.[18] For Taiwan the published investment series begins in 1951 and for South Korea in 1953. In general, I focus my analysis on the post-1966 period, allowing each economy thirteen or more years of investment data to establish the capital stock.[19]

Turning now to the measurement of labor inputs, my task is to estimate the working population, cross-classified by up to seven attributes, i.e., sex, age, education, industry, income, hours of work, and class of worker (i.e., employee, self-employed, etc.). Census and survey data frequently contain information on row and column sums in lower dimensions. Under the assumption that there are no interactions across attributes other than those present in the available subdimensional tables, I derive an approximation of the maximum likelihood estimate of each cell using the iterative proportional fitting technique suggested by Bishop, Fienberg, and Holland [1975]. In general, I make use of the information provided by additional worker characteristics, e.g., occupation, which, in their cross-tabulation with attributes of interest to me provide additional information. Thus, for example, I actually estimate the 1990 Singaporean working population cross-classified by sex × age × education × industry × income × class of worker × occupation, using all available census tabulations.[20] For my TFP estimates, I then sum across occupational categories to derive a reduced six-dimensional table of the variables of interest to me.

All four economies conduct occasional censuses and, on a more regular annual basis, surveys of labor force conditions. With regard to the overall size of the labor force, however, the labor force surveys provide little additional independent information over and above that derived from the census. Each survey is typically based upon a small sample[21] which must then be scaled up to a national estimate. The factors used to accomplish this scaling are usually drawn from the previous census. In essence, the reported survey results are a modified extrapolation of the previous census. Given the rapid transformation experienced by these economies, the results can, on occasion, be grossly inaccurate. Thus, the 1989 Labor Force Survey of Singapore (using scaling factors drawn from the 1980 census) estimated the working population at 1,277,254. The 1990 Census, however, found that the actual working population numbered 1,537,011 (i.e., 20 percent more than reported in the previous survey). The 1991 Labor Force Survey of Singapore (using updated 1990 scaling factors) then estimated the working population at 1,524,315. In the estimates below, I confine myself to census years, treating the census results as the appropriate measure of the "population" and the survey results as a "sample," making use of these, when they contain cross tabulations that are unavailable in the census, by conforming the survey row and column totals to those given by the census. Since, over the long run, the labor force surveys track (with large variance) the census, the long-term average rates of productivity growth reported below are not dependent on this choice of sources.[22]

Finally, I should note that to improve the accuracy of my labor force estimates I have acquired thousands of pages of unpublished census tabulations from the governments of Hong Kong and Singapore, while, in the case of Taiwan, I have made use of the Chinese language area and district census tabulations, which contain additional tabulations over and beyond those reported in the summary English language volumes. These additional tabulations provide valuable information. Thus, for example, unpublished Hong Kong tabulations provide information on income by age, sex, and education cross-tabulated by class of worker (e.g., self-employed, employee, etc.). In contrast, the published tabulations rarely cross-tabulate income with class of worker. Consequently, relying on the published tabulations alone pollutes one's estimates of the returns to different types of labor input with nonlabor capital income.

C Measuring factor shares

In order to estimate the share of labor and capital in total payments to factors of production, it is necessary to measure value added from the point of view of the producer. This requires removing all indirect business taxes on the value of output (including all sales and excise taxes), while retaining all subsidies and taxes on factors of production (such as license fees and profits taxes), a concept of value added midway between GDP at factor cost and GDP at market prices. In the case of Hong Kong, where indirect taxes are minimal, I simply take as my measure of value added the national accounts estimates of GDP at current factor cost. In the case of the other economies, where indirect taxes are more significant, I use published and unpublished data on tax revenues to separate out the "admissible" indirect taxes, i.e., those that are part of the value of output from the point of view of the producer, and allocate them to the different economic sectors.[23]

To estimate the share of labor in total factor payments, I begin by constructing estimates of the hourly incomes of employees cross-tabulated by industry, sex, age, and education. I then use these compensation data, and my estimates of hours of work cross-tabulated by industry, sex, age, education, and class of worker, to estimate the incomes of employees and the implicit labor income of employers, unpaid family workers, and the self-employed, under the assumption that the latter earn an implicit wage equal to the hourly wage of employees with similar sex, age, educational, and industrial characteristics. To determine the share of labor in each sector, I then multiply the sectoral compensation of employees data reported in the national accounts by one plus my sectoral estimates of the ratio of implicit to explicit labor income.[24] Combining my measures of implicit and explicit income provides an estimate of sectoral labor income cross-classified by the sex, age, and educational characteristics of workers and, hence, an estimate of the share of each labor subinput in total payments to labor by sector.

Turning to capital input, under the assumption of perfect competition and constant returns to scale, I take the aggregate share of capital by sector to be simply one minus the estimated share of labor. To allocate capital income by asset type, I note that with geometric depreciation, and perfect foresight, the rental price of a capital good k_i is given by[25]

$$P_{k_i}(T) = P_{I_i}(T-1)\, r(T) + \delta\, P_{I_i}(T) - \{P_{I_i}(T) - 1)\}, \tag{8}$$

where P_{I_i} denotes the investment price of capital good *i* and *r(T)* is the nominal rate of return between periods $T - 1$ and T. Under the assumption that all assets earn the same nominal rate of return, I vary *r(T)* until total payments to capital equal my estimate of the aggregate share of capital. This yields estimates of the rental price of each asset category and, by extension, its share of payments to capital.

6.III HONG KONG

Table 6.5 presents estimates of total factor productivity growth in Hong Kong. With the exception of the 1981–1986 period, when business activity was depressed by the Anglo-Chinese negotiations over the future of the colony, Hong Kong sustained total factor productivity growth rates of 2 percent or more in each of the five-year periods, averaging 2.3 percent over the 1966–1991 period as a whole. As one would expect, given the relative constancy of the post-1966 investment to GDP ratio, there is little evidence of capital deepening, with weighted capital input growing only 0.7 percent faster per annum than output during the 1966–1991 period. As the table shows, the weighting of capital and labor input raises, but only slightly, the estimated growth rate of these factors of production. In the case of capital, weighting raises the growth rate somewhat by placing a greater emphasis on the rapidly growing stock of machinery.[26] In the case of labor, adjustments for sex, hours

Table 6.5 Total factor productivity growth: Hong Kong

Time period	*Output*	*Raw capital*	*Weighted capital*	*Raw labor*	*Weighted labor*	*TFP*	*Labor share*
	Annual growth of:						
61–66	0.109	0.169	0.162	0.032	0.025	0.035	0.643
66–71	0.065	0.075	0.078	0.025	0.024	0.023	0.660
71–76	0.081	0.075	0.080	0.033	0.024	0.039	0.662
76–81	0.099	0.093	0.098	0.051	0.064	0.022	0.617
81–86	0.058	0.078	0.079	0.019	0.027	0.009	0.593
86–91	0.063	0.062	0.066	0.005	0.022	0.024	0.609
66–91	**0.073**	**0.077**	**0.080**	**0.026**	**0.032**	**0.023**	**0.628**

Notes: Raw inputs are the arithmetic sum of subcomponents, with no adjustment for hours of work. Weighted inputs are translog indices of factor input growth, with labor services measured by hours of work.

of work, and age (prior to 1976) lower the growth rate of effective labor input, while adjustments for education and age (after 1976) raise its effective growth rate, with the net effect being slightly positive on average. Weighting is, however, of substantial importance during individual periods, for example during the late 1980s, when the stabilization of female participation rates, aging of the labor force, and rising educational attainment, all served to increase measured labor input. These patterns are repeated in the other economies and, for reasons of space, will, in general, not be commented upon further.[27]

6.IV SINGAPORE

Table 6.6 presents estimates of total factor productivity growth in Singapore. Although the late 1960s appear to have been a period of rapid productivity growth, these gains were largely lost during the 1970s and 1980s. With weighted capital input growing an average of 2.8 percent per annum faster than output and output per unit of effective labor input growing only 3.0 percent per annum, the total factor productivity residual for the aggregate economy averages a rather low 0.2 percent per annum. Interestingly, although the growth of capital input has slowed down over time (as the investment rate has stabilized around 40 percent of GDP), the growth of human capital has accelerated. While weighted labor input grew 2.1 percent more slowly than raw labor in the late 1960s, it rose 3.0 percent faster in the 1980s (due to large increases in the age and educational attainment of the workforce). The changing role of physical and human capital accumulation in sustaining growth is reflected in the decline in the growth of output per effective worker, which went from 9.7 percent in the late 1960s, to 3.0 percent in the 1970s, to 0.3 percent in the 1980s.

Table 6.6 Total factor productivity growth: Singapore

Time period	*Annual growth of:* *Output*	*Raw capital*	*Weighted capital*	*Raw labor*	*Weighted labor*	*TFP*	*Labor share*
Economy:							
66–70	0.130	0.119	0.134	0.054	0.033	0.046	0.503
70–80	0.088	0.122	0.140	0.050	0.058	−0.009	0.517
80–90	0.069	0.091	0.084	0.036	0.066	−0.005	0.506
66–90	**0.087**	**0.108**	**0.115**	**0.045**	**0.057**	**0.002**	**0.509**
Manufacturing: *							
70–80	0.103	0.123	0.130	0.086	0.089	−0.009	0.423
80–90	0.067	0.090	0.094	0.021	0.051	−0.011	0.385
70–90	**0.085**	**0.107**	**0.112**	**0.054**	**0.070**	**−0.010**	**0.404**

Note:
* Only covering firms recorded in the Census of Industrial Production.

Although the Singaporean national accounts do not estimate capital formation by sector, it is possible to make use of the annual report on the *Census of Industrial Production* (CIP), which contains data on fixed assets, capital formation, employment, value added, output, and production costs, to derive total factor productivity growth estimates for the manufacturing sector. The CIP is the principal source of information on Singaporean manufacturing and, along with departmental data on prices, forms the basis of Singapore's Index of Industrial Production (IIP), which in turn is the basis of the national accounts estimates of the constant price growth of manufacturing value added. I regret to inform the reader, however, that (i) 40 percent or more of the output recorded in the IIP is *undeflated*, i.e., for many manufacturing subsectors the index is simply the growth of nominal output; and (ii) the Singaporean national accounts use this *undeflated output index* as their measure of the constant price growth of manufacturing value added. Nevertheless, following the lead of the Singaporean statistical authorities, I use the IIP as my measure of the growth of value added in the CIP firms.[28]

As shown in Table 6.6, over the 1970 to 1990 period as a whole total factor productivity growth in Singaporean manufacturing averaged −1.0 percent per annum, a performance slightly below that of the aggregate economy during the same period. As in the case of the aggregate economy, the principal source of low productivity growth in Singaporean manufacturing is the combination of a slow growth of output per weighted worker[29] (1.5 percent per annum) and a rapid fall in output per unit of capital input (−2.7 percent per annum). Given the IIP's questionable (i.e., nonexistent) deflators, these estimates are clearly grossly inaccurate and are simply meant to show what can be accomplished at the sectoral level given the current state of Singaporean data.

6.V SOUTH KOREA

Table 6.7 below presents total factor productivity growth estimates for South Korea. Although South Korea exhibits even more capital deepening than Singapore, with output per unit of effective capital input falling 3.4 percent per annum, the larger labor share and faster growth of output per effective worker (3.9 percent) combine to give the economy a considerably larger total factor productivity residual (1.7 percent). Productivity growth in the Korean economy appears to have improved over time, with the average 2.5 percent growth of the 1980s well above the 0.8 and 1.0 percent growth experienced during the 1960s and 1970s, respectively. Turning to the industry level analysis,[30] we see that manufacturing has had the highest average level of productivity growth. Productivity growth in manufacturing fluctuates dramatically from period to period, but averages 2 to 3 percent per decade. Productivity growth in other industry and services, while also volatile, has improved on a decade-by-decade basis, with, in particular, a dramatic rise in other industry from −2.0 percent in the 1960s to 1.9 percent in the 1970s and 4.0 percent in the 1980s. Although the results are not reported in the table, I should note that I have estimated productivity growth in the subsectors of other industry and services, finding average total factor productivity growth rates (during the 1966–1990 period) of −1.1 percent in mining, 5.2 percent in electricity, gas, and water, 2.2 percent in construction, 3.4 percent in transport, storage and communications, and −0.1 percent in finance, insurance, real estate and business services (1970–1990).

6.VI TAIWAN

Table 6.8 presents total factor productivity growth estimates for Taiwan. With output per unit of weighted capital input falling 2.9 percent per annum, but output per effective worker rising 4.5 percent per annum (the fastest growth in this sample of four economies), Taiwan exhibits an average rate of productivity growth comparable to that of Hong Kong (2.6 percent). As Table 6.8 shows, the sectoral pattern of productivity growth in Taiwan is markedly different from that in Korea. In the Taiwanese economy manufacturing and other industry appear to be productivity laggards (with average growth rates of 1.7 and 1.4 percent, respectively), while services seems to have played the role of the productivity powerhouse (with an average growth of 3.5 percent per annum). Strong differences in the performance of Taiwan and Korea are also apparent within the more detailed sectors of "other industry." Thus, over the 1966–1990 period total factor productivity rose 3.7 percent per annum in Taiwanese mining (as compared with a decline of −1.1 percent per annum in Korea) and fell −0.2 percent per annum in Taiwanese electricity, gas, and water (as compared with rapid growth of 5.2 percent per annum in Korea). Elsewhere, the performance of the two

Table 6.7 Total factor productivity growth: South Korea

Time period	Annual growth of: *Output*	*Raw capital*	*Weighted capital*	*Raw labor*	*Weighted labor*	*TFP*	*Labor share*
Economy—excluding agriculture:							
60–66	0.077	0.069	0.070	0.062	0.072	0.005	0.690
66–70	0.144	0.167	0.194	0.095	0.103	0.013	0.690
70–75	0.095	0.121	0.118	0.052	0.055	0.019	0.661
75–80	0.093	0.158	0.178	0.040	0.052	0.002	0.694
80–85	0.085	0.102	0.099	0.031	0.047	0.024	0.729
85–90	0.107	0.105	0.108	0.061	0.072	0.026	0.739
66–90	**0.103**	**0.129**	**0.137**	**0.054**	**0.064**	**0.017**	**0.703**
Manufacturing:							
60–66	0.123	0.105	n.a.	0.115	0.115	0.013	0.504
66–70	0.204	0.205	n.a.	0.104	0.108	0.048	0.504
70–75	0.165	0.133	n.a.	0.084	0.088	0.053	0.477
75–80	0.127	0.207	n.a.	0.047	0.062	–0.007	0.503
80–85	0.106	0.075	n.a.	0.019	0.039	0.051	0.547
85–90	0.118	0.147	n.a.	0.069	0.082	0.008	0.572
66–90	**0.141**	**0.151**	**n.a.**	**0.063**	**0.074**	**0.030**	**0.521**
Other industry:							
60–66	0.127	0.188	n.a.	0.082	0.097	–0.012	0.537
66–70	0.176	0.258	n.a.	0.165	0.166	–0.033	0.537
70–75	0.085	0.104	n.a.	0.006	0.014	0.028	0.528
75–80	0.117	0.180	n.a.	0.051	0.071	0.010	0.672
80–85	0.089	0.131	n.a.	0.051	0.051	0.014	0.693
85–90	0.119	0.058	n.a.	0.040	0.050	0.066	0.674
66–90	**0.115**	**0.142**	**n.a.**	**0.058**	**0.067**	**0.019**	**0.624**
Services:							
60–66	0.059	0.052	0.048	0.040	0.054	0.007	0.804
66–70	0.118	0.142	0.163	0.079	0.089	0.014	0.804
70–75	0.083	0.124	0.131	0.043	0.042	0.022	0.782
75–80	0.073	0.140	0.139	0.033	0.045	0.009	0.796
80–85	0.074	0.107	0.113	0.034	0.047	0.016	0.828
85–90	0.099	0.096	0.098	0.060	0.069	0.025	0.821
66–90	**0.088**	**0.121**	**0.127**	**0.048**	**0.057**	**0.017**	**0.806**

Note: Other industry combines mining, electricity, gas & water, and construction. Services combines wholesale & retail trade, restaurants & hotels, transport, storage & communictions, finance insurance, real estate & business services, and community & social services.

economies was more similar, with productivity in Taiwan rising 1.5 percent per annum in construction (2.2 percent Korea), 4.7 percent per annum in transport, storage, and communications (3.4 percent Korea), and 0.2 percent per annum in finance, insurance, real estate, and business services (–0.1 percent Korea).

Table 6.8 Total factor productivity growth: Taiwan

Time period	*Annual growth of:* *Output*	*Aggregate capital*	*Weighted capital*	*Aggregate labor*	*Weighted labor*	*TFP*	*Labor share*
Economy—excluding agriculture:							
66–70	0.111	0.152	0.171	0.043	0.044	0.034	0.739
70–80	0.103	0.137	0.144	0.068	0.068	0.015	0.739
80–90	0.078	0.085	0.083	0.024	0.032	0.033	0.749
66–90	**0.094**	**0.118**	**0.123**	**0.046**	**0.049**	**0.026**	**0.743**
Manufacturing:							
66–70	0.168	0.207	0.214	0.078	0.075	0.031	0.558
70–80	0.121	0.145	0.146	0.100	0.101	0.001	0.566
80–90	0.072	0.078	0.079	0.012	0.021	0.028	0.613
66–90	**0.108**	**0.128**	**0.130**	**0.059**	**0.063**	**0.017**	**0.579**
Other industry:							
66–70	0.104	0.177	0.190	0.100	0.096	0.031	0.702
70–80	0.112	0.165	0.169	0.063	0.066	0.001	0.691
80–90	0.059	0.058	0.060	0.012	0.018	0.028	0.692
66–90	**0.088**	**0.122**	**0.127**	**0.048**	**0.051**	**0.014**	**0.695**
Services:							
66–70	0.087	0.145	0.162	0.018	0.023	0.040	0.828
70–80	0.094	0.134	0.139	0.049	0.050	0.029	0.827
80–90	0.090	0.094	0.092	0.036	0.038	0.039	0.777
66–90	**0.091**	**0.119**	**0.123**	**0.038**	**0.040**	**0.035**	**0.811**

Note: Other industry combines mining, electricity, gas & water, and construction. Services combines wholesale & retail trade, restaurants & hotels, transport, storage & communictions, finance insurance, real estate & business services, and community & social services.

It is important to note that part of the extraordinary performance of Taiwanese services is due to the unusual approach taken by the Taiwanese national accounts to the measurement of public sector output. Whereas most national accounts authorities deflate public sector output by the wages of different types of public sector employees, leading to an approximately zero growth in output per effective worker, the Taiwanese national accounts incorporate a "quality adjustment," allowing for the growing (unmeasurable) productivity of public sector employees. According to my estimates, between 1966 and 1990 output per effective worker in the Taiwanese public sector grew 4.4 percent per annum (6.6 percent per annum if one includes military personnel in the denominator).[31]

Table 6.9 provides additional total factor productivity measures for Taiwan, where I have adjusted the national accounts measure of public sector output to conform to the more standard (zero growth) deflation technique. As the reader can see, this adjustment has a large impact on the aggregate nonagricultural economy, where productivity growth falls to an average of

Table 6.9 Adjustment of public sector output: Taiwan

	Annual growth of:						
Time period	*Output*	*Aggregate capital*	*Weighted capital*	*Aggregate labor*	*Weighted labor*	*TFP*	*Labor share*
Economy—excluding agriculture and with adjustment of public sector output:							
66–70	0.092	0.152	0.171	0.043	0.044	0.015	0.739
70–80	0.103	0.137	0.144	0.068	0.068	0.015	0.739
80–90	0.073	0.085	0.083	0.024	0.032	0.028	0.749
66–90	**0.089**	**0.118**	**0.123**	**0.048**	**0.049**	**0.021**	**0.743**
Services—with adjustment of public sector output:							
66–70	0.050	0.145	0.162	0.018	0.023	0.003	0.828
70–80	0.094	0.134	0.139	0.049	0.050	0.029	0.827
80–90	0.082	0.094	0.092	0.036	0.038	0.031	0.777
66–90	**0.082**	**0.119**	**0.123**	**0.038**	**0.040**	**0.026**	**0.811**
Economy—excluding agriculture and official public sector:							
66–70	0.120	0.173	0.187	0.069	0.073	0.012	0.699
70–80	0.112	0.141	0.145	0.072	0.073	0.017	0.693
80–90	0.080	0.083	0.081	0.024	0.033	0.033	0.715
66–90	**0.100**	**0.122**	**0.125**	**0.052**	**0.056**	**0.023**	**0.072**

2.1 percent, and an even stronger impact on services, where productivity growth now appears to have averaged 2.6 percent (which nevertheless remains higher than manufacturing and other industry).[32] Table 6.9 also presents estimates for the nonpublic sector nonagricultural Taiwanese economy, which sidesteps these measurement issues by excluding the public sector from consideration.[33] I find that total factor productivity growth in the nonagricultural private sector Taiwanese economy averaged 2.3 percent per annum between 1966 and 1990. Interestingly, the two sets of estimates for the aggregate economy, both with and without the public sector, show a substantial improvement in productivity growth during the 1980s, which is reminiscent of the results for Korea.

Finally, I remind the reader that in the results reported above I have excluded the large conscript armies of Korea and Taiwan in measuring the growth of labor input in these economies on the grounds that the measured output of these military personnel (i.e., their wages) is a negligible proportion of total output. In the case of Taiwan, census sources provide information on the sex, age, and educational characteristics of military personnel. To analyze the sensitivity of my results, I make use of this information to incorporate military personnel into my estimates. As shown in Table 6.10, including military personnel raises the rate of total factor productivity growth in the aggregate economy by 0.3 percent, to an average of 2.9 percent per annum.[34] However, if one considers military personnel as part of public sector employment, then the quality adjustment of public sector output in the Taiwanese

Table 6.10 Inclusion of military personnel: Taiwan

	Annual growth of:						
Time period	*Output*	*Aggregate capital*	*Weighted capital*	*Aggregate labor*	*Weighted labor*	*TFP*	*Labor share*
			Economy				
Excluding agriculture, including military:							
66–90	0.094	0.118	0.122	0.039	0.041	**0.029**	0.709
Exc. agri., inc. mil., with adj. of public sector output:							
66–90	0.086	0.118	0.122	0.039	0.041	**0.021**	0.709
			Services				
Including military:							
66–90	0.091	0.119	0.122	0.029	0.029	**0.037**	0.738
Inc. military, with adj. of public sector output:							
66–90	0.077	0.119	0.122	0.029	0.029	**0.235**	0.738

national accounts appears to be even more exaggerated. Adjusting public sector output to standard deflation techniques yields an average total factor productivity growth rate of 2.1 percent (Table 6.10), i.e., the same as that reported earlier (excluding military personnel) in Table 6.9. Similar estimates for services yield average rates of productivity growth of 3.7 and 2.3 percent, which are only 0.2 percent greater and 0.3 percent less, respectively, than the comparable figures reported earlier above. In sum, the estimates for Taiwan are not extremely sensitive to the inclusion of military personnel, particularly once one adjusts the growth of public sector output to international norms. The impact of military personnel in Korea, where they constitute a much smaller percentage of the working population, should be even smaller.

6.VII COMPARISON WITH EARLIER RESEARCH

This paper is by no means the first rigorous study of total factor productivity growth in the East Asian NICs. Of these, by far the most heavily examined has been South Korea, where, as shown in Table 6.11, different studies have produced a wide range of estimates. A review of the elements underlying the differing results of these studies of the Korean economy can provide some insight into the choices regarding methodology and data selection made in this paper.

The highest estimate of total factor productivity growth in the Korean economy is provided by Christensen and Cummings [1981], who report a private sector growth rate of 4.1 percent for the period 1960–1973. Christensen and Cummings do not separate out the agricultural sector and, consequently, include land input in their measure of the capital stock, which

Table 6.11 Studies of total factor productivity growth: South Korea (annual rates of TFP growth)

	Period	*Economy*	*Manufacturing*
This study	1966–1990	1.7	3.0
Christensen and Cummings [1981]	1960–1973	4.1	n.a.
Kim and Park [1985]	1963–1982	2.7	n.a.
Pyo and Kwon [1991]	1960–1989	1.6	n.a.
Pyo, Kong, Kwon, and Kim [1991]	1970–1990	1.3	1.1
Moon, Jo, Whang, and Kim [1991]	1971–1989	n.a.	3.7
Dollar and Sokoloff [1990)	1963–1979	n.a.	6.1

Note: n.a. = Not applicable.

Table 6.12 Estimated composition of the Korean capital stock (billions of 1970 won)

	Nonresid. structures	*Producer durables*	*Residential structures*	*Nonfarm inventories*	*Farm inventories*	*Consumer durables*	*Land*
1969	168.6	252.0	933.3	298.1	113.1	118.8	3627.3
1973	1495.3	1305.0	1288.8	485.1	341.0	269.0	3632.5
Growth	15.6%	11.7%	2.3%	3.5%	7.9%	5.8%	0.0%

Source: Christensen and Cummings [1981, Table 7].

is summarized in Table 6.12. As the reader can see, land input and agricultural inventories accounted for 68 percent of Christensen and Cummings' measured capital stock in 1959, but only 45 percent in 1973. Thus, while their aggregate capital stock was growing by only 3.4 percent per annum, the components of greatest importance to the nonagricultural economy, i.e., nonresidential structures and equipment, were growing at rates well in excess of 10 percent per annum.[35] Christensen and Cummings' capital stock estimates, when disaggregated, would probably suggest a record of high productivity growth in agriculture and moderate productivity growth in the nonagricultural economy, which would be in keeping with the results reported in this paper.[36]

Kim and Park [1985] report a somewhat lower estimate of 2.7 percent total factor productivity growth for the aggregate Korean economy during the period 1963–1982. Like Christensen and Cummings, Kim and Park include agriculture and measures of inventories. As they extend their analysis further into the 1970s, however, they derive lower estimates of total factor productivity growth, as the rapidly growing stock of structures and equipment accounts for a growing share of the capital stock. Thus, they estimate total factor productivity growth rates of 4.0 percent for 1963–1972 and 1.5 percent for 1972–1982.[37]

Pyo and Kwon [1991] estimate rates of total factor productivity growth for the private sector Korean economy, 1.6 percent for the period 1960–1989, comparable to those found in this study. Pyo and Kwon also include agriculture and a measure of land input in their estimates. Like Park and Kim, Pyo and Kwon's estimates exhibit a downward trend, as the role of land input in the capital stock declines, finding rates of total factor productivity growth of 2.4 percent for 1960–1973 and 1.0 percent for 1973–1989. Despite the inclusion of land input, Pyo and Kwon's estimates for the 1960s are substantially below those of Kim and Park and Christensen and Cummings. This is largely due to the fact that Pyo and Kwon make use of very early estimates of hours of work, which show a rise of almost 30 percent in hours of work during the 1960–1963 period. Excluding this anomalous period, Pyo and Kwon estimate an average total factor productivity growth rate of 3.5 percent per annum during 1963–1973. In the estimates presented in this paper, I do not make use of these early hours data, assuming that hours of work were constant in the 1960s.[38]

Pyo, Kong, Kwon, and Kim [1993] estimate an aggregate rate of total factor productivity growth for the 1970–1990 period of 1.3 percent per annum. This study includes agriculture in the measure of output, but excludes both land and inventories from the capital stock measure. Consequently, Pyo, Kong, Kwon, and Kim record extremely rapid growth in the capital stock, in a manner similar to this paper.[39] Unlike this paper, however, they estimate a considerably lower share of labor, on the order of 53 percent, which explains their lower estimate of total factor productivity growth.[40] Pyo, Kong, Kwon, and Kim assume that the implicit labor income of each self-employed or unpaid worker is only one-quarter that of the average employee. In contrast, I assume that each self-employed or unpaid worker earns an implicit wage equal to that of an employee in the same sector with similar age, sex, and educational characteristics. In general, most studies of Korean productivity growth have been unwilling to make this one-for-one assumption and, consequently, have lower estimates of the share of labor.[41]

Turning to studies of the manufacturing sector alone, the lowest estimate here, 1.1 percent per annum for the period 1970–1990, is provided by Pyo, Kong, Kwon, and Kim [1993]. The difference between their estimate and the 2.6 percent per annum for the same period reported in this paper stems from Pyo, Kong, Kwon, and Kim's use of the Mining and Manufacturing Survey for data on employment in manufacturing. As compared with the census, the Mining and Manufacturing Survey, which is restricted to firms with five or more workers, reports about 1 percent per annum faster growth in labor input and only a very small number of self-employed and unpaid workers (implying only a small adjustment for implicit labor income). The faster growth in labor input and smaller labor share lead Pyo, Kong, Kwon, and Kim to estimate a considerably lower rate of total factor productivity growth.[42]

Moon, Jo, Whang, and Kim [1991] estimate a 3.7 percent rate of total factor productivity growth in manufacturing for the period 1971–1989. This study, however, does not include adjustments for the age, sex, or educational characteristics of the working population in its estimates of labor input. These adjustments contribute to about 1.3 percent per annum more rapid growth in labor input in my estimates for the period 1970–1990 which, when multiplied by a share of labor of about one-half, explains the bulk of the discrepancy between Moon, Jo, Whang, and Kim's results and those reported in this paper.[43]

Finally, Dollar and Sokoloff's [1990] study of Korean manufacturing arrives at the spectacular estimate of 6.1 percent total productivity growth per annum for the period 1963–1979. This study draws its output measures from the Mining and Manufacturing Survey.[44] During the period covered by the study, the output of the firms reported in the Mining and Manufacturing Survey grew some 2.5 percent faster per annum than the output for the manufacturing sector reported in the national accounts. I have repeatedly questioned the Korean national accounts authorities on this issue, and they steadfastly maintain that the Survey is not representative of the entire manufacturing sector. Apparently their adjustment of the survey data, using alternative sources, leads to a considerably lower estimate of the growth of the manufacturing sector. If one subtracts two and a half percent excess output growth from Dollar and Sokoloff's estimates, one arrives at an estimated total factor productivity growth rate of about three and a half percent per annum which, if further adjusted for labor weighting (not included in their study), would yield an estimate close to that reported in this paper.[45]

6.VIII SUMMARY AND CONCLUSIONS

Underlying the pervasive influence of the East Asian NICs on theoretical and policy-oriented research in the economics profession lies a common premise: that productivity growth in these economies, particularly in their manufacturing sectors, has been extraordinarily high. The results of this paper, as summarized in Table 6.13, suggest that this premise is largely incorrect.

Table 6.13 Average total factor productivity growth (percent per annum)

	Hong Kong (1966–1991)	*Singapore (1966–1990)*	*South Korea (1966–1990)*	*Taiwan (1966–1990)*
Economy *	2.3	0.2	1.7	2.1
Manufacturing #	n.a.	−1.0	3.0	1.7
Other industry	n.a.	n.a.	1.9	1.4
Services	n.a.	n.a.	1.7	2.6
Private sector	n.a.	n.a.	n.a.	2.3

Notes:
n.a. = Not available.
* In the case of Korea and Taiwan, agriculture is excluded.
# In the case of Singapore, the years are 1970–1990.

Over the past two and a half decades, productivity growth in the aggregate nonagricultural economy of the NICs ranges from a low of 0.2 percent in Singapore to a high of 2.3 percent in Hong Kong, whereas in manufacturing productivity growth ranges from a low of −1.0 percent in Singapore to a high of 3.0 percent in South Korea. For the purposes of comparison, Table 6.14 reproduces the results of two detailed cross-country studies of productivity growth, with methodologies similar to that used in this paper. As the reader can see, it is not particularly difficult to find either developed or less developed economies whose productivity performance, despite considerably slower growth of output per capita, has approximated or matched that of the NICs. While, with the exception of Singapore, productivity growth in the NICs is not particularly low, it is also, by postwar standards, not extraordinarily high.[46]

Table 6.15 helps the reader reconcile the moderate estimates of total factor productivity growth found in this paper with the towering record of output growth in the East Asian NICs. The table begins by presenting a "naive" prior estimate of total factor productivity growth in these economies, one based solely upon observation of the growth of output per capita, the statistic most frequently encountered in broad international data sets. Assuming that the analyst's prior was that all other ratios (e.g., participation, capital-output, etc.) had remained constant, the naive estimate of total factor productivity growth would be the labor share (believed to be, say, 0.6) times the growth of output per capita.[47] These, rather extraordinary, estimates of 3.4 to 4.1 percent per annum are presented on line (1) of the table. If, in addition, the analyst was aware that participation rates had risen in these economies, the naive estimate would be the labor share times the growth of output per worker, or, as shown on line (2) productivity growth rates of between 2.5 and 3.4 percent per annum. Refocusing the analyst's view on the nonagricultural sector (i.e., noting the slower growth of output per worker in that sector) and informing him/her about the unusual Taiwanese approach to the measurement of public sector output,[48] would lead to the estimates presented on line

Table 6.14 Comparative total factor productivity growth (percent per annum)

Country	*Period*	*Growth*	*Country*	*Period*	*Growth*
Canada	1960–1989	0.5	Brazil	1950–1985	1.6
France	1960–1989	1.5	Chile	1940–1985	0.8
Germany	1960–1989	1.6	Mexico	1940–1985	1.2
Italy	1960–1989	2.0	Brazil (M)	1960–1980	1.0
Japan	1960–1989	2.0	Chile (M)	1960–1980	0.7
United Kingdom	1960–1989	1.3	Mexico (M)	1940–1970	1.3
United States	1960–1989	0.4	Venezuela (M)	1950–1970	2.6

Note: M-manufacturing alone; developed economies are from Dougherty [1991]; less developed economies from Elias [1990].

Table 6.15 Reconciling naive and detailed estimates of productivity growth

	Hong Kong	*Singapore*	*South Korea*	*Taiwan*
(1) Naive estimate: $0.6(\hat{Q} - \hat{P})$	3.4%	4.1%	4.1%	4.0%
Adjustment for participation: $0.6(\hat{P} - \hat{L})$	−0.6%	−1.6%	−0.7%	−0.8%
(2) Naive estimate: $0.6(\hat{Q} - \hat{L})$	2.8%	2.5%	3.4%	3.3%
Focus on nonagricultural sector: $0.6[(\hat{Q}_{NA} - \hat{L}_{NA} - (\hat{Q} - \hat{L})]$	n.a.	n.a.	−0.4%	−0.4%
Adjustment of public sector output: $0.6(\hat{Q}_{adj} - \hat{Q}_{NA})$	n.a.	n.a.	n.a.	−0.3%
(3) Naive nonagricultural estimate: $0.6(\hat{Q}_{NA} - \hat{L}_{NA})$	2.8%	2.5%	3.0%	2.6%
(4) Using actual factor shares: $\overline{\Theta}_L(\hat{Q}_{NA} - \hat{L}_{NA})$	2.9%	2.2%	3.5%	3.2%
Weighting of labor: $\overline{\Theta}_L(\hat{L}_{NA} - \hat{H}_{NA})$	−0.3%	−0.6%	−0.7%	−0.2%
Capital deepening: $\overline{\Theta}_K(\hat{Q}_{NA} - \hat{C}_{NA})$	−0.1%	−1.0%	−0.8%	−0.8%
Weighting of capital: $\overline{\Theta}_K(\hat{C}_{NA} - \hat{K}_{NA})$	−0.1%	−0.3%	−0.2%	−0.1%
(5) Estimated total factor productivity growth	2.3%	0.2%	1.7%	2.1%

Notes: Circumflexes (^) denote logarithmic growth rates. Q, P, L, H, C, and K denote output, population, workers, weighted labor input, aggregate capital, and weighted capital input, respectively. The subscripts n.a. and adj. denote nonagricultural and 'adjusted.' $\overline{\Theta}_K$ and $\overline{\Theta}_L$ denote the average (interperiod) share of capital and labor, as in equation (3) earlier.

(3). Thus, in simply moving from the common international data on output per capita to country-specific data on output per worker in the nonagricultural sector, the analyst's naive (i.e., still assuming that other ratios remained constant) estimates of productivity growth would fall to between 2.5 to 3.0 percent per annum.

Line (4) of Table 6.15, which can be considered the starting point of the estimates in this paper, modifies the naive analysis to include the actual, estimated, share of labor. Since these shares are generally estimated to be above 0.6, the starting point of my analysis is somewhat above the figures on line (3). The table then shows the contribution of various factors to lowering this estimate. Weighting of labor input, i.e., taking into account changes in the age, sex, and educational composition of the workforce and adjusting for hours of work, lowers the productivity estimates by a little over half a percent in Singapore and South Korea, but by only a minimal amount in Hong Kong and Taiwan, where the common increases in educational attainment were offset by declining hours of work. With the exception of Hong Kong, capital deepening, i.e., the increase in the crude capital-output ratio brought about by the rapid rise in the investment to GDP ratio, contributes to about 1 percent per annum reduction in productivity growth. Weighting of capital input, i.e., most specifically placing a greater weight on the rapidly growing machinery stock,[49] has a slight downward effect in all four economies, with the largest effect being in Singapore, where the capital share was greatest.

As Table 6.15 readily shows, the results of this paper derive from a confluence of small effects, each serving to chip away at the performance of the NICs, with no one estimate, in particular, being essential to the argument. One might dispute the estimates for the impact of increases in educational attainment; one might dispute the weighting of capital; or one might dispute the adjustment of Taiwanese public sector output. And yet, one must recognize that participation rates have risen; that output per worker grew more slowly in the nonagricultural sector than in the aggregate economy; that the educational attainment of the working population has risen rapidly; and that investment, particularly in machinery, has skyrocketed. Each of these elements must be taken into account, and each serves to lower one's estimate of total factor productivity growth.[50] While some of these factors have no doubt been present in other economies, in the rapidly growing East Asian NICs they are all, probably fairly uniquely, congruently present.

The results of this paper should be heartening to economists and policymakers alike. If the remarkable postwar rise in East Asian living standards is primarily the result of one-shot increases in output brought about by the rise in participation rates, investment to GDP ratios, and educational standards and the intersectoral transfer of labor from agriculture to other sectors (e.g., manufacturing) with higher value added per worker, then economic theory is admirably well equipped to explain the East Asian experience. Neoclassical growth theory, with its emphasis on level changes in income and its well-articulated quantitative framework, can explain most of the difference between the performance of the NICs and that of other postwar economies.

APPENDIX: SOURCES

Hong Kong. Estimates of Gross Domestic Product 1966 to 1992, *Estimates of Gross Domestic Product 1961 to 1975*, and unpublished tabulations from the Hong Kong government[51] provided data on Gross Domestic Product (GDP) and Gross Fixed Capital Formation (GFCF) by asset type at current and constant 1980 market prices for the period 1961–1991.[52] Estimates of 1947–1960 investment by asset type were derived from data on retained imports of machinery and equipment, private construction expenditures and government capital expenditure published in *Hong Kong Statistics 1947–1967*, deflated to 1961 prices using the nonfood retail price index (the only price index available) and then linked to 1980 prices using the 61/80 deflators by asset type from the national accounts. Compensation of employees as a percentage of GDP for all years except 1966[53] were taken from current and historical issues of *Estimates of Gross Domestic Product*, data provided by the Hong Kong government, and the pilot national income survey of Hong Kong [Chang, *Report on the National Income Survey of Hong Kong, 1969*].

Estimates of the working population cross-tabulated by class of worker, sex, age, education, income, and hours of work were derived from published and unpublished census tabulations. For earlier years hours of work and relative incomes by worker characteristic were assumed to be constant at the levels reported in the 1971 and 1976 censuses, respectively, the earliest dates for which detailed data of each type were available.

Singapore. Singapore National Accounts 1987, Yearbook of Statistics Singapore 1991, and *Economic and Social Statistics Singapore 1960–1982* provided data on GDP and GFCF by asset type at current and constant 1968 and 1985 prices for the period 1960–1990. 1947–1959 investment in buildings and structures was estimated from data on the construction of one-family equivalent residential units and retained imports of cement (linked to 1985 prices using the overlap of these data with the 1960–1962 GFCF data) taken from the monthly issues of *Malayan Statistics*. Data on compensation of employees as a percentage of output at basic values (i.e., excluding commodity taxes) for the years 1973, 1978, 1983, and 1988 from the *Singapore Input-Output Tables* were taken as the (unadjusted) share of labor for those years, with values for other years interpolated or extrapolated (at constant levels), as necessary.

Estimates of the working population cross-tabulated by industry, class of worker, sex, age, education, and income were derived from the published and unpublished tabulations of the *Sample Household Survey 1966* and 1970, 1980, and 1990 censuses. The 1966 Sample Survey and 1970 Census provide little data on the income of workers.[54] Average incomes by worker characteristic, for use in computing the income weights for these years, were derived from the *Household Expenditure Survey 1972/1973* and *Labour Force Survey 1973*. Average hours of work by industry for 1972–1990 were taken from annual issues of the *Yearbook of Statistics*, with hours of work prior to 1972 assumed to be constant at the level reported in 1972.

South Korea. National Accounts 1990 and *National Accounts 1991* provided data on GDP and GFCF at current and constant 1985 prices for the period 1970–1990 (the "New System" accounts), while *National Income in Korea 1982* provided the same data (at 1975 constant prices) for the period 1953–1981 (the "Old System" accounts). Although the (revised) New System accounts should be superior to the Old System accounts in their measures of output and capital formation, they unfortunately follow the 1968 United Nations System of National Accounts (SNA) in classifying capital formation by industry of ownership, rather than by industry of use (as was the case in the Old System accounts, which followed the 1953 SNA). Provided that the ratio of ownership to use remains roughly constant over time, the New System accounts still provide a reasonable measure of the growth of capital input by industry. A problem arises, however, in linking the Old and New System accounts, when the change in definition induces a dramatic change in measured capital input by sector. To ameliorate this problem, I use the Old System accounts to measure the growth of capital and output by industry for the 1960–1975 period and the New System accounts (initializing the capital stock with the 1969 Old System values) for the period 1975–1990.[55] Measures of indirect taxes, and their distribution by type, were taken from the national accounts sources and the annual issues of the *Economic Statistics Yearbook*. Data on compensation of employees by economic sector are provided in *National Accounts 1990*. Since the Old System accounts do not provide data with similar detail, I assume that the share of labor by sector in 1960 and 1966 equalled the ratio estimated for 1970.

Estimates of the working population cross-tabulated by class of worker, sex, age, and education were derived from published census tabulations, supplemented with data from the *Economically Active Population Survey* (where this contained tabulations unavailable in the census). Incomes and hours of work by worker characteristic were estimated from the published tabulations of the *Occupational Wage Survey* for the period 1971–1990. For earlier years hours of work and relative income's by worker characteristic were assumed to be constant at the levels reported in 1971.[56]

Taiwan. Unpublished data provided by the Taiwanese government included information on capital formation and output in current and constant 1986 prices, as well as compensation of employees and indirect taxes. The publication *National Income in Taiwan Area of the Republic of China* summarizes much of these data. Estimates of the working population by class of worker, industry, sex, age and education were derived from English and Chinese language census sources.[57] Employee incomes by worker characteristic for the years 1976, 1980, and 1990 were estimated from the data tapes of the *Survey of Personal Income Distribution* (summarized in the publication of the same name), with labor force estimates prior to 1976 weighted with the relative wages of that year. Hours of work data from 1970 on were estimated from the results of the monthly labor force survey,[58] with hours of work for earlier years assumed to be constant at the levels reported in 1970.[59]

ACKNOWLEDGMENTS

This paper was supported by a grant from the MIT-NTU Collaboration Agreement and an NBER Olin Fellowship. I am indebted to Christina Paxon for providing data tapes on Taiwan, to Chan Wing-Kwong, Chao Bi-Tsyr, Ho Kun-Lon, Peter Kisler, John Sharon, and Woo Hyun-Sook for help in gathering and entering data, and, most especially, to Ho Veng-Si and Yang Shin-Kyu for extraordinary research assistance. Thanks are due the governments of Hong Kong, Singapore, South Korea, and Taiwan for providing unpublished data and answering queries.

NOTES

1 The Appendix provides a full description of sources. All growth rates reported in this paper are logarithmic, rather than geometric, growth rates. The labor force estimates for Korea and Taiwan exclude their large (predominantly conscript) armies, whose measured output (in the form of wages) is comparatively small. Section 6.VI examines the sensitivity of the results reported in this paper to the inclusion/exclusion of military personnel.

2 Changes in age-specific male participation rates are minimal in all four economies, while, with the exception of Hong Kong and Taiwan (where they declined gradually), reported nonagricultural hours of work have remained roughly constant. This suggests that the increase in participation is genuine, and not some statistical artifact.

3 This intersectoral transfer was greatest in Taiwan during the 1970s, when the difference in the growth of output per worker was 2.1 percent (5.6 versus 3.5), and in Korea during the 1980s, when the difference in growth rates was 1.7 percent (6.7 versus 5.0).

4 Defined as junior college and above in Korea and Taiwan and matriculation/A levels and above in Hong Kong and Singapore.

5 Developed independently by Christensen, Jorgenson, and Lau [1971, 1973], Griliches and Ringstad [1971], and Sargan [1971], and in recent years applied to the study of productivity by, for example, Jorgenson, Gollop, and Fraumeni [1987].

6 With similar restrictions on parameter values.

7 Table 6.15 summarizes the quantitative contribution of each factor toward reducing the estimate of productivity growth.

8 With the exception of Singapore, the NIC labor shares are about two-thirds, i.e., consistent with the standard prior on the elasticity of output with respect to labor. Singapore's share is, however, substantially lower. Raising its share to that of say Hong Kong, raises the estimate of average total factor productivity growth from 0.2 to 0.8 per annum, which, while certainly more respectable, is not

spectacular. In this regard, I should note that in order to bias my estimates in favor of Singapore I make use of the labor income share reported in the *Singapore Input-Output Tables*, which is substantially greater than that indicated by unpublished data on labor income provided to me by the Singaporean government.

9 This is not to say, however, that the measure of technical progress is independent of the quantity of factors, or the path of factor accumulation. Consider an isoquant that shifts in nonuniformly (i.e., in a non-Hicks-neutral fashion). In this case, the measured improvement in productivity will vary according to the capital-labor ratio of the economy, and the degree to which that capital-labor ratio changes during the period under analysis. If one estimates the production function, one can avoid this problem by describing the full movement of the surface, rather than simply decomposing changes along a particular path of factor accumulation.

One referee queried, if technological improvement led to an improvement in capital goods quality, and hence in a reduction in real capital goods prices, would the increase in capital goods productivity show up in the growth accounting residual? If the capital goods are imported, then the answer is, quite appropriately, no. However, if the capital goods are domestically produced, then if the price indices for capital goods production are quality adjusted, then so are the quantity indices. Thus, the increase in quality in the capital goods sector would show up as a rise in value added per unit of input in that sector and, when aggregated with other sectors, in the aggregate economy. In this regard, it is interesting to note that between 1966 and 1990 the ratio of the capital goods to GDP deflator rose by 1.2 percent per annum in Hong Kong, but fell by −0.2 percent per annum in Singapore, −1.8 percent per annum in South Korea, and −1.1 percent per annum in Taiwan. The decline in relative capital goods prices in South Korea and Taiwan partially offsets the reduction in capital returns induced by the approximately 3 percent per annum rise in the capital-output ratio in those economies.

10 For example, Kim and Park [1985, table 5–13] estimate that during the 1960s and 1970s land input on average accounted for only about 4 percent of Korean nonagricultural nonresidential income.

I also do not include inventories. I have found that the "changes in stocks" series published by most of the NICS are either (i) outright gross fabrications used to conceal large discrepancies between the production and expenditure accounts; or (ii) based upon the flimsiest of data. In Young [1992] I made use of unpublished stocks data provided to me by the Singaporean and Hong Kong governments. Problems with the existence of accurate stocks data for the other economies, combined with a growing suspicion as to the accuracy of the Hong Kong numbers, have led to me to drop consideration of stocks from the analysis.

11 The depreciation rates are based upon Hulten and Wykoff [1981, table 2] and Jorgenson and Sullivan's [1981, table 1] estimates of geometric depreciation rates for detailed asset types (e.g., trucks, autos, mining machinery, service machinery, etc.). I derive the depreciation rate for each of the five broad asset types used in my analysis as the unweighted average of the depreciation rates of the detailed asset types likely to be found in each industry. This approach is crude, but the results are, in any case, not sensitive to moderate adjustments in the depreciation rates (see, for example, Young [1992]).

12 I cumulate the national accounts investment at constant prices of the date of the wealth survey. The gross values reported in the wealth surveys represent, similarly, the product of a purchase price times a price index reflecting asset inflation up to the time of the survey. The price indices for the wealth surveys are drawn from sources similar to those used by the national accounts, e.g., wholesale price

indices, and, when reported, as in the Korean national wealth surveys, roughly parallel the national accounts deflators for similar asset types. Thus, the incongruities noted below seem to be more related to differences in the original current price values recorded in the surveys and national accounts, rather than differences in the deflators used to adjust these values to a common standard.

13 In principle, because of scrapping, the wealth survey gross assets should actually be less than the cumulative national accounts investment.

14 The values for each survey and the cumulative investment are converted to common benchmarks using the national accounts deflators.

15 In essence, if one believes the wealth surveys one has to discard most of the information in the national accounts. I tend to favor the national accounts, since the flow values recorded there are at least subject to some consistency checks (e.g., between the expenditure and production accounts), while the stock values reported in the wealth surveys are basically answers to the open-ended question: what assets do you have, and what did you pay for them?

16 Specifically,

$$\text{where } C_j(0) = \sum_{i=0}^{\infty} I^j_{-i-1}(1-\delta_j)^i = \sum_{i=0}^{\infty} I^j_0(1+g_j)^{-i-1}(1-\delta_j)^i = I^j_0/(g_j+\delta_j),$$

where I^j_0 is the first year of investment data for asset j, δ_j is the depreciation rate for asset j, and g_i is the average growth of investment in asset j in the first five years of the investment series.

An exception is Singaporean manufacturing, where I use the Net Fixed Assets reported in the Census of *Industrial Production* (CIP) to initialize the capital stock in 1969. Prior to 1969 the coverage of the CIP was changing rapidly. Thus, cumulating the annual investment flows prior to that date provides a poor measure of the capital stock of the firms covered by the survey in later periods.

17 Singapore did not produce cement prior to 1961. See the *Malayan Digest of Statistics*.

18 The estimates using retained imports of cement are, admittedly, rather crude. These data, however, suggest a large surge in construction activity in the mid-1950s (which I have not been able to corroborate), with the real value of investment in durable structures in the mid-1950s exceeding the levels recorded in the early-1960s. Although I feel these data are somewhat suspect, I make use of them in order to raise the value of my initial 1966 capital stock estimates, thus biasing the results in favor of Singapore.

19 To analyze the sensitivity of the results to the value of capital used to initialize the series, I also tried initial values of (i) zero capital and (ii) double the capital implied by the procedure described above. The impact of these (substantial) adjustments on average total factor productivity growth during the 1966–1990 period was (–0.1 percent, +0.1 percent) per annum in Hong Kong, Singapore, and Taiwan, and (–0.4 percent, +0.3 percent) per annum in Korea (where the pre-1966 investment series is shorter).

20 Hours of work data are drawn from other, non-Census, sources.

21 For example, 25,000 housing units in the case of the 1989 Singaporean labor force survey and less than 15,000 households in the case of the 1980 Korean economically active population survey.

22 In fact, during the period emphasized in this paper (1966–1990) the labor force surveys actually imply faster growth in the nonagricultural working population in both South Korea and Taiwan (the labor force surveys for Hong Kong and Singapore began in the mid- to late 1970s and hence do not cover the entire period of analysis).

23 I should note that while I make this adjustment to value added for the purposes of measuring income shares, I use value added *at market prices* to measure the growth of output, under the assumption that these prices better reflect the relative scarcities and values of the component products of national output. In this sense, my approach parallels that of the national accounts, where income is typically measured at factor cost and output at market prices.

24 This rescaling using the national accounts data corrects for underreporting of income on the part of workers and, also, adjusts for labor taxes and nonmonetary compensation, all of which form a part of the cost of labor input from the point of view of the producer.

25 This equation can be modified to take into account taxes and depreciation allowances, and one can also relax the assumption of perfect foresight and incorporates measure of the "expected" change in asset prices. These adjustments, however, are relatively minor compared with the basic concept embodied in equation (8); i.e., that assets with high depreciation rates and declining relative prices (such as machinery and equipment) should command comparatively higher rentals and, by extension, factor shares. In the case of the NICs, where machinery and equipment is one of the most rapidly growing elements of the capital stock, this raises the growth rate of the aggregate (weighted) capital stock.

26 See footnote 25.

27 Tables detailing the impact of each adjustment (age, sex, etc.) in each subperiod for the four economies are available upon request from the author.

28 Although much of manufacturing output is undeflated, the reader should not jump to the conclusion that the IIP overstates the growth of the manufacturing sector. While the undeflated items include many products whose prices have probably been increasing (e.g., printing and transport equipment), they also include many electronics products, whose prices have undoubtedly been declining. Interestingly, at one point the Singaporean statistical authorities, who were concerned about their methodology, sought the assistance of the Japanese on this issue, but were assured that nondeflation of manufacturing output was also common practice in that economy (!).

29 Since the CIP does not contain any information on the age or educational characteristics of the workers in the firms surveyed, I use census data to adjust for the age and educational characteristics of the workforce under the assumption that the workers in the CIP shared the same age and education characteristics as similar sex persons reported as manufacturing workers in the census.

30 The Korean national accounts include data on capital formation by asset type and by industry, but not by asset type *and* industry. After removing residential investment from service investment (where all residential investment would occur), I estimate each sector's capital stock by cumulating the (indifferentiated) industry investment, using the average nonresidential depreciation rate in the economy (as computed from the asset type data). I then add residential capital back into the service sector. Since I am only able to differentiate capital input in services (where it is subdivided into residential and nonresidential capital), I only compute weighted capital measures for that sector.

31 The reason the Taiwanese national accounts make this adjustment is fairly obvious. With public sector employment stagnating and output per worker in all other sectors of the economy growing rapidly, backward extrapolation (at constant prices of the mid-1980s) using the standard deflation technique implies that the share of the government in total output was about 50 percent in 1966. A similar problem exists in the U.S. national accounts, but is ameliorated by the fact that public sector employment is expanding rapidly, while the growth of the other sectors of the economy is more gradual than in Taiwan. The solution I

employ (in Table 6.9), is to estimate the growth of aggregete output as a Tornqvist index of the growth of the one-digit ISIC sectors (plus the public sector), with the (chain-linked) current price share of each sector taken as its weight. This approach is analogous to that used by Griliches and Jorgenson [1967] for the measurement of the output of the U.S. economy.

32 The reader may note that, during the 1980s the measures of output growth reported in Tables 6.8 and 6.9 are identical. The Taiwanese national accounts exaggerate the growth of public sector output in every period, which should lower one's estimate of the growth rate of output. During the 1980s, however, the Tornqvist weighting of the other one-digit ISIC sectors cancels this reduction.

33 This approach is not entirely satisfactory either, since the public sector provides many unpriced services (e.g., roads and bridges) to the private sector. Variations across economies and across time in the quantity of capital and labor services provided (free of charge) by the public sector could potentially bias estimates of private sector productivity

34 The reader may note that including military personnel lowers slightly the estimated share of labor. This follows from the fact that including the military lowers the ratio of the self-employed to the employed in the economy, implying (for a given aggregate wage bill) a lower implicit wage for the self-employed. The growth of weighted capital also varies between Tables 6.9 and 6.10. Different shares of labor produce different estimates of residual capital income, which changes the estimate of $r(T)$ (equation (8) earlier) and, by extension, the weights assigned to each capital good.

35 According to Kim and Park's [1985, Tables 5–3 and 5–12] estimates, while land input accounted for an average of 87 percent of tangible fixed assets in agriculture during the period 1961–1981, it accounted for only 16 percent of similar assets in nonagricultural nonresidential business.

Unlike this paper, Christensen and Cummings also include consumer durables and nonfarm inventories in their measure of the capital stock. As noted in Section 6.II, I have found the inventory series published in these economies to be largely fictional. In the case of Christensen and Cummings' estimates, the ratio of nonfarm inventories to value added in manufacturing and wholesale and retail trade (at constant prices) falls from 1.01 in 1959 to 0.28 in 1973, i.e., a 9 percent per annum decline in the capital output ratio.

36 I should note that Christensen and Cummings make use of the 1968 National Wealth Survey to initialize their capital stock estimates, using the flow values of the national accounts to cumulate forward and backward. This choice is fortuitous. If, instead, they had used the 1977 National Wealth Survey to initialize their estimates and cumulated backwards, they would have found that, for most depreciation rates, the stock of transport equipment was negative before the early 1970s, since the gross investment in transport equipment reported in the national accounts during the years 1975–1977 alone exceeds the net stock of transport equipment at the end of 1977 as reported in the 1977 wealth survey. As noted in Section 6.II, the stock values reported in the various national wealth surveys are completely incompatible with the flow values of the national accounts.

37 Of the difference, 1.4 percent is due to the more rapid growth in factor and 1.1 percent to the slower growth of output during the latter period.

38 Pyo and Kwon draw upon the *Korean Statistical Yearbook* [KSY] for hours of work estimates for 1960–1962 and the Economically Active Population Survey [EAPS] for hours of work thereafter. Between 1960 and 1962 the Ministry of Home Affairs' Labour Force Survey estimated hours of work. In mid-1962 the

survey was transferred to the Economic Planning Board, where a new methodology was developed, and the survey was renamed the EAPS. The hours of work reported in the 1960–1961 editions of the KSY are drawn from the Labour Force Survey, while the hours reported in the 1962 edition are from the end-of-year 1962 EAPS. Together with the 1963 EAPS, these date imply a 13 percent rise in private sector hours of work in 1961–1962, and a further rise of 15 percent in 1963 [Pyn and Kwon 1991, table 6]. While GDP grew 9 percent in 1963, the growth of output during 1962 was only 2 percent. Furthermore, subsequent changes in hours of work (in the EAPS) are all quite gradual. It seems highly likely that these early increases are simply a statistical artifact born of linking differing surveys (the increase between 1962 and 1963, drawn consistently from the EAPS, is due to the fact that the 1962 data reported in the KSY concern only the end of the year, when hours of work are seasonally low in agriculture, whereas the 1963 data from the EAPS cover the full year).

39 In both studies mentioned above, Pyo and his coauthors make use of the national wealth surveys to estimate the capital stock. However, rather than selecting any particular year to initialize the series, they, instead, endogenously determine which depreciation rate (for net capital stock) and disposal rate or gross capital stock) is necessary to reconcile the stock values of the national wealth surveys with the flow values of the national accounts. In practice, this requires that depreciation disposal rates are substantially negative in one period (say when linking the 1968 and 1977 wealth surveys) and substantially positive in the next (say when linking the 1977 and 1988 wealth surveys) [Pyo, Kwon, and Kim 1993, p. 117]. In essence, this amounts to a rejection of the information in the national accounts in favor of the wealth surveys. As it so happens, this (consistent) approach yields estimates of capital stock growth comparable to those found in my analysis. As noted earlier, the stock values reported in the wealth surveys are incompatible with the flow values in the national accounts. The overall growth in the capital stock implied by the two sources, is, however, roughly the same.

40 Despite the great difference in factor shares, their estimates are only slightly below mine. This is because they draw upon the Establishment Survey for their measure of labor input in the nonagricultural nonmanufacturing sectors, estimating much slower growth in this factor of production. The Establishment Survey, however, is an unscaled survey biased heavily toward manufacturing, with minimal coverage of other sectors. Thus, the 1970 Survey reported that there were only 1 million workers (in an economy with 31 million people), of which 640,000 were in manufacturing (see *Yearbook of Labour Statistics* [1971]). This survey focuses on the distribution of firm sizes, and was not designed to provide estimates of the aggregate number of workers. In Pyo and Kwon [1991] some of the same authors made use of the Economically Active Population Survey, which is the scaled labor force survey (whose results parallel the census). In earlier years, however, this source does not provide the detailed breakdown of employment by industry sought by Pyo, Kong, Kwon, and Kim in their 1993 analysis.

41 Christensen and Cummings [1981, Table 3] use the one-for-one assumption for the self-employed and a four-to-one assumption for unpaid family workers, estimating an average labor share in the private sector economy of about 64 percent. Kim and Park [1985, table 4–1] use a one-for-one imputation, adjusting, however, for wages by firm size. Since, most nonwage labor is in smaller firms, where reported wages are considerably lower, this lowers the estimated share of labor in nonresidential business to an average of 60 percent of national income (i.e., following Denison's [1979]) methods, not counting depreciation as part of factor

income). Pyo and Kwon [1991, table 4], drawing upon the estimates of Kim and Park, but including depreciation in factor income, arrive at an average share of labor in the private sector economy of 51 percent. I have experimented with adjustments for implicit wages in Korea based upon firm size. I did not include these adjustments, however, because I found that the substantial impact of firm size adjustments on the labor share was largely dependent upon the relatively low wages of paid workers in firms with less than ten employees. It is unclear, however, whether these low wages reflect the low marginal product of such workers or, instead, an implicit investment by the worker in the capital of the small firm.

42 Pyo, Kong, Kwon, and Kim also make use of data in the *Occupational Wage Survey* on worker characteristics, hours, and incomes to weight by age, sex, and education, which adds about 2.3 percent per annum to their measure of the growth of labor input. The *Occupational Wage Survey* is not, however, a balanced sample. For my estimates I use census data to establish the characteristics of the working population, drawing on the *Occupational Wage Survey* for data on average hours and incomes by worker characteristic, under the assumption that the sample is more representative within cross-tabulated cells. My adjustments add 1.3 percent per annum to the growth of labor input during the 1970–1990 period, or 1.0 percent lass than Pyo, Kong, Kwon, and Kim.

43 Moon, Jo, Whang, and Kim also report, separately, adjustments for the characteristics of workers and the quality of capital as a means of explaining total factor productivity growth. After these adjustments, their residual amounts to only 0.6 percent per annum. These adjustments, however, use an unusual methodology, e.g., the productivity of capital equipment is assumed to be inversely related to its age, and are not comparable to the weighting procedures used in this paper.

44 Dollar and Sokoloff actually make use of the Korean output data reported in the United Nations' Yearbook of Industrial Statistics, which, however, is drawn from the Mining and Manufacturing Survey.

45 Interestingly, the discrepancy between the Survey and the National Accounts largely disappears during the 1980s. It is possible that the earlier inconsistency stems from improvements in the Survey coverage. During the late 1960s and early 1970s, if one benchmarks the capital stock using the net fixed assets reported in one survey year and then cumulates investment, the resulting estimated capital stock is invariably less than the net fixed capital stock reported in a later year. During the 1980s, however, the annual net fixed capital and investment series are broadly consistent. Even if one wishes to restrict one's analysis to the survey firms alone, changes in survey coverage make estimation of the capital stock (which no longer depends upon flow values of investment) quite difficult. I should note that changes in survey coverage are a typical problem in the NICs, e.g., in the Singaporean Survey of Industrial Production, and that the national accounts in those countries make adjustments for this. In the case of my estimates of Singaporean manufacturing, I have restricted my analysis to the period in which the survey coverage appears to have been stable.

With regard to the other NICs, the best study, by far, is Tsao's [1982] analysis of Singapore, which estimates an average total factor productivity growth rate for the economy as a whole of −0.3 percent per annum during the 1966–1980 period and an average rate of −1.2 percent per annum for 28 manufacturing industries between 1970–1979. My earlier estimates for Hong Kong and Singapore [Young 1992] are completely superceded by the numbers reported in this paper, which make use of additional unpublished census and national accounts data.

46 In this regard it is interesting to note that Lau and Kim [1994], using an

econometric approach to the study of productivity growth, find that productivity growth in the NICs over the past few decades was not significantly different from zero.

47 Recall that total factor productivity growth is simply the weighted average of the growth of output per unit of labor and output per unit of capital.

48 See Section 6.VI.

49 See footnote 25 above.

50 In fact, as can be seen from the literature review in Section 6.VII, some estimates of these effects far exceed my own.

51 The 1961–1975 GDP estimates lacked several components introduced in the later series (e.g., adjustment for the profit margins of real estate developers). The data provided by the Hong Kong government allowed me to adjust the old series.

52 The Hong Kong national accounts measure of GFCF includes the transfer (i.e., transactions) cost of (used and new) buildings and an adjustment for the profit margins of private real estate developers. I exclude the transfer cost from my measures of investment and capital, but include the margins of real estate developers (which I distribute across different types of private sector construction in proportion to their value).

53 Where the value was taken as the average of the 1961 and 1971 percentage shares.

54 The 1966 Sample Survey collected some data on the employee income of heads of households, but the published tabulations only cross tabulate this with occupation, which is of little use in estimating the full array by industry, sex, age, and education.

55 For the analysis of the aggregete nonagricultural economy, where the distinction between user and owner is less significant, I use the Old System for 1960–1970 and the New System (initialized with the Old System values of 1969) for 1970–1990.

56 Both the Economically Active Population Survey and the Monthly Wage Survey (reported in the *Yearbook of Labour Statistics*) contain data on hours of work (in the former case extending back to the early 1960s). The hours of work data reported by both sources, however, are uncorrelated with movements in output (and with each other), which is not the case with the occupational wage survey, which also provides considerably greater detail. In any case, no source shows any substantial trend in nonagricultural hours of work since 1966.

57 Since the national accounts data cover only the "Taiwan Area," I excluded those listed as working in Fujian province from my estimates of the working population.

58 Most recently published in the *Yearbook of Manpower Statistics*, but previously appearing in publications such as the *Monthly Bulletin of Labor Statistics*.

59 The labor force survey extends hack 1966 (the beginning of my analysis), the reported hours of work data are in extremely crude categories (e.g., "49 hours or more"), which makes estimation of average hours of work difficult. For 1970, hours of work by detailed category are only available for the second half of the year. For the purposes of estimating changes in hours of work between 1970 and 1980, I link these data to 1980 data for the latter half of the year. I should note that the industry level earnings survey has, historically, also produced data on hours of work, reported, for example, in the *Yearbook of Earnings and Productivity Statistics* and in the *Taiwan Statistical Data Book*. These data, however, have been subject to enormous revisions, as the survey was expanded and industry definitions were changed. It is difficult to construct a consistent series from this source.

REFERENCES

Bank of Korea, *Economic Statistics Yearbook*, (Korea: Bank of Korea), annual issues.

——, *National Accounts 1991* (Korea: Bank of Korea, 1991).

——, *National Accounts 1990* (Korea: Bank of Korea, 1990).

——, *National Income in Korea 1982* (Korea: Bank of Korea, 1982).

Bishop, Yvonne M. M., Stephen E. Fienberg, and Paul M. Holland, *Discrete Multivariate Analysis* (Cambridge, MA: MIT Press, 1975).

Chang, E. R., *Report on the National Income Survey of Hong Kong* (Hong Kong: Government Printer, 1969).

Christensen, Laurits K., and Diane Cummings, "Real Product, Real Factor Input, and Productivity in the Republic of Korea, 1960–1973," *Journal of Development Economics*, VIII (1981), 285–302.

Christensen, Laurits R., Dale W. Jorgenson, and Lawrence J. Lau, "Conjugate Duality and the Transcendental Logarithmic Production Function," *Econometrica*, XXXIX (1971), 255–56.

Christensen, Laurits R, Dale W. Jorgenson, and Lawrence J. Lau, "Transcendental Logarithmic Production Frontiers," *Review of Economics and Statistics*, LV (1973), 28–45.

Denison, Edward F., *Accounting for Slower Economic Growth* (Washington, DC: The Brookings Institution, 1979).

Dollar, David, and Kenneth Sokoloff, "Patterns of Productivity Growth in South Korean Manufacturing Industries, 1963–1979," *Journal of Development Economics*, XXXIII (1990), 309–27.

Dougherty, John C., "A Comparison of Productivity and Economic Growth in the G-7 Countries, Ph.D. thesis, Harvard University, 1991.

Elias, Victor J., *Sources of Growth: A Study of Seven Latin American Economies* (San Francisco, CA: Institute for Contemporary Studies Press, 1990).

Griliches, Zvi, and Dale W. Jorgenson, "The Explanation of Productivity Change," *Review of Economic Studies*, XXXIV (July 1967), 249–80.

Griliches, Zvi, and V. Ringstad, *Economies of Scale and the Form of the Production Function* (Amsterdam: North-Holland Publishing Company, 1971).

Hong Kong, Census and Statistics Department, *Hong Kong Statistics 1947–1967* (Hong Kong: Government Printer, 1969).

——, *Estimates of Gross Domestic Product 1961 to 1975* (Hong Kong: Government Printer, 1977).

——, *Estimates of Gross Domestic Product 1966 to 1992* (Hong Kong: Government Printer, 1993).

Hulten, Charles R., and Frank C. Wykoff, "The Measurement of Economic Depreciation," *Depreciation, Inflation, and the Taxation of Income from Capital*, Charles R. Hulten, ed. (Washington, DC: Urban Institute Press, 1981).

Jorgenson, Dale W., Frank M. Gollop, and Barbara M. Fraumeni, *Productivity and U.S. Economic Growth* (Cambridge, MA: Harvard University Press, 1987).

Jorgenson, Dale W., and Martin A. Sullivan, "Inflation and Corporate Capital Recovery," *Depreciation, Inflation, and the Taxation of Income from Capital*, Charles R. Hulten, ed. (Washington, DC: Urban Institute Press, 1981).

Kim, Kwang-suk, and Joon-kyung Park, *Sources of Economic Growth in Korea: 1963–1982* (Seoul: Korea Development Institute, 1985).

Lau, Lawrence J., and Jong-il Kim, "The Sources of Economic Growth of the East Asian Newly Industrializing Countries," *Journal of the Japanese and International Economies*, VIII (1994), 235–71.

Moon, Hee-waa, Byung-tahk Jo, Ihn-ho Whang, and Kyung-buhm Kim, *Total Factor*

Productivity in Korea: An Analysis of 27 Manufacturing Industries (Seoul: Korea Productivity Center, 1991).

Pyo, Hak-kil, and Ho-young Kwon, "Estimation of Real Factor Input and Factor Productivity in the Korean Private Sector," *Korean Economic Journal*, XXX (1991), 147–94.

Pyo, Hak-kil, Byung-ho Kong, Ho-young Kwon, and Eun-ja Kim, *An Analysis of the Causes of Growth and Productivity by Industry for the Republic of Korea, 1970–1990* (Seoul: Korean Economics Research Institute, 1993).

Republic of China, Council for Economic Planning and Development, *Taiwan Statistical Data Book* (Republic of China: Council for Economic Planning and Development), annual issues.

Republic of China Directorate-General of Budget, Accounting and Statistics, *Monthly Bulletin of Labor Statistics, Republic of China*, monthly issues.

——, *National Income in Taiwan Area of the Republic of China*, annual issues.

——, *Report on the Survey of Personal Income Distribution in Taiwan Area of the Republic of China*, annual issues.

——, *Yearbook of Earnings and Productivity Statistics, Taiwan Area, Republic of China*, annual issues.

——, *Yearbook of Manpower Survey Statistics. Taiwan Area, Republic of China*, annual issues.

——, *1988 National Wealth Survey of Taiwan Area of the Republic of China*. Republic of Korea, Economic Planning Board, *Korea Statistical Yearbook*, annual issues.

——, *National Wealth Survey of Korea*, 1968, 1977, and 1987 issues. Republic of Korea, Ministry of Labour, *Report on Occupational Wage Survey*, annual issues.

——, *Yearbook of Labour Statistics*, annual issues. Republic of Korea, National Statistical Office, *Annual Report on the Economically Active Population Survey*, annual issues.

Sargen, J. D., "Production Functions," *Qualified Manpower and Economic Performance*, P. R. G. Layard, J. D. Sargen, M. Eager, and D. J. Jones, eds. (London: Penguin Press, 1971).

Singapore, Department of Statistics, *Economic and Social Statistics Singapore 1960–1982* (Singapore: National Printers, 1983).

——, *Report on the Household Expenditure Survey 1972/1973* (Singapore: National Printers, 1974).

——, *Report on the Labour Force Survey* (Singapore: National Printers), various issues.

—— , *Singapore Input-Output Tables* (Singapore: National Printers), 1978, 1983, and 1988 issues.

——, *Singapore National Accounts 1987* (Singapore: National Printers, 1988).

——, *Yearbook of Statistics Singapore* (Singapore: National Printers), annual issues.

Singapore, Registrar of Malayan Statistics, *Malayan Statistics* (Singapore: Government Printer, monthly issues.

Singapore, Economic Development Board, *Report on the Census of Industrial Production* (Singapore: National Printers), annual issues.

Singapore, Ministry of National Development, *Singapore Sample Household Survey 1966* (Singapore: National Printers, n.d.).

Taso, Yuan, "Growth and Productivity in Singapore: A Supply Side Analysis," Ph.D. thesis. Harvard University, 1982.

Young, Alwyn, "A Tale of Two Cities: Factor Accumulation and Technical Change in Hong Kong and Singapore," *NBER Macroeconomics Annual 1992*, Olivier J. Blanchard and Stanley Fischer, eds. (Cambridge, MA: The MIT Press, 1992).

——, "Lessons from the East Asian NICs: A Contrarian View," *European Economic Review*, XXXVIII (1994), 964–73.

7

THE TOTAL FACTOR PRODUCTIVITY DEBATE

Determinants of Economic Growth in East Asia

Edward K. Y. Chen

7.1 EXPLAINING THE EAST ASIAN ECONOMIC MIRACLE

In the past three decades, economic success in East Asia has been by all standards remarkable. Hyper-growth (Chen 1979) first occurred in the Four Little Dragons or the Asian newly industrialised economies (NIEs: Hong Kong, Taiwan, Singapore and South Korea), then in the ASEAN-4 (Thailand, Malaysia, Indonesia and, to some extent, the Philippines) and more recently in China and other transitional economies. Earlier in the 1950s and 1960s, it was Japan which started this hyper-growth trend. The economic success of this group of Northeast and Southeast Asian economies has been told and retold. There have also been many attempts to offer explanations for the East Asian success or 'miracle'. A recent attempt is that by the World Bank (1993) which contains an elaboration on its earliest assertion of the importance of 'getting the prices right'. This neo-classical view of the World Bank, while supported by a large number of mainstream economists, has been criticised by revisionists who argue that the role of government is significant (Wade 1990).

There is now a general consensus that the most important reason for East Asian economic success is the adoption of an export-oriented industrialisation strategy. Other developing economies got trapped because of their persistent indulgence in import substitution. But the more important question is why these East Asian economies managed to implement export-oriented industrialisation so successfully Since these economies are at an earlier stage of economic development, they could not possibly have a competitive edge over industrialised or other more advanced developing countries in manufactured products.

The success story of East Asian economies has been used both by protagonists and by opponents of the neo-classical school. The neo-classical writers cite

Source: *Asian-Pacific Economic Literature*, Vol. 11(1), May 1997.

examples of the *laissez-faire* policy of Hong Kong and the liberalisation and deregulation policies undertaken by other Asian NIEs. The revisionists argue that economic success in East Asia is based on active and market-friendly intervention policies, particularly in the cases of Taiwan and South Korea (Amsden 1989; Wade 1990).

Adopting the right policies is, however, only one necessary condition for economic success. The sufficient condition is an institutional framework which favours the implementation of such policies and change of policies at the right time. Why did the Indian government not change its import substitution policy after years of failures while in Taiwan a change of policy from import substitution to export orientation happened after a mild economic setback in the early 1960s? There must be reasons over and above the different size of the two economies. Institutional factors such as culture and political structure could have played an important part. There is a considerable literature on the importance of Confucianism and a developmental state in the economic development of East Asia. Cultural factors are also given an important place in the New Institutional Economics (North, 1994).

It is not the objective of this paper to probe into these non-economic issues. It should be pointed out that while Confucianism has existed in East Asia for a few thousand years and that developmental states do exist from time to time in many parts of the developing world, the East Asian economic 'miracle' is a recent event. Why did the 'miracle' not happen earlier? Chen (1988) attempts to provide an answer to this question by arguing, first, that an interaction between economic and non-economic factors in some positive way is necessary and, second, that such a model cannot be universally true but is applicable only to a particular type of economic development, in this case the early stage of export orientation. In sum, the initial and earlier success of the East Asian economies was derived from an interaction between the economic (gradual market-conforming policies) and institutional (Confucian cultural values and development-oriented authoritarianism) factors in the adoption of an export-oriented industrialisation strategy based on labour-intensive products. The earlier success has been sustainable despite economic transformation because of the concomitant changes in institutions and policies.

In the end, economic growth must be related to the supply-side factors of production. The literature on economic growth has focused attention on the question of which factor of production is the most important in maintaining long-run sustainable growth. In earlier growth models—such as Harrod-Domar, Ranis-Fei, Rostow, and Big Push—investment and savings were considered to be crucial factors. In the 1960s and 1970s, when neo-classical models were in vogue, technological change was treated as the primary determinant of long-term growth. Given that capital is subject to diminishing returns, and capital and technology are mobile across countries, there will be a process of growth convergence between developed and developing countries over time. The new growth theory (Romer 1986; Lucas 1988) of the

1980s once again emphasised the importance which investment derives from increasing returns to capital. Knowledge was regarded as the most important form of capital and as a result the new growth theory pinpointed the importance of human capital in building up capital and enhancing economic development. The new growth theory also implied a divergence of growth between developed and developing countries over time because capital accumulation is more rapid in developed countries and subject to increasing returns.

Most recently, however, the empirical findings of Alwyn Young (1992, 1995) with reference to the Asian NIEs cast doubt on the new growth theory implications. It is found that Hong Kong and Singapore experienced similar rates of high economic growth despite Singapore's much higher rates of capital accumulation than Hong Kong. Once again, technological change is regarded as the determinant of sustainable long-term economic growth.

The relative importance of capital and technological change in economic growth goes beyond academic and classroom interests. It touches on policy formulation and the prospects of East Asian economies in the long run. On the basis of the growth accounting results of Kim and Lau (1994) and Young (1994), Krugman (1994) presents a pessimistic outlook for East Asian economies. The reason, says Krugman, is that the economic growth of East Asia, which has been input-driven and not technology-based. is not sustainable in the long run, by analogy to the Soviet experience.

This survey article examines these recent studies of technological change or total factor productivity (TFP) as a source of growth in East Asian economies. The major objective of this paper is to show that in the end the importance of technological change in economic growth depends largely on how TFP is defined and how factor input data are measured.

7.II FIFTY YEARS' STUDIES OF TOTAL FACTOR PRODUCTIVITY

What exactly is total factor productivity?

TFP is a very old and perhaps obsolete concept in economic growth and development. Most authors trace back its origin to Solow's (1957) empirical work. In fact, the concept of TFP, defined as the ratio between real product and real factor inputs, was first introduced by Tinbergen (1942) in an article written in German. Obviously Solow was not aware of Tinbergen's work when he wrote his 1957 article.[1] Many others had developed the TFP concept and measured TFP before Solow (1957).[2] That explains the remarks by Griliches (1996:1328) that Solow's 1957 paper was not so original, 'not the question, nor the data, nor the conclusion . . . the "new wrinkle" was the explicit integration of economic theory into such a calculation and the use of calculus'.

Generally speaking, there are two approaches to measuring TFP: the explicit use of an aggregate production function for econometric estimations, and the national income or growth accounting approach which uses discrete data and assumes an aggregate production function implicitly.

The econometric approach begins with the specification of a production function, say of the Cobb-Douglas constant-returns-to-scale type:

$$Y_t = A_t K_t^{\beta} L_t^{1-\beta} \tag{1}$$

Where Y_t, K_t and L_t are output, capital input and labour input at time t respectively. A_t is the technology parameter governing the shift of the production function. β is the output elasticity of capital and $(1-\beta)$ that of labour.

A simple starting point is to define A_t in the following way:

$$A_t = A_o e^{\lambda t} \tag{2}$$

which means that technology grows at a constant exponential rate of λ.

Then, we have

$$Y_t = A_o e^{\lambda t} K_t^{\beta} L_t^{1-\beta} \tag{3}$$

Taking the logarithm on both sides of (3), we have the following estimation equation:

$$\ln Y_t = \ln A_o + \lambda t + \beta \ln K_t + (1-\beta)\ln L_t \tag{4}$$

It will be a simple matter to estimate λ and the output elasticities if we have time-series data for Y, K and L. Knowing λ we can ascertain the contribution of technological change to the growth of output. However, the meaning of thus defined and estimated must be clearly understood. λ is disembodied, exogenous and Hicks-neutral. Disembodied technological change means that it is not embodied in factor inputs but takes place like manna from heaven in the form of better methods and organisation that improve the efficiency of both new and old factor inputs. Any technological change embodied in the factor inputs is assumed to be properly specified and accounted for it, the aggregation of each input. Technological change is exogenous when its occurrence is independent of the variables in the growth model. Time is the only factor. Endogenous models on the other hand specify that technological change is related to R&D expenditure, learning by doing (experience), education, investment activities, etc.[3]

Hicks-neutral technological change has the effect of increasing the efficiency of both capital and labour to the same extent. On the other hand, Harrod-neutral technological change is labour-augmenting and Solow-neutral technological change capital-augmenting. These qualifications show that λ is a narrow concept of technological change. We must interpret λ with great caution in the context of technological change as a source of economic growth. Even if λ is small, the role of technology could have been important because embodied technological change might have been significant. Alternatively, λ may be small because the production function is mis-specified, failing to take into consideration the endogenous aspect of technological change and alternative forms of neutrality. Conversely, a large λ may be due to significant effects of economies of scale and resources reallocation. Another possible source of bias is the missing variables in the production function. Intermediate inputs, energy, education, and R&D, etc. have been considered as inputs that should be explicitly included.

The growth accounting approach of measuring total factor productivity was first undertaken by Stigler (1947), Abramovitz (1956), and Kendrick (1956), and finally brought to fruition by Kendrick (1961b) and Denison 1962, 1967, 1972, 1974). This approach gives more room for decomposition of the contribution of factor inputs and technological change to economic growth. It also makes it possible to study cases where data are available for the beginning and end of a period only. It must however be pointed out that in essence there is no real difference between the Cobb-Douglas production function estimation and the growth accounting approach as far as the underlying methodology is concerned (Black 1962). The growth accounting method is to use the factor shares in national income as weights when combining the individual factor inputs to form an index of total factor input, and to define that part of output growth which cannot be explained by increases in factor input as total factor productivity. This TFP is therefore the same as λ—disembodied, exogenous and Hicks-neutral technological change.

Let us assume a general neo-classical production function of

$$Y = F(K, L, t) \tag{5}$$

Differentiating (5) with respect to time and rearranging, we have

$$\frac{dY/dt}{Y} = \frac{(\delta F/\delta K)K}{Y} \cdot \frac{dK/dt}{K} + \frac{(\delta F/\delta L)L}{Y} \cdot \frac{dL/dt}{L} + \frac{(\delta F/\delta t)}{Y} \tag{6}$$

$(\delta F/\delta t)/Y$ is the proportional rate of shift of the production function. It is therefore technological change (disembodied, exogenous and Hicks-neutral) or TFP. Under neo-classical assumptions, $(\delta F/\delta K)K/Y$ and $(\delta F/\delta L)L/Y$ are factor shares of capital and labour respectively. Denoting the growth rates of Y, K, and L respectively by Y, K and L, (6) becomes:

$$Y = S_K K + S_L L + TFP \tag{7}$$

where S_K and S_L are respectively capital and labour shares in income.

$$TFP = Y - S_K K - S_L L \tag{8}$$

Equation (8) can therefore be used to calculate the sources of growth, viz. the contribution to growth by capital, labour and TFP. It can easily be proved that (7) is in fact the same as the Cobb-Douglas production function expressed in log-linear form as long as the factor shares remain constant over the period of study. In other production function forms, the weights S_K and S_L will change over time, that is, different weights must be used in calculating TFP at different moments of time.

It is very important to bear in mind that TFP as calculated from equation (8) is a 'residual', a catch-all sum indicating that part of output growth that cannot be explained by increases in factor inputs. It is simply an 'index of our ignorance'. Studies on TFP per se came more or less to a halt after the mid-1970s. Attention was then diverted to the related studies of quality measurement of labour and capital inputs (see below). It is only since the early 1990s that we have seen a revival of studies on TFP.[4] Interestingly, many economists have now become interested in this 'obsolete' subject and policy-makers are concerned about the numbers and rankings their countries receive. It seems possible that many of the participants in the current debate on TFP (and its implications for the East Asian economic miracle) have not gone through the earlier literature of the subject thoroughly. It is for this reason that a review of the earlier literature[5] is presented in this survey article, which otherwise would focus principally on the current debate generated by Alwyn Young (1992, 1994, 1995), Kim and Lau (1994), and Paul Krugman (1994). It is argued that the current controversy over the numbers, technological change versus factor inputs, is not substantial, but largely a matter of data and definitional/conceptual problems. Nonetheless, the conclusion of Alwyn Young and Paul Krugman is most probably wrong.

A discourse on methodology

It is obvious that the measurement of TFP depends crucially on (1) the specification of the relationship between input and output, (2) the proper measurement of the factor inputs, and (3) the weights assigned to the different categories of an input in the aggregation of sub-inputs. Since data availability and reliability differ widely among countries, international comparison of TFP estimations is very difficult even if a uniform methodology is adopted. Inevitably, a researcher has to make some assumptions (very often bold ones) to fill in the data gaps.

By now, the most popular form of the production function in estimating TFP is the transcendental logarithmic production function or, more simply, the translog production function of Christensen et at. (1973). In the earlier literature, Cobb-Douglas, CES (constant elasticity of substitution), and occasionally VES (variable elasticity of substitution) production functions were used. The translog production function is specified as follows:

$$\begin{aligned} Y = \exp [\alpha_o + \alpha_L \ln L + \alpha_K \ln K + \alpha_T T \\ + ½\beta_{KK}(\ln K)^2 + \beta_{KL}\ln K \ln L + \beta_{KK} T \cdot \ln K \\ + ½\beta_{LL}(\ln L)^2 + \beta_{LT}\ln L \cdot T + \Omega\beta_{TT}T^2] \end{aligned}$$

This production function specifies that output is an exponential function of the logarithms of inputs.[6]

The translog production function is a more generalised function than the Cobb-Douglas and CES because it is not constrained by the restriction of constant elasticity of substitution. Yet, it provides a theoretical justification for the use of average factor shares in the calculation of productivity growth on the basis of data at discrete points of time. The findings of relatively low productivity growth in East Asia by Young (1992, 1994 and 1995) and Kim and Lau (1994) are derived from the growth accounting approach based on the translog production function.

The translog form can further be extended to treat aggregate output as a function of its components. For data of discrete time periods, the difference between successive logarithms of aggregate output can be calculated from a weighted average of differences between successive logarithms of individual output components using the average value shares as weights. This can be similarly applied to aggregate capital and labour inputs with individual components. It can also be said that appropriate quality adjustments are built into the aggregation process. This is because the growth of each component in the input is weighted by its average value share or under neo-classical assumptions its average marginal product.

The translog production function has provided some theoretical justifications for the commonly used procedures in growth accounting studies. But, in the end, there are the basic problems of factor input measurements. The greatest problem is the measurement of capital input.[7] The major issues are: the contents of capital input and the level of aggregation/disaggregation, the valuation of capital, the choice of capital deflators, depreciation methods, capacity utilisation adjustments. It is important to examine these issues because capital has invariably been found to be the major contributor to economic growth in East Asia in those studies which found little or no TFP growth. The peculiar finding on low TFP growth in East Asia could well be related to the improper measurement of capital input.

Since the amount of physical capital cannot be measured directly, it has to be measured indirectly by value. The first question is then whether capital input should be valued at resource-cost or user-value. The conventional approach is to value capital at resource-cost, largely because of data availability The change in cost should reflect the quality improvements in the capital input. But this approach has the tendency to understate the value of capital in the context of the 'non-proportionality' and 'embodiment' arguments. When 'non-proportional' quality improvements occur, the conventional approach will underestimate the value of capital input. This refers to a situation in which a technological innovation increases the revenue-generating ability of a capital good by an amount larger than the resulting increase in the selling price of the capital good.[8] It is suggested (Gordon 1990) that this difference should be added to the recorded nominal price change. Some economists, notably Denison, maintain that capital input should be valued at resource-cost. Any change in the quality of capital due to non-proportionality will be shown in the 'residual' or TFP rather than in the measurement of the capital output. Denison also argued that it would not be feasible to make adjustments for non-proportional quality improvements. There is another problem of valuing capital at resource-cost. 'It implies that an item which costs twice as much to produce as another item represents twice as much capital, which ignores scale economies, and increases in the efficiency of factors in the capital goods industries themselves are not reflected in the price index' (Kennedy and Thirlwall 1972:29).

An important part of quality change is technological change embodied in the newer capital input. This embodiment hypothesis received significant attention in the earlier literature on productivity studies. Soon after his 1957 seminal paper on TFP (disembodied technological change), Solow (1959) developed a vintage-capital model to deal with embodied technological change. This was followed by others (Phelps 1962; Matthews 1964; Bliss 1968; Bardhan 1973). Studies soon came to a halt because of the many inherent problems in the estimation of the rate of embodied technological change. In most cases, the estimations involved the assumption of some arbitrary values of the parameters. Sometimes, the method of trial and error was used.[9] Moreover, in terms of empirical results, the embodied technological change was usually insignificant (Wickens 1970; You 1976). If we follow Nelson's (1964) derivation that embodiment is represented by changes in the average age of capital, we find that in practice such changes are usually small and so the effect of embodiment cannot be of great significance.

A recent study by Hulten (1992), however, throws some new light on the subject of embodied technological change. It is noted above that Gordon (1990) has derived new price indexes for capital goods which show that the official deflator has an upward bias and therefore the effect of understating the capital input. The difference reflects mainly the 'non-proportional' quality improvements. Most but not all of such 'non-proportional' quality improvements are embodied technological change.[10] Hulten's (1992) findings indicate that 20 per cent or more of the 'residual' or TFP could be attributed to embodied technological change.

Similarly, the embodiment hypothesis can be applied to labour input. Most of the growth accounting studies have made adjustments to the age-sex composition of the labour force and also the level of educational attainment. It is to be noted that in making adjustments for education, the user-value approach is as a rule adopted.[11] The quality adjustments are based on the differential incomes earned by the different categories of the labour force with different levels of educational attainment. The weights used are, however, arbitrary. In the case of Denison (1962), it is assumed that 60 per cent of the difference in income can be explained by education, while in Griliches (1970), education is assumed to explain 100 per cent of the differences in income. In the latter case, the labour input growth becomes higher and the contribution of labour to economic growth becomes larger and that of TFP smaller.

From the above, it is clear that TFP as a residual in growth accounting is an arbitrary concept. Strictly speaking, it is confined to disembodied, exogenous and Hicks-neutral technological change. But in practice, if we do not measure capital and labour correctly, the quality changes (including embodied technological change) will also show up in the residual.[12] In this case, the residual is no longer purely disembodied technological change but includes also embodied technological change and other quality improvements. The more quality improvement adjustments are made to the factor inputs, the less will be left for the residual or TFP. Thus, to a large extent, the TFP in a given estimation depends on the extent and scope of quality improvements which are included in the measurement of factor inputs. This sounds very frustrating. But, in practice this problem can be reduced to a pure question of definition. If we assume all quality improvements are embodied technological change and that technological change is made up of disembodied and embodied technological change, then technological change consists of quality improvements in factor inputs plus the residual or TFP. If there are over-adjustments in quality improvements, the TFP will become small, but the total technological change will remain the same. In the study of developed economies, it is often asserted that there are under-adjustments in the quality adjustments to factor inputs, and as a result the TFP becomes larger than what it should have been. In the context of developing economies, it is possible that over-adjustments are made and in consequence the TFP is smaller than what it should have been. We shall further discuss this in the next section.

We can therefore argue that it is not really meaningful to examine the role of technological change in economic growth in the context of growth accounting if we identify technological change only with disembodied technological change or TFP. This is because the measurement of TFP is so sensitive to the measurement of the factor inputs, specifically to the extent and scope of the adjustments of quality improvements made to the factor inputs. However, if we accept that quality improvements also constitute technological change, then it is much easier to study the role of technological change in economic growth and make comparisons across industries and countries. In this light, it is not therefore really meaningful to draw conclusions from past experience and future prospects of East Asian economic growth purely on the basis of the measurement of TFP. This is true even if the measurement of factor inputs has been correct. The relatively small TFP growth found in East Asia might simply reflect the fact that the major component of technological change in East Asia is quality improvements in factor inputs or embodied technological change. It does not imply that technological change has not been significant in East Asian economic growth but only that disembodied technological change has not been important. Furthermore, if factor inputs are not measured correctly in those studies on East Asia, then there are biases in the measurement of the TFP and any conclusion drawn on the basis of such estimates must be interpreted with great caution. In the next section, some of the possible biases in the measurement of factor inputs in the East Asian context will be discussed.

There are also other problems in the measurement of factor inputs, especially in the case of capital. First, there is the problem of the composition of the capital input. We have to make a decision on what kinds of the capital input should be taken into consideration. For example, a decision has to be made as to whether land should be included, whether the capital input of the public sector and the non-profit-making private sector should be included, and whether inventories, durable consumer goods, and financial capital should be included.[13] The choice of the content of capital inputs, in turn, affects the type of price deflators to be used in making quality change adjustments. Value shares have to be estimated as weights and therefore factor prices have to be known. Very often such factor prices have to be estimated on the basis of various assumptions for lack of readily available data.

Second, the capital input should be adjusted for capacity utilisation. The use of capital input must be subject to cyclical factors such that in recession and the early phase of an upswing, there is excess capacity in the use of capital. In the earlier studies (Kendrick 1961a; Denison 1962), no specific adjustment was made for capacity utilisation of capital. Later, some (e.g. Solow and Jorgensen) used the unemployment rate as a measure of underutilisation of capital; others (e.g. Griliches) used the power utilisation rate as a measure. There is also the problem of making utilisation adjustment to all capital sub-inputs or only to some categories such as non-residential structures and producers' goods.[14] Various studies suggest that utilisation adjustment rates are sensitive to the methodology used, and that adjustment of capacity utilisation could significantly affect the relative importance of capital as a source of economic growth. Again, if excess capacity is understated, the residual or TFP will be understated. It is not easy to adjust the capital utilisation rate correctly, especially for developing economies.

Third, there is the problem of choice between capital gross or net of depreciation. Denison (1962) and Solow (1957, 1962) used gross capital but Kendrick (1961b) did not.[15] It is argued that if net measures of capital are used, there is a tendency to over-state depreciation because 'obsolescence rather than physical deterioration is the dominant feature of depreciation. Capital becomes economically obsolescent before it has outlived its physical usefulness, but obsolescent equipment is still capable of contributing to production. Thus the flow of capital services does not decline with age at the rate frequently suggested by allowances for depreciation' (Kennedy and Thirlwall 1972:30). Ideally one should adjust capital for physical depreciation but not for obsolescence. But this is generally impossible in practice. Any over-depreciation will overstate the residual or TFP. This is probably the case in studies on developed economies. Our concern, however, is with studies on East Asia.

It becomes clear that the measurement of TFP for any economy is subject to all kinds of conceptual and measurement errors. TFP is a catch-all phrase, and its meaning differs greatly with the methodology used and the ways that factor inputs are aggregated and measured. Jorgenson and Griliches (1967) have argued that TFP is a result of mis-measurement of factor inputs and therefore does not really exist. They made the following adjustments for contribution of input growth to output growth: (1) disaggregating the price index for capital to obtain a better measure of capital input; (2) correcting for capacity utilisation of capital; and (3) taking flow prices for capital and labour services into account to obtain better measures of capital and labour inputs. After these corrections, Jorgenson and Griliches (1967) found that very little residual (only 3.3 per cent of it) remained. [16] On the other hand, if one does not make any adjustment to the measurement of capital and labour inputs, all the quality improvements and measurement errors will show up in the residual or TFP.

In view of this arbitrariness of the measurement of TFP, its use in theoretical reasoning and policy formulation is necessarily limited. It can at best serve as a starting point for further analysis but should be used as a verdict on the growth experience of economies, especially for those fast-growing ones in which the conventional neo-classical assumptions and steady-state economic conditions might not apply.

7.III TOTAL FACTOR PRODUCTIVITY AND EAST ASIAN ECONOMIC GROWTH

Empirical results

In the sources-of-growth literature, there is a distinct difference between the findings for developed and developing economies. Almost all the studies of developed economies show that TFP is a far more important source of growth than factor inputs.[17] This is also true for Japan. Kanamori (1972) found that for the period 1955–68, 60 per cent of Japan's output growth was explained by TFP Oshima (1987) showed that for the period 1953–71, 4.9 per cent of Japan's average annual growth of 8.8 per cent was due to TFP. Chen (1977) estimated for the period 1955–70, 55.1 per cent of Japan's economic growth was due to TFP. More recently the World Bank (1993) showed that for the period 1960–89, 3.5 per cent of Japan's 5.9 percent average annual growth was due to TFP. Takenaka (1997) found that even for the recent period 1970–92, 2.2 per cent of Japan's 4.2 average annual growth was explained by TFP. These studies use different time periods up to the early 1990s. Yet the results seem to be quite consistent despite the fact that the average growth rates are different and the economy has obviously undergone dramatic structural changes.

Empirical studies of growth accounting for developing economies in both Asia and Latin America began in the late 1960s. In almost all these studies, the role of TFP in economic growth is much less important than in the findings for developed economies.[18] Specifically, capital input is invariably the major source of economic growth. The following is a brief review of the studies of sources of growth in East Asian economies. This paper does not deal with Latin American countries, but the findings for them are quite similar to those for Asian developing economies.[19]

Newly industrialised economies

Table 7.1 presents a summary of the findings of six studies which examine the four NIEs (Hong Kong, Korea, Singapore, and Taiwan) all together as a group. While there must have been some studies of sources of growth in developing economies after the Solow methodology became widely known, only a few appeared in international journals. Chen (1977) and Chen (1979) are probably the only published ones until the burgeoning of studies in the last few years (see Table 7.1).

All the six studies use a similar methodology. But they refer to different time periods and, more importantly, make adjustments to the data on the basis of very different assumptions. The estimation results are therefore not really comparable. Chen (1977) makes no adjustments to the official data but has to derive the capital stock data for Singapore and Hong Kong using the conventional approach of accumulating investment to an assumed or derived base year capital stock. The resources reallocation component in the residual is also identified. The definition of TFP in Chen (1977) includes the effects of resources reallocation. Thus, the quality changes of capital not reflected by

Table 7.1 TFP estimates (whole economy): Asia NIEs

	Chen (1977) 1955–70	*World Bank (1993) 1960–89*	*Drysdale and Huang (1995) 1950–88*	*Young (1995) 1966–90*	*Takenaka (1995) 1970–92*	*Kim and Cau (1994)*[a]
Honk Kong	4.3 (46.5)	3.6 (43.9)	3.1 (34.4)	2.3 (31.5)[b]	3.1 (46.3)[c]	2.4 (35.0)
Korea	5.0 (56.4)	3.1 (36.9)	2.1 (28.4)	1.7 (16.5)	0.8 (9.3)	1.2 (14.0)
Singapore	3.6 (55.2)	1.2 (15.0)	0.8 (10.4)	0.2 (2.3)	–2.4 (…)	1.9 (23.0)
Taiwan	4.3 (53.6)	3.7 (42.0)	2.9 (33.7)	2.6 (27.7)	1.8 (20.9)	1.2 (15.0)

Notes:
[a] Hong Kong, 1966–90; Korea, 1960–90; Singapore, 1964–90; Taiwan, 1953–90.
[b] 1966–91.
[c] 1978–92.
In percentage points with percentage contribution to output growth in parentheses.

the official price deflator, the quality change of labour, the effects of resources reallocation and economies of scale, interaction of factor inputs, etc. are all lumped together to constitute the residual or TFP. In this case, it shows that about 50 per cent of output growth can be explained by TFP which by assumption includes most of the quality changes in factor inputs. The World Bank (1993) study uses labour input adjusted for education attainment and capital input deflated by a modified deflator. In this case, the residual or TFP excludes most quality changes in factor inputs. In other words, if TFP is considered as technological change, much of the quality improvement in factor inputs is not counted as technological change, that is, TFP is largely a concept of disembodied technological change. In Young (1995), the data on factor inputs have been thoroughly adjusted for quality changes in the process of the aggregation of sub-inputs.[20] Young divides capital input into five categories (land not included) and cross-classifies labour by up to seven attributes. This means that the residual or TFP or technological change in Young's estimates largely excludes quality improvements in factor inputs. In other words, Young's TFP is by assumption largely disembodied technological change. Drysdale and Huang (1995), Takenaka (1997), and Kim and Lau (1994) do not give details regarding adjustments for quality improvements of factor inputs. Presumably, some such adjustments have been implicitly or explicitly made.

In view of these differences in the extent and scope of adjustments made to quality improvements in factor inputs, it is hardly surprising that different studies arrive at significantly different results for TFP estimates. Where significant and careful adjustments are made to quality improvements in factor inputs, as in Young's 1995 study, the residual or TFP is relatively small. This does not imply that technological change has not been a significant source of economic growth. It implies only that disembodied technological change is relatively unimportant while embodied technological change and other quality improvements could have been significant. What we can infer from the findings for developed and developing economies regarding their differences in the relative importance of TFP in economic growth is that in developing economies embodied technological change is more important than disembodied technological change when compared to developed economies. Thus, Young (1994, 1995) and Krugman (1994) are not correct in concluding that technological change or productivity growth has been slow in East Asia. Technological change in the embodied form has in fact been significant in East Asia.

There is now a considerable number of studies of TFP in individual Asian NIEs. Studies of Taiwan seem to be the most numerous. The earliest study of Taiwan is probably Shirley Kuo (1968). By using a Cobb-Douglas production function, she found that technological change grew at an average annual rate of 4.57 per cent during the period 1951–65, accounting for 63 per cent of output growth. A later study by Kuo (1983) shows that the relative importance of technological change decreased over time. For example, in the first period 1952–61, technological change accounted for 53 per cent, 42 per cent, and 51 per cent respectively for output growth in the non-agricultural, manufacturing and service sectors; but only for 12 per cent, 7 per cent and 17 per cent respectively in the second period 1961–80. No details, however, were given for any adjustments to quality improvement in factor inputs. It was pointed out that there was no decrease in the actual rate of technological change; the decrease in relative importance was due to the rapid output growth and the concomitant rapid increase in both capital and labour inputs. Liang (1989) adopts a more sophisticated methodology. Adjustments for quality improvements of factor inputs are made in the aggregation of factor sub-inputs.[21] The study covers two sub-periods, 1961–73 and 1973–81 of the manufacturing sector by industry. It was found that for the manufacturing sector as a whole, TFP accounted for 7.1 per cent of output growth in the period 1961–73 and 23.5 percent in the period 1973–81. For the period 1961–81 as whole, TFP accounted for 12 per cent of output growth, compared to 7 per cent for the same period and same sector in Kuo (1983). Significantly, different estimates are obtained for TFP in Taiwan's manufacturing also in Wang (1990) and Okuda (1994) indicating how the choice of time period and methodology could significantly affect the results. Huang (1985) estimated TFP for the whole economy of Taiwan for the period 1962–82. Capital and labour inputs were adjusted for quality changes, and TFP was decomposed into scale economies and technical change (residual of the residual). It was found that TFP accounted for only 19.4 per cent of output growth and that 60 per cent of TFP was due to scale economies. Thus the findings of Young (1994, 1995) for Taiwan and indeed for other NIEs are not new. When factor inputs are adjusted extensively for quality improvements, the resulting TFP will be small. In response to the Young and Kim and Lau studies, Liang (1995), using similar methodologies, came to the conclusion that TFP was a significant source of growth for the period 1982–93, accounting for 46.3 per cent of output growth for the whole economy of Taiwan during 1982–87 and 41.4 per cent during 1987–93. The contribution of TFP was small for the period 1961–82, particularly 1973–82. This indicates that TFP estimates are very sensitive to the periods chosen for the study.

The first published work in English on TFP in Korea is probably Kim and Roemer (1979). Before this, there were at least two working papers: Lee (1972) and Christensen and Cummings (1975). Kim and Roemer (1979) used readily available official statistics without much adjustment for quality changes in factor inputs. For the period 1960–73, it was found that the unexplained residual was about 50 per cent at most for the entire economy, but as low as 25 per cent if land and dwellings were excluded from the capital stock (which results in a high overall growth rate of capital input) and labour input is adjusted for educational attainment. Christensen and Cummings (1975) found a residual of 41 per cent for the entire private economy even after adjustments of quality changes in factor inputs. With some allowances for quality changes, Lee (1972) found that 54 per cent of manufacturing output growth for the period 1957–70 is TFP.

An improved and more careful study was undertaken by Christensen and Cummings (1981) on the basis of their 1975 working paper. After careful adjustments for quality improvements in factor inputs, they still found that TFP accounted for 42.3 per cent of output growth in the private economy of Korea during 1960–73. While 'Korea's ratio of productivity growth and input growth to output growth have been similar to those of the developed countries, the composition of its input growth has been quite different' (Christensen and Cummings 1981:301). Interestingly, it is found that in Korea, unlike developed countries, there has been little capital deepening but significant growth in educational attainment of the labour force and a rapid increase in capital capacity utilisation. Kwon (1986) decomposes TFP in Korean manufacturing for the period 1961–80 into (a) technical change or shifts of the cost function, (b) scale economies, and (c) capital utilisation. Adjustments to quality improvement in capital input are made on the basis of official deflators and therefore capture only some of the quality changes. Not much adjustment is made for quality changes in labour input. The factors of production also include energy and intermediate input. The results show that TFP accounts for 9.9 per cent, 22.3 per cent, and 15.2 per cent respectively of the total manufacturing output growth for 1961–72, 1972–78, and 1961–80. For the whole period 1961–80, 44.6 per cent of TFP is due to technical change, 38.1 per cent to scale economies, and 17.3 per cent to capacity utilisation. The studies on Korea again show that the estimation results for TFP can differ significantly because of the choice of the time period under study and the methodology employed. But, generally speaking, TEP is far from insignificant as a source of economic growth in Korea.

There were very few TFP studies of the two city economies, Hong Kong and Singapore, before the Young (1992) paper. Chen (1977, 1979) on Hong Kong and Tsao (1982,1985,1986) are probably the only published studies.[22] One major reason must be the lack of good data, especially capital input data, for these two economies. The Chen (1977, 1979) studies demonstrate that TFP was an important source of economic growth in Hong Kong for the period 1955–70, treating quality improvements as embodied technological change. Tsao, using the methodology of Gollop and Jorgenson (1980), found TFP to be almost negligible for the manufacturing sector of Singapore for the period 1970–79. Indeed, in many industries TFP was negative. In this methodology, factor inputs are adjusted for quality improvements, and hence embodied technological change does not show up in the residual. Tsao, like many others, found this surprising. Given the rapid growth of the Singapore economy, TFP should have been significant. Tsao gave a number of explanations for this surprising result: predominance of foreign investment, availability of low-skilled labour, scarcity of domestic industrial entrepreneurship, and low technological capability. The arguments are not entirely convincing. Tsao was incorrect in equating low TFP growth to slow technological change. Low TFP growth indicates only slow disembodied technological change. It is most likely that embodied technological change was significant in Singapore during the period of her study, the 1970s. That TFP has consistently been found very small in the case of Singapore should be interpreted as an indication that embodied technological change has been more important than disembodied technological change. In Chen (1977), TFP was a significant source of growth for Singapore when factor inputs are not adjusted for quality improvements. Rao and Lee (1995) find that TFP is significant (30 per cent of GDP growth) for the most recent period, 1987–94 even when factor inputs are adjusted for quality improvements in line with Gollop and Jorgenson (1980).[24] Education is found to be an important source of economic growth in Singapore. As pointed out by Sarel (1996), TFP estimates are often sensitive to the period chosen for the study.

China

Studies of TFP in China have become possible only recently as a result of more reliable data being made available. Chen et al. (1988) estimate TFP for China's state industrial sector for the period 1953–85. The factor inputs are quality adjusted, but not too comprehensively for lack of data. However, attempts are made to correct for the significant excess capacity of state-owned enterprises. The results are very interesting, showing that TFP was relatively unimportant during the earlier period (27.5 per cent and 14.2 per cent of output growth for the periods 1953–57 and 1957–78 respectively), but had become very significant (68.6 per cent of output growth) for the more recent period 1978–85. This study is a point of departure from the earlier studies (Field 1983; World Bank 1985; Chow 1985) which generally suggested that TFP has been declining after the First Five-Year Plan. An important reason for this must be the adjustments made for excess capacity of capital input and under-employment of labour input of the state-owned industrial enterprises. This illustrates the fact that the ways in which data are measured determine to a large extent the resulting estimates for TFP. The recent study of Borensztein and Ostry (1996) supports the assertion that TFP as a source of growth in China has been increasingly important since the late 1970s. It is found that TFP was −0.7 per cent per annum for the period 1953–78 but increased to 3.8 per cent (or 41.3 per cent of GDP growth) for 1979–94.[25]

In two recent studies however, the earlier findings of slow productivity growth in China are confirmed. Chow (1993) comes to the conclusion that 'technological change was absent in the growth of the Chinese economy from 1952 to 1980'. Capital constituted the major source of growth. Similarly,

Woo (1996) finds that for 1985–93, TFP growth was only 0.3–0.6 per cent out of the output growth of 9.7 per cent during that period. It is probable that these findings of low productivity growth in China after the First Five-Year Plan are related to under-pricing and under-depreciation of the capital input. Capital input data are problematic for the studies of TFP in any country, but particularly so in the case of China. Significantly different results on TFP estimates are therefore hardly surprising.[26]

Southeast Asia

There are very few published studies on Southeast Asia, although studies on the Philippines were among the first TFP studies on developing countries.[27] Table 7.2 summarises a few recent studies. Among the ASEAN-4, Indonesia and Thailand might be classified as productivity-driven economies because TFP accounts for over 25 per cent of economic growth in these two countries. A study of the industrial sector of Indonesia shows that TFP growth has increased rapidly over time since the early 1980s.[28] However TFP is certainly less significant as a source of growth compared with developed countries and many studies on NIEs. The Philippines is an investment-driven economy with little or no productivity growth. Earlier studies (e.g. Williamson 1969) found that all TFP in the Philippines could be explained by quality improvements in factor inputs. It is also apparent that TFP has not been a major source of growth in Malaysia despite its high rate of economic growth in recent years. It is difficult to assess the results of these studies because not much detail is given for the derivation and measurement of the data used.

Table 7.2 TFP estimates[a] (whole economy): ASEAN-4 and China

	Drysdale and Huang (1995) 1950–88	*Kawai (1995) 1970–90*	*World Bank (1993) 1960–89*
Indonesia	2.1 (31.3)[b]	1.5 (24.2)	1.2 (23.1)
Malaysia	−0.5 (−8.3)	1.6 (23.9)	1.1 (17.5)
Philippines	0.2 (4.1)	−0.7 (−19.4)	—
Thailand	1.7 (29.3)	1.9 (27.1)	2.5 (36.8)
China	2.0 (28.2)[c]	1.9 (24.4)	—

Notes:
[a] In percentage points with percentage contribution to output growth in parentheses.
[b] 1962–88.
[c] 1960–88.

The importance of TFP as a source of growth in East Asia

The concept of TFP is a useful one and the empirical studies of it are revealing. However, the limitations of its usefulness in the study of economic growth must also be recognised. TFP, strictly speaking, should be used only for disembodied technological change. But depending on how factor input data are measured, TFP can also include many other sources of growth because TFP is just a residual. In the context of developing countries, the reliability and availability of data, especially capital input data, are problematic. It is therefore difficult to make comparison of different studies, and interpretations of results must not be accepted without reservations.

Significant differences have been found in various studies on East Asian economies with regard to the importance of TFP as a source of economic growth. Generally speaking, studies conducted earlier, often owing to lack of data, tended to arrive at greater importance of TFP; while recent studies, based on more sophisticated approaches of making quality change and other adjustments, tend to conclude that TFP is relatively insignificant. These results are indeed expected, and consistent with one another. What the results indicate is that in East Asia (and probably in other fast developing economies too), embodied technological change is the predominant source of productivity growth. However, it is possible that 'over-adjustments' have been made to the factor inputs, resulting in under-estimation of TFP or the residual. The importance of the residual would be even smaller if capacity utilisation, depreciation, capital input deflators, etc. are also taken into account. The conclusion of Jorgenson and Griliches (1967) that the residual is close to zero after all kinds of adjustments and corrections is therefore not unreasonable. The results obtained in Young's recent studies can be seen in this light. At least five reasons may be given for possible over-adjustment of factor inputs in the fast-growing East Asia context.

First, the capital input data are likely to be under-deflated, meaning that price deflators used have an upward bias. In a developed-country context, it is commonly accepted that the capital input data (especially those for producers' durable goods) are over-deflated. This is because official deflators do not sufficiently take 'non-proportional' quality improvements into account. In the case of developing economies, 'non-proportional' change could be small or negative. Owing to transfer pricing or monopolistic market structure, the price increases in capital goods often outweigh the effect of any particular technological change on revenue-generation. Also, the domestic price deflators cannot accurately reflect the quality improvement of imported capital goods which are often predominant in developing countries.[29] The domestic price indexes may under-inflate the imported capital goods if the domestic capital goods market is in disequilibrium. If the capital input data are under-inflated, as is most likely in the case of developing countries, TFP or the residual would be under-estimated.

Second, it is likely that in developing countries the capacity utilisation of the capital stock is over-estimated, that is, excess capacity under-estimated. In this case, the contribution of capital is over-stated and TFP under-stated. The usual method of adjusting for excess capacity is to reduce the capital stock by the labour unemployment rate. However, in developing countries, abnormally capital-intensive techniques are often used, excess capacity therefore rises faster than unemployment because it is easier to shut down machines than to lay off workers.

Third, for developed countries, a potential source of error in the measurement of capital is over-depreciation (Kennedy and Thirlwall 1972:30). In slow-growing, mature economies many capital goods which have become economically obsolescent are still being used. But in fast-growing developing countries, capital goods are often discarded or relocated to overseas subsidiaries through foreign direct investment before they reach economic obsolescence. Structures are subject to much higher rates of depreciation in developing countries than in developed countries. Buildings demolished for redevelopment a few years after completion are commonplace in Hong Kong. In this case, capital is likely to be under-depreciated, contribution of capital to economic growth again over-stated and that of TFP under-stated.

Fourth, in the aggregation of sub-inputs, the weights are the value shares of each sub-input. The estimation of such value shares is often based on inappropriate assumptions and incomplete information. The choice of capital sub-inputs also affects the measurement of capital input. In Young's studies, with the exception of Singapore's manufacturing sector, land is not included in capital input. This could lead to biases in the measurement of capital because the growth of land as an input over time could be significant in the case of Hong Kong. In the measurement of labour, disaggregation is based on attributes such as industry, occupation, sex, age, education, etc. In deriving the value share for education, we have to make assumptions about how education affects earnings. Denison (1962, 1967) assumed that 60 per cent of income differentials can be explained by educational attainment. Griliches (1970), on the other hand, argues that income differentials should be explained completely by educational attainment. This assumption can be challenged on the ground that abilities, family connections, on-the-job training, etc. must also be important factors in explaining earnings differentials. In fast-growing economies where new opportunities emerge all the time, entrepreneurial spirit perhaps explains earnings differentials better than formal education. If labour input is adjusted for quality improvements on the basis that education explains all earnings differentials, then the contribution of labour is over-stated and that of TFP under-stated.

Fifth, while it is true that capital input grows at a faster rate and therefore contributes more to economic growth in developing countries than in developed countries, its contribution would be over-estimated if too large a weight is assigned to capital input growth. There are several reasons for thinking that such weight is usually over-estimated for developing countries. Conventionally, the factor shares in total output are used to estimate output elasticities and therefore the weights for factor inputs in the growth accounting exercise. It is likely that for developing countries the capital share is overstated because the factor market is not in equilibrium.[30] The capital share might be over-stated because of monopolistic profits. In this case the capital share is larger than the output elasticity of capital and the use of the capital share as the weight will over-state the contribution of capital to economic growth. For developing countries also the labour share may be under-estimated because of non-reported incomes (extra jobs or moonlighting are commonplace in East Asia). Again, it is not clear whether in Singapore firms' contributions to the Central Provident are already included in the labour income. Assuming constant returns to scale, an under-estimation of the labour share means a significant over-estimation of the capital share and therefore of the contribution of capital input to economic growth. Michaelopoulos (1969) shows that the estimates by Bruton (1967) of TFP for Latin American countries were under-stated by as much as 50 per cent because of the over-estimation of the capital share used as the weight.

Taking the above discussion into account, it is hardly a surprise to find that estimates of TFP suggest it is relatively insignificant in East Asian economies.

7.IV THE FUTURE OF EAST ASIAN ECONOMIC GROWTH

Pessimism about the economic future of East Asia is unwarranted. Krugman's (1994) analysis of East Asian economic growth rests on a simplistic interpretation of the sources-of-growth results and gives too little weight to the potential dynamic changes in East Asia. Krugman would be right if he was referring to the inability of East Asian economies to maintain double-digit growth rates in the future. Certainly no economies can do this for long. But this has little to do with whether economic growth is input-driven or not. Few predict sustained double-digit economic growth for East Asia in the coming decade. What most believe is that economic growth in East Asia will continue steadily at 5-6 per cent without repeating the Soviet and Eastern European experience.

Krugman has clearly taken the sources-of-growth methodology too seriously and has referred only casually to the empirical findings. As shown above, technological change as a residual is very sensitive to the ways in which inputs are measured and to the time period chosen. Most likely, the relatively low TFP found in East Asia in recent studies reflects the relative importance of embodied technological change, economies of scale, increased capacity utilisation, and structural transformation, etc. Indeed, some recent studies arrive at the opposite conclusion, that the economic growth of East Asia has been technology-driven. In the World Bank report (1993), two groups of economies are identified: the investment-driven group, comprising

Indonesia, Malaysia, and Singapore, and the technology-driven group, comprising Japan, South Korea, Hong Kong, Thailand and Taiwan. In Liang (1995), it is found that for the period 1982–93, about 45 per cent of Taiwan's economic growth can be explained by TFP even though factor inputs have been elaborately adjusted for quality improvements.

One must also not take a static view of the sources of growth of an economy. Past studies indicate that the relative importance of factor inputs as sources of growth would change over time depending on the type and stage of economic development. It is usually found that technological change is the major source of growth for industrialised economies, a minor source of growth for slow-growing developing economies. For fast-growing developing economies the importance of technological change falls in between these two groups. Even if East Asian economic growth was largely input-driven in the past two decades, one cannot preclude the possibility that this will change when their economies become more mature. Structural transformation from light industries to knowledge-intensive industries and high value-added services accompanied by heavy investment in human capital and rapid expansion of technological capability gives rise to acceleration of technological change, embodied and disembodied.

In the context of the new growth theory, input-driven economic growth can also be sustainable. For capital input can be subject to increasing returns and human capital is the main engine of growth.[31] Also in terms of the theory of endogenous technological change, increase in investment is the major determinant of technological change. Indeed, Scott (1989:19) goes so far as to say that 'there is no need to consider the rate of technical change separately from the rate of investment, for it cannot be done and it makes no sense to try'. If we accept this view, it is no longer meaningful to make a distinction between input-driven and technology-driven economic growth.

Lastly, one must not equate the investment-driven Soviet growth in the 1950s and 1960s with that of today's Asian economies. There are at least two major differences. First, the allocation of resources in today's Asia is much more efficient because of the predominance of market forces. Investment is largely private and not public. Second, today's Asian economies are widely open to international trade and investment while the Soviet Union was inward-looking and adopted import substitution policies in the 1950s and 1960s. International mobility of capital and technology is an important factor for sustaining Asian economic growth. International competition and co-operation have also given rise to efficiency and quick responsiveness to internal and external shocks. There were no 'flying geese' in East and Central Europe in the 1950s and 1960s.[32]

In considering the economic future of East Asia, it is more meaningful to examine the regional aspect or the development of intra-regional economic activities in the Asia-Pacific. The most remarkable phenomenon of East Asian economic growth is the spreading out of economic growth throughout the region. East Asian economic dynamism can therefore be explained on the basis of two virtuous circles, which explains how openness to foreign trade and investment gives rise to high rates of growth. First, domestic policy reforms lead to inflow of foreign direct investment (FDI) resulting in increases in the competitiveness of domestic production. Such FDI is trade-promoting. Increases in foreign trade result in further increases in foreign direct investment and eventually a high rate of economic growth.

The second virtuous circle is the regional virtuous circle which is related to the sub-regional division of labour emerging in the Asia-Pacific in the context of the flying-geese model of industrialisation. This asserts that one country takes the lead in industrialisation and there are different tiers of followers. Industries are passed down from one tier to the next tier when a country is graduated from the production of a particular commodity. This virtuous circle works as follows. In the course of economic development countries undergo changes in comparative cost. To maintain competitiveness at the domestic and international levels, firms have to relocate the production activities overseas through FDI. As a result, a sophisticated sub-regional division of industrial labour emerges, spreading industrialisation throughout the region.[33]

East Asian dynamism will continue in the foreseeable future on the basis of export-oriented industrialisation. On the one hand, sub-regional division of labour in the flying-geese pattern results in complementarity rather than competition. This makes possible a positive-sum game of export-oriented industrialisation even when many countries undertake this strategy at the same time. On the other hand, rising purchasing power and measures of trade liberalisation and facilitation in the East Asian region have increased intra-regional trade and reduced the dependence of the region on Western markets. East Asian economic growth is not a miracle but the result of hard work and good policies. Nor is Asian economic growth a myth; it is a reality.

NOTES

1 Tinbergen's paper was not published in English until 1959.

2 For example, Johnson (1950), Schmookler (1952), Kendrick (1956), Abramovitz (1956), Rutton (1956). For an interesting historical note published recently, see Griliches (1996).

3 For a survey on endogenous technological change, see Chen (1975).

4 The World Bank is largely responsible for this. See Elias (1992); World Bank (1993); Nehru (1994). For a study on transitional economies, see Falk et al. (1996).

5 For a survey of earlier literature, see Nadiri (1970, 1972); Kennedy and Thirlwall (1972). See also Nelson (1973, 1981).

6 For an excellent summary of the characteristics and use of the translog production function, see Christensen et al. 1980.

7 Creamer (1972) reviews the problems of the measurement of capital.

8 A most meticulous study was undertaken by Gordon (1990) to work out a new

producers' durable equipment deflator to take into account the 'non-proportional' quality improvements.

9 For a view, see Chen 1979: 55–6.

10 For more details, see Hulten (1992: 972–3).

11 This is the case even in Denison's studies in which the resource-cost approach is used for the valuation of the capital input.

12 It can be shown that if capital and labour are mis-specified each by a multiplicative factor which refers to quality of improvement over time, the residual becomes the weighted average of the quality changes embodied in the mis-specified inputs. See Yotopoulos and Nugent (1973: 156).

13 For further discussion, see Creamer 1972: 59–62).

14 See Creamer (1972: 59–62).

15 For a critical summary of their arguments, see Creamer (1972: 62–6).

16 Griliches (1964) 'explained' away all the TFP in US agriculture by simply making four adjustments to the measurement of inputs: education in the labour input; correction of the downward biases in capital deflators; the use of gross instead of net capital; and allowances for economies of scale. For a general critique of the growth accounting methodology, see Maddison (1972).

17 For example, Denison (1967) found that over 50 per cent of output growth could not be explained by increases in factor inputs for all eight European countries under study even after allowance for quality improvement in labour input.

18 For an earlier survey, see Nadiri (1972). The recent study of Kim and Lau (1994) comes to the same results when comparing the Asian newly industrialised economies and the G-5 (France, Germany, Japan, UK, and the USA). See also Kelly and Williamson (1972). For an attempt to explain the contrary patterns as revealed in empirical studies, see Chen (1977).

19 See Bruton (1967), Correa (1970), Elias (1975), and Elias (1992) for studies on Latin American Countries.

20 Star (1974: 126) asserts that ' The great advantage of using disaggregated data is that quality changes are transformed into quantity changes.'.

21 The methodology is therefore very close to that used by Young (1995).

22 For a survey of TFP studies on Singapore, see Lall et al. (1996). See also Goh and Low (1996).

23 Resource reallocation as a source of growth included in TFP is estimated separately. As expected, the impact is insignificant for the city economies but considerable for Taiwan and Korea.

24 Even for the earlier period. 1966–73, TFP was not totally insignificant; it accounted for 10 per cent of GDP growth.

25 Data are updated of those given in Li (1992). Borensztein and Ostry (1996) believe that TFP is overestimated because output is overestimated because of under-pricing of the output series.

26 Two forthcoming studies, Drysdale and Huang (1995) and Kawai (1995), find that TFP was moderately significant as a source of economic growth in China. See Table 7.2.

27 Those studies on the Philippines include Lampman (1967), Williamson (1969). Ezaki (1975).

28 Aswicahyona et al. (1996).

29 See Young (1995, footnote 9).

30 For an analysis of the consequence of factor market disequilibrium for the calculation of TFP, see Bruno (1968).

31 Sengupta (1993) provides some empirical support for the new growth theory in the Asian NIEs in general and Korea in particular. Lucas (1993) illustrates that

human capital (education and on-the-job training) is the main engine of growth in East Asia.

32 The flying-geese model was first used to describe the life cycles of industries in the course of economic development (Akamatsu 1962). The focus was on specific industries in specific countries. The model has now been extended to study the shift of industries from one country to another mainly through foreign direct investment resulting in regional and sub-regional industrial division of labour.

33 For a discussion of the future of economic growth in East Asia and a critique of the Krugman thesis, see Chen (1997).

REFERENCES

Abramovitz, Moses. 1956. 'Resource and output trends in the United States since 1870', *American Economic Review*, 46(2): 5–23.

Akamatsu, K. 1962. 'A historical pattern of economic growth in developing countries', *Developing Economies*, 1(1):3–25.

Amsden, Alice. 1989. *Asia's Next Giant: South Korea and late industrialization*, Oxford University Press, New York.

Aswicahyono, H. H.; Bird, Kelly and Hill, Hal. 1996. 'What happens to industrial structure when countries liberalise? Indonesia since the mid-1980s', *Journal of Development Studies*, 32(3): 340–63.

Bardhan, P. K. 1973. 'More on putty-clay', *International Economic Review*, 14(1):211–22.

Black, John. 1962. 'The technical progress function and the production function', *Economica*, 29(1):166–70.

Bliss, Christopher. 1968. 'On putty-clay', *Review of Economic Studies*, 35(1):105–32.

Borensztein, Eduardo and Ostry, Jonathan D. 1996. 'Accounting for China's growth performance', *American Economic Review*, 86(2):224–8.

Bruno, Michael. 1968. 'Estimation of factor contribution to growth under structural disequilibrium', *International Economic Review*, 9(1):49–62.

Bruton, H. J. 1967. 'Productivity growth in Latin America', *American Economic Review*, 57(4):1099–116.

Chen, Edward K. Y. 1975. *Endogenous technical progress: a survey*, Hong Kong Economic Papers No. 9, Hong Kong Economic Association, pp. 18–45.

—— 1977. 'Factor inputs, total factor productivity, and economic growth: the Asian case', *Developing Economies*, 15(2):121–43.

—— 1979. *Hyper-growth in Asian Economics: a comparative study of Hong Kong, Japan, Korea, Singapore, and Taiwan*, Macmillan, London.

—— 1988. 'The economics and non-economics of Asia's four little dragons', Supplement to the *Gazette*, Vol. 35(1), March 21, University of Hong Kong, Hong Kong.

—— 1997. 'Dynamic Asian economies: retrospect and prospect', in Chan Heng Chee (ed.), *The New Asia-Pacific Order*, Institute of Southeast Asian Studies, Singapore (forthcoming).

Chen Kuan; Wang Hongchang; Zheng Yuxin; Jefferson, Gary H. and Rawski, Thomas G. 1988. 'Productivity change in Chinese industry: 1953–1985' *Journal of Comparative Economics* No. 12, pp. 570–91

Chen Tian-Jy and Tang De-Piao, 1990. 'Export performance and productivity growth', *Economic Development and Cultural Change 38(3): 577–85*

Chow, Gregory C. 1985. *The Chinese Economy*, Harper and Row, New York.

—— 1993. 'Capital formation and economic growth in China', *Quarterly Journal of Economics*, 108(3); 809–42.

Christensen, L. R. and Cummings, D. 1975. *Real product, real factor input, and total*

factor productivity in the Republic of Korea, 1960–73, Discussion Paper No. 7057, Social Systems Research Institute, University of Wisconsin, Madison, Wisconsin.
—— 1981. 'Real product, real factor input, and productivity in the republic of Korea, 1960–1973', *Journal of Development Economics*, 8(1981): 285–302.
Christensen, L. R.; Cummings, D. and Jorgenson, Dale W. 1980. 'Economic growth, 1947–73; an international comparison', in Kendrick, John W. and Vaccara, B. N. (eds), *New developments in productivity measurement and analysis*, University of Chicago Press, Chicago, Illinois, pp. 595–698
Christensen, L. R.; Jorgenson, Dale W. and Lau, Lawrence J. 1973. 'Transcendental logarithmic production frontiers', *Review of Economics and Statistics*, 55(1):28–45.
Correa, Hector. 1970. 'Sources of economic growth in Latin America', *Southern Economic Journal*, 36(1): 11–31.
Creamer, R. 1972. 'Measuring capital input for total factor productivity analysis', *Review of Income and Wealth*, 18(1):55–78.
Denison, Edward F. 1962. *The Sources of Economic Growth in the United States and the Alternatives before Us*, Committee for Economic Development, New York.
—— 1967. *Why Growth Rates Differ: post-war experience in nine western countries*, Brookings Institution, Washington, DC.
—— 1972. 'Classification of sources of growth', *Review of Income and Wealth*, 18(1):1–25.
—— 1974. *Accounting for United States Economic Growth, 1929–1969*, Brookings Institution, Washington, DC.
Drysdale, Peter and Huang Yiping. 1995. Technological catch-up and productivity growth in East Asia, The Australian National University, mimeo.
Elias, Victor Jorge. 1978. 'Sources of economic growth in Latin American countries', *Review of Economics and Statistics*, 60(3):362–70.
—— 1992. *Sources of Growth: a study of seven Latin American economics*, ICS Press, San Francisco.
Ezaki, M. 1975. 'Growth accounting of the Philippines: a comparative study of the 1965 and 1969 input-output tables', *Philippines Economic Journal*, 14(4):399–435.
Falk, Martin; Raiser, Martin and Brauer, Holger. 1996. *Making sense of the J-curve: capital utilization, output, and total factor productivity in Polish industry 1990–1993*, Kiel Working Papers No. 723, Kiel Institute of World Economics, Kiel.
Field, R. M. 1983. 'Slow growth of labour productivity in Chinese industry', *China Quarterly*, 96(2):1870 641–64.
Goh Keng Swee and Low, Linda. 1966. 'Beyond "miracles" and total factor productivity', *ASEAN Economic Bulletin*, 13(1):1–13.
Gollop, F. M. and Jorgenson, Dale W. 1980. 'U.S. productivity growth by industry, 1947–1973', in Kendrick, John W. and Vaccara, B. (eds), *New Developments in Productivity Measurement and Analysis*, University of Chicago Press, Chicago, pp. 17–136.
Gordon, Robert J. 1990. *The Measurement of Durable Goods Prices*, University of Chicago Press, Chicago.
Griliches, Z. 1964. 'Research expenditure, education and the aggregate agricultural production function', *American Economic Review*, 54(6):961–74.
—— 1970. 'Notes on the role of education in production functions and growth accounting', in Hansen L. (ed.), *Education, Income and Human Capital*, Columbia University Press, New York, pp. 71–115.
—— 1996. 'The discovery of the residual: a historical note', *Journal of Economic Literature*, September, 34(3):1324–30.
Griliches, Z. and Jorgenson, Dale W. 1962. 'Capital theory: technical progress and capital structure, sources of measured productivity change: capital input', *American Economic Review*, 52(1):50–61.

Huang Tze-Tseng. 1985. 'Measurement of total factor productivity in the R.O.C.', in Yu Tzong-shian (ed.), *Raising Productivity Experience of the R.O.C.*, Asian Productivity Organization, Tokyo, pp. 21–54.

Hulten, Charles R. 1978. 'Growth accounting with intermediate inputs', *Review of Economic Studies,* 45(3):511–18.

—— 1992. 'Growth accounting when technical change is embodied in capital', *American Economic Review*, 82(4):964–80.

Jefferson. Gary. H. 1989. 'Potential sources of productivity growth within Chinese industry', *World Development*, 17(1):45–57.

Johnson, D. Gale. 1950. 'The nature of the supply function for agricultural products', *American Economic Review*, 40(4):539–64.

Jorgenson, Dale W. 1966. 'The embodiment hypothesis', *Journal of Political Economy*, 74(1):1–17.

Jorgenson, Dale W. and Griliches, Z. 1967. 'The explanation of productivity change', *Review of Economic Studies*, 34(2):249–83.

Kanamori, H. 1972. 'What accounts for Japan's high rate of growth', *Review of Income and Wealth*, 18(2):155–71.

Kawai, K. 1995. 'International comparison of economic growth', in Urata, H. (ed.), *Trade Liberalization and Economic Development*, Institute of Developing Economies, Tokyo, (in Japanese).

Kelley, Allen C. and Williamson, Jeffrey G. 1972. 'Sources of growth methodology in low-income countries: a critique', *Quarterly Journal of Economics*, 87(3):138–47.

Kendrick, John W. 1956. 'Productive trends capital and labor', *Review of Economics and Statistics*, 38(3):248–57.

—— 1961a. 'Some theoretical aspects of capital measurement', *American Economic Review*, 51(1):102–11.

—— 1961b. *Productivity Trends in the United States*, Princeton University Press, Princeton.

Kennedy, Charles and Thirlwall, A. P. 1972. 'Surveys in applied economics: technical progress', *Economic Journal*, 82(1):11–72.

Kim Jong-II and Lau, Lawrence J. 1994. 'The sources of economic growth of the East Asia newly industrialized countries', *Journal of the Japanese and International Economics*, 8(3):235–71.

Kim Kwang Suk and Roemer, Michael. 1979. *Growth and Structural Transformation*, Studies in the Modernization of The Republic of Korea: 1945–1975, Harvard University Press, Cambridge, Massachusetts.

Krugman, Paul. 1994. 'The myth of Asia's miracle', *Foreign Affairs*, 73(6):62–78.

Kuo, Shirley W. Y. 1968. 'The economic development of Taiwan: an overall analysis', in Chang Kowie (ed.), *Economic development in Taiwan*, Cheng Chung Book Company, Taipei, pp. 29–139.

—— 1983. *The Taiwan Economy in Transition*, Westview Press, Boulder.

Kwon, Jene K. 1986. 'Capital utilization, economies of scale and technical change in the growth of total factor productivity', *Journal of Development Economics*, No. 24, pp. 75–89.

Lall, A.; Tan. R. G. K. and Chew, S. B. 1996. 'Total factor productivity growth experience of Singapore: an interpretative survey', in Lim Chong Yah (ed.), *Economic Policy Management in Singapore*, Addison Wesley, Singapore, pp. 1–22.

Lampman, Robert J. 1967. The sources of post-war growth in the Philippines', *Philippines Economic Journal*, 6(2):170–87.

Lee Kyu Sik. 1972. *The Bruno production function, factor market disequilibrium, and factor contributions to growth in the Korea industrial sectors*, KDT WP7208, Korea Development Institute, Seoul.

Li Jingwen. 1992. 'Productivity and China's economic growth', *Economic Studies Quarterly*, 43(4):337–50.
Liang Chi-Yuan. 1989. *The sources of growth and productivity change in Taiwan's industries, 1961–1981*, Discussion Paper No. 8903, Institute of Economics, Academia Sinica. Taipei.
—— 1995. 'Production growth in Asian NIEs: a case study of the Republic of China, 1961–93, *APO Productivity Journal*, 3(Winter):17–40.
Lucas, Robert E. JR. 1988. 'On the mechanics of economic development', *Journal of Monetary Economics*, No. 22, pp. 342.
—— 1993. 'Making a miracle', *Econometrica*, 61(2):251–72.
Maddison, Angus. 1972. 'Explaining economic growth', *Banca Nazionale Del Lavoro Quarterly Review*, 22(102):211–51.
Matthews, R. O. C. 1964. 'The new review of investment: comment', *Quarterly Journal of Economics*, 78(1):164–72.
Michalopoulos, Constantine. 1969. 'Productivity growth in Latin America: comment', *American Economic Review*, 59(3);435–9
Nadiri, M. Ishaq. 1970. 'Some approaches to the theory and measurement of total factor productivity: a survey', *Journal of Economic Literature*, 8(4):1137–77
—— 1972. 'International studies of factor inputs and total factor productivity: a brief survey', *Review of Income and Wealth*, 18(2):129–54
Nehru, Vikram. 1994. *New estimates of total factor productivity growth for developing and industrial countries*, Policy Research Working Paper No. 1313, World Bank, Washington, DC.
Nelson, Richard R. 1964. 'Aggregate production function and medium-range growth projections'. *American Economic Review*, 54(5):575–605.
—— 1973. 'Recent exercises in growth accounting: new understanding or dead end?', *American Economic Review*, 63(3):462–68.
—— 1981. 'Research on productivity growth and productivity differences: dead ends and new departures', *Journal of Economic Literature*, 19(3):1029–64.
North, Douglass C. 1994. 'Economic performance through time', *American Economic Review*, 84(3):359–68.
Okuda, S. 1994. 'Taiwan's trade and FDI policies and their effect on productivity growth', *Developing Economies* 32(4):423–43
Oshima, Harry T. 1987. *Economic Growth in Monsoon Asia*, University of Tokyo Press, Tokyo.
Phelps, E. 1962. 'The new view of investment: a neo-classical analysis', *Quarterly Journal of Economics*, 76(4):548–67
Rao, B. V. V. and Lee, Christopher. 1995. 'Sources of growth in the Singapore economy and its manufacturing and service sectors', *Singapore Economic Review*, 40(1):83–115.
Romer, P. M. 1986. 'Increasing returns and long-run growth', *Journal of Political Economy*, 94(5):1002–38.
Rutton, V. M. 1956. 'The contribution of technological progress to farm output: 1950–75', *Review of Economics and Statistics*, 38(1):61–9.
Sarel, Michael. 1996. *Growth in East Asia: what we can and what we cannot infer*, IMF Working Paper 95/98, International Monetary Fund, Washington, DC.
Schmookler, Jacob. 1952. 'The changing efficiency of the American economy: 1869–1938', *Review of Economics and Statistics*, 34(3):214–321.
Scott, Mayrice F. G. 1989, *A New View of Economic Growth*, Clarendon Press, Oxford.
Sengupta, Jati K. 1993. 'Growth in NICs in Asia: some tests of new growth theory', *Journal of Development Studies*, 29(2):342–57.

Solow, R. M. 1957. 'Technical change and the aggregate production function', *Review of Economics and Statistics*, 39(3):312–20.
—— 1959. 'Investment and technical progress', in Arrow, Kenneth. J.; Karlin, S. and Suppes, P (eds), *Mathematical Methods in the Social Sciences*, Stanford University Press, Stanford, pp. 89–104.
—— 1962. 'Technical progress, capital formation and economic growth', *American Economic Review*, 52(2):76–86.
—— 1967. 'The explanation of productivity change', *Review of Economic Studies*, 34(2):249–83.
Star, Spencer. 1974. 'Accounting for the growth of output', *Amencan Economic Review*, 64(1):122–35.
Stigler, George J. 1947. *Trends in Output and Employment*, National Bureau of Economic Research, New York.
Takenaka, H. 1997. Changing Asia-Pacific and the Japanese economy, Keio University, mimeo (in Japanese).
Tinbergen, Jan. 1942. 'Zur Theorie der Langfirstigen Wirtschaftsentwicklung', *Weltwirts. Archiv*, No. 1, pp. 511–49.
Tsao Yuan. 1982. Growth and productivity in the Singapore economy: a supply side analysis, PhD dissertation, Harvard University Cambridge, USA.
—— 1985. 'Growth without productivity: Singapore manufacturing in the 1970s', *Journal of Development Economics*, No. 18, pp. 25–38.
—— 1986. 'Sources of growth accounting for the Singapore economy', in Lim Chong Yah and Lloyd, Peter (eds), *Singapore Resources and Growth*, Oxford University Press, New York, pp. 17–44.
Wade, Robert. 1990. *Governing the Market: economic theory and the role of government in East Asian industrialisation*, Princeton University Press, Princeton.
Wang Fang-yi. 1990. Reconsidering the East Asian model of development: the link between exports and productivity enhancement, evidence from Taiwan, 1950–87, PhD dissertation, University of California, Los Angeles.
Wickens, Michael R. 1970. 'Estimation of the vintage Cobb-Douglas production function for the United States 1900–1960', *Review of Economics and Statistics*, 52(2):187–93.
Williamson, Jeffrey G. 1969. 'Dimensions of postwar Philippine economic progress', *Quarterly Journal of Economics*, 84(1):93–109.
Wolff, Edward N. 1991. 'Capital formation and productivity convergence over the long term', *American Economic Review*, 81(3):565–79.
Woo Wing Thye. 1996. 'Chinese economic growth: sources and prospects', paper presented at The Australian National University, August.
World Bank. 1985. *China: long-term development issues and options*, Johns Hopkins University Press, Baltimore.
—— 1993. *The East Asian Miracle*, Oxford University Press, New York.
Yotopoulos, Pan A. and Nugent, J. B. 1973. *Economics of Development: empirical investigations*, Harper & Row, New York.
You, J. K. 1976. 'Embodied and disembodied technical progress in the United States, 1929–1968', *Review of Economics and Statistics*, 58(1):123–7.
Young, Alwyn. 1992. 'A tale of cities factor accumulation and technical change in Hong Kong and Singapore', in Blanchard, O. J. and Fisher, S. (eds), *NBER Macroeconomic Annual 1992*, MIT Press, Cambridge, Massachussetts, pp. 13–53.
—— 1994. 'Lessons from the East Asian NICs: a contrarian view', *European Economic Review*, 38:964–73.
—— 1995. 'The tyranny of numbers: confronting the statistical realities of the East Asian growth experience', *Quarterly Journal of Economics*, 110(3):641–80.

Part III

GOVERNMENT INTERVENTION AND INDUSTRIAL POLICY

8

THE POLITICAL ECONOMY OF INDUSTRIAL POLICY IN KOREA

Ha-Joon Chang

The rapid growth and structural change of South Korea (henceforth referred to as Korea) during the last three decades has spawned a large body of literature, which is becoming almost impossible to keep track of.[1] With the accumulation of research, it has been revealed that the state played an important role, and the proponents of Korea as a free market have been on the defensive for the last several years. The 'alternative' literature emphasising the role of the state in the Korean developmental experience is still in its infancy, despite some important contributions by Jones and Sakong (1980), Luedde-Neurath (1986), and most notably Amsden (1989). The present article provides some additional empiricial support to this alternative literature, and consolidates its theoretical basis by using some recent developments in economic theory such as the New Institutionalist Economics.

In Sections 8.1 and 8.2 of the article we review some mainstream interpretations of the Korean developmental process. It is argued that these explanations, which try to dismiss the role of the state in the Korean developmental process, have a weak theoretical and empirical basis. In Section 8.3 we examine *how* state intervention works in Korea. In Section 8.4 we attempt to explain *why* state intervention works in Korea. The concluding section draws out some of the implications of our discussion for a new view of the Korean developmental experience and for economic development in general.

8.1 A FREE MARKET?

Although the formerly common interpretation of the Korean developmental experience as a free-market and a free-trade economy (e.g. Ranis and Fei, 1975; Balassa, 1982) is rapidly losing its popularity, it is useful to discuss briefly its argument, since the more recent mainstream interpretations (examined below) can be seen as attempts to rescue the conclusions of the early interpretation.

According to the free-market view, the Korean economy was stagnating in the late 1950s after it had depleted the possibility of 'easy import

Source: *Cambridge Journal of Economics*, Vol. 17, 1993, pp. 131–57.

substitution' in non-durable consumer goods. This 'inward-looking' strategy was inefficient because of the 'distortions' generated by excessive state intervention in various markets. Such 'chaotic' import substitution with multiple exchange rates behind the wall of across-the-board protection, largely using discretionary quantitative restrictions rather than universal tariffs, allowed inefficient firms to survive and discouraged export activities. This, in turn, added to foreign exchange shortage and hence to the pressure for more import restrictions.

The phenomenal growth of the economy, the argument goes, started with the transition from an inward-looking, or import-substituting industrialisation, strategy to an outward-looking, or an export-led growth, strategy. The turning point in this transition was a series of policy reforms around 1965, whose most important ingredients included (i) the introduction of a unified, realistic exchange rate regime; (ii) trade liberalisation involving cuts in tariffs and the abolition of most quantitative restrictions; and (iii) a substantial increase in real interest rates. These policies are regarded as having radically improved the performance of the economy for the following reasons. First, realistic exchange rates, by making export activities as profitable as they should be, allowed Korea to follow her comparative advantage in labour-intensive industries, and therefore to reap the gains from foreign trade. Second, trade liberalisation improved the efficiency of the economy by exerting competitive pressures on domestic producers. Finally, the rise in interest rates enabled the economy to invest more by mobilising more savings, on the one hand, and to use capital more efficiently by restoring the relative price of capital to near its 'realistic' level, on the other.

In the words of Ranis and Fei (1975, p. 56), '[s]tabilisation plus dismantling of the various existing direct control measures, on trade, interest rate and foreign exchange . . . created a more market oriented economy most conducive to access for large numbers of domestic entrepreneurs seeking efficient utilisation of the economy's relatively abundant resources via embodiment in labour-intensive industrial exports'.[2]

There is abundant empirical evidence, however, which runs counter to these explanations. Concerning trade-related reforms, Luedde-Neurath (1986) shows that such reforms were not as thorough as is usually presented and were implemented half-heartedly.[3] First, tariffs were still quite high after the 'liberalisation' and the bureaucracy retained the power to impose 'emergency tariffs' (for items with 'excessively' fast import growth) without changing the relevant laws. In the second place, quantitative restrictions, usually under the name of various 'special laws' and import area diversification regulations, were still pervasive after the 'liberalisation'. As late as 1982, 93 per cent of total imports (in value terms) were subject to one or more of such restrictions (see Luedde-Neurath, 1986, p. 156, table 14.4). Third, prohibitive inland taxes were often used virtually to ban importation of luxury consumer items which were subject only to non-prohibitive tariffs.[4]

Fourth, there was extensive state support for import substitution: for example, subsidised credits to the import-substitutors and to the purchasers of some domestic products (especially machinery), which in effect acted as import restrictions. Lastly, and most importantly, there was widespread foreign exchange rationing, which meant that often the importation of a certain item was impossible, not because it was illegal but because it was impossible to get the foreign exchange to pay for it.

The effect of financial reform has also to be reinterpreted (for a detailed discussion, see Harris, 1987). As may be seen in Table 8.1, the post-reform high interest rates did not last more than a few years, and real interest rates were negative until the 1980s owing to inflation. Nevertheless, savings ratios have showed a rising trend for the last three decades, up from less than 10 per cent in the 1950s and the early 1960s to more than 30 per cent in the late 1980s. That is, 'Korea's saving responds little to interest rates. Overall, the Korean experience suggests that there is no need for high positive real interest rates to mobilise saving through the financial system; as long as large negative real interest rates are avoided, the real interest rate is relatively insignificant' (Dornbusch and Park, 1987, pp. 418–9).[5]

Even if 'liberalisation' in Korea was as comprehensive as the proponents of free markets insist, it is not necessarily true that a 'more market oriented economy' is more efficient even in the neoclassical sense, as the above quote from Ranis and Fei implies. As the theory of second best tells us, the removal of market distortions in some, but not all, markets does not guarantee that the economy achieves higher allocative efficiency (Lipsey and Lancaster, 1956). Moreover, even if it is true that the move to a 'more market oriented' economy improved the *static* allocative efficiency of the economy by moving it closer to its comparative advantage, it does not explain why Korea *grew faster* (also see Bruton, 1989, p. 1616). There is very little economic theory which supports the view that conforming more closely to comparative advantage leads to higher growth, as even the leading neoclassical trade theorists admit (e.g. see Krueger, 1980). More importantly, when growth involves

Table 8.1 Real interest rates in Korea, 1960–1984 (percent)

Period	*Curb market*[a]	*Deposits*[b]	*Export loans*
1960–1964	31.1	−6.7	n.a.
1965–1969	44.4	26.9	n.a.
1970–1974	28.2	−0.2	−16.3
1975–1979	24.0	−4.5	−12.5
1980–1984	19.7	2.4	1.3

Notes:
[a] Nominal interest rates less consumer price inflation.
[b] Nominal interest rates less inflation of the GNP deflator.

Source: Adapted from Dornbusch and Park (1987), p. 419, Table 14.

innovation, there may exist a conflict between the achievement of static allocative efficiency and growth. As Schumpeter (1987, ch. 8) emphasised, under conditions guaranteeing perfectly free entry and thereby allocative efficiency, there will be little incentive for innovation, because any monopoly rent, or what he calls 'entrepreneurial profits' in his earlier work (Schumpeter, 1961, ch. 4), will be instantly competed away. As far as innovation is important for growth, this means that growth may be damaged by an improvement in the static allocative efficiency of the economy (also see subsection 8.4.1).

8.2 MARKET-PRESERVING STATE INTERVENTION?

Evidence shows that state intervention has been pervasive in Korea during its rapid industrialisation period. As Bhagwati (1987) correctly argues, '[t]he key question then is not whether there is governmental action in the Far Eastern economies, but rather how have these successful economies managed their intervention and strategic decision making in ways that dominate those of the unsuccessful ones' (p. 285). And, naturally, some neoclassical economists, including Bhagwati himself, have put forward explanations of the Korean experience which try to reconcile the existence of an interventionist state with rapid growth of the economy.

One such argument is the theory of the virtual free trade regime, which suggests that various measures of state intervention in Korea cancelled each other out to produce a neutral incentive structure (Little, 1982; Lal, 1983; World Bank, 1987). Another is the theory of prescriptive state intervention, which argues that state intervention in Korea does not hinder growth because it leaves room for 'private initiatives' (Bhagwati, 1985, 1987, 1988). In effect, these theories argue that, whatever state intervention there may have been in Korea, it did not affect the workings of the market mechanism, because it was either self-cancelling (virtual free trade) or porous (prescriptive state intervention). Below, we examine these arguments in turn, and argue that they are neither theoretically convincing nor empirically correct.

8.2.1 Self-cancelling state intervention?

According to the proponents of the theory of virtual free trade regime, in Korea there existed widespread price distortions due to one set of state interventions (e.g. import protection), but these were cancelled out by another set of interventions (e.g. export subsidies), producing a neutral incentive structure between production for export and production for the domestic market. They emphasise the fact that Korean exporters had free access to imported inputs at world market prices, and consequently by-passed various import restrictions (Lal, 1983). The economic crisis in the early 1980s following the heavy and chemical industrialisation (HCI) drive during the 1970s (in 1980, Korea experienced negative growth for the first time since the industrialisation drive began in the early 1960s) is presented as proof that a departure from incentive neutrality was a disaster (Lal, 1983; for a different interpretation of the early 1980s crisis, see Chang, 1987).

At the theoretical level, it is not clear how meaningful it is to call the import-substitution-cum-export-incentives régime a virtual 'free trade' régime, because there is no reason why the structure of relative prices under this trade régime should be the same as the one under genuine free trade (Yusuf and Peters, 1985, p. 18, n. 49). And, if the relative price structures under the two régimes are different, we cannot say that the incentive structure under the former is 'neutral', because what matters in determining the relative attractiveness of export and production for the domestic market is the relative price structure, and not the 'average' incentive (for a more detailed discussion, see Wade, 1990, ch. 5).

Moreover, at the empirical level, it is not true that Korean exporters could freely get inputs (raw material and machinery) at world market prices. Luedde-Neurath (1986, ch. 4) shows that only raw materials can be described as relatively, but not absolutely, 'freely-importable' in the Korean trade régime. The importation of machines was heavily controlled to promote the domestic machinery industry, which was seen as the vital ingredient in building a well-integrated economy (see below). Credits were usually refused to the importers of domestically available machines and, instead, subsidised credits, which often amounted to 90 per cent of the product value, were provided to the purchasers of domestic machinery (KDB, 1981, pp. 473–4).

Moreover, it is quite incorrect to assert that the promotion of the heavy and chemical industries through a departure from the incentive neutrality was a failure. Table 8.2 compares the performance of Korean three industry groups—that is, light, chemical, and heavy industries—between 1979 and 1988 with those of some countries at comparable levels of development and, except for Brazil, of a similar size. While Korean performance in all industry groups has been far better than that of other countries, the difference is especially pronounced in the heavy industries, where Korean performance was truly spectacular.

The advance of the heavy and chemical industry products was not confined to the domestic market. Table 8.3 shows trade performance for commodities at 1-digit and 2-digit levels between 1977 and 1987. Almost all the items promoted through HCI—which roughly comprise Standard International Trade Classifications (SITC) 5, 67, 68, and 7—show (often dramatic) improvements in trade balances during this period. The export–import growth differentials [which show the rate at which the sectoral trade deficit (surplus) decreases (increases)] of these items are mostly higher than that between the overall exports and imports, although, again, the performance of chemical products does not particularly stand out. A detailed cost-benefit analysis of the HCI programme is beyond the scope of this paper, but the above evidence suggests that the HCI programme, far from being a failure,

Table 8.2 Korea's comparative industrial performance, 1979–1988 (annual real growth rates of production)

	Brazil	*Chile*	*Greece*	*Korea*	*Mexico*	*South Africa*	*Spain*
Heavy industries [a]	0.6	1.6	−0.8	17.2	2.7	0.4	2.1
Chemical industries [b]	2.6	0.6	2.2	7.5	3.4	1.3	0.8
Light industries [c]	1.5	2.6	0.3	7.8	1.8	2.7	1.6
Manufacturing	1.5	2.7	0.4	11.7	2.1	1.6	1.5
1986 per capita GNP (dollars)	1810	1320	3680	2370	1860	1830	4860

Notes:
[a] Includes the following industries: iron & steel, non-ferrous metal, metal products, machinery not elsewhere classified, electrical machinery, transport equipment, and professional goods.
[b] Includes the following industries: industrial chemicals, other chemicals, petroleum refineries, petroleum & coal products, rubber products, and plastic products not elsewhere classified.
[c] Includes the following industries: food products, beverages, tobacco, textiles, apparel, leather & leather products, footwear, wood products, furniture & fixtures, paper & paper products, printing & publishing, pottery & china, glass & glass products, non-metal products, and all other industries.

All figures are weighted averages unless otherwise stated. The weights are 1980 (except for South Africa, which is for July 1980–June 1981) output at producers' prices (including indirect taxes and excluding subsidies), except for Greece, South Africa, and Spain, which are at factor values (excluding indirect taxes and including subsidies).

Source: UN, *Industrial Statistics Yearbook* (1983, 1984, 1990).

produced impressive growth and trade performance, especially in the heavy industries.

8.2.2 Porous state intervention?

The theory of prescriptive state intervention proposed by Bhagwati (1985, 1987, 1988) tries to resolve the (neoclassical) dilemma of an interventionist state in a rapidly growing economy by characterising the Korean state as 'prescriptive' (one which identifies a number of 'dos'), in contrast to a 'proscriptive' state (one which declares a number of 'don'ts'), such as that of India. According to this theory, state intervention in Korea does not hinder growth because it is less 'stifling'. According to Bhagwati (1988), 'although a prescriptive government may prescribe as badly as a proscriptive government does, a proscriptive government will tend to stifle initiative, whereas a prescriptive government will tend to leave open areas (outside of the prescriptions) where initiative can be exercised' (pp. 98–9) that is, state intervention in Korea does not hinder growth because it is porous.

At a superficial level, it is hardly questionable that an obstructive state will not be very helpful for business and, by implication, economic growth. However, on closer examination, we find the theory both theoretically and empirically unconvincing.

Table 8.3 Trade performance by commodity groups in Korea, 1977–1987

SITC	*Commodities*	*Trade balance (1977)*	*Trade balance (1987)*	*Export growth*	*Export growth*	*Differential*
0	Food and live animals	1.1	0.5	9.2	8.5	−0.3
1	Beverages and tobacco	0.4	n.a.	−1.7	n.a.	n.a.
2	Crude materials, excluding fuels	−7.9	−6.2	4.3	11.7	−7.4
3	Mineral fuels (e.g. petroleum, petroleum products)	−9.9	−6.0	20.4	10.7	9.7
4	Animal, vegetable oil and fat	n.a.	n.a.	n.a.	5.0	n.a.
5	Chemicals and related products	−3.7	−3.7	19.6	16.6	3.0
6	Basic manufactures	7.2	4.5	12.9	15.2	−2.3
61	Leather, dressed fur, etc.	−0.5	−0.4	23.7	15.4	8.3
62	Rubber manufactures n.e.c.	n.a.	0.6	16.3	n.a.	n.a.
63	Wood and cork manufacture n.e.c. (e.g. plywood)	n.a.	n.a.	−14.1	n.a.	n.a.
64	Paper products	0.2	0.1	16.5	19.8	−3.3
65	Textile yarn, fabric, etc.	3.5	3.0	14.1	15.2	−0.9
66	Non-metal mineral manufactures n.e.c. (e.g. cement, glass)	1.0	0.2	8.5	22.2	−13.7
67	Iron & steel	−1.1	0.5	19.6	11.7	7.9
68	Non-ferrous metals	−0.8	−0.8	27.3	18.4	8.9
69	Metal manufacture n.e.c. (e.g. tools, cables, cutlery)	2.1	1.2	10.7	15.5	−4.8
7	Machines & transport equipment	−3.6	3.2	24.7	16.9	7.8
71	Power generating equipmeents	−1.5	−0.7	31.7	12.0	19.7
72	Machinery for special industries (e.g. textile machinery)	−2.0	−2.1	22.6	17.0	5.6
73	Metal working machinery	n.a.	n.a.	n.a.	11.2	n.a.
74	General industrial machinery n.e.c. (e.g. furnaces, pumps)	−2.4	−1.9	35.6	15.5	20.1
75	Office machinery (e.g. computers)	−0.0	0.8	39.3	28.5	10.8
76	Tel;ecommunication & sound equipment (e.g. TV, phone)	1.2	4.4	25.4	15.3	10.1
77	Electric machinery n.e.c. (e.g. transformers, microchips)	−0.2	−0.0	23.6	22.6	1.0
78	Road vehicles	−0.4	3.1	48.2	18.5	29.7
79	Other transport equipment (e.g. ships, aircrafts)	1.2	0.4	35.3	10.3	25.0
8	Miscellaneous manufactured goods	14.7	14.9	16.2	19.6	−3.4
9	Goods not classified by kinds	n.a.	n.a.	n.a.	n.a.	n.a.
Total		−3.8	7.0	16.8	14.3	2.5

Notes:

[a] All figures are measured in per cent.

[b] Data for each commodity group appear only if the value in each year is greater than or equal to 0.3% of the total trade for that year.

[c] Trade balance for commodity i is $(x_i - M_i)/\sum(X_j + M_j)$, where $X_i(M_i)$ is exports (imports) of commodity i and X (M) is total exports (imports).

[d] Export and import growth rates are average annual growth rates between 1977 and 1987 in current value terms.

[e] The differentials are the differential between the export and import growth rates.

Source: UN, *International trade Statistics* (1980, 1987).

In a world with scarce resources (and therefore with opportunity costs), doing something means not doing something else. In this world, saying 'do' A is equivalent to saying 'don't' do 'not A'. And there can be no presumption that saying 'do' A (= 'don't' do 'not A') will allow more initiatives than saying 'don't' do A (= 'do' 'not A'). A prescriptive state can be as 'stifling' as a proscriptive one, since it can make private enterprises do so many things against their will that they are left with few resources to do what they want, even if these activities are not explicitly forbidden. Likewise, a proscriptive state may allow a lot of initiative if it proscribes only a few things. In fact, if we adopt the Liberal concept of negative freedom, that is, 'freedom from' (on the different notions of freedom, see Berlin, 1969), we may say that one has less freedom under a prescriptive state than under a proscriptive one, because private enterprises with government prescription are coerced to execute the prescription, whereas the private enterprises with a state proscription are not coerced into any particular action and therefore can choose the best option from whatever is not forbidden by the state (and thereby exercise 'initiatives').

The Korean state's prescriptions were certainly 'stifling' in many ways. The Korean state prescription for private firms to invest in heavy and chemical industries in the 1970s was a proscription against investing in less risky and often more profitable consumer goods industries. The best example in this regard is the shipbuilding industry, which has grown literally from scratch to the world's second biggest in less than a decade.[6] The Korean shipbuilding industry was set up in direct response to a personal 'command' from the then president Park Chung Hee, against the will of the Hyundai group, the boldest of the Korean business groups, who are famous for their boldness (Jones and Sakong, 1980, pp. 119–20, 357–8). Moreover, if private firms could not be made to do something, the Korean state did not hesitate to set up public enterprises, making the share of public enterprises in GDP almost equal to that of India (Jones and Mason, 1982, pp. 22–3). In a country like Korea where private firms depend heavily on the state-run banking sector for their investment funds, the state's channelling of money into public enterprises can have a very visible impact on 'private initiatives'.

Moreover, the degree of proscriptive intervention by the Korean state has not been so minimal as to warrant the description 'prescriptive' without serious qualifications. In addition to the restrictions on prices of foreign exchange and credit, there was legally implemented direct price control over all marketed products up to 1973. And even after 1973, the state reserved the right to impose a price ceiling when necessary. No price change is conceivable without formal and/or informal state permission, except in some unimportant markets.[7] In addition to price controls, most important Korean industries have had restrictions on entry and capacity (see subsection 8.3.2). Frequently, the Korean state 'reorganises' industries which it thinks have 'too many' firms, through state-led mergers and market-sharing arrangements (see subsection 8.4.1). It is not clear to us what could be more 'stifling', if so many firms have to little freedom to decide what and how much to produce at what price.

8.3 HOW DOES STATE INTERVENTION WORK IN KOREA?

Some mainstream explanations of the Korean developmental experience were discussed above. Their attempts to play down the role of the state in Korea are clearly unconvincing, on theoretical and empirical grounds. In this section, we present an alternative account of the role of the state in the Korean developmental process. This account tries to draw both from the 'revealed' and the 'stated' policy objectives, which are found in various policy documents, and have hardly been investigated by researchers outside Korea.[8] The account will be highly stylised, partly due to lack of space, but mainly due to the fact that this article aims to raise new issues for future research, rather than to be a comprehensive and conclusive case study.

8.3.1 Themes of Korean state intervention

The basic theme of state intervention in Korea has been the making of an 'independent economy' (Jarip Gyongjé) (see various Five Year Plan documents and EPB, 1982). Until recently, the dependence on foreign savings for financing of investments was seen as the major economic problem by Korean policy-makers. They regarded the ultimate solution to this problem to be the construction of an economy with sufficient technological capability to permit a reasonable living standard without a chronic balance of payments deficit. It was believed that the cause of the balance-of-payments problems lay in the underdevelopment of capital and intermediate goods industries, and therefore that 'a shift towards heavy and chemical industries is imperative in order to increase the independence of the Korean economy' (WP, 1970, p. 340)—a principle known in Korea (and Japan) as 'upgrading' the industrial structure (also see, 2nd FYP, pp. 9–10; 3rd FYP, p. 1).

To Korean policy-makers, economic development required giving priority to investment, which was 'essential for growth' (WP, 1968, p. 48). Therefore, macroeconomic policy was geared towards the need to create an expansionary environment if necessary through inflationary measures—which was seen as vital for a sustained high level of investment. Until the late 1980s, of course, there existed a persistent savings gap, which had to be filled by foreign savings. Although the filling of the savings gap was believed to depend ultimately on rising income levels (a Keynesian savings assumption), serious attempts were also made to repress consumption demand through policy measures, expressed in unashamedly paternalistic terms like 'the need to establish a sound consumption pattern' (4th FYP, p. 27). The state-owned banks were instructed not to make consumer loans. The heavy reliance on indirect taxes was also justified (against the accusation that they are less equitable than income taxes) in terms of its discouraging effect on consumption (3rd FYP, p. 16). The control was even stricter when it came to consumption which involved foreign exchange expenditure. For example, foreign holidays were banned until the late 1980s, and imports of 'luxury' goods have been either banned or subject to high tariffs and inland taxes (see Section 8.1). One outcome of such anticonsumption policies is low passenger car ownership, discouraged until recently by high taxation and restrictions on consumer loans. Despite being citizens of a major exporter of passenger cars, Koreans until very recently owned far fewer passenger cars than other developing countries at a comparable income level. In 1985, there were 73.5 people per passenger car in Korea, whereas the corresponding figures in 1983 were 27.0 in Taiwan, 21.8 in Chile, 16.3 in Malaysia, and 15.2 in Brazil (see NRI, 1988, p. 190, table 9.8). Given such a clear (stated and revealed) anti-consumption bias, Korean macroeconomic policy may be more appropriately understood as 'investment management' rather than as 'aggregate demand management'.

Maintaining a high investment level through 'investment management' was, however, seen by the Korean policy-makers as necessary but insufficient to upgrade the industrial structure in a short period of time. Macroeconomic policy measures were seen as ineffective for the rapid upgrading of the industrial structure, owing to their uncertain impact on specific sectors, and were consequently given a status secondary to industrial policy. It was explicitly stated that 'the market mechanism cannot be entirely trusted to increase competitive advantage of industries', and therefore sectors with high productivity growth potential had to be identified by the state and designated as 'promising strategic industries' (WP, 1984, p. 123), or 'priority' sectors, and given custom-designed financial, technical, and administrative support (see later for details). Although macroeconomic constraints often set severe limitations on the conduct of industrial policy, the latter has been actively used whenever deemed necessary and practical. When the aim of macroeconomic stability clashed with the aim of upgrading the industrial structure, the latter was usually allowed to dominate, as testified to by the fact that preferential (subsidised) loans directed to the 'priority' sectors increase faster than general (non-subsidised) loans during recession periods, when the availability of financing can be a matter of life and death for firms (Ito, 1984; Chang, 1987). That is, even when the increase in the overall money supply is contained, the priority sectors are guaranteed financing, at the cost of non-priority sectors. The 'unfair' nature of such a policy has been subject to criticisms inside and outside Korea, but the dominant attitude in policy-making circles has been that being unfair in the short run is justified in the long run by the greater benefits generated by the priority sectors in the form of faster growth and more efficient structural change.

In moving towards high productivity sectors, the biggest concern for

Korean policy-makers was that these industries are often characterised by large-scale economies. (e.g. WP, 1968, p. 174).[9] The strong emphasis on scale economies is exemplified by EPB (1982), which diagnoses the cause of the troubles in the heavy and chemical industries in the early 1980s—an example which is often thought to be the classic case of overly ambitious investments (e.g. Lal, 1983)—as 'the lack of scale economies due to the participation of too many firms in each industry' (p. 222).

The prevalence of scale economics in many priority sectors posed two challenges to Korean policy-makers. One was that individual firms in these sectors needed to be large, in order to obtain the minimum efficient scale of production. Firms were often instructed by the state to build plants of efficient production scale, which compelled them to start exporting as soon as possible in order not to incur losses due to low capacity utilisation. And when firms were thought to be smaller than the minimum efficient scale, state-initiated or state-subsidised mergers were often implemented. The most dramatic example of this was the 1980 'industrial reorganisation' (see subsection 8.4.1). The mergers of two automobile producers in 1965, of five PVC firms in 1969 (see KDB, 1981) and the mergers within fertiliser, shipping, and overseas construction industries in the 1980s (see subsection 8.4.1; also Leipziger, 1988) are other examples. The other challenge from the presence of large scale economies was the high possibility of 'excessive competition', a term used among Korean (and Japanese) policy-makers to describe the well-known propensity of industries with large sunk costs to engage in price wars. As a result, serious attempts were made to restrict entry and regulate capacity expansion in such industries (see subsection 8.3.2).

The apparent antitrust implication of the above policies (merger, entry restriction, etc) was regarded as secondary, because the Korean policy-makers thought that 'excessive competition' can result in 'social waste' (e.g. WP, 1968, p. 173). In traditional textbook economics, where it is believed that large numbers guarantee competition and small numbers hamper it, the notion that there can be 'excessive competition' and that it can result in 'social waste' may not be readily accommodated.[10] However, as has been suggested by the Austrian/Schumpeterian economics and the New Institutional Economics, competition is not a costless process in the presence of 'specific assets' which may not be redeployed without serious loss in value in cases of investment failures (on the notion of asset specificity, see Williamson, 1985).

Although they were not able to articulate this idea very clearly in theoretical terms, Korean policy-makers have regarded competition as a means to achieve efficiency rather than as an end in itself (on the different notions of competition, see Hayek, 1949; McNulty, 1968; O'Driscoll, 1986). This view is exemplified by the 6th FYP document, which states that collusive behaviour should be allowed, and even encouraged, in 'promising industries' which need to 'increase R & D, improve quality, attain efficient production scale' and to 'declining industries' which need to 'scale down their capacities'

(p. 79). Likewise, the antitrust law (the Law for the Regulation of Monopoly and for Fair Trade), which came into being in 1981 after four abortive attempts at legislation (in 1964, 1966,1969, 1971), aimed to regulate anti-competitive *behaviour*, rather than market concentration itself, although the growing criticism of the concentration of economic power into the hands of conglomerates brought about an amendment (in 1986) with stronger restrictions on cross-investments between members of the same conglomerates (see Paik *et al.*, 1988, pp. 28–9, 40–2).

Another related theme of Korean state intervention is the policy-makers' attitude towards foreign firms. Korean policy-makers regarded assimilation of advanced technology by domestic firms as a vital condition for an effective industrial upgrading (for the issue of technology assimilation, see Rosenberg, 1982). To them, this meant tight state control over foreign direct investment.[11] Of course, the persistent savings gap had to be filled, but Korean policy-makers preferred (state-guaranteed) foreign loans to foreign direct investment. As a result, the share of foreign direct investment in total foreign capital inflow (except foreign aid) between 1962–83 was a mere 5 per cent (see Amsden, 1989, p. 92, table 5).

Although such restrictions have been weakening recently, even the latest version of the Law for Importation of Foreign Capital (amended 1988), which is regarded as a 'liberal' one by Korean policy-makers, specifies that foreign direct investment is subject to restrictions in 'priority' industries, infant industries, industries with high imported raw material contents, (especially luxury) consumer goods industries, polluting industries, and agriculture and fishery—which can mean practically all industries, if the state so wishes. Even when foreign direct investment was allowed, foreign majority ownership was practically banned, with some rare exceptions, outside the Free Trade Zones. The fact that only 6 per cent of MNCs in Korea are wholly-owned subsidiaries, compared to 50 per cent in Mexico and 60 per cent in Brazil, suggests a substantial degree of state control over foreign direct investment in relation to ownership (Evans, 1987, p. 208). Even technological licensing, which was preferred to foreign direct investment whenever feasible, was put under heavy restrictions. For example, the latest version of the Law for Importation of Foreign Capital clearly states that technological licensing is banned in industries where local technological capability is deemed to be promising—which, again, can effectively mean any industry.

8.3.2 Industrial policy

At suggested above, the dominance of industrial policy with a view to 'industrial upgrading' has been the most distinctive feature of Korean state intervention (for the seminal work in this line, see Amsden, 1989). The Korean state has chosen several industries at a time as the 'priority' sectors and provided massive support to them. Most of Korea's major industries were designated as priority sectors at some stage and were developed through a combination of massive support and heavy controls from the state. The 'designated' industries had priority in acquiring rationed (and often subsidised) credits and foreign exchange, state investment funds, preferential tax treatments (e.g. tax holidays, accelerated depreciation allowances) and other supportive measures, including import protection and entry restrictions. In return for these supports, they became subject to state controls on technology (e.g. production methods, products), entry, capacity expansion, and prices. The most important tool of such policy was the use of 'policy loans' [i.e. loans with subsidised interest rates and/or priorities in the (ubiquitous) credit rationing], which accounted for 57.9 per cent of total bank loans made between 1962 and 1985 (Lee *et al.*, 1987, p. 53, table III-1).[12]

The practice of giving priority to certain industries identified as important originated in the very early years of Korean development, with the designation of cement, fertiliser, and oil refining in the first FYP (1962-1966) as 'basic' industries.[13] In the second FYP (1967–1971), chemical steel, and machinery were designated as 'priority' sectors. And during the third and fourth FYP periods (1972–1981), especially through the HCI programme (announced in 1973), non-ferrous metals, shipbuilding, and electronics were added to the list of 'priority' sectors. The practice continued in the fifth and the sixth FYP periods (1982–1991), during which machinery, electronics, automobile, chemical, shipbuilding, and various high-tech industries (semiconductor, new materials, biotechnology) were designated 'priority' sectors.

Details of such support and control measures can be seen in Table 8.4, which summarises the measures employed in some selected Promotional Laws, enacted in the late 1960s and early 1970s (except for textiles) to provide legal backing for support for and controls over 'priority' sectors. The Korean policy-makers' concern for 'excessive competition' and the resulting 'social waste' (see subsection 8.3.1) is reflected in the laws in the form of entry restrictions and regulations on capacity expansion. Violators of such restrictions could be heavily punished with revocation of license, fines, and, in some serious cases, prison sentences. Another interesting feature of these laws is the tight performance monitoring system. The monthly export performance monitoring by the Korean state is already famous (see, e.g. Sakong and Jones, 1980, p. 97), but all firms in the 'promoted' industries were required to report on not just export performance but also on performance in other areas. The failure of regular reporting and/or false reporting could be punished with fines and prison sentences. Such a system provided the Korean state with up-to-date and detailed information concerning the state of business in priority sectors, something which is absolutely essential for an effective industrial policy.

More recently, various Promotional Laws were integrated into the Industrial Development Law (enacted in 1986). The novelty of the Industrial Development Law (IDL), compared to the Promotional Laws, is its emphasis

Table 8.4 Major content of promotional laws

Major content (year of enactment)	*Machinery (1967)*	*Shipbuilding (1967)*	*Electronics (1969)*	*Petro chemicals (1970)*	*Iron & Steel (1970)*	*Non-ferrous metals (1971)*	*Textiles (1979)*
Regulations							
Entry restriction	×	×	×	×	×	×	×
Capacity regulations							
Setting up facility standard	×	×					
Capacity expansion approval				×	×		×
Incentives to use domesticxally produced facilities	×		×				
Production regulation							
Regulation of material imports					×	×	
Production standard and its inspection	×	×	×		×	×	
Restrictions on technology imports	×		×				
Price control				×	×		
Reporting and inspection	×	×	×	×	×	×	×
Rationalisation							
Rationalisation programmes	×	×	×	×			×
R & D support							
Subsidies to R & D	×		×	×	×		
Joint R & D projects			×				
Financial support							
Special purpose fund	×	×	×		×	×	×
Financial assistance	×	×	×		×	×	×
Subsidies							
Direct subsidy	×					×	
Reduced public utility rates	×				×		
Tax preferences							
Special depreciation	×					×	
Tax reduction/exemption	×	×	×	×	×	×	
Special industrial complex	×		×	×			×
Administrative assistance							
Facilitating overseas activities			×		×		
Purchase of raw materials					×	×	
Producers' association	×	×	×				×

on 'rationalisation programmes' with *limited*, albeit extendible, lifetimes (usually 2–3 years). The rationalisation programmes are custom-designed to the needs of individual industries and aim to provide temporary boosts for industries which need import substitution, capacity upgrading, and improvements in international competitiveness, on the one hand, and temporary protection for 'declining' industries which need a smooth phasing-out, on the other. Rationalisation programmes based on IDL may be implemented on application from the industry, but may also be implemented by the government *without any such application*.

The measures employed by the IDL can be divided into three groups (for details, see Kim, 1989, pp. 36, 62; Paik *et al.*, 1988, pp. 46–47; Lee, 1989, pp. 64–73). In the first place, there are protective measures to ease the adjustment process, which include import restrictions on competing products, reductions in tariffs for raw materials, price controls, and outright subsidies. Second, there are measures related to the attainment of optimal production scale and the prevention of 'excessive' competition. These include restrictions on entry and capacity expansion, state-initiated mergers, co-ordinated capacity scrapping and/or exit, and market-sharing arrangements (i.e. subdivision of markets into non-overlapping segments). Third, there are measures which aim to raise productivity. These include provision of subsidised credits for such activities as capacity upgrading (or capacity scrapping for 'declining' industries), import substitution of inputs (e.g. machine parts), subsidies for expenditures on R & D and training programmes, and joint research programmes between private firms and government-funded research institutes. As we can see, except for the introduction of limited lifetimes for rationalisation programmes, absent in the Promotional Laws, the major characteristics of Korean industrial policy have changed very little with the introduction of the IDL. The policy measures used are virtually the same, and the discretion of the bureaucracy remains as great as before (because the eligibility criteria are deliberately made vague enough to entitle any industry). The custom-designed nature of individual programmes also remains strong.

Since the enactment of the IDL in 1986, cars, coal-mining, dyeing, ferro-alloys, fertilisers, heavy construction machinery, heavy electrical equipment, naval diesel engines, and textiles have undergone such rationalisation programmes (for details, see Lee, 1989, pp. 64–72; Kim, 1989). As we have mentioned before, the rationalisation programmes were custom-designed for the different needs of different industries. For industries which needed technical upgrading involving large sunk investment (cars, ferro-alloys, heavy construction machinery, heavy electrical machinery, and naval diesel engines), the emphasis was on creating a more stable environment for major new investments and R & D activities, supported by state-led arrangements for market-sharing along product line (among existing producers), entry restrictions, and subsidies to investment and R & D. For the textiles and dyeing industries, which were identified as industries with satisfactory technological capabilities but aging capital stocks, the priority was capacity upgrading, and therefore subsidies were given to producers for scrapping old machines and installing new ones. For the (largely state-owned) fertiliser industry, where the local technological capability was already substantially developed, the programme aimed to introduce more competition in the product market, by granting sales licenses to more distributors and by reducing tariffs on fertiliser imports (but at the same time reducing tariffs on raw material imports). Coal-mining, which was identified as a 'declining' industry, had been under a phasing-out programme, which involved restrictions on entry and capacity expansion, subsidised capacity scrapping, price controls, and import restrictions.

8.4 WHY DOES STATE INTERVENTION WORK IN KOREA?

In the previous section, we gave an account of how state intervention works in Korea. One interesting thing which emerges from this discussion is that the policy measures used by the Korean state are not radically different from those often associated with economic failures in developing countries. This is contrary to the widespread belief that the Korean state's role, 'apart from the promotion of shipbuilding and steel . . . has been to create a modern infrastructure, to provide a stable incentive system, and to ensure that government bureaucracy will help rather than hinder exports' (Balassa, 1988, p. S286), unlike the Latin American countries, where 'there are pervasive controls of investment, prices, and imports and decisions are generally made on a case by case basis, thereby creating uncertainty for business decisions' (Balassa, 1988, p. S287). Why does the seemingly disastrous recipe of heavy-handed intervention work in Korea and not in other countries? In this section, we attempt some answers to this difficult question, although a full response to it would require a comparative study of the role of the state in different countries.

8.4.1 State-created rents and industrial development

Schumpeter (1987) emphasised that those who are starting 'new things' (p. 87), or innovating, need to be provided with 'profits far above what is necessary in order to induce the corresponding investment', or what he called entrepreneurial profits, which provide 'the baits that lure capital on to untried trials' (p. 90). According to him, this is because of the riskiness of innovative activity which is 'like shooting at a target that is not only indistinct but moving—and moving jerkily at that' (p. 88). Schumpeter argued that entrepreneurial profits, or what modern economics calls '(quasi-) rents' may sometimes be provided by the difficulty of imitating the new technology (or organisation), but sometimes would have to be secured through 'restraints of trade' like cartel arrangements (p. 91). The thrust of

Schumpeter's argument is, then, that entry barriers of one form or another are necessary to provide incentives for innovation because it means doing 'new things'.

Establishing an industry in a late-developing country may not involve doing anything 'new' from a global point of view, but poses a similar incentive problem, because it still is a 'new thing' for the nation. In order to set up an industry, a late-developing country has to import technology, but making the imported technology work requires a period of 'learning', which is often a costly activity with highly uncertain returns (Rosenberg, 1982; Abramovitz, 1986; Dore, 1989). Such risk means that those who are starting new industries in a late-developing country have to be provided with some form of entry barrier and the resulting rents. Now, in the context of late development, the market mechanism may not provide such rents, if only because the firms who are borrowing technology from someone else cannot, by definition, set up an entry barrier with the help of the technology, as innovators on the frontier are able to do. Therefore, in a late-developing country, the state, as the ultimate guarantor of property rights, has to create some 'restraints of trade' and provide rents to those who are developing new industries (or even set up those industries itself). And this is exactly what the states in many late-developing countries, from Germany and Japan down to Korea and other currently developing countries, have tried to provide through tariff protection and other forms of state-created rents like subsidies and preferential loans.[14]

Of course, as the opponents of industrial policy correctly point out, there are certain dangers associated with industrial promotion through state-created rents. First of all, there is the risk of policy failure due to lack of information, because the state may not have the information necessary to 'pick the winners' (e.g. Burton, 1983; Grossman, 1988). Second, as the currently popular theory of rent-seeking argues, the existence of state-created rents can lead to 'social waste' by diverting entrepreneurial activities from productive activities into unproductive activities like lobbying (see, e.g. Krueger, 1974; Buchanan *et al.* (eds), 1980; Colander (ed.), 1984). Third, state-created rents, once implemented, are not easy to remove, unlike market-created rents. The existence of 'infant' industries which refuse to grow up is a testimony to such a danger (for some evidence on infant industry performance, see Bell *et al.*, 1984). Korea, like other countries, had to face all the above problems. Korean policy-makers, naturally, made mistakes. The abuse of bureaucratic power, political favouritism, and corruption are hardly rare in Korea. And the country by no means lacks stories of rent-seeking activity. The puzzle is to explain, then, why in the case of Korea these dangers did not inhibit rapid industrial development.

The informational problem, we agree, is often a very serious one, especially in developing countries where basic statistics and other information, which are routinely acquired in developed countries, are not available. However, we would argue that the informational problem can be exaggerated and that it is solvable.

First of all, it is simply not true that private firms operate on the basis of perfect knowledge while bureaucrats know nothing about business. Private firms themselves often operate on the basis of 'informed guesses' or 'animal spirits' when they make major investment decisions, especially in new industries. In addition, large private firms, and not just the state, suffer from informational problems in controlling their divisions and subsidiaries. And when the state maintains an efficient information network of its own, as in the case of Korea, the informational gap between the private sector and the state may be virtually non-existent. The Korean state has kept very close track of priority industries through the obligatory reporting system (see subsection 8.3.1). In some respects, the state may often be better informed than the private sector, as exemplified by the important role played by the information collected by Korean state agencies, including the diplomatic service and, more importantly, KOTRA (Korean Trade Promotion Corporation) in the penetration of new export markets by Korean firms (see Sakong and Jones, 1980, p. 97).

Further, the difficulties of identifying 'sunrise' industries is not as great as is often made out by opponents of industrial policy, except perhaps on the very frontier of technological development. There usually exists a widespread consensus as to which industries are 'sunrise' industries. For example, we all know that, say, the car and microelectronic industries are going to be important in the conceivable future.[15] Especially, in 'catching up' situations, it is fairly easy to identify which sectors to favour and what kind of support is required for success (Dore, 1986, p. 135). The fact that the Korean economic bureaucracy has been traditionally manned by lawyers (at least until the 1970s) also suggests that 'expert' knowledge in the conventional sense may not be necessary for solving the informational problem.[16]

Recently, the proponents of rent-seeking arguments pointed out that industrial policy may, by opening up opportunities to acquire wealth through unproductive activities such as influence-peddling, divert entrepreneurial efforts away from productive activities. However, if the 'waste' from rent-seeking activities has been an obstacle to growth in Turkey or India (e.g. Krueger, 1974; Mohammad and Whalley, 1984), why has this apparently not been the case in Korea?[17]

Rent-seeking costs are fundamentally 'transaction costs' expended in the process of *seeking* rents (which will involve activities like information collection, influence-peddling, and bargaining), and have to be strictly differentiated from the rent itself, which is a pure transfer (Chang and Rowthorn, 1990 and Chang, 1991, ch. 1). Therefore, the mere existence of state-created rents—and therefore the *opportunity* of rent-seeking—does not mean that resources will *actually* be spent on rent-seeking. The *realised* magnitude of rent-seeking costs in a society will depend on how state-created rents can be obtained (Khan, 1989). For example, it has often been suggested that less resources are spent on influencing the state in Korea, because there is not much point in spending resources to influence a 'hard' state (in the Myrdalian sense) like that of Korea (e.g. Bardhan, 1984). One difficulty with this view is that, as is well known to anyone familiar with Korean politics and business, the country by no means lacks stories of huge corruption scandals, a sign that the Korean state certainly *is* subject to influence, if less so than other, 'softer' states.[18] The explanation has to be more sophisticated.

We think one solution to this puzzle lies in the fact that the Korean state is subject to influence, but mainly to influence from a small, exclusive group of agents, that is, the *chaebols*.[19] Although this practice has produced some undesirable distributional consequences, it seems to have reduced rent-seeking costs in Korea in several ways. First, when a small number of people have exclusive access to rents, rent-seeking activities will be less frequent and of lesser magnitude, because others may not join the rent-seeking contest, knowing that they have little chance of success in influencing the state (this is what Bhagwati, 1988, calls the 'brother-in-law theorem'). Second, since the *chaebols* as a group have exclusive access, they need to spend few resources on finding out what kind of agent the present opponent is (e.g. his/her strategy and belief), because they are frequently confronted by the same adversaries in different rent-seeking contests. Third, the fact that the *chaebols* are conglomerates, with stakes in multiple markets, also reduces rent-seeking costs by the 'bundling of issues'. A bargaining solution can be more easily devised if there are other related bargains which allow more room for arranging side-payments (see Schelling, 1960, pp. 32–3).[20]

Moreover, rent-seeking costs are often of a once-and-for-all nature, because once a rent is granted, there will be an 'entry barrier' into the 'rent market' which will discourage the potential entrants from spending resources to dislodge the incumbent. The more serious danger associated with the use of state-created rents is that state intervention may protect or even encourage inefficient producers or production methods, with long-lasting consequences for efficiency. This problem is not explicitly discussed in the rent-seeking literature, which normally assumes that all rent-seeking agents are identical and use optimal production methods. However, in the real world, there is no guarantee that someone who is competent (or even lucky) at seeking rents is equally competent as a producer, although this may well be the case, if rent seeking takes the form of franchise bidding. In Korea, the assumption of 'equal competence' of agents is paradoxically met due to the limitation of access to state-created rents to the *chaebols* which, as conglomerates, are able to operate in almost any line of business equally well. That is, state-created rents in Korea may generate a certain amount of once-and-for-all 'transaction costs' (rent-seeking costs), which are likely to be small for reasons we provided above, but generates little long-lasting production inefficiencies (for a seminal argument in this line, see Khan, 1989).

Probably the most serious problem with industrial policy is that, once implemented, state-created rents may be difficult to withdraw owing to *political* pressure from the recipients of such rents. As was powerfully argued by Marx's theory of 'surplus profit' (1981, e.g. pp. 373–4) and Schumpeter's theory of 'entrepreneurial profit' (1961, ch. 4), the beneficial role of rents, as a means to lure (positive rents) and force (negative rents) firms into more productive activities, hinges on the fact that no rent accruing to 'the innovator' is permanent. In a situation where rents are created by the state, these rents may cease to be transitory and become semi-permanent, if the state is unable to withdraw them when necessary.[21]

Indeed, Korea is no different from other countries in that industrial policy has created many inefficient firms. However, what differentiates Korea from other countries is that the Korean state has been willing and able to withdraw support whenever performance has lagged (Khan, 1989; Amsden, 1989; Shapiro and Taylor, 1990). Such state discipline, when combined with the strategy of 'industrial upgrading' (which involves creation of new and often bigger rents in more productive industries), has acted as a powerful incentive for the firms to enhance their technological capabilities. The imposition of such discipline, of course, has not been a purely technocratic procedure whereby the impartial bureaucrats teach non-performers a lesson, nor has it been a smooth and consensual procedure. It has been, rather, a painful process of continuous bargaining and conflict between the state and the private sector, which, as we shall see below, sometimes had to be solved by forceful measures which are difficult to imagine in other countries.

In 1969, the proliferation of inefficient firms after the massive investment boom in the late 1960s prompted the Korean state to set up a task force accountable only to the Blue House (the presidential residence) to deal with the problem. Between 1969 and 1972, the task force forced dozens of inefficient firms (exact numbers not released) into mergers, sales, and liquidation (sometimes sweetened by debt roll-overs by the Korea Development Bank). The programme eventually ended with the notorious 8–3 Decree (after the date of its announcement, August 3, 1972) involving a total freeze on all curb market loans which were eating into the profits of many firms under financial distress, with subsequent reduction in their interest rates and/or in debt-equity swaps (for details, see Lee, 1985).

After the investment boom of the late 1970s, which led to temporary excess capacity in some major industries, the Korean state again stepped in with the Reorganisation of Heavy and Chemical Industries programme (for more details, see Chang, 1987). Four existing companies in the power-generating equipment industry were merged into Korea Heavy Industries and Construction Co. (KHIC), which was subsequently nationalised, on the ground that the state support needed to make KHIC profitable was too big to be given a single private firm.[22] In the passenger car industry, one of the three existing producers (Kia) was forced to exit and specialise in trucks and buses with a promise that it would be allowed in again when the demand condition improved (this actually occurred).[23] One of the three companies in the naval diesel engine industry (Daewoo) was forced to exit, and the other two were forced to split the market into two segments and specialise (Hyundai in over-6000 h.p. engines and Ssangyong in under-6000 h.p. ones). In the heavy electrical machinery industry, which consisted of eight companies, three (Hyosung, Ssangyong, Kolon) were merged into one (Hyosung) and allowed to produce only highly specialised and expensive products. A subsidiary of Hyundai was asked to produce only for its sister companies. Four other minor companies were forced to produce only less sophisticated and cheaper products. Each of the four companies in the electronic switching system industry (Samsung, Gold Star, OPC, and Daewoo) was forced to specialise in a different product. The two companies in the copper smelting industry were merged by forcing one to buy the other's equity, which was supported by equity participation of KDB and a moratorium on bank loans repayment.

Another round of state-led mergers and liquidations of inefficient firms occurred between 1984 and 1988 (see Lee *et al.*, 1988, pp. 60–2). This time, the shipping, overseas construction, and fertiliser industries, which were identified as declining industries, formed the focus of the programme. In 1984, three fertiliser producers were liquidated, and 63 shipping companies were merged into 17. In 1986, a major reorganisation of the overseas construction industry was implemented. And between 1986 and 1988, 82 inefficient firms (23 of them in shipping and overseas construction industries) were forced into liquidation and mergers.

What is notable in the conduct of such 'reorganisation' programmes is that even the economically and politically powerful conglomerates, *chaebols*, as individual *conglomerates*, were not immune to state discipline, although, as *a group*, they were certainly privileged in their access to various rents. To the Korean policy-makers, it seems to matter less who runs a business than that it is run efficiently. If a particular *chaebol* runs a plant well, fine; otherwise, the ownership has to be transferred to another *chaebol* or even to the public sector (e.g. nationalisation of KHIC). The fact that the *chaebols* as conglomerates are potentially able to move into any line of business (on the basis of their activities in related lines) makes it difficult for a *chaebol* to keep a particular industry as its fiefdom. Unless it remains reasonably efficient, other *chaebols* can easily persuade the state that they can do a better job and get state support in the next round of capacity expansion in that industry. Therefore, the *chaebols* had a powerful incentive to remain efficient, especially when the loss of state support can mean a sharp downturn in business in a few years' time, given the state control of credit and the high leverage of Korean firms. Many *chaebols* which lost state favour (for political and/or efficiency reasons) went into oblivion or were disbanded and their carcasses were distributed to other *chaebols*, as exemplified by the fact that only two of the ten biggest *chaebols* in 1966 were among the top ten in 1974; only five out of the 1974 top ten were in the 1980 top ten; only six of the 1980 top ten were in the 1985 top ten (Paik *et al.*, 1988, p. 352, table 35).

8.4.2 The bases of state power: history, politics, and economics

The Korean state played a central role in the country's economic development through its cunning use of state-created rents as an instrument for industrial development. Of course, such a result was only possible because the Korean state was a strong state which could discipline firms.[24] What was the basis for such state power?

It has often been suggested that the Korean state could become strong because the country's historical development left a social structure with no powerful social classes to contest state power (Hamilton, 1983; Lim, 1985; Evans, 1987; Amsden, 1989, ch. 2). The landed class was eliminated through land reform at the time of the Korean War, and the incipient political organisations of the working class and the farmers were also crushed during the war and the subsequent domination of Cold War politics. Moreover, it is argued that the country's Confucian tradition produced a society where the state commands the moral high ground and draws on the best talents (e.g. Luedde-Neurath, 1985).[25] The long tradition of centralisation in Korean history seems to have been another factor serving to legitimatise the power possessed by the central bureaucracy.[26]

We think these historical factors are extremely important, and perhaps what differentiates Korea most from, say, India or Latin America (on India, see Datta-Chaudhuri, 1990; on Latin America, see Fishlow, 1990, and Shapiro and Taylor, 1990). The weakness of social classes was certainly important in deciding the balance of power between state and society in Korea. The Confucian belief in the state as a legitimate social institution (if not necessarily in particular governments and individual political leaders), often lacking in other developing countries, also seems to have been an important factor in making state intervention effective in Korea.

However, we think that such historical factors are, in themselves, not enough to bring about a strong state. For example, if social classes had been weak since the end of the Korean War, why was the Korean state so weak and incompetent in the 1950s? Again, if Confucianism is conducive to a strong and competent state, why was the Kuomintang government before 1949 so weak and incompetent? Although a full discussion of the subject is beyond the scope of this article, we would argue that the strong state should be at least partly understood as an outcome of the conscious actions taken by the military régime of General Park Chung Hee, which fundamentally shaped the political economy of the country for decades to come. The strong Korean state was, as we shall see soon, as much, if not more, an outcome of calculated political moves and institutional innovations as of historical conditions and culture.

The political ideas of the top political decision-makers of the military régime were fundamentally shaped under the shadow of the Japanese variety of corporatism.[27] In terms of their economics, the early Korean top political decision-makers were no fans of the free market, although they had to pay constant lip service to the 'free enterprise economy', given the critical importance of US support for the political survival of the régime.[28] In addition, whatever little economic knowledge the early Korean economic bureaucracy had was not neoclassical economics but the economic theories of Friedrich List, Joseph Schumpeter, and Karl Marx, which dominated Japanese academia and policy-making circles in the first half of the twentieth century (see Morris-Suzuki, 1989). The major themes of Korean economic policy-making, for example, the concern with 'social waste' from 'excessive competition', the emphasis on scale economies (and large firms), the obsession with capital accumulation (reflected in the anticonsumption bias), and the desire to develop heavy and chemical industries, make more sense when we understand the intellectual background of the economic bureaucracy. Given such a background, it is more than natural that the political-economic agenda of the Park régime was summarised as 'guided capitalism' (Gyodo Jabon-Jui), where the state plays a guardian role.

As soon as it came to power, the Park régime moved swiftly to prepare some institutional ground for its political-economic agenda. One of the first moves of the Park régime was to nationalise all the banks, and therefore to gain control over the financial flows in the economy. Subsequently, new state-owned banks (e.g. the Korean Exchange Bank, the Bank for Medium and Small Firms, the Ex-Im Bank) were set up over a period of time, resulting in full state control over investment loans.[29] At the same time, the Park régime imprisoned many prominent businessmen on the charge of having accumulated wealth through 'illicit' means (e.g. using political connections) and later released them in return for their promises to 'serve the nation through enterprise', which basically meant building new plants in state-designated industries (the so-called 'Illicit Wealth Accumulation' episode; see Jones and Sakong, 1980, pp. 69–70, 281–2). With these two major political blows, the business community suddenly became, morally, like criminals on parole on condition that they 'served the nation through enterprise', and, economically, a paper tiger with little power to make investment decisions—the ultimate capitalist prerogative.

Another important institutional innovation made by the Park régime was the centralisation of economic policy-making power in the hands of the super-ministry headed by the deputy prime minister, namely, the Economic Planning Board (EPB) (see Whang, 1991, pp. 86–7). The integration of *both planning and budgeting authorities* within the EPB eliminated the conflict of interests, if at the cost of concentration of power within the government (which may be objected to on other grounds), between the planning and industrial ministries (which are usually more interested in long-term investments) and the finance ministry (which is usually more interested in short-term stability). Elimination of such conflict made the implementation of industrial policy in Korea more effective than in other 'industrial policy states' like Japan and France where such conflict has been a problem (see Johnson, 1982, for Japan; see Hall, 1987, for France).

Even the much-vaunted cultural and ideological homogeneity of Korean society was not purely a historical bounty which the nation accidentally stumbled on. The Park régime mobilised the nation with the ideology of 'Renaissance of the Nation' through the building of 'Jarip Gyongjé' (independent economy). Workers were described by the state-controlled media and state-issued school textbooks as 'industrial soldiers' fighting a patriotic war against poverty (although the labour movement was brutally suppressed) and businessmen were given medals for their achievement of export targets as if they were generals who won major battles. Farmers were mobilised into semi-compulsory (unpaid) labour for rural infrastructural development à la Mao Tse Tung, through the 'Sémaul (New Village) Movement' (Michell, 1982, pp. 205–8). Although not all such ideological mobilisations were successful (for example, the Sémaul Movement was much resented) and some may criticise them as 'militarising' society (e.g. Halliday, 1980), it is undeniable that they were important in promoting that society's ideological homogeneity.

The Korean state has continued to occupy the economic and moral commanding heights throughout the country's developmental period. State control over credit, which has been the most effective means of controlling private firms, given their high leverage (see above), continued, although some of the state-owned banks (the so-called 'city banks') were partially 'privatised' in 1982. Despite privatisation, the independence of these banks is almost nil, given their over-exposure to highly-borrowed firms and their consequent dependence on the central bank, which is under full control of the state.[30] Indeed, following the 'privatisation', the share of 'policy loans' has actually *increased*, from 56.0 per cent (1962–1981) to 67.6 per cent (1982–1985), making it very difficult to argue that state control over the banking sector has loosened. In addition to their freedom to make loan decisions, the banks' freedom to set interest rates has also been severely limited. Despite the legal deregulation of rates on loans and long-term deposits in December 1988, it is still reported in 1991 that '[i]nterest rates are still strictly controlled by guidance from the Bank of Korea and the Ministry of Finance, despite the legal deregulation' (FEER, 30 May, 1991, p. 52).

In addition to its control over domestic financial flows, the Korean state has maintained tight foreign exchange controls. The buying and selling of foreign exchange has been tightly regulated and, up to a few years ago, it was illegal (and subject to a prison sentence) to possess foreign exchange except for business purposes. The state's control over foreign loans and foreign direct investments has been near-absolute. Although foreign borrowing and, to a lesser degree, foreign direct investment has not been discouraged, the state has had the final say in deciding whether a certain loan or foreign direct investment would be permitted, and on what terms.

Albeit far less important than the control over financial resources, the state's control over material resources through public enterprises should not be ignored. The Korean state has owned various strategic industries, including oil, coal (partly), gas, fertilisers, steel, and electricity. The fact that such crucial intermediate inputs like oil, coal, gas, electricity, steel and fertilisers (used as a means to control farmers) are supplied by public enterprises is another important factor contributing to the power of the state.

Of course, the regular threat by the Korean state that it is going to use this power to discipline non-performers (e.g. that it will restrict loans to firms which do not comply with a particular policy) is not always carried out, partly because large business firms have a strong influence on policy formation and implementation. Nevertheless, such a threat is not an idle one and is often realised, as exemplified by the freezing of bank credit (on 8 May, 1991) to 14 subsidiaries of eight conglomerates that had not complied with state pressure to sell non-business land (EIU, 1991, p. 20). A still more dramatic example is the Kukje group incident in 1985, when the state deliberately bankrupted the inefficiently run Kukje group, then the seventh largest conglomerate in the country, by ordering its major lending bank not to honour its cheques (for details, see FEER, 21 April, 1988, pp. 58–60). Although it is believed that the decision to let Kukje go under was in part motivated by its lukewarm attitude in meeting the ruling party's financial demands, this is a good example of how far the Korean state can go, if it chooses.

CONCLUSION

The Korean experience shows first that a development strategy is a complex set of interrelated policies rather than a simple matter of trade régime, as is often implied by debates between the proponents of 'outward-looking' and of 'inward-looking' strategies. Without doubt, trade strategy is a crucial ingredient in a developmental strategy, especially because, as we have seen in the Korean case, the fastest way to build up an advanced industrial base in a developing country is to earn foreign exchange to import advanced technologies and the machines which embody them. Nevertheless, the Korean success was based on a conception of economic development which encompassed far more than mere trade strategy. Development strategy is a multidimensional problem involving such wide-ranging areas as the establishment of long-term targets for growth and structural change, investment in productive facilities and infrastructure, the supply of an adequate labour force with industrial competence and discipline, and technological catching-up and development. Development strategy should no longer be discussed in terms of the misconceived dichotomy between export-led (or outward-looking) and import-substituting (or inward-looking) strategies.

Second, the Korean experience shows the importance of a long-term dynamic perspective in managing industrial transition. The industrial transition in Korea was achieved not mainly through the attainment of short-term static efficiency ('getting the prices right'), but through the pursuit of long-term dynamic efficiency through the state's constant creation of rents (or Marxian/Schumpeterian profits). A constant upgrading of the industrial structure based on the development of local technological and managerial capabilities was seen by Korean policy-makers as the surest way to achieve sustained growth and efficient structural change, and hence higher living standards. The state's control over technological transfers and foreign direct investments, and the state's commitment to long-term lending through state-owned banks and various special investment funds, have been vital in this respect. Many individual instances of intervention in Korea might have appeared inefficient and sometimes even megalomanic from a short-term static point of view (e.g. the establishment of steel and shipbuilding industries), but when viewed from a long-term dynamic point of view, most, if not all, make sense.

Third, the Korean experience suggests that a rethinking of the concept of competition is necessary. Until recently, the obsession of Korean (and other, notably Japanese) policy-makers with 'excessive competition' and the resulting 'social waste' has, unfortunately, been regarded as a sign of the stupidity of the bureaucrats who lack a good education in economics. However, as we have pointed out earlier (subsection 8.3.1), such concerns are more than legitimate in a world with asset specificity, because, in such a world, competition is not a costless process. Ultimately, competition is a means to achieve efficiency, and not an end in itself. We value competition because it can produce more than it costs, and not simply because it is categorically good. And, if the technological and institutional conditions are such that there is going to be 'excessive competition', suppressing competition may be desirable. The Korean experience comes as a serious challenge to the mainstream conception of competition, which is unable to explain why the Korean policy-makers could use all those blatantly 'anti-competitive' (in the neoclassical sense) policies to generate some of the most rapid growth rates and structural change ever seen in human history.

Last but not least, the Korean experience may be 'unique' in the sense that it was supported by a set of idiosyncratic institutions, but this does not mean that it is irrelevant for other countries which have different histories.[31] Practically all successful industrialisation after the British one was based on conscious efforts to import and modify more advanced nations' institutions. Korea, and its predecessor, Japan, are classic examples of such 'institutional learning'. Even when an institution is not transplantable, it is often possible to create some, at least partial, functional equivalent for it.[32] And, if all else fails, there is still the possibility of institutional innovation through conscious design. For example, the famous Swedish 'concensus' between labour and capital was constructed from the most contested industrial relations systems in Europe of the 1920s (Korpi, 1983, ch. 3). Moreover, the construction of a new and well-functioning institution need not take a long time. The famous Japanese lifetime employment is basically a postwar creation (Johnson, 1982, p. 14). The French state, once regarded as one of the most 'archaic' in Europe, transformed itself into one of the most 'modernising' states in the world soon after the Second World War (Cohen, 1977, ch. 4). And, as we have tried to show, Korea is another example of how a well-functioning system can be constructed in a reasonably short period of time through conscious action.

ACKNOWLEDGMENTS

Faculty of Economics and Politics, University of Cambridge. I thank Bob Rowthorn for his willingness to discuss and clarify many difficult questions which emerged in the process of writing this paper. Continuous discussions with Hawon Jang, Mushtaq Khan, and Jong-il. You were also crucial in formulating many ideas in this paper. Peter Nolan and Terence Moll read two earlier versions of the paper and made detailed and enlightening comments. Pranab Bardhan, Geoff Harcourt, Alan Hughes, Paul Kattuman, Michael Landesmann, Nathan Rosenberg, Helen Shapiro, Ajit Singh, John Sender, and Richard Wright made helpful comments on various earlier versions of the paper. I also want to thank two anonymous referees of the *Journal* for some important suggestions.

NOTES

1 Between 1965 and 1986, Korea's annual per capita GNP growth was 6.7 per cent, compared to 2.9 per cent for the developing countries as a whole. Korea's manufacturing growth rate between 1965 and 1980 was 18.7 per cent, compared to 13.2 per cent for Singapore, 9.6 per cent for Brazil, 9.5 per cent for China, 7.4 per cent for Mexico, and 4.3 per cent for India. Between 1980 and 1987, the corresponding figure was 10.6 per cent in Korea, compared to 12.6 per cent in China, 8.3 per cent in India, 3.3 per cent in Singapore, 1.2 per cent in Brazil, and 0.0 per cent in Mexico (World Bank, 1988). This rapid growth was accompanied by major structural change. The production structure in Korea, which looked more like that of low-income countries like India and Kenya in the 1960s, had become more like that of upper-middle income countries like Argentina, Brazil, and Spain by the mid-1980s.

2 It is interesting to note that one of the authors has, by emphasising the importance of 'institutional/organisational changes orchestrated by the governments' in Korean and Taiwanese developments, in effect denied most of what they said earlier (see Ranis, 1989).

3 Although there has been more 'trade liberalisation' since Luedde-Neurath's study all of the following 'invisible' import restrictions are still in operation.

4 For instance, the domestic price of imported Scotch whisky, whose tariff was 100

per cent, was over nine times that of the c.i.f. price after various inland taxes, e.g. liquor tax, luxury consumption tax, and VAT (Luedde-Neurath, 1986, p. 130).

5 In other words, '[b]y paying depositors low real interest rates and by controlling capital outflows, the government implicitly taxed depositors, then channelled the proceeds to favoured sectors for investment' (Dornbusch and Park, 1987, p. 418).

6 The Korean shipbuilding industry raised its share of world shipbuilding output from nil in 1973 (when the first modern shipyard started production) to 4 per cent in 1980 and then to 21.6 per cent in 1986. Korea is now the second largest shipbuilding nation in the world (next to Japan), and produces more ships (in gross tonnes) than Western Europe as a whole, whose world production share was 12.2 per cent in 1986 (NRI, 1988, pp. 162–4).

7 Reading Korean newspapers, one usually finds that 'the government has allowed', and not that 'firm A has decided on', a certain percentage price rise of a product.

8 The most important policy documents include various Five Year Plan (FYP) documents and the White Paper on the Economy (WP), annually produced by the Economic Planning Board (EPB), the super-ministry with *both planning and budgeting authorities*. The 1st FYP (1962–1966) was issued in 1961, and was revised in 1964. Some of the later FYPs, for example, the fourth and the sixth, were also revised during the plan period, but the changes are mainly in macroeconomic forecasting, rather than in policy themes.

9 WP (1968) states that 'it is needless to say that the attainment or otherwise of efficient production scale is the most fundamental determinant of productivity' (p. 174).

10 Of course, the mainstream economists have not been unaware of the possibility that competition can be 'wasteful'. The recent growth of the literatures on 'wasteful R & D' (for a survey, see Tirole, 1988, ch. 10) and 'sunk cost' (for a survey, see Pindyck, 1991) attest to a growing disillusion with the traditional concept of competition even among mainstream economists. However, it seems fair to say that such developments have not been fully incorporated in the mainstream theory of competition in general.

11 Of course, this does not necessarily mean that it is impossible to develop national technological capability by inviting multinationals in. For example, Singapore has developed a sophisticated technological capability with a large multinational presence (see Evans, 1987, pp. 208–9). Likewise, there has been a substantial technological diffusion through subcontracting by multinationals in the Malaysian electronics industry in Penang (see Rasiah, 1990). The important question, then, seems to be what kind of policies are necessary to promote technological transfer by multinationals.

12 Credit availability becomes very important given the high leverage of Korean firms. The average equity participation ratio (as a proportion of total assets) of Korean manufacturing firms was 22.7 per cent during 1971–1979 (Cha, 1983, table V–30). The same figure for 1986 was 22.2 per cent, which is even lower than the Japanese figure for the same year (28.3 per cent). Compare this with 47 per cent of American firms (1986) or with 46.8 per cent of Taiwanese firms (1985) (See Patik *et al.*, 1988, p. 43, table 1–6).

13 The concept of 'basic' industries was also used in the early French planning practice (Cohen, 1977).

14 From a purely static point of view, the states in late-developing countries should not deliberately seek to develop new industries, because it means, *ceteris paribas*, a less efficient use of resources. This was perhaps what was in their minds when various international lenders, including the World Bank and KISA (Korea International Steel Associates)—a consortium formed by steel-makers from the US,

West Germany, the UK, and Italy—turned down Korea's three applications for loans to build an integrated steel mill in the 1960s (Amsden, 1989, p. 295; Watanabe, 1987, p. 69) or when the Bank of Japan was fiercely opposing MITI's effort to develop the car industry in the 1960s (Magaziner and Hout, 1980, p. 55). However, in a world where there is learning, the fact that an industry is unprofitable in a developing country at present prices does not mean that it should not be promoted, as the spectacular successes of Korea's (state-owned) steel mill and the Japanese car industry testify. After the above-mentioned three unsuccessful attempts to raise money for the steel mill, the Korean state was finally successful in securing funds through the war repatriation from the Japanese government and the loans from Japanese Ex-Im Bank (EPB, 1982, pp. 92–4). Ten years after it started operation, the state-owned steel mill (POSCO) became the fourth largest and one of the most cost-efficient steel makers in the world (Amsden, 1989, pp. 298–9). The success of the Japanese car industry is too obvious to merit further discussion.

15 The reaction of the Korean conglomerates to the recent move by the Korean state to increase specialisation among them is instructive in this regard. In 1991, the Korean state forced the top 30 conglomerates to choose three 'core' lines of activity, which are to be exempted from the credit restrictions imposed on the member firms of top conglomerates in 1984 (in a move to mitigate the increasing concentration of economic power) in return for higher investments in technological development. Twelve of the top 30 conglomerates, for example, chose petrochemicals as their core businesses. Cars and electronics were also a common choice (*Financial Times*, 23 April, 1991). This shows that there exists a broad consensus on which industries are 'sunrise' industries.

16 In terms of their theoretical sophistication, the earlier Korean planning documents do not compare with, say, the Indian ones, which were based on such advanced models as the Mahalanobis model.

17 Bhagwati (1988) has suggested that 'prescriptive governments provide fewer inducements for such unproductive activities, because the prescriptions leave large areas open for initiatives' (p. 100). Nevertheless, prescriptive policy is no less prone to rent-seeking activities, because the logic of rent-seeking activities is such that, even if there are large areas open for private initiatives, individuals will engage in such activities if their rate of return is higher than in those areas which are 'open for initiatives'. For example, it is well known in Korea that obtaining subsidised credits (by being a producer in a 'priority' sector) is a very profitable business in itself, because one can divert that money into the curb market where real interest rates can be more than 40 per cent points higher than that of the subsidised credit (see Table 1).

18 The head of one of the country's largest companies is reported to have recently complained that '[t]he government has all the power and you have to purchase approval . . . [and as a result] we pay as much in extortion—legal, semi-legal and illegal extortion— as we do in legitimate taxes' (FEER 30 May 1991, p. 54).

19 A *chaebol* is a diversified conglomerate which is usually controlled by one or two families, although professional managers have been becoming more influential recently. It is similar to the pre-war Japanese *zaibatsu*, except that it does not have its own bank, banks being mainly owned by the state in Korea.

20 In the 1980 industrial reorganisation, for example, Daewoo, the third largest *chaebol*, remained in the passenger car market as one of the duopolists, but was forced to exit from the diesel engine industry and to specialise in a cheaper variety of product in the electronic switching system industry; Hyundai, the second

largest *chaebol*, remained in the passenger car industry in return for forced specialisation in diesel engines and heavy electrical machinery.

21 The introduction of limited lifetimes for rationalisation programmes, with the implementation of IDL, may be understood as an attempt to increase the 'transitory' nature of rents.

22 In addition to rolling over KHIC's debt (details not released), that state tried to boost its activities by giving it monopoly rights to produce certain power-generation components and certain heavy construction equipment (FEER, 2 June 1983, pp. 67–8).

23 The history of the passenger car industry characteristically shows how the Korean state shapes up a targeted industry (the following account is based on KDB, 1981, pp. 501–6). The Korean passenger car industry started in 1962 as assemblage of imported semi-knock-down (SKD) kits. In 1965, there was a state-led merger between the two existing passenger car makers (Senara and Shinjin) into one (Shinjin). In 1968, there were two more entries (Hyundai and Asia), and, thereafter, new entry was banned until 1972, when a lorry producer, Kia, was allowed to enter. In 1974, the government announced the Long term Plan for Promotion of Automobile Industry to develop local passenger car models [at this point, passenger car producers were still assembling complete-knock-down (CKD) kits from Toyota, Ford, GM and Fiat] and forced Asia, which failed to submit a plan for a development of local passenger car models, to exit and its capacities to be bought by Kia. From 1974, local models were developed (Kia's Brisa in 1974, Hyundai's Pony in 1975, GMK's Gemini in 1977). In the mean time, Shinjin withdrew from GMK (its joint venture with GM since 1972) owing to a sales crisis in the newly introduced Chevrolet models. Shinjin's stake was bought by the Korea Development Bank (KDB) (hence a KDB-GM joint venture), which ultimately sold it to Daewoo in 1978 (hence a GM-Daewoo joint venture until 1992). In the 1980 reorganisation of the sector, the original plan was to force Kia to exit and to merge Hyundai and Daewoo, but it was aborted because the policy-makers would not accept Daewoo's plan to abandon local models in favour of GM 'world car' models. The market was maintained as a duopoly between Hyundai and Daewoo until 1987, when Kia was allowed in again.

24 The power of the Korean state has frequently been underrated, especially by some neoclassical economists (e.g. Balassa, 1988), on the ground that the 'size' of Korean state (defined in terms of public sector expenditure) is relatively small (but see Sachs, 1987, for some evidence to the contrary). However, what matters for the effectiveness or otherwise of state intervention is not where the boundary of the state as a legal entity lies, but how far it can exercise its influence. Public sector expenditure as usually defined is a very poor measure of this.

25 However, Confucianism in itself is not necessarily beneficial to economic development. Its contempt for commercial and industrial pursuits (the merchant and the craftsman occupied the two lowest castes in the traditional Confucian social hierarchy) could have acted as an obstacle to industrialisation. In fact, Confucianism, often hailed currently as the reason for the Korean success, was often blamed for the relatively poor economic performance in the 1950s.

26 Korea has traditionally been even more centralised than other Confucian countries. The Japanese feudal system was fairly decentralised until the Meiji Restoration, and the Chinese system, owing to the sheer size of the country, had a strong tendency to dissolve into a decentralised one except in the prime time of a dynasty.

27 Park was a fierce nationalist strongly influenced by corporatist ideas. His

education in the Japanese military academy in Manchuria, which he joined after a brief career as a school teacher, left him deeply influenced by the Japanese variety of corporatism, as is testified by his naming the 'October Restoration' in 1972, his own mid-career political coup to guarantee himself a lifetime presidency, after the Meiji Restoration. He was also strongly influenced by Communism. His brother was an influential local Communist leader, and he himself was sentenced to death (but earned an amnesty by publicly denouncing Communism) as one of the leaders of a Communist mutiny within the Korean army in 1949.

28 With the growing acceptance of 'private initiative', later policy documents (especially the fifth and the sixth FYP documents) emphasise the government's commitment to the 'private-led economy', but this testifies to the persisting dominance of the state (if the economy was already 'private-led', no comments of this sort would have been necessary).

29 Short-term working capital, given credit rationing, was mainly provided either by small non-bank financial institutions or by the curb market.

30 'The government [as of 1988] appoints senior bank officials and major credit allocation decisions have traditionally been cleared with government authorities' (FEER, 21 April, 1988, p. 58).

31 For a rare attempt to consider the importance of the idiosyncratic factors in the developmental experience of East Asian NICs in general (Korea, Taiwan, Singapore, and Hong Kong), see Nolan (1990).

32 For example, the Swedish system of state-guaranteed employment and Japanese lifetime employment are radically different from each other in many respects, but in so far as they create positive attitudes among workers towards the introduction of more mechanised (and hence generally more productive) technology, they are functionally equivalent to one another. It is no coincidence that these two countries are the most robotised economies in the world.

REFERENCES

Amsden, A. 1989. *Asia's Next Giant*, New York, Oxford University Press

Balassa, B. 1982. Development strategies and economic performance, in Balassa, B. *et al., Development Strategies in Semi-Industrial Economies*, Baltimore, Maryland, The Johns Hopkins University Press

—— 1988. The lessons of East Asian development: an overview, *Economic Development and Cultural Change*, vol. 36, no. 3, Apr. 1988, Supplement

Bardhan, P. 1984. *The Political Economy of Development in India*, Oxford, Basil Blackwell

Bell, M., Ross-Larson, B. and Westphal, L. 1984. Assessing the performance of infant industries, *Journal of Development Economics*, nos. 1/2

Berlin, I. 1969. Two Concepts of Liberty, in Berlin, I. *Four Essays on Liberty*, Oxford, Oxford University Press

Bhagwati, J. 1985. Foreign trade régimes, in Bhagwati, J. *Dependence and Interdependence*, Oxford, Basil Blackwell

—— 1987. Outward orientation: trade issues, in Corbo, V., Khan, M. and Goldstein, M. (eds), *Growth-Oriented Structural Adjustment*, Washington DC, IMF and World Bank

—— 1988. *Protectionism*, Cambridge, Massachusetts, MIT Press

BOK (Bank of Korea) 1987. *National Accounts*, Seoul, BOK

—— *Economic Statistics Yearbook 1988*, Seoul, BOK

Bruton, H. 1989. Import substitution, in Chenery, H. and Srinivasan, T. (eds), *Handbook of Development Economics*, vol. 2, Amsterdam, Elsevier Science Publishers

Buchanan, J., Tollison, R. and Tullock, G. (eds) 1980. *Toward a Theory of the Rent-Seeking Society*, College Station, Texas A&M University Press
Burton, J. 1983. *Picking Losers . . . ?: The Political Economy of Industrial Policy*, London, Institute of Economic Affairs
Cha, D. S. 1983. 'Öja Do-ip ui Hyokkwa Boonsok' (The Effects of Foreign Capital Inflow), Seoul, Korea Institute for Economics and Technology (KIET)
Chang, H-J. 1987. 'Crisis of Capital Accumulation in South Korea, 1979–82—An Analysis of Policy Solutions', unpublished M.Phil. thesis, Faculty of Economics and Politics, University of Cambridge
—— 1991. 'The Political Economy of Industrial Policy–Reflections on the Role of the State Intervention', unpublished Ph.D. dissertation, Faculty of Economics and Politics, University of Cambridge (forthcoming from Macmillan)
—— and Rowthorn, R. 1990. 'Rent-Seeking, Transaction Costs, and State Intervention—Towards a New Institutionalist View of State Intervention', mimeo., Faculty of Economics and Politics, University of Cambridge
Cohen, S. 1977. *Modern Capitalist Planning: The French Model*, 2nd edition, Berkeley, California, University of California Press
Colander, D. (ed.). 1984. *Neoclassical Political Economy*, Cambridge, Massachusetts, Ballinger Publishing Co.
Cumings, B. 1987. The origins and development of the Northeast Asian political economy: industrial sectors, product cycles, and political consequences, in Deyo, F. (ed.), *The Political Economy of the New Asian Industrialism*, Ithaca, Cornell University Press
Datta-Chaudhuri, M. 1990. Market failure and government failure, *Journal of Economic Perspectives*, vol. 4, no. 3
Dore, R. 1986. *Flexible Rigidities: Industrial Policy and Structural Adjustment in the Japanese Economy 1970–80*, London, The Athlone Press
—— 1989. Latecomers' problems, *European Journal of Development Research*, vol. 1, no. 1
Dornbusch, R. and Park, Y. 1987. Korean growth policy, *Brookings Papers on Economic Activity*, no. 2
EIU (Economist Intelligence Unit) 1991. *South Korea—Country Report*, no. 2
EPB (Economic Planning Board) 1982. Gaebal Nyondae ui Gyong-je Jonngchek (Economic Policy in the Developmental Era), Seoul, EPB
EPB (Economic Planning Board) 1989. *Major Statistics of Korean Economy*, 1989, Seoul, EPB
Evans, P. 1987. Class, state, and dependence in East Asia: lessons for Latin Americanists, in Deyo, F. (ed.), *The Political Economy of the New Asian Industrialism*, Ithaca, Cornell University Press
FEER (*Far Eastern Economic Review*), various issues
Fishlow, A. 1990. The Latin American state, *Journal of Economic Perspectives*, vol. 4, no. 3
FYP (Five Year Plan) various years. Seoul, Republic of Korea Government
Grossman, G. 1988. Strategic export promotion: a critique, in Krugman, P. (ed.), *Strategic Trade Policy and the New International Economics*, Cambridge, Massachusetts, The MIT Press
Hall, P. 1987. *Governing the Economy*, Cambridge, Polity Press
Halliday, J. 1980. Capitalism and Socialism in East Asia, *New Left Review*, no. 124
Hamilton, C. 1983. Capitalist industrialisation in East Asia's four little tigers, *Journal of Contemporary Asia*, 1983, no. 1
Harris, L. 1987. Financial reform and economic growth: a new interpretation of South Korea's experience, in Harris, L. (ed.), *New Perspectives on the Financial System*, London, Croom Helm

Hayek, F. 1949. The meaning of competition, in Hayek, F. *Individualism and Economic Order*, London, Routledge & Kegan Paul

Ito, K. 1984. Development finance and commercial banks in Korea, *The Developing Economies*, vol. 22, no. 4

Johnson, C. 1982. *MITI and the Japanese Miracle*, Stanford, Stanford University Press

Jones, L. and Mason, E. S. 1982. Role of economic factors in determining the size and structure of the public-enterprise sector in less-developed countries with mixed economies, in L. Jones (ed.), *Public Enterprise in Less-Developed Countries*, Cambridge, Cambridge University Press

Jones, L. and Sakong, I. 1980. *Government, Business and Entrepreneurship in Economic Development: The Korean Case*, Cambridge, Massachusetts, Harvard University Press

KDB (Korea Development Bank) 1981. 'Palship Nyondae ui Jonryak Sanup' (Strategic Industries of the 1980s), Seoul, KDB

Khan, M. 1989. 'Clientelism, Corruption, and Capitalist Development: An Analysis of State Intervention with special reference to Bangladesh', Unpublished Ph.D. Thesis, Faculty of Economics and Politics, University of Cambridge

Kim, J. H. 1989. 'Korean Industrial Policies for Declining Industries', Korea Development Institute (KDI) Working Paper no. 8910, Seoul, KDI

Korpi, W. 1983. *The Democratic Class Struggle*, London, Routledge & Kegan Paul

Krueger, A. 1974. The political economy of the rent-seeking society, *American Economic Review*, vol. 64, June

Krueger, A. 1980. Trade policy as an input to development, *American Economic Review*, 1980, Papers and Proceedings

Lal, D. 1983. *The Poverty of Development Economics*, London, The Institute of Economic Affairs

Lee, S. H. 1985. Gookka, Kyegup mit jabon chookjok (The state, classes and capital accumulation), in Choi, J. J. (ed.), *Hangook Jabonjui a Gookka* (Korean Capitalism and the State), Seoul, Hanwool

Lee, S. H., Kim, S. D. and Hahn, S. H. 1989. *Hangook ui Sanup Jongchek—Sanup Goojo Jongchek Gwanryon Jaryojip* (Korean Industrial Policy—Policies concerning Industrial Structure), Seoul, Korea Institute for Economics and Technology (KIET)

Lee, Y. S., Lee, J. H. and Kim, D. H. 1987. *Sanup Goomyoong Jongchek ui Hyoyool-hwa Bang-ahn* (A Proposal for Improving the Efficiency of Industrial Financing Policy), Seoul, Korea Institute for Economics and Technology (KIET)

Leipziger, D. 1988. Industrial restructuring in Korea, *World Development*, vol. 16, no. 1

Lim, H-C. 1985. *Dependent Development in Korea*, Seoul, Seoul National University Press

Lipsey, R. and Lancaster, K. 1956. General theory of the second best, *Review of Economic Studies*, vol. 24, no. 63

Little, I. 1982. *Economic Development*, New York, Basic Books

Luedde-Neurath, R. 1985. State intervention and exported-oriented development in South Korea, in Wade, R. and White, G. (eds), *Development States in East Asia*, Brighton, IDS

Luedde-Neurath, R. 1986. *Import Controls and Export-Oriented Development; A Reassessment of the South Korean Case*, Boulder and London, Westview Press

Maddison, A. 1989. *The World Economy in the 20th Century*, Paris, OECD

McNulty, P. 1968. Economic theory and the meaning of competition, *Quarterly Journal of Economics*, vol. 82, November

Marx, K. 1981. *Capital*, vol. 3, Harmondsworth, Penguin Books

Michell, T. 1982. South Korea: vision of the future for labour surplus economies? in Bienefeld, M. and Godfrey, M. (eds), *The Struggle for Development: National Strategies in International Context*, New York, John Wiley & Sons Ltd

Mohammad, S. and Whalley, J. 1984. Rent seeking in India: its costs and policy significance, *Kyklos*, vol. 37, no. 3
Morris-Suzuki, T. 1989. *A History of Japanese Economic Thought*, London and New York, Routledge
Nolan, P. 1990. Assessing economic growth in Asian NICs: some thoughts on the conclusions drawn from their experience, *Journal of Contemporary Asia*, 1990, no. 1
NRI (Nomura Research Institute) 1988. *Sekai ni Hiyakusuru Kankoku Sangyo* (Korean Industries are Joining the World Class), Tokyo, NRI; Korean language edition, Seoul, Panmun Book Company
O'Driscoll, G. 1986. Competition as a process: a law and economics perspective, in Langlois, R. (ed.), *Economics as a Process*, Cambridge, Cambridge University Press
Paik, N. K., Chang, S. I. and Lee, D. H. 1988. *Hangook ui Sanup Jongchek—Sanup Jojick Jongchek Gwanryon Jaryojip* (Industrial Organisation Policies of Korea), Seoul, Korea Institute for Economics and Technology (KIET)
Pindyck, R. 1991. Irreversibility, uncertainty, and investment, *Journal of Economic Literature*, vol. 29, no. 3
Ranis, G. 1989. The role of institutions in transition growth: the East Asian newly industrialising countries, *World Development*, vol. 17, no. 9
Ranis, G. and Fei, J. 1975. A model of growth and employment in the open dualistic economy: the cases of Korea and Taiwan, in Stewart, F. (ed.), *Employment, Income Distribution and Development*, London, Frank Cass
Rasiah, R. 1990. 'Electronics Industry in Penang', mimeo., Faculty of Economics and Politics, University of Cambridge
Rosenberg, N. 1982. The international transfer of technology: implications for the industrialised countries, in Rosenberg, N., *Inside the Black Box: Technology and Economics*, Cambridge, Cambridge University Press
Sachs, J. 1984. Comment on C. Diaz-Alejandro, Latin American debt: I don't think we are in Kansas anymore, *Brookings Papers on Economic Activity*, 1984, no. 2
Sachs, J. 1987. Trade and exchange rate policies in growth-oriented adjustment programs, in Corbo, V., Khan, M. and Goldstein, M. (eds), *Growth-Oriented Structural Adjustment*, Washington DC, IMF and World Bank
Schelling, T. 1960. *The Strategy of Conflict*, Cambridge, Massachusetts, Harvard University Press
Schumpeter, J. 1961. *The Theory of Economic Development*, London, Oxford University Press
Schumpeter, J. 1987. *Capitalism, Socialism, and Democracy*, 6th edition, London, Unwin Paperbacks
Shapiro, H. and Taylor, L. 1990. The state and industrial strategy, *World Development*, vol. 18, no. 6
Tirole, J. 1988. *The Theory of Industrial Organisation*, Cambridge, Massachusetts, The MIT Press
UN (United Nations) various years. *Industrial Statistics Yearbook*, New York, UN
UN (United Nations) various years. *Trade Statistics Yearbook*, New York, UN
Wade, R. 1990. *Governing the Market*, Princeton, New Jersey, Princeton University Press
Watanabe, T. 1987. *Venture Capitalism* (translated from Japanese), Seoul, The Korea Economic Daily
Whang, I. J. 1991. Government direction of the Korean economy, in Caiden, G. and Kim, B. W. (eds), *A Dragon's Progress—Development Administration in Korea*, West Hartford, Connecticut, Kumarian Press
Williamson, O. 1985. *The Economic Institutions of Capitalism*, New York, The Free Press

World Bank 1987. *World Development Report 1987*, New York, Oxford University Press

World Bank 1988. *World Development Report 1988*, New York, Oxford University Press

WP (White Paper on the Economy) various years. Seoul, Economic Planning Board (EPB)

Yusuf, S. and Peters, R. 1985. 'Capital Accumulation and Economic Growth: The Korean 'Paradigm', Washington, DC, World Bank Staff Working Paper no. 712

9

ANOTHER LOOK AT THE EAST ASIAN MIRACLE

Gustav Ranis

The key elements of East Asia's development success story have become shrouded in a controversy between supporters of the "Washington Consensus," generated by the World Bank and the International Monetary Fund (IMF), and its heterodox critics.[1] The controversy focuses almost exclusively on the importance of recent government industrial policy, mainly in the form of directed credit. The Bank has offered olive branches in the form of "market friendly interventions" followed by "reversible nonmarket contests" (World Bank 1991, 1993). These have not been accepted by either the heterodox critics or the Japanese government, and the argument continues to rage.

The main purpose of this article is to help move the discourse away from such ahistorical and relatively narrow industry-focused "markets versus government" arguments. Instead, it examines what I believe to have been the critical elements of the overall success of development in East Asia, especially Taiwan (China), over the longer run. Not surprisingly, there is no single key ingredient. Instead, what is critical and persuasive is the continuing flexibility of policymakers who have responded on a broad front to the changing demands of the economy during each of the identifiable subphases of the transition growth effort over the past four decades. As a result of this flexibility, the system was able to avoid running out of steam and to be in a position to shift onto new rails at the end of each subphase.

In the 1950s, East Asia, like virtually all developing regions, initially chose an import substitution package, but it was an exceptionally mild and brief version that was less destructive of agricultural incentives in comparison with versions adopted in other regions. Consequently, once the domestic market for labor-intensive nondurables had become exhausted in the early 1960s, it was much easier to overcome the resistance of vested interests to macro and structural policy changes aimed at facilitating an increasingly outward-oriented, labor-intensive industrialization effort. The next major challenge, the gradual exhaustion of that labor by the early 1970s, once again met an anticipatory response, this time in the form of public policies focused

Source: *The World Bank Economic Review*, Vol. 9 (3), 1995, 509–34.

on human capital and technology-oriented investments. These policies enabled East Asia to flexibly overcome the external shocks of the 1970s and to participate as an ever more equal partner in the continuously changing product cycle of the industrial countries. Ultimately, the economies of East Asia themselves approached mature-economy status.

Each decade had its challenges, and each decade produced government policy responses that turned out, in Kuznets's terms, to have been accommodating rather than obstructive of changes required by mainly private agents. If there is one key to developmental success, it is avoiding the encrustation of ideas. This has been achieved by continuing policy reforms aimed at an ever-increasing reliance on the responsiveness of large numbers of dispersed decisionmakers.

Section 9.I briefly describes the distinguishing initial conditions that set off East Asia's development efforts. Section 9.II analyzes the unusually mild version of the import substitution subphase (1953–63) that permitted the system to avoid the neglect of its agricultural sector that usually occurs during such a phase. Section 9.III highlights the classical behavior of Taiwan (China)'s dualistic labor market, which was critical for the generation of an initially vigorous domestic, subsequently export-oriented, process of balanced growth (1963–72). Section 9.IV analyzes the importance of flexible policies with respect to the formation of human capital and technological infrastructure in the 1980s and 1990s. Section 9.V presents conclusions and briefly explores the elements of this experience that may be relevant to other economies.

9.I INITIAL CONDITIONS

A developing economy's policy space and its performance over time are constrained by the initial conditions bestowed upon it by nature and the economy's colonial past. Differences in these conditions yield important typological distinctions among developing countries and are instructive for analytical as well as comparative purposes (for more on this theme, see Ranis 1984).

Both Taiwan (China) and the Republic of Korea were relatively small societies with labor surpluses and poor natural resources in the early 1950s. Both had been part of the Japanese colonial network for which they produced mainly agricultural products (for example, 95 percent of Taiwan (China)'s sugar production and 52 percent of its rice production were exported to Japan [Wu 1972]). The colonial administration expended substantial resources on rural infrastructure (roads, drainage, irrigation, and power) as well as on institutional infrastructure (agricultural research, experiment stations, and farmers' associations). Those investments led to a significant, early "green revolution" in rice (based on the ponlai variety) yields that were raised by 4 percent a year between 1921 and 1937. By the early 1950s the multiple cropping index stood already at 137, and 33 percent of all households had electricity.

Taiwan (China) had also benefited from colonial policies ensuring unusually high literacy rates; in the early 1950s, 60 percent of the population was literate (for a full account of the colonial period in Taiwan (China), see Ho 1978). A colonial (1905) land reform was early on reinforced by another major reform (1949–53), and a similar substantial redistribution of land took place in Korea (1949) under U.S. prodding (see Kuo, Ranis, and Fei 1981 and United Nations, various years a).

The Japanese maintained ownership over large-scale industry. Taiwanese were not admitted into higher education, but the priority given to primary schooling encouraged their expanding participation in small and medium-size industrial and service activities. The already-respectable initial stock of human capital of independent Taiwan (China) was, moreover, substantially enhanced by the massive influx of small traders and entrepreneurs from China in 1949. Also at that time, some very large-scale activities that had been taken over from the Japanese, for example, mining, cement, and pulp and paper, landed in the public sector. Many of these activities were soon divested in connection with the land reform program; the continuing shift to predominantly private industrial activity on Taiwan (China) is illustrated in Table 9.1. In Korea most large-scale industry had originally been located in the North; the South was preponderantly agricultural, with less public sector industrial activity at the outset and no evidence of an increase over time (Tables 9.1 and 9.2).

Table 9.1 Private and public sector industrial output in Taiwan (China), 1952–87, and Korea, 1963–72 (percent)

Taiwan (China)			*Korea*		
Years	*Private*	*Public*	*Year*	*Private*	*Public*
1952–61	48.7	51.3	1963	88.4	11.6
1962–71	64.2	35.8	1964	87.4	12.6
1972–81	80.8	19.2	1971	86.2	13.8
1982–87	83.8	16.2	1972	86.1	13.9

Source: Taiwan, China (various years a); for Korea, Jones (1975).

Table 9.2 Average annual growth in agricultural and nonagricultural output in Taiwan (China) and Korea, 1952–89

	Agricultural output		*Nonagricultural output*	
Years	*Taiwan (China)*	*Korea*	*Taiwan (China)*	*Korea*
1952–60	4.2	2.2	11.7	9.7
1960–70	4.3	4.9	18.5	17.6
1970–80	2.6	3.4	12.9	19.2
1980–89	–0.8	0.7	9.8	6.4

Source: Taiwan, China (various years a); for Korea, Das (1990).

Thus Taiwan (China) inherited relatively favorable initial conditions; so did Korea, although it had invested less in agricultural infrastructure during the colonial period. Moreover, in both countries there were relatively few landed or industrial vested interest groups to overcome. These factors, plus the perceived threat from China and the Democratic People's Republic of Korea, to Taiwan (China) and the Republic of Korea, respectively, gave these relatively autocratic governments unusual freedom of action in the sphere of economic policy.

9.II THE IMPORT SUBSTITUTION SUBPHASE, 1953–63

The import substitution syndrome as it played itself out in Taiwan (China) had some unusual features: government policies were not unduly discriminatory of the agricultural sector, encouraged rural nonagricultural activities as part of a balanced growth process, avoided intervention in labor markets, built on the foundations of substantial pre-existing human and physical overheads, and ensured early macroeconomic stabilization.

The agricultural sector

A dynamic agricultural sector is not frequently encountered during the typical initial import substitution subphase in developing countries. Yet if the concept of an early "leading sector" has any validity, here it clearly was agriculture, especially in the case of Taiwan (China). In 1952 the agricultural sector generated 33 percent of the net domestic product, 60 percent of total employment, and 90 percent of still relatively modest exports. By 1988 these figures had declined to 6, 14, and 6 percent, respectively. Nevertheless, agriculture played a critical historical role, not only as a provider of savings, foreign exchange, and labor but also as a contributor to the dynamic nonagricultural sector in rural areas (Taiwan, China, various years a).

Agricultural output in Taiwan (China) had regained pre-war levels by 1951 and increased at roughly 4.2 percent a year during the 1950s (Table 9.2). The output of traditional crops rose by about 50 percent and that of nontraditional crops, especially cotton, fruits, and vegetables, approximately doubled. Even more significant, agricultural employment increased by 12 percent during the decade, worker-days deployed rose by 17 percent, and the multiple cropping index increased to 188 by 1964. Nontraditional crops were much more labor-intensive and more subject to changes in labor-using technology over time. Working days per hectare increased from 170 just after World War II to 260 in the early 1960s (Ho 1978).

Forty-five percent of the growth of agriculture during the 1950s can be attributed to a change in total factor productivity, largely a result of government-supported research and technology diffusion activities (Fei,

Ranis, and Kuo 1979). Some of these activities focused on new strains of rice and sugar, but most of them focused on new crops—cotton, fruits, vegetables, and, during the 1960s, asparagus and mushrooms. Agricultural output growth in Korea was much more modest in this early period, but accelerated later on (Table 9.2) as the government belatedly recognized its neglect of the rural economy and sought to redress it.

Arthur Lewis's classic concept of organizational dualism is empirically relevant to societies whose relatively preponderant agricultural sectors are initially characterized by heavy population pressure on scarce land (Lewis 1954, 1979). This means that, with the marginal product of agricultural labor at very low levels, real wages on largely family-operated farms are determined by an initial average product-related sharing mechanism, side by side with a commercialized, profit-maximizing nonagricultural sector in which wages (for unskilled workers) are tied to those in agriculture. Such extended family-related sharing has its roots in the agrarian tradition and serves as a form of insurance for those living not far from the margins of subsistence (see, for example, Scott 1976).

The increasing gap between changes in the average product of agricultural labor and agricultural wages (Figure 9.1) permitted substantial agricultural surpluses to be generated, especially in Taiwan (China). Although labor productivity grew by 3.7 percent a year between 1955 and 1964 in Taiwan (China) (Kuo 1983), in Korea it grew at a more modest 2.4 percent a year over the same period (Das 1990). Growth was lower in Korea for several reasons. The initial conditions, including climate and soil fertility, were less favorable. Infrastructural investments during the Japanese period were less

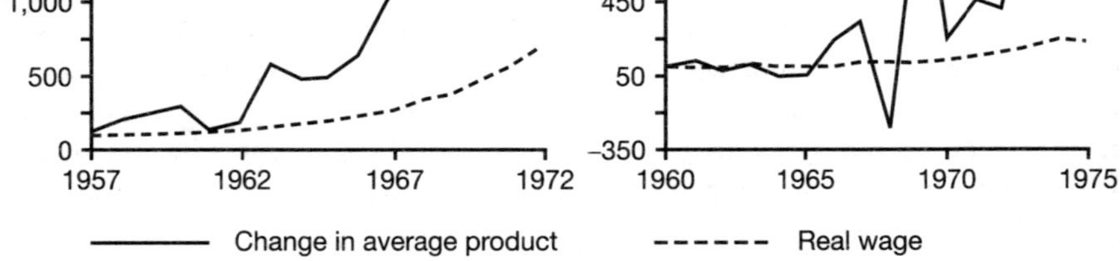

Figure 9.1 Real Wages and the Change in Average Product of Agriculture Labor in Taiwan (China), 1957–72, and Korea, 1960–70

Source: Das (1990); Mason and others (1980); government of Korea (1978); United Nations (various years b); Kuo (1983); Taiwan, China (various years a).

substantial. And the Korean government initially paid less attention to rural development.

Nonagricultural activities

Taiwan (China)'s agricultural surpluses went partly into the coffers of the government through land taxes, a fertilizer-rice barter program that represented a hidden tax on agriculture, and procurement by the armed forces at below-market prices. But an increasing proportion of the surplus that found its way into rural nonagricultural activities was contributed by private household savings. The household savings resulted from a combination of fast growth, the absence of a need to spend privately on education, the growth of financial institutions, and a major interest rate reform that took place in the 1950s. It is estimated that 15 to 20 percent of total agricultural output was transferred in the 1950s and 1960s, 3 percent of which was in the form of private savings in the 1950s, and raised to 12 to 15 percent in the 1960s (Ho 1978).

Given the equal distribution of land on Taiwan (China), plus the shift toward more labor-intensive crop mixes and technologies, the demand for nonagricultural products was increasingly directed toward small- and medium-scale enterprises. These enterprises were largely in the rural areas, thus strengthening the mutual backward and forward linkages between changes in agricultural and nonagricultural output (see Ranis and Stewart 1993). The preponderance of small- and medium-scale firms clearly represented a central feature of the landscape, helping to explain the multidimensional success of the system in terms of growth, employment generation, and enhanced equity.

In employment terms, for example, a remarkable shift occurred in the allocation of rural household labor from agricultural to nonagricultural activities: the latter made up 29 percent of total employment in 1956, 47 percent in 1966, and 67 percent in 1980 (Taiwan, China, various years a). In income terms, the proportion earned by rural households outside of agriculture rose from 25 percent in 1962 to 43 percent in 1975 to 60 percent in 1980 (Fei, Ranis, and Kuo 1979). Taiwan (China)'s industrialization pattern thus clearly avoided the customary relative (sometimes absolute) decline in postcolonial rural nonagricultural activities. Rural nonagricultural activities were not—as so often occurs—competed out of existence by favored urban industry and services. In Korea, agriculture was not as dynamic and, partly as a consequence, industrialization was substantially more urban-oriented and large scale.

As a result of land reform and the increasingly labor-intensive mix of agricultural outputs, the distribution of rural incomes in Taiwan (China) also improved dramatically, with the rural income Gini declining from close to 0.50 in 1950 to 0.35 in 1957, 0.35 in 1966, and 0.31 in 1970.[2] As incomes rose, farmers' demand for both domestically produced consumer goods (forward linkages) and intermediate inputs (backward linkages) rose. At the same time, farmers' ability and willingness to take advantage of new investment opportunities outside of agriculture increased. Both trends further encouraged the growth of rural, small- and medium-scale industries and services.

Taiwan (China)'s nonagricultural output increased at the rate of about 12 percent during the 1950s (Table 9.2). Korea's nonagricultural growth rate in the same period was not very different, but more of it was urban and financed by a combination of industrial reinvestment and foreign capital. Moreover, although exports began to play an increasing role in both systems, in Taiwan (China) 60 percent of overall growth between the early 1950s and mid-1960s was still domestically oriented, a fact that is often overlooked when the East Asian experience is cited (Taiwan, China, various years a). During this relatively mild import substitution subphase, the close contact between agriculture and rural industry and services induced mutually reinforcing changes in productivity.

Labor markets

As long as labor was in surplus, nonagricultural wage rates in Taiwan (China) and Korea were at a modest margin above agricultural wage rates. Both rates moved up only slowly throughout the 1950s and 1960s (Figure 9.2). Nonagricultural wages are represented by unskilled wages rather than average

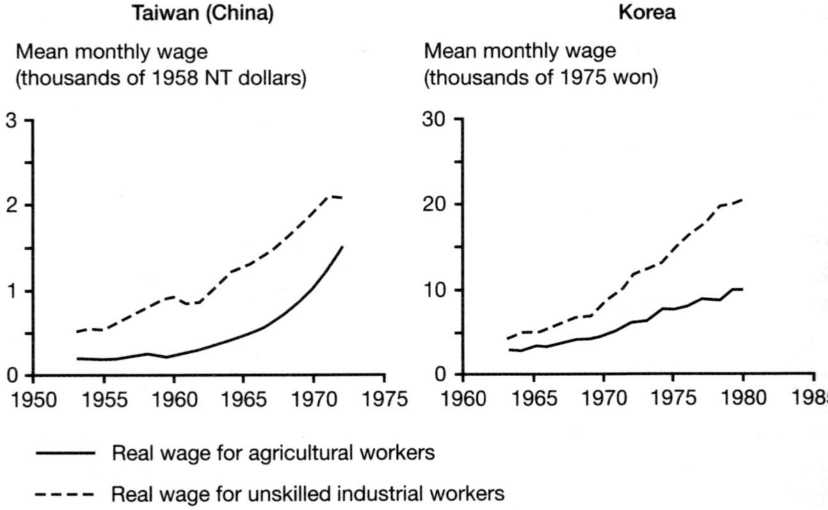

Figure 9.2 Real Wages for Agricultural and Unskilled Industrial Workers in Taiwan (China), 1950–1975, and Korea, 1960–85

Source: Kuo (1983); Taiwan, China (various years a); Das (1990); Mason and others (1980); government of Korea 1978.

wages, which would distort the picture by incorporating changes in the output and therefore the skill mix. Capital accumulation and changes in technology in a labor-using direction rapidly raised industrial employment and incomes. Unskilled wages, tied to agricultural incomes, rose only modestly, and substantial nonagricultural profit margins also became available for savings and reinvestment.

Employment increased at more than 3 percent a year, even during the 1950s and early 1960s (Taiwan, China, various years a). Thus, the nonagricultural wage bill did not decline, in spite of the fact that the ample supply of labor kept wages from rising very much. This fact, plus the improvement in the distribution of agricultural incomes following land reforms and the marked changes in the composition of agricultural output in the direction of greater labor intensity, permitted the overall distribution of income to improve continuously (Table 9.3). Private savings, generated largely by households and small businesses, contributed substantially to the high, and rising, national savings rate (Table 9.4) as early as the 1950s and 1960s. The contrast with Korea's substantially lower domestic savings rate and consequently greater reliance on foreign savings is marked (Table 9.5).

The gap between the real wages of industrial skilled and unskilled workers in Taiwan (China) and Korea (Figure 9.3) was relatively modest by the standards of most developing countries, especially those in Latin America and Africa. There is little evidence of government intervention in the nonagricultural labor market through minimum wage legislation, public sector wage setting, or support of union activities. "Repressed" labor markets, as they are sometimes erroneously referred to, are really no more than an unwillingness

Table 9.3 Comparative performance in overall development, Korea and Taiwan (China), 1953–90

	Average annual growth in real GNP per capita (percent)		*Equity (Gini coefficient)*[a]		*Long-term foreign debt*[b] *(millions of dollars)*	
Years	*Korea*	*Taiwan (China)*	*Korea*	*Taiwan (China)*	*Korea*	*Taiwan (China)*
1953–60	1.80	4.63	—	.440	25	—
1960–70	8.71	9.61	.357	.330	447	226
1970–80	1.46	10.92	.313	.289	10,681	2,864
1980–90	9.12	8.85	.301	.296	20,239	11,315

Notes:
— Not available.
[a] Data for Korea are for 1967, 1975, and 1984. Data for Taiwan (China) are for 1959, 1966, 1976, and 1986.
[b] Data are for the end of the decade, for example 1960 for Korea for the 1953–60 period.

Source: Taiwan, China (various years a); Government of Korea (various years); United Nations (various years b); Mason and others (1980).

Table 9.4 The rate and composition of savings in Taiwan (China), 1952–88 (percent)

Year	*Gross domestic savings as a percentage of GNP*	*Source*		
		Private sector	*General government*	*Public enterprises*
1952	15.3	50.93	35.58	13.49
1960	17.8	54.72	22.45	22.83
1965	20.7	69.55	12.64	17.80
1970	25.6	68.03	13.94	18.02
1980	32.3	60.35	24.49	15.16
1985	32.6	65.61	16.81	17.58
1988	34.9	64.22	22.76	13.02

Source: Taiwan, China (various years a).

Table 9.5 The rate and composition of savings in Korea, 1945–88

Year	*Gross domestic savings as a percentage of GNP*	*Source*	
		Private sector	*Public sector*
1945	4.63	92.27	7.73
1960	6.79	63.90	36.10
1965	7.40	76.78	23.22
1970	17.30	62.37	37.63
1975	19.10	78.48	21.52
1980	21.90	68.94	31.06
1984	27.40	76.14	23.86
1988	30.00[a]	—	—

Notes:
— Not available.
[a] Percentage of GDP.

Source: Government of Korea (various years); United Nations (various years c).

by the government to support an elite organized labor force at the expense of foregone employment opportunities for the rest. The fact that wage bills held steady or increased, while wage rates continued to reflect the underlying labor surplus condition during the 1950s and 1960s, actually helped improve the relative position of the working poor.

Building on pre-existing physical and human overheads

Taiwan (China) and, once again to a lesser extent, Korea continued to build on the favorable rural infrastructure left by the Japanese. Taiwan (China)'s rural road network was further extended, and access to infrastructure climbed rapidly. Electricity coverage, especially critical for decentralized industrial growth in the rural areas, increased from 33 percent of households in 1952 to

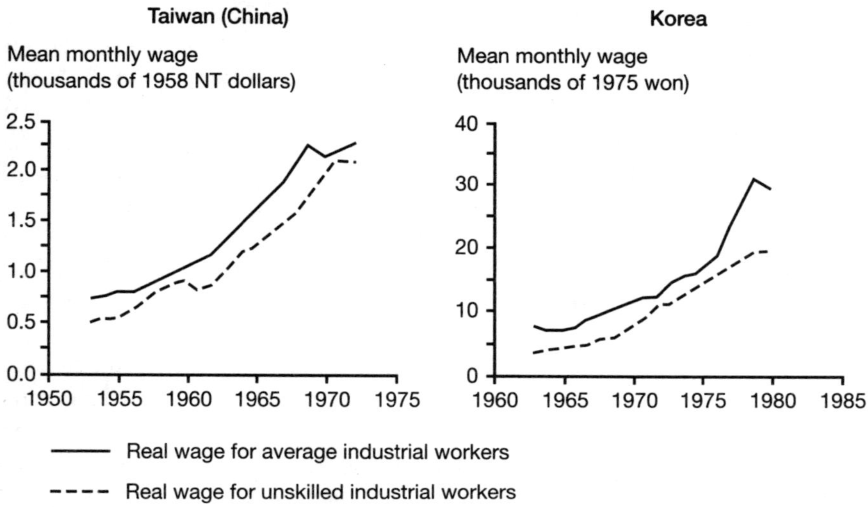

Figure 9.3 The industrial wage gap in Taiwan (China), 1950–1975, and Korea, 1960–85

Source: Kuo (1983); Taiwan, China (various years a, b); government of Korea (1978); Kim (1990).

99.7 percent in 1979. In 1952, 2 percent of households had telephones and 14.4 percent had piped water, compared with 71.1 percent and 63.8 percent, respectively, in 1979 (Taiwan, China, various years c). Moreover, with respect to the institutional infrastructure, Taiwan (China)'s Joint Commission on Rural Reconstruction (JCRR), supported by U.S. aid, was deployed to provide financial and technical assistance to decentralized farmers' associations left behind by Japan. Very similar associations were initially used for "top-down" instruction and taxation by the more centralized government in Korea. Both this and the fact that Korea let its agricultural terms of trade deteriorate were among the reasons for not only the referenced differential performance of agriculture in the two economies but also for a very different pattern of nonagricultural growth.

In Taiwan (China) most farmers' associations were focused on rice and sugar production, others specifically on irrigation, and still others on fishing. In addition to providing all-important research and extension services, the JCRR assisted with purchasing, marketing, warehousing, and processing. Farmers' associations organized cooperative banks and used positive real interest rates to induce members to deposit their own savings and receive locally supervised loans. Over time, the JCRR provided information and technical assistance on new crops and on linked nonagricultural activities in rural areas. Food processing, for example, came to represent the fastest-growing nonagricultural activity by the early 1960s.

Korea started with a less favorable initial base and neglected its agricultural sector during the 1950s and early 1960s in both the infrastructural and institutional dimensions. The relative contribution of total factor productivity to the lower growth of agricultural output in Korea was 36 percent in 1954–65 compared with 49 percent in Taiwan (China) in 1957–67. Until as late as 1970, Taiwan (China) spent twice as much as Korea on agricultural research as a percentage of agricultural output. The situation was reversed with the advent of the "New Village Movement" in the 1970s. The contribution of total factor productivity rose to 86 percent in 1970–77 in Korea and fell to 18 percent in 1973–77 in Taiwan, China (Chi-Ming and Yu 1982).

As for human capital formation, the emphasis in both countries during this period continued to be mainly on further improving literacy through compulsory universal primary education, as Table 9.6 indicates. Total enrollment rates rose especially rapidly between 1953 and 1965, faster for women than for men. It is worth noting that Taiwan (China) not only had a substantial advantage in primary education and literacy early on but also that it held on to it over time.

Table 9.6 Population by level of education in Taiwan (China), 1952–88, and Korea, 1944–85 (percentage of population)

Year	*Higher education*	*Secondary education*	*Primary education*	*Illiterate*	*Others*[a]
Taiwan (China)					
1952	1.4	8.8	43.5	42.1	4.2
1960	1.9	12.4	54.1	27.1	4.5
1966	2.5	15.8	54.8	23.1	3.8
1970	3.7	26.5	51.8	14.7	3.3
1974	4.8	29.1	49.9	13.3	2.9
1980	7.1	36.9	43.3	10.3	2.4
1988	10.1	44.2	37.0	7.4	1.3
Korea					
1944	0.3	1.7	11.3	86.7	n.a.
1960	2.6	17.5	36.2	43.7	n.a.
1966	4.5	24.7	40.0	30.8	n.a.
1970	5.6	31.8	39.2	23.4	n.a.
1974	5.7	38.0	36.0	20.3	n.a.
1985	7.4	48.7	32.3	11.6	n.a.

Notes:
n.a. Not applicable.
[a] Includes people who have not completed primary education.
Data are end-of-year values for percentage of population age six and over.

Source: Taiwan, China (various years a): for Korea, McGinn and others (1980) and Government of Korea (1983).

Early macroeconomic stabilization

Government policies during this subphase not only moved both systems toward positive real interest rates, breaking the back of inflation with the help of foreign aid inflows, but also began to gradually open them to foreign trade and investment. Quantitative controls began to be replaced by tariffs, and as early as 1956 a system of customs duty rebates for exports was instituted on Taiwan (China), followed by a major devaluation, unification of the exchange rate, and maintenance of a relatively realistic rate after 1960. Indeed, by the early 1960s, the well-known "Nineteen Points" of macroeconomic reform had liberalized much of Taiwan (China)'s economy, facilitating its entry into the next, export-oriented subphase of development. A similar package of fairly orthodox macroeconomic and structural reforms was introduced a few years later in Korea.

In summary, Taiwan (China) began to get its macroeconomic budgetary and financial house in order in the 1950s, with the help of a temporary ballooning in foreign aid. Its relatively mild import substitution phase meant avoidance of the customary severe discrimination against agriculture and permitted a remarkably balanced process of rural growth. The major, foreign trade—oriented liberalization package of the early 1960s was once again helped by U.S. aid commitments. In the political economy sense, it was also assisted by the (1961) announcement that the United States intended to terminate such assistance by 1965. The combination of an intrinsic natural resources poverty and the impending end to economic aid by its major donor undoubtedly helped focus the minds of Taiwan (China)'s policymakers on the famous Nineteen Points of reform, permitting the economy to shift relatively smoothly into its competitive export-oriented subphase of development.

In the Republic of Korea these macro and structural policy shifts took place a little later. The aftermath of the Korean War, the continued confrontation with the Democratic People's Republic of Korea, plus the fact that the U.S. economic as well as military presence remained a feature of the landscape reduced the pressure on the Republic of Korea to undertake thoroughgoing reforms at the same pace. These factors led to a relatively greater neglect of the rural sector early on and to a greater concentration on large-scale urban industry partly financed with private foreign capital. However, in spite of these differences, and certainly in comparison with the standards in other developing countries, both these East Asian systems had been eminently successful by the mid-1960s in making a politically difficult transition to a vigorous, labor-intensive, industrial export subphase.

9.III THE LABOR-INTENSIVE EXPORT SUBSTITUTION SUBPHASE, 1963–72

The decade 1963–72 in Taiwan (China) was witness to a remarkable performance of rapid growth coupled with enhanced equity. Such a performance was made possible by the complementary effects of balanced, domestic, intersectoral growth and an increasingly powerful export drive. The contours of this new and more competitive development subphase and the policies that accommodated it are analyzed in this section.

The overall economic record is quite clear: during the 1960s, rapid growth, heavily supported initially by agriculture and then fueled increasingly by labor-intensive industrial expansion, resulted in a rapid generation of employment and an increasingly favorable income distribution. Savings and growth rates soared (not only in Taiwan, China, but also in Korea), and total factor productivity rates in industry increased with enhanced openness. The economy witnessed a rapid rise in the importance of exports as well as rapid change in their composition. Emerging nonagricultural output mixes and technologies now permitted the reallocation at a 6 percent annual rate of the relatively unskilled, although increasingly literate, numerate, and therefore high-quality agricultural labor force. As a consequence, by the early 1970s even the combination of increased, especially female, participation rates (see Liu 1992), offshore (Southeast Asian) investment sourcing, and some (largely illegal) immigration of Southeast Asian workers could not postpone the advent of a labor shortage.

Changes in output, labor allocation, and the distribution of income

Taiwan (China)'s agricultural output increased at an average rate of 4.3 percent during the 1960s (Table 9.2). Labor productivity rose even faster, with the total agricultural labor force beginning to decline absolutely after 1965 (Taiwan, China, various years a). Most of the increase in agricultural output came through higher yields at the intensive margin because of a burst in agricultural research combined with dramatic changes in the composition of agricultural output, illustrated in Table 9.7.

Nonagricultural output boomed in both Taiwan (China) and Korea (Table 9.3). In Taiwan (China) the rate of increase in nonagricultural employment doubled to 6 percent annually (Das 1990; Taiwan, China, various years a). The role of agricultural savings in helping to finance this rapid expansion of nonagricultural output remained important, especially in Taiwan (China). With 15 to 20 percent of its agricultural output transferred as agricultural surplus, the sector continued to be a major, although gradually declining, source of fuel for the overall growth of the economy during the 1960s. By 1972 its contribution to gross national product (GNP) had fallen to 14 percent, from 36 percent in 1952, and its contribution to employment to 33

Table 9.7 Composition of agricultural output in Taiwan (China), 1960–88 (percent)

Year	*Rice*	*Other traditional crops*	*Nontraditional crops*
1960	57.0	15.8	27.3
1970	45.0	12.9	42.1
1980	41.8	7.4	51.0
1988	27.1	7.9	65.0

Note: Numbers may not add to 100 because of rounding.

Source: Mao and Schive (1992, Table 2.6).

percent, from 56 percent. Manufacturing output had increased from 11 percent in 1952 to 32 percent, and employment in manufacturing from 12 percent to 25 percent (Taiwan, China, various years a).

This was clearly the decade when export-oriented industrialization—concentrated initially on processed agricultural goods and later increasingly on labor-intensive commodities based on imported raw materials—began to soar. The 1960s embody the best example of a mutually reinforcing relationship between the two blades of successful development: domestic balanced growth and labor-intensive industrial exports. Taiwan (China)'s exports as a percentage of a rapidly rising GNP increased from 10 percent in the early 1960s to more than 23 percent by 1972 (Taiwan, China, various years a). Table 9.8 provides evidence of the continued dramatic shift in the composition of these rapidly growing exports, a shift from more than 90 percent agricultural to more than 90 percent nonagricultural, in less than three decades (Taiwan, China, various years a).

Much of the labor reallocation in Taiwan (China) consisted of people not

Table 9.8 Composition of exports in Taiwan (China) and Korea, 1952–88 (percent)

	Taiwan (China)		*Korea*	
Year	*Agricultural*	*Industrial*	*Agricultural*	*Industrial*
1952	91.9	8.1	—	—
1960	67.7	32.3	85.8	14.2
1970	21.4	78.6	22.6	77.4
1980	9.2	90.8	9.5	90.5
1988	5.5	94.5	6.2	93.8

Notes:
— Not available.
Agricultural exports are raw and processed agricultural products. Numbers may not add to 100 because of rounding.

Source: Taiwan, China (various years a); for Korea, Bank of Korea (various years) and Government of Korea (1980).

actually leaving rural households. Only 17 percent of the so-called migrants actually departed from the rural areas in 1963, and even as late as 1968 only 26 percent of newly absorbed industrial workers had actually physically migrated to urban centers (Ho 1976). This feature underlines the continued, remarkable expansion, not only absolutely but also relatively, of rural industry and services. As Table 9.9 shows, the percentage distribution of employed persons by locality in manufacturing and services actually shifted in favor of the rural areas.

The two main factors that rendered such rapid growth in the 1960s consistent with an increasingly equitable distribution of income were already at play earlier and continued to assume an important role. One was that the smallest, that is, the poorest, farmers participated more than proportionally in the economy's booming rural industrial and service activities. The other was that these rural industries and services were increasingly labor-intensive, especially in the mid-1960s, when food processing still played a prominent role. As a consequence, the Simon Kuznets–Arthur Lewis prediction—that during a period of labor surplus the profit share would have to rise and the labor share fall and that the size distribution of income would therefore worsen—was not borne out. Employment increases in Taiwan (China) made up for the continued low level of unskilled industrial wages and permitted the wage share to rise and the Gini coefficient to fall into the 0.29 range during a period of very rapid growth (Fei, Ranis, and Kuo 1979). Counter to the usual assumptions, the shift that took place was not from an egalitarian agricultural sector to a less egalitarian nonagricultural sector, but from an egalitarian agricultural sector to an even more egalitarian nonagricultural sector.

The situation in Korea was not quite as favorable. Less success in mobilizing agriculture meant a lower savings rate, an earlier resort to food imports,

Table 9.9 Distribution of employed persons by locality in Taiwan (China), 1956 and 1966 (percent)

	1956			*1966*		
Sector	*Cities*	*Towns*	*Rural areas*	*Cities*	*Towns*	*Rural areas*
Manufacturing	42.68	10.06	47.26	37.02	10.80	52.18
Construction	44.84	11.45	43.71	43.92	12.27	43.81
Utilities	51.30	9.74	38.96	47.25	9.89	42.86
Commerce	44.36	9.98	45.66	42.34	10.56	47.10
Transport and communications	54.27	8.92	36.81	50.74	9.50	39.76
Services	41.16	9.73	49.11	34.44	9.38	56.17

Notes: Cities are the seven largest cities. Towns are the nine largest towns. Rural areas are all other locations.
Source: Ho (1976, Table 4) and data from the 1956 and 1966 population censuses.

and a greater reliance on foreign savings. The nonagricultural sector was more urban-oriented, large-scale, and capital-intensive. Thus, although Korea clearly still figures prominently as one of the success stories, both its Gini coefficients and its foreign debt levels were substantially higher than those of Taiwan (China) (Table 9.3).

The role of government policy

As a semipublic, semiautonomous agency of the government of Taiwan (China), the JCRR was relatively isolated from political pressures. It was able to respond to local needs in research, extension, credit, and marketing at provincial, county, and township levels. The government also continued to build on the initial conditions by making substantial investments in power, transport, and communications throughout the island. Infrastructural investments were not directed to the support of particular regions or industries; indeed, there appears to have been a conscious effort by the government to be evenhanded and to permit fairly decentralized decisions in setting priorities. Rural and urban electricity rates were maintained at parity, so the power system, although not subsidized overall, was subject to internal cross-subsidization. After 1960 the government began to establish industrial districts, providing infrastructure, other overhead facilities, and horizontal linkages specifically to encourage decentralized industrial activities. By 1986, eighty-eight such districts were operational.

Booming nonagricultural growth was still heavily rural but also increasingly export-oriented. It was further facilitated by such policy inducements as the streamlining of previously established tariff rebates for exports (in lieu of fuller import liberalization) as well as the construction of several export-processing zones in the mid-1960s, supplemented by bonded factories dotting the landscape. In support of Lucas's (1993) theoretical note on Taiwan (China)'s success, this rapid change in East Asian exports and export composition was the result of an accelerating learning-by-doing process.

These useful transition devices for economies moving from a domestic to an external orientation proved especially relevant in the electronics and other light assembly industries that were part of the rapid output and employment generation spurt of the 1960s. Over the years the zones provided no more than 1 percent of total employment and 3 percent of investment, but they contributed 6 percent of exports (Fei, Ranis, and Kuo 1979). More important, they permitted entrepreneurs to compete abroad while the bulk of the domestic economy continued substantially protected. Gradually, as competence grew, additional forward or finishing stages were added, intermediate inputs were procured from, and final sales made into the domestic economy. Once labor surplus had come to an end, by the late 1960s and early 1970s, the historical mission of the zones had been accomplished and they began to atrophy. Thus, in a number of specific ways, beyond the accommodating shift in macro policies, the government provided direct institutional support. This support permitted Taiwan (China) both to explore domestic rural niche markets and to successfully enter growing international markets.

Taiwan (China)'s unusually decentralized industrialization effort was helped by its initially high literacy rates and early in-migration of a substantial number of small entrepreneurs from China. Then, as the economy moved through the 1960s and the industrial output mix changed, the government's educational emphasis shifted from compulsory primary to compulsory secondary education. Overall, expenditures on education rose from 2.1 percent of GNP (11 percent of the budget) in 1955 to 4.6 percent of GNP (20 percent of the budget) in 1970 (Figure 9.4). In Korea, expenditures on education first fell and then rose, going from a low of 1.7 percent of GNP in 1965 to a high of 3.5 percent in 1970 (Figure 9.4). As for quality, in both countries expenditures per student increased consistently over time for each level of education. Taiwan (China)'s expenditures on education per student increased sixfold between 1960 and 1975 (Taiwan, China, various years b). Those of Korea almost doubled over the same period (Mason and others 1980; see also Taiwan, China, various years b, and United Nations, various years a). Recurring expenditures were unusually high in relation to nonrecurring expenditures, as indicated in Figure 9.4.

East Asian governments clearly understood the importance of human capital and, even more important, were flexible in shifting the emphasis of the educational structure as changes in the economy demanded. Although general literacy and numeracy objectives seem to have dominated at the outset, the six years of compulsory primary education in Taiwan (China) were

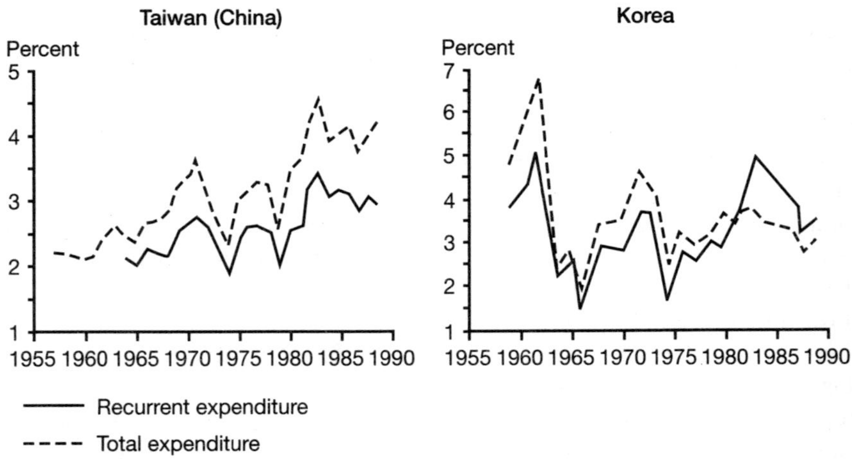

Figure 9.4 Total and Recurrent Expenditures on Education in Taiwan (China) and Korea, 1955–90

Source: Taiwan, China (various years b); United Nations (various issues a).

extended to nine years in 1968, just when scarcity of unskilled labor, indexed by the first pronounced rise in unskilled real wages, appeared imminent. In addition, female participation rates increased sharply after 1967. This "turning point" also coincided with a much increased emphasis given to vocational as opposed to academic training at the secondary level. Vocational training increased sixfold between 1966 and 1974, a time when the nonagricultural labor force increased by 80 percent (Taiwan, China, various years a). Only 40 percent of Taiwan (China)'s high school students were in the vocational track in 1963, but by 1972 that percentage was 52 percent and by 1980 almost 70 percent (Taiwan, China, various years a). This pattern was much less pronounced in Korea, for both level and trend.

Approximately half the vocational education in Taiwan (China) was administered by private enterprises and half by government agencies. Public sector policies influenced the mix between academic and vocational or technical high schools by using differential tuitions as a carrot. Within the vocational schools, agriculture, commerce, and the industrial arts were combined. Offerings, unlike those in many other developing countries, were highly diversified, flexible, and responsive to changing market demands.

Both Taiwan (China) and Korea were able to count on a cheap and unskilled, yet efficient and literate labor force, extremely important ingredients for any competitive, export-oriented development drive. The percentage of population of ages sixteen to twenty-four with primary education in Taiwan (China) rose from 40 percent in 1953–54 to 60 percent by the early 1970s. The increase was even faster for women; the average number of years of schooling for women over age fifteen rose from 2.8 to 6.9 (Taiwan, China, various years a). Similar figures can be cited for Korea.

Education as a public sector responsibility represents a very strong cultural tradition in East Asia. Even as private sector schooling above the primary level—both secondary and higher education—increased in relative importance (from 10 percent in 1950 to 60 percent in 1980), demand continued to be strongest for entry into the higher-quality elite public institutions. Expenditures per public school student ran at 2.5 times those in private schools, and in public universities the student-teacher ratio was twelve to one, compared with twenty-nine to one in private universities (Taiwan, China, various years b; Mason and others 1980; Taiwan, China, various years a). Moreover, parents had to pay 50 percent of total costs in private schools, but only 7 percent in public high schools and universities (Taiwan, China, various years b; Mason and others 1980). Throughout the public school system, competitive examinations—part of the cultural heritage derived from the imperial examinations system of China—rather than ability to pay or family connection, determined entry.

The labor market

As indicated in Figure 9.1, agricultural wages continued to lag considerably behind the increase in agricultural productivity, thus setting the baseline for the remuneration of unskilled labor as long as the labor surplus persisted. Also, as shown in Figure 9.2, unskilled nonagricultural wages, relatively undistorted by minimum wage legislation or union activity, continued at a reasonably small margin above agricultural wages. Unions concentrated heavily on working conditions, not collective bargaining on wages. Strikes were either illegal or officially frowned upon, and work stoppages were rather rare.

Unionization has had little effect on labor market conditions—at least until very recently. The percentage of the nonagricultural labor force unionized in Taiwan (China) (28 percent in 1988, from 18 percent in 1973) was consistently larger than in Korea (where it peaked at 16 percent), even though unions have to date played a substantially more prominent political role in Korea (Taiwan, China, various years a; United Nations 1990). In Taiwan (China), minimum wage legislation has been on the books since the 1950s, but these wages have been consistently at 40 to 60 percent of the actual manufacturing wage, that is, not "biting," even for unskilled labor (Taiwan, China, various years a). In both Korea and Taiwan (China), wages across different skill levels seem to have converged more as a result of supply-side changes brought about by more education and increased access rather than as a consequence of demand-induced changes in the industrial structure. The wage gap between skilled and unskilled labor in Taiwan (China) was only about 20 percent in 1953, approximately 30 percent in the mid-1960s, and once again 20 percent in 1970, very low by developing-economy standards (Figure 9.3; Kuo 1983; Taiwan, China, various years a, b).

9.IV THE SCIENCE AND TECHNOLOGY SUBPHASE—THE MID-1970s, 1980s, AND BEYOND

The latest subphase of development in Taiwan (China) and Korea may be characterized as dominated by three major phenomena. First, agriculture, having performed its mission—although less well and more belatedly in Korea—is no longer a major catalyst and source of saving, and has instead become a subsidized appendage of the economy. Second, the increasing shortage of labor has caused a marked shift in the industrial output and export mix. Electronics, information, science, and technology-intensive exports soar and now substantially exceed those of textiles, garments, and other light industry. Third, the government is paying vastly increased attention to infrastructure related to science and technology and to institutional changes encouraging additional activity in research and development (R&D).

It is, of course, difficult to assess the impact of the combination of human capital accumulation, institutional construction, and R&D activity on bottom-line performance. In the mixed economy much depends on the competitiveness of the private sector and the support of public good externalities. In the absence of workably competitive conditions, the existence of large, unearned rents can be expected to lead to satisficing behavior and a reduced incentive for product and process innovations (see, for example, Otsuka, Ranis, and Saxonhouse 1988). Where workable competition does exist—more true for Taiwan (China) than for the *chaebol*-dominated industries of Korea—the externalities provided by the government can have a substantial payoff. One way to assess this issue is to examine the contribution of total factor productivity to growth. As expected, East Asia has done markedly better in this respect than, say, Latin America, and Taiwan (China) levels exceed those of Korea (see Page 1994; Young 1993; Pack 1992; Kim and Roemer 1979). Counter to current revisionism, high investment rates alone do not tell the full story.

As clearly demonstrated in Table 9.2, the underlying, longstanding poverty of land and natural resources in Taiwan (China) and Korea has gradually reasserted itself. The "New Village Movement" in Korea gave a somewhat belated spurt to the agricultural sector there, but both Taiwan (China) and Korea are now net importers of agricultural goods. Farmers are being subsidized rather than taxed. Although 15 to 20 percent of Taiwan (China)'s agricultural output was transferred into nonagricultural investments during the 1950s and 1960s, the direction of resource flows reversed after 1973 (Ho 1978). A second land reform, involving land consolidation, increased mechanization, and the advent of specialized-cultivating firms, represented rational policy responses to the changing role of agriculture. Policies protecting and subsidizing farmers, by contrast, reflect political pressures of the kind familiar to most advanced industrial countries and represent an equally predictable but less rational response.

East Asia is still trying to prolong the life of its labor-intensive industries by investing in such low-wage neighbors as China, Indonesia, the Philippines, and Thailand. It is also closing its official eye to a limited number of unskilled, largely illegal, immigrants from these countries. An absolutely large volume of labor-intensive exports continues to flow predominantly to the industrial countries. As international trade theory predicts, however, an increasing proportion of East Asia's rapidly expanding high-tech and capital-intensive exports are destined for neighboring developing countries.

Government policy has accommodated shifts in the output mix in four main ways: first, by placing marginally greater reliance on public enterprises, given the still relatively underdeveloped domestic financial markets;[3] second, by focusing public policy on creating the necessary externalities on the human capital side; third, by considering institutional investments in science and technology as a high-priority public good; and fourth, by providing directed credit to export-oriented industries on an across-the-board basis.

Human capital formation has accommodated the accelerating shift in nonagricultural output mixes and technologies. By 1988 total expenditures on education in Taiwan (China) had risen to a new high of 5.2 percent of GNP. Moreover, in the 1950s, 50 percent of the total expenditures on education were spent on primary education, 35 percent on secondary education, and 15 percent on higher education; more recent figures are 30, 40, and 30 percent, respectively (Taiwan, China, various years b; Mason and others 1980). In addition, by 1989 fully 70 percent of the high schools in Taiwan (China) were vocational, representing a marked acceleration of earlier trends (Taiwan, China, 1989).

In both Taiwan (China) and Korea, higher education has continued to shift toward engineering and the natural sciences and away from the traditional humanities and agricultural concentrations. The human capital foundation for this shift clearly had been laid earlier. International comparisons for 1990, provided by the International Assessment of Educational Performance, indicate that Taiwanese and Korean students already occupied the two top positions in the sciences and mathematics at the age of thirteen.

The government intervened at the university level partly by shifting entry quotas, but partly also by using financial support as incentives favoring such new departments as industrial engineering, industrial design, automatic controls, and petro-chemistry. As a result, enrollments in graduate engineering and material science programs in Taiwan (China) virtually doubled (to 40 percent of total graduate enrollments) between the mid-1960s and late 1980s (Taiwan, China, 1989). It seems that policymakers recognized that more engineering and science-oriented investments were now required. The countries were no longer able to depend for their total factor productivity increases either on the shift from agriculture to nonagriculture or on the adaptation of relatively simple imported technologies and designs associated with labor-intensive output mixes (see, for example, Westphal 1985). The increased need to shift to domestically generated Schumpeterian-type innovative responses meant an accelerating shift toward more high-tech labor as well as R&D.

Every year from 1960 to 1967 approximately 15 percent of Taiwan (China)'s college graduates went to the United States for postgraduate study, two-thirds of them in science and engineering, but only 4.5 percent of them returned each year. After 1973 the government initiated a major effort to encourage the reverse flow of this high-talent labor by actively recruiting in such locations as California's Silicon Valley and offering Taiwanese graduates substantial financial incentives to return. Although only a handful of highly trained graduates returned before 1970, by 1986 more than 90 percent did so. It is estimated that in recent years almost 10,000 Taiwanese graduates of U.S. universities have returned to take up positions related to science and technology. Many have become venture capitalists in their own right (Taiwan, China, various years b).

The construction of complementary science and technology infrastructure in Taiwan included the establishment of a Cabinet Committee on R&D

(1965), the National Science Council (1967), the Chung Shan Institute of Science and Technology (1965), the Industrial Training and Research Institute (ITRI; 1973), the Institute for Information Industry (1979), and the Shin Chu Science-Based Industrial Park (1979). Most prominent of these has been the last mentioned, which has encouraged new ventures in high-tech export-oriented areas by providing public facilities to private firms on favorable terms. These terms include five-year tax exemptions, a ceiling on taxes at 22 percent thereafter, subsidized rent and credit facilities, and other amenities. The Industrial Park, moreover, guaranteed close physical and intellectual contacts with academic and private commercial interests; in recent years fully 70 percent of the companies in the park have been managed by repatriated Chinese.

ITRI, located nearby, carries on basic industrial research in areas that might otherwise be underrepresented because of the continued predominance of small- and medium-scale firms. ITRI's $400 million annual budget permits a substantial volume of in-house product and process research in adapting foreign technology through both reverse engineering and the generation of original patents. ITRI also sells technical assistance and market information to small- and medium-scale firms and, although it is still heavily focused on government basic research, private contracts are growing gradually.[4]

Overall, 60 percent of Taiwan (China)'s industrial R&D is carried out by the private sector and 40 percent within various public sector institutes. The government funds 60 percent and the private sector 40 percent of the total expenditure on R&D (Taiwan, China, various years a). In other words, formal private sector R&D is generally carried out within large firms whereas the government supports R&D and training-related activities of benefit to the large population of small- and medium-scale firms.

During the 1980s, both Korea and Taiwan (China) increased their formal R&D expenditures from approximately 1 percent to 2.5 percent of GNP. That was a substantial expansion symptomatic of the new subphase of growth they had entered, although still substantially less than what mature economies allocate. Moreover, these figures do not capture the informal, blue-collar tinkering type of R&D that takes place in the machine shops and on the factory floors of many small- and medium-scale establishments. Basic research is still carried on largely by the public sector and applied research by the private sector. But product development, which comprised only 40 percent of R&D in 1970 and is virtually exclusively the province of private firms, now constitutes more than 70 percent of the total R&D expenditure. New patents, although an admittedly imperfect indicator of innovative activity, increased from 2,770 in 1980 to 10,379 in 1990 (Taiwan, China, various years a). Over the same decade there has been an almost tenfold increase in paper citations, a measure of the quality of the basic research output of government-sponsored institutes and universities.

9.V SOME CONCLUSIONS

If any common ground exists between adherents of the Washington Consensus, as purveyed by the IMF and the World Bank, and its heterodox critics, it is that developing economies, to be successful, must get their "fundamentals" right. That is, they must practice fiscal and monetary restraint and maintain a reasonably realistic exchange rate. By contrast, disagreements have focused on industrial policy, including what the appropriate role for governments and markets should be and on how micro structural reforms should be sequenced. What is still required, in my view, is a broader multisectoral view with typological and historical sensitivity, that is, concern with a country's initial conditions as well as the subphase of the transition growth process that has been reached.

The East Asian economies were, at the outset, relatively small, poor in natural resources, rich in human resources, and endowed with relatively good physical and institutional infrastructure. All this was as important as the fact that their newly independent governments continued to actively build on that base. It is also important that the typically interventionist, import substitution subphase was relatively mild and relatively short-lived. What proved critical, especially for Taiwan (China)'s success, was the early avoidance of agricultural neglect, the encouragement of the agricultural sector's mutually beneficial interactions with a dispersed nonagricultural sector, and the timely shift from land-based to human resources. The controversy swirling around *The East Asian Miracle* study (World Bank 1993) focused unduly on recent vintage industrial credit policy.

Korea's long-run pattern was broadly similar to Taiwan (China)'s, but there were also important and instructive differences. For example, Korea paid relatively less attention to the agricultural sector and to rural industry early on and was more tempted by the notion that large-scale, urban, export-oriented activities could pull the economy along. High growth rates comparable to Taiwan (China)'s were indeed achieved. However, because the financing of that growth received less support from agricultural savings, it required a larger volume of foreign capital, leading to a more capital-intensive industrialization path and a much larger foreign debt than was the case in Taiwan (China) (table 9.3).

Both Taiwan (China) and Korea initially highlighted literacy and numeracy by concentrating on primary education. They then moved flexibly to emphasizing vocational and, still later, graduate-level science and technology-oriented education—always in line with the system's continuously changing requirements. Labor markets were permitted to behave competitively; that is, there was very little intervention either through government support of unions or through minimum wage legislation with any "bite." Public policy was instead clearly focused on easing the path of an early transition from inward- to outward-oriented development.

The East Asian experience, moreover, confirms the usefulness of government actions in support of agricultural research and small- and medium-scale industrial development. There were critical government interventions in fashioning the appropriate organizational and institutional infrastructure, reducing transactions costs, and providing the necessary facilities and policies to ease the transition. Finally, there was the need to create temporary innovation profits in the hands of private industrialists through R&D and the strengthening of patents and other intellectual property rights.

Moreover, success did not lead the government to become excessively active in promoting growth. The importance of prudence in sequencing, and flexibility in implementing, reforms becomes even more evident when put to a stronger test during times of adversity. Unlike many other developing economies, Taiwan (China) was willing to accept temporarily lower growth rates in the face of negative external shocks such as the oil crisis, but maintained the direction of reforms without major zigzags in the various policy arenas. The avoidance of periods of relatively doctrinaire interventionism alternating with equally doctrinaire free market episodes was a key ingredient of its success.

Both macro and structural policies tended to oscillate more in Korea, although around an overall favorable trend, partly as a consequence of greater political instability, but largely because of a less consistent set of domestic policies. There were indeed times when Korea's behavior temporarily resembled that of the more "typical" developing economy, characterized by growth activism, resort to large-scale monetary expansion, deficit financing, and high levels of inflation. However, such deviations were temporary, with the system always able to return to its underlying trend toward liberalization. Consequently, the long-run performance of Korea, like that of Taiwan (China), has nevertheless been outstanding by any international standard—even if the results, in terms of foreign debt and income distribution, were not as favorable. What clearly marks off East Asia from the average developing-economy case is the remarkable ability of the authorities to recognize mistakes and quickly take appropriate corrective action.

In brief, public policies in East Asia consistently accommodated the changing needs of the economy, rather than specifically directing its path. Over time, East Asia has shown the necessary entrepreneurial and policy flexibility to weather inevitable exogenous shocks and turning points and thus managed to "stay the course" en route to economic maturity. It refused to retreat to stop-go restrictionist regimes at times of crisis and continuously adopted accommodating policy mixes that recognized the ever more critical reliance on human capital and technology in navigating the transitional growth process.

ACKNOWLEDGMENTS

Gustav Ranis is with the Department of Economics at Yale University. An early version of this article was prepared as a background paper for the World Bank's *The East Asian Miracle* (World Bank 1993). The author gratefully acknowledges the research assistance of Ryan Schneider and the comments of three anonymous referees.

NOTES

1 The Washington Consensus is summarized in Williamson (1990). For examples of the heterodox critics, see Amsden (1989) and Wade (1990).
2 The 1950 and 1957 figures are based on farm size as a proxy for income (see Fei, Ranis, and Kuo 1979) and are therefore less reliable than the post-1964 figures based on data from Taiwan, China (various years b).
3 This reliance continues to be reflected in Taiwan (China)'s current six-year plan, which permits the small savings of many individuals to be channeled into large investment projects.
4 A recent visit to ITRI convinced me that a major explicit contribution of the institute, in addition to providing information and venture capital to medium- and small-scale entrepreneurs, has been the generation in-house of a group of technologically oriented venture capitalists, who, given ITRI's remarkably high staff turnover rate, make their way each year into the private sector.

REFERENCES

The word "processed" describes informally reproduced works that may not be commonly available through library systems.

Amsden, Alice. 1989. *Asia's Next Giant: South Korea and Late Industrialization*. New York: Oxford University Press.

Bank of Korea. Various years. *Economic Statistics Yearbook*. Seoul.

Chi-Ming, Hou, and T. S. Yu, eds. 1982. *Agricultural Development in China, Japan, and Korea*. Taipei, Taiwan (China): Academia Sinica.

Das, Dilipk. 1990. *Korean Economic Dynamism*. Paris: Macmillan.

Fei, John, Gustav Ranis, and Shirley Kuo. 1979. *Growth with Equity: The Taiwan Case*. Oxford: Oxford University Press.

Government of Korea. 1978. *Major Statistics of the Korean Economy*. Seoul: Economic Planning Board.

——. 1980. *Statistical Yearbook of Foreign Trade*. Seoul: Office of Customs Administration.

——. 1985. *Supplementary Tables, Census of Population*. Taiwan: National Bureau of Statistics, Economic Planning Board.

——. Various years. *Korean Statistical Yearbook*. Economic Planning Board, Seoul.

Ho, Samuel. 1976. "The Rural Non-Farm Sector in Taiwan." World Bank Studies in Employment and Rural Development. Working Paper 32. World Bank, Washington, D.C. Processed.

——. 1978. *Economic Development of Taiwan, 1860–1970*. New Haven, Conn.: Yale University Press.

Jones, Leroy. 1975. *Public Enterprise and Economic Development*. Seoul: Korea Development Institute.

Kim, C. 1990. "Labor Market Development." In Jene K. Kwow, ed., *Korean Economic Development*. New York: Greenwood Press.

Kim, Kwang Suk, and Michael Roemer. 1979. "Growth and Structural Transformation." In *Studies in the Modernization of the Republic of Korea: 1945–1975*. Cambridge, Mass.: Harvard University Press.

Kuo, Shirley. 1983. *The Taiwan Economy in Transition.* Boulder, Colo.: Westview Press.

Kuo, Shirley, Gustav Ranis, and John Fei. 1981. *The Taiwan Success Story: Rapid Growth with Improved Distribution in the Republic of China, 1952–1979*. Boulder, Colo.: Westview Press.

Lewis, W. A. 1954. "Economic Development with Unlimited Supplies of Labor." *The Manchester School* 22(2):139–91.

——. 1979. "The Dual Economy Revisited." *The Manchester School* 47(3):211–29.

Liu, Peter. 1992. "Science, Technology, and Human Capital Formation." In Gustav Ranis, ed., *Taiwan: From Developing to Mature Economy*. Boulder, Colo.: Westview Press.

Lucas, Robert. 1993. "Making a Miracle." *Econometrica* 61:251–72.

Mao, Y. K., and Chi Schive. 1992. "Agricultural and Industrial Development of the Republic of China." Council of Agriculture, The Executive Yuan, Taipei, Taiwan (China). Processed.

Mason, Edward, M. Kim, Dwight H. Perkins, Kwang Suk Kim, and David Cole. 1980. *The Economic and Social Modernization of the Republic of Korea*. Cambridge, Mass.: Harvard University Press.

McGinn, Noel F., Donald Snodgrass, Yung Bong Kim, Shin-Bok Kim, and Quee-Young Kim. 1980. *Education and Development in Korea*. Cambridge, Mass.: Harvard University Press.

Otsuka, Keijiro, Gustav Ranis, and Gary Saxonhouse. 1988. *Comparative Technology Choice: The Indian and Japanese Cotton Textile Industries*. London: Macmillan.

Pack, Howard. 1992. "New Perspectives on Industrial Growth in Taiwan." In Gustav Ranis, ed., *Taiwan: From Developing to Mature Economy*. Boulder, Colo.: Westview Press.

Page, John. 1994. "The East Asian Miracle: An Introduction." *World Development* 22(April):615–25.

Ranis, Gustav. 1984. "Typology in Development Theory: Retrospective and Prospects." In Moshe Syrquin, Lance Taylor, and Larry Westphal, eds., *Economic Structure and Performance: Essays in Honor of Hollis B. Chenery*. Orlando, Fla.: Academic Press.

Ranis, Gustav, and Frances Stewart. 1993. "Rural Nonagricultural Activities in Development: Theory and Application." *Journal of Development Economics* 40(1):75–101.

Scott, J. C. 1976. *The Moral Economy of the Peasant*. New Haven, Conn.: Yale University Press.

Taiwan (China). 1989. *Educational Statistics of the Republic of China*. Taipei: Ministry of Education.

——. Various years a. *Taiwan Statistical Data Book*. Taipei: Ministry of Finance and Directorate-General of Budget, Accounting, and Statistics, Council for Economic Planning and Development.

——. Various years b. *Statistical Yearbook of the Republic of China*. Taipei: Directorate-General of the Budget, Accounting, and Statistics.

——. Various years c. *Taiwan Statistical Abstract of Transport and Communication*. Taipei: Ministry of Transportation and Communications.

United Nations. Various years a. *UNESCO Statistical Yearbook*. New York.

——. Various years b. *United Nations Statistical Yearbook*. New York.

——. Various years c. *National Income Accounts Statistics Yearbook*. New York.

Wade, Robert 1990. *Governing the Market: Economic Theory and the Role of the Government in East Asian Industrialization*. Princeton, N.J.: Princeton University Press.

Westphal, Larry. 1985. "Reflections on the Republic of Korea's Acquisition of Technological Capability." In Nathan Rosenberg and Carlos Frischtak, eds., *International Technology: Concepts, Measures, and Comparisons*. New York: Praeger.

Williamson, John. 1990. "What Washington Means by Policy Reform." In John Williamson, ed., *Latin American Adjustment: How Much Has Happened?* Washington, D.C.: Institute for International Economics.

World Bank. 1991. *World Development Report 1991*. New York: Oxford University Press.

——. 1993. *The East Asian Miracle: Economic Growth and Public Policy*. New York: Oxford University Press.

Wu, Rong-I. 1972. "Some Aspects of Export Trade and Economic Development in Taiwan." University of Louvain, Department of Economics, Louvain, Belgium. Processed.

Young, Allyn. 1993. "Lessons from the East Asian NIC's: A Contrarian View." NBER Working Paper 4482. National Bureau of Economic Research, Cambridge, Mass. Processed.

10

GETTING INTERVENTIONS RIGHT

How South Korea and Taiwan Grew Rich

Dani Rodrik

10.1 INTRODUCTION

To any economist interested in growth, the East Asian experience since the early 1960s poses enduring challenges. In 1960, South Korea was poorer than many sub-Saharan African countries, and Taiwan not all that much richer (Table 10.1). Since then, these two countries have experienced average increases in per-capita income of 6.8% and 6.2% respectively, with the result that they have left far behind not only these African countries, but also others like Mexico and Argentina which had been much richer. How these two countries managed to transform themselves from economic basket cases into economic powerhouses remains something of an enigma.

The standard story to which most orthodox economists subscribe is one of export-led growth (see, for example, Tsiang, 1984; Kreuger, 1985; World Bank, 1993; Little, 1994). During the 1950s, the story goes, both of these

Table 10.1 Comparative growth experience

Country	*Per-capita GDP, 1960 (1985 dollars)*	*Per-capita GDP, 1989 (1985 dollars)*	*Per-capita GDP, growth, 1960–89 (%)*
South Korea	883	6206	6.82
Taiwan	1359	8207	6.17
Ghana	873	815	−0.54
Senegal	1017	1082	0.16
Mozambique	1128	756	−2.29
Brazil	1745	4138	3.58
Mexico	2798	5163	2.36
Argentina	3294	3608	0.63

Source: Penn World Table 5.5.

Source: *Economic Policy*, No. 20, April 1995, pp. 55–107.

countries engaged in traditional import substitution policies, with multiple exchange rates, high levels of trade protection, and repressed financial markets. By the late 1950s, each country had exhausted the 'easy stage' of import substitution. This, together with the impending reduction in US aid – which had been the main source of foreign exchange for both economies – led policy-makers in the two countries to alter their economic strategy and adopt export-oriented policies. These policies included the unification of exchange rates accompanied by devaluations, various other measures to stimulate exports (including most significantly duty-free access for exporters to imported inputs), higher interest rates, and some liberalization of the import regime. As a consequence of these measures, as well as a broadly supportive policy environment (encompassing macroeconomic stability and public investment in infrastructure and in human capital), exports took off in the mid-1960s. Export orientation led both economies to specialize according to comparative advantage, resulting in rising incomes, investment, savings and productivity.

This orthodox account has been criticized for downplaying the active role of governments in Taiwan and South Korea in shaping the allocation of resources. Observers like Amsden (1989) and Wade (1990) have argued that the reforms of the 1960s went considerably beyond giving markets and comparative advantage free rein. According to these authors, governments in both countries had clear industrial priorities and they did not hesitate to intervene (through subsidies, trade restrictions, administrative guidance, public enterprises or credit allocation) to reshape comparative advantage in the desired direction. Interestingly, however, the orthodox and revisionist accounts converge on the importance of the export-oriented strategy in having disciplined firms and enhanced productivity growth. The World Bank's detailed recent study, *The East Asian Miracle* (1993), has attempted to incorporate some of the revisionist objections (particularly on the role of directed credit) into the standard account.

I will argue in this paper that the standard story, as sketched above, is incomplete and quite misleading on the importance it attaches to the role of export orientation in the growth performance. It also has backward the causal relationship between exports, on the one hand, and investment and growth on the other. As I will show, the increase in the relative profitability of exports around the mid-1960s was modest in both countries, and can account fully neither for the initial jump in the export–GDP ratio at that time nor for the subsequent steady increase in this ratio.

A much more plausible explanation for the economic take-off is the sharp increase in investment demand that took place in the early 1960s. The reason for this investment boom is the key issue addressed in this paper. I will argue that in the early 1960s and thereafter the Korean and Taiwanese governments managed to engineer a significant increase in the private return to capital. They did so not only by removing a number of impediments to investment and establishing a sound investment climate, but more importantly by alleviating a coordination failure which had blocked economic take-off. The latter required a range of strategic interventions – including investment subsidies, administrative guidance and the use of public enterprise – which went considerably beyond those discussed in the standard account. That government intervention could play such a productive role was conditioned in turn by a set of advantageous initial conditions: namely, a favourable human capital endowment and relatively equal distribution of income and wealth.

I will elaborate on these arguments below. It is useful to set the stage first by reviewing some of the key elements of the Taiwanese and Korean miracles (Section 10.2). Next, I discuss the shortcomings of the export-based explanations of these miracles (Section 10.3). I then turn to some of the distinctive initial conditions – relative abundance of human capital and equitable income and wealth distribution – which appear to have played a role in both countries' economic performance (Section 10.4). Section 10.5 lays out the paper's central arguments on coordination failure and the governments' role in removing it. Section 10.6 discusses the investment-stimulating policies followed by the two governments in light of the preceding analytical framework. Section 10.7 asks how it became possible for detailed interventions to be carried out efficiently and with little rent seeking. In Section 10.8, I discuss a number of objections to the arguments. Section 10.9 closes the paper by offering some concluding remarks. The formal model providing the foundation for the central argument is presented in the appendix.

10.2 THE CONTOURS OF A MIRACLE

We begin by reviewing some of the key facts about the two countries' economic performance over the last three decades. Figure 10.1 shows their spectacular growth performance since the early 1960s. We note that economic growth has fluctuated widely around a high mean. Both economies were particularly hard hit by the two oil shocks of the 1970s, but in each case output recovered remarkably quickly.

Figure 10.2 is the chief exhibit for the export-led growth hypothesis. The export–GDP ratio rose from virtually zero in Korea to more than 30% by the early 1980s, and from around 10% in Taiwan to over 40%. In both countries, the increase in export orientation was particularly rapid in the decade from the mid-1960s to the mid-1970s, and has abated somewhat since then.

Less discussed but certainly more important is the spectacular increase in the investment effort, shown in Figure 10.3. Investment rose from around 10% of GDP in the late 1950s in both countries to 30% in 1980. Since 1980, investment has continued its upward trend in Korea, but has declined somewhat in Taiwan. This investment effort has been matched by a roughly equivalent increase in savings. Consequently, the net resource transfer from abroad has been either small (Taiwan) or moderate but manageable (Korea).

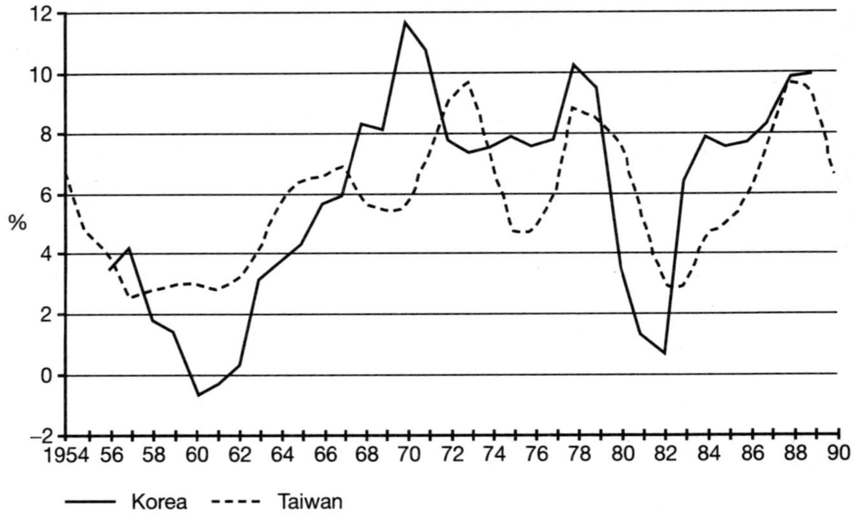

Figure 10.1 Per-capita growth rates (three-year moving averages), 1954–90
Source: Penn World Table 5.5.

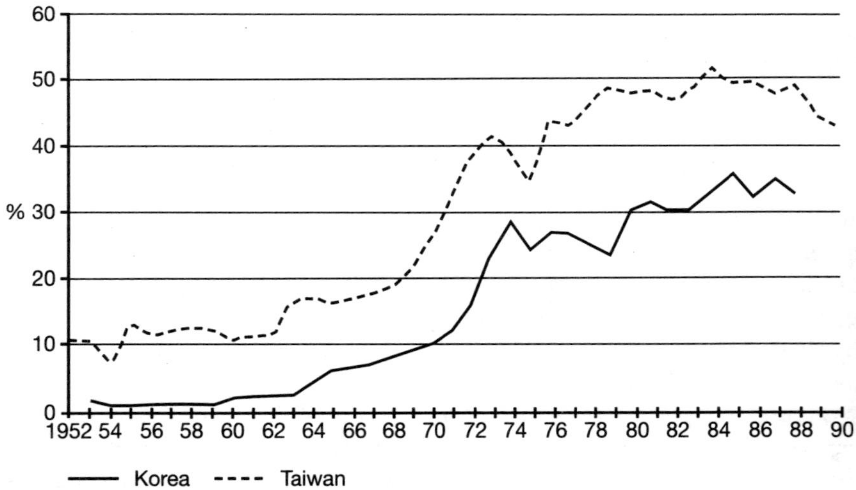

Figure 10.2 Export/GDP ratios, 1952–90
Source: Council for Economic Planning and Development, *Taiwan Statistical Data Book*, 1982 and 1992; Economic Planning Board, *Major Statistics of the Korean Economy*, various issues; IMF, *International Financial Statistics*.

Finally, to round out our discussion of the main outlines of the Korean and Taiwanese experience, productivity performance has been respectable in both countries, but hardly spectacular. Table 10.2 shows the results of Young's (1994) careful calculations of changes in total factor productivity (TFP) for

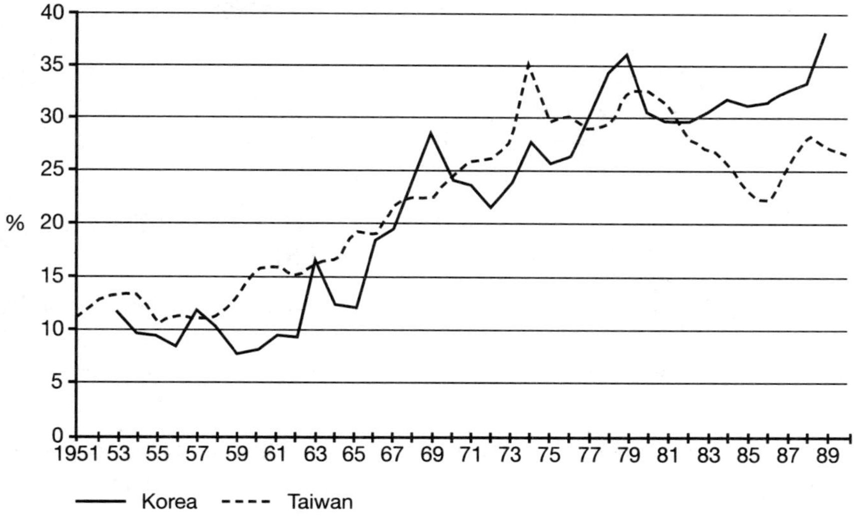

Figure 10.3 Investment/GDP ratios, 1951–90
Source: Penn World Table 5.5.

Table 10.2 Comparative productivity growth statistics

		Total factor productivity growth (% per year)	
Country	*Period*	*Economy*	*Manufacturing*
South Korea	1966–90	1.2*	2.7
Taiwan	1966–90	1.8	1.4
Argentina	1940–80	1.0	n.a.
Brazil	1950–80	2.0	n.a.
	1960–80	n.a.	1.0
Chile	1940–80	1.2	n.a.
Colombia	1940–80	0.9	n.a.
Mexico	1940–80	1.7	n.a.
	1940–70	n.a.	1.3
Venezuela	1950–70	n.a.	2.6

Note:
* Non-agricultural economy.

Source: Young (1994). Latin American statistics are originally from Elias (1990).

Korea and Taiwan, along with similar numbers for Latin American countries. The East Asian TFP figures do not stand out in comparison with those for Latin American countries. A paper by Kim and Lau (1992), based on an econometric estimation of a 'meta-production function' across countries, presents an even more dramatic finding: the rate of technical progress in South Korea and Taiwan has been essentially nil.[1] Surprising as these results may seem, they reflect the simple fact that once the phenomenal rate of factor accumulation (primarily in capital) is taken into account, there is very little growth 'residual' left over to explain. The inescapable conclusion is that the proximate determinant of the East Asian miracle is capital accumulation rather than an increase in industrial factor productivity.[2]

10.3 WHAT IS WRONG WITH THE EXPORT-LED GROWTH HYPOTHESIS?

As pointed out in the introduction, the standard account gives priority to the role of export orientation in explaining the economic performance summarized in the previous section. A particularly clear statement comes from Ian Little (1994):

> the outstanding success of Korea and Taiwan from the early 1960s to the mid-1970s was based on a phenomenal growth of labour-intensive manufactures. This branch of manufacturing took off because exports were highly profitable once the bias against manufacturing for export was removed. The high profitability also depended on a relatively well-educated hard working docile labour force which was, apart from the natural rate of increase, fed by a large movement out of agriculture . . . High profits and increased earnings for recruits to the industrial labour force led to a very rapid rise in savings. There was thus a virtuous circle.

Upon a closer look, however, this account is not quite convincing for a number of reasons discussed below.

10.3.1 The switch in relative incentives towards exports in the early 1960s was not significant enough to account for the export boom

Countries that have experienced sustained export growth outside of East Asia have almost always done so as a consequence of a sharp increase in the relative profitability of exports. What is striking about the experience of South Korea and Taiwan is how stable the relative price of their exportables was around the time of export take-off. In both countries, most of the important export incentives had already been in place for several years before the export boom started. Once the boom got under way, it picked up speed, even though the measured profitability of exports did not increase further. Moreover, exports continued their inexorable rise, often in the context of deteriorating incentives for exporting activities. The following paragraphs elaborate on these points in greater detail.

10.3.1.1 Korea

Under the Rhee government of the 1950s, Korean policy was preoccupied by largely political considerations, and the government attached no particular importance to either economic growth or exports (Jones and Sakong, 1980). There were multiple exchange rates and a haphazard, ineffective programme of export subsidies (Frank *et al.*, 1975). However, exporters could retain a share of their export earnings to import certain items for home consumption, a system which translated into a large export subsidy whenever the free-market exchange diverged greatly from the official rate. After 1958, export incentives were increased. Exporters were given tariff exemption on imports of raw materials and spare parts in 1959. Subsidized credit was made available to exporters for up to 75% of their production costs, also in 1959. And a devaluation of the currency in 1961 brought the official exchange rate close to the free-market rate.

Later, after President Park took over in a military coup on 16 May 1961, the scope of export subsidization was greatly enlarged. The subsidy on export credits was increased and exporters were exempted from the commodity tax and the business activity tax. The income tax on export earnings was reduced. There were also direct cash grants on exports, but these were phased out by 1965 (Frank *et al.*, 1975). However, the incentive effects of the devaluations and the cash grants were eroded by expansionary macroeconomic policies that led to rising inflation in 1962–3 and a renewed gap between official and parallel exchange rates in 1963. A large devaluation in May 1964 served once again to unify the currency. After 1965, export subsidy programmes were expanded further. In that year, the existing practice of giving priority to exporters in acquiring import licences was formalized and expanded. Exporters were allowed automatic access to duty-free imports of raw materials and intermediate inputs up to a limit. This limit was determined administratively, on the basis of firms' and industries' input–output coefficients plus a margin of 'wastage allowance' (Frank *et al.*, 1975). Since the imports acquired under the wastage allowance could be sold in the domestic market, this was a significant subsidy and was consciously used as such. Subsidized credit to exporters became particularly important after 1966. Frank *et al.* estimate that the wastage allowance alone provided an export subsidy of 4.6% in 1968 on average, and up to 17–21% in certain fabrics and footwear. Bureaucrats had virtually unrestricted discretion in setting wastage allowance, and their generosity varied from time to time.

There is no doubt that these measures increased the relative profitability of exporting compared to the situation that had prevailed during most of the 1950s. However, it also seems clear that the greatest impact of the incentives was felt around 1959–60, rather than in the mid-1960s when the export boom began. This is largely due to two reasons: (1) the export subsidy implicit in the export–import link system was particularly significant in

1959–60 when the gap between the official and parallel exchange rates was large;[3] and (2) inflation eroded many of the export incentives between 1961 and 1964. The devaluation of 1964 and the widening scope of export subsidies could offset the deterioration of incentives since 1960 only partially.

This can be seen in Figure 10.4, which plots the real effective rate for Korean exports. This is a measure of the real exchange rate which includes the monetary equivalent of all the subsidies on exports (export premia through the import link, cash grants, tax incentives, duty-free imports, export credits and the like), and which is therefore an appropriate index of the profitability of exporting relative to other activities in the Korean economy.[4] As the denominator of this index is the domestic price level, subsidies or protection of non-export activities is captured to the extent that such policies raise the domestic price level *relative* to prices of export activities.

We note that, even with the devaluation of 1964, the level of export incentives in 1964–5 was no more than 10% higher than in the preceding couple of years, and actually *below* the level attained in 1959–60. Even though exports rose very fast from 1964 onward, they were not to regain their 1959–60 level of profitability until the early 1970s, and then again only briefly. By the mid-1970s, the export–GDP ratio was nearly ten times larger than in the early 1960s, yet the relative profitability of exports was lower! The argument that export-oriented policies were responsible for the increase in exports is often made in a different guise (see, for example, Page, 1994) by pointing out that trade and exchange rate policies in the 1960s were not overtly discriminatory against exports (as they commonly have been in other developing countries). The evidence for this comes from taking the ratio of the effective

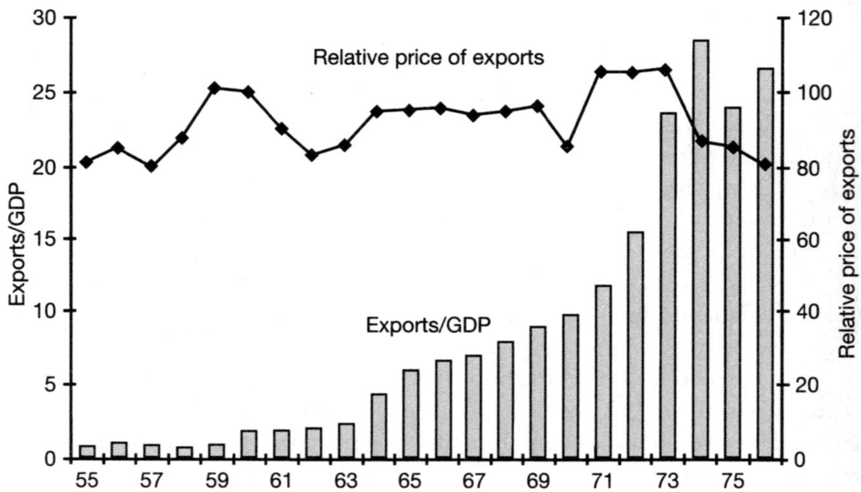

Figure 10.4 Relative price of exports: Korea, 1955–76
Source: Frank *et al*. (1975), Kim (1988) and Bank of Korea.

exchange rate for exports to the effective exchange rate for imports (both calculated by Frank *et al.*, 1975), and noticing that the resulting number is around 1 or somewhat larger during the 1960s. However, it turns out that the comparable number for the second half of the 1950s is much larger, suggesting (if the numbers are to be believed) a much greater export bias in the earlier period (see Frank *et al.*, 1975, Tables 5-10, 8-10D, 8-10E, 8-10C).

Hence the export spurt was not associated with a significant increase in the relative profitability of exports. This has been noted by others. In their authoritative study of Korean development, Mason *et al.* explicitly state that 'the industrial policy changes that took place in the first half of the 1960s did not clearly result in a significant increase in the measurable incentive to export'. Frank *et al.* (1975) attempt to estimate the sensitivity of Korean exports to exchange rates and export subsidies, and note that 'the main difficulty [in doing so is] that from 1955 to 1970 the effective exchange rate for exports remained remarkably steady'. The same point is noted by Jones and Sakong (1980) as well.

In resolving the apparent paradox, these authors resort to arguments that are not entirely satisfactory. Mason *et al.* suggest that it was the stability of incentives that was responsible for the export boom (see also Frank *et al.*, 1975). But since the incentive in question is the profitability of exports relative to other activities, there is no clear reason why enhanced stability should have favoured exports over other activities.[5] Jones and Sakong (1980) resort to a range of explanations, including greater stability, reduction in rent-seeking opportunities, simpler input acquisition, clear political leadership, a more favourable 'business climate', and non-pecuniary incentives such as presidential awards for successful exporters. Once again, the more compelling among these factors are not specific to exporting activities, and therefore cannot account for why exports increased faster than other activities.[6]

With regard to the import regime, there was no significant import liberalization until 1967, when the switch from a positive list to the negative list was implemented. Under the new regime, the regulations began to specify only those items that were prohibited, rather than those that could be imported subject to restrictions (as in the past). In the period 1961–3, the number of items positively listed as importables subject to government licensing, quotas, foreign currency allocation and other regulations ranged between 1000 and 1600. Under pressure from the balance of payments, the government actually reduced the number of importable items to fewer than 500 in late 1964. The 1961–3 level was restored in 1965, and further increased later, until 1967 when the switch occurred (Hong, 1993).

10.3.1.2 Taiwan

In Taiwan most of the export incentives were put in place in the mid- to late-1950s, even earlier than in Korea, and the currency was unified during

1958–61. By 1954–5, the system of import duty and commodity tax rebates for exportable production had already been implemented. In 1956, manufacturers were allowed to retain up to 80% of the foreign exchange they earned from exports and use it for their own import needs. (This ratio was raised to 100% of export earnings for most items after the exchange rate reform of 1958.) In 1957, a relatively generous export credit programme was started. Finally, the multiple exchange rate system was unified during 1958–61 in several stages: (1) in April 1958, the multiple buying rates were consolidated into two buying rates, in parallel with two selling rates; (2) in November 1958, exports and imports under the lower rate were brought up to the higher rate; and (3) further minor devaluations and simplifications were undertaken during the following two years (Hong, 1993; Lin, 1973). By July 1960, the difference between the official exchange rate and the market price of foreign currency had become insignificant.

Unlike in Korea, we do not have a synthetic measure of an effective exchange rate for exporters. So we have to content ourselves with a simple real exchange rate index (not inclusive of export subsidies), which is plotted in Figure 10.5. However, as discussed above, we know that all the significant export subsidies had already been deployed by the late 1950s. Therefore Figure 10.5 should give us a fairly accurate idea of the trend in the relative profitability of exports since 1960. The diagram shows that the initial export spurt (in 1963–4) was actually associated with a decrease in export incentives, indicated by a real appreciation of around 10% (the product of a fixed exchange rate). After 1964, the relative profitability of exports increased steadily until 1973. But it was not until 1969 that the export–GDP ratio resumed its climb. By the early 1980s, the relative profitability of exports

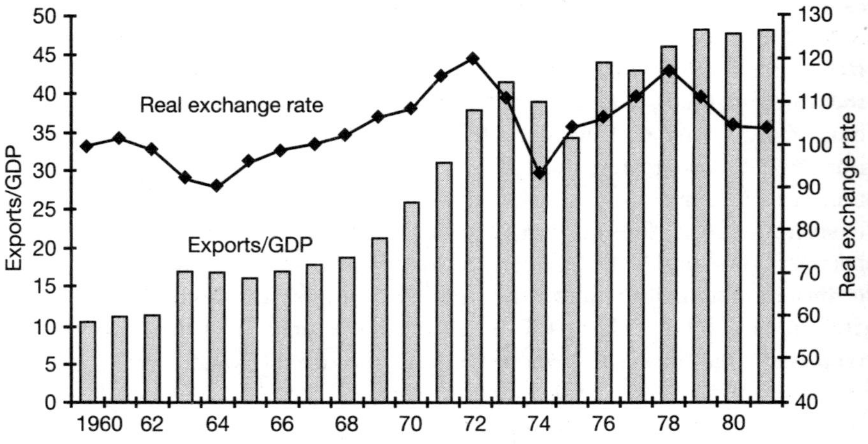

Figure 10.5 Real exchange rates and exports: Taiwan, 1960–81
Source: Kuo (1983, Table 14.4) and Council for Economic Planning and Development, *Taiwan Statistical Data Book*, 1982 and 1991.

stood roughly at its level of 1961, yet the export–GDP ratio was more than four times as large. It is a safe guess that no international economist, presented with a real exchange rate chart such as the one in Figure 10.5, would have predicted a fourfold increase in the exports–GDP ratio. (The real exchange rate in question is the domestic price of tradables, more specifically exportables, relative to the price of non-tradables. This ratio can change considerably even in a 'small' country with no market power in international trade.)

With regard to import liberalization, the Taiwanese pattern is again similar to Korea's. There is a trend towards liberalization after 1964, but this is very much the consequence of the increase in exports and the improvement of the balance of payments position. In any case, the opening up is hardly drastic. As in Korea, one could not possibly ascribe the export boom to import liberalization.

Could the boom of the mid-1960s have been a delayed response to the shift in incentives towards exports during the late 1950s in both countries? Comparative evidence indicates that exports tend to react quite quickly to changes in incentives. The examples of Turkey and Chile will be discussed briefly below. Moreover, this comparative experience is instructive in another respect as well: in cases like Turkey and Chile, sustained export booms generated by export-oriented policies have been associated with real exchange rate depreciations that are much larger than any experienced in Korea or Taiwan. The stability of relative prices in the latter is particularly striking in comparative context, and does suggest that much more than export incentives was involved in boosting exports.

Of course, export incentives (and in particular a relatively free-trade regime for exporters) must have been a necessary condition for exports to take off in Korea and Taiwan: it is hard to imagine the export performance of these countries taking place in the presence of grossly overvalued currencies or high barriers to trade in imported inputs used in exportables. Nonetheless, the delay suggests that the export incentives were not sufficient in themselves.

10.3.2 Export orientation versus investment boom

It is not clear why export orientation (or the increase in exports) should have led to an investment boom. The standard account rarely confronts the question of why either the export incentives or the export boom should have led to an investment boom. We have many cases where even more sizeable increases in the profitability of exports either have not led to increases in investment or have done so only after considerable lag. This is obviously important, in so far as exports (unlike investment) do not directly lead to economic growth.

Consider two important examples, Turkey and Chile. In Turkey, there was a massive increase in the profitability of exports in the early 1980s (of more than 50%), with considerable import liberalization as well. These reforms were accompanied by an impressive increase in the export–GDP ratio (Figure 10.6). Yet, as Figure 10.6 shows, private investment actually fell in this period, and did not recover until the second half of the 1980s. In Chile, a fall in the relative profitability of exports in the late 1970s was accompanied by an investment boom. Investment collapsed in 1982–3 as a result of a major financial crisis. Export incentives increased significantly after 1982, but private investment responded sluggishly until 1989 (Figure 10.7).

We should not be surprised to find that export incentives and investment can covary in different ways. In theory, there is no reason to suppose that export orientation should be associated with an increase in investment demand. Export orientation makes some sectors more profitable and others

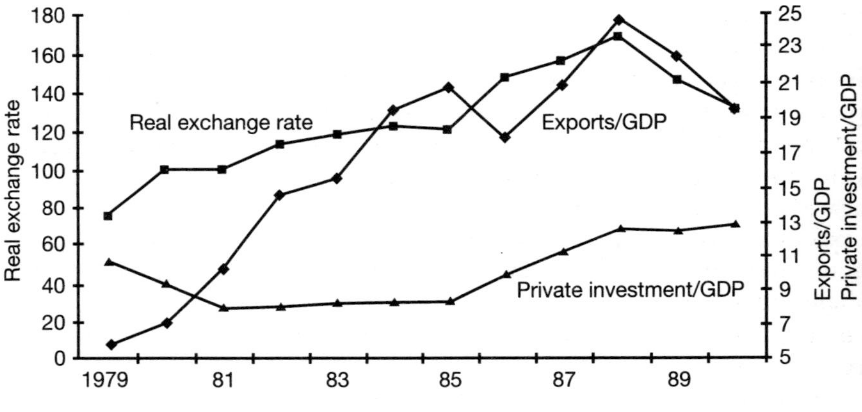

Figure 10.6 Turkey, 1979–90
Source: OECD, *Economic Surveys: Turkey*, various issues.

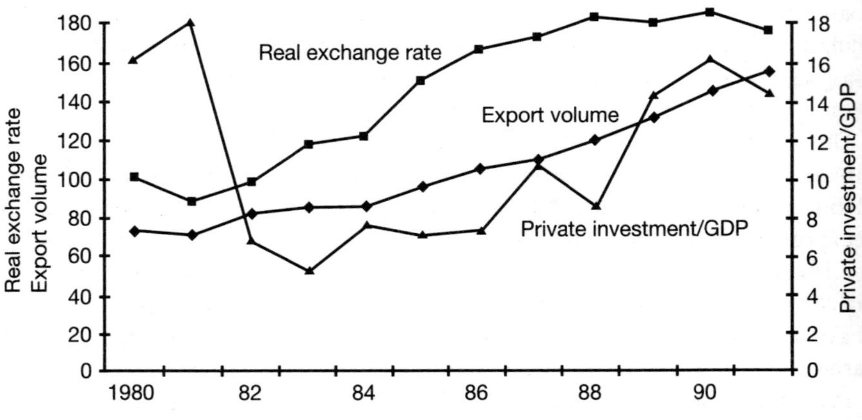

Figure 10.7 Chile, 1980–91
Source: Bosworth *et al*. (1994).

(import-competing activities and non-tradables) less so. The same is true of import liberalization.

The net effect on investment demand is indeterminate. If anything, the logic of relative factor endowments and the Stolper–Samuelson theorem suggests an opposing presumption: in capital-poor countries like Taiwan and South Korea during the 1950s and 1960s, an increase in the relative price of exports should have been associated with a *decline* in the return to capital, and hence reduced investment!

10.3.3 The contribution of exports

Since the export base was so small early on (especially in Korea), the contribution of exports to GDP growth could not have been very high until the mid-1970s at least. Exports were less than 5% of GDP in Korea around 1960, and barely over 10% in Taiwan. In a purely accounting sense, exports could have been responsible for only a small fraction of the initial growth spurt in both countries, in view of the small base from which they sprang. This comes out clearly in demand-side decompositions of output growth (which break down growth into increases in domestic demand, import substitution, exports and changes in input–output coefficients). For example, Hong (1976) calculates that export expansion could not have accounted for more than 10% of Korea's growth in 1966–70. Kuo (1983) reports a higher contribution of exports to Taiwan's growth (but still below that of domestic demand until the 1970s), in large part because the Taiwanese economy was more open at the beginning of the transition.

Such demand-side decompositions of the 'sources of growth' are in themselves unsatisfactory because the methodology is vague as to the mechanism, if any, that relates exports growth to GDP growth. In a fully employed, small open economy with marginal products of productive factors equalized among different activities, an increase in exports cannot raise output. Of course, an increase in exports caused by an external terms of trade improvement could be associated with an increase in real income. However, terms of trade movements cannot account for any significant part of Korea's and Taiwan's success. During much of the 1960s, Korea and Taiwan had some unemployment as well as a productivity gap between the modern and traditional sectors of their economies. Under such conditions, an increase in exports can be expansionary, but the question is how much.

A useful first approximation is provided by a computable general equilibrium (CGE) model constructed by Trela and Whalley (1992) for Korea. These authors treat the agricultural sector differently from the other sectors of the economy, in that they assume labour is paid its average (rather than marginal) product in the agricultural sector. Consequently, as labour is drawn into the modern sectors of the economy (including exportables), total output rises. Even so, they find that export-oriented policies can explain in their model only a very small fraction of Korean growth during 1962–82. In their words, 'the results seem to imply that outward-oriented policies in Korea have little significance in driving growth' (1992). This is a consequence of the facts already discussed: exportables were a small part of the economy and there was only a relatively small change in measured incentives towards exportables.

10.3.4 Productivity spillovers from exports?

It is not clear that export growth was, or should have been, associated with cumulative productivity spillovers to the rest of the economy. The previous arguments can be countered by claiming that the contribution of exports to growth came not from the demand side or through investment, but from widespread technological spillovers and cumulative productivity benefits deriving from export performance. This is indeed a common presumption. The World Bank's (1993) East Asian report gives it top billing in its exposition of the 'dynamic' benefits of outward orientation. See also de Melo and Robinson (1992). These authors use a CGE model with export externalities to account for those stylized features of East Asian development that standard CGEs are unable to 'explain'.

The trouble is there is virtually no evidence that exports or outward orientation were associated with technological externalities. The World Bank's report does not provide any. It bases its arguments on a number of a priori reasons, which are in themselves quite problematic (see Rodrik, 1994, for a critique of the report, and Rodrik, 1992, for a general discussion of the ambiguous theoretical case in favour of productivity spillovers from exports). It is common in this literature to point to correlations between export growth and TFP performance across firms or industries as evidence for technological spillovers. Such correlations obviously say nothing about the direction of causality, if any. The most plausible way to interpret such findings is that firms and industries which are successful in improving their productivity are better able to compete in world markets. Perhaps most telling on this score is that, as we have seen, overall productivity growth in industry has not been spectacular in either country, and can explain only a small part of total growth. As Young (1994) puts it, 'it is not particularly difficult to find either developed or less developed economies whose productivity performance, over time periods spanning two decades or more, has matched or rivalled that of the NICs [including Korea and Taiwan]' (see also Young, 1993). Hence, we should be suspicious of any argument that gives pride of place to the (assumed) presence of technological spillovers from exports.

Moreover, the argument about technological spillovers from exports is usually made in the context of manufactured, rather than aggregate, exports (World Bank, 1993; Page, 1994). That constitutes another problem, in view of the meagre base from which the externalities in question are presumed to have come. In both countries, manufactured exports accounted for a quarter or less of total exports around 1960, and consequently they were an even smaller share of national income. It is not easy to see how the spillovers from such a puny source could be so strong as to set a process of aggregate economic growth into motion.

10.3.5 The rising share of exports in GDP is consistent with investment-led growth

As mentioned previously, the apparent clincher for the export-led growth hypothesis is the steady increase in the exports–GDP ratio that both countries have experienced. If, as argued above, exports are unlikely to have played much of a causal role in growth, why did this ratio increase so much? The answer is provided by thinking in general equilibrium terms, with a formal illustration provided in Box 10.1.

Box 10.1 Endogenous response of exports to an investment boom

The initial levels of consumption and production are represented in Figure 10.8 by points C_0 and Q_0 respectively. We represent the increase in investment demand as a shift in preferences, which biases home demand towards the more capital-intensive importables. The relevant indifference surface now becomes U_1, with the associated consumption and production levels of C_1 and Q_1 respectively. (Note that the production mix remains the same, as the external terms of trade are taken to be fixed.) The economy's imports and exports both expand. The impact effect of an increase in investment is to render the economy more open to trade. The longer-run effect is shown on the right panel. As the economy's capital stock expands, the transformation frontier moves outward in a fashion that is biased towards the capital-intensive importable. This has the effect of reducing trade over time, but, as drawn, the trade triangle remains larger than in the initial equilibrium.

The figure also clarifies how, following an increase in investment (and import) demand, an increase in exports can develop *without* any change in the relative price of the exportable. The mechanism that enables this is the switch in domestic expenditures away from the exportable, allowing in turn an increase in exports. In the absence of non-tradables (as in the diagram), the increase in exports exactly matches the increase in imports, with no change in relative prices. In the presence of non-tradables, some of the increased demand for the importables would come at the expense of non-tradables, calling for a reduction in the price of non-tradables (relative to tradables) to equilibrate the market for non-tradables. The magnitude of the equilibrium real exchange rate depreciation would then depend on the parameters of the model.[7]

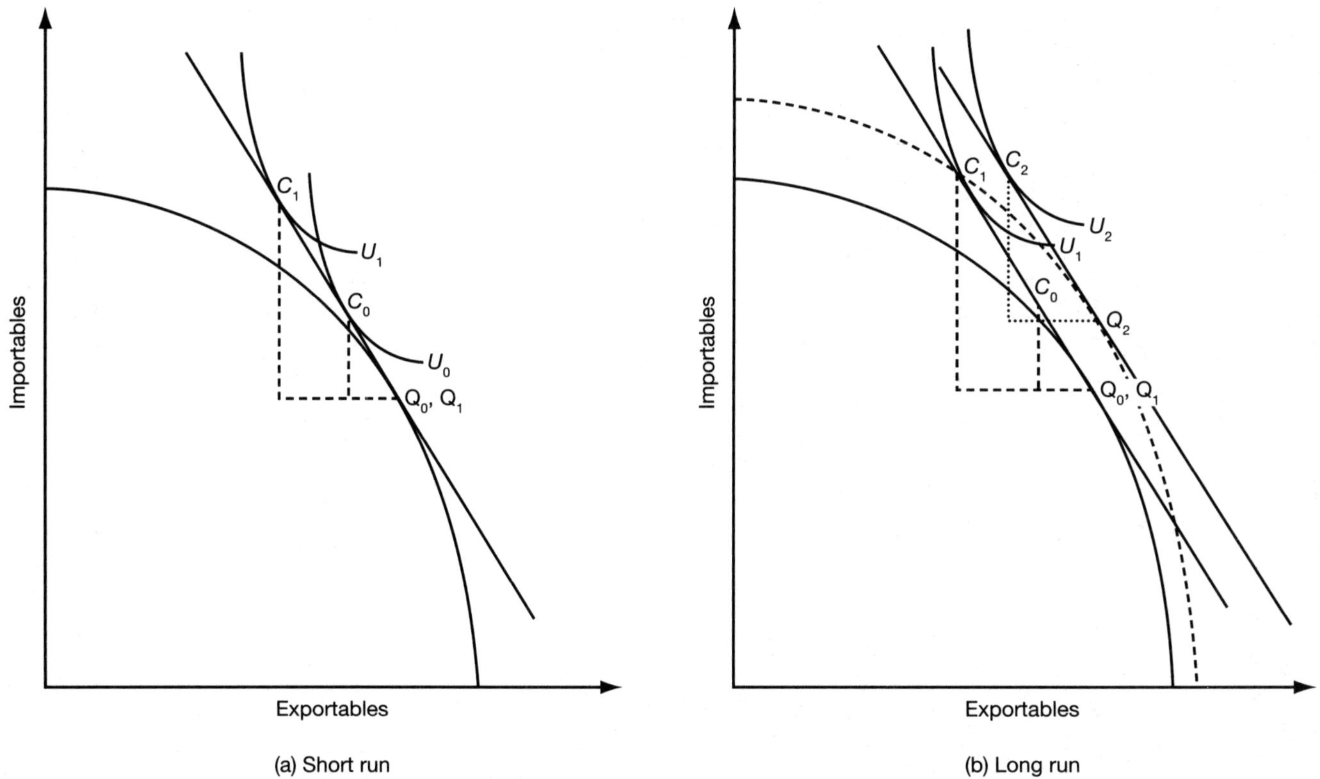

Figure 10.8 Consequences of an increase in investment demand

Consider an (exogenous) increase in the profitability of investment, followed by an increase in the share of investment in GDP. Suppose that the country in question (like Korea and Taiwan during the 1960s) has a comparative disadvantage in producing capital goods. The investment boom will require a commensurate increase in imports (also as a share of GDP). And if international borrowing is not unlimited, exports must rise (as a share of GDP) to pay for the imports. Hence, we will observe an increasing trade orientation alongside the boom in investment. This story reverses the causality between growth and exports. Exports orientation enables growth (by allowing imports to increase), but it is not its ultimate determinant. Ultimately, the reasons for growth must be traced back to reasons why it became profitable to invest.

This story is quite consistent with the Korean and Taiwanese experiences. First, a casual look at the data shows that in both cases investment and imports are closely related. As Figures 10.9 and 10.10 make clear, the behaviour of imports tracks quite closely the behaviour of investment. In Korea, investment and imports both rise (as a share of GDP) until around 1980, and then stabilize somewhat. In Taiwan, investment and imports rise in tandem until the late 1970s, and then both decline somewhat. Figures 10.11 and 10.12, showing the composition of imports, make clear the connection. Since the mid-1960s, the share of capital goods (machinery and transport equipment) in both countries' imports has risen sharply. In fact, it is mainly the increase in capital goods that accounts for the rise in the imports–GDP ratio. Hence, the increasing export orientation of the economy

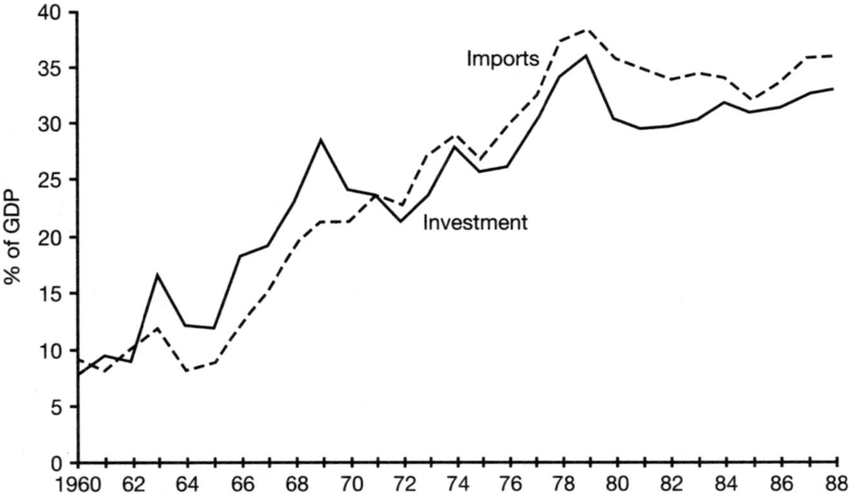

Figure 10.9 Imports and investment: Korea, 1960–88
Source: Penn World Table 5.5 and Economic Planning Board, *Major Statistics of the Korean Economy*, various issues.

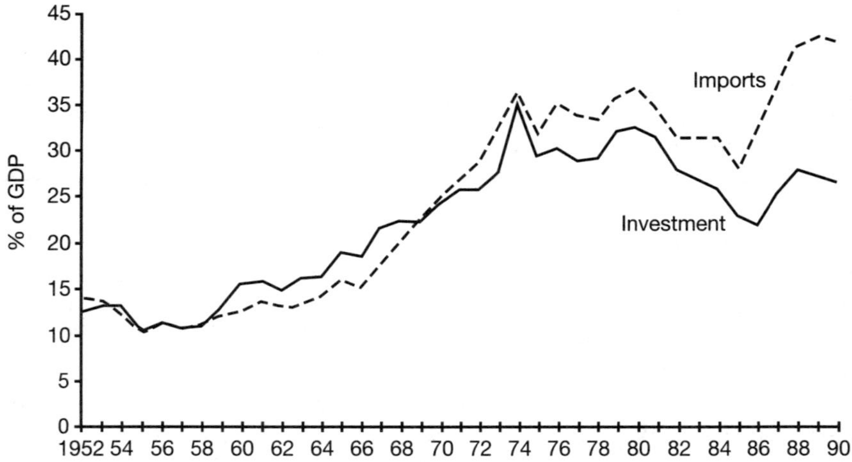

Figure 10.10 Imports and investment: Taiwan, 1952–90
Source: Penn World Table 5.5 and *National Income in Taiwan Area of the Republic of China* (1993).

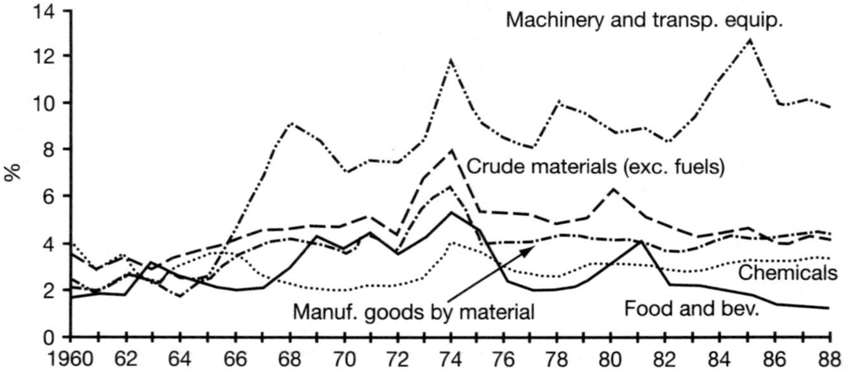

Figure 10.11 Imports as a share of GDP: Korea, 1960–88
Source: Economic Planning Board, *Major Statistics of the Korean Economy*, 1976, 1989.

is quite consistent with investment-led growth, with causality running from investment to imports and from imports to exports.[8,9]

10.3.6 The role of savings

In both countries, savings rose alongside investment, and therefore enabled growth to proceed without hitting balance of payments constraints. This is important as it constitutes another part of the explanation of how a large export surplus could develop without substantial contemporaneous changes in the relative price of exportables. Most accounts view the increase in savings

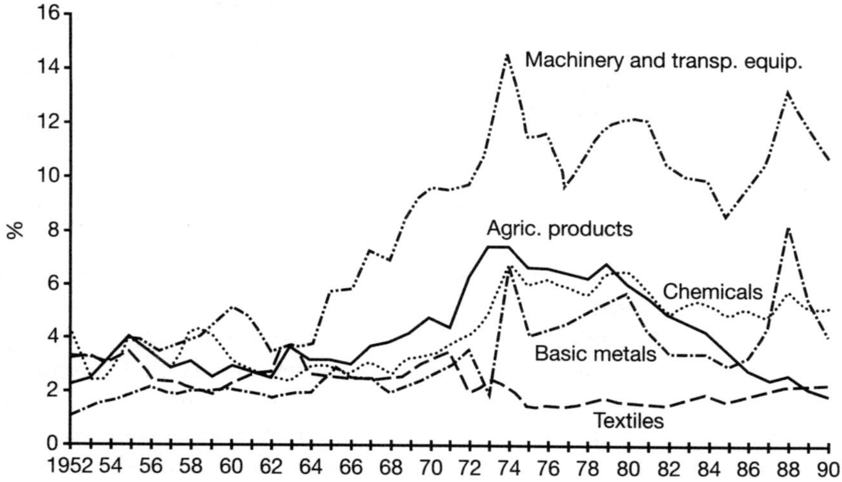

Figure 10.12 Imports as a share of GDP: Taiwan, 1952–90
Source: Council for Economic Planning and Development, *Taiwan Statistical Data Book*, 1982, 1991.

in Korea and Taiwan as having been the result of economic growth itself and of a comparatively early demographic transition (Collins and Park, 1989; Collins, 1991; World Bank, 1993).

Government policy was helpful as well. Real interest rates were raised for depositors to levels that were either positive or only mildly negative (Taiwan in the 1950s and Korea in the 1960s). In addition, an increase in public savings made an important contribution to total savings in both countries. In Taiwan, the increase in the savings rate in the early 1960s coincided with a sharp increase in government saving after 1961 (Kuo, 1983). This was enabled in turn by a reduction in government consumption. And in Korea, 'it was the rapidly increasing contribution of government savings and the steady inflow of foreign savings which enabled Korea to achieve the very high rate of investment during the 1962–73 period' (Hong, 1976).

10.3.7 Recapitulation

The proposition that Korea's and Taiwan's economic performance can be ascribed to export orientation faces serious difficulties. The switch towards export-oriented policies cannot account for the sustained export boom since the mid-1960s, and even less for the equally impressive and sustained investment boom. Export growth itself can explain only a limited part of the early growth in output. The increasing share of exports in GDP is quite consistent with a story of investment- rather than export-led growth. These problems should lead us to search for more direct explanations for the apparent increase in the profitability of private investment around the mid-1960s in both countries. The rest of this paper argues that the explanation has to do with government policies that go considerably beyond export incentives, and that Korea and Taiwan shared some rather special initial conditions that made such government policies possible.

10.4 IMPORTANCE OF INITIAL CONDITIONS

While South Korea and Taiwan were both quite poor around 1960, their social indicators placed them among the ranks of countries at several times their income levels. Table 10.3 shows Adelman and Morris's (1967) index of socioeconomic development for a range of countries, as measured around the late 1950s and early 1960s. This index is derived from factor analysis and is based on a large number of indicators meant to capture characteristics of social structure and social organization. (The indicators include the extent of dualism, urbanization, importance of an indigenous middle class, social mobility, literacy, mass communications, cultural and ethnic homogeneity, fertility, national integration and sense of national unity, and modernization of outlook.) Adelman and Morris place Taiwan and Korea in their most advanced group, even though their per-capita incomes are considerably below average.

If we focus specifically on indicators of educational attainment, we see the same discrepancy with the level of per-capita income. Table 10.4 displays data on three educational indicators which are commonly employed as explanatory variables in cross-country growth regressions. The table shows the actual school enrolment and literacy rates in Korea and Taiwan in 1960, as well as the corresponding rates that would have been expected on the basis of these countries' per-capita income levels alone. The latter are derived from cross-section regressions of educational indicators on per-capita income and its square. We find that both countries had virtually universal primary school

Table 10.3 Socioeconomic development and income

	Index of socioeconomic development, c. *1960*	*Per-capita GNP, 1961 ($)*
South Korea	0.85	73
Taiwan	1.05	145
Brazil	0.79	186
Cambodia	−0.55	101
Ivory Coast	−0.98	184
Morocco	−0.57	150
Cyprus	1.08	416
Jamaica	1.06	436

Source: Adelman and Morris (1967, Table IV-5).

enrolment, while the norm for countries at their income levels stood at around 60% only. Korea had more than double the literacy rate compared to the norm, and Taiwan's literacy rate was one-and-a-half times as high. It is clear that both countries had a labour force that was considerably better educated than would be predicted from their income levels.

The other respect in which Korea and Taiwan stood out by 1960 was their exceptionally equal distribution of income and wealth. This was due in part to long-standing historical reasons, and in part to the serious land reforms undertaken in both countries during the 1950s. Figure 10.13 plots Gini coefficients for income and land distribution for 41 countries for which both measures are available for a year around 1960. Korea and Taiwan are the two countries closest to the origin: that is, with the lowest overall inequality.

These initial conditions can account, in a statistical sense, for a large part of the two countries' economic performance since 1960. Table 10.5 shows the results of regressing growth and investment rates on initial primary

Table 10.4 Educational indicators

	Primary enrolment ratio		*Secondary enrolment ratio*		*Literacy rate*	
	Predicted	*Actual*	*Predicted*	*Actual*	*Predicted*	*Actual*
Korean	0.57	0.94	0.10	0.27	0.31	0.71
Taiwan	0.62	0.96	0.12	0.28	0.36	0.54

Source: See text.

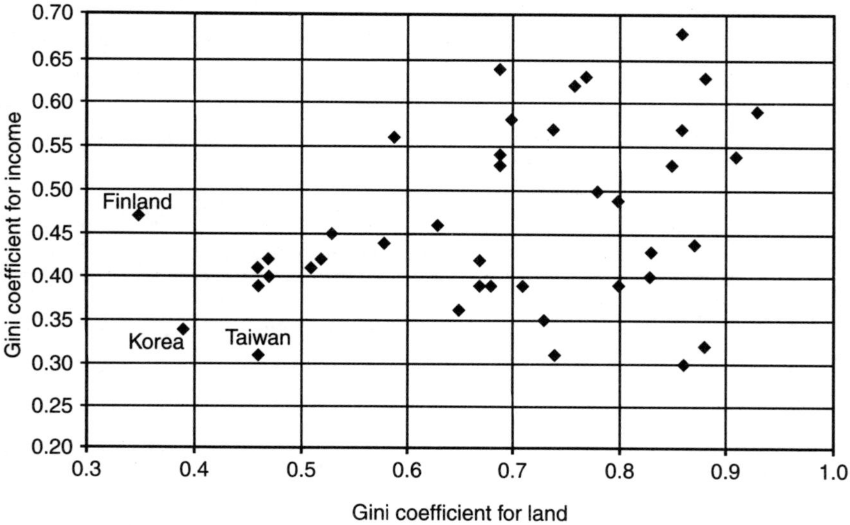

Figure 10.13 Measures of income and land distribution, *c.* 1960
Source: Alesina and Rodrik (1994).

enrolment and inequality indicators (as well as initial per-capita income) in the sample of countries for which inequality data are available. The primary enrolment rate has a positive and statistically significant coefficient (as expected). In addition, there is a strong negative association between inequality (particularly in land distribution) and subsequent growth. Despite the parsimonious specification (most notably, the exclusion of investment as an explanatory variable from the growth equation), these regressions do rather well, and explain around half or more of the cross-national variation in growth and investment rates.

Table 10.6 shows that almost 90% of the two countries' growth experience since 1960 can be 'explained' by these initial conditions. When Korea and

Table 10.5 Growth regressions

	Dependent variables			
	Per-capita GDP growth, 1960–85		*Investment/GDP, 1960–85*	
Independent variables	*(1)*	*(2)*	*(3)*	*(4)*
Intercept	6.22*	3.71*	16.06*	18.06*
	(4.69)	(3.86)	(2.64)	(4.32)
Per-capita GDP, 1960	−0.38*	−0.38*	0.94	0.49
	(−3.25)	(−3.61)	(1.76)	(1.08)
Primary enrolment, 1960	2.66**	3.85*	11.01**	14.11*
	(2.66)	(4.88)	(2.40)	(4.11)
Gini coeff, for land	−5.22*	−5.50*	−21.04*	−16.59*
	(−4.38)	(−5.24)	(−3.85)	(−3.64)
Gini coeff, for income	−3.47		14.44	
	(−1.82)		(1.66)	
$\bar{R}^2$	0.53	0.53	0.43	0.50
Sample size	41	49	41	49

Notes: Numbers in parentheses are *t*-statistics. Asterisks denote level of significance:
* Significant at the 1% confidence level.
** Significant at the 5% confidence level.

Table 10.6 Proportion of growth explained by initial conditions

	Actual growth (1960–85)	*Predicted growth*	*Proportion explained (%)*
South Korea	5.95	5.24	88
Taiwan	5.68	4.96	87
Argentina	0.48	1.58	329
Brazil	3.52	1.96	56
India	1.37	3.46	253
Kenya	0.96	1.46	152

Note: Predicted growth rates are from regression (1) in Table 5.

Taiwan are excluded from the original sample from which the predicted values are generated, the percentage of actual growth predicted by the regression is a bit lower (82% for Korea and 81% for Taiwan), but still striking. In a statistical sense, then, there is nothing 'miraculous' about their experience. The real outliers are countries like Argentina and India (whose actual growth is vastly overpredicted) or Brazil (whose growth is vastly underpredicted). Of course, while these results may be interesting, they do not amount to an explanation. We still need a theory on why these initial conditions mattered as much.[10] That is the task of the next section.

10.5 THE COORDINATION FAILURE INTERPRETATION

10.5.1 The argument

What we need is an explanation that can account for the main outlines of Korean and Taiwanese economic performance, and which also has a role for the special set of initial conditions discussed in the previous section. Such an explanation can be constructed along the following lines.

First, by 1960 Taiwan and South Korea shared a set of advantageous initial conditions relating to social infrastructure. In particular, both economies had a skilled labour force, relative to their physical capital stock and income levels. These initial conditions made both countries ready for economic take-off, in the sense that the latent return to capital accumulation was high.

Second, for a number of reasons, the economic take-off could not take place under decentralized market conditions. Chief among these reasons are the imperfect tradability of key inputs (and technologies) associated with modern-sector production, and some increasing returns to scale in these activities. These conditions created a situation of coordination failure. In other words, while the rate of return to coordinated investments was extremely high, the rate of return to individual investments remained low.

Third, governments in both countries undertook a set of measures starting in the late 1950s that not only removed some policy-induced distortions, but also served to coordinate and subsidize private investment. These measures included: credit subsidies, tax incentives, administrative guidance and public investment.

Fourth, this active government role helped remove the coordination failure that had blocked industrial growth. As private entrepreneurs responded to these measures, the resulting investments turned out to be profitable not only in financial terms, but in social terms as well.

Fifth, government intervention could be implemented in an effective manner (without leading to rent-seeking behaviour) because initial conditions, once again, had endowed the government in each country with an extraordinary degree of insulation from pressure groups, and with leadership capability over them. Among these initial conditions, a relatively equal distribution of income and wealth was critical.

Sixth, as investment rose as a share of GDP, so did imports of capital goods, as neither country had a comparative advantage in such goods. Thanks to appropriate macroeconomic and exchange rate policies, export supply was adequate to meet the increase in import demand, and rose alongside imports.

Seventh, as a consequence, the increase in exports played a critical role in paying for the imports of capital goods. But it is more appropriate to view this increase in exports as a consequence of the increase in investment demand, rather than the other way around.

10.5.2 A framework of analysis

There are two critical claims in this story: (1) both countries were ready for economic take-off by the early to mid-1960s, but economic growth was blocked by a coordination failure; (2) governments in both countries were able to undertake the measures needed to override this coordination failure. The evidence on the presence of a coordination failure is necessarily circumstantial. I think the case is reasonably compelling in view of the likelihood that all of the prerequisites for the existence of a coordination failure were met in the two countries. The appendix presents an analytical framework which makes explicit what these prerequisites are. Here I rely on an intuitive exposition of the economic logic.

Imagine a small open economy, initially specializing in the production of traditional goods. Alongside there exists a relatively capital-intensive modern sector, which yields higher factor returns when it is viable. The modern sector relies on specialized inputs (e.g. particular labour skills, technologies, intermediate inputs or capital goods). These inputs share the following features: (1) they require well-educated workers but at low cost; (2) they exhibit scale economies; and (3) they cannot be perfectly traded in international markets. The viability of the modern sector requires the local presence of these inputs, which in turn depends (in part) on the existence of a sufficiently well-educated workforce.

Such an economy is ready for take-off if there is enough skilled labour that the modern sector would be viable if a large enough share of the economy's resources were devoted to producing the specialized inputs. Yet there is no certainty that labour and capital move from the traditional sector to the modern sector, leading to specialization in the latter and to higher incomes. The reason is that, because of scale economies, only a large-scale movement of resources is guaranteed to be profitable. From the perspective of an individual investor, it will not pay to invest in the modern sector unless others are doing so as well. The profitability of the modern sector depends on the simultaneous presence of the specialized inputs; but the profitability of producing these inputs in turn depends on the presence of demand from a pre-existing modern sector. It is this interdependence of production and investment decisions that creates the coordination problem.

Coordination failure is least likely to happen when the economy is well endowed with both skilled labour and physical capital, for then production in the modern sector is profitable even when entrepreneurs act in an uncoordinated manner. For economies at the other end of the spectrum – lacking both skilled labour and capital – the coordination issue is moot because the modern sector is not viable in the first place. It is in the intermediate economies most reminiscent of Korea and Taiwan in the early 1960s – well endowed with skilled labour but poor in physical capital – that the coordination problem is most severe.

Markets are known to handle resource allocation poorly in the presence of scale economies and non-tradability: market prices reflect the profitability of different activities only as they are currently undertaken; they do not provide any signals about the profitability of activities that would require a large-scale reallocation of resources within the economy (which, after all, is what economic development is all about). These are, of course, old ideas that go back to Scitovsky's (1954) analysis of pecuniary externalities and Rosenstein-Rodan's (1943) advocacy of big-push policies. More recently, the arguments have been formalized in papers by Faini (1984), Pack and Westphal (1986), Murphy *et al.* (1989), Krugman (1991), Matsuyama (1991), Ciccone and Matsuyama (1993), Rodríguez-Clare (1993) and Rodrik (1993).

One problem with this literature has been that coordination failure is often presented as a generic problem affecting all kinds of economies. The present framework is more specific about the prerequisites. It highlights the following three prerequisites for a coordination failure to become a serious issue: (1) some degree of non-tradability in the technologies and/or goods associated with the modern sector; (2) economies of scale; (3) a reasonably skilled labour force (but a low endowment of physical capital). The last one clearly applies to the case of Korea and Taiwan. Scale economies are also plausible in many of the modern-sector activities. Hence, non-tradability is the feature that requires additional discussion.

Upon a moment's reflection, it should be clear that some degree of non-tradability is necessarily associated with the types of goods produced by rich countries. Otherwise poor countries would not remain poor for long: arbitrage through trade would eliminate the disparities. In practice, the non-tradability of modern-sector inputs is observed in a number of different ways. Labour services are for the most part effectively non-traded, so that skilled and specialized workmanship must be locally available. The fixed costs often required to develop these skills lead to scale economies. Intermediate and capital goods are in principle tradable, but they sometimes require either geographic proximity to the final user (as when they are manufactured to suppliers' specifications) or the use of complementary local inputs before they can be put to use (as when skilled workers are needed to operate sophisticated imported machinery). Often, the requisite technologies also have a non-tradable element, in so far as much of the technological capability is tacit and not explicitly codified in designs and blueprints. As Pack and Westphal (1986) put it:

> The tacitness of technology leads to problems in its communication over long distances and across social differences, problems which can be overcome – if at all – only at some cost . . . Moreover, knowledge that exists (somewhere in the world) does not exist everywhere simultaneously because there are costs in advertising its mere existence or in discovering its existence through search. Only knowledge that is 'close by' is known to exist . . . Another significant channel for inter-industry externalities is the exchange of technological elements in transactions involving intermediate products and capital goods. Indeed many such exchanges leading to better utilization of local resources and to improvements in the design of capital goods have been observed. A salient aspect of these exchanges is the dependence of their outcome on extensive interaction between suppliers and users in iteratively changing both process and product characteristics.

Some examples drawn from the East Asian experience may help bring these points to life.

10.5.3 Case studies: Hyundai and Lucky-Goldstar

The importance of specialized labour skills and the complementarities they generate across manufacturing activities is illustrated by the experience of Hyundai, one of Korea's huge conglomerates (*chaebol*). Hyundai first entered manufacturing in 1964 by building a cement plant. According to Amsden (1989):

> Hyundai used its cement plant as a laboratory to train its managers with background in construction, before assigning them to other manufacturing affiliates. Trainees gained experience in inventory management, quality and process control, capacity planning, and so on, thus spreading basic production skills throughout the Hyundai organization. After Hyundai Cement, the next manufacturing affiliate in the group was founded in 1967 and named Hyundai Motors. Twenty years later it became the first independent automaker from a late-industrializing country to export globally. The first president of Hyundai Motors was a former president of Hyundai Cement.

Korean government policies were highly partial to conglomerates like Hyundai. By giving them access to subsidized capital, the government allowed them to internalize many of the labour market spillovers in the fashion described in the quote.

Hyundai's experience with shipbuilding provides a concrete instance of the imperfect tradability of technology (and its interaction with scale economies). The company started out by importing its basic design from a Scottish firm, but soon found that this was not working out. The Scottish design relied on building the ship in two halves because the original manufacturer had enough capacity to build only half a ship at a time. When Hyundai followed the same course, it found out that the two halves did not quite fit. Subsequent designs imported from European consulting firms also had problems, in that the firms would not guarantee the rated capacity, leading to costly delays. Engines were available from Japanese suppliers, but apparently only at a price higher than that obtained by Japanese shipyards. Moreover, ship buyers would often require design modifications, which Hyundai would be unable to undertake in the absence of an in-house design capability. Only with large enough capacity would it pay for Hyundai to integrate backwards (into design and engine building). In a highly volatile business, scale in turn depended on having access to a steady and reliable customer (a merchant marine). The Korean government provided Hyundai with substantial assistance, as well as an implicit guarantee of markets. Hyundai eventually integrated both backwards and forwards. The government's guarantee came in handy in 1975 when a shipping slump led to the cancellation of foreign orders. President Park responded by forcing Korean refineries to ship oil in Korean-owned tankers, creating a captive demand for Hyundai (Jones and Sakong, 1980).

The chairman of the Lucky-Goldstar group explains the success of his company in this way:

> My father and I started a cosmetic cream factory in the late 1940s. At the time, no company could supply us with plastic caps of adequate quality for cream jars, so we had to start a plastic business. Plastic caps alone were not sufficient to run the plastic-moulding plant, so we added combs, toothbrushes, and soap boxes. The plastics business also led us to manufacture electrical and electronic products and telecommunication equipment. The plastics business also took us into oil refining which needed a tanker-shipping company. The oil-refining company alone was paying an insurance premium amounting to more than half the total revenue of the then largest insurance company in Korea. Thus, an insurance company was started. This natural step-by-step evolution through related businesses resulted in the Lucky-Goldstar group as we see it today. (cited in Amsden, 1989)

The quotation clearly illustrates the importance of local inputs and customers as well as of scale economies in fuelling the growth of *chaebol*. While the *chaebol* could thus internalize some of the coordination issues, they were greatly assisted in doing so by government policies which will be discussed in the next section.

In both Korea and Taiwan, the rate of return to capital and profitability in key manufacturing activities rose significantly from the late 1950s on. In Korea, Jones and Sakong (1980) report (based on Hong, 1977) steadily rising real rates of return to capital in manufacturing: the range is 9–18% in mid- to late-1950s, 9–26% in 1962–6, 16–38% in 1967–72, and 17–40% after 1972. The rate of profit in manufacturing steadily rose from 9% in 1951–3 to 16% in 1954–6, to 28% in 1957–62, and to 35% in 1963–70 (Hong, 1993, p. 347). Apparently, investment became more profitable as the investment rate rose.[11] In Taiwan, profitability rates rose in most of the private manufacturing industries after the late 1950s, with the notable exception of textiles and wood products, two major exporting industries (Lin, 1973). Interestingly, the greatest increase in profitability in the post-1963 period (outside food, beverages and tobacco) was experienced by public-sector manufacturing. As will be discussed in the next section, it was public enterprises that supplied many of the key intermediate inputs in Taiwan. This is how Lin (1973) explains the increase in their profits:

> The domestic consumption of the output of these non-food industries (which produce petroleum products, chemical fertilizers, industrial chemicals, etc.) increased tremendously during the 1960s, due to increased demand from chemical-using industries (such as those making polyvinylchloride, monosodium glutamate, and paper and pulp for both the export and domestic market), as well as from the agricultural sector and the transportation industry.

In other words, intermediate industries became profitable thanks to expanding linkages downstream.

We note finally that in both Korea and Taiwan the way policy-makers viewed the economy and their role in it has parallels with the logic of the coordination failure. As the discussion in the following section will make clear, the Korean government has always perceived itself as a mediating agent and a facilitator for bringing about industrial change, through arm-twisting, subsidies or public enterprises as the circumstances may demand. In the words of Pack and Westphal (1986):

> In Taiwan, the basic philosophy underlying [the government strategy] is that an economy will undergo certain stages of development, and at each stage there are certain key industries (such as integrated steel mill, large shipyard, and petrochemical plants) which through various linkages will bring about development of the entire economy. This strategy also assumes that government officials know what those key industries are and what policy measures should be adopted to develop these industries. (Hou, 1988, cited in Hong, 1993)

Indeed, Taiwan's Fourth Plan (1965–8) stated:

> For further development, stress must be laid on basic heavy industries (such as chemical wood pulp, petrochemical intermediates, and large-scale integrated steel production) instead of end product manufacturing or processing. Industrial development in the long run must be centred on export products that have high income elasticity and low transportation cost. And around these products there should be development of both forward and backward industries, so that both specialization and complementarity may be achieved in the interest of Taiwan's economy. (quoted in Wade, 1990)

Hence, what these governments thought they were doing has much in common with the ideas discussed here.

10.6 GOVERNMENT POLICIES TO SUBSIDIZE AND COORDINATE PRIVATE INVESTMENT

Under the conditions discussed in the previous section, there exists a large role for government intervention. Such intervention can take many different forms. Most directly, policy-makers can coordinate private-sector production and investment decisions through their control over credit allocation, the tax regime and trade policy, as well as through 'administrative guidance'. Government policies to subsidize investment in the modern sectors of the economy have a large payoff because they get the private sector to internalize the coordination externalities. The same outcome can also be obtained through investments by public enterprises themselves. The Korean and Taiwanese governments used a combination of these interventions, thereby raising the private return to capital in the modern sectors to the level of the social return.

10.6.1 Improving the investment climate

As indicated above, both governments actively subsidized and coordinated private investment. However, one of the most important changes that took place in the late 1950s in Taiwan and the early 1960s in Korea was a substantial improvement in the investment climate overall, brought about by a reorientation of government priorities. We can view this as an important prerequisite to the effectiveness of the interventions themselves.

During much of the 1950s, economic goals did not rank particularly high with the Taiwanese leadership. The government was preoccupied instead with the reconquest of the mainland. By the end of the decade, it became clear that the communist regime was firmly entrenched: '[Taiwan's] party elders came to see that economic development could be a better guarantee of the party's survival' (Wade, 1990). Thereafter, the government turned its energies to eliminating many investment-deterring distortions (such as multiple exchange rates and macroeconomic instability). An important turning point was the Nineteen-Point Reform Programme instituted in 1960. This contained a wide range of subsidies for investment, and will be discussed further below. What is more important at this juncture is that this programme signalled a major shift in government attitudes towards investment: Lin (1973) notes that '[with] the announcement of the nineteen-point reform programme of 1960, the improvement of investment climate became a catchword. The simplification of administrative procedures and the liberalization of regulative measures with regard to economic matters became an official goal.' And in 1965, many of the remaining administrative controls on new plants or capacity expansion were removed altogether.

The story in South Korea is quite similar. President Park, who took power in a military coup in 1961, could not have been more different from Syngman Rhee, his predecessor (not counting the short-lived Chang Myon regime). Rhee's attention had been focused on national consolidation and on political goals; economic growth was never a priority. Park, on the other hand, gave precedence to economics over politics, and to economic growth over other economic concerns. These priorities were reflected in the amount of time he spent on economic matters, and in his support of growth-oriented bureaucrats and businessmen (Jones and Sakong, 1980). Park made very clear early on in his rule that entrepreneurs who undertook investments in line with his priorities would be richly rewarded, while others were penalized. In fact, one of the first acts of Park was to arrest most of the nation's leading businessmen, under a Special Law Dealing with Illicit Wealth Accumulation, and to charge them with profiteering under the previous regime. The businessmen were eventually set free, after Park had extracted a commitment from them to undertake specified investments. While locking up businessmen may seem an odd way of enhancing the investment climate, the episode served to underline the expectation that entrepreneurs were to invest in productive activities rather than rent seeking.

10.6.2 Investment subsidies

In Korea, the chief form of investment subsidy was the extension of credit to large business groups at negative real interest rates. Korean banks were nationalized after the military coup of 1961, providing the government with exclusive control over the allocation of investible funds in the economy. 'Allocation of under-priced credit [became] by far the most important single instrument of government microeconomic control' (Jones and Sakong, 1980). Korean firms were highly dependent on external credit, as borrowing made up two-thirds of their cash flow during 1963–74. According to Jones and Sakong, 'the general bank [lending] rate has typically been half of the curb-market rate; and second, the real bank rate has often been negative and generally below even the most conservative estimates of the opportunity cost of capital'.

With bank lending rates below market clearing rates, a rationing mechanism was needed. Under the Rhee regime, political motives apparently played a key role in the allocation of scarce credit. Under Park, however, credit was allocated on the basis of 'economic' criteria: namely, the priority given to different economic activities. Deserving users were judged on the basis of their investment plans, technology, domestic linkages and scale economies. Since credit was more likely to be awarded to those with some track record, the loan allocations necessarily favoured established firms, and the *chaebol* in particular. This explains why, unlike in Taiwan, expansion of the manufacturing sector has come primarily through the growth of existing firms, rather than the entry of new firms. Between 1966 and 1971, the value added share of firms with 200 or more employees rose from 58% to 72% (Table 10.7). In the 1970s, Korean credit policy became even more partial to *chaebol* as the government decided to use them as instruments for the government's industrial diversification strategy (Pack and Westphal, 1986).

Another important manner in which investment was subsidized in Korea was through the socialization of investment risk in selected sectors. The government – most notably President Park himself – provided an implicit guarantee that the state would bail out those entrepreneurs investing in 'desirable' activities if circumstances later threatened the profitability of these investments. 'The Korean government had extensively socialized the investment risk for selected entrepreneurs, and such an arrangement invigorated the *animal spirit* of the big business groups, inducing them to indulge in aggressive expansion through the *fail-safe* government-sponsored investment activities' (Hong, 1993). The shipbuilding industry is a good example. Without the personal involvement and encouragement of President Park, Hyundai would not have embarked on or completed what eventually became one of the world's best shipyards. The government guaranteed the firm's external borrowing, provided extensive subsidies for the infrastructure, and

Table 10.7 Size distribution of manufacturing firms: Korea

	1966			*1971*		
Number of employees	*Number of firms*	*Percentage of workers*	*Percentage of value added*	*Number of firms*	*Percentage of workers*	*Percentage of value added*
5–49	21 013	39.4	24.9	21 045	27.9	12.8
50–199	1326	20.8	17.6	1605	18.3	15.2
200 and above	379	39.8	57.5	762	53.8	72.0

Source: Hasan (1976).

supplied financial guarantees to get Hyundai its first order (Amsden, 1989). As discussed above, when the world shipping industry collapsed in 1975, Hyundai could activate the government's contingent subsidy. The subsidy took the form of a regulation forcing Korean refineries to ship oil in Korean-owned tankers. Such implicit investment subsidies were greatly reduced during the 1980s, as a consequence of the financial difficulties experienced by some of the investments undertaken in the second half of the 1970s (the period of so-called heavy and chemical industries).

In Taiwan, investment subsidies took different forms. Real lending rates were generally positive and credit subsidies were much less important. However, public enterprises did get credit at more favourable terms, and they also served to socialize investment risk. The most important direct subsidies in Taiwan came in the form of tax incentives. The Statute for Encouragement of Investment (enacted in 1960 in conjunction with the Nineteen-Point Programme mentioned above) represented a 'sweeping extension' (Lin, 1973) of the prevailing tax credit system for investment. The maximum business income tax paid by enterprises was reduced to 18% of annual income (from a previous maximum of 32.5%); the tax holiday for new investments was extended from three to five years; tax exemption was given to undistributed dividends for reinvestment, to 2% of foreign exchange earnings, and to proceeds of export sales; 'productive' real estate was made either exempt from stamp tax and deed tax, or taxable at reduced rates; and payments of import duties on plant equipment were made deferrable, and payable in instalments after starting operations. These incentives were further expanded in 1965, at which time the business income tax was reduced in all priority sectors listed in the investment law, and specified manufacturing sectors (in basic metals, electrical machinery and electronics, machinery, transportation equipment, chemical fertilizers, petrochemicals and natural gas pipe) were given complete exemption from import duties on plant equipment. (Information in this paragraph is taken from Lin, 1973; and Kuo, 1983.)

The quantitative significance of these tax incentives for investment can be observed from Table 10.8, which shows the ratio of tax credits or rebates to the relevant tax base. We observe a sharp rise around 1960 and another one in 1965, associated with the original statute and its revision, respectively. Not coincidentally, these increases are also associated with jumps in the investment–GDP ratio around the same time.

10.6.3 Direct co-ordination of investment decisions

In addition to providing subsidies, the Korean and Taiwanese governments played a much more direct, hands-on role by organizing private entrepreneurs into investments that they may not otherwise have made. In Taiwan, it was the government that took the initial steps in establishing such industries as plastics, textiles, fibres, steel and electronics. In Korea, in the words of

Table 10.8 Tax credits and reimbursements as a share of the relevant tax base: Taiwan

Year	*Percentage*
1955	0.4
1956	0.7
1957	0.8
1958	1.5
1959	3.4
1960	5.6
1961	9.8
1962	8.5
1963	12.4
1964	12.4
1965	13.1
1966	14.9
1967	18.0
1968	17.2

Source: Lin (1973, Table 6-5).

Amsden (1989), '[t]he initiative to enter new manufacturing branches has come primarily from the public sphere. Ignoring the 1950s . . . every major shift in industrial diversification in the decades of the 1960s and 1970s was instigated by the state.'

Wade (1990) describes how Taiwan's first plastics plant for PVC was built under government supervision, and handed over to a private entrepreneur upon completion in 1957. In 1966, three more private firms began producing PVC. All four relied on an imported intermediate. Meanwhile, the state-owned Chinese Petroleum Corporation (CPC) produced ethylene, from which an intermediate suitable for processing into PVC could be derived at a cheaper price than the imported intermediate. 'So the government forced the four private producers of PVC to merge in a joint venture with the Chinese Petroleum Corporation and another state-owned chemical company, in order to adopt a more efficient ethylene-using production method' (Wade, 1990). (While Wade is not explicit on this, there must have been some scale economies or complementarities that prevented CPC from unilaterally moving into the production of the ethylene-based intermediate, without waiting for a commitment from the downstream producers.) The story illustrates nicely the coordinating role of the government.

A similar account is given regarding fibres:

> The government . . . decided to oversee the creation of a rayon-making plant as part of a plan to diversify the textile industry away from cotton fibre. With much help from US advisors it brought together an American synthetic fibre company with several local textilers from both public and private firms, and oversaw negotiations on the terms of the joint

> venture . . . The resulting corporation . . . was the largest 'private' firm on the island at the time [1957] . . . In 1962, this same state-sponsored rayon company, together with a state financing agency, created another company to make nylon. It started production in 1964. (Wade, 1990)

Private firms soon followed after this state-led entry into synthetic fibres.

Finally, the role of the Taiwanese state was crucial in the early stages of the electronics industry. In 1974 the publicly owned Electronic Research and Service Organization (ERSO) was formed to bring in foreign technology and disseminate it to local firms. ERSO built the country's first model shop for wafer fabrication and centered a technology transfer agreement with RCA. It trained engineers, who later moved to private firms. The strategy led to many private-sector offshoots that commercialized the technology developed by ERSO (Wade, 1990).

It is interesting to note that the Taiwanese authorities' approach to selecting industries to nurture in this fashion was based on what Wade calls 'engineering concepts', such as take-off, linkages, gaps, substitutions and incremental extensions – concepts which have little place in conventional welfare economics. Wade mentions that the justification for building a stainless steel plant in the early 1980s was to 'fill a gap in Taiwan's infrastructure'. Similarly, '[d]evelopments in electronics are being promoted with the aid of an input–output map which highlights gaps in the production structure within Taiwan'. This concern with linkages may sit awkwardly with neoclassical development theory, but it does resonate with our emphasis on coordination failures.

In Korea, as we have seen, the presence of large conglomerates helped internalize some of the industrial complementarities that Taiwanese policy-makers had to nurture through more direct interventions. But the Korean government was not hesitant to intervene in order to solve what it perceived to be larger-scale coordination problems:

> The state masterminded the early import-substitution projects in cement, fertilizers, oil refining, and synthetic fibres, the last greatly improving the profitability of the overextended textiles industry. The government also kept alive some unprofitable factories inherited from the colonial period, factories that eventually provided key personnel to the modern general machinery and shipbuilding industries, which the state also promoted. The transformation from light to heavy industry came at the state's behest, in the form of an integrated iron and steel mill . . . [The government] was responsible for the Big Push into heavy machinery and chemicals in the late 1970s. (Amsden, 1989)

The case of shipbuilding has already been discussed in some detail. As in Taiwan, the government proceeded on the understanding that some industries and products were more 'strategic' than other because they were the source of linkages with the rest of the economy. A recent account about how Daewoo got into the shipbuilding business provides yet another example: 'Mr Kim [the founder of Daewoo] found himself in shipbuilding in 1978, when the government twisted his arm to take over a near-bankrupt project to build a giant shipyard at Okpo, on Koje island near the southern port of Pusan. "I did not have a chance to say no," says Mr Kim. Indeed, the government simply announced the move when he was out of the country' (*The Economist*, 26 November 1994, p. 81). The Okpo shipyard is now 'at the heart of . . . [Korea's] achievement' in shipbuilding.

10.6.4 Use of public investment and public enterprise

Public enterprises played a very important role in enhancing the profitability of private investment in both countries (perhaps more so in Taiwan than in Korea). They did so by ensuring that key inputs were available locally for private producers downstream. In Taiwan, as we have seen, it was common for the state to establish new upstream industries and then either hand the factories over to selected private entrepreneurs (as happened in the case of glass, plastics, steel and cement) or run them as public enterprises. In Korea, the government established many new public enterprises in the 1960s and 1970s, particularly in basic industries characterized by a high degree of linkages and scale economies. In both countries, public enterprises were the recipient of favourable credit terms, as well as direct allocations from the government budget.

Not only did public enterprises account for a large share of manufacturing output and investment in each country, their importance actually increased during the critical take-off years of the 1960s. This can be seen clearly in Table 10.9, where data on three comparator countries are also listed. Public enterprises actually accounted for a larger share of GDP in Taiwan than in such 'socialist' developing countries as India and Tanzania.

Jones and Sakong (1980) have analysed in detail the expansion of the public enterprise sector in Korea. They find that the Korean government had a coherent set of preferences with respect to where public enterprises should be set up. They summarize their results thus: 'the industries chosen for the public-enterprise sector [were] characterized by high forward linkages, high capital intensity, large size, output-market concentration, and production of non-tradables or import substitutes rather than exports'. These are exactly the characteristics associated with a high potential for coordination failure.

The case of POSCO, Korea's state-owned integrated steel mill, is instructive (if not entirely representative). In the early 1970s, the Korean government was turned down by the World Bank when it applied for a loan to construct a steel plant. The World Bank's argument was that Korea did not have a comparative advantage in steel. The government was undeterred and went ahead nonetheless. The government provided POSCO with capital

Table 10.9 The importance of public enterprise in GDP and investment (%)

		Public enterprise share of	
	Year	*GDP*	*Capital formation*
South Korea	1963–4	6.7	31.2
	1971–2	9.1	21.7
Taiwan	1954–7	11.7	34.3
	1958–61	13.5	38.1
	1962–5	14.1	27.7
	1966–9	13.6	28.0
	1970–3	13.3	30.5
	1974–7	13.6	35.0
India	1966–9	6.5	29.6
Tanzania	1970–3	12.7	48.2
Argentina	1978–80	4.6	19.6

Sources: Wade (1990, Table 6.2), from original data in Short (1983), except for public enterprise share in GDP for Korea, which is from Jones and Sakong (1980, Table 24).

assistance as well as infrastructure subsidies (for the construction of water supply facilities, port facilities, an electricity generating station, roads and a railway line). In addition, the government supported downstream industries to ensure demand for POSCO's production. POSCO eventually became, by the World Bank's reckoning, 'arguably the world's most efficient producer of steel' (cited in Wade, 1990), supplying Korean mini-mills with steel at below world prices. Moreover, the presence of POSCO stimulated in turn a wide range of upstream industries, ranging from capital goods to spare parts. Between 1977 and 1984, the local content of POSCO's output rose from 44 to 75%.

10.7 HOW COULD INTERVENTION BE IMPLEMENTED EFFECTIVELY?

To any economist with experience in the developing world, what is striking about the policies discussed in the previous section is their similarity to those commonly employed in many other, considerably less successful economies. Why have these interventions, along with many others not specifically discussed (such as quantitative trade barriers or local content requirements), been successful in Taiwan and Korea and not elsewhere? One part of the answer to this question has already been given: the imbalance between a well-educated labour force and a low endowment of physical capital meant that the return to coordinated investments – and therefore government policy aimed at coaxing these investments – was quite high.

This is an important part of the story, but not the entire story. While the initial human capital advantage may have been a necessary condition for intervention to work, it was not sufficient. On top, what was required was a competent, honest and efficient bureaucracy to administer the interventions, and a clear-sighted political leadership that consistently placed high priority on economic performance. In Korea and Taiwan, unlike in so many other developing countries, these additional requirements were present. Why? One important factor was clearly the availability of relatively skilled labour, enabling the formation of a competent bureaucracy. In addition, an exceptionally high degree of equality in income and wealth – one of the other initial conditions mentioned earlier – was important as well.

How exactly did the latter help? The absence of large inequities meant several things. First, neither government had to contend with powerful industrial or landed interest groups. Such powerful groups had been decimated by the Japanese occupation (Korea), the settlement by the mainland Chinese (Taiwan), and land reform (both countries). Therefore, policy making and implementation could be insulated from pressure group politics. In both countries, the implementation of growth-oriented policies required a number of institutional reforms, including the centralization of functions previously distributed among multitudes of ministries and agencies, and the creation of new bureaucracies (see Haggard, 1990). These institutional reforms could be undertaken relatively autonomously, and with little pressure from the push and pull of daily politics. Economic laws and regulations could be written by technocratic élites, with little concern for their effect on organized pressure groups.

Second, the absence of large-scale inequities meant that governments felt no immediate need to undertake redistributive policies. The analytical literature on the political economy of growth suggests that regimes which inherit large inequalities are constantly under pressure to implement growth-retarding policies (Alesina and Rodrik, 1994; Persson and Tabellini, 1994). An example is the pursuit of populist fiscal and microeconomic policies (as in much of Latin America) which engender high inflation, stop–go cycles and low growth. The political leadership in Taiwan and Korea could concentrate on expanding the pie instead. Third, and related to the above, the fact that the top political leaders were free to focus on economic goals meant that they could supervise the bureaucracy closely. This is important because interventionist regimes are prone to two fatal problems having their origin in the bureaucracy. The first is that interventions naturally generate opportunities for rent seeking. A weak or poorly supervised bureaucracy is incapable of reining in rent seeking (or becomes part of it). A strong bureaucracy, on the other hand, can choke off entrepreneurial incentives by sticking too closely to the letter of the law and imposing too many cumbersome restrictions aimed at rooting out rent seeking. In both Taiwan and Korea, the top political leaders closely monitored the bureaucracy to make sure that the bureaucrats assisted rather than hindered private entrepreneurship. President Park, in particular, was famous for his daily involvement in the implementation of his economic policies, and his willingness to override the bureaucracy at a moment's notice when businessmen had legitimate complaints.

Hence, the initial advantage with respect to income and wealth distribution played an important role in shaping the political landscape in both countries. This is probably the single most important reason why extensive government intervention could be carried out effectively, without giving rise to rampant rent seeking.

10.8 SOME FREQUENTLY ASKED QUESTIONS

The arguments I have made in this paper are naturally controversial. I have challenged one of the most widely held beliefs in development economics: namely, the view that South Korea and Taiwan owe their growth to export-oriented policies. I have also argued that both economies on balance greatly benefited from extensive government intervention in markets, a proposition which neoclassical economists are trained to regard with suspicion. The professionally correct response to these arguments is, and perhaps should be, a high degree of scepticism.

All the more so since some of my arguments, regarding the existence of a coordination failure in particular, lack direct empirical confirmation, even if they are suggestive and broadly consistent with the evidence. Without more detailed micro- and industry-oriented studies, we will not know with any degree of confidence whether the hypothesis I have put forward has great relevance to these two cases. My hope is that this paper will stimulate such research, as well as providing some clues and a set of organizing principles to guide it.

This section addresses some of the more common reasons for scepticism.

10.8.1 Can we really distinguish between export and investment strategies?

One objection is that the distinction between a trade-oriented strategy and investment policies is too sharp, that these governments were preoccupied with both exports and investment. It is argued that the potential distortions of investment incentives and other interventions were kept in check by the requirement that enterprises eventually become competitive in world markets. Indeed, some of the investment subsidies were in practice contingent on export performance. Besides, since so much of investment went into exportables, exports must indeed have been profitable.

Nothing I have said in this paper should be taken to imply that exports did not play a facilitating role in Korea's and Taiwan's growth miracles. In fact, an implication of my argument is that without the increase in exports the investment boom would probably not have taken place. It is possible, as the above indicates, that exports also made a contribution by acting as a disciplining device on subsidy-receiving firms.[12] However, none of this is very helpful in understanding what made these countries take off. An adequate analysis has to confront the questions: why did investment and exports respond so vigorously to government policies, and which of these served as the driving force behind economic growth? My view is that the investment booms would not have been possible in the presence of gross policy biases against exports, but that these booms were compatible with a wide range of trade policy options.

10.8.2 Doesn't the experience of many other countries show that investment is not enough for sustained growth?

Investment-led growth irresistibly invites comparison with the Soviet Union and other Soviet-type economies. Doesn't this experience show that accumulation is far from enough for sustained growth? It is not appropriate to compare economic systems lacking markets and private property, and in which both the level and allocation of investment are determined by central planners, to market systems where investment decisions are made on the basis of profitability. For all the government interventions, it is not possible to confuse South Korea and Taiwan with the German Democratic Republic or the former Czechoslovakia.

Overlooking Soviet-type economies, the causal relationship between investment and growth should be one of the least controversial propositions in economics. The empirical correlation is clear enough, as can be seen from the scatterplot in Figure 10.14. Conceptually as well, all theories of growth are based at least in part on capital accumulation. That is not to say that all countries which invest a lot have experienced high growth: Figure 10.14 shows a number of outliers. But in view of the overall correlation, it is these exceptions that require explanation, not the cases (like South Korea and Taiwan) which have followed the general rule.

10.8.3 Isn't the evidence on coordination failures too weak in view of failed government interventions elsewhere?

As already noted, the case for coordination failures is based on circumstantial, rather than direct, evidence. This is not the kind of evidence that will move anyone with strongly held priors on the inefficiency of government intervention. Traditional arguments against it abound. The 'big push' ideas of the 1950s have led nowhere. How is it possible for governments to 'pick the winners'? And what about the example of free-market, yet successful, Hong Kong?

Without disagreeing on the need for more evidence, I would point out a number of things. First, I have tried to be explicit about the conditions under which a coordination failure is most likely to exist, and have not treated it as a

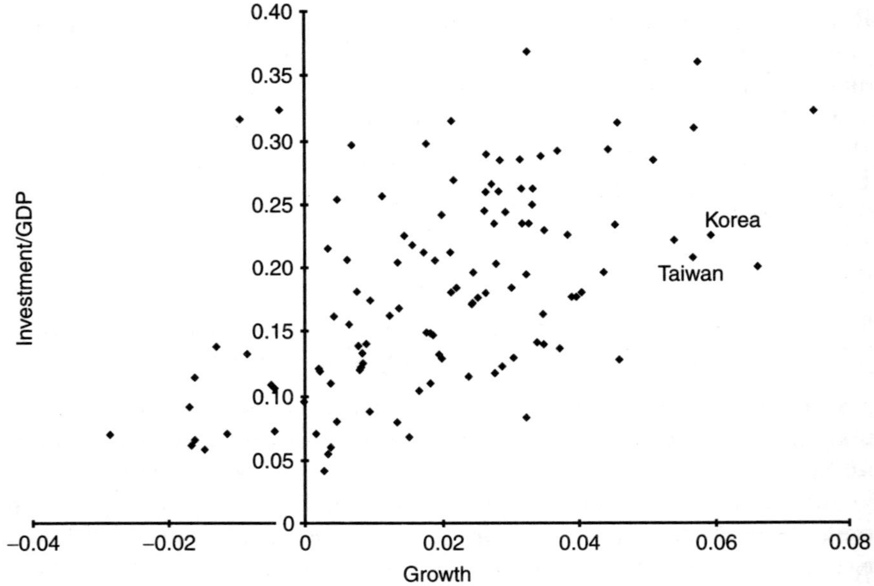

Figure 10.14 Relationship between growth and investment, 1960–85

generic issue, as in much of the early (and current) literature. There is nothing implausible about the presence of these conditions in the South Korea and Taiwan of the 1960s. Second, I have tried to bring a considerable amount of case study evidence to bear on these issues. In fact, so voluminous is the case study literature on government interventions (and their apparent success) in these countries that one may as well regard the main problem as being one of finding an adequate theory on which to hang this evidence, rather than locating the evidence to support a particular theory. The framework I have proposed here helps us make sense of the findings of this case study literature, something that is hard to do with the conventional approach.[13]

This approach also clarifies why 'picking winners' was not so difficult in the early years of the Korean and Taiwanese experience. Policy-makers in these countries only had to look at Japan and more advanced countries to see their future. Of course, once the catch-up is nearly complete, it becomes more difficult to play the same game.

Finally, Hong Kong's experience is not as telling as it may seem at first glance – and not only because Hong Kong is a small city state, with significant geographical and historical advantages in foreign trade. Hong Kong was already a high-investment country by 1960: its investment ratio stood above 20% (of GDP) in 1960, almost double the figure for Korea and Taiwan at the time. Consequently, Hong Kong never faced the challenge of raising investment. And the absence of government policy in this regard reveals itself in an investment ratio that has remained virtually flat since 1960. Therefore, one might as well read the Hong Kong evidence as suggesting that an increase in domestic investment requires government action.

10.8.4 Doesn't the initial imbalance between human and physical capital suggest an even simpler story of catch-up, with little role for government policy?

Recent theories of growth show that an initial imbalance between human and physical capital speeds up growth (Mulligan and Sala-i-Martín, 1993). That growth is higher in economies where human capital is large relative to physical capital holds even in the absence of increasing returns to scale or other possible market failures. This applies well to South Korea and Taiwan, and perhaps we do not need the role of government policy to explain fast growth in these two countries.

Table 10.10 suggests, however, that such an imbalance does not necessarily translate into high growth. I have listed in the table four countries which had roughly the same human capital advantage (as measured by educational indicators) in 1960 as did Korea and Taiwan: Dominican Republic, Philippines, Paraguay and Sri Lanka. None of them experienced the kind of growth rates that Korea and Taiwan did. It would seem plausible that the difference in outcomes has much to do with differing government policies in the two sets of countries.

10.9 CONCLUDING REMARKS

The role of government policy in Korea and Taiwan is open to diverse interpretations. In principle, one could argue in favour of any of the following propositions:[14] (1) government policy was a hindrance, but these countries

Table 10.10 Countries with human capital 'imbalance', *c.* 1960

	Per-capita growth, 1960–89	*Primary enrolment ratio*		*Secondary enrolment ratio*		*Literacy rate*	
		Predicted	*Actual*	*Predicted*	*Actual*	*Predicted*	*Actual*
Dominican Republic	2.48	0.64	0.98	0.13	0.07	0.39	0.65
Philippines	1.58	0.62	0.95	0.12	0.26	0.36	0.72
Paraguay	2.72	0.65	0.98	0.14	0.11	0.40	0.75
Sri Lanka	1.83*	0.65	0.95	0.14	0.27	0.39	0.75

Note:
* 1960–85.

Source: Same as Table 4.

overcame it nonetheless; (2) it was irrelevant, not helping growth but not hindering it either; (3) it was helpful, though not essential (that is, it speeded up a process which would have happened anyway); (4) it was necessary for the growth experience of these countries. Propositions (1), (2) and (3) are hard to sustain because the experience of Taiwan and South Korea was far from exemplary throughout the 1950s, prior to the concerted efforts made by governments in both countries to make their economies grow. In fact, it was not uncommon for visiting economists to despair that these economies would remain basket cases for the foreseeable future. Hence, the real debate should be over which government policies made the difference, not whether policy made a difference or how much.

I have argued in this paper that the South Korean and Taiwanese 'miracles' can best be understood by taking seriously what the two governments thought and said they are doing: namely, coordinating and encouraging private (and public) investments with a high degree of linkages within the modern sector. Such policies had a high payoff because they helped remove coordination failures in economies where the latent return to investment was already high. A relatively skilled and educated workforce was a necessary condition. So was a relatively equal distribution of resources, which endowed the political leadership with insulation and allowed it to focus on economic growth as the top priority. Export-oriented policies (and chief among them exchange rate policies) were important in so far as they enabled a steady rise in imported capital goods. But viewing export orientation as the clue to the growth puzzle misses the mark by a wide margin.

This approach can explain why so many other developing countries have failed miserably with government interventions that bear more than a passing resemblance to those employed by the East Asian countries. South Korea and Taiwan shared a number of special initial conditions – high levels of educational attainment relative to income, and equal distribution of income and wealth – that these other countries lack. Consequently, the relevance of their experience with government intervention to other developing economies may well be limited.

DISCUSSION

Gene Grossman

Woodrow Wilson School, Princeton University

It is always a pleasure to read one of Dani Rodrik's papers. They are clear, well organized and well argued. And they are always provocative.

This paper is no exception. Dani challenges the view that trade policy 'explains' the success of South Korea and Taiwan. In fact, he takes the orthodoxy head on, and tries to demolish it entirely. Export orientation could not deserve pride of place in these stories, he argues, because: the timing of the export booms was not right to account for the growth experiences; the changes in relative prices were not large enough to have such a dramatic effect on growth performance; export orientation itself has no obvious implications for the rate of investment, which surely shot up in both countries and evidently played a major role in spurring growth; and there is no real evidence of productivity spillovers from export activities to the rest of the economy. For each of these arguments, Dani musters empirical evidence from the raw data and by referring to the studies of others.

Having disposed of the traditional explanation, Dani sets out to build a new one to replace it. He argues that Korea and Taiwan had (1) favourable initial conditions thanks to the high levels of human capital in their labour forces and the relative equality in their income distributions, and (2) good policy, which overcame a coordination failure that otherwise would have impeded investment in the modern industrial sector. He lays out a theoretical structure (informally in the text, more formally in the appendix) that explains how such a coordination failure could arise, how the preconditions for its existence are consistent with the initial conditions that prevailed in these countries in the late 1950s, and how government policy could in principle be used to overcome the market failure. Finally, he discusses the policies that were actually used, argues that their intended purpose in the eyes of the policy-makers was exactly the one suggested by the theory, and shows that the evidence is at least consistent with the view that they were successfully implemented.

I find the rejection of the export-led growth story to be rather convincing. How could the trade sector have been the driving force? What was the exogenous change? The relative price changes were surely too small to affect such a large movement in resources. And even if productivity in the exportable sector improved dramatically, this sector was much too small to begin with to generate a large boost in the growth rate.

Barro and Lee (1993) provide additional corroborating evidence. They estimate a relationship between growth in per-capita income and a number of country-specific variables for the decades from 1965 to 1975 and 1975 to 1985. These regressions, which use data for 85 countries in the first period and 95 in the second, are similar to those reported by Rodrik in his Table 10.5, except that the list of regressors is different. Barro and Lee use as explanatory variables: the beginning of period log of real GDP per capita; measures of educational attainment by males and females (entered separately); the log of life expectancy; the investment/GDP ratio; the ratio of government consumption to real GDP less the ratio of nominal spending on defence and non-capital expenditures on education to GDP; the log of (one plus) the black market premium on foreign exchange; and the average number of successful and unsuccessful revolutions per year. Recognizing the possible endogeneity of many of these regressors, Barro and Lee estimate their growth relationship using instrumental variable techniques. Note that the black market premium here is intended as a proxy for the size of marked distortions.

Using the estimated coefficients from the growth regression, Barro and Lee can decompose a country's growth experience into its proximate 'sources'. Table 10.11 shows the results of this decomposition for Korea and Taiwan.[15] The table shows the contribution of each variable to the fitted growth rate of real per-capita GDP, expressed relative to the sample mean for all countries. The 'net convergence effect' is the combined impact from the initial values of log (GDP), male and female educational attainment, and log (life expectancy); it corresponds roughly to what Dani terms 'the initial conditions'.

The table shows that, with the possible exception of Taiwan in the period from 1975 to 1985, the short list of regressors 'explains' most of these two countries' growth experience; perhaps there is no 'miracle' here. Moreover, the biggest contribution to growth comes from the 'net convergence effect', i.e. the fact that these countries had low initial per-capita GDP levels, but high initial levels of human capital per worker (and thus, by implication, low initial physical capital to worker ratios). The relatively modest levels of government consumption also seemed to play a role. Apparently, the elimination of price distortions, to the extent that this is captured in the change in the black market premium, is not a big part of the story.

The argument that there existed coordination failures that inhibited investment in the modern manufacturing sectors in Korea and Taiwan until the government intervened to overcome them is intriguing, but requires further elaboration and empirical investigation. I am not sure how one would definitively establish the existence of a coordination failure, let alone the potential for one in a counterfactual world where government policy was different. I am naturally inclined to be suspicious of any argument that says, 'there are important non-traded inputs that are critical to an entire sector's

Table 10.11 Sources of growth in Korea and Taiwan

	Korea		*Taiwan*	
	1965–75	*1975–85*	*1965–75*	*1975–85*
Net convergence effect	0.028	0.023	0.026	−0.017
Investment/GDP ratio	0.002	0.008	0.003	0.008
Government consumption	0.007	0.014	−0.008	−0.003
Black market premium	0.001	0.005	0.003	0.006
Number of revolutions	−0.003	−0.003	0.002	0.002
Fitted value	0.081	0.061	0.060	0.040
Actual per-capita growth	0.078	0.063	0.061	0.057

Note: Contributions to per-capita GDP growth measured as deviations from sample means.

Source: Barro and Lee (1993) and additional calculations by Robert Barro.

being whose production entails such substantial scale economies that profitability requires a very large *local* market'. But this suspicion is nothing more than the usual suspicion economists have when reference is made to unmeasured, and perhaps unmeasurable, externalities.

Dani briefly addresses the possibility that the experiences of Korea and Taiwan could be explained by a much simpler story, such as the one told by Mulligan and Sala-i-Martín (1993). These authors investigate an endogenous growth model where the production technology for final output is homogeneous of degree one in physical and human capital, but there are no non-convexities or multiple equilibria. Mulligan and Sala-i-Martín show that in the transition phase, the growth rate rises with the magnitude of the gap between the ratio of physical to human capital and its steady-state value. This 'imbalance effect' arises from the fact that gross rates of investment in each type of capital must be non-negative. Dani rejects this possible alternative explanation because it would have also predicted 'miraculous' performances in countries like the Dominican Republic and the Philippines. This is true, but on the other hand, the alternative may be somewhat more consonant with the results reported in Table 10.1. The table shows that, after taking account of the initial high levels of human capital accompanied by the initial low levels of real GDP, the high ratios of investment to GDP in these countries apparently did not contribute much extra to growth. I would guess that the 'imbalance effect', even if not the entire story, is an important part of it.

I would also draw attention to the recent argument put forward by Ventura (1994), which seems relevant as well. Ventura notes that in an integrated world economy, small countries like Korea and Taiwan can accumulate capital at very high rates for long periods of time without driving down the marginal product of capital, because they can continually reallocate resources among sectors with different factor intensities. In this context, he shows, a small country that is a little more patient than others can have dramatically faster capital accumulation and superior growth performance for a prolonged period, until it eventually ceases to be small.

In the concluding section of his paper, Dani lists the various roles that government policy might have played in the Korean and Taiwanese experience. My own personal assessment (which has a large standard error) is described by (3): I suspect that the governments of Korea and Taiwan implemented wise policies that speeded up a process that would have happened anyway. But Dani dismisses this view with reference to the 1950s: if it would have happened, why did it not start sooner? In one sense he is surely right. Governments can always find policies that will interfere with growth, and Korea and Taiwan probably had such policies in place in the early post-war period. So, by removing the impediments, the change in government policy made growth possible. What I wonder is whether the targeted industrial policies, such as the selective investment subsidies, the direct coordination of investment decisions, and the strategic use of public enterprises, were necessary for the successful performance. I suspect not, but I really do not know the answer. Dani's paper highlights this question; future researchers will surely be inspired by his challenge to provide definitive answers.

Victor Norman

Norwegian School of Economics and Business Administration

There are two main arguments in this paper. One is that the success of South Korea and Taiwan had little to do with export orientation. The other is that government intervention, to overcome a coordination failure, had a lot to do with their success. The arguments are linked, but it is useful to consider the two separately.

Export orientation and growth

To a traditional trade theorist, the idea of export-led growth might be comforting and politically appealing, but intellectually puzzling. If growth stems from a growing resource base or better technology, there is no obvious link between trade and growth, except in so far as a static gain from trade, by producing higher income, could give higher savings. And even that link is weak, since the gain from trade is a permanent one, with a correspondingly low marginal propensity to save.

In that perspective, it is not Rodrik's argument which is surprising. The surprising assertion is the conventional one that Korea and Taiwan (and a number of other countries) have taken off industrially through large-scale exports.

A puzzle remains, however. Why is the belief in exports as a source of growth so persistent? And why is a strong correlation between export orientation and growth apparently observed in so many countries?

The answer is, I think, that there are good reasons to expect – at least for small countries – a strong correlation between exports and growth, even in the absence of a simple causality between the two. The correlation derives from perhaps the oldest observations in economic theory: namely, Adam Smith's assertion that the division of labour is limited by the extent of the market. If there are economies of scale – internal or external to firms – efficient production is only possible if there is access to markets of sufficient size. In countries such as South Korea and Taiwan, that simply was not the case. To take one of Rodrik's own examples: the Korean shipbuilding industry has a world market share of 25%, and much of its efficiency derives from its scale. Three firms (Hyundai, Daewoo and Samsung) account for 93% of production; and Hyundai alone builds 10% of all new tonnage in the world (Nagatsuka, 1994). Clearly, production units of this size could not have been developed on the basis of the internal Korean market for transport equipment.

In the Adam Smith view then, market size is a prerequisite for growth. It is not the *cause* of growth, however. Access to large markets is of no help unless the internal conditions, such as the quality of the labour force, market infrastructure, savings, etc., are right. The point is simply that internal conditions are not sufficient, unless the market is large enough. That may explain why exports and growth are strongly correlated for small countries, while countries such as Germany and the USA could combine industrialization with protection.

Rodrik suggests an entirely different explanation for the correlation between exports and growth – that growth generated import demand, which in turn generated exports. That cannot be correct. As shown in Rodrik's Figures 10.4 and 10.11 (for Korea) and 10.5 and 10.12 (for Taiwan), the export boom preceded the import boom. For Korea, for example, the ratio of exports to GDP trebled from the early to the mid-1960s – from a level of around 2% to 6% in 1965, and roughly 7% in 1966–7. Imports of capital goods, on the other hand, did not take off until the second half of the decade. They amounted to between 2 and 4% of GDP from 1960 to 1966, then rose to around 7% in 1967 and more than 9% in 1968. It takes exceptional belief in the foresight of policy-makers if this is to be seen as consistent with the view that 'thanks to appropriate macroeconomic and exchange rate policies, export supply was adequate to meet the increase in import demand, and rose alongside imports'.

Investment and coordination

If my interpretation of the role of exports is correct, it is easier to accept the rest of Rodrik's story. There could well have been a coordination failure which prevented industrial take-off and rapid export growth in the 1950s, and it might be that government intervention to overcome the failure was important. One should ask, however, why he argues for a complex intervention story (direct intervention to overcome a coordination failure) when a simple one – a high saving and investment rate – suffices. As he demonstrates, in the 1960s the rate of investment rose sharply in both South Korea and Taiwan. He also shows that saving by publicly owned firms was a major source of higher investment. In Korea, for example, public enterprises in 1963–4 accounted for 31.2% of capital formation, while only contributing 6.7% of GDP. Furthermore, the governments in the two countries stimulated private savings and investment through credit subsidies and tax incentives. One can argue that these measures were sufficient to initiate a self-reinforcing process of industrialization. In fact, in Rodrik's own model they would be sufficient. Why then add a less convincing story about government coordination of investment projects?

The complex story is particularly puzzling when contrasted with the examples cited. Rodrik cites Jones and Sakong, who argue that the Korean government had a 'coherent set of preferences' for public enterprises, favouring industries with 'high forward linkages, high capital intensity, large size, output-market concentration, and production of non-tradables or import substitutes rather than exports'. He then takes the steel mill POSCO as an example, saying that it is instructive, but not representative. The examples of *private* firms that he cites are also curious relative to the stated government preferences. He makes a point of government promotion of shipbuilding, which has no forward linkages, is labour intensive, sells in an almost perfectly competitive market, and is export oriented. The other Korean example, the Lucky-Goldstar group, was successively in cosmetics, plastics, telecommunications, oil refining, tanker shipping and insurance. How that fits in with the 'clear government preferences' is unclear to me. The story could be made consistent if the private firms were dependent on inputs from public enterprises with the Jones–Sakong characteristics; but that is equally unclear in the Hyundai and Lucky-Goldstar cases – Korean shipbuilders, for example, import steel and main engines from Japan or Western Europe.

A central part of Rodrik's explanation is that successful government intervention was possible in South Korea and Taiwan because the governments were insulated from pressure groups. He then describes President Park, pointing out that he spent a lot of time on economic matters and supported growth-oriented bureaucrats and businessmen. To me, that does not sound like insulation from pressure groups. On the contrary, policy-makers who are insulated from public opinion, and who depend on a small group of 'prominent' associates, must be prime candidates for regulatory capture. Did Edward IV control the Woodvilles? Was the military–industrial complex in the USA easier to control before it came under public scrutiny?

The assertion of successful industrial policies in South Korea and Taiwan to me remains unproven.

GENERAL DISCUSSION

Several Panel members wondered under exactly which conditions the results claimed by Rodrik would obtain. Thus there were discussions about whether it was a story about two sectors (one backward, one modern) or about capital accumulation. The role of human capital was often explicitly mentioned.

In establishing a favourable climate for investment, George Alogoskoufis pointed out, the political regime is important. It is essential to have a regime that guarantees that there will not be expropriation. David Begg made a similar point regarding the role of the exchange regime, including restrictions to capital movements, and the risk of partial expropriation through devaluation and inflation as well as limits to where to hold incomes from profit. Mathias Dewatripont stressed the importance of the initial distribution of wealth, which is one of the preconditions listed by Rodrik. Unequal distribution of wealth may create pressure for redistribution and thereby discourage investment. He also wondered whether the more recently successful Asian countries had followed the same pattern of growth and government intervention, or whether South Korea and Taiwan are exceptions.

Hans-Werner Sinn thought that the paper dismissed too quickly the Hecksher–Ohlin theory. He observed that this theory is compatible with the stylized facts used by Rodrik. If the economy starts from a situation where only the labour-intensive commodity is produced, then allowing capital movements immediately triggers capital inflows. These inflows have nothing to do with government intervention; they simply reflect natural scarcities.

Assaf Razin raised another issue. He questioned the treatment of relative prices of exports as exogenous. On the contrary, he expected that a push for exports would lead to an exchange rate appreciation. Dani Rodrik responded that it is possible to treat that relative price as exogenous as long as it is acceptable to treat Korea as a small country with no market power. Inderjit Singh wondered about the role of the size of military spending. He noted that a country with less military expenses should perform better. He also thought that the paper should have looked at the importance of the homogeneity of society. Much as with equality, a homogeneous society is often characterized by less social conflict. Alessandra Casella questioned measures used to evaluate equality. She further asked whether the policy which had been carried out had increased inequality.

Xavier Vives drew a parallel with Japan. In this case, he felt that the coordination of investment had indeed been important, as stressed by Rodrik. Yet, in his view, the role of public subsidies has been mostly symbolic as their size has been quite modest. He was seconded by Michel Keen, who asked Rodrik to provide more information on the size of investment subsidies.

APPENDIX

The model discussed here is taken from Rodrik (1993), to which the reader is referred for further details (see also Rodríguez-Clare, 1993). We focus on a small, open economy that can produce two tradable final goods. Both of these goods are produced under constant returns to scale. The first of these is a labour-intensive good, requiring labour and capital, which we associate with the 'traditional' sector. Its unit cost function is given by $\theta(w, r)$, with w and r standing for the wage and rental rates prevailing in the economy. The other good, produced in the 'modern' sector, uses capital and a range of intermediate goods (producer services and specialized inputs) that are imperfect substitutes for each other. We use the Dixit–Stiglitz–Ethier specification for the way that these intermediates enter the production function of the modern good. In a symmetric equilibrium in which n intermediate goods are available at price p, the unit cost function of the modern good is given by $\varphi(r, pn^{-1(\sigma-1)})$, where $\sigma > 1$ is the elasticity of substitution between any two of the intermediate goods. Note that the productivity of the modern sector is linked to the number of input varieties available: as n increases, unit costs in the modern sector decline.

As discussed in the text, a key assumption is that the intermediates are non-tradable. They are produced using labour and under increasing returns to scale. Intermediate-good production is assumed to be intensive in labour skills, so that the educational attainment of the workforce is taken to be an important determinant of costs in this sector. The unit cost function of the representative intermediate is expressed as $w\lambda(h)c(z)$, where h is an index of the skill level of the workforce (so that $\lambda'(h) < 0$), and z is the output level of the representative intermediate. Due to increasing returns, $c'(z) < 0$. The presence of scale economies implies that each intermediate will be produced by a single firm under monopolistically competitive conditions. Therefore, when the intermediate sector is active, $p = w\lambda(h)c(z)$. In addition, marginal costs equal (perceived) marginal revenue, so that $[p - MC]/p = 1/\sigma$. These two conditions, together with the separability of the intermediates' cost function, imply that the ratio AC/MC depends only on z, and can be written as $AC/MC = \mu(z)$. The result is that the equality between marginal cost and marginal revenue can be written in a simple form:

$$\mu(z) = \frac{\sigma}{\sigma - 1} \tag{A1}$$

This fixes the output level of each intermediate as a function of the elasticity of substitution alone. Hence, any change in the scale of the intermediate sector will have to come from a change in n. Let X and Y stand for the output levels of the modern and traditional goods, and K and L for the economy's (fixed) endowments of capital and labour. Let the world prices of the modern and traditional goods be π and 1, respectively. The remaining equations of the model can be expressed in the following form:

$$\theta(w, r) \geq 1,\ Y \geq 0,\ Y[\theta(w, r) - 1] = 0 \tag{A2}$$

$$\varphi(r, pn^{-1/(\sigma-1)}) \geq \pi,\ X \geq 0,\ X[\varphi(r, pn^{-1/(\sigma-1)}) - \pi] = 0 \tag{A3}$$

$$w\lambda(h)c(z) \geq p,\ z \geq 0,\ z[w\lambda(h)c(z) - p] = 0 \tag{A4}$$

$$\theta_w(w, r)Y + \lambda(h)c(z)nz = L \tag{A5}$$

$$\varphi_r(w, r)Y + \varphi_r(r, pn^{-1/(\sigma-1)})X = K \tag{A6}$$

$$\varphi_p(r, pn^{-1/(\sigma-1)})X = nz \tag{A7}$$

The first three equations are the appropriate complementary slackness conditions that relate domestic costs to prices. The next two equations are the full-employment conditions, where we have used the fact that the partial derivatives of the unit cost functions with respect to factor prices yield unit factor demands. The last equation is the market-clearing condition for the intermediate-goods sector. There are seven endogenous variables in this system (w, r, p, n, z, X, Y) to be determined by the seven equations above.

A key feature of the model is that the competitiveness of the modern sector depends on both the skill level of the workforce (h) and the range of domestically produced intermediate varieties (n). For sufficiently low levels of h and K, the modern sector will not be competitive even when the economy produces the maximum feasible number of intermediates (which is reached when the entire labour force is employed in the intermediate-goods sector). When h and K are sufficiently large, on the other hand, the modern sector will be competitive even when a very small number of intermediate goods is produced.

But when h is large and K is low, the economy can have two equilibria: one in which the economy specializes in the traditional sector and the modern sector remains uncompetitive, and another one in which the modern sector is competitive and becomes active. The possibility of multiple equilibria arises from a coordination problem. If the economy is initially specialized in the traditional sector, it will not pay for any single firm to enter the modern (or the intermediate-goods) sector at the prevailing factor prices, even though a large-scale shift of resources in that direction can be both privately and socially profitable. The reason, in turn, is that there will be demand for intermediates only if a sufficiently large number of them is being produced. Hence the profitability of being in the intermediate-goods sector depends on the number of other firms already there.

When there are two competing equilibria, specialization in the modern sector produces at least as high a level of real income as specialization in the traditional sector (and generally the inequality is strict). And the rate of return to capital (r) is necessarily higher in the equilibrium with specialization in the modern sector. This is so for two reasons: (1) as just explained, the modern sector produces higher incomes and can pay out higher factor returns; and (2) the modern sector is capital intensive. Government policies that push resources into the modern sector will improve resource allocation as well as increasing the return to capital. These results form the basis of the argument in the text.

ACKNOWLEDGMENTS

I am grateful to Jagdish Bhagwati, Paul de Grauwe, Ann Harrison, Arvind Panagariya, Andrés Rodriguez-Clare, Robert Wade, Adrian Wood, Alwyn Young, Panel members and especially Gene Grossman and Charles Wyplosz for helpful comments, Eytsung Kim for excellent research assistance, and the CEPR MIRAGE project for financial assistance.

NOTES

1 The World Bank (1993) study mentioned above reports high TFP growth in these countries, but its analysis has been seriously challenged by Young (personal communication) and Little (1994).

2 This statement does not contradict the fact that both countries have managed to increase greatly the sophistication of the manufactured goods they produce, from toys and apparel to consumer electronics and semiconductors. What it suggests is that this transformation has been fully paid for by investments in physical and human capital.

3 At first sight it may seem strange that a multiple exchange rate system, with an overvalued official exchange rate, would act as an export subsidy. But the import–export link (i.e. the ability of exporters to retain some of their dollar earnings to import for the home market) meant that exporters received some of the scarcity rents created by the system.

4 The subsidy equivalent of the export incentives are taken from Kim (1988). This, and the earlier Frank *et al*. (1975) study on which these estimates are based, are the most authoritative and widely cited sources on the quantitative aspects of Korea's trade regime.

5 It is true that, in the presence of sunk costs associated with exporting, uncertainty in the pre-1964 period may have prevented entrepreneurs from switching *existing* production from the home market to world markets. However, the export boom that took place was not a matter of switching production: it entailed the establishment of *new* capacity specifically oriented towards foreign markets. With greater stability in relative incentives, the first-order effect should have been to enhance the profitability of investing in new capacity for both foreign *and* home markets.

6 In discussing the same issue, Frank *et al*. (1975) draw what is in my judgement the correct conclusion: 'it is plausible to hypothesize that South Korean exports were constrained more by the capacity to produce goods than by the relative profitability of producing for export instead of domestic markets'. To extend this to its logical conclusion, we must therefore search for explanations for why it became profitable to invest and expand productive capacity.

7 The general case with non-tradables is analysed formally in Rodrik (1995) in the context of an explicit intertemporal model. In such a model, there are two offsetting effects on the price of exportables relative to non-tradables. The substitution effect (as expenditure switches towards the importable) tends to depress the price of non-tradables and raise the relative price of exportables. The income effect (from the increase in the profitability of investment) goes in the opposite direction.

8 According to Box 10.1, the openness of the economy must necessarily decline once the investment ratio stabilizes. However, there are a number of confounding features in the Korean and Taiwanese experiences. Foremost among these is the large-scale import liberalization that has taken place in both countries during the 1980s.

9 As Robert Wade has reminded me, the argument about investment-led exports is not new. However, I have had difficulty locating sources in the published literature which place priority on investment demand *and* at the same time explain the rising export–GDP ratio. Bradford (1990), for example, seems to suggest a causal role for investment, but it is unclear as to why the investment was allocated disproportionately in export-oriented sectors.

10 Another possibly important initial condition, emphasized by Adrian Wood in personal correspondence, is the lack of a good natural resource base in Korea and

Taiwan. This is in part related to the high educational attainment ratios relative to income: as Wood points out, countries with the same level of education per worker but more land would have had a higher GNP per capita and lie closer to the regression line. But in addition, the meagre natural resources gave these countries a clear comparative advantage in manufactures, allowing them to enjoy both rapid industrialization and rapid trade expansion.

11 Little (1994) calculates that the annualized return to investment in Kórea was 31.1% during the period 1963–73. However, his calculations also show a reduction in the rate of return subsequently, to 18.3% during 1974–9. He attributes the decline to the HCI drive.

12 However, the analytical basis for this argument has, to my knowledge, never been properly laid out. If fulfilling an export target is the price to be paid for hefty subsidies, many firms will willingly pay the price. There is nothing inherently efficient or desirable about the resulting exports.

13 A clear example is the need to square the Korean and Taiwanese governments' emphasis on inter-industry linkages with the complete neglect of such linkages in standard welfare economics.

14 With thanks to Gene Grossman, for laying out these different positions. I am borrowing his wording here.

15 The Barro and Lee paper does not report the decomposition for individual countries. The table here is based on calculations performed by Robert Barro, to whom I am grateful.

REFERENCES

Adelman, I. and C. Taft Morris (1967). *Society, Politics and Economic Development: A Quantitative Approach*, The Johns Hopkins Press, Baltimore, MD.

Alesina, A. and D. Rodrik (1994). 'Distributive Politics and Economic Growth', *Quarterly Journal of Economics*.

Amsden, A. H. (1989). *Asia's Next Giant: South Korea and Late Industrialization*, Oxford University Press, New York.

Barro, R. J. and J.-W. Lee (1993). 'Losers and Winners in Economic Growth', NBER Working Paper No. 4341.

Bosworth, B., R. Dornbusch and R. Laban (1994). *The Chilean Economy: Policy Lessons and Challenges*, Brookings Institution, Washington, DC.

Bradford, C. I., Jr (1990). 'Policy Interventions and Markets: Development Strategy Typologies and Policy Options', in G. Gereffi and D. L. Wyman (eds.), *Manufacturing Miracles: Paths of Industrialization in Latin America and East Asia*, Princeton University Press, Princeton, NJ.

Ciccone, A. and K. Matsuyama (1993). 'Start-up Costs and Pecuniary Externalities as Barriers to Economic Development', NBER Working Paper No. 4363.

Collins, S. (1991). 'Saving Behavior in Ten Developing Countries', in B. D. Bernheim and J. B. Shoven (eds.), *National Saving and Economic Performance*, University of Chicago Press, Chicago, IL.

—— and W.-A. Park (1989). 'External Debt and Macroeconomic Performance in South Korea', in J. Sachs and S. Collins (eds.), *Developing Country Debt and Economic Performance*, vol. 3, University of Chicago Press, Chicago, IL.

de Melo, J. and S. Robinson (1992). 'Productivity and Externalities: Models of Export-Led Growth', *International Trade and Economic Development*.

Elias, V. (1990). *Sources of Growth: A Study of Seven Latin American Economies*, ICS Press, San Francisco, CA.

Faini, R. (1984). 'Increasing Returns, Non-Traded Inputs, and Regional Development', *Economic Journal*.
Frank, C. R., Jr, K. S. Kim and L. Westphal (1975). *Foreign Trade Regimes and Economic Development: South Korea*, Columbia University Press, New York.
Haggard, S. (1990). *Pathways from the Periphery: The Politics of Growth in the Newly Industrializing Countries*, Cornell University Press, Ithaca, NY.
Hasan, P. (1976). *Korea: Problems and Issues in a Rapidly Growing Economy*, The Johns Hopkins University Press, Baltimore, MD, and London.
Hong, W. (1976). *Factor Supply and Factor Intensity of Trade in Korea*, Korea Development Institute, Seoul.
—— (1977). 'Trade, Distortions and Employment in Korea', Korea Development Institute, Seoul.
—— (1993). 'Trade and Development: The Experience of Korea and Taiwan', in G. Hasson (ed.), *International Trade and Development*, Routledge, London.
Hou, C.-M. (1988). 'Strategy for Economic Development in Taiwan and Implications for Developing Economies', paper presented at the Conference on Economic Development Experiences of Taiwan, Taipei, 8–10 June.
Jones, Leroy and H. Sakong (1980). *Government, Business, and Entrepreneurship in Economic Development: The Korean Case*, Harvard University Press, Cambridge, MA.
Kim, J.-I. and L. J. Lau (1992). 'The Source of Economic Growth of the Newly Industrialized Countries on the Pacific Rim', unpublished manuscript, Stanford University, CA.
Kim, K. S. (1988). 'The Timing and Sequencing of Trade Liberalization Policy: The Case of Korea', unpublished manuscript, World Bank.
Krueger, A. O. (1985). 'The Experience and Lessons of Asia's Super Exporters', in V. Corbo *et al.* (eds.), *Export-Oriented Development Strategies: The Success of Five Newly Industrializing Countries*, Westview Press, Boulder, CO, and London.
Krugman, P. (1991). 'History versus Expectations', *Quarterly Journal of Economics*.
Kuo, S. (1983). *The Taiwan Economy in Transition*, Westview Press, Boulder, CO.
Lin, C.-Y. (1973). *Industrialization in Taiwan, 1946–72: Trade and Import-Substitution Policies for Developing Countries*, Praeger, New York.
Little, I. M. D. (1994). 'Trade and Industrialization Revisted', unpublished paper, Nuffield College, Oxford.
Mason, E. S., M. J. Kim, D. Perkins, K. S. Kim and D. Cole (1980). *The Economic and Social Modernization of the Republic of Korea*, Harvard University Press, Cambridge, MA.
Matsuyama, K. (1991). 'Increasing Returns, Industrialization and Indeterminacy of Equilibrium', *Quarterly Journal of Economics*.
Mulligan, C. and X. Sala-i-Martín (1993). 'Transitional Dynamics in Two-Sector Models of Endogenous Growth', *Quarterly Journal of Economics*.
Murphy, K., A. Shleifer and R. Vishny (1989). 'Industrialization and the Big Push', *Journal of Political Economy*.
Nagatsuka, S. (1994). 'Recent changes in the South Korean shipbuilding industry and its future prospects', JAMRI Report No. 49, Japan Maritime Research Institute.
Pack, H. and L. E. Westphal (1986). 'Industrial Strategy and Technological Change: Theory versus Reality', *Journal of Development Economics*.
Page, J. (1994). 'The East Asian Miracle: Four Lessons for Development Policy', in S. Fischer and J. Rotemberg (eds.), *NBER Macroeconomics Annual 1994*, Cambridge, MA.
Persson, T. and G. Tabellini (1994). 'Is Inequality Harmful to Growth?' *American Economic Review*.

Rodríguez-Clare, A. (1993). 'The Division of Labor and Economic Development', unpublished manuscript, Stanford University, CA.
Rodrik, D. (1992). 'Closing the Technology Gap: Does Trade Liberalization Really Help?', in G. K. Helleiner (ed.), *Trade Policy, Industrialization and Development: New Perspectives*, Oxford University Press, Oxford.
—— (1993). 'Coordination Failures and Government Policy in Intermediate Economies: A Model with Applications to East Asia and Eastern Europe', unpublished manuscript, Columbia University, New York.
—— (1994). 'King Kong Meets Godzilla: The World Bank and *The East Asian Miracle*', in A. Fishlow, C. Gwin, S. Haggard, D. Rodrik and R. Wade, *Miracle or Design? Lessons from the East Asian Experience*, Overseas Development Council, Washington, DC.
—— (1995). 'Trade Strategy, Exports, and Investment: Another Look at East Asia', Institute of Policy Reform Discussion Paper, Washington, DC.
Rosenstein-Rodan, P. (1943). 'Problems of Industrialization of Eastern and South-Eastern Europe', *Economic Journal*.
Scitovsky, T. (1954). 'Two Concepts of External Economies', *Journal of Political Economy*.
Short, R. (1983). 'The Role of Public Enterprises: An International Statistical Comparison', International Monetary Fund, Washington, DC.
Trela, I. and J. Whalley (1992). 'The Role of Tax Policy in Korea's Economic Growth', in T. Ito and A. Krueger (eds.), *The Political Economy of Tax Reform*, University of Chicago Press, Chicago, IL, and London.
Tsiang, S. C. (1984). 'Taiwan's Economic Miracle: Lessons in Economic Development', in A. C. Harberger (ed.), *World Economic Growth*, ICS Press, San Francisco, CA.
Ventura, J. (1994) 'Growth and Interdependence', mimeo., Harvard University, Cambridge, MA.
Wade, R. (1990). *Governing the Market: Economic Theory and the Role of Government in East Asian Industrialization*, Princeton University Press, Princeton, NJ.
World Bank (1993). *The East Asian Miracle: Economic Growth and Public Policy*, Oxford University Press for the World Bank, Washington, DC.
Young, A. (1993). 'Lessons from the East Asian NICs: A Contrarian View', NBER Working Paper No. 4482.
—— (1994). 'The Tyranny of Numbers: Confronting the Statistical Realities of the East Asian Growth Experience', unpublished paper.

11

GOVERNMENT INTERVENTION, RENT DISTRIBUTION AND ECONOMIC DEVELOPMENT IN KOREA

Yoon Je Cho

As part of their economic development strategies, most governments in developing countries intervene in the market to affect resource allocation. In the process, economic rent is created. The creation of economic rent and its distribution provide government with perhaps its greatest leverage for affecting the economic behavior of the private sector. In every economy, developing or industrialized, economic rent is created and rent seeking is ubiquitous. The difference among economies may be the relative size of rent created and the way it is distributed—and this seems to have important consequences for the performance of the economy.

Korea is a country where government intervention in the market, especially in the financial market, was extensive, and where substantial economic rent was created and allocated in the course of economic development. However, the areas where major rent was created and the rules by which it was distributed changed over time, with the changes in political regimes and economic policy goals. In retrospect, this brought remarkably different outcomes in the course of Korea's postwar economic development. In the 1950s, rent was created mainly in relation to import restriction and overvalued foreign exchange rates. The sale of government assets, which had been owned by the Japanese during the Japanese occupation period (1910–45), to the private sector also entailed substantial rent. During this period, the government did not have a clear vision for economic development and the development goal was overshadowed by the political agenda related to nation-building. Thus, the creation and distribution of rent was done largely with political considerations in mind rather than clear economic goals.

Change occurred in the 1960s and 1970s in the main area where rent was created. As the Korean government shifted to an export-oriented

Source: *The Role of Government in East Asian Economic Development*, M. Aoki, H-K Kim and M. Okuno-Fujiwara (Editors), Oxford: Clarendon Press, 1997.

development strategy, the rent involved with overvalued exchange rates almost disappeared and that involved with the restriction of import quotas diminished. Instead, rent was created mainly in relation to financial allocations—allocation of domestic bank loans as well as foreign loans to priority sectors (e.g., the export sector in the 1960s and the heavy and chemical industries in the 1970s). The government, during this period, created rent with a clear vision of providing incentives to the priority sectors (mainly exports), thereby striving to accelerate economic development. It had a comprehensive development strategy in which credit policies were well coordinated with other economic policies. Although the amounts of rent created and distributed were equally substantial in both periods, the economic performance in the 1960s and 1970s differed widely from that of the 1950s.

This chapter discusses how economic rent was created and distributed in the course of the economic development of Korea, and how the government used this rent to achieve its economic goals. In discussing rent, the chapter focuses mainly on government intervention in the financial market. This study thus attempts to shed some light on the role of government in the early stages of economic development.

The first section briefly discusses the main features of Korean economic policies during the aforementioned periods and the main policy instruments used to achieve economic goals. In this context, it focuses on the areas where economic rent was created and how it was distributed during the 1950s, 1960s, and 1970s. The experience of the 1950s is contrasted with that of the 1960s and 1970s in order to highlight how the areas of rent creation and methods of distribution can have significantly different consequences on economic performance. Section 11.1 also attempts to estimate the relative size of this rent over time. Section 11.2 attempts to assess whether or not government intervention in the market (i.e., the creation and distribution of rent intended to affect industrial behavior) can have a positive impact on economic development in its initial stages by examining the Korean experience. The chapter concludes with brief summary remarks.

11.1 RENT CREATION AND DISTRIBUTION OVER TIME

The 1950s: import restriction and foreign exchange allocation

With the end of World War II, Korea gained independence from the Japanese occupation (1910–45). Soon thereafter, it was divided into the two countries of North Korea and South Korea (hereafter, 'Korea" refers to the latter). The first Korean government was led by President Rhee Syng-Man. Rhee devoted much of his agenda to building the nation, securing a United States military commitment to ensure Korean security, guiding the country's involvement in the Korean war (1950–53), stabilizing war inflation, and securing US grants for the war-devastated economy.

In the 1950s, the government did not have a comprehensive economic development strategy and economic policy during this time was characterized by an assortment of government regulations that lacked a clear vision or set of policy goals. Since the government's economic policy came under strong US influence, the government did not systematically intervene in the market, and a relatively independent central bank was established following the model of the US Federal Reserve Board, resulting in the private control of banks. Although interest rate regulations and preferential credit programs existed, bank operations were not subject to much government regulation.

However, the government did enact strong regulations with respect to external transactions. It maintained import restrictions and highly overvalued exchange rates. The import restriction policy was adopted not necessarily in accordance with an industrial development strategy, but rather in consideration of the shortage of foreign exchange and the political agenda. Korea did not have any significant exports and the major source of foreign exchange at that time was foreign aid and the local expenditures of the US ground forces. Korea also maintained restrictions on imports, as did most developing countries at that time, for nationalistic reasons. In particular, the government rejected the purchase of Japanese manufactured products. Thus, the government had to ration the scarce foreign exchange mainly to alleviate the shortage of daily necessities and to build factories to produce them. In order to maximize foreign exchange revenues derived from the local expenditures of the US ground forces, the Korean currency remained highly overvalued.

The allocation of import quotas under the strong import restriction that accompanied foreign exchange allocation entailed substantial rent. Importers received windfall gains and prospered; some of the Korean *chaebol* operating in the 1990s were established during this period as major recipients of this rent. The amount of rent that accompanied foreign exchange allocation is estimated to have been roughly 10–14 per cent of annual GNP during this period (see Table 11.1).[1]

In the 1950s, the government had no comprehensive economic development strategy and did not create rent to drive private business in the direction of its economic policy goals. There were no established rules for the allocation of rent or for the explicit and formal institutions in charge of making decisions regarding allocation. The ruling political party and strong political figures intervened in the allocation process. Consequently, there was no clear link between rent distribution and economic considerations for development (Yoon 1991). The allocation of rent was mainly discretionary, and those who received these allocations benefited from windfall gains, portions of which were shared with politicians and bureaucrats.

Table 11.1 Exchange rate of the US Dollar and economic rent in relation to overvalued exchange rates (million won, %)

Year	*Official rate*[a]	*Parallel market rate*[a]	*Total rent (A)*[b]	*A/GNP*
1953	18.00	37.90	6,873.5	14.3
1954	18.00	43.60	6,228.5	9.3
1955	50.00	96.40	15,841.0	13.6
1956	50.00	96.60	17,992.3	11.8
1957	50.00	103.30	23,569.3	11.9
1958	50.00	118.10	25,755.4	12.4
1959	50.00	125.50	22,936.9	10.4
1960	65.00	145.30	27,583.1	11.2
1961	130.00	150.00	6,535.6	2.1
1962	130.00	134.00	1,687.2	0.5
1963	130.00	174.50	24,933.4	5.1
1964	255.77	290.07	13,870.9	2.0
1965	271.78	323.68	24,050.5	3.0
1966	271.18	302.58	22,495.0	2.2
1967	274.60	305.70	30,981.8	2.5
1968	281.50	309.00	40,229.8	2.6
1969	304.45	339.85	64,555.4	2.6
1970	316.65	348.75	63,686.4	2.5

Notes:
[a] Exchange rates are averaged on an annual basis.
[b] Total rent = total imports × exchange rate gap. Imports are valued at CIF and the exchange rate gap is the gap between the official rate and the parallel market rate.

Source: Bank of Korea.

The 1960s: rent creation and distribution through credit market intervention

Korea's rapid economic growth began in the 1960s. In May 1961, Park Chung Hee, a military general, grasped control of the government in a *coup d'état*; in 1963, he became president in a popular election. His regime continued until his assassination in 1979. When Park took power, he—and many other Koreans—harbored little confidence in the free market system. He and his economic staff believed the government should guide important prices, such as interest rates, and oversee the allocation of resources. But they gradually began to see the merits of price reforms that allowed important prices such as interest rates and the exchange rate to become closer to market prices. So they implemented price reforms that strengthened guidance in resource allocation.

In the early 1960s, Park's military government established new priorities for Korea's economy by shifting its policy stance from stabilization to growth and from import substitution to export promotion. The overvalued exchange rate was devalued by approximately 100 per cent. Consequently, rent associated with foreign exchange allocation in the 1950s almost disappeared, as indicated in Table 11.1.

The government believed it could accelerate economic growth by taking the lead in mobilizing and allocating resources. In pursuit of this goal, the government launched its first five-year economic development plan and implemented two measures to strengthen state control of the financial market: nationalizing commercial banks, and amending the Bank of Korea (BOK) Act to subordinate the central bank under the government. In addition, it introduced three significant policy reforms: the overhaul of the export credit program, the reform of interest rates, and the facilitation of foreign capital inflow. The government strengthened its control over the financial system and used credit allocation as the major industrial policy instrument. However, it also streamlined relative prices to correspond more closely to market levels during this period; interest rates were substantially increased and the exchange rate overvaluation was corrected.

The rent generated in relation to credit allocation was substantial during the 1960s, not necessarily because the government heavily repressed interest rates, but because the total volume of credit (both bank loans and foreign loans) to be allocated expanded as a result of interest rate reform and government effort to mobilize foreign borrowing.

Expansion of export credit programs

An export credit program to support the export industry was in place as early as the 1950s, but the size of loans then was negligible. When the military government initiated the export-led strategy for economic growth, it naturally strengthened export credit programs to support exporters. Until the mid-1980s, when Korea ran a current account surplus,[2] the system of export financing played a critical role in promoting the export industry.

The short-term export credit system was streamlined in 1961. The essence of the new system was the "automatic approval" of loans by commercial banks to prospective borrowers holding export letters of credit (L/C). Initially, the program covered certain portions of the production costs of goods slated for export. Its coverage expanded rapidly, extending to sales to United Nations forces in Korea in 1961; to exports on a documents-against-payment (D/P), documents-against-acceptance (D/A), or consignment basis in 1965; to construction services rendered to foreign governments or their agencies in 1967; to imports of raw materials and intermediate goods for export-related use or to purchases from local suppliers in 1967; and so on. In each case, the expanded coverage was intended to promote the exploration of new export opportunities and the diversification of export items. These new programs were established after close consultation between the government and exporters.

General trading companies were introduced in the new export-financing system and were provided with financing on the basis of their export performance. To be eligible for financing, these companies had to exceed a specified level of exports which increased year to year, thus linking their export performance to their access to credit. The general trading companies had favorable access to export credit but were required to renew their licenses each year. Those whose exports did not exceed the specified level had their licenses revoked.

The interest rate on export loans was subsidized heavily. When the 1965 interest rate reform was implemented with the doubling of nominal rates (see below), the interest rate on export credit remained untouched. Consequently, the gap between export loans and general loans widened sharply. Interest rates on loans to exporters remained at 6.5 per cent while the general loan rate rose to 26 per cent (see Table 11.2). The rent associated with export credit alone is estimated to have been about 0.5–1.0 per cent of GNP during the 1960s, and about 2–3 per cent of GNP during the 1970s (see Table 11.3).

Interest rate reform

The government drastically changed its interest rate policies in 1965. Overnight, it raised the nominal interest rate on (one-year) time deposits from 15 per cent per year to 30 per cent, and the general loan rate from 16 to 26 per cent. However, the reform only partially helped draw the interest rates offered by the banks closer to market rates. Loan-rate increases were selective, excluding export-related, agricultural, and many other categories of investment loans. This action was intended to spur domestic saving to finance ambitious investment programs for economic development. To protect industrial firms from increasing costs incurred from overborrowing, a "negative interest margin" was introduced. At the same time, to protect the profitability of banks, the central bank provided cheap credit to commercial banks, which depended heavily on this credit in the extension of loans to firms.[3] On the other hand, the central bank placed high reserve requirements on commercial banks to contain inflationary pressure due to the expansion of its credit, but it paid interest on this reserve to protect commercial banks' profitability.

The reform successfully attracted private saving. In the first three months, the level of time and savings deposits increased by 50 per cent; over the next four years the level grew at an annual compounded rate of nearly 100 per cent. The stock of M2 relative to GNP increased from 8.9 per cent in 1964 to 31.8 per cent in 1971. Total bank loans increased by an equivalent amount. The annual growth rate of bank loans rose from 10.9 per cent during 1963–64 to 61.5 per cent during 1965–69.

More importantly, the reform helped shift funds from the unregulated informal sector to the banking sector, over which the government tightened its control. This allowed the government to increase controls on financial

Table 11.2 Comparison of various interest rates and rent created in the financial sector (%)

Year	*Bank loan rate* General loan (A)	*Bank loan rate* Export loan (B)	*Curb market rate (C)*	*Corporate bond Rate*	*Inflation*[a]	*A – B*	*C – A*	*Rent/GNP*[b]	*Rent/GNP*[c]
1968	25.8	6.0	55.9	—	16.1	19.8	30.1	5.6	—
1969	24.5	6.0	51.2	—	14.8	18.5	26.7	5.5	—
1970	24.0	6.0	50.8	—	15.6	18.0	26.8	7.0	—
1971	23.0	6.0	46.3	—	12.5	17.0	23.3	6.3	—
1972	17.7	6.0	38.9	22.9	16.7	11.7	21.2	6.1	1.5
1973	15.5	7.0	39.2	21.8	13.6	8.5	23.7	7.2	1.9
1974	15.5	9.0	37.6	21.0	30.5	6.5	22.1	8.7	2.2
1975	15.5	7.0	41.3	20.1	25.2	5.8	25.8	9.5	1.7
1976	17.5	8.0	40.5	20.4	21.2	8.5	23.0	8.0	1.0
1977	19.0	9.0	38.1	20.1	16.6	10.0	19.1	6.3	0.4
1978	19.0	9.0	41.7	21.1	22.8	10.0	22.7	8.2	0.8
1979	19.0	9.0	42.4	26.7	19.6	10.0	23.4	9.2	3.0
1980	20.0	15.0	45.0	30.1	23.9	5.0	25.0	10.8	4.4
1981	16.4	15.0	35.4	24.4	17.0	1.4	19.0	8.8	3.7
1982	10.0	10.0	33.1	17.3	6.9	0.0	23.1	11.8	3.7
1983	10.0	10.0	25.8	14.2	5.0	0.0	15.8	8.4	2.2

Notes:
[a] GNP deflator.
[b] Rent = total loans × (curb market rate – bank loan rate).
[c] Rent = total loans × (corporate bond rate – bank loan rate).

Source: Bank of Korea.

Table 11.3 Rent created in export loans (billion won, %)

Year	*Export loans*[a] *(A)*	*(A)* × Interest gap[b] *(A)*	*Rent (B)/GNP*
1963	3.9	1.4	0.3
1964	10.0	4.6	0.7
1965	12.1	4.0	0.5
1966	16.6	5.4	0.5
1967	32.4	9.8	0.8
1968	43.4	13.1	0.8
1969	80.7	21.5	0.9
1970	161.6	43.3	1.7
1971	248.5	57.9	1.8
1972	231.8	49.1	1.3
1973	416.2	98.6	2.0
1974	652.6	144.2	2.1
1976	1,042.7	269.0	3.0
1976	1,511.5	347.6	2.9
1977	2,616.0	499.7	2.9
1978	3,764.8	854.6	3.7
1979	5,642.8	1,320.4	4.5
1980	6,957.4	1,739.4	4.7
1981	6,957.4	1,321.9	2.9
1982	8,192.0	1,892.4	3.7
1983	9,232.0	1,458.8	2.5

Notes:
[a] Outstanding loans at the end of the year.
[b] Interest gap = curb market rated – export loan interest.

Source: Bank of Korea, *Economic Statistics Yearbook*, various issues.

flow. It increased the total volume of capital to be distributed under government influence. Despite the interest rate reform, bank interest rates were still substantially lower than market rates (Table 11.2). Thus, the allocation of bank credit was accompanied by substantial rent. The rent associated with domestic credit allocation is estimated to have been around 4–6 per cent of GNP in the 1960s when bank interest rates were significantly high.[4] Real interest rates were very positive in the 1960s. However, interest rates were reduced to support the heavy and chemical industries in the 1970s, and accordingly the rent generated also increased to 6–12 per cent of GNP (Table 11.2).

The interest rate reform of the 1960s has been described by many economists as financial liberalization.[5] This is correct in the sense that the degree of government repression on the interest rate level was substantially reduced. In price terms, therefore, it was substantial liberalization that brought rapid growth of the financial sector. However, as mentioned earlier, liberalization in fact helped to enhance government influence over the total financial flow of the economy by expanding the formal banking sector, which was already under tight government control. Funds shifted from the informal credit market, which lay beyond government control. Therefore, the interest rate policy in the 1960s can be assessed as one of financial restraint.[6] On the other hand, government policy in the financial sector shifted toward more financial repression in the 1970s, as the government reduced interest rates, tightening its control over credit allocation.

However, financial repression in Korea was somewhat different from that usually found elsewhere or that defined in Chapter 6 by Hellmann, Murdock, and Stiglitz in this volume. In Korea, financial repression was not the mechanism for the nonproductive transfer of wealth from the household sector to the government. Rather, that mechanism was the implicit taxation of depositors to subsidize priority industrial sectors. Cheap credit for industrial firms was supported by interest rate control on deposits and the central bank's cheap credit to commercial banks, which sometimes reached 20–30 per cent of the latter's total lending. The interest rates on these loans were very low in order to sustain the profitability of banks.[7]

Most of the central bank credit to commercial banks was to support the policy-based lending of commercial banks such as export bills. In Korea, a substantial part of policy loans was supported by the expansion of high-powered money rather than fiscal funds, as was the case in postwar Japan. This was a fundamental reason why Korea had a relatively unstable inflation rate compared to Japan or Taiwan, despite its conservative fiscal stance. The financial resources to support industrialists in the priority sector were mobilized through implicit taxation on depositors. In Korea, through this implicit taxation, the transfer of wealth took place within the private sector rather than from the private to the public sector as was the case in many other developing countries.

Facilitating the flow of foreign capital

The Korean saving rate remained very low in the 1960s. In order to compensate for the shortage of domestic capital and declining foreign aid, the government normalized its relations with Japan in 1965 and amended the Foreign Capital Inducement Act in 1966, allowing state-owned banks to guarantee foreign borrowing by the private sector. This measure prompted a large inflow of foreign capital, especially from Japan. Since few Korean firms had direct access to foreign borrowing in the 1960s, the government's repayment guarantees to private borrowers through state-owned banks facilitated and reduced the cost of private foreign borrowing. Because domestic interest rates were high, private firms perceived foreign borrowing as a very attractive alternative. Yet each foreign loan had to be approved and allocated by the government, and foreign loans were used selectively to support industrial policy goals. The *ex post* rent associated with foreign loans fluctuated with

Table 11.4 Cost of foreign loans and domestic market rates (%, % point)

Year	Cost of foreign loans: Nominal (A)[a]	Cost of foreign loans: Effective (B)[b]	Bank loan rate	Curb market rate (C)	Corporate bond yield (D)	C – A	D – A	C – B	D – B
1968	7.13	15.28	25.8	55.9	—	48.77	—	40.62	—
1969	10.06	14.07	24.5	51.2	—	41.14	—	37.13	—
1970	6.57	24.61	24.0	50.8	—	44.05	—	26.19	—
1971	5.81	12.70	23.0	46.3	—	40.49	—	33.60	—
1972	6.19	5.84	17.7	38.9	22.9	32.71	16.71	33.06	17.06
1973	10.03	31.79	15.5	39.2	21.8	29.17	11.77	7.41	–9.99
1974	10.19	10.19	15.5	37.6	21.0	27.41	10.81	27.41	10.81
1975	6.63	6.63	15.5	41.3	20.1	34.67	13.47	34.67	13.47
1976	5.38	5.38	17.5	40.5	20.4	35.12	15.02	35.12	15.02
1977	7.50	7.50	19.0	38.1	20.1	30.60	12.60	30.60	12.60
1978	12.31	12.31	19.0	41.7	21.1	29.39	8.79	29.39	8.79
1979	14.44	50.78	19.0	42.4	26.7	27.96	12.26	–8.38	–24.08
1980	16.75	22.90	20.0	45.0	30.1	28.25	13.35	22.10	7.20
1981	14.81	21.59	16.4	35.4	24.4	20.59	9.59	13.81	2.81
1982	9.50	15.85	10.0	33.1	17.3	23.60	7.80	17.25	1.45
1983	10.06	13.86	10.0	25.8	14.2	15.74	4.14	11.94	0.34

Notes:
[a] Labor-based cost of borrowing.
[b] Nominal cost adjusted for the annual fluctuation rate of the exchange rate.

Source: Bank of Korea.

changes in exchange rates but was quite substantial (Table 11.4). Estimations are presented in Table 11.5.

Rent distribution in the 1960s

Following the creation of substantial rent in relation to credit allocation, rent distribution was used more effectively as an industrial policy instrument in

Table 11.5 Rent created in foreign loan allocation (million $US, %)

Year	*Total foreign loans (A)*	$B \times A$[a]	$C \times A$[b]	$D \times A$[c]	$E \times A$[a]
1968	1,199	548.8	—	487.0	—
		(11.2)	—	(9.3)	—
1969	1,800	740.5	—	668.4	—
		(11.2)	—	(10.1)	—
1970	2,277	1,003.0	—	596.4	—
		(12.6)	—	(7.5)	—
1971	2,984	1,208.2	—	1,002.7	—
		(12.9)	—	(10.7)	—
1972	3,580	1,171.0	598.2	1,183.6	610.8
		(11.1)	(5.7)	(11.2)	(5.8)
1973	4,257	1,241.8	501.0	315.4	−125.3
		(9.2)	(3.7)	(2.3)	(−3.1)
1974	5,955	1,632.3	643.7	1,623.3	643.7
		(8.8)	(3.5)	(8.8)	(3.5)
1975	8,547	2,932.0	1,139.2	2,932.0	1,139.2
		(14.1)	(5.5)	(14.1)	(5.5)
1976	10.635	3,735.0	1,597.4	3,735.0	1,597.4
		(13.0)	(5.6)	(13.0)	(5.6)
1977	12,649	3,870.6	1,593.8	3,870.6	1,593.8
		(12.3)	(5.1)	(12.3)	(5.1)
1978	14,823	4,356.5	1,302.9	4,356.5	1,302.9
		(8.4)	(2.5)	(8.4)	(2.5)
1979	20.287	5,672.2	2,487.2	−1,700.7	−4,885.7
		(9.1)	(4.0)	(−2.7)	(−7.8)
1980	27,170	7,675.5	3,627.2	6,003.0	1,955.6
		(12.7)	(6.0)	(10.0)	(3.2)
1981	32,433	6,678.0	3,110.3	4,478.7	911.1
		(10.1)	(4.7)	(6.8)	(1.4)
1982	37,083	8,751.6	2,892.5	6,396.7	537.6
		(12.6)	(4.2)	(9.2)	(0.8)
1983	40,378	6,355.5	1,671.6	4,822.6	138.8
		(8.4)	(2.2)	(6.3)	(0.2)

Note:
[a] B = curb market rate — nominal Libor (London interbank offer rates) rate.
[b] C = corporate bond yield – nominal Libor rate.
[c] D = curb market rate – effective Libor rate.
[d] E = corporate bond yield – effective Libor rate.

Numbers in parentheses are ratio to GNP.

the 1960s than in the 1950s. Credit allocation (both domestic and foreign), especially export credit allocation, was linked with the performance of rent seekers: those who were more successful in the export market were rewarded with more allocated credit. In the 1950s, harboring close ties with government officials or politically powerful figures often proved to be enough to receive rent allocations. However, such practices and conditions changed in the 1960s. In addition, industrialists were required to prove they could perform in the international market and meet the criteria set by the government. If they did not perform up to the standards, they faced the revocation of favorable treatment. In the 1950s, the volume of items to be allocated with rent (i.e., foreign exchange) was quite small, but the price subsidy (degree of overvaluation) was significant and the rules for distribution were not clear. In the 1960s, however, the degree of the price subsidy was reduced, the volume of items to be allocated credit (both domestic and foreign) was large, and rent distribution was more closely linked to the performances of rent seekers.

The 1970s: intensified rent creation associated with development of the heavy and chemical industries

In the 1970s, the government reverted to lower interest rates while intensifying its controls on credit allocation. Credit policies were made more "selective." This reversion was marked by a Presidential Emergency Decree in 1972, which bailed out many financially insolvent firms by placing an immediate moratorium on all loans in the informal credit markets, and reduced the bank loan rate from 23 per cent to 15.5 percent.[8] Furthermore, approximately 30 per cent of short-term high-interest commercial bank loans to businesses were converted into long-term loans with concessional terms for repayment on an installment basis, over a five-year period, at an 8 per cent annual interest rate, with a three-year grace period. The lapse back to more repressive financial policies was motivated by the policy shift toward the promotion of the heavy and chemical industries (HCI), which required enormous amounts of cheap financing and constituted a significant departure from the export-oriented, non-sectoral-biased strategy adopted throughout the 1960s.

The government adopted two other important measures to support the HCI drive: it established the National Investment Fund (NIF), and it expanded BOK discounts. HCI development required a large amount of term financing. In December 1973, the government established the NIF to finance long-term investments in HCI plants and equipment.[9] The NIF was mobilized from a combination of funds from private financial intermediaries and the government, but predominantly from the former. Although the NIF did not comprise a large share of total bank loans, it provided more than 60 per cent of term financing for HCI equipment investment in the years 1975–80

(Cho and Kim 1995). BOK also expanded its rediscount facility to support the HCI. Considering the long maturation period of investments in the HCI, BOK also increased the maximum loan period for equipment investment. Furthermore, BOK brought out the "Guide to Bank Loans," adding HCI to the list of high-priority industries for financial support to induce more lending by banks to the HCI. The Guide curbed, or in some cases prohibited, some service industries from receiving bank financing (Cho and Kim 1995).

As the government pursued HCI development, rent was generated through the restriction on entry and selection of manufacturers in specific industries (since there were economies of scale in production for most HCI) in addition to the allocation of credit. Choosing market entrants and providing financial support were packaged. Since great uncertainty accompanied HCI investment, in the opening stages of the HCI drive, industrialists were reluctant to enter these industries, even with the large rent generation. Later, when the government's determination to stand behind selected market entrants at whatever cost was confirmed, these industrialists competed fiercely to receive selection as HCI manufacturers.

In accordance with the nature of this kind of industrial policy, rent distribution became more discretionary in the 1970s than it had been in the 1960s. Although most selected entrants were already established industrialists (and thus their management capability was proven), there was no explicit criterion for the selection of a specific industrialist or *chaebol* as an entrant to a specific industry. There was substantial room for the discretionary allocation of rent and favoritism. Since the HCI required an immense scale of investment, most of the firms that entered these industries with strong government support, in terms of credit allocation, were the already well-established *chaebol*. Consequently, rent distribution in the 1970s increased the degree of economic concentration in the Korean economy, later becoming a serious burden on economic policy.

11.2 DID GOVERNMENT INTERVENTION AND ECONOMIC RENT PROMOTE RAPID DEVELOPMENT?

In Korea, as discussed earlier, government intervention in the financial market was extensive: the government controlled interest rates and supervised the allocation of bank credit. Economic rent associated with credit allocation (and foreign exchange allocation) was substantial, and its distribution constituted the major government tool for corporate governance and industrial policy. The export drive in the 1960s and the HCI drive in the 1970s were supported by various preferential credit programs and the government's discretionary allocation of credit.

To what extent, then, did credit spur growth in the priority sectors and/or support industrial development? A direct answer to this question is not possible. Since credit supports were provided in conjunction with other incentives, it is not easy to isolate the impact of the credit supports from the other incentives. Thus, we can address this issue only in an indirect manner. We can first examine the impact of credit supports on the take-off of exports in the 1960s; second, we can discuss the impact of credit supports on the HCI in their rapid growth during the 1970s, to determine their merit and whether rent allocation had occurred.[10]

The impact on export growth

In order for exporters to respond to foreign demand, they should have access to the trade financing necessary to fill export orders (Rhee 1989). In many developing countries, financing mechanisms that are taken for granted in industrial countries, such as short-term money markets and bill discount markets, are rudimentary or nonexistent; such was the case in Korea in the 1960s. Thus, one way to provide a market for bill discounts to exporters was to establish the central bank's rediscount facility (Rhee 1989). Although exporters in Korea in the 1950s received some selective credit supports through lending by the central bank, export credit programs were formalized only in the 1960s. The total amount of credit supported by export credit programs increased from 4.5 per cent of total bank credit in the years 1961–65 to 7.6 per cent (196–72), and further to 13.2 per cent (1973–81). In addition, as shown in the previous section, interest rate subsidies for export credits were substantial. In the years 1966–72, the interest rate for export credit was 17.1 per cent lower, on average, than the general loan rate. Exporters also received support from various other credit programs (such as equipment funds for export industries) and favorable credit allocations in conformity with government directives or administrative guidance. During Korea's export expansion period, credit subsidies comprised the major component of total export subsidies (Figure 11.1), which peaked in 1967 when the total interest rate subsidy was 2.3 per cent of the total value of exports,[11] far exceeding the fiscal subsidy of 1.0 per cent in the same year.

The extent to which credit subsidies contributed to the take-off of Korean exports in the 1960s is unclear (Figure 11.2 shows the export growth rate throughout the economic development period). A competitive exchange rate (with a major devaluation of the won in 1964) and various institutional supports also contributed to export growth. The expanded accessibility of credit (subsidized by low interest rates) was crucial in enabling Korean exporters to fill foreign orders and to explore foreign markets. In general, access to credit seems to have been more essential for supporting the continuous growth of exports than were interest rate subsidies. But, because export marketing requires substantial fixed costs in the initial stages and involves tremendous externalities,[12] government subsidies may also have made a large contribution because private efforts and investment in the exploration of external markets might not have been sufficient to fuel rapid

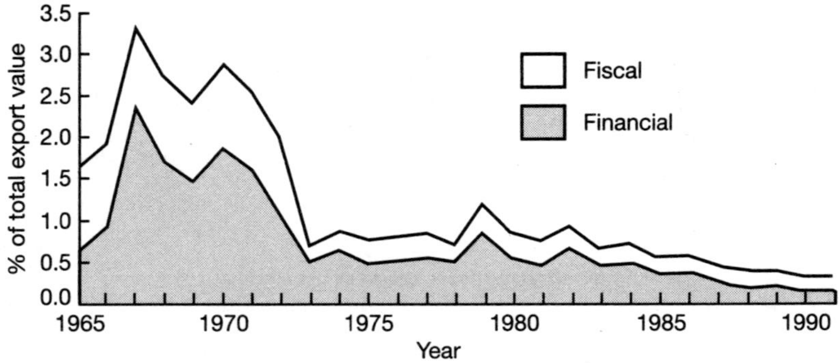

Figure 11.1 Subsidies to Export, 1965–1991

Note: The amount of financial subsidies is the size of export-related loans multiplied by the interest rate differential between the average loan rate for the manufacturing industry and interest rates for export-related loans. The tax subsidy ratio is the amount of tax subsidies from export reserves and special depreciation systems divided by the total value of exports. If the amount of the financial subsidy were based on the gap between the market interest rate and the export loan rate, the credit subsidy would be much larger. The tax subsidy from the export reserve system is the amount of tax savings that comes from corporate tax exemptions on the export reserve in a given year. That is, it is calculated by subtracting the net present value of the deferred tax on the export reserve that would be paid over a three-year period after a two-year grace period from the tax on the export reserve that should have been paid in a given year. The tax subsidy from a special depreciation system is the net present value of the tax savings from the added depreciation that is allowed within 30 per cent of the normal depreciation on fixed assets purchased by an exporter.

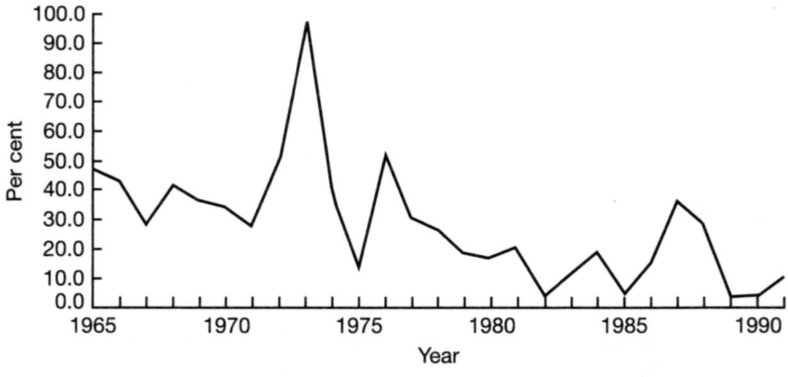

Figure 11.2 Growth of Exports, 1965–1991

growth. Alternatively, export marketing could have been subsidized by the budget. But given the poor budgetary situation in the 1960s when total tax revenue fell within the range of 6.8–12.4 per cent of GNP (as discussed earlier), the use of fiscal subsidies was clearly limited. It was also true that using subsidized credit through implicit taxation on the banking system (and consequently on depositors) was politically easier.

Impact on HCI development

As discussed in the previous section, bank loans were allocated favorably to the HCI in the 1970s. The manufacturing sector received 46.1 per cent of total domestic bank loans in 1970 but contributed only 21.3 per cent to GDP.[13] Within the manufacturing sector, the HCI received 22.6 per cent of total bank loans but contributed only 8.6 per cent to GDP. In 1980, after a decade of the HCI drive, the share of bank credit to the HCI increased further to 32.1 per cent, while its contribution to GDP also rose to 16.5 per cent.

The NIF was the major credit support program for the HCI, providing preferential maturities and interest rates. Credit support was provided not only by explicitly designated credit programs such as the NIF, but also by government directives to banks to provide more credit. The allocation of foreign loans was also a large part of total credit support. In the years 1972–76, for example, industries in the manufacturing sector claimed 66.1 per cent of the total amount of foreign commercial loans. Of this amount, 64.1 per cent went to the HCI (Table 11.6 provides a breakdown of the composition of foreign commercial loans).

The massive credit support made it possible to invest heavily in the HCI during the 1970s. During the late 1970s, almost 80 per cent of all fixed investment in the manufacturing sector went to the HCI. Consequently, the industrial structure and export composition of Korea changed drastically (Table 11.7). The expansion of the HCI in the 1970s is striking. Within a

Table 11.6 Composition of public and commercial loans by industry (%)

Year	Type of loan	*Agriculture, Forestry, & Fisheries*	*Manufacturing*		Service[a]	Total
			HCI	*Light*		
1959–66	Public	7.5	11.7	8.3	72.4	100.0
	Commercial	22.3	43.4	31.4	2.9	100.0
1967–71	Public	42.2	6.8	1.6	49.4	100.0
	Commercial	3.6	31.6	23.9	40.8	100.0
1972–76	Public	18.2	6.1	0.0	75.8	100.0
	Commercial	2.2	42.4	23.7	31.7	100.0
1977–82	Public	17.0	1.5	0.3	81.2	100.0
	Commercial	0.6	46.0	10.6	42.8	100.0
1959–82	Public	19.0	3.0	0.4	77.6	100.0
	Commercial	1.6	43.6	15.4	39.5	100.0
	Total	9.6	24.9	8.5	57.0	100.0

Note:
[a] Service includes construction, electricity, transportation, etc.

Source: Cha (1986).

Table 11.7 Industrial structure and export composition: HCI trends, 1970–1988 (%)

	1970	*1975*	*1980*	*1985*	*1988*
Industrial structure					
Agriculture/fisheries	17.0	12.8	8.3	7.7	6.3
Mining	1.1	0.9	0.8	0.7	0.6
Manufacturing	40.3	50.4	51.0	50.0	52.7
Light	28.4	29.5	24.6	21.7	21.4
HCI	11.9	20.9	26.3	28.3	31.3
Petrochemical	5.9	10.8	12.6	11.4	10.0
Base metal	2.0	3.4	5.1	4.9	5.3
Metal/machinery	4.0	6.7	8.6	12.0	16.1
Power/gas/construction	9.8	7.7	10.2	10.4	9.3
Service	31.8	28.2	29.7	31.2	29.4
Total	100.0	100.0	100.0	100.0	100.0
Composition of exports					
Light	49.4	45.6	35.2	30.0	29.1
HCI	12.8	29.0	38.3	47.5	51.4
Petrochemical	5.4	9.2	9.9	12.4	11.0
Base metal	1.5	4.0	8.1	5.8	5.1
Metal/machinery	5.9	15.8	20.3	29.3	35.4

Source: Bank of Korea, 'Input-Output Tables,' various issues.

decade, the HCI share of total industrial output grew more than two and half times, and their share of exports tripled. Moreover, HCI shares of bank credits, output, and exports within the manufacturing sector also expanded rapidly over time (see Figure 11.3). It is obvious that without government intervention in the allocation of credit, the quick transformation of the industrial composition and discrete jump in the level of industrial development would not have been possible.

Impact on overall economic growth

Did the growth of these credit-supported sectors contribute to the rapid economic growth of Korea? In response to this question, we can only make tentative conclusions. In a sense, it is too early to answer, since Korea is still undergoing economic development and may not yet have fully realized the costs or benefits of financial policies. One solid conclusion pertains to the growth of exports, which was the main engine of rapid growth in Korea during the 1960s and 1970s. To the extent that credit support was indispensable to export growth, credit support, in turn, must have acted as the catalyst for rapid economic growth; but whether the extent of the subsidization implemented was necessary to propel the growth of exports remains questionable. However, the impact of credit support on the HCI drive and its subsequent effect on growth remains controversial (e.g., Amsden 1989; Stern

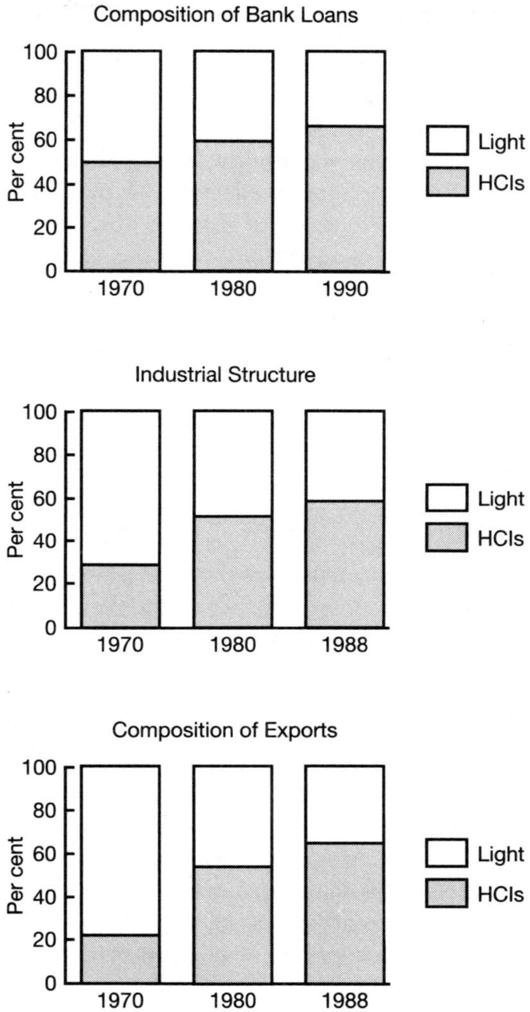

Figure 11.3 Significance of the HCI and Light Industries in the Manufacturing Sector: Trends

et al. 1992; Leipziger and Petri 1992; and World Bank 1987a). Although credit supports were influential in spurring the rapid development of the HCI, credit allocation might have been more efficient had it been allocated more equitably between the HCI and light industry—particularly given the labor endowment in the 1970s.[14] However, by the mid-1980s, the HCI did become the leading export industries in Korea; currently, HCI exports such as steel, metal, general machinery and equipment, electrical and chemical products, etc. constitute 66.1 per cent of Korea's total exports.

The effectiveness of credit policy as an industrial policy instrument

The impact of credit policies on economic growth is not limited to their effect on the cost of and access to credit. In an economy such as Korea's, in which the expansion of investment was financed by bank credit and foreign loans, the financial structure of firms was highly leveraged. By controlling financing, the government could become an effective risk partner for industrialists and motivate the latter's development of risk ventures and entrepreneurship. It could induce industrialists to adopt long-term business perspectives, while a competitive financial market might have prompted firms to take a shorter-term view (Cho and Hellmann 1993). In other words, by controlling financing, the government established a government-industry-bank coinsurance scheme to protect industrial firms from any unexpected circumstances. This indirect effect of government credit policy may also have been an important factor in the rapid industrialization of Korea.

Credit policy as an instrument for corporate governance

In Korea, state control over financing was the most powerful tool for inducing cooperation and compliance among businesses in the promotion of exports and industrialization. One of the distinct advantages of credit supports over other policy measures, such as fiscal subsidies, is that it gives the government greater leverage for implementing industrial policy (Cho and Hellmann 1993). Control over financing confers on the government some explicit right of governance over the borrowers for the entire period of their loans. Credit policies allow the government to allocate subsidies flexibly, according to the performance of supported firms or industries. In turn, such control extends to refinancing decisions—whether or not existing debt should be rolled over or new debt extended, and, if so, under what conditions. Well-measured refinancing decisions provide incentives: good performance can be rewarded with continued or expanded support; or inappropriate use of funds can be punished with a reduction in or even termination of support, an action that could make a firm's survival untenable. This carrot-and-stick policy underlying credit programs makes them effective tools of government industrial policy, being more effective than fiscal incentives, which stem from legislative initiation and are subject to the rigidity of the implementation process.[15]

But credit policies carry their own risk—the "risk of government failure." In Korea, the government's continuous communication with business leaders and close monitoring of firms through various channels (such as monthly export promotion meetings) helped reduce its risk of failure. Moreover, by controlling the banks, the government created incentives for firms to maximize their assets and growth, rather than to strive for immediate profitability. As long as they satisfied the government by expanding exports and successfully completing the construction of plants, firms ensured their continued credit support and survival. The government thus mitigated the risk of failure by adopting a sounder, more stable investment environment.

Credit control as an instrument for risk management

Industrial investment in Korea was financed largely by debt, especially during the period of rapid economic growth. Fiscal incentives and low interest rates allowed some firms to accumulate retained earnings, but, in the absence of a well-functioning domestic equity market, huge investment requirements for rapid industrial expansion had to be financed largely with bank loans and foreign debt. In the years 1963–71, the debt ratio of the Korean manufacturing sector increased more than fourfold, from 92 per cent to 394 per cent. Even in the 1990s, Korean firms remain highly leveraged, although their debt ratio in the second half of the 1980s declined somewhat with the expansion of the stock market. Consequently, Korean firms became more vulnerable to internal and external shocks.[16] In fact, Korea could have undergone several financial crises had the government not become actively involved in risk management through credit intervention.

The government implemented major corporate bail-outs in 1969–70, 1972, 1979–81, and 1984–88 to ride out recessions and avoid major financial crises. In the credit-based economy, the government made these bailouts by intervening in credit markets. The government's involvement in restructuring firms and industries and in redistributing losses made risk sharing possible among the members of the economy. Depositors usually incurred the lion's share of this cost, but were also beneficiaries, reaping subsequent rewards from the steady economic growth, increased job opportunities, and higher wages (Woo 1991). The overall size of the financial sector and the total saving rate grew rapidly in Korea although the banking system, subject to heavy government intervention, remained stagnant (Table 11.8).

11.3 AN OVERALL ASSESSMENT

In Korea, government intervention in the financial market was extensive during the process of economic development. The government owned the banking institution, controlled its interest rates, and directed a substantial portion of its loans. This allocation of credit was accompanied by substantial rent, and it constituted a major industrial policy instrument and tool for government control of industrial firms. This strategy—often called financial repression—is viewed by most economists as an ineffective way to achieve high economic growth. It is true that this policy stance in Korea also caused many problems. From time to time it led to the allocation of large amounts of credit to unsuccessful ventures, forcing the government to bail out firms and banks through monetary expansion. It inhibited the development of an efficient banking system and fostered economic concentration. However, the

Table 11.8 Growth of the financial sector (%)

Year	*M2/GNP*	*M3/GNP*	*Financial intermediation ratio*[a]	*Domestic saving ratios to GNI*[b]
1968	26.4	—	—	15.1
1969	32.7	—	—	18.8
1970	32.2	10.0	2.22	15.8
1971	31.7	37.4	2.23	14.7
1972	34.6	40.2	2.36	16.3
1973	36.8	44.5	2.43	22.2
1974	32.4	40.1	2.29	20.2
1975	31.1	38.5	2.26	18.7
1976	30.3	38.1	2.18	24.0
1977	33.0	42.2	2.28	27.4
1978	33.0	42.4	2.28	29.3
1979	32.0	43.3	2.29	28.8
1980	34.0	48.7	2.56	24.8
1981	34.3	51.4	2.71	25.1
1982	39.7	59.6	3.04	26.3
1983	36.9	61.3	3.07	29.6
1984	34.8	54.4	3.72	32.1
1985	36.0	69.9	3.94	32.4
1986	36.4	77.1	3.83	35.9
1987	36.7	85.3	3.79	38.5
1988	37.3	91.6	3.79	40.0
1989	39.6	104.0	4.25	36.8
1990	38.5	111.0	4.33	36.4
1991	39.1	113.9	4.40	36.7
1992	40.3	123.5	4.67	35.4
1993	42.5	132.4	—	35.3

Note:
[a] Domestic stock of financial assets/GNP (at current prices).
[b] Domestic saving ratio = GDP – final consumption expenditure.

Source: Bank of Korea.

Korean government targeted industrialization and achieved it by allocating cheap credit to large industrialists, forcing them to build industries and increase their exports, while threatening to withdraw the credit if they did not perform up to par. As an additional result, depositors were paid lower rates of return on their deposits but they were rewarded as wage-earners with the expansion of job opportunities and the increase in real wages. Rapid income increases contributed to the accumulation of domestic savings and the subsequent expansion of the financial market. What made this approach work in Korea, while similar policy initiatives led to unsuccessful developmental experiences elsewhere?

This question cannot be answered completely. Only a tentative conclusion can be asserted based on observations on the thrust of policy measures and the overall economic environment prevailing during the process of Korea's economic development. From the observations in this chapter, it is quite obvious that government intervention and the creation of economic rent as such does not contribute to rapid economic development. It could simply nurture widespread corruption in relation to rent-seeking behavior and help sustain economic backwardness, as was manifested in Korea in the 1950s. However, government intervention through the creation and distribution of rent could also be an effective industrial policy measure to help spur economic development, when it is managed carefully as part of a comprehensive economic development strategy with a clear vision.

The major difference between the experiences of Korea in the 1950s and those in the 1960s lay in the areas where rent was created (i.e., import versus export) and the ways it was distributed (i.e., discretionary versus rule based). Providing subsidy (rent) to the export sector, the development of which presented substantial externalities to the economy through the rapid upgrading of technology, etc., can contribute positively to growth in the early stages of development. Rent distribution linked to the performance of exporters in the international market helped expose domestic firms to international competition and encouraged mobilization of high-powered human as well as physical capital in the export sector. Despite the fact that interest rate control entailed substantial subsidies, the level of interest rates remained positive in real terms, and this allowed the rapid growth of financial savings in the 1960s. Although the government's intervention in the financial market and its control over financial institutions afforded it discretion in decision making on rent distribution, the criterion of distribution was monitored reasonably according to the economic development goals. However, when the focus of industrial policy was shifted to HCI development in the 1970s, more room was created for the discretionary allocation of rent, and the extent of rent (or financial repression) was also increased with the widened gap between controlled interest rates and the market rate. This also increased the cost of government intervention. The government was able to partially compensate for the consequently negative impact on financial sector growth by allowing the expansion of nonbank financial institutions and the securities market, which were less regulated during the 1970s.

Overall, what contributed most to the effectiveness of government intervention from the economic development standpoint seem to be effective economic management and the competitive business environment. In Korea, close consultation between government and business and the government's risk partnership with business made what could have been a very distorted investment approach into quite an effective developmental strategy. When the risk capital market was poorly developed, the Korean government controlled banks and effected a close relationship between government, banks, and industry, and thereby made itself an effective risk partner with industry. This implicit coinsurance scheme among the government, industries, and banks allowed the credit-based economy and its highly leveraged corporate firms to explore risky investment opportunities and to operate without the danger of major financial crisis.

However, the Korean experience also suggests that the cost of this approach can be substantial and can be exacerbated as economic development advances. The Korean policy strategy fueled rapid industrialization, but it also dampened efforts to develop an efficient banking system. The government's risk partnership with industrial firms placed a heavy burden on the banking system, loading it with large nonperforming loans, and raised social equity issues. Extensive government intervention in financing, especially in relation to low interest-rate ceilings, slowed the growth of financial savings. Korea was able to overcome this negative impact of government intervention by relying heavily on foreign borrowing. Korea's special relationship with the United States and Japan gave the country access to foreign loans. Furthermore, the perpetuation of strong government intervention in credit allocation when the industrial sector was well established and when economic organizations had become sophisticated placed Korea at greater risk of distorting the allocation of financial resources. The coinsurance scheme among government, industries, and banks fostered a moral hazard for banks and firms, despite contributing to the development of entrepreneurship and the expansion of industrial investment. Consequently, the government became captive to a vicious cycle of intervention. It also became captive to its own bureaucratic interests.

The overall lesson from the Korean experience is that it is possible for governments to intervene productively and effectively in the early stages of economic development. The balance between the role of government and market forces should reflect the financial market, industrial organization, market structure, and political and international environment that face the country. But as economic development advances, the role and scope of government intervention must be reappraised with a view toward fostering greater reliance on market forces.

ACKNOWLEDGMENTS

I am grateful for helpful comments from Masahiko Aoki, Hyung-Ki Kim, Masahiro Okuno-Fujiwara, and participants of seminars held for this project in Tokyo and Stanford.

NOTES

1 This estimate, however, should be qualified. In a sense, it is purely indicative because there is some doubt whether parallel market rates were at the equilibrium

rate. Furthermore, import restrictions allowed importers to monopolize the supply of certain goods, entailing additional rent.

2 The export credit program has been substantially reduced since the mid-1980s.

3 Central bank credit to commercial banks constituted 20–30 per cent of total loans extended by the latter during the 1970s.

4 Again the rent estimate here may have been exaggerated because it is doubtful that the curb market rate was the equilibrium rate when the financial market was liberalized.

5 For example, McKinnon (1973) and Shaw (1973).

6 See Hellmann, Murdock, and Stiglitz, Chapter 6 in this volume.

7 For instance, the central bank's rediscount rate for export bills was 3.5 percent in the years 1964–75.

8 See Cho and Kim (1995) and Kim (1990,1994) for detailed discussion on the two impacts of the decree.

9 According to Nam, then Minister of Finance, he was compelled to establish the NIF, given the importance of the heavy industry program, for project financing, thereby attempting to minimize the burden on banking operations.

10 This part relies on the analysis by Cho and Kim (1995).

11 Here, the export subsidy is estimated based on the gap between average bank loan rates and the export loan rate. If it was estimated based on the gap between the curb market rate and the export loan rate, as done in this volume by Hellmann, Murdock, and Stiglitz (see Chapter 6), the amount of the subsidy would be much higher.

12 It is asserted that since Korean export growth was based on the expansiön of manufactured exports, the technological effect of export marketing and the informational externality was substantial (see Kim and Roemer 1979, World Bank 1987b).

13 This reflects the fact that the Korean government's credit allocation favored the manufacturing sector over other sectors.

14 But in terms of dynamic efficiency, heavy HCI investment might have had some merits.

15 However, the benefits of the flexibility of credit policies cannot be taken for granted. In particular, poor information on behalf of creditors may turn their potential effectiveness into a large hazard, because renegotiations and refinancing decisions involve delicate trade-offs. In order to use credit effectively as a selection and incentive device, creditors should have the ability to understand two crucial aspects of a firm's performance. First, in order to provide an effective incentive scheme, the creditor should be able to distinguish external factors from managerial performance. Second, in order to make effective selection decisions among external factors, creditors should be able to distinguish cyclical influences from structural ones; in particular, they should have good information on whether financial distress is due to temporary or permanent problems.

16 This is, to some extent, the result of the government-led industrial financing strategy.

REFERENCES

Amsden, A. (1989), *Asia's Next Giant: South Korea and Late Industrialization*, Oxford University Press, Oxford.

Cha, D.-S. (1986), *Waekuk Jabon Doyip Hoykya eui Bonseok* (An analysis of the effect of foreign capital inflow), Korean Institute for Economics and Technology, Seoul.

Cho, Y. J. and Kim, J.-K. (1995), "Credit Policies and Industrialization of Korea," World Bank Discussion Papers, No. 286.

—— and Hellman, T. (1993), "Government Intervention in Credit Markets in Japan and Korea: An Alternative Interpretation from the New Institutional Economics Perspective," PRE Working Paper Series No. 1190, World Bank, *Seoul Journal of Economics*, 7(4).

Kim, C.-Y. (1990), *Hankuk Kyungje Jeongchaek Samship yeon sa* (A 30-year history of Korean economic development policy: a memoir), Seoul Joong-ang and Ilbosa, Seoul.

—— (1994), "Policy Making on the Front Lines: Memoirs of a Korean Practitioner, 1945–1979," EDI Retrospectives in Policy Making, World Bank, Washington.

Kim, K. S. and Roemer, M. (1979), *Growth and Structural Transformation*, Harvard Institute for International Development, Cambridge, Mass.

Leipziger, D. M. and Petri, P. A. (1992), 'Korean Industrial Policy: Legacies of the Past and Directions for the Future," unpublished manuscript.

McKinnon, R. (1973), *Money and Capital in Economic Development*, Brookings Institution, Washington.

Nam, D.-W. (1979), "Korea's Economic Take-off in Retrospect," paper presented at the Second Washington Conference of the Korea-America Association.

Rhee, Y.-W. (1989), "Trade Finance in Developing Countries," Policy and Research Series, No. 5, World Bank.

Shaw, E. (1973), *Financial Deepening in Economic Development*, Oxford University Press, New York.

Stern, J. *et al.* (1992), *Industrialization and the State: The Korean Heavy and Chemical Industry Drive*, Harvard Institute for International Development, Cambridge, Mass.

Woo, J.-E. (1991), *Race to the Swift: State and Finance in Korean Industrialization*, Columbia University Press, New York.

World Bank (1987a), *Korea: Managing the Industrial Transition*, World Bank, Washington.

—— (1987b), *World Development Report 1987*, Oxford University Press, Oxford.

Yoon, Y.-J. (1991), "Hankuk eui Kyungje Sungjang Kwajung aesu ei Jungbu Gaeyip Jidae Chuku Hwaldong ae kwanhan Yeonku" (A study on government intervention and rent-seeking behavior in Korean economic development), master's thesis, School of Public Administration, Seoul National University, Seoul.

12

TAIWAN'S INDUSTRIAL POLICY IN THE 1980s

An Appraisal

Heather Smith

12.I Introduction

The rapid postwar economic growth of Taiwan has raised many questions relating to its possible causes. While populist debate on the relationship between industrial policy and economic growth has traditionally dwelt on the Japanese experience, there has been a progressive shift towards examining the role of government in the economic growth of other East Asian economies.

This paper focuses on Taiwan's industrial policy during the 1980s and the government's attempt to shift the economy away from a reliance on labour-intensive industries towards the development of technology-intensive products and industries. Though widely used, the term "industrial policy" has no standard definition. Yue (1993, pp. 16–17) provides a broad definition of industrial policy as one that aims to promote new and/or sunrise and strategic industries, protect adjustment assistance of ailing and declining industries, upgrade existing industries and promote technological development, exports, regional dispersion, and so on. A narrower definition sees industrial policy as targeting or "picking winners". In reviewing Taiwan's industrial policy, this paper employs the latter definition.

12.I.1 The structuralist model

During the 1980s two sources of heterodoxy – the governed-market model and new trade or strategic trade model – emerged to challenge the mainstream neo-classical explanation of East Asian development.[1] According to the governed-market model, East Asia's rapid industrialization has "resulted from the state deployment of a range of industrial promotion policies, including ones to intensify the growth of selected industries" (Wade, 1990a, p. 370). Wade argues that in Taiwan, as well as in Northeast Asia generally,

Source: Asian Economic Journal, Vol. 11(1), March 1997.

governments have guided or governed market processes of resource allocation so as to produce production and investment outcomes different from those that would have occurred in a free market. Government intervention of a "leadership" kind is considered to have focused on industries which are capital intensive, or which use technology that must be imported from a small number of potential suppliers (Wade, 1990a, p.303). The state is thought to have anticipated shifts in comparative advantage and intervened aggressively to develop national champions for international markets (Wade, 1984, p.65). Leadership is thus applied to a shifting band of industries (Wade, 1990b, p.249). In turn, sector-specific interventions are supported by a certain kind of organization of the state and the private sector. In particular, the corporatist and authoritarian political arrangements of East Asia are said to have provided the basis for market guidance.

In the case of Taiwan, it is argued, Taiwan's industrial policy since the 1950s has been characterized as having had two objectives – encouraging exports and promoting infant industries (Wade, 1990a, 1990b). Exports have been promoted using policies largely thought to be neutral (Lee and Liang, 1982), exhibiting an absence of differential effects on the allocation of resources among activities relative to free trade. Non-neutral policies have focused on promoting infant industries. In so far as government policies have affected economic outcomes, improved industrial performance and export growth are believed to have resulted from the coordinated use of both kinds of policy. While asserting the object of industrial policy has been quite different in each development phase, the governed-market model argues that, in general, it has worked to change comparative advantage in anticipation of changing market conditions. In the 1980s, Taiwan's government is considered to have continued its role as facilitator of industrial growth in response to the pressures of technological upgrading. Implicit then is a rejection of the notion that government became less dirigiste as industrialization proceeded, at least at this stage of development.

On this view, an emphasis on trade considerations is secondary to technological ones in searching for an understanding of industrialization that is relevant to policy making. When technological change rather than trade is emphasized as the centrepiece of industrialization, an economic rationale for selective industrial promotion then follows for two reasons. First, because comparative advantage is not simply the result of given endowments, but also rests on the accumulated capital and skills which can be enhanced by a long-term national strategy. Secondly, because some sectors and products are more important to the economy's future growth prospects than others (Wade, 1988, pp. 152–153). Industry policy interventions are thought to have been motivated by the belief that shifting the industrial structure towards increasingly sophisticated sectors would increase the opportunities for capturing dynamic scale economies that result from learning. The presence of externalities or "spillover" effects is thought to have provided the grounds for industry-specific interventions so that the incentive structure was correcting for such market failures.

Similarly, Amsden (1990), in arguing that Taiwan represents a successful case of etatism, has also emphasized the role that state capitalism played in the emergence of Taiwan's economy. It is suggested that the reason East Asian economies have grown faster than other late-industrializers is not because of markets operating more freely and because they "got relative prices right", but rather that governments have intervened more effectively.[2] These economies are thus thought to have succeeded by "getting relative prices wrong", by deliberately distorting prices with a variety of subsidies when extensive currency devaluations and other policies to liberalize the price mechanism failed to create competitiveness (Amsden, 1990).

While the government market model was gaining prominence, some economists were developing a new theoretical rationale for active intervention by government to pursue a "strategic trade policy". Krugman (1984, 1987) sought to encapsulate empirically what Givens (1982) referred to as the Japanese "narrow moving band". The government, it was said, targets a series of new industries in succession, leaving subsidies in place just long enough for long-run competitiveness to be assured. In this way, industries are "sliced off" one after another. Baldwin and Krugman (1988) suggest that this policy may have been adopted by Japan as a means of overcoming the "early start" advantage of the United States semiconductor industry and enabling Japan's industry to become a significant exporter of the 16K random access memory chip. Other East Asian economies are said to have used similar policies to establish export industries.

From the mid-1980s, much of the more informal academic discussion of strategic trade theory increasingly emphasized externalities as a reason for protecting or promoting strategic sectors. Krugman (1992, p. 436) and other, predominantly US, academics raised the possibility that a country could advance its standard of living at the expense of other countries by systematically promoting industries subject to external economies of a particular kind.[3] They cited the importance to modern industrial competition of economies of scale, of learning-by-doing, and of externalities stemming from research and development. These "dynamic effects" associated with the development of "strategic" high-technology industries were said to provide productivity-enhancing spillover effects. Such industries were also said to show rapid growth in productivity, to be marked by rapid reductions in cost over time, to exhibit high value added per worker, and to have substantial barriers to late entrants and first-mover advantages which tend to create imperfectly competitive market structures. Support for industries possessing these characteristics was therefore crucial if a country was to stay at the technological frontier (Tyson, 1990).

Much of this research emerged from the United States at a time of increasing American fears of an East Asian challenge in trade and technology. A number of authors argued that the Japanese government's targeting of industries on the basis of their technological potential was the foundation of Japan's dramatic competitive success in world markets (Dosi, Tyson and Zysman, 1989, pp. 3–34). Other East Asian governments were considered to have been accomplished practitioners of such policies through the course of their industrialization (Tyson, 1992, p.4). Richardson (1991, p.38) in a survey of the new trade literature and its relevance to the Pacific region notes that

> American and European perceptions are that selected Asian technological protectionism and trade-policy activism have actually succeeded . . . [they] have come to believe that Japan, Korea, and probably Singapore and Taiwan as well, have been the most accomplished practitioners of new-view trade policies. Out of that perception comes the desire to establish new ground rules, to "even the playing field".

New trade theories, emphasising the role of scale, learning, and market structure, have also been said to be more relevant to the developing countries, because of their small and imperfect markets, than to the industrialized world for which most of the writing on them has been intended (Krugman, 1986; Rodrik 1988). Yet while increasingly being applied in the context of developing countries, the theoretically-based new trade literature has by and large not focused on the debate surrounding East Asian industrial development. The governed-market model on the other hand has sought support for selective government intervention, by drawing on the insights of the new trade literature.[4]

12.I.2 The neoclassical model

In characterizing East Asia's experience, the mainstream neoclassical approach has been to argue that, while interventionist at varying stages, these economies ensured their trade regimes were more neutral between import substitution and export activities than most economies. This facilitated specialization on the basis of comparative advantage. In other words, local prices of traded goods, on average, departed much less from world prices than in other developing regions, even though there were substantial variations for some individual items and for some countries. Neoclassicists stressed that the economically successful economies were by and large those that had "got their prices right" and had not greatly inhibited market signals driving resource allocation. Great importance is attached to the ongoing process of trade liberalization and strengthening of the market mechanism in maintaining the growth momentum.

On this view, government industrial policy interventions are not the *sine qua non*. Rather good macroeconomic management is thought to account for superior economic performance. Specifically, the soundness of underlying policies – fiscal, monetary, financial, trade, labour and infrastructure – determined the speed, sustainability and equity of growth (Hughes, 1993).

In highlighting the disadvantages of interventionist industrial policy the neoclassical school did not argue that the state had no role to play in the process of economic development. Mainstream neoclassical economists stressed that "dynamic" effects, such as learning-by-doing and externalities arising from R&D, provided the strongest, if not the only valid, reason for promoting industrialization in the sense of allocating resources between industries on a discriminatory basis (Corden, 1974). Functional measures, such as across-the-board R&D incentives, provision of training facilities and incentives to develop a broad-based venture capital market, were advocated rather than industry and firm-specific interventions (Baldwin, 1969).

In the case of Taiwan, Ranis and Mahmood (1992, pp. 116–117) contend that the government has been active in the creation of a favourable environment for economic growth, but has successfully resisted the temptation to push growth beyond its "natural levels", maintaining policy flexibility in response to changing economic conditions. Fiscal and monetary policy remained restrained and flexible, with the government refraining from intervening heavily and, to the extent that it did intervene, exhibiting political courage by relying on overt rather than covert means of transferring resources either to itself or private interest groups. The end result was not only a consistent increase in Taiwan's external orientation, but also much higher average rates of growth, achieved with an egalitarian distribution of income.

The market guidance by the Taiwan government was thus of a special form. This involved: guiding the market economy in response to world demand and supply changes by maintaining control over the money supply and avoiding deficit spending; maintaining a proper exchange rate, enabling market forces to equilibrate around a pegged rate; and the continual encouragement of economic structural change to help deployment of resources, again in accordance with market forces.

While the initial choice of appropriate labour-intensive technologies and sectors in response to relatively undistorted price signals was important in increasing both output and employment in the early decades of rapid growth, the ability to adjust to a rapidly growing capital to labour ratio, growing real wages and changing international product markets, required considerable flexibility. The shift to new industries characterized by more capital- and technology-intensive processes and the adoption of new technologies was facilitated by a simultaneous growth in the level of education (Pack, 1992, p. 102).

According to both the new-trade and governed-market models, the role of the state in Taiwan during the 1980s was one of orchestrating the technological upgrading of the economy. To evaluate this proposition, this paper focuses on the Taiwan government's adoption in the early 1980s of a "strategic industrial policy" designed to provide preferential finance to high technology industries. This is used to assess whether the incentive structure was specifically designed to promote strategic industries? Was the allocation of resources to the "strategic" industries important in influencing this sector's development? Answering these questions can in turn provide an insight into whether the Taiwan government became more or less *dirigiste* over the 1980s.

The Section 12.II of this paper discusses the structure of incentives to industry over 1980s. The Taiwan government's policy response to changing economic circumstances was quite different from that of past decades as it came under increased external pressure to liberalize, and was faced with the domestic problem of declining industries. While addressing these concerns via a programme of trade liberalization, the government also sought to foster specific industries to shift the economy away from a reliance on labour-intensive industries towards the development of technology-intensive industries. This section discusses this dual policy, evaluates the effectiveness of preferential fiscal and financial measures directed to industry during the 1980s and assesses whether the incentive structure discriminated among traded-goods industries. Section 12.III then evaluates the government's implementation of a strategic industrial policy. This provides an interesting test case for the evaluation of the propositions put forth by new-trade theory. In Section 12.IV the Taiwan experience is drawn on to highlight the practical limitations and shortcomings of new-trade theory when various policy implications are taken into account. In particular, the problems associated with identifying what constitutes a high technology and strategic industry are considered, as are the criteria used by the government to select strategic industries. This discussion informs the question of whether the government's policy possessed a forward-looking rational view on how the industrial structure should evolve. Conclusions follow in Section 12.V.

12.II EVALUATION OF TRADE AND INDUSTRIAL INCENTIVES

Despite rapid export expansion in the 1960s and 1970s, by the early 1980s the Taiwan economy was facing a number of structural pressures. Persistent trade surpluses were placing heavy upward pressure on the exchange value of the New Taiwan (NT) dollar and intensifying trade friction with the United States. In response to US pressure and several other factors, such as US retaliatory actions against Japan, the passage of the US Omnibus Trade and Competitive Act in 1988, and withdrawal of Generalized System of Preference (GSP) trade concessions treatment, Taiwan announced in 1989 the adoption of an official policy of diversifying its export trade away from the United States.[5]

However, Taiwan's trade surpluses have created pressures to liberalize quite separately from US pressure. Haggard (1988) notes that the surpluses gave new impetus to trade liberalization on purely economic grounds and that

Taiwan became a target of US attention precisely as a result of domestic policies that contributed to external imbalance. Hence the adjustment process demanded went beyond exchange rate adjustments to encompass broader reforms.

By the 1980s the industrial sector was subject to a number of domestic pressures. A labour shortage had been gradually apparent in the manufacturing sector since the late 1970s, and more so after the mid-1980s, resulting in firms relocating industrial activities offshore to mainland China and Southeast Asia. Labour costs rose as a result of this labour shortage, following the introduction in 1984 of the Labour Standard Laws, which were designed to improve working conditions. The average monthly wage, which increased in real annual terms by 6.5% during 1981–86, increased by 11.4% between 1986 and 1990. Rising living standards led to a greater community awareness of environmental concerns with the government imposing increasingly stringent pollution control standards. Requirements on firms in polluting industries to meet these standards also contributed to cost pressures.

In addition to domestic pressures, a number of external factors were affecting the industrial sector. Developing countries in Southeast Asia and mainland China began to move into producing light industrial products, placing pressure on Taiwan to upgrade its export composition. In the early 1980s, rising protectionism in US markets towards Taiwan's exports of textiles and consumer goods induced Taiwan to change the composition of its exports and diversify its markets by seeking other trading partners. This, in turn, required Taiwan's export industries to increase competitiveness without the burden of protection and subsidies to inefficient industries.

In recognizing that structural adjustment of the economy required a more liberal environment, the government in 1984 announced its intention to promote a strategy of economic liberalization and internationalization of the economy (see Schive, 1994, 1995). A trade surplus reduction programme was announced. This included the relaxation of foreign exchange and interest rate controls, the lifting of foreign investment restrictions and tariff reductions. These measures were aimed at ensuring that domestic demand, rather than foreign demand, became the driving force behind future industrial development.[6]

The rapid development of science-based technology in developed countries meant that industrial upgrading required a more liberal policy with regard to direct foreign investment. As an increasing number of domestic producers became foreign subsidiaries, the rationale for protecting domestic producers no longer held. Policies to support domestic producers could end up supporting foreign subsidiaries, contrary to the government's desire to increase technology transfer as a means of enhancing indigenous technological capabilities. Table 12.1 shows how technology-intensive industries gradually took over the role of traditional industries in exports with this trend accelerating after 1986.

Table 12.1 Distribution of exports by industry, Taiwan: 1982–94

Year	*1982*	*1983*	*1984*	*1985*	*1986*	*1987*	*1988*	*1989*	*1990*	*1991*	*1992*	*1993*	*1994*
Total	100	100	100	100	100	100	100	100	100	100	100	100	100
Agriculture, forestry and fishing	2.2	2.1	1.8	1.7	1.7	1.4	1.6	1.0	0.8	0.9	0.9	0.8	0.7
Processed food	5.0	4.5	4.0	4.3	4.7	4.5	3.7	3.6	3.5	3.6	3.3	3.2	3.2
Beverages and tobacco	0.1	0.1	0.0	0.0	0.0	0.0	0.0	0.0	0.0	0.0	0.1	0.1	0.1
Energy and minerals	0.0	0.1	0.1	0.1	0.1	0.1	0.1	0.1	0.1	0.0	0.0	0.1	0.0
Construction materials	0.7	0.8	0.6	0.5	0.4	0.3	0.4	0.3	0.2	0.2	0.2	0.2	0.1
Intermediate products A*	8.8	7.9	7.5	8.7	7.4	6.9	8.7	9.0	9.5	9.5	9.4	10.0	11.3
Intermediate products B*	25.7	26.5	26.4	26.8	26.0	26.5	27.7	31.0	34.9	37.0	39.1	41.2	43.5
Consumer non-durable goods	35.5	35.7	36.5	35.5	35.3	33.3	29.7	27.4	23.7	22.0	19.8	17.0	14.6
Consumer durable goods	12.3	12.7	11.6	10.3	11.7	11.9	11.2	10.3	8.9	8.5	8.0	7.8	7.3
Machinery	6.5	7.6	9.8	10.3	10.8	13.1	15.4	15.5	16.3	16.1	17.2	17.4	16.8
Transportation equipment	3.2	2.0	1.7	1.7	1.9	1.9	1.5	1.9	2.1	2.1	2.0	2.3	2.3
Share of technology-intensive exports	25.3	26.0	27.2	27.0	27.6	30.0	33.7	33.9	35.9	36.3	37.9	40.1	42.1

Notes: Intermediate products A are products that can be used for consumer goods or producer goods after processing.
Intermediate products B are products that can be used for consumer goods or producer goods without processing.

Source: The Republic of China; Department of Statistics, Ministry of Finance, Taipei. *Monthly Statistics of Exports and Imports, Taiwan Area*, Table 7; February 1992, pp. 327–328; October 1995, pp. 353–354.

12.II.1 Trade policy measures

Although a policy of economic liberalization was announced in 1984, actual implementation took several years to gain momentum. Under the pressure of excess foreign exchange reserves and the threat of US "Super 301" retaliatory action, the process of trade reform speeded up after 1986.[7] The reduction of tariffs and removal of remaining import restrictions was considered necessary to smooth trading relationships, to foster the upgrading of the industrial structure and to strengthen international competitiveness. On the other hand, the tariff structure has at times been adjusted fragmentarily in response to foreign pressure with little attempt to revise and simplify the entire tariff structure based on a clear conception of the economic rationale in view (Lee et al., 1975). Trade liberalization measures have also met with resistance from various interest groups, particularly from within the agricultural sector and sectors within manufacturing, such as the automobile industry (Tu and Wang, 1988).

Table 12.2 indicates that the average nominal tariff rate remained above 40% throughout the 1950s, 1960s and 1970s. Despite gradual liberalization, tariff rates in fact still remained relatively high until the mid-1980s. In 1974 the average nominal tariff rate for all importables was 55.7%. The pace of liberalization accelerated after 1985 with the nominal rate falling from 30.8% to 8.9% between 1985 and 1990 for the so-called Column II countries.[8] The average tariff burden (total tariff revenue as a percentage of the total value of imports)[9] fell from 7.9% to 5.9% over the same period (Hsueh, 1992, p. 9). As a result, 96% of tariff rates on industrial items were lower than 15% by 1990 compared with 34% in 1986. Moreover, 58% of the rates were lower than 5%. Under the government's "Four-Year (1989–92) Tariff Reduction Plan", the effective real tariff rate was further reduced to 4.2%, which is the average of the OECD countries.

Non-tariff barriers began to be lowered from the early 1970s. The percentage of permitted import items, or the import liberalization ratio, rose from 57.1% in 1970 to 97.0% by the late 1980s. However, as Table 12.3 shows, of the permissible imports, only 11% were free from import licences, with many other items subject to other forms of import restriction.[10] After 1985 items free from import licences increased to 31.4%, reaching 65.7% by 1991. Also, the number of items restricting applicants who could qualify, and the origin of the imported products criteria, were sharply reduced over the period. While non-tariff barriers are no longer used as instruments to protect domestic industries, some restrictions still apply to particular sources of origin, and the status of applicants.

In the past Taiwan has imposed local content requirements which have affected parts of such industries as machinery (tractors), electrical equipment (colour televisions, video recorders and refrigerators), and transport equipment (motorcycles, bicycles and heavy sedans). These restrictions were

Table 12.2 List of tariff changes, Taiwan (percentages)

	Average nominal tariff rate (%)			*Amended items*			
Year	*Column I countries*		*Column II countries*	*Reduction*	*Free*	*Increase*	*Average tariff burden*
1955	"	"	"	"	"	"	38.2
1965	"	"	"	"	"	"	16.5
1970	"	"	"	"	"	"	16.1
1971	"	"	"	242	39	171	14.1
1972	"	"	"	415	0	53	12.1
1973	"	"	"	94	4	16	12.6
1974	"	55.65	"	202	2	7	11.7
1975	"	52.69	"	71	0	13	9.9
1976	"	49.13	"	44	11	19	11.4
1977	"	46.17	"	159	4	14	10.4
1978	"	43.58	"	996	16	119	11.3
1979	"	39.14	"	432	21	16	11.6
1980	35.96	n.a.	31.17	1604	23	10	9.0
1981	35.96	n.a.	31.17	0	0	0	7.5
1982	35.95	n.a.	31.03	106	5	124	7.6
1983	35.95	n.a.	31.04	0	0	0	7.6
1984	35.95	n.a.	30.81	281	2	23	7.7
1985	32.79	n.a.	26.46	1058	35	1	7.9
1986	21.77	n.a.	22.83	777	25	11	7.7
1987	"	n.a.	19.37	1599	15	6	7.5
1988	"	n.a.	12.57	3377	142	"	6.2
1989	"	n.a.	9.73	4738	"	"	5.1
1990	"	n.a.	8.90	"	"	"	5.9

Notes:
1. Average tariff burden is defined as the collected tariff revenue weighted by total import value.
2. Column I countries refer to those countries that do not grant preferential tariffs to Taiwan, while Column II countries do grant preferential tariffs to Taiwan.

Sources:
a. Table 4, Kuo (1991, p. 135). Derived from Customs Import Tariff Table, The Inspectorate General of Customs, Ministry of Finance, Republic of China.
b. Table 2, Tu and Wang (1988, p. 67).
c. Figures for 1990 are from Hsueh (1992, p. 9).

designed to foster linked parts and components industries but have also resulted in the maintenance of higher prices and lower quality relative to imports (Wu, 1991). From 1989, local content requirements have applied only to the automobile industry.

12.II.2 Fiscal incentives

The most influential fiscal incentive scheme for investment was the Statute for the Encouragement of Investment (SEI). Available to both domestic and

Table 12.3 Type of permissible imports, Taiwan

	Total permissible imports		*Free of import licences*		*Restricting applicants' qualifications*		*Restrictiong origins of imported products*	
	No. of items	*% of total*	*No. of items*	*% of total*	*No. of items*	*% of total*	*No. of items*	*% of total*
1983, 8	25.640	96.4	2,805	10.5	628	2.4	1,610	6.1
1983, 12	25,827	97.1	2,986	11.2	372	1.4	124	0.5
1984, 12	25,968	97.1	2,937	11.0	339	1.3	125	0.5
1985, 12	26,065	97.4	8,412	31.4	330	1.2	99	0.4
1986, 12	26,270	98.1	11,477	42.9	271	1.0	64	0.2
1987, 12	26,426	98.3	11,457	42.6	226	0.8	58	0.2
1988, 12	26,472	98.5	11,454	42.6	165	0.6	58	0.2
1989, 1	8,519	97.0	5,849	66.6	93	1.1	41	0.5
1989, 1	8,610	97.3	5,887	66.5	86	1.0	42	0.5
1989, 12	8,715	97.2	5,928	66.2	43	0.5	51	0.6
1991, 1	8,758	97.3	5,918	65.7	43	0.5	46	0.5

Notes:
1. There was a change of classifications in January 1989.
2. Since January 1990, import licences have been abolished.

Sources:
a. Table 6, Kuo (1991, p. 138), Derived from the Board of Foreign Trade, Ministry of Economic Affairs, Republic of China; and Kuo (1991).
b. Table 1, Tu and Wang (1998, p. 66).

foreign firms, the SEI was in force between 1961 and 1990, during which period it was revised several times. The primary purpose of this statute was to encourage and channel investment into areas considered important for economic development. The emphasis of the statute in the 1960s was to encourage the establishment and enlargement of exporting industries; in the 1970s to encourage capital-intensive industries; and in the 1980s to encourage technology-intensive industries. Over time, however, the objectives and incentive measures available under the SEI have become more complex, with the statute serving as a policy instrument guiding enterprise economic behaviour in such areas as export, pollution control, R&D and energy conservation. As a result of these additions, the targets for encouragement have continuously been increased and the items receiving encouragement have been enlarged, resulting in a complicated tax reduction system.

Under the statute, a "productive enterprise" conforming to certain categories of, and criteria for, encouragement were eligible for several major fiscal incentives during the 1980s. "Newly established" and "newly expanded" productive enterprise could choose from either a tax exemption of four or five years respectively, or accelerated depreciation on machinery and equipment. Under the accelerated depreciation option offered, an enterprise could reduce the service life of machinery and equipment to five years for machines whose service life was more than ten years, or by half for those whose service life was less than ten, and by one-third for buildings, construction, communications and transportation facilities.

The accelerated depreciation option served as an alternative to tax exemption, but very few enterprises chose to take it up. Prior to 1987 only twenty-one enterprises applied for accelerated depreciation, while thousands of enterprises applied for tax exemption (Chung-hua Institution for Economic Research, 1987). While the accelerated depreciation option was expected to become more popular as the economy underwent industrial restructuring and more capital and technology-intensive production techniques were adopted, the number of applicants did not increase significantly. This option was obviously beneficial for a firm engaged in capital-intensive production with heavy investment in long-service-life machinery or equipment. However, most enterprises in Taiwan are small and medium-sized enterprises, operating under labour-intensive production technology.

The income tax rate for "ordinary" productive enterprises was reduced in 1977 from 30% to 25% and since 1987 "important productive enterprises" have been eligible for an income tax ceiling of 20%.[11] A productive enterprise could also apply for a tax credit for the purchase of machinery and equipment ranging from 5% to 20%. The tax credit was introduced in 1981 and discontinued between 1984 and the first half of 1985. The effectiveness of the tax credit was somewhat controversial and the measure was discontinued in 1990.

In addition, a productive enterprise could be exempted from import duties or had the option to use an instalment plan for paying duties on machinery purchased from abroad.[12] This helped enterprises to lower capital costs to some extent when import duties were high, but the importance of the measures diminished as tariff rates and other surcharges were progressively lowered (Chou and Wu, 1991, p. 13).

Other tax benefits included incentives: for research and development; for promoting the rationalization of enterprises through merger and consolidation; for acquisition of land for industrial use; and for the purchase of machinery and equipment for energy conservation.

In 1987 the Taiwan government initiated a long-term research project to evaluate the effectiveness of the SEI.[13] Research institutions were contracted to conduct a series of studies on Taiwan's industrial organization, to evaluate industrial policy measures and to review government incentive schemes. The study concluded that, while extensive tax relief might have been useful in speeding up economic development in the past, it was no longer suitable for a maturing economy. The intervention was seen as resulting in distorted resource allocation, and it was considered highly questionable whether the results of government intervention justified the costs in lost taxes. The report concluded that:

- excessive tax exemptions and deductions were causing an unfair distribution of the tax burden;
- complications of the law were creating insurmountable difficulties in tax administration;
- the incentives had created entrenched interest groups that were hampering the establishment of a fair tax system; and
- the correlation between favoured enterprises and their productivity and profitability was low (Chung-Hua Institution for Economic Research, 1987).

The majority of the tax revenue losses due to the enforcement of the SEI occurred during the 1980s. This tax revenue loss of NT$290.5 billion was equivalent to 6.8% of the total tax revenue collected over the period 1981–90.[14]

More specifically, the report noted[15] that in the initial stages of industrial development the statute was quite effective in encouraging an increase in investment but that the effectiveness of tax reductions had lessened over time. While the five-year tax exemption was estimated to have reduced the investment costs for firms by some 20%, and the number of firms benefiting from tax exemptions or reductions had increased, the growth rate of total investment had not been obviously enhanced. Moreover, measures used to accelerate depreciation were found not to be as effective as tax exemptions and reductions, while measures to encourage business mergers, R&D and environmental protection were also all thought to have had limited effectiveness for the following reasons:

- the motivation behind encouraging R&D was based on the potential for expected development and the pursuit of profit-making, so that preferential tax reductions and exemptions had not been a major element;
- the motivation behind merging of enterprises, in seeking to reduce expenses, coordinate manpower and technology, and control access to marketing, had little to do with tax reductions and tax exemptions;
- the effect of encouraging the prevention of industrial pollution had not been significant, given that the equipment for curbing pollution was not capital that generated profits;
- measures for encouraging energy saving were considered insignificant since the price of energy still did not reflect real cost; and
- investment credits, while stimulating investment, particularly during a period of recession, could not be employed as a long-term instrument (Yu, 1988).

At the time of promulgation the basic philosophy underlying the SEI was that an economy will undergo certain stages of development, and at each stage there are certain key industries which through various linkages will bring about development of the entire economy. This strategy assumed government officials knew what those key industries were and what policy measures should be adopted to develop those industries (Hou, 1988, p. 48). In recent years, though there has been an increasing awareness among government officials that it is difficult to pick the right industries or winners, if indeed such winners can be identified in advance; and that selective protective measures may not be effective. This view has been reinforced by several other studies into government incentives to industry. One study, for example, based on input–output tables for the 1970s and 1980s, found no significant relationship between tariff protection and growth rates of industries when industries are classified according to market orientation (for export or for the domestic market) or according to value added (Hou, 1988, p. 49).[16] Another study (Sun, 1985) suggested that government measures designed to encourage investment in certain selected industries had little effect. Rather it was found that investment decisions were primarily determined by persistent increases in sales which government officials were not in a position to determine beforehand. Interest burden and tax deductions were found to be insignificant in influencing investment decisions.

Consensus was reached by the Taiwan government in 1990 that the encouragement of targeted products and industries should be discontinued. A substantial modification was made to the system of fiscal incentives and the more function-oriented Statute for the Upgrading of Industry (SUI) was adopted in 1990 to replace the specific industry-oriented SEI. The SUI does not single out any specific industry for special tax treatment, but provides tax benefits to all industries for certain generic types of investment, such as R&D, manpower training and anti-pollution measures. Hence it is not a targeting measure, since all benefits are available to all industries. The following incentives are available under the SUI:

- industries using selective technologies are eligible for accelerated depreciation and tax credits of 5 to 20% relating to R&D, manpower training, pollution control, industrial equipment, energy conservation and international marketing;
- in the case of merger or consolidation, a company is exempted from stamp tax and deed tax;
- tax benefits are available for acquisition of land for industrial use;
- exemption is allowed from personal income tax for royalties derived from patents or computer software;
- companies which invest overseas may set aside a tax free reserve of up to 20% of their total outward investment to cover investment losses; and
- tax incentives are provided for the encouragement of purchase of machinery and equipment for energy conservation.

12.II.3 Financial incentives

The Taiwan government has also at various times adopted selective credit rationing policies to accommodate the financing needs of some specific industries, economic activities or borrower groups, in order to promote economic growth or to equalize to some extent the availability of bank loans among borrower groups (Yang, 1990, p. 19). The most important of these have been the export financing policy[17] and the strategic industry financing policy. The export financing policy is discussed briefly below while the strategic industry financing policy is discussed in greater detail in the following section.

Since the 1960s, export activities have been granted special low interest loans to provide pre-shipment finance and for the importation of raw materials.[18] The difference between the export loan rate and the minimum interest rate for secured loans is illustrated in Table 12.4. With continuous trade surpluses and accumulated foreign exchange reserves, the interest rate differential has narrowed over the past decade and the margin of preference for exports has diminished. Other forms of finance available to exporters have also been considerably wound back since the mid-1980s.

But while the financial system in Taiwan is considered to have effectively mobilized domestic savings, its performance in allocating funds during the 1980s was subject to criticism. It was claimed that collateral was emphasized rather than profitability of the firm in determining allocation of funds; that public enterprises and large firms were favoured, while private enterprises and medium and small enterprises were discriminated against; and that exporting industries enjoyed privileged access to bank loans and preferential loans, compared with import-competing industries and the non-tradables sector (Shea and Yang, 1990, p. 13).

In testing these criticisms, and in determining which industries have been favoured, Shea and Yang (1990) estimated a "bank finance equation" by applying pooling data of twelve manufacturing industries over the period 1974–87. Their results provide support for the claim that larger firms have found it easier to obtain financing from financial institutions, while the smaller the asset scale of a firm, the greater the dependence on curb market finance. Thus, to the extent that export finance has been regarded as stimulating exports and economic growth, it has also distorted the fund allocation among exporting, import-competing, and the non-tradables sectors, and contributed to the problem of large trade surpluses in recent years.

The study found also that food and beverage, paper, printing and publishing, chemicals, basic metals, and transport equipment have been favoured in applying for access to loans, while wood and bamboo products, non-metallic mineral products, fabricated metal products, electrical and electronic machinery and equipment, and miscellaneous products have been discriminated against. The preference order of bank financing to manufacturing industries was found to be unrelated to the order of production growth rates of

Table 12.4 Export loan subsidy, Taiwan

Year	*Export loan rate (%)* (1)	*Minimum interest secured loans (%)* (2)	*Interest rate difference (%)* (3) = (2) – (1)	*Export loans of manuf. industries by domestic banks (millions of NTS)* (4)	*Exports of Manuf. industries (millions of NTS)* (5)	*Export loans subsidy (%)* (6) = ((3) * (4))/(5)
1963	7.50	14.94	7.44	..	..	..
1964	7.50	14.04	6.54	..	..	..
1965	7.50	14.04	6.54	..	..	..
1966	7.50	14.04	6.54	..	..	..
1967	7.50	13.63	6.13	..	..	..
1968	7.50	13.32	5.82	..	28,460	..
1969	7.50	13.32	5.82	..	38,252	..
1970	7.50	13.30	5.80	..	53,429	..
1971	7.50	12.25	4.75	3,983.14	75,019	0.2522
1972	7.50	11.63	4.13	6,200.25	113,869	0.2249
1973	8.17	11.81	3.64	8,304.08	162,744	0.1857
1974	10.99	15.89	4.90	8,094.75	207,104	0.1915
1975	7.80	13.48	5.68	6,761.58	190,804	0.2013
1976	7.00	12.83	5.83	8,934.83	296,727	0.1755
1977	6.62	10.91	4.29	9,924.00	339,278	0.1255
1978	6.50	10.50	4.00	10,750.58	453,043	0.0949
1979	8.75	11.89	3.23	12,609.42	565,724	0.0722
1980	10.53	13.50	2.97	12,597.08	693,953	0.0539
1981	11.55	14.19	2.64	15,345.67	807,134	0.0502
1982	9.79	11.18	1.39	19,151.67	843,147	0.0316
1983	8.05	8.60	0.55	20,981,75	979,856	0.0118
1984	7.86	8.31	0.45	20,593.25	1,178,811	0.0079
1985	7.41	8.08	0.67	20,422.08	1,197,951	0.0114
1986	5.79	7.20	1.41	17,427.67	1,475,760	0.0167
1987	5.50	6.75	1.25	15,162.33	1,674,866	0.0113
1988	5.50	6.87	1.37	16,374.99	1,731,804	0.0129

Note: 1. .. not available.

Sources:
a. Table 19, Shea and Yang (1990, p. 45). Derived from *the Central Bank of China, Financial Statistics Monthly, Taiwan District, The Republic of China.*

manufacturing industries, suggesting that the financial institutions have not allocated loans according to the growth potential of industries.

12.II.4 Informal credit markets

The curb market (informal financial system) is composed of all markets where borrowing and lending activities occur without being subject to the supervision and regulation of financial authorities. It is generally believed that the active curb market, which the government has never tried to suppress vigorously, has played an important role in Taiwan by attracting household saving and financing the investment needs of private enterprises.

Table 12.5 shows that curb market finance (enterprises and households) grew from 20% of total domestic financial assets in 1965 to more than 30% in 1980, and then fell to around 17% by the end of the 1980s. At its peak in 1980, curb market finance was roughly equal to that of all regulated financial institutions taken together, indicating a very large diversion of savings from the regulated financial institutions to the unregulated curb market.

During the period 1964–87, financial institutions provided the business sector with 58% of total financing from the financial system, while the informal curb market, capital market and money market accounted for 25%, 14% and 7% respectively. Between 1981 and 1987, financial institutions provided 51% of financing, while the curb, capital and money market contributed 26%, 14% and 9% respectively (Shea and Yang, 1990, p. 30). Over the period 1964–87 public enterprises obtained 95% of their borrowings from financial institutions and 2.1% of their borrowings from the curb market. This compared with private sector shares of 60% and 30%

Table 12.5 Composition of domestic financial assets, Taiwan, 1965–89 (percentages)

	1965	*1970*	*1975*	*1980*	*1985*	*1989*
Loans by:						
Financial institutions	31.1	28.5	36.8	33.0	32.7	43.0
Enterprises and households	19.6	29.0	28.6	32.2	26.8	16.6
Government agencies	9.7	4.6	1.7	1.7	1.7	0.9
Securities:						
Government enterprises	2.6	2.7	0.8	0.6	1.2	2.2
Long-term	35.4	32.3	28.6	26.1	28.0	29.8
Short-term	0.0	0.0	0.0	2.1	3.5	1.9
Other domestic assets (net)	1.5	2.9	3.5	4.3	6.1	5.6
Total	100	100	100	100	100	100

Note: Loans made by enterprises and households include suppliers' credits as well as direct borrowing from households through various informal financial channels.

Source: Derived from the Central Bank of China, *Flow of Funds in Taiwan District*, December (1990, Table 1, pp. 115, 125, 135, 145, 155, 163).

respectively. Over the sub-period 1981–87, public enterprises' share of borrowings from financial institutions was 88.7%, compared with 3.7% from the curb market. Private enterprises' share was 53.5% and 35.2% respectively (Shea and Yang, 1990).

Table 12.6 compares various types of bank interest rates with a curb market interest rate and consumer price inflation rate. In real terms, the bank deposit rate yielded a fairly consistent and positive rate of return (except for high inflation years). However, compared to the returns that seem to have been available in the curb market – the loan rate minus an undetermined, presumably high, profit margin – the bank deposit rate was probably not very attractive for many savers (Cheng, 1986).

Export loans were extended by banks at interest rates lower than the savings deposit rate. A special rediscount facility at the central bank made this possible and effectively meant that the central bank financed exports while commercial banks collected a fee for initiating and servicing the loans

Table 12.6 Interest rates and inflation rates in Taiwan: 1956–89 (percentages)

Year (end)	*Bank rates*			*Curb market unsecured loans*	*Consumer price inflation*
	Savings deposits *	*Unsecured loans*	*Export loans*		
1956–62	17.00	20.90	11.20	41.10	8.35
1963–73	10.10	14.10	7.70	25.40	3.40
1974	13.50	15.50	9.00	29.30	47.47
1975	12.00	14.00	7.00	26.40	5.24
1976	10.75	12.75	7.00	27.60	2.50
1977	9.50	11.50	6.50	25.60	7.04
1978	9.50	11.50	6.50	27.20	5.77
1979	12.50	15.25	10.50	30.10	9.75
1980	12.50	16.20	10.50	31.30	19.01
1981	13.00	15.25	11.00	30.10	16.34
1982	9.00	10.75	8.25	27.70	2.96
1983	8.50	10.25	8.00	26.80	1.35
1984	8.00	10.00	7.75	25.90	–0.02
1985	6.25	9.50	6.25	24.48	–0.07
1986	6.25	9.00	5.50	21.96	0.70
1987	6.25	9.00	5.50	21.60	0.52
1988	6.25	9.00	5.50	21.60	1.28
1989	6.25	12.00	6.50	21.96	4.41

Note:
* One-year savings deposits.

Source: Data for 1956–84 are from Cheng (1986, p. 151, Table 11.6). Data for 1985–89 are from Tsai (1993, p. 56, Table 5). Derived from the Central Bank of China, *Financial Statistics Monthly*, various issues; and Council for Economic Planning and Development, *Taiwan Statistical Data Book*, 1990.

and bearing the credit risk. Cheng (1986, p. 151) notes that these separate arrangements created a three-tiered credit market.

Exporters enjoyed a heavily subsidized loan rate, other privileged borrowers (mostly large enterprises) paid the bank loan rates, and the rest sought high-cost finance in the curb market. Given the significant size of the curb market, the average cost of capital in Taiwan was probably much higher than indicated by the bank loan rates.

12.III OTHER MEASURES FOR INDUSTRIAL UPGRADING

12.III.1 Technology policy

While over the course of the 1980s Taiwan continued to maintain competitiveness in some of the labour-intensive industrial sectors, the government, in recognizing the need for industrial restructuring, announced in 1979 the adoption of a Science and Technology Development Programme. The programme, which was later integrated into the Eighth Four-Year Economic Plan (1982–85), sought to raise R&D expenditure and focus attention on private sector technology development. A further sub-plan in 1982 called attention to the development of the following eight strategic areas: information, automation, materials science, energy, optoelectronics, food processing technology, biotechnology and hepatitis prevention. This was followed in 1984 by the formulation of the Ten-Year National Science and Technology Development Plan (1986–95), a major goal of which was the improvement of the general environment for science and development. The government's aim was to raise R&D expenditure by 1995 to 2% of GNP – 40% from government (including public enterprises) and 60% from private enterprises. The government also established the Hsinchu Science-based Industrial Park in 1980 to attract high technology industries with high R&D content.

The heavy dependence on the government to finance R&D activities is due to the lack of research capabilities of small and medium-sized enterprises (SMEs). But investment in private domestic R&D has become essential for the maintenance of future competitiveness. R&D expenditure as a percentage of GNP rose from 0.7% in 1978 to 1.4% by 1989 (compared with 1.9% for Korea and 2.7% for Japan). Between 1978 and 1989, the government accounted for between 50 and 65% of total R&D spending (35 to 47% by government agencies, 10 to 25% by public enterprises). By 1989, nearly 50% of R&D spending was being undertaken by private enterprise, indicating that the government was achieving its aim of increasing private sector R&D. However, private sector spending on R&D as a percentage of sales was only 0.1% in 1978, compared with 2% and 3% in the United States and Japan respectively. By 1989 this had risen to 0.7%, but was still much lower than that of Korea (1.9%) and Japan (2.7%). Throughout the 1980s, R&D spending by the foreign sector has largely remained under 1%.

12.III.2 Strategic industry financing policy

In 1982, in order to promote industrial development and restructure industry, the Taiwan government adopted a policy of identifying "strategic" industries and products for promotion. Apart from factors already mentioned, the policy was largely adopted as a means of addressing the structural imbalance apparent in the manufacturing sector since the early 1980s, and the associated reliance of Taiwan on Japan for imported intermediate goods of machinery and equipment.

Selection of strategic industries was based on the following six criteria, as identified by the government (Council for Economic Planning and Development, 1981): high technology intensity, high market potential, high rate of value added, low energy intensity, low pollution, and large linkage effects. The selected products were drawn from the mechanical, information and electronics industries in the original promulgation. The list was revised four times during the 1980s, with additional products added after 1986 to include biotechnology and material technology industries.

The government offers two measures to subsidize strategic industries – preferential medium- and long-term low interest loans, and technology and management guidance. The interest-rate difference between the strategic loans and the prime rate is around 1.75–2.75%. The loans are managed by the government's development bank, and were disbursed in five phases from 1982 to 1991. The actual amounts extended are listed in Table 12.7. By the end of 1988, 32% of the total preferential loans, were directed to the strategic industries. In addition to financing strategic industries, preferential loans have been expanded to finance the purchase of automated equipment, domestically produced machines and pollution prevention equipment, the production of exports and the development of new products (Yang, 1990, p. 2). Under the technology and management guidance incentives, the government subsidizes 60% of total consulting expenses of firms, up to NT$1 million. Strategic industries were also eligible for the incentives contained under the SEI.

Since implementation, the strategic loan policy has been subject to two major criticisms. The first relates to its distortionary effects. The second is that the various criteria used by government to determine what constitutes a strategic product are inconsistent with each other and lack a clear rationale.

A study by Yang, Jen and Chou (1990) is the only research to date which has sought to review the effectiveness of the policy.[19] Based on questionnaire data sent to some 3,000 firms, of which 357 responded, the authors attempted to answer the following questions:

Table 12.7 Medium- and long-term low-interest loans for strategic industries and major industries and loans for strategic projects, Taiwan

Credit type	*Period*	*Size of loan*	*Interest rate*	*Function of project*	*Approved loans No. of applicants*	*Amount*
Phase I	May 1982–Dec. 1983	NT$10 billion	Av. interest rate minus 2%	1. Production of strategic industry 2. Procurement of local made machinery and equipment 3. Project approved by the CEPD	433	NT$10 billion
Phase II	Jan 1984–June 1985	NT$20 billion	,,	Supplementary project: Procurement of automatic machinery	451	NT$22 billion
Phase III	July 1985–June 1987	NT$20 billion	Prime rate minus 1.75% to 2.75%	Supplementary project: Procurement of pollution-control equipment	465	NT$24 billion
Phase IV	July 1987–Aug 1988	NT$20 billion	,,	Supplementary project: 1. Production of pollution-control equipment and plant relocation 2. Implementation of good manufacturing process project	447	NT$28 billion
Strategic investment project Phase I	March 1989–Feb 1990	NT$20 billion	Prime rate minus 1.75%	Supplementary project: 1. Procurement of the energy conservation equipment 2. Parking lot construction	245	NT$25 billion
Phase II	Aug 1990–Dec 1991	NT$30 billion	Prime rate minus 2%	Supplementary project: Procurement of mass transportation vehicles	236	NT$26 billion
Total		NT$120 billion				

Source:
(1) Compiled on request of author by the Loan Department, Bank of communications 1992.
(2) Table 1, Bank of Communications (Chiao Tung) *Annual Report* (1991), p. 11).

- To what extent has government intervention changed the pattern of investment from what free market prices would have generated, so as to carry out a planned pattern of sectoral growth?
- To what extent has government intervention made for faster economic growth?
- To what extent have the processes of and measures for executing policy been effective in improving the investment position and performance of firms?

The authors' sample included firms which had acquired strategic preferential loans, firms which acquired technical and management assistance, and firms in the mechanical, information and electronic industries which did not receive preferential loans.

The authors then applied principal component analysis[20] to test the following hypotheses:

- the characteristics of the firms influence the probability of their receiving the loans;
- strategic loans cause a greater level of fixed asset accumulation in subsidized firms than in non-subsidized firms;
- strategic loans help decrease the interest burden of firms; and
- strategic loans increase the operational performance of subsidized firms compared with that of non-subsidized firms.

Five OLS regression equations were estimated based on the following dependent variables representing the various hypotheses – subsidize or not, interest burden, growth of fixed capital, operational efficiency, and productive efficiency. The explanatory variables included the aforementioned plus technology level, scale of firm, sufficiency of funds, investment mood, and credibility.

The results of this research indicated that the most significant item influencing the availability of preferential loans was the firm's investment mood, evaluated on the basis of the following categories – frequency of firm investment, the depth of the evaluation employed in the investment decision-making process, and the importance of investment in the firm's growth. Other factors, such as technology level, scale, sufficiency of funds and credibility (evaluated by the availability of short-term, medium and long-term credit to the firm) were shown not to be important factors in the issuance of loans. In the electronic, information and mechanical products industry preferential loans were also found not to significantly influence interest burdens, or to stimulate fixed capital formation or operational performance (Yang, Jen and Chou, 1990).

The effects of technological and management guidance on the firms' operational performance were also evaluated. Higher technology firms were found to rely more heavily on non-government support than on government assistance. It was shown also that government aided in the dissemination of technology, but not in the upgrading of technology. Thus, whether a firm obtained assistance through government or other institutions was not a key factor influencing the production performance of firms. The study also found that most subsidized firms would have continued with their investment projects and would have sought funds from other institutions in the absence of preferential support from the government.

12.IV POLICY LESSONS FROM THE TAIWAN EXPERIENCE

12.IV.1 The identification problem: defining a high technology industry

High technology usually refers to those technologies at the cutting edge of science which have a great potential for commercial use or are already involved in commercial production. However, a comparison of country classifications reveals that there is neither a uniform standard nor a formula for identifying what constitutes a high technology industry. Some classifications relate to standard industry codes; other high technology industries, particularly in OECD classifications, cover many standardized products. Japan, for example, lists the following nine high technology industries: industrial robots, integrated circuits, office automation, new industrial materials, biotechnology, computers, information, optoelectronics and aerospace. It is often unclear though how these industries have been chosen.[21] Some industries, such as new industrial materials and biotechnology, are still at the development stage, without mass production, yet the technological and market potential is thought to have been thoroughly analysed. There are also "strategic-transformative" technologies or industrial technologies which are not necessarily bonded to any specific product. Thus there is a problem of how to distinguish among the many high technology industries and their sub industries.

In popular discussions, the delineating aspects of a strategic industry are rarely identified. The attitude of many observers is that they know one when they see one (OECD, 1991, p. 36). Strategic industries are considered "good" industries for a nation to have or defined as industries that a country feels "it has to have". Within the literature there would appear to be at least some consensus that major positive externalities and large economies of scale based on learning by doing should be involved. But some industries are regarded as strategic by all governments, not only in the static sense of oligopolistic games as suggested by new trade theory, but also in terms of their dynamic potential for future growth. The problem thus remains of how to identify the industries in which opportunities for dynamic gain may exist. The examples are largely based on ex post identification, and the theoretical models do not suggest a strong definition of the required characteristics of such industries.

12.IV.2 The information problem

It seems doubtful that, in designing policy, bureaucrats are particularly conscious of the mechanism behind the criteria. The Taiwan government, for example, identifies strategic industries as "industries that have to grow at an accelerated pace in order to promote improvements or breakthroughs in the present industrial structure", while key industries are identified as being "indispensable to continued economic growth" (Council for Economic Planning and Development, 1981, p. 8). Thus when the policy was first announced the information industry was considered a strategic industry, whilst its software component was not. Basic metals and metal products on the other hand are considered to be key industries but not strategic industries.

As mentioned previously, government selection of a strategic industry was judged according to the criteria of great market potential and linkages, high technology intensity and value-added ratio, a low level of energy consumption and low pollution. While each criterion may have some economic justification, together they appear to have little consistency.

As the priority accorded to each criterion has not been explicitly spelt out, it is difficult to identify which industries meet all the criteria, given that any industry may exhibit one or more of the characteristics. In practice, though, there would appear to be few oligopolistic-type firms which readily conform to all the characteristics put forth by the theory. Schive and Hsueh (1987, pp. 150–1), in assessing the criteria applied by the government in Taiwan, point out that encouragement of investments with great market potential is redundant if the market signal is clear. A similar argument can be applied to the low energy requirement. A high value-added ratio reveals nothing about the efficient use of resources, as is true for the rule for high technology intensity. As far as linkages are concerned, though more investment can be induced by the initial investment if there are linkages, there is no guarantee of success of such an investment. Moreover, the failure of the investment of great linkages implies that the negative impact upon other industries will be greater. There also exist great difficulties in determining the positive spillovers that may accrue to end users and related industries.

12.IV.3 Implementation

By the end of March 1987, of the 199 strategic products defined and eligible for preferential loans, only 72 had asked for technological assistance in production, and 46 for management consulting. Only 82, less than half of the total, applied for preferential loans. Two results concerning the distribution of preferential loans are worth mentioning. First, the ratio of transmitted loans for the strategic industries – machinery and information – over total funds at the end of March 1987 was around 21%. The ratio rises only to 31%

when the electrical and automobiles and parts industries are added. Second, the highest ratio of funds went to the textiles industry, which received 28.6% of total loans transmitted. From this information, it is somewhat difficult to determine the theoretical rationale behind the strategic industry policy where the textile industry enjoyed the largest share of preferential loans originally designed for high technology industries. Though a comprehensive empirical study is necessary for a thorough evaluation of the policy, preliminary findings show that implementation of the policy is far from satisfactory (Schive and Hsueh, 1987, p. 131). In particular, it appears that changes in the incentive structure during this period were not concerned with directing resources towards the development of high technology "strategic" industries.

12.IV.4 Was the policy necessary?

It could be argued that the preferential loans are too small to have a significant impact, and incentives should be channelled directly to R&D activities, instead of production, as far as the externalities are concerned. This then begs the question of whether the policy was necessary at all.

Small and medium-sized enterprises (SMEs) are generally regarded as having provided the backbone for economic development in Taiwan. These SMEs have made a greater contribution to the development of foreign trade than have the larger enterprises and, unlike the larger firms, have not on the whole been major recipients of government protection and incentives.[22] Almost 99% of total manufacturing enterprises are SMEs, employing in 1986 around 68% of the manufacturing workforce (compared with 43% in 1966), and contributing almost 45% of manufacturing output in 1989 (compared with 27% in 1971). Table 12.8 shows that, economy-wide, large enterprises on average exported 37% of their production between 1976 and 1988. SMEs, however, exported more than 64% during the same period.

The contributions of SMEs to Taiwan's economic development can also be illustrated by the export shares of SMEs in manufacturing. The share of SME exports in manufacturing ranged from 62.5% to 73.5% between 1981 and 1988, with precision instruments, textiles, plastic products, leather and electrical machinery and appliances as the major export industries. However, since 1982, SMEs have experienced a decline in their export contributions, indicating that they have been under fairly competitive pressures.

Small and medium-sized enterprises are by and large price takers, being heavily influenced by, and adapting to, the overall environment rather than relying on their individual strategies or efforts. In the past, SMEs have shown considerable flexibility and adaptability in response to changing market decisions, though this challenge has become more difficult since the early 1980s as product cycles have shortened. But the predominantly labour-intensive SMEs have gradually been losing their international competitiveness as a result of increases in production and marketing costs. Moreover,

Table 12.8 Export ratios of small and medium enterprises (economy-wide), Taiwan (percentages)

Year	*Large enterprises*	*Small and medium enterprises*
1976	39.1	56.8
1977	36.8	53.5
1978	40.9	56.7
1979	40.2	59.0
1980	40.1	66.7
1981	41.9	74.8
1982	39.3	75.9
1983	35.0	73.3
1984	36.6	71.8
1985	34.2	70.0
1986	32.4	66.5
1987	32.3	61.9
1988	32.5	47.0
Annual average		
1976–88	37.0	64.2
1981–88	35.5	67.7

Source: Table 10, Lee (1992, p. 47). Derived from *Industrial Finance Situation Survey* (various issues).

maintenance of traditional practices of operating on small profit margins with attention to costs and cost adjustment have become more difficult as capital deepening and technology have grown more important in maintaining niche markets and market shares both domestically and abroad.

In responding to this challenge, SMEs have either changed their traditional lines of business or invested abroad. While flexible in meeting market demand, the SMEs are still characterized as having labour-intensive technologies and thus being largely incapable of conducting intensive R&D other than basic research, as having lower capabilities in marketing and after sales service, and as having few brand name products (Kuo, 1992). Thus how these firms undertake restructuring in response to both domestic and global pressures is seen as crucial to Taiwan's future industrial development. The bottleneck to further industrial upgrading though is not seen as being one of capital *per se* but acquisition of design and processing technology. Over the 1980s the SMEs have adopted the following strategies in seeking to overcome these limitations: overseas mergers, outward investment, joint efforts for the upgrading of technology, technology alliances in acquiring design and processing technology and a mixture of economy of scale and economy of scope approaches.

A question not sufficiently dealt with in the new trade literature then is whether the anticipated benefits of high technology can be realized through foreign direct investment (FDI) rather than strategic policies. The fundamental rationale for FDI lies in the transfer of firm- and industry-specific intangible assets, such as the knowledge embodied in both new products and new processes and managerial skills. A related question concerns the strategic benefits of FDI by domestically owned producers. Often the presumption is that domestically-owned firms are necessary to obtain the national strategic benefits of high technology production. However, in this respect Taiwan has always had an open door policy towards foreign investment. This has been particularly fruitful for the electronics industry, where local electronic firms are importers and distributors of foreign high-tech products, and as an industry where Taiwan firms are becoming more international in design, production and marketing. Between 1952 and 1988, of the US$8.5 billion total of FDI realized by foreign nationals and overseas Chinese, 28% of this went into the electronics industry – the majority in the latter half of the 1980s. This foreign investment has been an important channel for the rapid diffusion of technology into these export industries as well as for industrial upgrading.

The Taiwan government has also played a major supportive role in developing high technology industries through the provision of training, equity loans, research support and science parks, and in providing the institutional structures for technical support. Such policies are not concerned with picking winners, but have created support by offering better information conditions, reducing uncertainties and sustaining organizational change and skill formation. It is thus difficult to see how strategic policies have been the main force behind this sector's rapid growth.

The Taiwan case thus reveals a significant paradox in the actual emergence and growth of domestic strategic industrial policies and their theoretical foundations, given that the "domestic" firms at which such policies are aimed are becoming increasingly global, are themselves involved in so-called "strategic alliances", and are increasingly sourcing on an international scale "strategic" science and technology inputs.

A major constraint on the effectiveness of strategic policies then is the emergence of the multi-domestic corporation, where governments cannot be sure of the domestic competitive effects. The trend among major players in so-called "strategic sectors" is to strengthen their competitive position, share the burden of R&D costs, or gain access to foreign markets via an intricate web of joint ventures, cooperative agreements and so on. This has further blurred the distinction between "home" and "host" country, and complicated any definition of national economic interest. National technology policy to support specific firms or activities may thus become increasingly meaningless given the leakages, in terms of both financial advantages and research results, to foreign enterprises (OECD, 1991, p. 100). Industrial policy measures to support domestic production may end up supporting foreign production facilities and subsidizing foreign subsidiaries while programmes to increase domestic production may subsidize goods that have largely been produced abroad through offsets and subcontracting arrangements. Investment incentives and domestic policies may thus in fact transfer income to trading partners and help strengthen rival industries. Moreover, policies to isolate and build technology through domestic strategies may in fact slow progress by reducing the scale of the market and blocking cross-fertilization of ideas.

12.V CONCLUSION

In focusing on Taiwan's industry policy in the 1980s, this paper has highlighted the special form of liberalization that took place, whereby general trade liberalization, including the winding back of export incentives, occurred in conjunction with an industrial policy of identifying and favouring certain industries over others. This latter policy was gradually abandoned in response to various studies showing the policies to be inefficient and difficult to implement successfully. In fact, the considerable progress in trade liberalization that took place after 1985 suggests that industrial upgrading appeared to be driven largely by economic forces (both internal and external) rather than by industry policy initiatives. This suggests that the government became less rather than more *dirigiste* over the period.

A survey of the available evidence does not support the view that strategic policies were a major factor in furthering Taiwan's industrialization during the 1980s. Most of the changes in the incentive structure over this period were not concerned with the promotion of strategic industries. It is important to distinguish the economic impact from changes in the internal economic environment in the 1980s – such as the exchange rate appreciation and the policy of economic liberalization including reductions in tariffs and import controls – from the impacts due to the selective fiscal and financial incentives and measures. The former provided the opportunity for the mechanism of comparative advantage to operate and is the crucial factor explaining the industrialization and structural change during the past four decades of Taiwan's development. The latter, in discriminating between traded goods industries, led to the distortion of resource allocation. In fact, the policy of allocating funds to strategic industries in order to stimulate economic growth contradicts the objective of equalizing the availability of bank loans among borrower groups based on equity considerations. It is also contrary to the liberalization programme announced in 1984 and to Taiwan's progress in trade liberalization as a prelude to admission to GATT.

This paper has also sought to highlight that the circumstances under which strategic policies might pay off are difficult to detect in practice. Given Taiwan's industrial structure, composed predominantly of small and medium-sized enterprises, with a reliance on informal channels of financing, it is doubtful whether the policy was significant in furthering industrial growth over the period. Moreover, it is difficult to determine the economic rationale behind the implementation of the policy given that the high technology "strategic" industries did not appear to be the major recipients of preferential finance. In implementing the policy, it is not apparent that the government had a clear perception on how the industrial structure should be evolving. It is thus difficult to determine the rationale behind the government's designing of the policy. An assessment of the extent to which the government appeared to be directing resources to "strategic" industries finds that incentives were not important in this sector's development and, in fact, it appears that the government did not possess a "strategic" view on how this sector should be evolving.

ACKNOWLEDGMENTS

I am grateful to Ross Garnant, Peter Drysdale, Richard Pomfret and an anonymous referee for helpful comments and suggestions.

NOTES

1 For a survey of the competing models see Smith (1995).

2 The impressive body of empirical research on trade and industrialization undertaken in the 1970s by Little, Scitovsky and Scott (1970), Balassa (1971), Krueger (1978) and Bhagwati (1978) related the economic success stories of the export-oriented East Asian NIEs, noting that their development accelerated as they liberalized their foreign trade regimes and adopted an outward-looking strategy of export promotion.

3 But proponents of the more recent theoretical literature are not dogmatic on the issue of intervention to capture technological externalities. In arguing that the presence of externalities in high technology industries may provide a legitimate case for intervention, some new trade theorists have stressed that the circumstances giving rise to such externalities are likely to be very limited.

4 See, for example, Wade (1990a) and Komiya, Okuno and Suzumura (1988).

5 Up until 1992, Taiwan had been named in seven cases for investigation under Section 301 of the Trade Act of 1974 (as amended). Four of these cases were in manufacturing, two in agriculture and one covering intellectual property rights. Three of the seven cases led to explicit threats of retaliatory measures by the United States. Friction centred mostly on market access for major agricultural and food products, including wine and cigarettes, and intellectual property rights (Bayard and Elliott, 1992).

6 Financial liberalization was also accelerated, whereby interest rates were decontrolled and a new Banking Law, enacted in 1989–90, removed all interest rate restrictions. Foreign exchange controls were lifted on trade-related transactions and residents were allowed to hold and use foreign currencies after July 1987 (although remittances of foreign exchange were still subject to quantitative limitations).

7 The accumulation of foreign exchange reserves increased from less than US$11 billion in 1981 to over US$73 billion in 1990. Appreciation of the US dollar in the first half of the 1980s made the US market relatively attractive to Taiwan

exports. From 1980 to 1986 the percentage of exports to the United States rose from 34 to 48%. Since 1985, the US dollar has fallen against the NT dollar, the yen, and other major currencies. The US share in Taiwan's exports has declined throughout this period following the appreciation of the NT dollar by 40% against the US dollar in the period 1986–88.

8 From 1980, Taiwan adopted a two-column tariff schedule. Column I countries refer to those countries that do not grant preferential tariffs to the ROC, while Column II countries do grant preferential tariffs to the ROC. Column II preferential rates apply to goods imported from most countries, with 119 countries or areas eligible for applying the Column II preferential rates.

9 As is well known, averaging tariffs by means of import values introduces a downward bias since high tariffs are given a small weight and low tariffs a large weight. The simple average of tariffs will also be overstated because of the various tax exemptions and the tax rebate system, with the same true of the frequency distribution of actual tariffs.

10 Imported commodities are classified into three groups: one, commodities that may be imported but only under strict controls; two, commodities that may be imported but only with the consent of certain branches of government or with restrictions imposed on the qualifications of importers or country of origin; and three, commodities that Cannot be imported at all by private importers.

11 The income tax rate for all "other" enterprises was reduced to 35% in 1975, to 30% in 1985, and to 25% in 1986.

12 The size of rebates expanded as the items covered expanded and exports grew. Rebates have applied to customs duties, the defence surtax on customs duties, harbour construction dues, commodity taxes and the salt tax. These rebates made up 1.2% of total relevant tax receipts in 1955, 30% in 1964, and 62% in 1972. In 1983, as part of the trade liberalization strategy, the government announced a five-year programme to abolish tax rebates. By 1986, their level had fallen to 21% (Wu, 1991, p. 319).

13 This study was undertaken by the Industrial Development Bureau (IDB) and the Chung-Hua Institution for Economic Research. The IDB is the major governmental agency dealing with industrial development. The IDB is responsible for initiating industrial policies and strategies for overall industrial development, as well as for specific industries such as electronics, information, aviation and automotive.

14 Tax revenue includes taxes collected at all levels of government, but excludes monopoly revenue.

15 The following findings are taken from the work of Yu (1988), which in turn has been taken from the Summary Report: An Evaluation of the Statute for the Encouragement of Investment, Chung-Hua Institution for Economic Research, August 1987.

16 Based on Hou's (1988) study on the problem of Taiwan's trade surplus by a research team at the Chung-Hua Institution for Economic Research.

17 As McKinnon (1991, p. 37) notes, although some financial repression existed in the form of preferential interest rates for exporters, these rates were generally kept positive and substantial in real terms; nor was this commitment to finance exporters sufficient to undermine the central bank's control over the monetary base.

18 As Wu (1991, p. 319) in quoting Lin (1973) notes, credit has generally been of the revolving, short-term type; for example, for three months covering the period between receipt of letter of credit and shipping. The letters of credit were discounted by the central bank at a lower rate than a commercial bank would charge,

if the bank would even advance money at all. This provided firms, especially small and medium-sized ones, with needed working capital to fill orders without resorting to the high-cost black market, and thus promoted smaller enterprises as well as exports.

19 See Smith (1994) for subsequent research into the effectiveness of this policy.

20 Principal component analysis involves combining several variables that represent each characteristic of the firms to form a representative variable. For example, the growth of sales and profitability are combined to form a term to represent operational performance, and the variables of productivity of labour and capital are combined to represent productivity performance.

21 Accordingly, MITI used the following criteria in determining key industries for promotion in the 1960s and early 1970s: productivity growth, income elasticity, and employment relatedness (Okuno-Fujiwara, 1992).

22 Yen (1984) has calculated the percentages of loanable funds of the whole banking system extended to SMEs between 1977 and 1981. While SMEs accounted for 95% of all firms in the economy, they received around 32.5% of preferential total loans in 1981 (28% in 1977).

REFERENCES

Amsden, A., 1990, *Taiwan in International Perspective.* Paper presented at the Columbia University Conference on Taiwan, New York, September.

Baldwin, R. and P. R. Krugman, 1988, Market access and international competition: a simulation study of 16K random access memories. In R. Feenstra, Ed., *Empirical Methods for International Trade.* MIT Press, Cambridge, Mass.

Baldwin, R. E., 1969, The case against infant-industry tariff protection. *Journal of Political Economy*, 77, pp. 295–305.

Balassa, B., 1971, *The Structure of Protection in Developing Countries*, Johns Hopkins University Press, Baltimore.

Bank of Communications, 1981, 1982, 1989, *Annual Report*, various years, Taiwan.

Bayard, T. O. and K. Elliott, 1992, Aggressive unilateralism and Section 301: market opening or market closing? *The World Economy*, 15(6), pp. 685–706.

Bhagwati, J. N., 1978, *Foreign Trade Regimes and Economic Development: Anatomy and Consequences of Exchange Control Regimes.* Ballinger Press, Cambridge, Mass.

Brander, J. and B. Spencer, 1985, Export subsidies and international market share rivalry. *Journal of International Economics*, 18, pp. 83–100.

Cheng, Hang-Sheng, Ed., 1986, Financial policy and reform in Taiwan, China. In *Financial Policy and Reform in Pacific Basin Countries.* Lexington Books, Lexington, Mass.

Chou, Ji and De-Min wu, 1991, The cost of capital and the effective tax rate in Taiwan: 1961–1985. Chung-Hua Institution for Economic Research Discussion Paper No. 9110, Taiwan.

Chung-Hua Institution for Economic Research (CIER), 1987, *An Economic Cost–Benefit Analysis Evaluation of Regulations to Encourage Investment.* Taipei (in Chinese).

Cole, D. C. and H. T. Patrick, 1986, Financial development in the Pacific Basin market economies. In A. H. H. Tan and B. Kapur, Eds, *Pacific Growth and Financial Interdependence.* Allen and Unwin, Sydney.

Corden, W. M., 1974, *Trade Policy and Economic Welfare.* Clarendon Press, Oxford.

Council for Economic Planning and Development (CEPD), 1981, *Four-Year Economic Development Plan for Taiwan, Republic of China (1982–1985)*, Taiwan.

Deardorff, A. and R. Stern, 1987, Current issues in trade policy: an overview. In R. Stern, Ed., *US Trade Policies in a Changing World Economy.* MIT Press, Cambridge, Mass.

Dixit, A., 1984, International trade policy for oligopolistic industries. *Economic Journal* (supplement), 94, pp. 1–16.
Dosi, G., L. D. Tyson and J. Zysman, 1989, Trade technologies and development: a framework for discussing Japan. In C. Johnson, L. D. Tyson and J. Zysman, Eds, *Politics and Productivity: the Real Story of Why Japan Works.* Ballinger Press, Mass.
Givens, N. L., 1982, The U.S. can no longer afford free trade. *Business Week*, 15, November 22, p. 11.
Grossman, G.M. and J. D. Richardson, 1985, Strategic US trade policy: a survey of issues and early analysis. *Princeton University Special Papers in International Economics*, No. 15, April.
Haggard, S., 1988, Policy, Politics and Structural Adjustment: the U.S. and the East Asian NICs. Paper presented at the Columbia University Conference on Taiwan, New York, September.
Helpman, E. and P. Krugman, 1985, *Market Structure and Foreign Trade.* MIT Press, Cambridge, Mass.
——, 1989, *Trade Policy and Market Structure.* MIT Press, Cambridge, Mass.
Hou, Chi-ming, 1988, Relevance of the Taiwan Model of Development. Paper presented at the Conference on Successful Economic Development Strategies of the Pacific Rim Nations, Taiwan, 14–18 November.
——, 1992, Strategy for Economic Development in Taiwan and Implications for Developing Countries. Paper presented at the Conference on the Economic Development Experience of Taiwan and its Role in an Emerging Asia-Pacific Area, Vol. II., Academia Sinica, Taiwan, 8–10 June.
Hsueh, Li-Min, 1992, Taiwan's industrial policies for industrial restructuring in the 1990s. Proceedings of the Joint Conference on the Industrial Policies of the ROK and ROC, Korea Development Institute, Seoul, 2–3 April.
Hughes, H., 1993, *Is There an East Asian model?* Economic Division Working Papers No. 4, Research School of Pacific Studies Canberra, The Australian National University.
Johnson, C., 1982, *MITI and the Japanese Miracle: The Growth of Industrial Policy. 1925–1975*. Stanford University Press, Stanford.
Komiya, R., M. Okuno and K. Suzumura, Eds., 1988, *Industrial Policy of Japan.* Academic Press, Tokyo.
Krueger, A. O., 1978, *Foreign Trade Regimes and Economic Development: Liberalization Attempts and Consequences*, Vol. 10. National Bureau of Economic Research, Ballinger Press, New York.
Krugman, P. R., 1984, Import protection as export promotion: international competition in the presence of oligopoly and economies of scale. In H. Kierzkowski, Ed., *Monopolistic Competition and International Trade.* Oxford University Press, Oxford.
——, Ed., 1986, *Strategic Trade Policy and the New International Economics*. MIT Press, Cambridge, Mass.
——, 1987, The narrow moving band, the Dutch disease, and the competitive consequences of Mrs Thatcher. *Journal of Development Economics*, 27, pp. 41–55.
——, 1992, Does new trade theory require a new trade policy? *World Economy*, 15(4), pp. 423–441
Kuo, Wen-Jeng, 1991, *Effects of External Protectionism and Internal Liberalisation: the Case of Taiwan*. Paper presented at the Conference on the Industrial Policies of The ROC and ROK, Taiwan, 8–9 April.
——, 1992, The marketing of small and medium enterprises in Taiwan. Paper presented at the Seminar on the Development of Small and Medium Enterprises in the ROC, Chung-Hua Institution for Economic Research, Taiwan.

Lee, C. J., 1992, *The Role of Small and Medium Enterprises in the Process of Economic Development*. Paper presented at the Conference on Economic Restructuring and Growth, Chung-Hua Institution for Economic Research, Taiwan, 1–2 May.

Lee, T. H., Kuo-shu Liang, Chi Shive and Ryh-song Yeh, 1975, The structure of effective protection and subsidy in Taiwan. *Economic Essays*, 6, pp. 55–175.

Lee, T. H. and Liang, Kuo-shu, 1982, in Balassa, B. et al. Ed., *Development Strategies in Semi-industrial Economies*, Johns Hopkins University Press, Baltimore.

Liang, Kuo-shu, 1992, *Evolution of Foreign Trade from Protection to Liberalization in Taiwan, the Republic of China*. Paper presented at the Conference on Economic Restructuring and Growth, Chung-Hua Institution for Economic Research, Taiwan, 1–2 May.

——, 1993, The evolution of Taiwan's economy in the emerging Asia-Pacific century. *Industry of Free China, LXXX(3)*, pp. 33–48.

Lin, Ching-yuan, 1973, *Industrialization in Taiwan, 1946–72*. Praeger, New York.

Little, I., T. Scitovsky and M. Scott, 1970, *Industry and Trade in Some Developing Countries*. Oxford University Press, London.

McKinnon, R. I., 1991, *The Order of Economic Liberalization*. Johns Hopkins University Press, Baltimore.

National Science Council, 1989, *Science and Technology Yearbook*. Taipei.

——, 1991, *Indicators of Science and Technology*. Republic of China Taiwan. OECD, 1991, *Strategic Industries in a Global Economy*. OECD, Paris.

Okuno, M. and K. Suzumura, 1986, The economic analysis of industrial policy: a conceptual framework through the Japanese experience. In H. Mutoh et al., Eds., *Industrial Policies for Pacific Economic Growth*. Allen and Unwin, Sydney.

Okuno-Fujiwara, M., 1992, Industry policy in Japan. In P. R. Krugman, Ed., *Trade with Japan*. University of Chicago Press, Chicago.

Pack, H. 1992, New perspectives on industrial growth in Taiwan. In Ranis, Ed., *Taiwan: From Developing to mature Economy*. Westview Press, Boulder.

Pai, Pei-Ying, 1991, *Tax Policy and Economic Development in the Republic of China*. Paper presented at the CIAT Technical Conference on the Role of Tax Policy and Tax Administration in the Course of Economic Development, 21–25 Taiwan, October.

Ranis, G. and S. A. Mahmood, 1992, *The Political Economy of Development Policy Change*. Blackwell, Cambridge, Mass.

Reidel, J., 1992, International trade in Taiwan's transition from developing to mature economy. In G. Ranis, Ed., *Taiwan: From Developing to Mature Economy*. Westview Press, Boulder.

Richardson, J. D., 1989, Empirical research on trade liberalization with imperfect competition: a survey. *OECD Economic Studies*, No. 12, Spring, pp. 7–50.

——, 1991, *"New" Trade Theory and Policy a Decade Old: Assessment in a Pacific Context*. Paper presented at the First Australian Fullbright Symposium, *Managing International Economic Relations in the Pacific in the 1990s*, Australian National University, Canberra, 16–17 December.

Rodrik, D., 1988, Imperfect competition, scale economies, and trade policy in developing countries. In R. E. Baldwin, *Trade Policy Issues and Empirical Analysis*. National Bureau for Economic Research, University of Chicago Press, Chicago.

Schive, C., 1994, How did Taiwan solve its Dutch disease problem? In M. Dutta and R. Shiratori, Eds, *Asian Economic Studies, Vol. V, Asia-Pacific Economies: 1990s and Beyond*. JAI Press, London.

——, 1995, *Taiwan's Economic Role in East Asia*. The Center for Strategic and International Studies, Washington, D.C.

—— and Kuang-tao Hsueh, 1987, *The Experience and Prospects of High-tech*

Industrial Development in Taiwan, R.O.C. – The Case of the Information Industry. Paper presented at the Joint Conference on the Industrial Policies of the ROC and the ROK, 16–17 February; and Chung-Hua Institution for Economic Research, Occasional Paper No. 9001, Taiwan.

Scott, M., 1979, *Foreign trade*. In W. Galenson, Ed., *Economic Growth and Structural Change in Taiwan: The Postwar Experience of the Republic of China*. Cornell University Press, Ithaca.

Shea, J. D. and Ya-Hwei Yang, 1990, *Financial System and the Allocation of Investment Funds*. Chung-Hua Institution for Economic Research, Taiwan.

Simon, D. F., 1992, Taiwan's strategy for creating competitive advantage: the role of the state in managing foreign technology. In N. T. Wang, Ed., *Taiwan's Enterprises in Global Prespective*. M. E. Sharpe, New York.

Smith, H., 1994, *The Role of Government in the Industrializalion of Taiwan and Korea in the 1980s*. Unpublished PhD dissertation, The Australian National University, Canberra.

——, 1995, Industry policy in East Asia. *Asia Pacific Economic Literature*, 9(1), pp. 17–39.

Sun, Keh-nan, 1985, An economic evaluation of the Statute for Encouraging Investment. Chung Hua Institution for Economic Research Economic Papers No. 17, Taiwan (in Chinese).

Tsai, Chi-yuan, 1993, The causes of Taiwan's current account surplus in the 1980s. *Industry of Free China, LXXX(3)*, pp. 49–83.

Tu, Chaw-hsai and Wen-thuen Wang, 1988, Trade liberalisation in the Republic of China and the economic effects of tariff reductions. In *Industrial Policies of Korea and the Republic of China*. Korea Development Institute, Seoul

Tyson, L. D., 1990, Managed trade making the best of the second best. In R. Z. Lawrence and C. L. Schultze, Eds. *An American Trade Strategy*. Brookings Institution, Washington, D.C.

——, 1992, *Who's Bashing Whom?* Institute for International Economics, Washington, D.C.

Wade, R., 1984, Dirigisme Taiwan-style. *Institute of Development Studies Bulletin*, 15(2), pp. 65–70.

Wade, R., 1988, The role of government in overcoming market failure: Taiwan, Republic of Korea and Japan. In H. Hughes, Ed., *Achieving Industrialisation in East Asia*. Cambridge, Cambridge University Press.

——, 1990a, *Governing the Market: Economic Theory and the Role of Government in East Asian Industrialization*. Princeton University Press, Princeton.

——, 1990b, Industrial policy in East Asia: does it lead or follow the market? In G. Gereffi and D. Wyman, Eds., *Manufacturing Miracles, Paths of Industrialization in Latin America and East Asia*. Princeton University Press, Princeton.

Wu, Hui-lin and Tein-chen Chou, 1988, Small and medium enterprises and economic development in Taiwan. *Industry of Free China*, Council for Economic Planning **LXXIX** (3), pp. 15–30.

Wu, Rong-I, 1991,Taiwan: adjustment in an export-oriented economy. In H. Patrick and L. Meissner, Eds, *Pacific Basin Industries In Distress*. Columbia University Press, New York.

Yang, Ya-Hwei, 1990, *The Influence of Preferential Policies on Strategic Industries: an empirical study of Taiwan*. Chung-Hua Institution for Economic Research Discussion Paper No. 9003, Taiwan.

——, Li-Chung Jen and Rong-Chien Chou, 1990, An evaluation of the effects of preferential policies for strategic industries. *CIER Modern Economic Studies Series*, No. 17, Taiwan (in Chinese).

Yen, Gi-il, 1984, *Industrial Policies as They Relate to SMBs – a Financial Perspective*. Paper presented at the Joint Conference on the Industrial Policies of the ROC and the ROK, Chung-Hua Institution for Economic Research, Taiwan, 27–28 December.

Yu, Tzong-shian, 1988, *The Role of Government in Industrialization*. Paper presented at the Columbia University Conference on Taiwan, New York, September.

Yue, Chia Siow, 1993, *The Dynamics of East Asian Growth – Reform and Government Management*. Paper presented at *Sustaining the Development Process, A Festschrift Seminar held in honour of Helen Hughes*, Australian National University, Canberra, 19–20 August.

Part IV

FOREIGN TRADE, FOREIGN INVESTMENT AND TECHNOLOGY TRANSFER

13

ECONOMIC INTEGRATION WITHIN GREATER CHINA

Trade and Investment Flows between China, Hong Kong and Taiwan

Robert F. Ash and Y. Y. Kueh

Economic integration is essentially a process of unification – the means whereby coherence is imposed upon previously separate, even disparate, geographical regions. It may be pursued as a domestic or international goal, although the simultaneous attainment of both may prove elusive. Recent efforts towards the creation of formal trans-national, regional economic identities, whether North American (NAFTA), European (EC) or Asian-Pacific (APEC), have sometimes been perceived as a threat to the establishment of a truly integrated *global* economy. By contrast, the remarkable degree of economic integration already achieved between southern China and Hong Kong (and, latterly, Taiwan) might ironically have a fissiparous effect on China's *domestic* economy. From this point of view, there is a danger that increasing economic integration within Greater China[1] could threaten China's national economic identity, or at least compel its re-definition.

Cultural and linguistic affinities have no doubt helped to facilitate the economic integration of China, Hong Kong and Taiwan. But international trade and foreign investment have been its most potent stimuli. The rapid development of trade has generated familiar static and dynamic gains, which have enhanced economic growth within the region. These have been complemented, especially for China, by the benefits of rapidly-expanding foreign investment. Overcoming their technological backwardness is a cornerstone of developing countries' growth strategies and it is no coincidence that the Chinese government has increasingly used foreign investment to encourage productivity-enhancing technical progress. After all, inflows of capital promise to obviate resource bottlenecks, especially capital shortages and skill deficiencies. China's willingness to accept such overseas participation, including foreign direct investment (FDI), in its domestic economic development is a measure of the real significance of its post-1978 open-door strategy.

Source: *The China Quarterly*, No. 136 (December 1993), pp. 711–45.

The different resource endowments and levels of development of China, Hong Kong and Taiwan suggest how all stand to benefit from greater economic integration. Economic growth in Hong Kong and Taiwan has derived overwhelmingly from trade-orientated strategies, characterized by a decline in the export shares of resource-based goods in favour of those of labour and (later) capital-intensive products. Such developments have been accompanied by worsening shortages of land and labour, which have generated upwards pressure on rents and wages.

In China too the export sector, originally dominated by resource-based goods, has shifted towards the production of labour-intensive commodities. But land and labour remain plentiful and their accessibility has made the extension of Hong Kong and Taiwanese industrial facilities to the Chinese mainland an increasingly attractive proposition. For China, short of capital and technologically immature, such a relationship promises enormous benefits. This complementarity has generated an economic symbiosis between the constituent elements of Greater China.

Through their effects on resource allocation and their stimulus to technology transfer, the expansion of merchandise trade and investment has had a profound impact on the economies of Hong Kong, Taiwan and southern China. The same forces have generated new employment and production opportunities. They have also been the source of important structural changes, associated with the re-allocation of resources. Above all, they have caused accelerated economic growth, in recent times unmatched almost anywhere else in the world.

These considerations define the main themes of this article. In it we seek to assess, through an examination of the pattern and level of trade and investment flows, the extent to which Greater China has become economically integrated. We are also concerned to analyse some of the economic implications of this process. For reasons of convenience, trade and investment are treated separately. The reality is of course more complicated and less artificial. Each encourages and facilitates the other and it is the combined effect of both which makes their stimulus to economic growth so powerful.

MERCHANDISE TRADE

Trade flows between China, Hong Kong and Taiwan

The rapid expansion of China's foreign trade after 1978 is one of the most remarkable features of the impact of the reform programme (in this case, the open-door strategy). Between 1978 and 1991 China's merchandise trade grew, on average, by over 14 per cent per annum – almost twice as fast as global trade, marginally faster than Taiwan's, but a little more slowly than that of Hong Kong.[2] The outcome was that all three countries and regions dramatically increased their share of global trade during this period: China and Taiwan by almost 100 per cent each, and Hong Kong by almost 200 per cent. Imports and exports contributed about equally to Hong Kong's trade expansion, whereas the increasing contribution of China and Taiwan to world trade owed more to export expansion than to import growth.[3]

The historical context of the most recent (post-1978) expansion in Hong Kong's trade with China has been rehearsed elsewhere[4] and will not receive detailed consideration here. Suffice to say that between 1949 and the end of the 1970s, China's share of Hong Kong exports fell to a negligible level, although its role as an importer of Chinese goods remained significant. In the latter connection, it is worth recording that by the beginning of the 1970s Hong Kong's role as a channel for the re-export of Chinese goods had become insignificant.[5] In 1970, for example, the value of retained imports of Chinese products was 13 times higher than in the 1930s, whilst that of re-exported commodities was only 57 per cent more.[6] A striking feature of developments during the 1980s was a reversal of this position to one approximating that of the pre-war years.

Table 13.1 contains estimates of the average annual rate of growth of bilateral trade flows between 1980 and 1991. They highlight the process whereby Hong Kong and China have each become the other's most important trading partner.

Analysis of the data from which these estimates are derived suggests the critical contribution which China has made to Hong Kong's overall trade performance. For example, in 1978 exports[7] to China accounted for less than 1 per cent of Hong Kong's total exports. By 1983, the corresponding figure was 11.45 per cent, and by 1985 it had risen to 26.03 per cent. Thereafter, after a temporary decline, it remained (on average) in excess of 26 per cent. Without access to the Chinese market, Hong Kong's export growth in the 1980s would have been significantly slower,[8] although it would also have displayed a more sharply accelerating trend during the second half of the 1980s.

The symbiosis which has come to characterize the economic relationship between China and Hong Kong is highlighted in the British Colony's role as a re-distribution channel for goods passing through the territory.

Table 13.1 The expansion of trade between Hong Kong and China (average annual growth rate (%))

	HK exports to China			*HK imports from China*		
	Total	*Domestic*	*Re-exports*	*Total*	*Retained*	*Re-exports*
1980–91	31.86	32.03	31.79	23.57	8.96	32.98
1980–85	45.65	44.95	45.88	19.76	14.38	28.34
1985–91	20.36	21.26	20.06	26.74	4.44	36.83

Sources: Hong Kong Census and Statistics Department, *Hong Kong Monthly Digest of Statistics*, various issues.

Domestic exports and re-exports from Hong Kong to China grew strongly, but in tandem throughout the period. By contrast, the global picture reveals slower export growth, but a differential performance in favour of re-exports. The share of re-exports in Hong Kong's total shipments to China remained stable at around 75 per cent throughout the 1980s, while the corresponding figure for countries other than China rose steadily from 30 to 70 per cent.[9]

Hong Kong's import profile shows that the growth of imports from China consistently outstripped that from the rest of the world.[10] Moreover, in contrast to the pattern of export growth, the expansion of imports – already strong during the first half of the 1980s – accelerated quite sharply after 1985. The increasing share of imports from China subsequently re-exported from Hong Kong is particularly striking. Between 1980 and 1985, this rose from 31 to 47 per cent; by 1991 it had reached an astonishing 86 per cent.[11] The true measure of this transformation is indicated by the changing ratio between re-exports of imports from China and from elsewhere: in 1978 it was 0.35:1.00, but by 1990 it had been reversed to 1.26:1.00.[12] Meanwhile, not only has the share of Chinese imports retained in Hong Kong declined, but – since 1988 – the absolute level of such shipments has also fallen.[13]

The growing importance of Hong Kong as a channel for the redistribution of goods originating from, or destined for, China is the single most significant finding to emerge from Table 13.1. This fact, perhaps more than anything else, highlights the integration of the region into the southern Chinese economy.[14]

Between 1978 and 1983, Hong Kong's trade deficit *vis-à-vis* China increased from US$10.25 to 24.42 million.[15] A sharp but temporary reversal took place in 1984 and 1985 (the only post-1978 year in which Hong Kong enjoyed a bilateral surplus), but thereafter the deficit reasserted itself and steadily increased to reach US$85.63 million in 1991. During the same period, Hong Kong consistently enjoyed a surplus in its trade with the rest of the world.[16] This was not always sufficient to nullify the bilateral deficit, the net result being that Hong Kong's global trade balance was sometimes in surplus, sometimes in deficit, without any clear pattern emerging.

Trade relations between Taiwan and the Chinese mainland were historically very close[17] and at the beginning of the 1930s, during the Japanese occupation of the island, its trade with the mainland accounted for half or more of total trade with countries other than Japan.[18] Such relations were interrupted after the removal of the Kuomintang government to Taiwan in 1949 and only officially resumed some three decades later. But as the estimates in Table 13.2 suggest, two-way trade subsequently expanded rapidly.[19]

The estimates leave no room for doubt about the dramatic nature of trade expansion across the Taiwan Straits during the 1980s and into the 1990s. At first it was subject to considerable instability, mainly because of strong annual fluctuations in Taiwanese exports to the mainland (only in 1985 did shipments in the opposite direction fail to record positive growth). Major

Table 13.2 Changing trends in trade between Taiwan and the Chinese mainland: indirect trade through Hong Kong

	Taiwan exports			*Taiwan imports*		
	Annual growth rate of global exports (%)	*Annual growth rate of exports to PRC (%)*	*Exports to PRC as global % global imports*	*Annual growth rate of global imports (%)*	*Annual growth rate of imports from PRC (%)*	*Imports from PRC as % global imports*
1980–91	12.25	26.90	3.41	10.55	24.22	0.99
1980–85	8.78	28.08	1.61	0.36	7.79	0.48
1985–91	15.14	25.92	4.09	19.04	37.92	1.17

Sources: *HKMDS*, various issues; and *IFSY 1992*, pp. 111 and 113.

increases between 1979 and 1981 gave way to absolute declines in 1982 and 1983, and recovery during 1984 and 1985 was again halted in 1986. In short, only since 1987 has relatively stable growth become apparent.

Until mid-1981 a no-tariff policy was a major incentive to Taiwan exporters to the PRC. But it also encouraged market saturation by inviting others to disguise their products as being of Taiwan origin. The subsequent abandonment of preferential treatment and imposition of stricter controls were the factors behind the negative growth of Taiwanese exports in 1982 and 1983. Recovery was, however, rapid and only momentarily interrupted in 1986, when import restrictions were introduced in an effort to halt the sharp decline in China's foreign exchange reserves.

For the post-1980 period as a whole, the average annual rate of growth of Taiwanese imports from the Chinese mainland almost matched that of exports to the PRC. However, legal restraints on such imports, especially during the early 1980s, were responsible for the much slower rate of expansion during the first half of the decade.

Table 13.2 also quantifies the increasing involvement of Taiwan and the PRC in each other's overall trade after 1980. At the start of the decade, mainland exports accounted for 1.22 per cent of Taiwan's global exports, the corresponding figure for imports being less than 0.5 per cent. By 1991 these figures had risen to 6.13 and 1.6 per cent respectively.[20] From the mainland's perspective, Taiwan's share in total exports rose more modestly from 0.43 to 1.57 per cent during 1980–91.

The indirect nature of trade between Taiwan and the PRC highlights the paramount role which Hong Kong has played in the evolution of bilateral trade relations. That it will continue to do this is suggested by the finding that in 1992 almost 49 per cent of shipments from Taiwan to Hong Kong were destined for the Chinese mainland, and 29.5 per cent of goods exported to Taiwan from Hong Kong originated in the PRC.[21]

Since 1980 Taiwan has maintained a favourable balance in its indirect trade with the PRC, the second half of the decade witnessing a consistent increase in its surplus. Indeed, between 1985 and 1991, Taiwan's cross-Straits surplus rose from 8 to 27 per cent of its global surplus.[22] Such estimates are one measure of the extent to which Taiwan's remarkable record in accumulating foreign exchange reserves has increasingly become linked to the expansion of trade with its neighbour.[23]

Measuring trade intensity between China, Hong Kong and Taiwan

Estimates of the trade intensity ratio (TIR) between two countries provide a formal measure of the changing strength of their trade relationship – the extent to which each is becoming more (or less) dependent upon the other.[24] A value of TIR greater than unity is significant in the sense that the share of country A's exports to country B in the former's export portfolio is higher than B's import share as a proportion of aggregated global imports. The larger the value of TIR, the stronger the trade links between any two countries.

Table 13.3 sets out TIR estimates in selected years for China, Hong Kong and Taiwan in the twin contexts of Sino-Hong Kong and Sino-Taiwanese merchandise trade. The figures highlight some of the implications of China's implementation of an open-door strategy after 1978. They suggest that from a Chinese export perspective, trade with Hong Kong has remained "significant,"[25] albeit – especially in the early reform years – at a declining rate. From the Hong Kong perspective, the open-door policy had a marked impact, the TIR rising sharply up to the mid-1980s and then stabilizing somewhat.

If, however, re-exports of Chinese goods are excluded, the calculations show China's TIR to have fallen more sharply and consistently.[26] This would seem to suggest that an increasingly small proportion of exports to Hong

Table 13.3 TIR estimates: China, Hong Kong and Taiwan

	China–Hong Kong		*China–Taiwan*	
	With China as exporter	*With Hong Kong as exporter*	*With China as exporter*	*With Taiwan as exporter*
1978	24.43	0.62	0.53	0.0005
1980	20.92	6.23	0.43	1.20
1985	16.62	11.41	0.39	1.41
1989	17.68	13.21	0.64	2.24
1990	—	—	0.78	3.20
1991	—	—	0.90	3.48

Sources: *HKMDS*, various issues: *IFSY 1992*, pp. 111 and 113; United Nations, Economic and Social Commission for Asia and the Pacific, *Statistical Yearbook for Asia and the Pacific, 1991*, pp. 85 and 127–28.

Kong was retained in the territory. The results of similar calculations based on Hong Kong as the exporting region are much more closely in line with those in Table 13.3 and indicate an increasingly important role for the territory as direct and indirect supplier of goods to China after 1978.[27]

In the wake of the open-door strategy, China's trade ties with Taiwan rapidly assumed significance. But it is noteworthy that this process was driven more by the expansion of exports from Taiwan than from the PRC. With China (PRC) as the exporting country, the value of TIR has not yet reached unity, although if recent trends are maintained attainment of this level cannot be long delayed.[28]

The changing composition of merchandise trade

The export experiences of the countries in North-east Asia, including the constituent regions of Greater China, reveal a common pattern. In the early stages of economic development, exports derive largely from natural resource-based products. Only later is there an increasing role for labour-intensive manufactured goods – and ultimately for capital-intensive, high-technology commodities.[29]

The decline in the share of Chinese exports retained in Hong Kong is reflected in the changing structure of bilateral trade. One contributory factor has been the fall in food exports from the mainland, consequent upon rising per capita income.[30] More generally, Hong Kong consumers' perception of Chinese goods as cheap, but inferior in quality and design, has encouraged demand to shift towards other overseas sources of goods (especially manufactures).[31] Meanwhile, the share of re-exported Chinese goods has been rising. Between 1979 and 1987, for example, the ratios of retained to re-exported Chinese crude materials, chemicals and manufactures were reversed in favour of re-exports.[32]

Hong Kong's role as a direct supplier of goods to China has expanded markedly since 1978. The fact that domestic exports of producer goods (especially machinery and transport equipment) have outstripped those of consumer goods makes Hong Kong's trade with China unique and reflects the increasingly important role of Hong Kong-based industrial operations on the Chinese mainland.[33] Thus, the expanding share of Chinese imports of Hong Kong-produced machinery and components highlights the growing importance of outward-processing activities in southern China. This emerging pattern is further evidence of a cross-border economic symbiosis and growing regional integration.

Similar factors have determined the changing composition of Taiwan's exports to China. During 1985–90, for example, these were dominated by machinery, transport equipment and industrial materials for manufacturing purposes,[34] with the contribution of chemicals and related products also expanding rapidly.[35] These are precisely the goods needed by the subsidiaries of parent Taiwan companies, located in China. The simultaneous acceleration of exports and FDI from Taiwan to the Chinese mainland after 1987 suggests that the cross-Straits export expansion has been no less intimately related to investment considerations than in Hong Kong.

The composition of Chinese exports to Taiwan has been limited by government restrictions emanating from Taipei.[36] But available evidence points to the declining importance of agricultural products, fuels and raw materials at the expense of industrial materials for manufacturing, machinery and transport equipment, and miscellaneous manufactures.[37]

The role of Guangdong and Fujian in trade integration within Greater China

Hong Kong and Taiwan entrepreneurial activity has been heavily concentrated in Guangdong and Fujian provinces and the nature and level of the trade flows analysed above have been critically influenced by the process of economic integration between Hong Kong, Taiwan and southern China. This process has dictated the changing composition of shipments of goods to and from the Chinese mainland, not least as outward processing activities have come to dominate the operations of Hong Kong and Taiwanese manufacturers in China.[38]

The economic rationale of the integration of Greater China lies essentially in the complementarity of factor endowments throughout the region. In recent years, the continued economic expansion of Hong Kong and Taiwan has been constrained by shortages of land and labour – and associated pressures on rents and wages. In contrast to unemployment rates in these regions of well under 2 per cent,[39] the labour force in Guangdong and Fujian was growing, respectively, by 2.85 and 3.35 per cent during the second half of the 1980s.[40] Such figures mean access to cheap labour and land for overseas entrepreneurs who are prepared to re-site their operations in southern China.

Guangdong and Fujian's trade growth after 1978 was significantly faster than that of China as a whole, and of Hong Kong and Taiwan.[41] Such rapid expansion was reflected in an increasing contribution by both provinces to China's overall trade, even though Guangdong's share of national exports only reattained the previous peak level (1970) in 1991.[42] Their contribution to China's trade balance throughout the 1980s was also positive and significant.[43] Meanwhile, one corollary of these regional developments was the spectacular decline of Shanghai's export role in domestic trade, its contribution to all exports falling from 23.55 to 7.98 per cent between 1980 and 1991.[44]

Such figures set the trade performances of Guangdong and Fujian in a national context. They do not, however, show the debt which they owed to evolving relationships with Hong Kong and Taiwan. Table 13.4 seeks to encapsulate these emerging trade relations. Between 1980 and 1991 Guangdong's exports to Hong Kong grew by 21.2 per cent annually – a performance

Table 13.4 Trade flows between Guangdong, Fujian, Hong Kong and Taiwan

	1980		*1985*		*1989*		*1990*		*1991*	
	Value US$ m.	*%*	*Value US$ m.*	*%*	*Value US$ m.*	*%*	*Value US$ m.*	*%*	*Value US$ m.*	*%*
Guangdong										
Total exports	2,194.72	100	2,952.67	100	8,167.67	100	10,560.24	100	13,687.87	100
Hong Kong	1,126.80	51.4	2,168.20	73.4	6,514.32	79.8	8,709.11	82.5	11,593.06	84.7
Taiwan	—	—	—	—	6.96	0.1	8.95	0.1	36.52	0.3
Total imports	356.12	100	2,426.64	100	4,831.21	100	5,748.88	100	8,510.09	100
Hong Kong	—	—	2,210.64	91.1	3,554.17	73.6	4,152.16	72.2	6,294.13	74.0
Taiwan	—	—	—	—	28.44	0.6	53.78	0.9	134.11	1.6
Fujian										
Total exports	363.66	100	491.48	100	1,661.77	100	2,238.13	100	2,925.67	100
Hong Kong	116.76	32.1	200.76	40.8	761.69	45.8	1,065.35	47.6	1,075.58	36.8
Total imports	141.77	100	599.90	100	735.31	100	933.24	100	1,407.76	100
Hong Kong	37.25	26.3	318.23	53.1	373.23	50.8	459.94	49.3	747.23	53.1
Taiwan	—	—	13.20	2.2	20.41	2.8	41.58	4.5	103.84	7.4

Note: The figures shown here are based on export and import trade statistics. Notice that a different set of estimates of Fujian's total exports and imports are available from "customs statistics," as follows: exports: 1989 – 1,828.36, 1990 – 2,448.82, 1991 – 3,147.46; imports: 1989 – 1,594.45, 1990 – 1,897.18, 1991 – 2,608.51.

Sources: *Guandong*. *GDTJNJ 1992*, pp. 343–45 (1980, 1985, 1990 and 1991); *GDTJNJ 1991*, pp. 303–305 (1989); and p. 334 (imports from Hong Kong, 1985).

Fujian. Export and import trade statistics *FJTJNJ 1992*, p. 330 (1980–85, 1989, 1990 and 1991) and pp. 332–33 (Hong Kong, exports and imports, 1980), 1985, 1989, 1990 and 1991; and Taiwan, imports, 1985, 1990 and 1991).

Customs statistics: *FJTJNJ 1991*, p. 314; *FJTJNJ 1992*, p. 337.

which owed most to accelerated expansion after 1985.[45] The result was to raise Hong Kong's share in Guangdong's exports to so dominant a position that by 1991 such shipments constituted 85 per cent of total provincial exports and accounted for more than one-third of all exports from *China* to Hong Kong. This remarkable expansion also brought about a dramatic improvement in Guangdong's trade balance, the figures in Table 13.4 indicating that a minor deficit in 1985 was transformed into a healthy surplus by the end of the decade.[46]

Hong Kong also became an important destination for goods from Fujian during the 1980s. During the first half of the decade, exports to the British colony grew by almost 11 per cent p.a., but this figure accelerated to 28 per cent between 1985 and 1991.[47] This differential performance no doubt reflects the availability of new markets in Taiwan, as restrictions on cross-Straits trade were relaxed and entrepreneurs increasingly exploited new investment opportunities on the Chinese mainland. The same factors are no doubt responsible for the marked impact which Hong Kong and, latterly, Taiwan, had on Fujian imports. Taken at face value, the figures in Table 13.4 suggest that Hong Kong's share of provincial imports doubled between 1980 and 1985, but thereafter stabilized; by contrast, imports from Taiwan grew by more than 34 per cent annually during the next six years. their share rising almost three-and-a-half fold.[48]

The economic symbiosis inherent in integration counsels caution in interpreting these figures. Shipments of commodities between the Chinese mainland, and Hong Kong and Taiwan do not all derive from self-contained, indigenous activities. Rather, they have increasingly reflected the integrative impact of FDI and outward-processing operations. Such considerations make it desirable to distinguish between conventional merchandise trade and commodity movements related to FDI (*sanzi*[49]) or outward processing and compensation trade (*sanlai yibu*[50]). The significance of these distinctions is highlighted in Table 13.5.

These figures highlight the changing structural composition of the two provinces' exports and imports and thereby suggest the impact of regional integration with Hong Kong and Taiwan upon their foreign trade profiles. In the immediate wake of the new open-door policy, for example, virtually all Guangdong's exports remained conventional "merchandise exports" *(maoyi chukou)*.[51] Their share fell from 96 to 83 per cent during the first half of the 1980s, but thereafter declined much more rapidly to reach a mere 55 per cent in 1991. Initially, the role of exports generated through *sanzi* funding took second place to those facilitated by *sanlai yibu* activities, But under the impact of China's strategy of export-orientated foreign investment, this relationship changed dramatically during the second half of the decade. Increased capital inflows were reflected in a rapid growth of *sanzi* exports (on average, by 53 per cent p.a. between 1985 and 1991). As a result, by the beginning of the 1990s foreign sales of FDI-related products accounted for more than a

Table 13.5 FDI-related exports and imports of Guangdong and Fujian Provinces

	1980		*1985*		*1989*		*1990*		*1991*	
	Value US$ m.	*%*	*Value US$ m.*	*%*	*Value US$ m.*	*%*	*Value US$ m.*	*%*	*Value US$ m.*	*%*
Guangdong										
Total exports	2,194.72	100	2,952.67	100	8,167.67	100	10,560.24	100	13,687.87	100
Commissioned processing	82.33	3.8	272.50	9.2	578.17	7.1	583.32	5.5	799.72	5.8
Compensation trade	6.65	0.3	8.70	0.3	62.67	0.8	77.78	0.7	95.06	0.7
FDI ventures	—	—	221.16	7.5	2,276.71	27.9	3,723.83	35.3	5,327.48	38.9
Total imports	356.12	100	2,426.22	100	4,831.21	100	5,748.88	100	8,510.09	100
FDI ventures	—	—	336.56	13.9	1,950.92	40.4	3,297.44	57.4	4,513.02	53.0
Fujian										
Total exports	—	—	—	—	1,828.36	100	2,448.82	100	3,147.46	100
Commissioned processing	—	—	—	—	178.07	9.7	208.54	8.5	293.31	9.3
Compensation trade	—	—	—	—	12.49	0.7	11.29	0.5	5.53	0.2
FDI ventures	—	—	—	—	687.14	37.6	1,115.52	45.6	1,376.95	34.8

Table 13.5 (Cont.)

	1980		*1985*		*1989*		*1990*		*1991*	
	Value US$ m.	*%*	*Value US$ m.*	*%*	*Value US$ m.*	*%*	*Value US$ m.*	*%*	*Value US$ m.*	*%*
Total imports	—	—	—	—	1,594.45	100	1,897.18	100	2,608.51	100
Commissioned processing	—	—	—	—	163.54	10.3	161.87	8.5	251.25	9.6
Compensation trade	—	—	—	—	9.90	0.6	4.20	0.2	5.04	0.2
FDI ventures	—	—	—	—	168.35	10.6	237.63	12.5	282.80	10.8
Export processing	—	—	—	—	584.25	36.6	895.97	47.2	1,278.55	49.0

Notes:
Guangdong. "Commissioned processing" is a translation of the Chinese phrase *lailiao jiagong*. It refers to the processing (*jiagong*) of materials from outside (*lailiao*) for re-export. This category usually includes assembly (*zhuanpei*) of product parts which have been similarly imported. Export through "compensation trade" (*buchang maoyi*) involves not only the provision of raw materials, semi-finished manufactures and/or parts, but also the supply of machinery and equipment, to be "compensated" for by reducing or relinqushing processing fees or land rents. Note that the term *sanlai yibu* embraces both *lailiao jiagong* and *buchang maoyi*. "FDI ventures" refer to the activities of the "three foreign-funded enterprises" (*sanzi qiye*): equity, contractual and wholly-foreign-owned ventures. Because of Chinese restrictions on domestic sales, the bulk of these enterprises' output is destined for the world market. A large proportion of exports generated through "commissioned processing" or "compensation trade" also involves FDI firms.

Fujian, "Export processing" translates the Chinese phrase *jinliao jiagong* (literally "imported materials for processing"). The term is clearly similar to *lailiao jiagong*, although it is not clear whether the activities under this heading constitute a broader category, which also embraces "commissioned processing." "FDI equipment" refers to imports via FDI of machinery and equipment as part of their investment.

Sources: As Table 13.4. Estimates for Fujian are derived from customs statistics.

third of all Guangdong's exports.[52] (On the import side the dominance of FDI-related activities emerges even more dramatically.) Although a detailed breakdown of Fujian's exports and imports is only available for the most recent years, the evidence points to the emergence of a similar pattern.[53]

The symbiotic economic relationship between the constituent parts of Greater China is well reflected in their trading position *vis-à-vis* the United States. Figure 13.1 seeks to illustrate this by showing the changing trade surpluses of Hong Kong, Taiwan and China (including Greater China) with the United States between 1981 and 1991.[54] It is clear that since the mid-1980s China's trade surplus with the United States has risen dramatically. By contrast, during 1987–91 the large surpluses enjoyed by Hong Kong and –

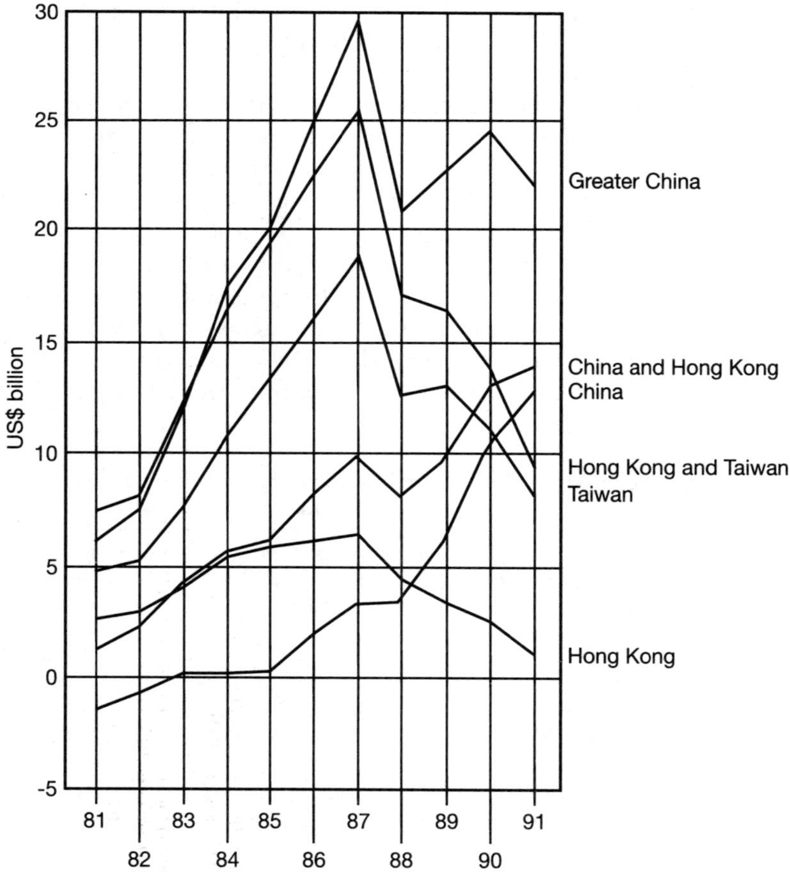

Figure 13.1 Annual Trade Surpluses of Greater China with the United States 1981–91

Source: 1981–90: Ian K. Perkin, "Greater China trade area surplus with the U.S." in *SCMP*, 29 January 1992; Hong Kong and China 1991: *SCMP*, 21 February 1992; Taiwan 1991: *Taiwan Statistical Data Book 1992*.

especially – Taiwan declined no less significantly. There can be no doubt that these contrary trends precisely reflect the accelerated relocation, since the middle of the 1980s, of export-orientated Hong Kong and Taiwanese firms to mainland China (above all, the Pearl River Delta).[55]

The impact of the relocation of Hong Kong manufacturing activities in China, and associated "outward processing" operations for re-export through Hong Kong, is suggested by the estimates in Table 13.6. The figures reveal that between 1989 and the first half of 1992 some 71–77 per cent of Hong Kong's exports to China were destined for outward processing and related to FDI ventures. On the conservative assumption that the processing fee (including transport costs) constituted 20 per cent of the value of exports to China, the finished manufactures accounted, on average, for 68 per cent of Hong Kong's total exports to the United States during the same period. This clearly reflects the transfer of Hong Kong manufacturing enterprises to mainland China during recent years.

The evidence presented in this section suggests that the open-door strategy has facilitated the establishment of a framework to accommodate increasing involvement by Hong Kong and Taiwan entrepreneurs in the southern Chinese economy. The outcome has been to alter both the level and pattern of trade within Greater China. Especially striking are the changes which have taken place since the mid-1980s and which at present show no sign of abating. Such changes have of course had important implications for economic growth and structural change throughout the region. Before examining these implications in greater detail, however, further consideration must be given to the nature of investment flows from Hong Kong and Taiwan to Guangdong and Fujian.

Table 13.6 The implications of the re-location of Hong Kong manufacturing enterprises in China

	Hong Kong exports to China (US$ m.)	*Hong Kong exports to China for outward processing (US$ m.)*	*%*	*Hong Kong exports to United States (US$ m.)*
1988	38,043	—	—	72,884
1989	43,272	32,262	74.6	72,162
1990	47,470	36,418	76.7	66,370
1991	54,404	40,369	74.2	62,870
1992				
Jan.–June	28,499	20,323	71.3	28,038

Source: *TKP*, 30 December 1992.

FOREIGN INVESTMENT[56]

Investment flows between China, Hong Kong and Taiwan.

Changes in the level of investment flows from Hong Kong and Taiwan to southern China provide a further measure of the growing economic integration of the region. Capital flows from mainland China to Taiwan for the time being remain largely non-existent, although accelerated increases in Chinese investment in Hong Kong – especially from Guangdong – have been a notable feature of the recent past. Political factors may have played a part in this recent expansion. But from an economic perspective, it is as well to remember that capital flows from Japan and the United States continue to dominate foreign investment in the colony. There is no question of the archetypal market economy of Hong Kong (or, for that matter, of Taiwan) becoming integrated with those of Guangdong and Fujian under the impact of increased Chinese investment in Hong Kong.

Table 13.7 summarizes trends in capital flows between Hong Kong and Taiwan and the Chinese mainland between 1985 and 1991. Where possible, estimates for Shanghai have also been included in order to introduce a comparative perspective. The table shows that Guangdong has remained by far the largest recipient of investment from Hong Kong, whether measured in terms of FDI flows or, more broadly, of AFI. Except for 1987, the provincial intake of FDI increased consistently after 1985, the gross stock rising on average by 51.2 per cent p.a. The comparable percentage for AFI was 47.1, the slightly lower figure perhaps reflecting the downturn in 1990 as well as in 1987.

Fujian's intake of capital from Hong Kong has been much less impressive than that of Guangdong (*cf.* an average annual rate of growth of AFI of 41 per cent). It is telling too that the cumulative level of AFI into Fujian from Hong Kong during 1985–91 was little more than half that received by the tiny enclave of Shenzhen Special Economic Zone (SEZ).[57] But Fujian's profile still compares favourably with most other FDI/AFI recipient provinces, including – see Table 13.4 – Shanghai.

After 1985 Hong Kong investment in China as a whole grew even more rapidly than in Guangdong.[58] Such a comparison is, however, misleading in at least one important respect. As a pioneer in the search for foreign capital, Guangdong was by 1985 already well-established as a recipient of investment from the British colony. Subsequently an increasing number of eastern coastal provinces emerged as competitors for the same pool of capital.[59] Even so, in 1991 Guangdong still accounted for more than half of total Hong Kong investment in China (54 per cent of FDI, 59 per cent of AFI). If Fujian were included (9 per cent of FDI, 8 per cent of AFI), the two provinces were in receipt of some two-thirds of foreign investment from the colony.

It is difficult to estimate with accuracy the level of Taiwanese investment

Table 13.7 Shares of Guangdong, Fujian, Shanghai and all China in realized foreign investment from Hong Kong and Taiwan, 1985–91 (US$ million)

	1985	*1986*	*1987*	*1988*	*1989*	*1990*	*1991*	*1985–91*
From Hong Kong								
Guangdong								
FDI	450.20	622.65	502.67	836.54	952.72	1018.59	1448.60	5831.97
	(47.11)	(46.86)	(27.79)	(34.45)	(40.68)	(48.08)	(54.42)	(42.75)
AFI	845.63	1095.45	884.09	1537.96	1544.89	1298.46	1724.80	8931.28
	(83.20)	(69.65)	(42.28)	(49.46)	(53.04)	(53.40)	(58.97)	(55.61)
Shenzhen								
FDI	146.05	328.87	219.54	225.61	212.66	177.99	227.81	1538.52
	(15.28)	(24.75)	(12.14)	(9.29)	(9.08)	(8.40)	(8.56)	(11.28)
AFI	272.42	385.87	256.32	281.98	287.29	262.91	323.75	2070.54
	(26.80)	(24.53)	(12.26)	(9.07)	(9.86)	(10.81)	(11.07)	(12.89)
Guangzhou								
FDI	—	—	—	—	—	125.71	187.07	—
	—	—	—	—	—	(5.93)	(7.03)	—
AFI	136.63	120.85	49.72	111.47	104.16	125.57	—	—
	(13.44)	(7.68)	(2.38)	(3.58)	(3.58)	(5.16)	—	—
Fujian								
FDI	95.07	—	—	80.56	195.28	160.91	225.77	—
	(9.95)	—	—	(3.32)	(8.34)	(7.60)	(8.40)	—
AFI	141.97	70.23	36.67	177.48	204.23	249.45	225.77	1105.80
	(13.97)	(4.47)	(1.75)	(5.71)	(7.01)	(10.26)	(7.72)	(6.89)
Xiamen								
FDI	58.83	—	—	31.77	—	45.08	—	—
	(6.16)	—	—	(1.31)	—	(2.13)	—	—
AFI	*	*	*	*	153.91	107.27	—	—
					(5.28)	(4.41)	—	—

Shanghai								
FDI	—	—	—	—	—	—	47.44	—
	—	—	—	—	—	—	(1.78)	—
AFI	—	31.30	312.83	—	178.96	—	—	—
	—	(1.99)	(14.96)	—	(6.14)	—	—	—
All China								
FDI	955.68	1328.71	1809.05	2428.05	2341.77	2118.48	2661.81	13643.55
	(48.86)	(59.22)	(68.35)	(64.93)	(62.06)	(56.42)	(57.04)	(60.67)
AFI	1016.37	1572.85)	2091.24	3109.44	2912.78	2431.68	2924.96	16059.32
	(22.78)	(21.67)	(24.74)	(30.40)	(28.96)	(23.63)	(25.32)	(25.95)
From Taiwan								
Guangdong								
FDI	—	—	—	3.24	22.72	70.33	109.56	—
	—	—	—	—	—	(31.36)	(23.32)	—
Shenzhen								
FDI	—	—	—	3.16	10.06	3.71	2.16	—
	—	—	—	—	—	(1.65)	(0.46)	—
Guangzhou								
FDI	—	—	—	—	4.37	22.69	28.79	—
	—	—	—	—	—	(10.12)	(6.13)	—
Hainan								
FDI	—	—	—	—	—	5.68	—	—
	—	—	—	—	—	(2.53)	—	—
Fujian								
FDI	—	0.57	0.72	11.01	106.66	—	—	—
	—	—	—	—	—	—	—	—
Shanghai								
FDI	—	—	—	—	—	—	—	—
	—	—	—	—	—	—	—	—

Table 13.7 (Cont.)

	1985	*1986*	*1987*	*1988*	*1989*	*1990*	*1991*	*1985–91*
All China								
FDI	—	—	—	—	—	224.26	469.89	—
	—	—	—	—	—	(5.97)	(10.11)	—

Notes:
* The cumulative total AFI (1985–88) was US$240.46 million (3.09%).
FDI = foreign direct investment.
AFI = all foreign investment (including FDI and loans).

Figures in brackets show the percentage share of total investment to China from Hong Kong and Taiwan, except for those under "All China," which show the share of Hong Kong and Taiwan in China's total intake for foreign capital. Some of the absolute US$ estimates for Hong Kong have been obtained by applying the FDI or AFI ratio to the total FDI or AFI intake for the relevant region. For example, Shenzhen's FDI (1991) is derived from the AFI ratio and total FDI (from Hong Kong and elsewhere). For some areas – notably Guangzhou (1985–88) and Shanghai (1986–87) – the ratio from the pledged, rather than realized, investment series has been used.

The figures for Taiwan are all from official mainland Chinese sources. For Fujian the estimates appear to constitute a complete series. The source from which they are taken (*FJTJNJ 1990*) also gives a cumulative total for 1979–89 as US$120.19 million. This is only marginally more than the US$118.96 million cited for 1986–89. It is curious that annual estimates for 1990 and 1991 are absent from the 1991 and 1992 editions of *FJTJNJ* – precisely when the national *Statistical Yearbook* made available such estimates for the country as a whole. The estimates for Shenzhen for 1988–91, which generate a cumulative total of US$19.09 million, seem to constitute another complete series, since the figure is almost identical to that given in *SZTJSC 1991* (p. 43).

Sources:
Hong Kong. Kueh, "Foreign investment and economic change," p. 674 and 682–83; *Guangzhou tongji nianjian 1992 (Guangzhou Statistical Yearbook 1992)* (hereafter *GZTJNJ*), p. 315; and *SHTJNJ 1992*, p. 358.

Taiwan. GDTJNJ 1992, p. 360; *Shenzhenshi qiwu shiqi guomin jingji he shehui tongji ziliao (1960–90) (National Economic and Social Statistical Material for Shenzhen Municipality during the Seventh Five-Year Plan Period (1986–90))*, p. 405; *Shenzhen tongji nianjian 1992 (Shenzhen Statistical Yearbook 1992)* (hereafter *SZTJNJ*), p. 397; *GZTJNJ 1991*, p. 305; *GZTJNJ 1992*, p. 315; *Hainan tongji nianjian 1991 (Hainan Statistical Yearbook 1991)*, p. 433; *FJTJNJ 1987*, p. 331; *FJTJNJ 1988*, p. 429; *FJTJNJ 1990*, p. 295; and *ZGTJNJ 1992*, p. 642.

in mainland China. The fragmentary data shown in Table 13.4 are all that can be found in official mainland publications. What is not in doubt is that Taiwanese investment in the two southern provinces has increased dramatically in recent years in the wake of informal contacts and, since 1991, the formal authorization by the Taipei government of "indirect investment" through third parties.[60] With US$469.89 million invested in 1991 (twice as much as in the previous year), FDI of Taiwanese origin accounted for some 10 per cent of China's total intake. Although this was far behind the contribution of Hong Kong, it placed Taiwan only marginally behind Japan as a supplier of FDI to the Chinese mainland. By the end of 1992, Taiwan had in fact overtaken Japan to rank second as a source of FDI to the PRC.[61]

Estimates of Fujian's intake of FDI from Taiwan in 1991 are apparently not available. But assuming that it was no smaller than the US$109.56 million invested in Guangdong, there can be little doubt that the combined share of the two provinces in FDI flows from Hong Kong and Taiwan was no less than 60 per cent – and cumulatively (1985–91) much more. Such figures demonstrate clearly the locational choice made by Hong Kong and Taiwanese entrepreneurs and signal the trend towards greater economic integration within Greater China,

There is, however, a qualification to be entered here. A survey conducted by the Ministry of Economic Affairs (MOEA) in Taipei in April 1991 suggested that the level of Taiwanese FDI in mainland China was more substantial than that indicated in official PRC sources. The survey, based on the responses of 2,503 firms which had voluntarily registered their investment interests with the government in Taipei, revealed a cumulative FDI stock of US$750 million.[62] Although it is impossible to reconcile the statistical discrepancy, there is no doubt that a significant part of FDI flows to China from Hong Kong, Japan, the United States and South-east Asia reflect the activities of Taiwanese firms in disguise. It is unlikely, however, that such flows from places other than Hong Kong have exceeded the colony's own investment involvement and we are confident that the combined contribution of FDI from Hong Kong and Taiwan to mainland China (or Guangdong and Fujian) shown in Table 13.7 requires little modification.

In line with the findings of official PRC statistics, the MOEA survey reveals that accumulated FDI stock of Taiwanese origin was, as of April 1991, heavily concentrated in Guangdong and Fujian (see Table 13.8). On the basis of such evidence, the distribution of Taiwanese FDI between the two provinces seems less unbalanced than that of Hong Kong (see Table 13.7), although it remains heavily skewed towards Guangdong. In any case, current press reports indicate that new FDI from Taiwan continues to favour Guangdong ahead of Fujian.

Table 13.8 Distribution of cumulative FDI of Taiwanese origin within mainland China (as of April 1991)

	FDI		*No. of firms*	
	US$ m.	*%*	*Units*	*%*
Guangdong	342.6	45.7	1,253	50.1
Shenzhen	111.6	14.9	378	15.1
Guangzhou	55.9	7.5	146	5.8
Fujian	179.5	23.9	598	23.9
Xiamen	92.2	12.3	275	11.0
Shanghai	87.0	12.3	78	3.1
Others	140.9	18.8	574	22.9
Total	750.0	100.0	2,503	100.0

Source: Kao, Lee and Lin, *Taiwan tupuo*, p. 12.

FOREIGN INVESTMENT, TRADE AND ECONOMIC GROWTH

It is difficult to estimate exactly how foreign investment from Hong Kong and Taiwan has translated into economic growth in Guangdong and Fujian provinces.[63] As a proxy, it is likely that Hong Kong contributed no less than 16 per cent of total fixed capital formation in Guangdong between 1985 and 1990 – and 28 per cent in Shenzhen. The comparable figure for Fujian is probably around 7 per cent.[64] Even more important is the fact that every dollar of foreign investment will generate a multiplier effect in terms of complementary domestic investment expenditure (expressed in *yuan*). In short, the overall level of investment associated with FDI and AFI has become very substantial.[65]

A summary of the growth performance of Guangdong and Fujian since 1980 is given in Table 13.9. For comparative purposes, data for Hong Kong, Taiwan and Shanghai are also included. Most foreign investment (FDI and AFI) has been directed towards high growth sectors and it is reasonable to suppose that the impressive GNP growth recorded in Guangdong and Fujian (including Shenzhen, Guangzhou and Xiamen) after 1985 owed much to capital contributions from Hong Kong and Taiwan. The contrast between Hong Kong and Taiwan – both, after all, mature economies with a sustained record of high growth – and the two southern Chinese provinces is less significant than that between those same provinces and Shanghai. It is no coincidence that Shanghai has fallen far short of Guangdong and Fujian as a recipient of foreign capital. The data in Table 13.9 thereby suggest the influence of overseas involvement in the Chinese economy and its impact upon domestic growth.

Table 13.9 The growth performance of Hong Kong, Taiwan and selected areas of China – trends in gross domestic [national] product, 1980–91 (average percentage annual rates of growth)

	1980–85	*1985–91*	*1980–91*
Hong Kong	5.60	7.20	6.47
Taiwan	6.71 [7.09]	8.34 [8.63]	7.69 [7.92]
Guangdong	12.16	13.30	12.80
Shenzhen	54.54	25.95	38.22
Guangzhou	12.71	10.83	12.51
Fujian	11.91 [11.93]	9.71 [9.96]	10.71 [10.85]
Xiamen	16.24	29.00	23.04
Shanghai	9.08	5.90	7.34

Sources: Hong Kong: *HKMDS*, September 1992, p. 10: Taiwan: *Taiwan Statistical Data Book 1992*, p. 25: Guangdong: *GDTJNJ 1992*, p. 83: Shenzhen: *SZTJNJ 1992*, p. 170, Guangzhou: *Guangzhou tongji nianjian 1992* (*Guangzhou Statistical Yearbook 1992*), p. 14 and p. 20, Fujian: *FJTJNJ 1992*, p. 20. Xiamen: *FJTJNJ 1992*, p. 447; Xiamen Statistical Bureau, *Fenjinde Xiamen (Advancing Xiamen)* 1989), p. 46, Shanghai: *SHTJNJ 1992*, p. 34.

TRENDS TOWARDS ECONOMIC INTEGRATION

The factors which have led Hong Kong and Taiwanese firms to re-locate their manufacturing activities to mainland China are already the subject of a considerable literature. The most familiar argument is that against the background of high indigenous wage costs and land rents, entrepreneurs have sought increasingly to transfer their labour-intensive operations across the border, or Taiwan Straits, in order to take advantage of an abundant supply of cheap labour and land. The accelerated appreciation of the NT Dollar against the U.S. dollar since the mid-1980s has been a further contributory factor, prompting many Taiwanese firms to move to the mainland in an attempt to reduce export costs. More stringent government legislation to control pollution, as well as greater self-awareness and even militancy on the part of the labour force, have been further reasons for the accelerating trend, especially amongst Taiwanese entrepreneurs.

In an attempt to measure the impact of the transfer of manufacturing activities from Hong Kong and Taiwan to the Chinese mainland, estimates of sectoral contributions to national income and employment in all three countries and regions, as well as of labour productivity, are set out in Tables 13.10A, 13.10B and 13.10C. There is no doubt that the re-location of manufacturing operations from Hong Kong and Taiwan to the Chinese mainland has been a catalyst in effecting remarkable structural changes in national income and employment within the constituent economies of Greater China. In 1991, for example, Hong Kong investors were reported to be employing some 3 million workers in Guangdong (especially in the Pearl River Delta).[66] This constituted a labour force about four-and-a-half times greater than the colony's own manufacturing workforce. Transferring industrial activities across the Shenzhen River meanwhile resulted in a decline in manufacturing employment in Hong Kong in both absolute and relative terms. Table 13.10A shows that the employment share of the industrial sector (including building construction) fell from 50 per cent (1980) to 44 per cent (1985) to a mere 36 per cent (1991), whilst that of services rose from 48 to 54 to 63 per cent.

The corresponding changes in Taiwan's employment structure appear at first glance to have been less spectacular. But the reality is that employment in many branches of light industry (notably electrical engineering, footwear, plastics and textile production) has fallen dramatically as a result of the transfer of such labour-intensive activities to the PRC. Indeed at times the government in Taipei has expressed its concern about a "hollowing out" of the island's industrial structure.

The re-location of manufacturing firms to China has also been accompanied by striking changes in the structure of output in Hong Kong and Taiwan. Table 13.10A shows that the service sector's share in Hong Kong GDP

Table 13.10A Measuring the impact of re-locating manufacturing activities to the Chinese mainland – the changing contributions of agriculture (A), industry (I) and services (S) to gross domestic product and employment in greater China, 1980–91 (%)

	1980			*1985*			*1991*		
	A	*I*	*S*	*A*	*I*	*S*	*A*	*I*	*S*
GDP									
Hong Kong	1.0	31.8	67.2	0.7	29.6	69.7	0.3	24.9	74.8
Taiwan	7.7	45.7	46.6	5.8	46.3	47.9	3.7	42.3	54.0
Guangdong	33.8	41.1	25.1	31.1	40.8	28.1	23.4	42.1	34.5
Shenzhen	28.9	26.0	45.1	7.9	46.8	45.4	4.6	60.2	35.2
Guangzhou	10.9	54.5	34.6	9.7	52.9	37.4	7.3	46.5	46.2
Fujian	37.2	41.5	21.3	35.7	38.0	26.3	31.2	39.8	29.0
Xiamen	21.1	58.6	20.3	12.7	56.3	31.0	10.4	53.7	35.9
Shanghai	3.2	75.7	21.1	4.2	69.8	26.0	4.0	64.3	31.8
Employment									
Hong Kong	2.0	49.6	48.3	1.8	43.8	54.4	1.0	35.9	63.1
Taiwan	19.5	42.4	38.1	17.5	41.4	41.1	12.9	40.1	47.0
Guangdong	73.7	13.9	12.5	60.1	21.3	18.6	51.0	25.9	23.1
Shenzhen	—	—	—	—	—	—	6.1	69.8	24.1
Guangzhou	40.2	33.6	26.2	31.3	37.7	31.1	27.6	36.8	35.6
Fujian	73.0	11.8	15.2	61.5	19.4	19.0	57.8	20.9	21.3
Xiamen	—	—	—	46.6	26.8	26.6	42.4	28.8	28.8
Shanghai	29.6	48.7	22.1	16.6	57.9	25.5	10.7	60.0	29.3

increased by almost 8 per cent between 1980 and 1991, mostly at the expense of industrial activity. Similar structural "upgrading" has apparently taken place in Taiwan, although the smaller scale of its FDI involvement may mean that the principal reason for this lies elsewhere The more significant consequence for Taiwan may have been in terms of changes in its *intra*-industrial structure. According to the Head of the Industry Bureau in Taipei, the large-scale transfer of "sunset industries" to the PRC has more than anything else accounted for the rapid increase of heavy industry's share in total manufacturing output in recent years (from 47 to 56 per cent between 1986 and 1991).[67]

There is no doubt that Guangdong and Fujian have benefited most from the increased economic integration of Greater China. As a result of accelerated GDP (GNP) growth and more rapid industrialization, the structure of output and employment in both regions – but above all in sub-provincial units such as Guangzhou, Shenzhen and Xiamen – has changed markedly. This process of structural change has been characterized by gains for the industrial and service sectors at the expense of agriculture, and by a reduction in inter-sectoral relative levels of labour productivity (Tables 13.10B and 13.10C). The significance of the latter achievement is highlighted by the experience of China's pre-reform era, when – accelerated industrialization notwithstanding – agriculture carried almost the entire burden of absorbing increases in labour supply, thereby exacerbating inter-sectoral productivity differentials.[68]

The tertiary sector's increased share of total output and employment since 1980 has been a noteworthy feature of the recent development experience of both Guangdong and Fujian.[69] This no doubt reflects the increased provision of banking, insurance and financial services, transport and telecommunication facilities, and expertise in processing export and import orders. An expansion of tourism and rise in real estate transactions also underlie the same trend. The growing contribution of the tertiary sector in the southern Chinese economy is of course paralleled in the experience of other industrializing countries.

Table 13.10B Relative product per worker, 1980–91

	1980			*1985*			*1991*		
	A	*I*	*S*	*A*	*I*	*S*	*A*	*I*	*S*
Hong Kong	0.50	0.64	1.39	0.39	0.68	1.28	0.30	0.69	1.19
Taiwan	0.39	1.08	1.22	0.33	1.12	1.17	0.29	1.05	1.15
Guangdong	0.46	2.96	2.01	0.52	1.92	1.51	0.46	1.63	1.49
Shenzhen	—	—	—	—	—	—	0.75	0.86	1.46
Guangzhou	0.27	1.62	1.32	0.31	1.40	1.21	0.26	1.26	1.30
Fujian	0.51	3.52	1.40	0.58	1.96	1.38	0.54	1.90	1.36
Xiamen	—	—	—	0.27	2.10	1.17	0.25	1.86	1.25
Shanghai	0.11	1.55	0.95	0.25	1.21	1.02	0.37	1.07	1.09

Table 13.10C Total inequality amongst sectors

	1980	*1985*	*1991*
Hong Kong	0.37	0.30	0.24
Taiwan	0.24	0.24	0.18
Guangdong	0.80	0.58	0.55
Shenzhen	—	—	0.22
Guangzhou	0.59	0.43	0.41
Fujian	0.72	0.52	0.53
Xiamen	—	0.68	0.64
Shanghai	0.54	0.25	0.14

Sources: Hong Kong: Census and Statistics Department, *Estimates of GDP, 1966–91*, p. 38; *Hong Kong Annual Digest of Statistics* (1991 edition). Yin-ping Ho, *Trade, Industrial Restructuring and Development in Hong Kong* (London: Macmillan Press, 1992), p. 36. Taiwan: *Taiwan Statistical Data Book, 1992*, p. 17 and p. 41. Guangdong: *GDTJNJ 1992*, p. 85 and p. 142. Shenzhen: *SZTJNJ 1992*, pp. 161 and 182; *Shenzhenshi guomin jinghi he shehui tongji ziliao. 1979–85* (*National Economic and Social Statistical Data for Shenzhen Municipality, 1979–85*), pp. 10–11; *SZTJNJ 1992*, pp. 168–69; *Shenzhenshi qiwu shiqi guomin jingji he shehui tongji zilao, 1986–90*, p. 21. Guangzhou: *Guangzhou tongji nianjian 1992*, p. 28 and p. 358. Fujian: *FJTJNJ 1992*, p. 15 and p. 53; *Fujian shehui tongji ziliao, 1986* (*Fujian Social Statistics, 1986*), p. 43. *Fenjinde Xiamen*, p. 44; *FJTJNJ 1992*, p. 447; *Fujian shehui tongji ziliao, 1986*, p. 48; *Xiamen jingji tequ nianjian, 1990* (*Xiamen SEZ Yearbook, 1990*), p. 171. Shanghai: *SHTJNJ 1991*, pp. 34 and 72; *SHTJNJ 1992*, pp. 33 and 86.

THE ECONOMIC INTEGRATION OF GREATER CHINA: ISSUES, PROBLEMS AND PROSPECTS

The experience of economic integration in Greater China differs significantly from that which has occurred elsewhere in the world. For example, the EC and ASEAN are two economic groupings which have sought to create a single common market, designed to enhance the free movement of goods and factors of production to members' mutual advantage. By contrast, the establishment of closer ties between Hong Kong, Taiwan and the Chinese mainland is the result of the internationalization of manufacturing production, based on joint production and/or the division of labour and geared towards third-party countries (rather than member countries themselves). A large proportion of output so generated has been destined for overseas locations and most inputs similarly derive from abroad. The movement of factors of production, as well as of finished products, within Greater China meanwhile remains limited; and much Hong Kong and Taiwanese FDI is still heavily concentrated in SEZs, geographically isolated from the rest of the PRC. Backward and forward linkages have thereby been minimized.[70]

The creation of closer trade and investment ties between Hong Kong, Taiwan, Guangdong and Fujian and the process of economic integration which it has facilitated are in any case not free of risk. An example is that associated with the vulnerability of the Hong Kong and southern Chinese (especially Guangdong) economies to their export dependency on American markets. From this perspective, an increase in export tariffs following cancellation of China's MFN status would have serious consequences for both regions. It has, for example, been estimated that the loss to Hong Kong could be as much as US$15.7 billion in overall trade and 60,000 jobs; re-exports from China might meanwhile fall by US$4.6–6.2 billion, leading to massive job losses in Guangdong.[71] Such data highlight the importance to China *and Hong Kong* of a resumption of Chinese membership of GATT. They also suggest how failure to resolve trade issues between China and the United States could undermine the very process of regional economic integration by leading investors to lessen their involvement in the southern Chinese economy and re-direct their investment elsewhere (say, to other countries in South-east Asia).

If the rapid expansion of cross-Straits trade has boosted Taiwan's export growth, it has also led to increasing dependence on Chinese markets. This has obvious dangers in a situation in which cross-Straits political relations remain uncertain. Meanwhile, Taiwanese enterprises must face up to increased competition from their overseas subsidiaries, now sited in southern China. Other things being equal, the access to cheaper land and labour which such firms enjoy should enable them to produce cheaper goods and may thereby threaten parent firms' competitiveness in international (and even local) markets.[72]

Nevertheless, as the estimates in Table 13.11 suggest, there also remains considerable scope for even closer economic integration within Greater China. The marked economic differences between Hong Kong, Taiwan and southern China in terms of the major measures shown above suggest that before full integration and equalization of per capita income, productivity and degree of industrialization[73] can be achieved, many economic and political barriers to cross-border labour mobility will have to be removed. However, the political unification which such an outcome would seem to demand is clearly far beyond anything conceivable within the foreseeable future.

The data in Table 13.11 indicate that within China, only Shenzhen can lay claim to approaching the advanced standards of Hong Kong and Taiwan in terms of per capita income, productivity and degree of industrialization. But even that gap remains considerable and in any case Shenzhen SEZ can perhaps be more usefully regarded as a "satellite town" of Hong Kong than an integral part of Guangdong.[74] If the SEZ's "second line," north of the enclave, replaced the Shenzhen River as the border with Hong Kong, no doubt economic equalization would rapidly come about. Whether or not this would be to the benefit or detriment of the British colony is an open question.

In any case, with or without Shenzhen, Hong Kong has now become inseparable from the economy of Guangdong. With the tertiary sector now contributing about three-quarters of GDP (see Table 13.10A), its process of

Table 13.11 Economic disparities within greater China, 1991

	Population (m.)	*GNP (US$ m.)*	*Per capita GNP (US$)*	*GVIO (US$ m.)*	*Per capita GVIO (US$)*	*Capital/labour ratio (US$)*	*Trade volume (US$ m.)*	*Trade GNP ratio*
Hong Kong	5.82	81,157	13,945	—	—	4,339	107,439	1.32
Taiwan	20.56	180,270	8,815	155,000	7,546	4,832	139,035	0.77
Guangdong	63.49	33,452	527	47,422	747	2,597	22,198	0.66
Shenzhen	2.39	3,284	1,491	5,303	2,223	4,951	5,967	1.82
	(1.20)	(2,546)	(2,306)	—	—	—	—	—
Guangzhou	6.02	7,265	1,214	10,887	1,808	3,998	5,382	0.74
	(3.62)	(5,977)	(1,660)	—	—	—	—	—
Fujian	30.39	10,480	340	12,378	402	1,761	4,334	0.41
Xiamen	1.15	1,168	1,016	1,936	1,683	—	2,406	2.06
Shanghai	13.40	16,114	1,203	36,583	2,730	2,822	8,044	0.50

Notes: Bracketed figures are for Shenzhen and Guangzhou cities "proper," i.e. excluding the outlying counties.

Population: the estimates for Shenzhen embrace "temporary" and "permanent" residents.

GNP: the figures for Hong Kong, Shenzhen, Guangzhou and Xiamen are measures of GDP. Per capita GDP estimates for Shenzhen and Guangzhou are given independently in Chinese sources and are slightly different from figures which can be obtained from the estimates of population and GDP shown in Table 13.11.

GVIO: gross value of industrial output.

Capital-labor ratio: this refers to capital stock (K) per industrial employee (L). For Hong Kong and Taiwan K means, respectively, to gross domestic capital formation and gross fixed capital formation. For China, K is the net value of fixed assets (i.e. net of depreciation); and K/L refers to industry in general in Guangdong, Fujian and Shanghai, but only those enterprises which have an independent-accounting (*duli hesuan*) identity in Shenzhen and Guangzhou.

Trade volume: This embraces only domestic exports and imports (i.e. it excludes exports originating from, and imports destined for, other places). However, the data for Xiamen appear to include re-exports.

Exchange rates: US$1.00 is assumed to equal HK$7.80 (under the linked system). NT$25.75 (interbank closing rate, December 1991) and *RMB* 5.323 (official annual average, 1991).

Sources: Hong Kong: Hong Kong Government Census and Statistics Department, *Estimates of GDP, 1966–1991*, p. 10: *HKMDS*, August 1992, p. 105 and September 1992, pp. 1–2 and 19. Taiwan: Council for Economic Planning and Development, *Taiwan Statistical Data Book, 1992*, pp. 1, 17, 49 and 192. Guangdong: *GDTJNJ 1992*, pp. 68, 183 and 341. Shenzhen: *SZTJNJ 1991*, p. 2; *SZTJNJ 1992*, p. 163; and *GDTJNJ 1992*, pp. 81, 93 and 105. Guangzhou: *GDTJNJ 1992*, pp. 91, 93, 104, 138 and 199; *Guangzhou tongji nianjian 1992*, p. 307. Fujian: *FJTJNJ 1992*, pp. 8–9, 53 and 146. Xiamen: *FJTJNJ 1992*, pp. 444–48; Y. Y. Kueh, 'Foreign investment and economic change,' pp. 689–690. Shanghai: *ZGTJNJ 1992, p. 79: SHTJNJ 1992*, pp. 33, 86, 112, 144 and 349.

"de-industrialization" seems to have reached a point at which it has become irreversible. The most unequivocal evidence of the two regions' inseparability are the estimates of the potential economic impact of a withdrawal by the United States of China's MFN status, cited earlier.

If Hong Kong has wholly succumbed to the principle of comparative advantage in pursuing regional economic specialization, Taiwan has adopted a more cautious approach vis-à-vis the Chinese mainland. Various econometric studies have been undertaken in an attempt to assess the security implications of its closer trade and investment relations with the PRC. One of these suggests that against the background of increased exports to mainland China in recent years, an embargo by the authorities in Beijing would, on average, have reduced Taiwan's GDP and total employment by 1.46 and 3.42 per cent respectively (1987–91).[75] Such losses would have to be regarded as fairly minor in their impact. By contrast, another study has argued that the reduction in Taiwan's GDP consequent upon reduced domestic capital formation might offset FDI-related exports to the PRC to generate a significant net income loss. To those who would use such estimates to highlight the threat posed by Taiwan's allegedly increasing dependency, it has, however, been argued that in the absence of investment opportunities on the Chinese mainland, Taiwanese entrepreneurs would merely have directed their funds elsewhere. Nor could there be any guarantee that the funds involved would have been used for productive purposes on Taiwan itself.[76]

Clearly, it is not easy to estimate the economic costs and benefits associated with Taiwanese investment in mainland China. But it would be surprising if the government in Taipei were not to act prudently to safeguard its security. To this extent, it is significant that when "indirect investment" to the PRC was officially sanctioned in 1991, it was deliberately restricted to 3,679 product categories. It was also specified that such investment should only involve labour-intensive undertakings to which the PRC could contribute necessary raw materials and in areas which, in terms of the domestic Taiwanese economy, had low inter-industrial linkages; and should embrace the production of goods which might enjoy a competitive advantage against Taiwanese exports.[77]

Whether Taiwanese investors will be able to overcome what are essentially political restrictions on their activities as successfully as they circumvented earlier restraints on investment contacts with mainland firms – and if so, how – remains to be seen. What is not in doubt, however, is the potentially explosive nature of the current situation, should continuing embargoes on direct commercial, navigational and postal links (the *santong*) be lifted. If this were to happen, a dramatic realignment of investment and trade flows within Greater China would certainly result. Such a prospect may at present seem remote. But it behoves the government and business community of Hong Kong to be on constant alert and ready to adjust their plans in anticipation of such an eventuality.

The various problems outlined in this final section suggest that the undoubted benefits of closer economic integration within Greater China are not to be taken for granted. The experience of the 1980s is evidence enough of the substantial gains to be derived from closer economic – and by implication, political – relations. But many obstacles remain to be overcome if the growth and structural benefits are to be sustained. To the extent that the economic well-being of Guangdong and Fujian determines the economic direction and health of the rest of the Chinese economy, resolving these issues assumes the greatest urgency in China itself.

ACKNOWLEDGMENTS

Some of the points raised at the workshop in Hong Kong in January 1993 have been incorporated into the revised version of this paper and we are grateful to participants, especially Joseph C. H. Chai, for their helpful observations. Y. Y. Kueh is also indebted to Yee-yen Chua, Li Fang and Sandy Chau for their assistance in obtaining valuable statistical materials relating to foreign investment.

NOTES

1 For most purposes of this article we define "Greater China" in terms of the two southern provinces of Guangdong and Fujian, Hong Kong and Taiwan. Occasionally, however, our analysis extends to mainland China as a whole.

2 Global trade grew by 7.93% p.a., Taiwan's by 13.61%, Hong Kong's by 16.00%. See International Monetary Fund (IMF), *International Financial Statistics Yearbook, 1992* (hereafter *ISFY 1992*) (Washington, D.C.: IMF, 1992), pp. 108–115. Note that in 1992 China's merchandise trade expanded by a further 22% (State Statistical Bureau (hereafter SSB), *Zhongguo tongji zhaiyao 1993* (*Statistical Survey of China. 1993)* (Beijing: State Statistical Publishing House, 1993), p. 101.

3 IMF data for China reveal a reversal of the pattem of trade expansion in the first and second halves of the 1980s. In the earlier period, import growth sharply exceeded that of exports; latterly, the opposite was the case. In Hong Kong and Taiwan the second half of the decade witnessed an acceleration of growth of both exports and imports.

4 See, for example, Yun-wing Sung, *The China-Hong Kong Connection: The Key to China's Open Door Policy* (Cambridge: Cambridge University Press, 1991).

5 This role is a major complicating factor in compiling and interpreting trade statistics between China and the region. Goods flowing from (to) Hong Kong to (from) China comprise some which are part of a purely bilateral trade flow and others which have their origin or destination in a third country. It is important to distinguish between the two categories and to allow for a "re-export margin," added to goods which have passed through Hong Kong. In this article re-exported Chinese imports into Hong Kong are discounted on the basis of an assumed re-export margin of 25%; for commodities coming from other countries, a rate of 14% is thought more appropriate.

6 These estimates are derived from 1930s data, cited in Yun-wing Sung, *The China-Hong Kong Connection*, p. 19.

7 Including re-exports.
8 Calculations suggest that it would have declined by about 3 percentage points.
9 Hong Kong Census and Statistics Department, *Hong Kong Monthly Digest of Statistics* (hereafter *HKMDS*), January 1981, pp. 19–21, January 1987, pp. 19–22, and December 1991, pp. 19–22. By the beginning of 1993 re-exports accounted for 78% of Hong Kong's total exports (Hong Kong, *South China Morning Post* (hereafter *SCMP*), 14 May 1993, which also noted that ". . . the market in China for goods re-exported through Hong Kong is now almost double the size of the Unitest States market . . .").
10 China's share of Hong Kong imports rose in every single year between 1978 and 1991, from 19% to 38%. *HKMDS*, January 1981, pp. 19–21, January 1987, pp.19–22, and December 1991, pp. 19–22.
11 Re-exported imports to countries other than China showed a similar surge during the first half of the decade, but thereafter stabilized. *Ibid.*
12 To state it differently, in 1980 re-exports of Chinese imports accounted for 26% of all Hong Kong's re-exports; by 1990 the figure had risen to 56%.
13 The extent of the decline depends critically on assumptions made about the value of the re-export margin.
14 The very fact of such integration does, however, make interpretation of re-export data hazardous. Conventional practice regards any movement of goods across a border as trade. But cross-border shipments for processing purposes will lend an inflationary bias to measures of the volume of trade. Take the case of imported components from Taiwan, re-exported from Hong Kong to Guangdong, and subsequently shipped back in processed form (as Chinese exports) for re-export elsewhere (perhaps even to China itself!). Such a process will earn several separate entries in customs statistics, threatening to disguise the true value-added element embodied in each stage. The extent of the underlying interpretative problem is suggested by the finding that by 1991 the share of outward-processing trade in Hong Kong's gross imports from China had reached 67.6%
15 These and other estimates cited in this paragraph are derived from statistics in *HKMDS*.
16 It increased from US$1.11 to 72.54 million between 1978 and 1991.
17 In the early 18th century some 3,000 small-scale boats plied across the Taiwan Straits, carrying large quantities of sugar and rice to the mainland in exchange for cotton cloth, silk, paper and timber. See Zhou Shulian *et al.* (eds.), *Haixia liangan ji Xianggang jingji hezuo qianjing* (*Prospects for Economic Co-operation across the Taiwan Straits and with Hong Kong*) (Beijing: Economic Management Publishing House, 1991), p. 156.
18 *Ibid.* pp. 156–57.
19 The estimates are "suggestive" in the sense that they are derived from data which only show *indirect* trade between Taiwan and the Chinese mainland, conducted through Hong Kong. Such trade dominates transactions across the Taiwan Straits, but also underestimates their true extent by excluding indirect trade through other countries (for example, Japan and Singapore), as well as genuinely direct – but minor – trade with coastal mainland ports. See Gao Chang, Yan Zongda *et al.* (eds.), *Liangan jingji jiaoliu jin xiankuang ji fazhan chushi yanjiu* (*A Study of Economic Exchanges Across the Taiwan Straits: the Current Situation and Prospects for Future Developments*) (Taipei: Zhonghua Institute for Economic Research, 1992), pp. 14–16.
20 Notice that in 1991 alone the PRC's share of all Taiwan's exports rose from 4.89% to 6.13%.
21 Hong Kong, *Ta Kung Pao* (*Ta Kung Daily*) (hereafter *TKP*), 30 December 1992.

22 Sources as in Table 4.

23 Since the late 1980s Taiwan's trade balance has also improved with ASEAN countries. but deteriorated against the United States. The changing pattern is not coincidental. On the one hand, growing American protectionism has forced Taiwan to diversify its export markets; on the other, increasing FDI by Taiwanese entrepreneurs in both the Chinese mainland and ASEAN countries has given added impetus to trade expansion with these countries.

24 TIR is given by the following formula:

$$\text{TIR} = X_{ij}/X_j \div M_J/M_W$$

where X_{ij} are the exports of country i to country J; X_i are the total exports of country i; M_J are the total imports of country J: and M_w are global imports.

25 That is, TIR $\geq$ 1. See above.

26 From 18.9 (1980) to 8.52 (1989).

27 By the end of the 1980s such shipments included a large proportion of goods destined for outward processing.

28 Also relevant are data cited in *TKP*, 31 May 1993.

29 Between 1980 and 1991 the share of primary products in China's total exports fell from 50.2% to 22.5%, whilst that of manufactured goods (mainly produced by labour-intensive methods) rose from 49.8% to 77.5% (SSB, *Zhongguo shangye waijing tongji ziliao, 1952–1988* (*Statistical Materials Relating to China's Internal and External Trade, 1952–1988*) (hereafter *ZGSYWJTJZL*) (Beijing: State Statistical Publishing House, 1990), p. 430; and State Statistical Bureau, *Zhongguo tongji nianjian, 1992* (*Chinese Statistical Yearbook, 1992)* (hereafter *ZGTJNJ*) (Beijing: State Statistical Publishing House, 1992), p. 630). Since 1970 the share of labour-intensive manufactures in *Hong Kong's* exports has fallen steadily (e.g. from 75% to 55% during 1970–87) in favour of an expansion of capital-intensive goods (up from 21% to 41%) (data cited in Ross Garnaut, *Australia and the Northeast Asian Ascendancy* (Canberra: Australian Govemment Publishing Service, 1989), p. 54). The same period saw the simultaneous expansion of the export shares of labour and capital-intensive products in *Taiwan*, although it is only in recent years that the latter category has come to predominate *(ibid.)*.

30 During the 1980s the proportion of total Chinese food exports retained in Hong Kong fell by more than half.

31 Ironically, more and more goods labelled "Made in China" have in fact been produced by subsidiaries of Hong Kong parent companies, sited in Guangdong.

32 Yun-wing Sung, *The China-Hong Kong Connection*, ch. 7.

33 A kind of technological complementarity is also evident. That Hong Kong's textile machinery does not embody the most up-to-date technology makes it appropriate for use in labour-intensive operations, such as China's resource-endowment favours.

34 Although their relative importance did decline, in 1990 such products still accounted for 76.69% of Taiwan's exports to China.

35 The share of chemicals and related exports rose from 2.24% to 12.65% between 1985 and 1990.

36 See Maruyama Nobuo (ed.), *Kanan keizaiken: Hirakareta chiiki shugi* (*The South China Economic Region*) (Tokyo: Institute of Developing Economies, 1992), pp. 299–302 for a useful summary of cross-Straits trade policies emerging from Beijing and Taipei between 1977 and 1991.

37 As a proportion of total PRC exports to Taiwan, goods under SITC 0 and 2 fell from 74.93% to 31.85% (1985–90), whilst those under SITC 6, 7 and 8 increased from 13.39% to 54.26%.

38 Notice too that as Taiwan has become increasingly involved in southern China, its investment in Hong Kong hat risen dramatically (in 1991 Hong Kong was the destination of 43% of all Taiwanese FDI in Asia). This sharp rise no doubt reflects the need to make appropriate servicing arrangements in Hong Kong for the operations of subsidiary companies in China.

39 See, for example, Alan J. Day (ed.), *The Annual Register, 1992* (Harlow, Essex: Longman Group, 1991), p. 360; and British Broadcasting Corporation, *Summary of World Broadcasts, Part 3: The Far East* (*Weekly Economic Report*), FE/W0244, 19 August 1992, p. A/l.

40 SSB, *Quanguo gesheng zizhiqu zhixiashi lishi tongji ziliao huibian, 1949–89* (*Compilation of Historical Statistics for Every Province, Autonomous Region and Directly-Administered Municipality in China, 1949–89*) (Beijing: State Statistical Publishing House, 1990), pp. 434 and 618. These figures imply an average addition of some 400,000 (Fujian) and 800,000 (Guangdong) labour recruits each year. Notice too that secondary and tertiary-sector employment growth in both provinces has easily outstripped that of the primary sector (*ibid.*).

41 Guangdong recorded an average annual rate of growth of 20.27% during 1978–91 (Guangdong Provincial Statistical Bureau, *Guangdong tongji nianjian 1992* (*Guangdong Province Statistical Yearbook 1992)* (hereafter *GDTJNJ 1992*) (Beijing: State Statistical Publishing House, 1992), p. 342); the corresponding figure for Fujian was even higher (Fujian Provincial Statistical Bureau, *Fujian tongji nianjian 1992* (*Fujian Province Statistical Yearbook 1992)* (hereafter *FJTJNJ 1992)* (Beijing: State Statistical Publishing House, 1992)). Fujian's faster trade growth needs to be set against a much smaller base level than in Guangdong. Compare these figures with the estimates for Hong Kong and Taiwan presented earlier (see n. 2).

42 In 1970 Guangdong accounted for 19.2% of all China's exports; in 1991 the corresponding figure was 19.0% (*GDTJNJ 1992*, p. 342 and *ZGSYWJTJZL*, p. 502). Note that preliminary estimates indicate that Guangdong exports grew by a further 32% in 1992 (*TKP*, 1 January 1993).

43 To cite just one example: available evidence suggests that without Guangdong and Fujian, China's trade surplus in 1990 would have been reduced by 70%!

44 During the same period Shanghai's share of imports rose from 1.2% to 3.6%. By way of comparison, Guangdong's share of China's trade increased from 1.78% to 13.34% (imports), and from 12.11% to 19.03% (exports). The corresponding increases in Fujian were from 0.71% to 2.21% (imports), and from 2.01% to 4.07% (exports). (National data from *ZGSYWJTJZL*, pp. 432–33 and 438–39; Shanghai data from Shanghai Municipal Statistical Bureau, *Shanghai tongji nianjian 1992* (*Shanghai Statistical Yearbook, 1992*) (Beijing: State Statistical Publishing House, 1992), pp. 349 and 352. The sources for Guangdong and Fujian estimates are shown at Table 13.4 (p. 453). However, these figures conceal the fact that the shares of both Guangdong and Fujian in total exports declined between 1980 and 1985, thereafter rising in a spectacular fashion. Given the more consistent downward trend in Shanghai, it is clear that during the early 1980s the export performance of other parts of China outstripped that of all three regions. In this respect, it is noteworthy that in 1985 *Liaoning's* export share was the highest in the country (19.34%), even though just three years later its contribution had almost halved. Shandong was another province which experienced a significant relative decline (*ZGSYWJTJZL,* p. 510).

45 Average growth during 1985–91 was 27.94% p.a. The estimates show imports to have grown by 17.44% pa. during 1985–91.

46 Guangdong's export surplus vis-à-vis Hong Kong almost doubled in two years, rising from US$2,960 to $5,290 million between 1989 and 1991.

47 For 1985–90 the corresponding figure is over 33% p.a.
48 Average annual growth of imports from Hong Kong was only 14.23% during 1985–91, compared with 42.90% during 1980–85
49 This phrase (literally "three foreign funded") refers to the activities of equity and contractual joint ventures and firms wholly under foreign ownership
50 That is, processing operations based on the provision of raw materials, assembly operations based on the supply of components, and manufacturing based on supplied designs (*sanlai*); and exchange through the practice of compensation trade (*yibu*)
51 The difference between total exports and those associated with commissioned processing, compensation trade and FDI ventures provides a measure of merchandise exports
52 No doubt the figure would be even higher if provincial exports to Hong Kong alone were considered.
53 The available evidence also suggests that Taiwan's relationship with southern China has mirrored that of Hong Kong. Since shipments between Guangdong and Fujian, and Taiwan must formally pass through Hong Kong, the extent of Taiwan's linkages with the two Chinese provinces is partly concealed within the British Colony's own statistical records.
54 *TKP*, 1 January 1993, stated that China's trade balance with the USA had declined by 5% in 1992. However, another Hong Kong source subsequently revealed that the American deficit had further widened during the early months of 1993 (*SCMP*, 20 May 1993).
55 In the context of the accelerated re-location of manufacturing activity on the Chinese mainland, specific mention should he made of the Plaza Accord (1985), which forced Japan and Asian NIEs to appreciate their currencies against the U.S. dollar and thereby encouraged large-scale transfers of manufacturing operations within the Asia-Pacific Region.
56 For a detailed analysis of quantitative trends in foreign investment and its distribution amongst "economically opened coastal areas" in China, as well as consideration of its impact on output and income growth, see Y. Y. Kueh. "Foreign investment and economic change in China," *The China Quarterly*, No. 132 (September 1992), pp. 637–690.
57 But in terms of AFI stock growth, Fujian and Shenzhen are almost identical.
58 The figures for investment in all China are 53.2% p.a. (FDI stock) and 55.2% p.a. (AFI stock).
59 For an elaboration of this point, see Kueh, "Foreign investment and economic change," pp. 652–55.
60 The momentum of Taiwanese investment in mainland China accelerated after an official government declaration (Taipei, November 1987) that Chinese from Taiwan would be allowed to visit relatives across the Taiwan Straits. The continued and active interest shown by Taiwanese entrepreneurs in seeking investment opportunities in the PRC eventually brought official approval (1991) of investment conducted "through a third country." For further details, see T. B. Lin, "Economic nexus between the two sides of the Taiwan Straits" (paper presented at Conference on the Economic Development of ROC and the Pacific Rim in the 1990s and Beyond: Taipei, 25–29 May 1992); and Charng Kao, "Economic interaction between the two sides of the Taiwan Straits" (paper presented at Conference on the Evolution of Taiwan within a New World Economic Order: Taipei, May 1993).
61 *TKP*, 2 June 1993.
62 See Charles H. C. Kao, Joseph S. Lee and Chu-chia Steve Lin, *Taiwan tupuo:*

liangan jingmao zhuizhong (*An Empirical Study of Taiwanese Investment in Mainland China*) (Taipei: Taipei Commonwealth Publishing Company Ltd.), p. 12. The actual number of Taiwanese firms then operating in mainland China was thought to be between 3,000 and 3,500. Different estimates again are available in other Taiwanese sources. For example, the prestigious Chung-Hua Institution for Economic Research suggested that as of April 1993, some 2,700 Taiwanese firms were operating on the mainland with a total investment of US$3.7 billion (King Pei and Hsu Chia-xian, "Trends and prospects of economic interaction between the two sides of the Taiwan Straits" (paper presented at a Symposium on the Current State of Economic Management in the Mainland, Taiwan and Hong Kong: Hong Kong, December 1991)). King and Hsu also give a cumulative total of US$100 million in Taiwanese investment in mainland China for 1979–87. This figure increased by US$300 million (1988) and 600 million (1989) (see Lin, "Economic nexus") to raise the cumulative total to US$1 billion. None of these figures is compatible with the official PRC statistics. The discrepancy is likely to reflect differences in the definition of FDI of Taiwanese origin (which may or may not include investment originating in Taiwanese firms based outside Taiwan – e.g. in Hong Kong or South-east Asia – and which have become detached from their parent companies). The cumulative total given in the MOEA 1991 survey (US$750 million) seems most reconcilable with the incomplete official PRC estimates shown in Table 13.7.

63 For example, any attempt to estimate FDI's contribution to China's domestic capital formation and GNP growth should take account of possible distortions arising out of erratic exchange rate adjustments in converting foreign capital into *renminbi* (*RMB*) equivalent. See Kueh, "Foreign investment and economic change," p. 657.

64 These estimates were obtained by applying Hong Kong's shares (HKS) in the total intake of foreign investment of all kinds (FDI and capital borrowing) received by Guangdong, Shenzhen and Fujian to the respective percentage contributions of *all* foreign investments to total investment in fixed assets (CFA) in the corresponding areas. HKS are calculated from the absolute dollar figures shown in Table 13.7 and in Kueh, "Foreign investment and economic change," Appendix A, p. 683. CFA are given in *ibid*. p. 656.

65 For an elaboration of this point, see Kueh, "Foreign investment and economic change," p. 658.

66 K. Y. Tang, "Outward processing in China and its implications for the Hong Kong economy" (paper presented at Symposium on Asian Newly-Industrializing Economies: Past Success and Future Challenge: Hong Kong, May 1991).

67 Kao, Lee and Lin, *Taiwan tupuo*, pp. 90–91.

68 See Y. Y. Kueh, "The Maoist legacy and China's new industrialization strategy," *The China Quarterly*. No. 119 (September 1989), pp. 422–24.

69 Shenzhen seems to be the only exception, its tertiary share in GDP having fallen from 45% (1980 and 1985) to 35% (1991). This decline was offset by a rapid increase in industry's GDP share (from 26% to 60%, 1980–91).

70 We are grateful to Joseph C. H. Chai for raising the points outlined in this paragraph.

71 These are the Hong Kong government's own estimates, made in March 1992 in the wake of the annual U.S. review. The same report predicted that China's loss of MFN status would reduce Hong Kong's GDP growth in 1992 (forecast at 5%) by half. See *SCMP*, 14 March 1992; also *The China Business Review*, May–June 1992, p. 14. For consideration of the impact on the USA of a decision to revoke China's MFN status, see *SCMP*, 23 May 1993.

72 But see also below.
73 The capital/labour ratio provides one measure of the extent of industrialization.
74 See Yin-ping Ho, *Trade, Industrial Restructuring and Development*, ch. 10.
75 Yuh-jiun Lin and Chin-shu Huang, "Development of trade and investment between the two sides of the Taiwan Straits" (paper at Conference on Global Interdependence and Asia-Pacific Cooperation: Hong Kong. 8–10 June 1992). pp. 8 and 10.
76 See Kao, Lee and Lin, *Taiwan tupuo*, p. 42.
77 *Ibid.*p. 65.

14

TAIWAN'S OUTWARD DIRECT INVESTMENT

Has Domestic Investment been Hollowed Out?

T. J. Chen et al.

INTRODUCTION

Conventional theory states that foreign direct investment (FDI) is undertaken only by firms that possess some level of intangible asset (Hymer 1976; Caves 1971). These firms invest in a foreign country in order to exploit the firm-specific advantage embodied in the intangible asset. Examining Taiwan's FDI in recent years reveals that most FDI has been undertaken by firms that are export-oriented (Chen 1992). These firms venture into a foreign country because their competitiveness is undermined by rising wages coupled with an appreciating currency at home. If they possess any intangible asset, this asset must be associated with the ability to export—such as a production technology that delivers products in a timely and flexible manner, and at a reasonable cost—or good customer relations with international buyers. The rationale for these firms to engage in FDI is that a good market for their intangible assets does not exist. Therefore, direct investment is sought to supersede the market.

Generally speaking, when a firm's export market position is threatened, two reactions are possible, which, in turn, lead to two types of FDI. One reaction is cost-cutting, which happens when a firm relocates its production base to a lower-wage country in an effort to regain its competitive edge. The other reaction is product differentiation, done to enhance the value of a product by differentiating it from similar products on the market. Differentiation often involves local production that necessitates FDI. Local production enables producers to better cater for the local market demand, and to provide product-related services that a pure exporter usually is not able to accommodate. Cost-cutting is a defensive action; and the FDI associated with such a reaction may be termed "defensive FDI". Product-differentiation, on the other hand, is aggressive, its aim being to expand production into the export market; the related FDI may thus be termed "expansionary FDI". Similar

Source: *The New Wave of Foreign Direct Investment in Asia*, Singapore: Institute of Southeast Asian Studies (1995), pp. 87–110.

distinctions were made by Kojima (1973), who called defensive FDI "labour-oriented" and expansionary FDI "market-oriented".

The distinction between defensive and expansionary FDI is particularly useful for a country such as Taiwan, whose major export markets are high-wage countries. Defensive FDI typically moves production to countries where the wage rate is lower than that of Taiwan. Expansionary FDI, on the contrary, typically moves production to countries where the wage rate is higher than that of Taiwan. Via FDI, international division of labour is effected, and such division of labour is meaningful only if the wage gap between Taiwan and the host country is large enough to create significant economic benefits. Therefore, Taiwan should not be expected to invest a great deal in countries with a similar wage level. In fact, we do not observe Taiwanese firms investing much in Korea or Mexico. There is some investment in Hong Kong and Singapore, but this is mainly to facilitate trade rather than to manufacture goods. However, this does not imply that large economic benefits can always be derived from FDI between countries whose wage differential is large. There are things other than wage rate that determine profits, such as political stability and infrastructure.

The fact that Taiwan invests substantially in high-wage countries, for example, the United States and Western Europe, as well as low-wage countries, for example, Southeast Asia and mainland China, provides a good contrast between the two types of FDI. The two types of FDI may be motivated by different factors, characterized by different operating strategies, and exert a different impact on the home country's industries. The purpose of this chapter is to examine these differences and relate them to the characteristics of Taiwan's industries.

TRENDS OF TAIWAN'S FDI

Taiwan's FDI expanded rapidly after 1986, with rising wages and an appreciating currency at home. Foreign direct investment reached its peak in 1991 and then started to decline, indicating that the industrial restructuring process set off in 1986 was gradually coming to an end. Table 14.1 lists the distribution of Taiwan's FDI since 1959. It can be seen that Asia (primarily Southeast Asia) and North America (primarily the United States) are major destinations of Taiwan's FDI. It must be noted, however, that official statistics reported in Table 14.1 may substantially under-estimate the actual amount of investment. The discrepancy arises because many firms, mainly small and medium-sized ones, go abroad to invest without notifying their government. The more concentrated the small-sized firms in FDI, the larger the discrepancy. Hence, while FDI statistics for North America and Europe are close to actual investment, those for Asia may represent no more than one fifth of actual investment, and those for mainland China only one-tenth. The prevalence of small and medium-sized firms in FDI in Southeast Asia and

Table 14.1 Taiwan's outward FDI (million US$)

Year	*Asia*	*North America*	*Europe*	*Mainland China*	*Others*	*Total*
1959–79	43.1	14.6	0.1	—	1.5	59.3
1980	3.2	35.1	1.0	—	2.8	42.1
1981	6.7	1.8	2.2	—	0.0	10.8
1982	9.1	2.5	0.0	—	0.0	11.6
1983	6.6	2.8	0.0	—	1.1	10.6
1984	6.6	32.2	0.0	—	0.5	39.3
1985	4.2	35.8	0.9	—	0.4	41.3
1986	8.4	46.2	0.2	—	1.6	56.9
1987	21.3	70.3	10.2	—	1.0	102.8
1988	69.3	125.3	17.0	—	7.1	218.7
1989	296.4	553.4	73.3	—	7.9	931.0
1990	602.9	669.0	265.9	—	14.4	1,552.2
1991	929.6	369.2	350.2	174.2	7.0	1,830.2
1992	369.9	202.2	292.8	247.0	22.3	1,134.3

Note: All data are proposed investment projects approved by the Taiwan Government.

Source: Statistics on Overseas Chinese & Foreign Investment, Technical Co-operation, Outward Investment, Outward Technical Co-operation, Indirect Mainland Investment (Investment Commission, Ministry of Economic Affairs).

mainland China is a unique characteristic that distinguishes Taiwan's FDI from other countries'. A similar pattern was observed in Japanese FDI in earlier years where Japanese small and medium-sized firms concentrated their outward FDI in East Asia, particularly Taiwan.

Small firms have limited managerial resources that constrain their scope of international diversification. They are unable to undertake investment projects that require extensive adjustment in production techniques. They are also unable to run a cross-country operation that requires extensive co-ordination among different production units. Therefore, small and medium-sized firms normally invest only in countries where the industrial infrastructure and the culture are similar to that of their home country. Small Taiwanese firms are particularly fond of Thailand and Malaysia precisely because of industrial and cultural proximity. Despite the great political risk, this proximity also attracts a large amount of Taiwanese FDI into mainland China. The recent rush of small Taiwanese firms into Vietnam was driven by the same factors.

To small and medium-sized firms, their choice of host country is limited. Because of limited managerial resources, they can usually handle only one production site outside Taiwan. Since they rarely make an extensive search for a production site, the FDI decision is usually based on the limited information available. Therefore, FDI by small and medium-sized firms usually moves in flocks. It first rushed to Thailand (and to Malaysia and the Philippines to a lesser extent), then to mainland China, and then to Vietnam. Since the firms' possession of production technology is often unsophisticated and easy to duplicate, and they often invest in the same country *en masse*, their competitive edge based on cost advantage evaporates very quickly. Therefore, the investment "fever" in a particular country often does not last very long.

Compared with small and medium-sized firms, large firms have a longer investment horizon. Their scale of investment is larger and therefore can afford a larger transaction cost in assessing and implementing investment projects. They make a more extensive search for a production site, and upon locating one considered desirable, are capable of engaging in multiple investment projects in various countries. For example, they may simultaneously make an expansionary type of FDI in the United States and a defensive type of FDI in Southeast Asia. The former investment enables them to differentiate their products, while the latter action enables them to reduce the cost of homogeneous products. Hence, both large and small firms have been observed to be investing in low-wage countries, but small firms have rarely been observed to be investing in high-wage countries.

MOTIVATIONS AND OPERATIONAL CHARACTERISTICS

Given the distinction between expansionary and defensive FDI, one ought to examine the motivations of Taiwanese investment in high-wage and low-wage countries. Table 14.2 lists the motivations of Taiwanese investment in the United States, Southeast Asia, and mainland China. It shows that the primary motive for investing in the United States is to expand the local market as well as third-party market (for example, Canada). The secondary motive is to acquire new technology. The third is to collect market information. Both the second and third motives imply an effort towards differentiating and upgrading products. These two motivational factors, together with the market expansion motive, account for 64 per cent of the motivational factors for FDI. Other motives include risk diversification and securing the supply of raw materials. Utilizing local labour is only a minor motivational factor, accounting for a negligible 2.3 per cent. Avoiding trade barriers is also of insignificant importance (1.3 per cent).

In contrast, FDI in Southeast Asia is mainly motivated by low-cost labour, which accounts for 35.4 per cent of the motivational factor. Market expansion is of secondary importance, accounting for 23.7 per cent. Other motivational factors include risk diversification (14.6 per cent), low-cost land (4.2 per cent), and tax incentives (4.2 per cent). The comparison is reminiscent of Kojima's (1973) distinction between market-oriented and labour-oriented FDI. We must be cautious, however, in interpreting labour-oriented FDI because with investment into low-wage countries, the potential of the local market is also an important attraction. A pure labour haven often does not last long because the influx of foreign capital bids up wages. In our study of

Table 14.2 Rankings of motivational factors for Taiwan's FDI towards different locations

	United States	*ASEAN*	*Mainland China*
To expand local or third-party markets	1 (36.1%)	2 (23.7%)	3 —
To acquire or develop new technologies	2 (14.8%)	 (0%)	— —
To collect market information	3 (13.1%)	8 (1.4%)	—
To diversify risks, including exchange-rate risks	4 (7.5%)	3 (14.2%)	—
To secure raw material supply	5 (2.9%)	6 (3.6%)	4
To utilize local labour	6 (2.3%)	1 (35.4%)	1
To circumvent trade restrictions	7 (1.3%)	7 (3.1%)	—
To access cheap land	7 (1.3%)	4 (8.8%)	2
To capitalize on tax incentives or other trade preferences	9 (0.4%)	5 (4.2%)	5
Others	(20.3%)	(5.6%)	
Sample size	46	102	368

Note: Percentages in parentheses indicate the average weights of motivational factors; weights are assigned to each factor in line with its ranking by individual firms: the *i*th rank factor weights $(n - i + 1)/n!$. Such information is not available for foreign direct investment (FDI) in mainland China.

Source: Statistics on the United States and ASEAN are from the Council for Economic Planning and Development (1992), those on mainland China, from Kao and Yen (1992), which draws on a survey conducted by the Chinese National Federation of Industries (CNFI) in 1991. The factor of 'linguistic and cultural proximity', which ranks second in the CNFI survey, was discarded because it explains the locational choice of FDI rather than what motivates FDI.

Taiwan's FDI, mainland China is the closest to a labour haven, but even that status is changing. In Table 4.2, we see that FDI in mainland China is motivated mainly by cheap labour and low-cost land. Market expansion is of tertiary importance.

The importance of the market-expansion factor depends on the nature of the product and the income level of the host country. Since most Taiwanese FDI made during the 1986–92 period was undertaken by firms that had previously exported to U.S. and European markets, the products they introduced to the host country were designed primarily for high-income society. Market potential for such products in Southeast Asia is limited, even more so in mainland China. Product outlets in various regions prove this point.

Table 14.3 lists the product outlets for Taiwanese FDI in the United States, Southeast Asia, and mainland China, based on survey data. It shows that in the United States, 83.5 per cent of the products are sold locally. In Southeast Asia, 33.0 per cent are sold locally. In mainland China, only 2.3 per cent are sold locally. The difference is remarkable. It is evident that mainland China offers very little attraction as a market. When the local market is small, a third-party market becomes important. In mainland China, for instance, 84.6 per cent of the product is exported to third-party markets. There is also a substantial proportion of products moving from Southeast Asia and mainland China back to Taiwan (14.3 per cent for Southeast Asia and 13.1 per cent for mainland China). This largely represents intra-firm transactions whereby subsidiaries ship semi-finished products back to Taiwan for further processing before they are re-exported or marketed in Taiwan. Thus, via vertical integration, investing firms are able to reap the benefits of international division of labour. In the case of investment in the United States, vertical integration goes in the other direction: semi-finished products or major components and parts move from parent firms to their subsidiaries for assembly or further processing before they are sold locally. Both market orientation and the pattern of vertical integration suggest that expansionary and defensive FDI exploit different types of intangible assets.

Empirical studies of FDI based in Western countries have revealed that the tendency for a firm to become involved in multinational production is related to the industries in which the firm operates (for example, Caves 1974). Therefore, one way to explore the difference in intangible assets associated with expansionary and defensive FDI is to examine the industrial composition of FDI for different host countries. This result is presented in Table 14.4 where the industry distributions of FDI in the United States, Southeast Asia (including Thailand, Malaysia, Indonesia, and the Philippines), and mainland China are tabulated.

Table 14.3 Destination of product sales (percentages)

	United States	*ASEAN*	*Mainland China*
Local market	83.5	33.0	2.3
Taiwan	2.6	14.3	13.1
(Parent firm)	—	(13.1)	—
Third-party country market	13.9	52.7	84.6
Total	100.0	100.0	100.0

Source: Statistics for the United States and Southeast Asia are from the Council for Economic Planning and Development (1992); statistics for mainland China are from Yen et al. (1992).

Table 14.4 Industry distribution of Taiwan's FDI in the manufacturing sector (percentages)

	United States	*Indonesia*	*Malaysia*	*Thailand*	*Philippines*	*Mainland China*
Food processing	0	4.5	3.9	6.3	0.6	4.3
Textiles and apparel	0	57.4	6.5	30.1	42.6	10.4
Leather	0	0	0.1	—	—	0.1
Footwear	0	12.5	—	—	0.1	8.8
Wood and furniture	0	4.8	5.9	0	0.7	2.8
Pulp and paper	0	0.1	0	—	2.7	2.4
Chemicals and plastics	23.8	5.3	5.1	12.3	29.8	8.3
Rubber	1.2	0	3.1	5.7	—	0.1
Non-metal minerals	2.6	0.1	2.0	1.4	13.3	3.6
Basic metals	3.0	1.5	37.1	—	—	0
Metal products	0.1	2.2	4.2	1.7		4.5
Machinery	1.1	1.8	2.0	0	—	1.4
Electrical and electronics	68.0	5.3	25.2	17.6	6.4	17.3
Transport equipment	0	2.1	0.1	0	0.1	12.1
Precision instruments	0	0	0	0	—	1.5
Miscellaneous	0	2.3	4.9	21.9	3.2	20.5
Total	100.0	100.0	100.0	100.0	100.0	100.0

Notes: All data on ASEAN countries are based on the host country's approved projects; percentages are calculated in terms of the value of proposed investments. Data on mainland China are based on cases registered with the government of the Republic of China. The Indonesia data cover 1985 to September 1990; the Malaysian data, 1987–90; the rest, 1986–90.

Source: Statistics for Indonesia are calculated from Watanabe (1992), for Malaysia, from Sekiguchi (1992), for Thailand, from Tsunekawa (1992), for the Philippines, from Tecson (1992), and for China, from Chung (1992).

First, FDI in the United States is predominated by the electrical and electronic products industry (68.0 per cent), followed by the chemicals industry (23.8 per cent). Little investment is made outside these two industries. It is noticeable that both electronic and chemical products were the mainstay of Taiwan exports to the United States prior to 1986. It is apparent that investing firms use local production to differentiate their products when their export market is threatened by competition from lower-wage countries. Their differentiation efforts include establishing their own brand names, employing local experts for product design, utilizing local assembly lines to cater to consumer needs, and performing after-sales service. How fruitfully this differentiation effort will pay off depends on the nature of the product. Some products may be easier to differentiate than others. Among traditional Taiwanese exports to the United States, textile products are conspicuously missing from the ranks of FDI into the United States. Textile products must be so homogeneous and the related technology so standardized that such a differentiation effort is not considered beneficial.

In fact, most textile firms choose to make FDI in Southeast Asia, resorting to low-cost labour to regain their competitive edge. The textile industry is the primary area in which Taiwanese FDI operates in Southeast Asia, accounting for 57.4 per cent of Taiwanese FDI in Indonesia, 42.6 per cent of Taiwanese FDI in the Philippines, and 30.1 per cent of Taiwanese FDI in Thailand. In mainland China, the textile industry also accounts for 10.4 per cent of FDI from Taiwan. This pattern suggests that only defensive FDI is feasible in the textile industry.

In contrast, the electronics and chemicals industries are major areas of FDI in the United States as well as Malaysia, Thailand, and mainland China, accounting for, respectively, 25.2 per cent, 17.6 per cent, and 17.3 per cent of total Taiwanese investment. Electrical and electronic products and chemical products seem to be more diversified, such that both differentiated and standardized products coexist in the same industries. Firms may move production into the United States to upgrade their product value or move into Southeast Asia to lower their production cost. Our conjecture is that the choice is dictated by the firm's technological capability and the depth of its managerial resources. Product upgrading requires technological knowledge and the financial resources to support such an endeavour. While small firms can choose only one route to protect their export market due to resource constraints, large firms may choose both for risk diversification.

In addition to textiles, electronics, and chemicals, some other industries stand out as significant areas of FDI. These include, for example, footwear in Indonesia, basic metals in Malaysia, and non-metal minerals in the Philippines. Similar to the textile industry, footwear is an industry typified by the defensive type of FDI. Basic metals and non-metal minerals are related to natural resources. In fact, the amount of investment in Malaysia in the basic metals industry is inflated by a steel-mill project which has not yet materialized.

Another feature that emerges from Table 14.4 is that the industry distribution of FDI in mainland China is the most dispersed among all regions. This is because small firms from all industries consider mainland China as the most desirable place to relocate their production. The leading sector among Taiwanese FDI in mainland China is the "miscellaneous" manufacturing industry which covers toys, sporting goods, travel gear, and so forth. This is followed by the electrical and electronic products industry, and next by the transport equipment industry, which consists mostly of bicycle producers. The statistics on mainland China record investment up to April 1991. Up to that time, FDI aimed at the local market had been largely prohibited by mainland Chinese authorities.

The fact that FDI in mainland China is dominated by small firms can be verified by Table 14.5, in which the registered capital and sales for both parent firms and subsidiaries are listed. It can be seen that the average capital registered for the subsidiaries in mainland China is US$1.44 million, much smaller than the average capital for FDI made in Southeast Asia. Based on investment projects approved by the Taiwanese Government in 1959–92, the average investment in Thailand, Malaysia, Indonesia, and the Philippines was US$40.1 million. Although the government approval-based data are upwardly biased, the conclusion that FDI in Southeast Asia is made by larger firms probably can be substantiated.

From Table 14.5 it can also be seen that the average turnover of Southeast Asian subsidiaries amounts to US$11.5 million while that of mainland Chinese subsidiaries is only US$4.8 million. A comparison between the parent firms shows a similar pattern, that is, those investing in Southeast Asia are larger firms. The pattern of employment is slightly different, however. While the average employment in the parent firms is much larger in the Southeast Asia group, the average employment in the subsidiaries is almost the same in the two regions. It is particularly interesting to find that the subsidiaries in mainland China actually employ more workers than their

Table 14.5 Average operating scales in Southeast Asia and mainland China

	Southeast Asia		*Mainland China*	
	Parent firm	*Subsidiary*	*Parent firm*	*Subsidiary*
Registered capital (thousand US$)	—	—	1,367	1.437
Sales (thousand US$)	15,620	11,484	6,349	4,814
No. of employees	729.5	360.2	108.7	354.4

Source: Statistics on Southeast Asia are calculated from the Council for Economic Planning and Development (1992), those on mainland China are from Yen et al. (1992, Table 4.2.0-1, p. 119).

parent counterparts. This suggests that the investing firms shift labour-intensive product lines to mainland China, resulting in a cutback in employment at home. In contrast, employment cutback is not common among those investing in Southeast Asia. These firms usually introduce new product lines to replace ones that have been relocated to Southeast Asia. This restructuring broadens the scope of product lines and, therefore, can only be undertaken by relatively large firms. Small firms can hardly handle such a complicated international production scheme. In fact, a survey conducted by Yen et al. (1992) reveals that 12.8 per cent of the firms that had invested in mainland China closed their Taiwan operation altogether.

INVESTMENT PATTERN OF LARGE FIRMS

Since large firms are capable of making multiple investments, their decision regarding investment in low-wage and high-wage countries reveals the strategic choice between cost reduction and product differentiation. This study is based on Taiwan's top 674 firms whose annual sales in 1986 exceeded NT$500 million (approximately US$14 million at the time) and were cited in China Credit Information Service Company's *The Largest Corporations in the Republic of China 1987* (which provides 1986 statistics).

We identified these firms and followed their FDI history in 1986–91. The first question we asked was how many of them made FDI during the period and how this pattern was related to their industries. The statistics related to this question are listed in Table 14.6, where the number of firms in each industry is tabulated along with the proportion of the group that made FDI in 1986–91. The FDI literature based on the experience of Western countries has suggested that large firms have a higher tendency to venture abroad. Taiwan's experience seems to indicate a similar pattern. The incidence of FDI decreases significantly when the scale of the firm decreases.

As can be seen from Table 14.6, out of the 674 top firms in Taiwan, 150 have made some FDI since 1986, amounting to 22.3 per cent of the total. In other words, roughly one out of five top firms have responded to changing macroeconomic conditions since 1986 by investing abroad. The tendency to invest differs greatly among industries, however. Among all industries, the plastics industry has the highest propensity to invest: 38.9 per cent of the firms in the group have engaged in FDI. This is followed, in order, by electrical and electronic products, and chemical materials, all of which are above 30 per cent. Coincidentally, these industries also constituted Taiwan's mainstay of exports prior to 1986. They are also the areas that have attracted the most inward foreign investment to Taiwan. There is little reason to believe that this outward move of FDI was engineered by multinational firms which own subsidiaries in Taiwan. It suggests rather that the most crucial factor among all determinants for FDI is probably the industry's characteristics, regardless of the origin of capital flow (Horst 1972).

Table 14.6 FDI by the top 674 firms in Taiwan

Industry	*Total no. of firms (A)*	*No. of firms that made FDI (B)*	*Proportion of FDI (%) (A/B)*
Food	74	7	9.5
Drinks and tobacco	10	1	10.0
Textiles	97	17	17.5
Apparel	33	7	21.2
Leather	10	2	20.0
Wood products	14	4	28.6
Paper and paper products	17	4	23.5
Chemical materials	35	11	31.4
Chemical products	20	4	20.0
Petroleum and coal	0	0	—
Rubber	11	3	27.3
Plastics	36	14	38.9
Non-metal minerals	10	2	20.0
Basic metals	51	4	7.8
Metal products	21	5	23.8
Machinery	14	2	14.3
Electrical and electronic products	148	48	32.4
Transport equipment	29	6	20.7
Footwear	21	4	19.1
Miscellaneous manufacturing	23	5	21.7
Total	674	150	22.3

Source: China Credit Information Service Co. and Foreign Investment Commission.

At the other end, basic metals is the most apathetic to FDI: only 7.8 per cent of firms in this group made the move. Similarly, low proportions of FDI are observed for the food and drink and the tobacco industries, both of which are below 10 per cent. These industries are typically domestic market-oriented with little export experience. When wage rates increased and the local currency value rose after 1986, these domestic-oriented industries felt little pressure from international competition. In fact, as the local currency appreciated, their competitiveness *vis-à-vis* imports improved. It is fair, therefore, to say that the purpose of FDI in these industries is primarily for market expansion rather than export defence. Unlike export-oriented industries, investment in these sectors is made in low-wage countries rather than high-wage countries despite its expansionary nature. This investment usually involves products that command reasonable demand even in low-wage countries. In comparison, expansionary FDI in the high-wage countries usually involves products that cater to high-income economies. Therefore, in identifying investment in low-wage countries as defensive FDI, one runs the risk of overestimating defensive investment. In other words, FDI in low-wage countries is not always labour-seeking. In industries where exports are a rarity, FDI in low-wage countries is often market-oriented.

In other major export industries, namely textiles, apparel, and footwear, the propensity to invest abroad is close to, but slightly below, the industry average. This indicates that although exports may be a precondition for FDI, the tendency to invest abroad may differ substantially among export industries. The textile, apparel, and footwear industries are characterized by more or less homogeneous products where price competition dominates the international market. Product differentiation in these industries is mainly achieved by advertisement. After-sales service is almost unnecessary. Local production in these industries, therefore, serves little purpose in product differentiation. Therefore, FDI in these industries is primarily geared towards cost reduction and destined for low-wage countries. Lack of the expansionary type of investment may explain why the proportion of FDI in these industries falls behind that of the plastics and electronics industries.

Having reviewed industry differences in terms of FDI patterns, we now examine the allocation of investment between high-wage and low-wage countries in the course of FDI. Table 14.7 lists the distribution of FDI in these two categories in 1986–91. It can be seen that FDI in high-wage countries increased steadily after 1986 and peaked in 1989. In contrast, FDI in low-wage countries also increased steadily after 1986 but was still on the rise in 1991. Although six years is too short a period from which to infer FDI behaviour, the pattern seems to suggest that expansionary FDI occurs intermittently, subject to macroeconomic shocks that disturb the portfolio balance. In Taiwan's case, it is the sudden appreciation of the currency that made the cost of acquiring foreign assets lower than before. Many firms took this opportunity to venture into advanced countries to establish production-related facilities, including R&D units, distribution warehouses, and sales networks. On the other hand, defensive FDI seems to occur continuously, driven by rising wages at home and the evolution of the product life-cycle.

Table 14.7 FDI in high-wage and low-wage countries by the top 674 firms

	FDI in high-wage countries		*FDI in low-wage countries*	
Year	*Amount (thousand US$)*	*Share (%)*	*Amount (thousand US$)*	*Share (%)*
1986	3,582	48	3,878	52
1987	15,244	63	8,947	37
1988	49,340	78	13,841	22
1989	362,822	78	104,252	22
1990	142,024	41	205,183	59
1991	98,271	27	259,866	73

Source: As for Table 14.6.

Although the currency appreciation which commenced in 1986 reinforced the effect of wage increases, setting off a big boom in this kind of investment, the activity did not die out even after the currency value stabilized. Although we believe that defensive FDI will also eventually reach a peak, without further currency appreciation or other major external shocks its volume will probably remain above that of expansionary FDI. Recently, however, mainland China opened its doors for foreign investment to produce goods chiefly for local consumption. Accessibility to its lucrative domestic market will probably induce another wave of the expansionary type of investment in the coming years.

EFFECTS OF FDI ON DOMESTIC INDUSTRIES

Whether FDI will lead to a hollowing-out of the domestic industry (de-industrialization) has been debated for quite some time without coming to a conclusion. Theoretically speaking, if FDI results in a relocation of domestic industries without compensating effects, it will contribute to de-industrialization. On the other hand, if FDI results in a "restructuring" of industries, de-industrialization should not occur. Any defensive type of FDI involves relocation of production activities. Restructuring, however, may take place immediately following the relocation. This may occur through three channels. First, some firms, particularly the large ones, may introduce new product lines to replace old ones in an effort to exploit the power of their firm-specific asset, which is often embodied in their employees. Laying off employees runs the risk of leaking special knowledge. This is intra-firm restructuring. Second, relocated production may be forwardly or backwardly linked to domestic industries. Through this linkage, overseas production may nourish thriving downstream or upstream industries at home. This is intra-industry restructuring. For example, the relocation of the Taiwanese garment industry to Southeast Asia and mainland China in recent years has benefited the domestic textile industry, leading to an expansion of production in areas in which Taiwanese firms possess a comparative advantage. Synthetic fibres, for instance, are sold not only to Taiwanese subsidiaries in mainland China in large quantities, but also to local firms that compete with Taiwanese subsidiaries. Third, resources that are released from relocation can be transferred to new industries. This follows the classical argument that resources find their own way to full employment as long as the market functions well. This is inter-industry restructuring. Among the three channels, inter-industry restructuring seems to be the most treacherous and unreliable because if the newly created industry does not carry new technology with it, the productivity of the reallocated resources will not increase and the economy will become stagnant even if full employment can be maintained. Stagnation is synonymous with de-industrialization.

Since expansionary FDI is an effort to differentiate products, it is indicative of intra-firm restructuring. Defensive FDI, on the other hand, may or may not be associated with any type of restructuring. We shall, therefore, put forth a hypothesis that the ratio of defensive to expansionary FDI in a particular industry indicates the risk of de-industrialization. The following exercise tests this hypothesis empirically against the Taiwan data.

Despite a possible measurement error, we first categorize all FDI in high-wage countries as expansionary investment and all FDI in low-wage countries as defensive investment. Low-wage countries include Turkey, Thailand, Malaysia, Indonesia, the Philippines, India, Sri Lanka, African and Latin American countries, and mainland China. The rest are classified as high-wage countries. Cumulative FDI in 1986–91 is calculated and presented in Table 14.8.

As shown in Table 14.8, out of sixteen manufacturing industries, defensive FDI is greater than expansionary FDI (indicated by A/B being greater than one) in nine industries. According to our hypothesis, these industries are at a high risk of de-industrialization. We expect some "hollowing-out" to emerge. Examining changes in domestic production between 1986 and 1992, however, we found that only four industries, namely textiles, apparel, leather, and wood products suffered a decline in domestic production. The other five industries experienced an upward trend in domestic production. Upon closer examination, three of the five industries going against our prediction depend heavily on natural resources for production, namely, paper and paper products, non-metal minerals, and basic metals. Firms in these three industries ventured into low-wage countries, particularly Southeast Asia, mainly to secure a supply of natural resources rather than cheap labour. Another industry, the food industry, as discussed above, is local market-oriented. The purpose of investment in this area, whether in low-wage or high-wage countries, is to explore local demand. The products involved in FDI in low-wage countries, such as instant noodles and animal feed, are prepared for local consumption. In the outlier industry, miscellaneous manufacturing, domestic production increased by 4.7 per cent during the period despite a modest defensive-to-expansionary FDI ratio of 1.1. Growth in domestic production, however, is largely attributable to growth in the sub-industry of precision instruments. If we exclude precision instruments from the miscellaneous manufacturing category, the industry actually declined by 5.7 per cent between 1986 and 1992. Foreign direct investment in this sector rarely involves precision instruments.

Therefore, if we exclude natural resources–intensive industries, refine the industry definition of miscellaneous manufacturing, and take into account the fact that FDI in low-wage countries in the food industry is not of the defensive type, our hypothesis that the ratio of defensive FDI to expansionary FDI predicts the likelihood of de-industrialization is substantiated. Our prediction, however, is good only for the direction of change in industrial output, not for the magnitude of change. For example, the largest decline in industrial output occurs in the wood products industry (33.0 per cent), which

Table 14.8 FDI and corresponding change in domestic production in the manufacturing industry

Industry	*(A) 1986–91 FDI in low-wage countries (thousand US$)*	*(B) 1986–91 FDI in high-wage countries (thousand US$)*	*(A)/(B)*	*Change in domestic production,[a] 1986–92 (%)*	*Ratio of FDI to domestic capital stock (%)*
Food	39,350	8,052	4.9	62.9	0.7
Drinks and tobacco	0	0	—	47.3	0
Textiles	81,936	15,523	5.3	−5.0	0.9
Apparel	20,537	1,967	10.4	−12.8	1.3
Leather	3,965	2,994	1.4	−10.4	0.6
Wood products	17,785	7,986	2.2	−33.0	0.9
Paper and paper products	12,520	545	22.9	35.3	0.3
Chemicals[c]	74,195	329,809	0.2	22.6	3.3
Petroleum and coal	0	0	—	11.1	0
Rubber and plastics	84,973	82,554	1.0	8.7	2.2
Non-metal minerals	66,253	3,100	21.4	59.0	1.3
Basic metals and metal products	410,040	10,362	39.6	43.9	2.7
Machinery	26,903	56,667	0.5	65.4	2.6
Electrical and electronic products	275,297	320,600	0.9	49.2	4.2
Transport equipment	2,932	0	—	100.8	0
Miscellaneous manufacturing[d]	3,623	3,295	1.1	4.7	0.2

Notes:
[a] Changes in Industrial output based on current National Taiwan (NT) value.
[b] The ratio is the sum of A and B to the stock of operational capital in 1986. Foreign direct investment (FDI), which is measured in terms of US$ dollars, is converted to NT value, using the year-end exchange rate in 1988 (1US$: 28.2NT$).
[c] Including chemical materials and chemical products.
[d] Including precision instruments.

Source: FDI statistics are from the Statistics on Overseas Chinese and Foreign Investment, Technical Co-operation, Outward Investment, Outward Technical Co-operation, Indirect Mainland Investment, on basis of approval (Investment Commission, Ministry of Economic Affairs); Industrial output statistics are from the Monthly Industrial Production Statistics (Bureau of Industrial Development, Ministry of Economic Affairs).

has a modest defensive-to-expansionary ratio of 2.2. The highest ratio occurs in the apparel industry whose domestic production declined by 12.8 per cent. This suggests that although defensive and expansionary FDI is indicative of the possibility of intra-firm restructuring, other forms of restructuring may be unrelated to this distinction. In particular, the possibility of intra-industry restructuring is related to the degree of vertical integration within the industry. For example, there seems to be a higher degree of vertical integration within the textile and apparel industry than the leather and wood products industry. In the former sectors, production moves from fibre, to yarn, to fabrics, then to dyeing, and finally to clothing. Different factor intensities and functions are required in different stages of the production. Division of labour across the country may be desirable given different factor prices and technological levels. In addition, transport of textile products does not impose heavy costs on producers because the products are light. This makes vertical integration across national borders possible. In comparison, leather and wood products do not require long series of distinctive processing but transport costs are high. Vertical integration across national borders is less feasible. The lack of cross-country, vertical integration may partially explain why the leather and wood products sectors suffer a relatively serious decline in domestic production despite relatively small ratios of defensive-to-expansionary FDI.

The possibility of inter-industry restructuring is determined by the nation's technological capability as well as domestic market demand conditions. For example, due to a rise in personal income, demand for passenger cars has increased remarkably in Taiwan since 1986. This led to a boom in the automobile market, contributing to an increase in the transport industry by 100.8 per cent between 1986 and 1992, despite a small amount of defensive FDI made in the areas of bicycles and auto parts.

Also listed in Table 14.8 is the ratio of cumulative FDI to operating capital at home, which is indicative of the importance of overseas production. Since the data used in Table 14.8 only cover officially approved FDI, the ratio greatly underestimates the share of overseas production. For example, the electrical and electronic products industry, which has the highest FDI–to–domestic capital ratio of 4.2 per cent, would have an overseas-to-domestic production ratio of 21.0 per cent if actual FDI is five times the official statistics, as is generally believed to be the discrepancy in low-wage countries. Given the importance of overseas production, the Taiwan economy can no longer be judged in isolation. Its linkage to overseas operations has become a crucial determinant of Taiwan's economic health. Nevertheless, such a large scale of overseas production does not prevent the electrical and electronic products industry from growing steadily at home.

CONCLUSION

Whether FDI causes de-industrialization is an unsettled economic issue. This chapter distinguishes defensive FDI aimed at reducing production costs from expansionary FDI aimed at differentiating products, and proposes a hypothesis which states that when defensive FDI is greater than expansionary FDI, the industry runs a high risk of being de-industrialized. Expansionary FDI is often associated with intra-firm restructuring while defensive FDI may be a relocation of production activity without beneficial feedback to domestic industries. The evidence based on Taiwanese FDI seems to support the hypothesis at large.

The nature of FDI, however, is probably more complicated than we have suggested. Many investment projects are undertaken for multiple objectives and the importance of each objective may shift over time. Therefore, an FDI project initially aimed at reducing labour costs may end up serving that local market. The demarcation line between expansionary and defensive FDI can never be drawn scientifically. Nevertheless, the distinction is useful in conceptualizing the motivation of FDI and in analysing the effect of FDI on domestic industries.

The major roadblock in analysing the effect of FDI on domestic industries is the lack of knowledge on the linkage between domestic and overseas production. Not only do we know little about intra-firm transactions between parent firms and their subsidiaries, we also know little about the sourcing policy of subsidiaries in general. While more research in this area is required, this chapter suggests that study at the industry level can be beneficial even when firm-level data are not available.

REFERENCES

Caves, Richard. "International Corporations: The Industrial Economics of Foreign Investment". *Economica* 38 (1971): 1–27.

——. "Causes of Direct Investment: Foreign Firms' Shares in Canadian and United Kingdom Manufacturing Industries". *Review of Economics & Statistics* 56 (1974): 279–93.

Chen, Tain-Jy. "Determinants of Taiwan's Direct Foreign Investment: The Case of a Newly Industrializing Country". *Journal of Development Economics* 39 (1992): 397–407.

Chung, Chin. "Impacts on Domestic and Host Economies of Taiwan's DFI toward Mainland China". Occasional Paper no. 9202. Taipei: Chung-Hua Institution for Economic Research, 1992.

Council for Economic Planning and Development (CEPD). "*Tui-wai tou-tzu cheng-che ping-ku pao-kao*" [A study of Taiwan's direct foreign investment]. Mimeographed. Taiwan, 1992.

Horst, Thomas. "Firm and Industry Determinants of the Decision to Invest Abroad: An Empirical Study". *Review of Economics and Statistics* 54 (1972): 258–66.

Hymer, Stephen. *The International Operation of National Firms: A Study of Direct Foreign*

Investment. Ph.D. dissertation, Massachusetts Institute of Technology, 1960. Cambridge, MA: MIT Press, 1976.

Kao Charng and Chung-ta Yen. "*Tai-shang tsai ta-lu tou-tzu chi-yeh ying-yun ching-kuang chih tiao-cha fen-hsi*" [A survey analysis of the operations of Taiwanese subsidiaries in mainland China]. Mimeographed. Chung-Hua Institution for Economic Research, Taipei, 1992.

Kojima, Kiyoshi. "A Macroeconomic Approach to Foreign Direct Investment". *Hitotsubashi Journal of Economics* 14 (1973): 1–21.

Sekiguchi, Junko. "Japan and NIEs' DFI in Malaysia and Industrialization" (in Japanese). In *Chokusetsu Toshi To Kogyoka* [Direct investment and industrialization], edited by Hirohisa Kohama. Tokyo: Japan External Trade Organization, 1992.

Tecson, Gwendolyn. "The Changing Pattern of Foreign Direct Investment in the Philippines". Paper presented at the Pacific Economic Outlook Task Force Meeting under the Pacific Economic Co-operation Conference (PECC), 25–26 March 1992, Osaka, Japan.

Tsunekawa, Jun. "Industrialization and Foreign Direct Investment in Thailand: Focus on the Second Half of the 1980s" (in Japanese). In *Chokusetsu Toshi To Kogyoka* [Direct investment and industrialization], edited by Hirohisa Kohama. Tokyo: Japan External Trade Organization, 1992.

Watanabe, Machiko. "Japan and NIEs' DFI in Indonesia and Industrialization" (in Japanese). In *Chokusetsu Toshi To Kogyoka* [Direct investment and industrialization], edited by Hirohisa Kohama. Tokyo: Japan External Trade Organization, 1992.

Yen Chung-ta, Yu-chun lin, and Chin Chung. "*Tai-shang ta-lu tou-tzu chi mao-yi chi yen-chou*" [A study on Taiwanese direct investment in mainland China]. Mimeographed. Taipei: Chung-Hua Institution for Economic Research, 1992.

15

STAYING GLOBAL AND GOING REGIONAL

Singapore's Inward and Outward Direct Investment

Pang Eng Fong

INTRODUCTION

Among fast-growing countries in the Asia-Pacific region, Singapore stands out in its early and exceptional ability to attract foreign direct investment (FDI) and to the contribution of this investment to its economy. In the mid-1960s, it was one of the few countries in the region that courted foreign investors assiduously and allowed them to set up wholly owned subsidiaries. In the 1980s, it received an average annual FDI inflow of US$2.3 billion, the largest among developing countries. This large inflow amounted to a third of the island's gross domestic capital formation, a proportion much higher than that for other developing countries in the region.

A large and growing outflow of FDI by Singapore-based companies has paralleled the steady rise in FDI inflows since the late 1980s. Driven in part by expanding opportunities in the region and strongly supported by government policy, this outflow is creating "an external wing" in Singapore's capital-surplus, labour-short economy.

The changing patterns of inward and outward FDI flows since the late 1980s have profound implications for the upgrading of Singapore's economy. This chapter analyses these patterns with particular reference to the electronics industry. It examines how inward and outward investments are influencing the development of regional networks by foreign and Singaporean firms, including government-linked companies, venturing abroad.

INWARD FDI FLOWS

Trends and patterns

Between 1980 and 1989, foreign firms tripled their equity investment in Singapore to S$47 billion, which was equal to 38 per cent of all equity

Source: *The New Wave of Foreign Direct Investment in Asia*, Singapore: Institute of Southeast Asian Studies (1995), pp. 111–29

investment in the country. In 1989, manufacturing accounted for 42 per cent of the foreign equity investment and the largest investor was the United States with 19.5 per cent of the foreign equity investment, followed by Japan (18.3 per cent) and the United Kingdom (11.9 per cent).

Net investment commitments by foreign firms in Singapore's manufacturing sector have risen from S$1.2 billion in 1982 to S$2.8 billion in 1992. The relative shares of the three major investing countries—the United States, Japan, and Europe—have changed since 1982. The U.S. share peaked at 44.1 per cent in 1984. Japan's share rose rapidly from 1982, peaking at 34.4 per cent in 1988, three years after the sharp yen revaluation in 1985, a development that triggered a surge of Japanese investments in developing Asian countries. European investment commitments too have increased in absolute terms since the early 1980s, but relative to other investing countries, their share has also fallen.

In cumulative terms, total investments by U.S., Japanese, and European firms do not differ greatly. In 1990, U.S. firms had cumulative investments of S$7.6 billion (representing 23.8 per cent of total manufacturing investment including local investments) compared with S$7.5 billion for Japanese firms, and S$7.2 billion for European firms (Table 15.1).

In the early 1980s, investments in the electronics industry were mostly in consumer electronics and semi-conductors. Since then, the industry has expanded and diversified, attracting investments in many new sectors including computer peripherals, computer systems, telecommunications equipment, passive electronics, display devices (including cathode ray tubes and liquid crystal displays) and office automation equipment (including printers, electronic typewriters, and facsimile machines).

Determinants and role of government policy

The changing flow and pattern of foreign investments in Singapore since the early 1980s is the outcome of the interactions of many global, industry, and national developments. One general factor is the state of the world economy and the economic vitality of its key players. Developments in individual industries have also affected the flow and pattern of foreign investments. But where a particular investment is made depends on conditions and policies in host countries. Few countries have been as effective as Singapore in attracting high-quality investments and in devising policies, programmes and incentives to meet the changing needs of foreign investors.

Singapore's enduring attraction to foreign investors is the result of a total approach to ensuring a business environment characterized by transparent, predictable rules and in which both local and foreign businesses can operate efficiently. Many policies and projects the government initiates are intended not only for foreign investors, but to meet larger societal and developmental goals. These include heavy investments in physical infrastructure (for

Table 15.1 Singapore: cumulative investment in manufacturing, by major region of origin, 1980–90 (percentage of total)

	1980	*1981*	*1982*	*1983*	*1984*	*1985*	*1986*	*1987*	*1988*	*1989*	*1990*
USA	19.8	20.9	21.5	21.7	21.4	23.0	24.6	25.6	25.3	24.2	23.?
Japan	11.2	11.2	11.1	11.2	14.7	14.5	16.1	18.3	20.0	22.4	22.?
Europe	28.3	27.4	26.1	25.2	22.7	22.1	22.0	21.1	21.1	22.3	21.?
Others	7.7	7.8	7.5	7.5	6.3	5.3	4.9	4.8	4.6	3.9	4.?
Local	32.9	32.6	33.8	34.4	35.0	35.0	32.5	30.2	28.9	27.2	27.?
Total (million S$)	10,561	12,443	14,528	16,423	19,450	20,259	20,924	22,782	25,785	29,513	32,815

Notes: Data excludes rubber processing. Coverage includes only establishments with ten or more workers. Data for 1980–89 have been revised to trace the ultimate source of capital.

Source: Economic Development Board, *Yearbook 1991/1992* (1992), p. 11.

example, public housing, internal and international transportation and communications facilities, and public services), and in education at all levels, from pre-school to post-tertiary. These investments in social overhead capital have contributed to general efficiency, low costs, greater labour productivity, and human capital accumulation.

Other policies have been targeted specifically at industry. The government builds industrial estates, including high-tech science parks, supports industrial research institutes, provides state equity or loan capital at favourable interest rates, organizes or subsidizes worker training and retraining programmes, and gears the educational and training system to meet the manpower needs of industry and the state.

Singapore's heavy public investments in infrastructure and education have benefited the domestic economy. The increasingly well-educated population has been able to absorb ever higher industrial skills, a development that has encouraged foreign investors to transfer more sophisticated and higher-value operations to Singapore, and to spawn local supporting industry. Where Singapore's performance has been weak—in comparison with Hong Kong, Taiwan, and South Korea—is in the development of an independent local entrepreneurial class in manufacturing, a weakness the government recognizes and has been working hard to remedy since the recession of the 1970s revealed the risks of depending on government-linked and multinational companies to power Singapore's economic growth and transformation.

The experience of Singapore suggests that such efforts are less important in attracting foreign investment than factors such as political and financial stability, responsible government, a good local business environment, adequate infrastructure and services, availability of low-cost skilled and unskilled labour and other resources, availability of local suppliers, and location in or near major markets or sources of supply.

Singapore does not have cheap labour or other resources, or a significant domestic market, or a well-developed local supplier base. Its government shows a strong interventionist bent, though mostly in ways that support rather than obstruct market forces. Free trade, free capital flows, and no restrictions on foreign ownership are powerful attractions which few other countries offer, and fiscal incentives—though offered by most other developing countries seeking foreign investment—are more selective and finely tuned and probably more generous here.

OUTWARD FDI FLOWS

Official survey data show that Singapore's direct investment abroad rose from S$1.7 billion in 1981 to $7.5 billion in 1990 (Table 15.2). At the beginning of the 1980s, 60 per cent of the FDI outflow went to Malaysia, another 10.8 per cent to Hong Kong, these being the two biggest recipient economies. By 1990, Malaysia's proportion had dropped to 22.2 per cent as other countries

Table 15.2 Singapore's direct investment abroad, by country, 1981–90 (percentage of total)

	1981	*1982*	*1983*	*1984*	*1985*	*1986*	*1987*	*1988*	*1989*	*1990*
Asian countries										
ASEAN	0.2	0.3	0.4	2.0	2.3	1.9	1.8	1.9	1.3	0.9
Brunei	2.4	1.9	2.0	2.3	2.9	2.6	2.0	2.0	1.5	1.3
Indonesia	60.0	55.7	52.1	50.4	43.1	37.9	34.1	34.4	26.9	22.2
Malaysia	1.1	0.8	0.8	0.7	1.0	0.9	0.5	0.8	1.0	0.8
Philippines	0.6	0.5	0.4	0.4	0.9	1.2	1.5	1.5	2.7	2.8
Thailand										
Hong Kong	10.8	15.2	16.0	16.3	20.4	19.2	18.2	18.2	15.8	12.3
Japan	0.0	0.0	0.0	0.0	0.2	0.2	0.5	0.6	0.5	0.9
China	0.0	0.0	0.0	0.0	2.6	3.6	3.4	2.6	2.1	1.9
Taiwan	0.8	0.7	1.1	1.1	1.5	1.5	0.9	1.8	2.8	2.7
Others	1.0	1.0	1.7	1.9	1.4	1.7	1.5	1.7	2.3	2.6
Europe	3.0	2.8	2.6	3.0	4.0	6.4	12.1	10.1	5.8	12.2
Australia	3.7	4.3	5.4	5.5	7.8	6.8	7.4	5.5	6.3	6.9
USA	1.9	2.1	2.1	2.3	2.9	2.5	2.3	3.6	5.5	4.4
Others	14.5	14.7	15.4	14.0	9.0	13.6	13.8	15.1	25.4	28.2
Total (million S$)	1,677.7	2,086.9	2,233.1	2,399.3	2,257.2	2,597.7	2,961.5	2,993.9	5,288.7	7,473.8

Source: Department of Statistics, *Singapore's Investment Abroad, 1976–1989* (October 1991a), Table A5; Department of Statistics, *Singapore's Investment Abroad, 1990* (February 1993), Table A19–A20 (for 1989 and 1990 data).

including developed countries began to attract more Singapore investments. Although Singapore investments in the Asian region rose absolutely in the 1980s, their share of the total fell from about four-fifths to half.

One source (*Kay Hian James Capel*, 1993, p. 8) estimates Singapore's total investments abroad in 1993 to be S$15.9 billion—S$9.8 billion by listed companies and S$6.1 billion by unlisted companies and individuals. With 38 per cent of the total, Malaysia is the largest recipient of Singapore's outward investments by listed firms, followed by Indonesia (11 per cent) and China (10 per cent). Listed companies earn an average of 12.5 per cent return on their overseas investment, a rate that is much higher than the cost of capital in Singapore. The country distribution of overseas investments by individuals and unlisted firms differs greatly from that of listed firms. The two largest hosts of these investments were China (with 43 per cent of the total), and Vietnam (22 per cent).

Singapore's investments in China have surged since 1992. China now ranks as the third most important offshore investment location (after Malaysia and Indonesia) for Singapore-based manufacturers. With Singapore's policy emphasis on growing "an external wing" to complement its domestic economy, and official encouragement to invest overseas, China's large market and low-cost labour will attract much more investments by government-linked and private firms from Singapore. Already, government-linked companies have signed many contracts with Chinese firms and provinces.

Outward investment flows from Singapore are adding to the fast-expanding flows of intra-regional investments by capital-surplus, labour-short countries in the region. One source (*Kay Hian James Capel*, 1993, p. 2) estimates that outward investments could help raise Singapore's sustainable gross national product (GNP) growth rate by three percentage points, from 6 to 9 per cent.

REGIONAL INTEGRATION AND FDI FLOWS

The regional and domestic factors that have encouraged intra-regional investments in the late 1980s will remain important in the 1990s. Japan, Singapore, other Asian NIEs, and, increasingly also the near-NIEs will continue to be the major sources of intra-regional investment. Firms from these countries will invest in neighbouring countries to serve Western markets as well as their own home markets. China, already a major investor in Hong Kong, will likely become an increasingly important investor in the region if its breathtaking economic progress continues.

The NIEs, near-NIEs, and China are being joined by other countries in the region, especially Vietnam, as major recipients of foreign investments, from within and outside the region. Among recipient countries, China will likely receive the most investments because of its unmatched attractions of low-cost, abundant labour, a large domestic market, and cultural similarities with capital-surplus countries in the region.

Investments in the region by U.S. companies rose 7 per cent in 1992, and were projected to increase another 20 per cent to US$13.0 billion in 1993. Rapidly growing consumer markets in the Asia-Pacific region for U.S. products and services are the reason for the large increases in planned U.S. investments. Though preoccupied with the single European market and Eastern Europe, European Community (EC) countries are also increasingly aware of the opportunities in the Asia-Pacific region. Their investments in the region have also been increasing.

The expanding flows of intra-regional trade and investments have led to the rapid evolution of regional production and trade networks. Japanese manufacturers such as Sony, Matsushita, and Aiwa increasingly treat the region as an economic integrated unit, locating plants to service Asian and Western markets in the region's economies according to their comparative advantage. Non-Asian multinationals, particularly U.S. firms, are making linked investments in the region, generating new trade and capital flows among host countries. Throughout the region, Chinese businesses (including those from Taiwan as well as those from South-east Asia) are responding to new opportunities and the liberalization of investment rules in developing host countries, particularly China.

Expanding regional linkages have reinforced Singapore's emerging role as a regional headquarters and "hub-city" for multinational investors. The city's growing importance to global firms has led multinationals to change their traditional structure of a single home-country head office controlling branches the world over to a more complex one with decentralized decision-making centres. Interviews with subsidiaries of large Japanese firms with operational headquarters (OHQs) in Singapore indicate that decentralization has increased their influence on decisions made by their head office.

Impact and implications of intra-regional FDI flows

For Singapore, as for other source and host countries, the impact of intra-regional (and inter-regional) investment depends on many factors. Most of all, it depends on the magnitude of the foreign investment relative to the size of the country. For large recipients of foreign investment like Singapore and Malaysia, the impact of foreign investment on production, export, employment, and skill generation has been great.

Second, the impact of intra-regional investment (and also direct investment from outside the region) varies with the type of investment. Export-oriented foreign investments increase export earnings and improve the balance of payments. Investments in high-technology sectors transfer more skills, but investments in mature, low-tech industries spawn more local linkages. As intra-regional investments are increasingly in export-oriented industries, their impact is positive. But they may not expand linkages within countries if they reflect a regional investment strategy where a company allocates its chain of value-added activities according to the comparative advantages of host countries.

Third, the effects of investments on technology transfer change over time, being small in the early stages and becoming more prominent as skills accumulate and linkages develop. Singapore's experience and also that of other countries suggests that complaints about slow technology and skill transfer by foreign investors usually decline over time as countries gain experience with foreign investments and as their capacity to absorb foreign technology grows. Profit-seeking investors, unless deterred by host-country restrictions, will transfer higher levels of technology only if the host country can absorb it. This does not mean a host country must be a passive recipient of foreign capital. As Singapore's experience suggests, a host country can actively strengthen its capacity to absorb more sophisticated technology by investing in education and training, and by supporting the development of scientific and engineering research.

Fourth, external factors also influence the effects of foreign investment on a host country. Small developing countries in particular are likely to figure only marginally in the changing global strategies of giant multinationals. Their strategies determine whether a foreign investment project is likely to export, reinvest, have high local content, upgrade skills, or develop indigenous technology.

Fifth, intra-regional investments affect not only output, exports, and employment in host countries; they also influence industrial restructuring in source countries. Outward investments allow source countries to concentrate resources in higher value-added activities. While these investments enable source countries to specialize, they may have negative effects. In Singapore, the issue is of increasing concern as outward investment flows are growing rapidly. The government is seeking to ensure that regional investments do not result only in income from abroad, but also strengthen local companies, transforming some of them into multinationals and interlocking them with the Singapore economy.

Sixth, the macroeconomic growth, employment, and balance of payments effects of foreign investment are important in the early stages of development. However, as host countries in the region develop their industrial skills and accumulate more capital and expertise, the dynamic benefits of foreign investment on entrepreneurship and technology transfer multiply.

Seventh, the new wave of intra-regional investments has resulted in new types of joint ventures between local and foreign firms. These ventures more closely resemble the global strategic alliances forged by multinationals from industrialized countries with each other. Alliances with foreigners are sought less for capital input than for the sharing of risks and technology, and for access to world markets.

Besides economic effects, outward investments also have political consequences. Singapore is concerned about the political implications of its growing investment and economic links with China. It does not want these links to overshadow its strong ties with its neighbours, Indonesia and Malaysia. Accordingly, it has encouraged Singapore firms to invest not only in the Asia-Pacific region, but also in other countries including India.

FOREIGN INVESTMENTS IN THE ELECTRONICS INDUSTRY

Singapore's electronics industry began in the mid-1960s with two local firms assembling black-and-white TV sets for a tariff-protected domestic market under licence from Japanese consumer electronics firms. The industry was transformed in the late 1960s with the influx of U.S. semi-conductor firms. By the early 1970s, these semi-conductor firms had been joined by Japanese, European, and other American firms mainly engaged in producing electronics components and consumer products for export to the world market. The electronics industry became the largest employer in Singapore.

In the early 1980s computers and computer peripherals replaced semi-conductors as the dominant segment of Singapore's electronics industry. American disk-drive companies, which were much less labour-intensive and had much higher value-added than semi-conductors, other components or consumer products, established themselves in Singapore beginning in 1980. Within a few years, Singapore became the world's leading supplier of disk drives. Major foreign companies were attracted to Singapore by the presence of major customers who manufacture electronic equipment locally or in the neighbouring Asian region, where demand for semi-conductors is growing rapidly.

Singapore is also becoming the world's largest producer of computer tape drives, which are used to store computer data and are a back-up for disk drives. They are used in personal computers and workstations, mini-computers, and mainframes. The world leader in this industry, Archive Corp. of California, which produces 45 per cent of the global supply of quarter-inch tape drives, 95 per cent of them in two Singapore factories, has doubled its investment in Singapore and set up a research and development (R&D) unit.

Singapore is likely to remain the world's fifth largest semi-conductor producer, with a 4 to 5 per cent share of world production, after the United States, Japan, Malaysia, and South Korea. The consumer electronics sector has also grown since the late 1980s, though at a much slower rate than the other electronics sectors. In 1992, the sector exported S$4.24 billion, two-thirds that of the disk drive and tape drive sector.

Suppliers to the electronics industry which have located here include firms in other sectors, such as glass, engineering, and chemicals.

Many electronics multinationals, including those without local manufacturing facilities (such as IBM) as well as those with such facilities have established international purchasing offices (IPOs) in Singapore which purchase parts and supplies for their world-wide operations. For these and other companies, Singapore increasingly functions as a purchasing, warehousing, distribution, and transshipment centre for parts, components, and finished products destined for regional factories or world markets.

In the late 1980s, the Singapore Government offered new tax breaks to encourage multinationals to establish regional OHQs in Singapore. To qualify, companies must base their regional R&D, distribution, service network and financial system in Singapore. A growing number of electronics companies have obtained OHQ status.

To sum up, the electronics industry is Singapore's most important manufacturing industry. It accounts for 36 per cent of manufacturing value-added, employs 25 per cent of the work-force in manufacturing and contributes 12 per cent to the island's gross domestic product (GDP). Its transformation since the late 1960s has been remarkable. The main change is the shift begun in the 1970s from labour-intensive assembly activities mainly in semiconductors, components, and consumer products, to capital-intensive, high-tech manufacturing and related high-value services in these sectors but also in telecommunication equipment, display devices, office automation equipment, computers and computer peripherals, particularly disk drives, in the 1980s and 1990s. The industry remains heavily dominated by foreign-owned enterprises, mainly from the United States, but with sizeable and growing contingents from Europe and Japan as well. Over time, large, mature multinationals which are household names the world over have given way in the ranks of new investors to smaller, newer, more inexperienced high-tech firms at an early stage of their life-cycle, many of whom are first internationalized by their investment in Singapore, from which they then begin to venture to other countries in the region. In Singapore itself, the average foreign electronics firms now employs more capital but fewer workers, more of whom are in highly skilled categories, than before. Value added per worker has increased dramatically, in some cases to levels found in the United States and Japan.

The electronics industry has contributed greatly to Singapore's industrial growth, exports, employment and incomes, and perhaps most importantly, to skills and learning as well. Linkages have been created in many directions, to local supporting industries which themselves may become exporters, and to the services sector and further overseas ventures of multinationals and local firms, revitalizing Singapore's traditional entrepôt and service role in the Southeast Asian region. Despite sharply rising costs and labour scarcity in Singapore itself, multinationals have not left, but rather have diversified and expanded their investments. A pool of experienced indigenous scientific, technical, and managerial personnel has been created, and the multinationals have spawned local entrepreneurs from the ranks of their own employees (some of whom have left to set up independent related businesses) and local suppliers (some of whom have parlayed the connection and experience into broader business ventures).

These developments have favoured Singapore because of its political and financial stability, free trade, and efficient business environment, and excellent social and physical infrastructure and its location in a region where world electronics production and markets are increasingly concentrated. The main attractions today are accessibility to cheap but good-quality material inputs (mostly from the Asian region), and proximity to the world's fastest-growing regional market.

But these industry-derived advantages would not be enough to attract a constant stream of new multinational investments had the Singapore Government not also improved the quality and quantity of domestic resources (including infrastructure and trained manpower), fine-tuned investment incentives, and aggressively promoted the country to the kind of foreign companies it wished to attract

THE EXPERIENCE OF JAPANESE ELECTRONICS FIRMS

Japanese electronics firms have been important to the expansion and transformation of Singapore's electronics industry since the late 1960s. A small survey of nine Japanese electronics firms in late 1993 in Singapore confirms findings of earlier studies (for example, Natarajan and Tan 1992; Lim and Pang 1991) which found a trend among both large and small Japanese (and non-Japanese) firms to "decant" their labour-intensive operations into neighbouring economies while upgrading their operations in Singapore. In many cases, this upgrading was accompanied by the strengthening or diversification of the Singapore operations into service, sales, and support activities.

All the large firms (Aiwa, Hitachi, JVC, Matsushita, Sanyo, and Sony) have upgraded their operations, bringing in higher value-added products and phasing out or relocating labour-intensive assembly operations to sister plants in Southeast Asia. Because of the transfer of new product lines and despite automation, none has seen a reduction in their Singapore work-force, but many have expanded employment and output in their other Southeast Asian plants.

Most of the sample firms have already moved a significant proportion of their production overseas, a competitive move impelled by rising costs in Japan and facilitated by the greater availability and lower costs of inputs and labour in Southeast Asia. Aiwa, for example, produces only 20 per cent of its global output of audio and video products in Japan. The proportion is even lower for Sanyo, which makes only 10 per cent of its products in Japan.

All nine firms report buying an increasingly large proportion of their inputs from sources outside Japan (including Japanese suppliers that have moved to Southeast Asia). Aiwa, for example, purchases 90 per cent of its inputs from the region, including 25 per cent from Japanese suppliers with operations in the region. Only inputs such as integrated circuits and optical laser pick-ups are still sourced from Japan directly.

The backward linkages the nine firms are building extend beyond Singapore to the region. These firms buy inputs from not only suppliers in Singapore but also suppliers located in other countries. The survey reveals no evidence that the nine firms prefer to buy inputs mainly from sister plants or affiliates in the region.

All nine firms indicate an interest or have plans to expand operations in Southeast Asia, China, or Vietnam. Several have opened or will open soon new plants in various parts of China to cater to that country's potentially huge domestic market. Matsushita and Sony, for example, have established manufacturing facilities in Shanghai, while Mitsumi has a plant in Guangdong and will build two more in Qingdao and Tianjin.

CONCLUSIONS

Since the early 1980s, Singapore has continued to attract a disproportionate amount of the FDI flows to developing countries. But Singapore would have failed to attract more than its share of these flows had it not maintained a business-friendly domestic environment that encouraged firms to upgrade and diversity their operations. It has also been fortunate in being located in a region where neighbouring economies have complementary resources of land and labour, and to which Singapore-based firms can "decant" labour-intensive activities.

Since the early 1980s, the regional dimension in Singapore's FDI flows has become increasingly prominent. There have been greater inflows from economies in the region, particularly Japan whose firms, like those from outside the region, are using Singapore more and more as a production base for high value-added activities and as a regional service and support centre. FDI outflows have also expanded rapidly, as Singapore-based firms, both local and foreign, increase their investments in the region, partly to escape rising costs at home, but increasingly to take advantage of growing market opportunities in the region. As with inward FDI flows, outward FDI flows have also been influenced by government policy initiatives. The Growth Triangle provided an impetus for Singapore-based firms to locate more activities in neighbouring Johor and the Riau islands, while the regionalization push begun in 1991 has encouraged firms to invest in new areas, particularly, China, Vietnam, and other reforming socialist economies.

Inward FDI flows, including those from Japan, have created employment, boosted incomes, transferred technology, and strengthened Singapore's global and regional linkages. Outward flows have extended the island's regional and international connections. But there are risks. To begin with, the interests of

Singapore firms with large investments abroad may become less congruent with those of Singapore. They may not necessarily buy Singapore-made products or services, remit incomes to Singapore, or expand their linkages with the home base. Much will depend on how government policy encourages them to be interlocked with Singapore. There is also a risk that outward FDI flows may "hollow out" Singapore's manufacturing base. This phenomenon has yet to develop, but it could if Singapore loses its ability to induce existing firms to upgrade and new firms to invest in higher value-added activities, including manufacturing-related support and service activities because in the long run its labour-short economy cannot sustain a large employment-intensive manufacturing sector. Maintaining this ability—which means ensuring a stable, predictable environment conducive to profit-making by both local and foreign enterprises—is critical to Singapore's further economic progress in the 1990s, as it was in the 1970s and 1980s.

REFERENCES

Business Times. "Indonesia Maintains Momentum with US$3b Foreign Investment in 4 Months", 3 June 1993*a*.

——. "China Becomes Top Asian Investor in the Philippines in First Quarter", 3 June 1993*b*.

——. "Foreigners Invest Record Amount", 3 June 1993*c*.

——. "Malaysian Companies Step Up Investments in China", 3 June 1993*d*.

——. "US Companies to Increase Asian Investment by 20pc This Year", 3 November 1993.

Chen, Edward K. Y. "Foreign Direct Investment in East Asia". *Asian Development Review* 11, no. 1 (1993): 24–59.

Chia Siow Yue. "The Role of Foreign Trade and Investment in the Development of Singapore". In *Foreign Trade and Investment in the Newly-Industrializing Asian Countries*, edited by Walter Galenson, pp.259–97. Madison, Wisconsin: University of Wisconsin Press, 1985.

——. "Foreign Direct Investment in the Singapore Economy". In *Evolution of Asia-Pacific Economies: International Trade and Direct Investment*, edited by Ippei Yamazawa and Fu-Chen Lo, pp. 183–232. Kuala Lumpur: Asian and Pacific Development Centre, 1993*a*.

——. "Foreign Direct Investment in ASEAN Economies". *Asian Development Review* 11, no. 1 (1993*b*): 60–102.

Department of Statistics. *Singapore's Investment Abroad, 1976–1989*. Singapore, October 1991*a*.

——. *Foreign Equity Investment in Singapore, 1980–1989*. Singapore, 1991*b*.

——. *Singapore's Investment Abroad, 1990*. Singapore, February 1993.

——. *Yearbook of Statistics 1992*. Singapore, 1992.

Dobson, Wendy. *Japan in East Asia: Trading and Investment Strategies*. Singapore: Institute of Southeast Asian Studies, 1993.

Economic Development Board. *Yearbook 1991/1992*. Singapore, 1992.

Kay Hian James Capel. "Singapore Inc. Going Global: Brighter Horizons Ahead?", June 1993.

Krause, Lawrence B., Koh Ai Tee, and Lee (Tsao) Yuan. *The Singapore Economy Reconsidered*. Singapore: Institute of Southeast Asian Studies, 1987.

Lee Tsao Yuan, ed. *Growth Triangle: The Johor-Singapore-Riau Experience*. Singapore: Institute of Southeast Asian Studies and Institute of Policy Studies, 1991.

Lim, Linda Y.C. and Pang Eng Fong. *Foreign Direct Investment and Industrialisation in Malaysia, Singapore, Taiwan and Thailand.* Paris: OECD Development Centre, 1991.

—— and N. Siddall. "Foreign Investment, Trade and Technology Linkages in Asian Developing Countries in the 1990s". Paper prepared for United Nations Centre on Transnational Corporations Project on Globalisation and Developing Countries, December 1992.

Low, Linda et al. *Challenge and Response: Thirty Years of the Economic Development Board.* Singapore: Times Academic Press, 1993.

Ministry of Trade and Industry. *Economic Survey of Singapore 1992*. Singapore, February 1993.

Natarajan, S. and Tan Juay Miang. *The Impact of MNC Investments in Malaysia, Singapore and Thailand.* Singapore: Institute of Southeast Asian Studies, 1992.

Pang Eng Fong. "Foreign Investment and the State in Singapore". In *Developing with Foreign Investment*, edited by Vincent Cable and Bishnodat Persaud, pp. 84–100. London: Croom Helm, 1987.

——. *Labour Flows and Regionalisation in Pacific Asia*. Paris: OECD Development Centre, 1993.

—— and Rajah Komaran. "Singapore Multinationals". *Columbia Journal of World Business* xx, no. 2 (Summer 1985): 35–43.

Singapore Investment News. Special Sectoral Supplement, March 1993.

——. Electronics and Design Development Supplement, October 1993.

Straits Times. "Singapore Investments in China Set to Top $1.5b This Year", 30 October 1993.

——. "China Reports Rise in Foreign Investment", 5 November 1993.

United Nations. *World Investment Report 1992: Transnational Corporations as Engines of Growth*, New York, 1992.

United Nations Centre on Transnational Corporations (UNTNC). *World Investment Directory 1992*. New York: United Nations, 1992.

16

CHARTING TAIWAN'S TECHNOLOGICAL FUTURE

The Impact of Globalization and Regionalization

Denis Fred Simon

There is now general agreement among observers of international economic and technology affairs that the world has entered a period characterized by the interplay of two potent and possibly dialectical forces – globalization and regionalization. Globalization, which is clearly manifested in the changing nature of competition in industries ranging from textiles to telecommunications, is being driven by a combination of diverse forces, including the communication and transportation revolutions, the growing trends towards liberalization, privatization and deregulation, and the rapid diffusion of technologies around the world.[1] Multinational companies (MNCs) have become the principal purveyors of globalization as they seek out new markets and search the world for access to critical R&D, production and distribution assets irrespective of where they may be found.[2] Regionalization, on the other hand, has primarily been driven by macro-political forces, with governments as the initiating agents, as in the case of the formation of the European Union and the North American Free Trade Association. Where regionalization is driven by explicit and overt government actions and policies it can more often than not be seen as an anathema to globalization; politically-induced regionalization in these cases is driven, in large part, by concerns about loss of national competitiveness and a decline in economic welfare.[3]

The major exception to this characterization of the nature and thrust of regionalization can be found in the Pacific Rim. From a comparative perspective, regionalization in the Asia-Pacific region has been primarily a market-driven phenomenon with cross-border investment, technology flows and trade being vehicles for expanded regional integration. Intra-regional trade now accounts for over 40 per cent of the total trade of these economies and the largest sources of foreign investment continue to come from within rather than outside the region.[4] While the governments, via such entities as APEC and PECC, are trying to give some degree of formality to efforts at regional

Source: *The China Quarterly*, No. 148 (December 1996), pp. 1196–223.

co-operation, the process of institutionalization has been slow. In a world where the imperatives of global competition have not abated so far as most industries are concerned, most of the economies in the region see little virtue in moving too far too fast for fear of inducing greater fragmentation of global markets and industries. Simply put, Asian economies would be the big losers in a world where regionalization thwarted the forces of market openness and liberalization associated with the increasingly borderless globalizing international economy.[5]

Another reason why greater formalization of this process in the Pacific Rim might not be in the interest of its economies is that the manufacturing and R&D assets of the leading firms in the region have come to assume a steadily more critical role in global competition, especially in industries such as microelectronics, computers, telecommunications and more recently aerospace and software development.[6] This indicates that the technological assets within the region will only become more important in the years ahead as multinational firms from around the globe seek out reliable and capable partners from among companies such as Samsung (Korea) and Acer (Taiwan) as well as Hitachi and Toshiba.[7] In fact, one of the consequences of the steadily improving technological base among the Pacific Rim economies is the growing proliferation of strategic alliances between OECD-member companies and Asian firms. These alliances can be viewed as part of the globalization process as firms from the United States, EC and Japan seek, for example, a hedge against actual and potential competition from domestic as well as foreign competitors.[8]

Collaborative agreements between Taiwan and the world's leading MNCs seem to be growing quite rapidly, raising many questions about the evolving pattern of competition and co-operation in the Asia-Pacific region. Moreover, as the number of these agreements increase, they could reach some critical threshold in terms of Pacific Rim regionalization. Will expanded industrial and technological co-operation between Taiwan and American or EC firms, for example, serve as a bulwark against Japanese companies both inside and outside the region? Are there enough technological assets on Taiwan to add substantial competitive advantage to the capabilities of OECD firms? Even more provocative is the possibility that expanded technological collaboration with Taiwan will serve as an impetus for a fundamental re-thinking by Japanese firms of their technology transfer policies towards the island, especially if Japanese companies view competition for access to Taiwan's manufacturing and R&D assets in a more strategic fashion.[9] This has already occurred to some degree among firms such as Matsushita, Canon, Sony and Fujitsu, all of whom have moved away from their traditionally hierarchical approach to foreign investment and technology transfer in respect of Taiwan. The recent collaborative agreement between Nan Ya Plastics and Oki Electric in the semiconductor field reflects the beginning of a new Japanese perspective.[10]

This article examines the emerging architecture of Taiwan's growing technological prowess, aiming to highlight the implications in terms of globalization and regionalization within the Pacific Rim. The case of Taiwan's microelectronics industry is examined to underscore the growing role of the island's technological assets in international business. The general argument focuses on those emerging economic and technological factors – within the context of global competition – that are driving Taiwan companies to seek more substantial partnerships with foreign firms and vice versa. It is argued that these technological alliances hold much more strategic value in terms of the evolving patterns and thrust of globalization than they do for regional integration. In other words, technological collaboration with Taiwan must first and foremost be viewed as a product of globalization, as both Taiwan and MNCs seek to enhance their respective positions in the larger international division of labour. Taiwan firms remain committed to playing a more central role in global competition, and view co-operation with MNCs primarily as a means to acquire needed technologies – thereby enhancing their own self-reliance – and to offset Japanese technological influence over Taiwan industry.

CHARTING TAIWAN'S EMERGING TECHNOLOGICAL TRAJECTORY

One of the most notable aspects of Taiwan's economic experience over the last four decades has been its ability to re-invent and re-engineer itself to respond to the changing demands of the domestic and international economy.[11] Starting from the ravaged state of the Taiwan economy in the immediate aftermath of the Communist takeover of the Chinese mainland in 1949, the government has been able to orchestrate a number of critical transitions in economic orientation and emphasis. In the 1950s, with the help of the U.S. Agency for International Development, Taiwan officials put in place a successful programme of import substitution.[12] During this period, beginning with the launching of the Ten Major Development Projects in 1973, a new economic infrastructure was constructed, including roads, ports, power plants and communications. In the 1960s and 1970s, the government helped to initiate and implement a programme of export promotion.[13] This provided the backdrop for the upgrading of Taiwan's manufacturing firms and the achievement of quality standards that helped make the export drive a success. It also served to stimulate the initial influx of foreign investment, which has proved to be a critical factor in further areas such as technology transfer and management training.[14]

The 1980s, however, brought a broad array of problems so far as Taiwan's ability to compete in overseas markets was concerned. A principal problem was that the low-cost labour that had at one point been a major source of competitive advantage for the island's numerous manufacturers was no longer available. With improvements in living standards among the island's residents and a continued strengthening of the overall economy, prices and wages both rose, thereby detracting from the attractiveness of Taiwan as a site for foreign investment.[15] In addition, questions arose about the overall business environment, especially with respect to such matters as intellectual property protection, labour turnover and government bureaucracy. Taiwan's private sector also revealed an apparent hesitancy to make new capital investments in the face of an uncertain political future. Lacking the technological wherewithal to compete head-on with the leading firms from the OECD nations and deprived of the cost advantages that in the past had helped drive exports and attract appreciable levels of American and Japanese foreign investment, many questions arose about the ability of the Taiwan economy to sustain any appreciable growth in the future. Add to this economic situation the growing isolation of Taiwan in international affairs engendered, in large part, by the policies of the People's Republic of China (PRC) government, and it becomes clear why a quasi-crisis atmosphere began to emerge in Taiwan at this time.[16]

The beginning of the 1990s brought into sharp relief a set of new economic and technological imperatives that had begun to make their presence felt during the latter part of the previous decade. In particular, as the dynamics of international competition shifted away from a variable-cost to a fixed-cost model – where technology rather than the "variable costs" of production inputs became more critical in determining overall competitiveness – and as the era of the energy-intensive economy began to give way to the era of the information economy, Taiwan officials recognized that another new economic foundation would have to be built.[17] Fortunately, the crisis of Taiwan's faltering sovereignty was abated by the continued, wide-scale participation of MNCs within the island's economy.[18] Although a combination of diplomatic manoeuvring and other factors had seemingly weakened the Taiwan state internationally, the reality in terms of domestic and foreign economic and technology relations seemed just the opposite. The government on Taiwan was able to weather the apparent storm and initiate a shift into new, knowledge-intensive industries as exemplified by the opening and operation of the Hsinchu Science and Industry Park in 1979 and the emergence of Taiwan as a major player in the global computer and microelectronics industry.[19] A key factor in this regard was the ability of the government on Taiwan to continue its quest to attract prominent MNCs to the island to make substantial investments in areas consistent with the shifting needs of the local economy.[20] In particular, the government was adept at facilitating and upgrading the transfer of technology into Taiwan by MNCs. Over time, this has led to a consolidation and further enhancement of Taiwan's place within the evolving international division of labour.

TAIWAN'S EVOLVING TECHNOLOGY STRATEGY

The key technological challenges faced by Taiwan are in two principal domains. First, Taiwan officials must establish a viable industrial structure and set of support mechanisms to move the economy further into the knowledge-intensive age. This requires assisting local firms to shift from dependence on traditional, labour-intensive industries as well as creating a vibrant R&D system capable of meeting the growing technological needs of both large, and small and medium enterprises (SMEs) on the island.[21] The second challenge is the need to devise a strategy for managing external technology relationships, especially with the world's leading corporations (see below). Taiwan officials must establish a pattern of relationships that will allow local firms, both big and small, the maximum room for manoeuvre with respect to the deployment of local R&D and manufacturing resources and capabilities. In other words, the government on Taiwan must strive for higher levels of technological sophistication domestically so that it remains attractive to MNCs as a collaborative partner.[22]

Taiwan's attempt to create a capable and responsive R&D and manufacturing infrastructure reflects the common effort in the Asian newly industrialized economies (NIEs) to strengthen indigenous science and technology resources.[23] Initially, Taiwan officials have adopted a two-pronged strategy for promoting rapid and sustained technological development. One element has been to use the process of technological upgrading as part of a strategy for building what David Teece has called "technological complementarities" with key high technology companies from around the world.[24] In many ways, the essence of this has been to enhance the island's linkages with major MNCs as well as with some critical second-tier firms in a range of priority technology fields. Heretofore, rather than competing head-on with firms from the industrialized world, as has been the case for South Korea, Taiwan adopted a strategy that essentially seeks to build products designed and offered by foreign firms. The strategy has been developed in recognition of the limited willingness of many local firms to invest an appreciable percentage of their revenues in R&D. Ideally, through this variety of linkages with MNCs, Taiwan officials have hoped to stimulate the diffusion of technology that will eventually, albeit gradually, strengthen local capabilities.[25] A recent example of such a relationship involves the decision by Boeing to set up a US$48 million quality assurance laboratory on Taiwan to test aircraft components.

The second prong of Taiwan's technology strategy is to increase the island's self-sufficiency in this area through industrial and technological deepening. To accomplish this goal, the government on Taiwan has offered a large number of financial and tax incentives to local companies to expand their R&D investments. These include accelerated depreciation allowances, investment tax credits, deferral of income tax payments, and duty-free import of selected machinery and equipment. The overall design of the strategy rests in the hands of the Science and Technology Advisory Group (STAG) under the Executive Yuan. The STAG, which was founded in 1979, is responsible for assessing global trends in science and technology and formulating relevant policies in conjunction with the National Science Council, the Council for

Economic Planning and Development, and the Industrial Bureau of the Ministry of Economic Affairs.[26]

While the 1990s have witnessed the coming together of the various strands of a so-called overall technology strategy, the reality is that many of the policies in place today have their roots in the late 1970s when Li Kwo-ting, then a minister without portfolio, assumed responsibility for designing an entirely new industrial architecture for the island.[27] One of the key goals was to enlarge total R&D spending, which in 1978 was about US$111 million, representing only 0.48 per cent of GNP. At the time, the government provided approximately 56 per cent of the total, while the private sector contributed between 30 and 35 per cent. Most important, within the private sector, R&D spending averaged only 0.12 per cent of sales for domestic firms compared with 2–3 per cent in Japan and the United States, reflecting the generally small size of local firms and their tendency to ignore the potential, long-term value of R&D. By 1984, things began to improve when national R&D expenditure apparently reached the 1.0 per cent of GNP mark (US$540 million). By 1990, it represented 1.65 per cent of GNP and has continued to grow, reaching 1.79 per cent of GNP in 1992 and 1.82 per cent in 1994.[28] Starting from 1983, the growth of R&D spending has surpassed 15 per cent per annum on average, slower than South Korea but faster than Japan. The goal stated in the Ten-Year Science and Technology Development Plan (1986–95) was to reach the 2.0 per cent mark by 1995, though this was not attained.[29]

In June 1995, the government released its first White Paper on science and technology affairs. It is focused on matching together world technological trends with Taiwan's S&T policies and programmes, and is conspicuous by the ambitious nature of its R&D spending goals. According to the 12-year national S&T development plan now in effect, R&D spending will reach 2.8 per cent of GNP in 2002, reflecting a 14.2 per cent growth over the ten-year period starting in 1992. The release of the plan coincided with a new initiative designed to attract more young engineers into careers in the government. Young engineers may skip their compulsory military service if they make a six-year commitment to work within government-sponsored research institutes and think-tanks.

While increasing the overall level of expenditure allocated for R&D has been an important goal, to make an appreciable difference in the orientation of the economy there must also be a concomitant shift in the role of the private sector. Based on data from the National Science Council, the government provided 61.2 per cent of R&D funds in 1983. That amount declined to 45.8 per cent in 1990, but has grown to 52.2 per cent in 1992. Unlike South Korea, where the private sector has assumed almost 80 per cent of the expenditure for R&D, Taiwan still suffers somewhat from an industrial structure dominated by small and medium-sized firms. In 1982, Taiwan's SMEs accounted for 69.7 per cent of the island's exports, but by 1994 that percentage had decreased to 52.6; at the same time, SMEs have accounted for over 96 per cent of all the firms on Taiwan. The shift in the role of SMEs in exports reflects their inability to compete technologically from their present situation and the decision among a growing number to move their operations to places such as the PRC, Vietnam and Malaysia rather than invest in technological upgrading.[30]

Nevertheless, this acknowledged, the impact of the industrial structure has helped to create a unique R&D system on the island, but one that should not necessarily be thought of despairingly because it departs from the private sector model present in most industrialized nations. The government on Taiwan has had to adopt a more activist role to overcome the specific inadequacies that continued to affect the potential for innovation on the island. At the core of government efforts to promote innovation is the Industrial Technology Research Institute (ITRI) located in Hsinchu, the site of the Hsinchu Science and Industry Park.[31]

The role of ITRI, which was founded in 1973, resembles that of the Korean Advanced Institute for Science and Technology (KAIST) insofar as its main purpose is industrially oriented research and development. It has a budget of about US$500 million and a staff of 6,000. Even though ITRI is not considered to be a government organization, it receives government assistance to a far greater extent than KAIST. Additionally, it is less independent than KAIST in the sense that contract research and revenues from royalties form a much smaller percentage of overall revenue.[32] ITRI's most important role is as a partner in high priority government-inspired projects.[33] For example, in the late 1970s, the Electronics Research Service Organization (ERSO), which is one of the ITRI laboratories, was the local recipient in a major microelectronics technology transfer project with RCA of the United States. Once ERSO had received and absorbed the technology from RCA, it worked with a local firm to diffuse that technology into the local market. United Microelectronics Corporation was the prime beneficiary. It was formed as a local joint venture involving ERSO's technology and a 25 per cent equity position from the government's Bank of Communications, in keeping with the government's role of sometime facilitator and sometime initiator.[34]

While ITRI is composed of several functionally distinct institutes, the most important is ERSO. ERSO has become the premier research institute on the island in terms of Taiwan's current and future advances in integrated circuits and other complex microelectronics components. It provides technical support to over 40 local integrated circuit manufacturers and wafer makers on Taiwan. Even more critical, ERSO serves as the training ground for young engineers, some of whom eventually leave the organization to start up their own firms. In many ways, this informal training and technology transfer function may have a more profound effect on the development of the integrated circuit industry in Taiwan than one of the more explicit programmes of activity occurring within the ERSO laboratories.

The role of ERSO also can be appreciated by examining its involvement in the island's ongoing ultra-large scale integrated circuit development programme. The project also exemplifies the government's efforts simply to provide the spark for a range of activities with the expectation that the private sector will assume the larger responsibility once the viability of the endeavour is assured. In co-operation with the Ministry of Education, the National Science Council and several private companies, ERSO has set up a joint design centre in Hsinchu to help accelerate the development of Taiwan's semiconductor industry. More recently, it was the force behind the creation in 1987 of the Taiwan Semiconductor Manufacturing Corporation, which serves as a foundry for the manufacture of foreign and domestic designed application specific integrated circuits. The project involved an initial investment of US$206 million, the largest ever made in the domestic electronics industry. This corporation has become one of the largest and most profitable foundries in the world and is currently considering establishing its fourth fabrication facility to meet growing demand from both inside and outside Taiwan. The major foreign partner in the project is Philips of Holland (which owns 27.5 per cent of the equity in the project).

As mentioned, the centre for the high-technology push on Taiwan has been the Hsinchu Science and Industry Park.[35] Its development was led by Li Kwo-ting, the man who is most frequently cited as the principal architect behind Taiwan's economic growth in the 1960s and 1970s. Li's most important legacy, however, may be in the foundation that he created at Hsinchu for the re-structuring of the Taiwan economy. In its broadest sense, the park represents Taiwan's move into the next stage of economic development, where industries are characterized by their skill and knowledge intensity rather than their labour intensity. Just as the three export processing zones in Kaohsiung and Tainan served as the engines of Taiwan's export drive 20 years ago, the Hsinchu Park is now the new engine of growth.[36]

In its initial phase in the early 1980s, the idea of the park was primarily to attract high technology companies from abroad. As at December 1993, it was home to 165 companies which had been approved and were already in operation, with total revenues of US$6.7 billion (see Table 16.1). Some

Table 16.1 High technology industries in Hsinchu Park, 1994

Industry	*No. of plants*	*Sales (US$ million)*
Computers and peripherals	39	2,712
Integrated circuits	51	3,171
Telecommunications	28	555
Opto-electronics	23	178
Precision machinery	15	73
Biotechnology	9	14
Total	165	6,705

40,600 people were employed, over 50 per cent of whom had college degrees with 12 per cent holding advanced degrees. At the beginning most of the firms entering the park were small in size, but more recently there has been a significant increase. Selection is based on a company's design, development and manufacturing capabilities. In the past, the goal was to attract firms with the plans and skills to improve products already developed in the industrialized nations rather than those planning to develop new technologies. Today, there is a greater concern with attracting the potential for innovation and new products. This is entirely in keeping with the philosophy in place when the park was established, namely to adjust and elevate the criteria for admission each year so that the park remains at the forefront of technological innovation and development. In this regard, it is interesting to note that as of later 1993, the average ratio between R&D spending and production value among the firms inside the park was 5.4 per cent compared with around 1.0 per cent for firms outside the park (see Table 16.2).[37]

Another fundamental purpose of Hsinchu Park is to capture the spillover from the presence of high-tech firms in terms of training, technology transfer and direct co-operation with local firms. Taiwan officials hope that the private sector will view the presence of high technology firms in the Hsinchu Park as "opportunity creating," thus inspiring some of them to move into those industries that the government hopes will become Taiwan's future source of competitive advantage. The geographic setting of the park is important because of the agglomeration dynamics that are present; it is situated near three major universities and ITRI as well as the Chiang Kai-shek International Airport. Many of the high-technology entrepreneurs in Hsinchu Park were formerly employees at ITRI institutes.

The location of Hsinchu Park and its steadily improving infrastructure are some of the reasons it has become a catalyst in facilitating the return of over 1,000 engineers and technicians who now work there. (Government officials estimate that in 1993 over 6,000 overseas Chinese returned to Taiwan to work in government and private companies; the National Science Council statistics indicate that between 1990 and 1994 some 23,000 Chinese

Table 16.2 R&D spending ratios in Hsinchu Park, 1993

Industry	*R&D spending*	*Production value*	*Ratio (%)*
Computers/peripherals	1,580	38,638	4.1
Integrated circuits	1,950	30,310	6.4
Telecommunications	578	10,135	5.7
Opto-electronics	178	1,344	13.3
Precision machinery	133	1,270	10.5
Biotechnology	39	463	8.4
Total	4,458	82,160	5.4

Source: National Science Council, Luper, 1994.

returned with a Ph.D. or Masters degree.) According to Hsinchu Park officials, 73 of the enterprises in the park have been set up by returning overseas Chinese.[38] The reverse of the brain drain, while clearly not complete, has helped to facilitate the overall development of high technology industry on the island. It is estimated that there are over 200 ex-AT&T Bell Labs and over 150 ex-IBM former employees working at the Science and Industry Park.

There is now no more space available within the Hsinchu Park boundaries, but its success has led to the decision to establish a new US$600-million science and industry park near Tainan county.[39] The Tainan site was selected because the local farmers in the Hsinchu area were not willing to accept the level of compensation offered by the government to buy their land. In addition, Hsinchu Park has recently experienced shortages of electricity, water and land. The new park will have three special industry zones: biotechnology, semiconductors and precision machinery. The decision to move in this direction reflects the fact that Taiwan's microelectronics industry is poised to expand, with current investment plans calling for the establishment of 10–12 major new production facilities over the next three to five years.

The formation of these new parks is just one piece of a new concerted effort by Taiwan to bring the island into the 21st century with a bang rather than a whimper.[40] Numerous concerns have developed regarding the possible "hollowing out" of the economy. Things, however, seem to be improving. According to a survey of 5,975 local firms conducted by the Ministry of Economic Affairs in mid-1995, 54 per cent indicated that they had maintained their original level of operations even after they made an overseas investment, 22 per cent said they even expanded their domestic operations, while only 22 per cent said they scaled down their operations and 2 per cent indicated that they would close their local operations. Moreover, in 1995, capital-intensive and technology-intensive industries will account for 65.7 per cent of overall manufacturing, an increase from 59.3 per cent in 1991. For the first time in seven years, in 1995 Taiwan's industrial production growth is expected to exceed that of the service sector. To keep the economy moving in this direction, the Ministry of Economic Affairs, in conjunction with both the Executive Yuan and the National Science Council, has announced a number of new measures to strengthen manufacturing and upgrade the industrial technology base. These include adopting the so-called "Singapore model" of training technology professionals, whereby the government will assist financially the training of scientists, engineers and technicians by research institutes; increasing R&D investments in government-run businesses such as Taiwan Power and China Steel; opening access to the defence-oriented Chung Shan Institute of Science and Technology so that local industry can take advantage of existing equipment and expertise; and expanding the overall scale and operation of technology development projects.[41]

TAIWAN'S EMERGING INFORMATICS AND MICROELECTRONICS INDUSTRIES

> The key to the new business environment is disintegration. After WWII, economists promoted the theory of vertical integration in which manufacturers would take all the stages of production, from processing the raw material to distributing the finished item. This approach was popular with the corporations for forty years. However, the current direction has turned, esp. for the IT industry. Now the emphasis is now on continuous technological enhancement to make products that appeal to better educated customers who have an awakened sense of product quality.[42]

Today, Taiwan continues to exhibit ambitions to play a major role in the global informatics and microelectronics industries. This is one of the main reasons why the government and local industry have decided to enter the semiconductor race, to ensure an even supply of microchips, especially DRAMs, to the growing computer industry. In 1991, semiconductors surpassed crude oil to become Taiwan's largest import item with a value of US$2.53 billion. By 1994, while oil imports reached US$2.7 billion, microchip imports shot up to US$7.2 billion. Estimates are that chip demand in Taiwan totalled 6 per cent of the world market; domestic producers turned out only US$3.1 billion and only supplied US$900 million to local end-users. Some suggest that the island's self-sufficiency rate for semiconductors may be as low as 16 per cent.

This helps to explain why there are plans to build as many as 18 new semiconductor facilities over the next few years, with a value of US$13 billion.[43] At present, while Taiwan is the fourth largest producer of integrated circuits in the world, it holds only 2.3 per cent of the global chip market. Even with its ambitious plans for chip production, *The Financial Times* (London) suggests that the self-sufficiency level will only reach 37 per cent by the year 2000. At that time, total semiconductor production on Taiwan will top US$19 billion. Nevertheless, the momentum is building and numerous projects are under way (see Table 16.3). One of the most important is the joint venture initiated in 1989 between Acer and Texas Instruments, in which 56 per cent is owned by the Taiwan firm, 26 per cent by the American firm and 16 per cent by the China Development Corporation. The two companies recently launched a second major facility on Taiwan to product 16MB and 64MB DRAM chips based on 8″ wafers, the prevailing state-of-the-art. Another important project involves the start-up of a second major integrated circuit subcontractor that will compete with the Taiwan Semiconductor Manufacturing Corporation. In May 1995, the government approved the application of the Asia-Pacific Semiconductor Manufacturing Corporation to set up a facility in Hsinchu Park. The key local firm in the project is Syntek, a local integrated circuit design company.

Table 16.3 Major semiconductor projects planned for Taiwan

Companies	*Country*	*Project*
Texas Instruments–Acer	United States	DRAM
Taiwan Semiconductor	Local expansion	Integrated circuit foundry
United Microelecronics–ATI	United States	Memory chips
Umax (Powerchip)–Mitsubishi	Japan	DRAM
Mosel–Vitelic–Mitsubishi	Japan	DRAM
Vanguard	Local	DRAM (sum-micron)
Nan Ya Plastics–Oki	Japan	DRAM
Macronix–Oki	Japan	Memory chips
Winbond	Local	SRAM, logic
Holtek	Local	Micro components
Hualon	Local	Micro components
Tatung	Local	Foundry??
Syntek	Local	Foundry

Source: *The Financial Times*, 15 May 1995.

As a recent *Business Week* article suggested, "Taiwan isn't just for cloning anymore."[44] By early 1994, it ranked fifth in the world in terms of computer hardware product value, accounting for approximately 4 per cent of total world production, behind the United States and Japan. Total output value was about US$15 billion. Production of microcomputer systems climbed from about 1,440 in 1981 to 2.4 million in 1991. Taiwan is the largest supplier of computer monitors in the world with a 56 per cent share of the market. Manufacture of monitors for computers grew from 39,000 in 1980 to 8.4 million in 1991 and 24 million in 1994. It was expected to reach 30 million by the end of 1995. Two years ago, with the help of ITRI, eight of Taiwan's leading computer firms invested close to US$200 million to establish a CRT plant to develop a new generation of computer monitors that will diminish the dependence of the island's firms on Japanese technology. (The plant will also serve as a first step in the effort to get into the high definition television race.)[45] Low end manufacturing for monitors has already begun to move offshore; in 1994, offshore production of monitors grew 130 per cent, about 1.67 times the growth of domestic output.[46]

The most interesting feature of the industry, however, is its rapid growth over the last decade. Informatics exports have grown from less than 10 per cent of electronics exports in the early 1980s to over one-third in 1988. Moreover, over 96 per cent of the production value of informatics products is exported into the world market. Today, in addition to being the world's biggest exporter of colour monitors, Taiwan also leads in exports of keyboards, mouses and image scanners.

As suggested, in the electronics industry Taiwan has moved from being a technological imitator to an innovator. Total electronics production in 1994 was US$14.7 billion.[47] According to data supplied by the Institute for

Information Industry in Taipei, for example, foreign invested firms account for less than 40 per cent of total exports. In addition, while many Taiwan firms got their primary start as OEM producers, more and more firms are manufacturing and marketing products under their own brand names, such as MITAC and Acer.[48] In 1992, for example, information products exported under local brand names grew to over 35 per cent of total exports, up from just 23 per cent two years earlier. A sort of division of labour seemed to be emerging between South Korea and Taiwan in the mid-1980s in this regard, with the latter seemingly focusing more on computer products and the former more on semiconductors. For example, in 1986 South Korea's exports of computers totalled US$707 million while Taiwan's exports exceeded US$2.1 billion. Yet in semiconductors, Korea's performance (US$1.3 billion) greatly surpassed that of Taiwan (US$707 million). More recently this seems to have faded with both economies vying for an increasing share of the highly competitive informatics market.[49] One major problem for Taiwan, however, is that it still imports almost 50 per cent of its personal computer components. In addition, markets are changing so fast that Taiwan is losing its job as a final assembler, especially as a result of the new manufacturing models adopted by American computer companies such as Compaq, Gateway and Dell.

The rapid changes in technology and markets have provided the main impetus for the decision by the Taiwan government to organize a consortium of semiconductor producers to advance the level of process technology on the island. ITRI will work with a range of local companies and universities in a research effort similar to the Sematech project in the United States several years ago. The goal of the effort will be to develop key technologies and quickly diffuse them to local industry, so firms such as Acer-TI and United Microelectronics can develop the commercial processes. Towards the same end, the Taiwan government also announced in mid-1995 a programme to develop a "domestic" computer processing unit that will compete with Intel's pentium chips. Taiwan hopes to overcome Intel's dominance over microprocessors and diminish its growing influence in the areas of motherboard and chip set production. Taiwan officials hope to follow the United Microelectronics model for CMOS; utilizing project teams within ITRI and National Chiaotong University, they hope to transfer the "know-how" to local producers for domestic manufacture. This will help Taiwan overcome its present deficiency which means it has to ship over half its motherboards without processors.

TAIWAN'S RESPONSE TO GLOBAL COMPETITION: THE PROLIFERATION OF STRATEGIC ALLIANCES

One of the notable responses of firms in the globalizing industries has been the formation of strategic alliances with other firms – domestic and/or foreign – to share costs, minimize risks and combine complementary assets among themselves.[50] This new pattern of business strategy is most prevalent in industries with large economies of scale, shortened technology cycles and heavy R&D intensity. The semiconductor and aircraft industries are good examples.[51] According to Ohmae and others, the keys to success in such alliances seem to lie in four main areas: skill complementarities among the partners, co-operative corporate cultures, high compatibility of goals, and sharing commensurate levels of risk and return.[52]

Traditionally, the motives for international collaboration in most industries are threefold: access to markets, access to technology, access to capital. Standard forms of foreign direct investment and licensing are becoming less critical, especially in high-technology sectors. The growth in strategic alliances reflects the fact that companies are looking for new ways to compete in the current international business environment: share risks, reduce costs, exchange knowledge. They appear willing to accept a whole series of possible new business risks and managerial challenges to obtain the alleged benefits of these alliances, only to find out, in many cases, that they have selected the wrong partner or that their partner is not capable of performing its assigned tasks. Recent studies have suggested that less than 50 per cent of these alliances ever succeed from the perspective of both partners.[53] Still, firms seem willing to venture into these collaborative arrangements in increasing numbers as a way to help their organizations overcome inhibitions about risk-taking and resource sharing. While alliances cannot solve the problems of weak management or lack of strategic focus, they can provide a critical mechanism for companies to enhance their competitive position and acquire new knowledge.[54]

International aeronautics is an excellent example of an industry that has been shaped significantly by the forces of globalization.[55] Accordingly, it is no surprise to find a proliferation of strategic alliances among the major aeronautics firms from the United States, Japan and Europe in both the airframe and aeroengine segments. In fact, it would not be an exaggeration to suggest that the rules of the game have shifted from a pure "lone-ranger type" of competition to a new form characterized by higher and higher levels of inter-firm collaboration and co-operation.[56] The future survival of each of the key firms in the industry seems increasingly dependent on the nature and quality of the alliances it has or will form with other firms. Partnering – being able to identify, develop and sustain working partnerships with "quality" partners – has already become one of the critical success factors in this industry.[57]

In the case of industrial and technological collaboration involving Taiwan, similar forces have been important. For the MNCs, access to production assets and capital has been central to their thinking; for Taiwan firms, access to technology has been most important.[58] In response to what they see as increasing techno-nationalism in the world, Taiwan firms, like their counterparts in Korea, feel that licensing and other forms of arm's-length transactions in the international technology marketplace are becoming more limited.[59]

They point to the fact that despite the claims about globalization of technology, in the early 1990s American based MNCs conducted only 12.7 per cent of their R&D abroad (up from 8.7 per cent in 1982). Companies such as Texas Instruments now generate sizeable revenues simply from enforcement of their patents rather than from actually creating the next generation technology.[60] The main problem for Taiwan, however, has not been the United States or EC; in fact, American and European firms had apparently become the main Taiwan hope. The real culprit is Japan. Heretofore, strategic alliances with firms from the United States or Europe have represented a means to reduce Taiwan's significant technological dependence on the Japanese.[61] Since the early 1980s, it has been the stated policy of the Taiwan government to engage the United States and Europe in a broad-based programme of technological co-operation with Taiwan firms.

Recently, however, the situation concerning Japan has begun to change. Faced with the appreciation of the yen and the need for fundamental restructuring inside Japan, Japanese companies have re-focused their attention on economies such as Taiwan with respect to their higher valued-added manufacturing operations.[62] During the first period of the endaka in the late 1980s, Japanese firms responded to their rising costs at home by re-locating much of their lower-end manufacturing to South-East Asia; a great deal of Japanese consumer electronics industry found a new home in the ASEAN economies. At present, however, Japanese firms have taken a dramatically different approach, perhaps in recognition of the achievements Taiwan has made in such industries as computers and peripherals.[63] The need to be near those firms that are actually designing and producing the components and final products in the information industry has stimulated a new Japanese strategy towards Taiwan.

Taiwan's technology linkages with the U.S.

These are significant for Taiwan's pattern of technological development because American firms have been and will continue to be a primary source of advanced technology to local firms. In terms of overall dollar value, the United States also has been the principal source of foreign investment into Taiwan. And, from a technology transfer perspective, just as Taiwan has changed the central focus of its economic activity away from simple, low-cost labour assembly type operations and begun to concentrate on high-technology sectors such as informatics and microelectronics, the technological nature of American investments have shifted in the same direction. Many Taiwan firms have become enmeshed in the global sourcing and subcontracting of American multinational firms, serving as critical suppliers of key components and final products – often on an OEM basis.[64]World-class companies such as Hewlett-Packard, NCR, Motorola and Texas Instruments have placed a great deal of emphasis on their Taiwan-based facilities and activities, seeing them as a central part of their overall global strategic operations.[65] In this context, the recent decision by AT&T/Lucent to set up two joint ventures on Taiwan is significant, as part of AT&T's strategic goal of generating 50 per cent of its revenues from overseas markets by the year 2000. One venture will utilize Taiwan's strong industrial design and manufacturing capabilities to develop new products and technology. The other will provide financial support to telecommunications firms in the Asia-Pacific region.

The American link is also significant because its market has been the traditional target for a large percentage of Taiwan exports. Even though local companies are diversifying away from dependence on the United States – approximately 50 per cent of Taiwan's exports in 1992 went to countries in the Asia-Pacific region – the fact remains that many of Taiwan's key exports are designed for use in the American market. The United States also receives a significant portion of overseas investment by Taiwan companies such as Formosa Plastics, which has invested in the American chemicals processing industry. Perhaps even more important, however, is the fact that within California's "Silicon Valley," many Taiwan entrepreneurs have either set up their own companies or made investments in existing companies. In some cases, the U.S.-based operations of these small, Taiwan-invested firms constitute high-technology listening posts for local firms on the island. Important technical and commercial information about new product developments and so on are frequently transmitted – legally and illegally – from California to Taiwan via these companies and their employees. In this context, it should also be remembered that the United States provides the main training ground for Taiwan's future engineers and scientists, a larger and larger percentage of whom now return home after receiving their education at the graduate level in America.

Taiwan's technology linkages with Japan

The impact of Taiwan's links with Japan on the island's technology orientation has been significant. Although 50 years have passed since the island was returned to China by Japan in the aftermath of the Second World War, the reality is that the Japanese continue to have a major influence on the Taiwan economy. If one looks simply at the total number of cases of foreign investment and formal technical co-operation agreements since the 1960s, Japanese firms have been predominant. As of 1994, even though the value of approved American investment on Taiwan has been approximately equal to that of Japan, Japanese companies have had more than twice as many cases of foreign investment. Statistics regarding technical co-operation agreements as of the end of 1993 reveal a similar pattern, with the number of Japanese cases exceeding American cases by almost a factor of three.

In almost all areas of the economy, the participation of companies from

Japan has been critical to the growth of Taiwan exports, many of which entered world markets through the distribution channels of Japanese trading companies. Taiwan government officials and companies have often been critical of Japanese firms for their almost explicit efforts to forestall technology transfer. Since the 1960s, Japan has been said to transfer "show-how" but not "know-how," often refusing to provide or sell certain critical information or components to Taiwan companies that are seeking to minimize dependence on their Japanese counterparts. This is not to suggest that the contribution of Japanese industry has been negligible; in fact, Taiwan officials probably excessively play down its level, both formal and informal. Nevertheless, the fact remains that many opportunities for fruitful collaboration have been bypassed because potential Japanese partners were hesitant to transfer the desired levels of technology.

In this context, it is perhaps no accident that, until recently (apart from a few isolated examples), Japanese firms were conspicuous by their absence from important government initiatives such as the Hsinchu Science and Industry Park. While there is no evidence that this was the result of intentional discrimination, the reality is that given Japan's past track-record, the principal targets were the United States, Europe and overseas Chinese investors. The fact that Japan continues to run a tremendous trade deficit with Taiwan has not helped the situation; it reached almost US$15 billion in 1994. Taiwan firms have disproportionately relied on Japanese companies as the source for the equipment and components that are needed to upgrade the technological base of the economy. As one scholar remarked, "Taiwan's exports are mostly built on imports from Japan!" Japanese firms have not been in the forefront of purchasing Taiwan exports, except in such areas as processed foods and clothing. Manufactured goods exported to the United States in 1994, for example, constituted over 90 per cent of total Taiwan exports to that country, but for Japan, manufactured products accounted for less than 60 per cent of total exports. Even with the expansion of imports from the Asian NIEs in the aftermath of the Plaza Accords in 1985 and the tremendous growth of Japanese investment in East and South-East Asia, this situation did not change in any fundamental way.[66]

More recently, due to a combination of competitive considerations and political pressures, some Japanese companies are changing their attitudes about engaging in higher value-added operations on Taiwan (see Table 16.4.)[67] Sharp, for example, has now set up an integrated circuit design centre for consumer appliances; a similar type of facility has also been set up by NEC. Matsushita is steadily expanding its R&D activities on the island, moving into computer software as well as engaging in design activities linked to its large joint venture in consumer electronics. Sony has established an international procurement centre on Taiwan. Other Japanese firms such as Mitsubishi are making major investments in Taiwan's semiconductor industry. In the Mitsubishi case, it appears the company wants to use the foundry

Table 16.4 Recent Japanese high-tech initiatives on Taiwan

Japanese firm	*Taiwan partner(s)*	*Focus*
Oki Electric	Nan Ya Plastics and Mosel-Vitelic	DRAM production
Mitsubishi	Umax-Elite Group/Powerchip	DRAM production
NEC	Taiwan Semiconductor Manufacturing Company	Chip subcontracting
Komatsu and Shin Etsu	NA	Silicon water materials
NKK	Macronix	Utilize production capacity in Japan

at the Taiwan Semiconductor Manufacturing Company to provide capacity for memory production; Mitsubishi will serve as an intermediary between this company and Japanese chip producers. In February 1993, a high-level group of Taiwan and Japanese executives met to promote technology transfer from Japan to Taiwan's component industries. This followed an earlier visit in May 1991 by a 156-member delegation from the Keidanren to Taiwan to discuss trade and technology transfer issues. These activities suggest some change in the approach of Japanese companies to the island.

Taiwan's technology linkages with the PRC

The opening up of trade and commerce with the PRC has clearly helped to contribute to continued growth of the local Taiwan economy, though some important questions remain in terms of the impact on overall technological development. Because of rapidly rising labour costs and a shortage of workers for low-skilled jobs, many small and medium-sized Taiwan companies have transplanted their operations to Fujian and southern China, where labour is in ample supply and wages are considerably lower than Taiwan. China has also become an attractive market for Taiwan-made products, including consumer electronics, textiles, chemicals and computers. In addition, companies such as Formosa Plastics, faced with an increasingly hostile domestic situation in terms of activist environmental groups, have sought investment projects on the China mainland to bypass newly installed pollution laws.

The economic pulls from the Chinese mainland on the Taiwan economy are indeed very strong and ever present. They are part of the emergence of what some call "Greater China," a manifestation of the coming together of the economies of Hong Kong, the mainland and Taiwan. Government officials on Taiwan have made repeated efforts on several occasions to control, manage and even halt the expansion of investment and trade, but these have not succeeded as local companies have found numerous ways to sidestep official pronouncements and regulations. The reality is that the emergence of the mainland market for Taiwan has been a blessing in many ways, helping to offset the actual and potential loss of markets overseas and rising costs at home. Nevertheless, a number of critical issues have emerged. One problem is that while the opportunity to trade with and invest in the PRC has had some immediate positive effects, there is a danger that excessive focus on the Chinese mainland will pre-empt government efforts to upgrade the industrial technology base on the island. Over 10 per cent of Taiwan's total trade is with the PRC; as much as 15 per cent of its total exports may go to the Chinese mainland, primarily through Hong Kong. And while the mainland does provide some short-term relief for local firms, it could produce a degree of technological complacency that reduces rather than enhances these companies' interest in making new technological investments at home. This is especially true given the industrial structure on Taiwan, where small and medium-sized firms with limited capital availability continue to be predominant.

Another problem is related to larger firms, many of which see very lucrative opportunities opening up on the Chinese mainland – and only more and more bureaucratic entanglements at home. Of course, this does not only apply to the PRC but also to other parts of South-East Asia, Eastern Europe and so on. Nevertheless, because of the historical and cultural links between Taiwan and the mainland, doing business in the PRC seems remarkably less complex – an irony in comparison with the experiences of many Western firms doing business in China. Thus these two problems – forestalling new investment in technological upgrading and siphoning off existing investment – could serve to damage government attempts to attract larger private sector involvement in Taiwan's high technology development programmes. Moreover, given the apparent technological gap that exists between the PRC and the United States, it remains to be seen whether the former can provide the same type of technological stimulation that the latter has and will continue to provide in the future.

This is not to deny that the potential for technological synergies does exist between the scientific and technical communities on Taiwan and the Chinese mainland. The decision in 1992–93 by the authorities on Taiwan to permit acquisition of technology from the PRC does open up some very interesting possibilities.[68] This is especially true when one considers the idea of "Greater China." Within areas such as biotechnology, computer software and materials, some collaborative activities have already begun on an informal basis. In August 1992, "the 1992 Workshop on Scientific and Technical Co-operation and Exchange Between Industries on Both Sides of the Strait" was held for two days in Beijing. Agreement was reached on five areas of co-operation, with special emphasis on computer science and information technology: protection of intellectual property rights; establishment of common information technology standards; joint technical development with regard to products distinctively related to Chinese fields of application; co-operative development of a large, possibly integrated, national information system; and establishment of a research and development centre and exchanges of skilled personnel. As a follow-up, the first science and technology delegation from the mainland since 1949 visited Taiwan in early 1993 to discuss possible areas of co-operation. And in October 1995, some 70 metrology experts from both sides met in Beijing to begin work on harmonization of standards.[69] In this regard, Taiwan would seem to hold the upper hand and greatest leverage since its interconnections with the West in high technology go far beyond those of the PRC. Recognition of this fact has prompted Taiwan authorities to caution local firms about providing technologies that could have military applications. Similarly, in fields such as information technology and consumer electronics, consideration must also be given to possible completion from PRC enterprises, many of which are anxious to enter an export market which is currently occupied, in part, by Taiwan companies.

Taiwan's technology linkages with the Asian NIEs

Although frequently grouped together for purposes of analysis, the four NIEs are highly competitive with one another over attracting foreign investment and technology and gaining an expanded market share in overseas markets. Unlike Taiwan's relationships with the United States, Japan and Europe, where there is a great deal of complementarity in terms of markets, technology capabilities, human resources and so on, the Asian NIEs are embarked on very similar paths of technological development. This requires careful understanding and constant monitoring of each of the economies. For example, just as Singapore and Hong Kong pushed ahead with their plans to serve as operational centres for the Asia-Pacific operations of many MNCs, Taiwan embarked on a similar course, having recently recruited Imperial Chemical Industries, AT&T and Microsoft to set up significant production and/or R&D facilities on the island. Philips, one of the world's leading electronics companies, has made plans to use Taiwan as its base for production of tubes for high definition televisions. While some might suggest that each of the Asian NIEs has developed its own particular areas of specialization in industries such as computers – with Taiwan focusing on monitors, Korea on semiconductors, Singapore on hard disk drives and Hong Kong on peripherals – there is little doubt that each hopes to move into higher value-added products even if it is at the expense of its neighbours. Competition from the other Asian NIEs provides a healthy stimulus to Taiwan firms in terms of investing in R&D and new equipment, but it also adds an element of fragility to the situation, thus preventing even key players such as Acer and UMC from feeling secure for too long.

Taiwan's technology linkages with ASEAN

In many respects, the ASEAN represents an important outlet for the export of intermediate technologies and related equipment from Taiwan. With operating costs spiralling on the island, many Taiwan firms even in so-called high technology sectors have sought competitive refuge by investing in one or several of the ASEAN economies. This includes Acer, Taiwan's leading producer of personal computers, which has set up a factory in Malaysia to cut costs and provide needed capacity so that the Taiwan-based operations of the company can focus on higher value-added products. Acer's Malaysia operations now account for two-thirds of that company's total monitor output. Taiwan's investments in the ASEAN countries have proved to be of great significance in terms of building economic bridges, with Taiwan serving as a supplier of technology rather than as a recipient. Of course, Taiwan firms are well aware of the potential "boomerang effect" that could come from being too forthcoming in terms of technology transfer. Nevertheless, these relationships continue to expand, thus further integrating Taiwan into the regional division of labour in the Pacific Rim (see Table 16.5).

Taiwan's other technology linkages

Technology ties between Taiwan and the EU, Eastern Europe and the former Soviet Union have been growing as well. Taiwan officials have expressed a willingness to hire scientists and engineers from the former Soviet Union. Efforts are also under way to expand ties with Australia and New Zealand. Yet, in spite of these efforts, the fact remains that the shape of the Taiwan economy continues to be defined principally by the pushes and pulls associated with the five sets of linkages above. The benefits and dangers of becoming too involved in any one relationship have been identified, with the most significant danger coming from the growing pulls of the Chinese mainland. In some respects, therefore, an interesting four-sided dynamic is emerging: one set of forces that has the United States pulling at Taiwan – with a concerted push from several elements in the Taiwan government – to be a player in its global R&D and manufacturing networks; a second set that has the Japanese pulling to ensure that the Taiwan economy continues to articulate and move in tandem with the economic and technological

Table 16.5 Taiwan's Activities in South-East Asia

Country	*Amount invested*	*Major targets*	*Outcome*
Vietnam	US$2.5 billion	Infrastructure	Low-cost labour but must face 'red tape'
Indonesia	US$7.7 billion	Labour-intensive industry	Abundant cheap labour
Philippines	US$740 million	Labour-intensive industry	Poor infrastructure
Malaysia	US$7.3 billion	Computer/peripherals	Close to many MNCs
Thailand	US$5.1 billion	Electronics manufacture	Highly skilled labour but rising labour costs

Source: *Business Week*, 6 November 1995.

re-structuring occurring in Japan; a third set, largely politically induced, that has the Chinese mainland pulling for closer economic and technological integration with Taiwan, perhaps even at the expense of short-circuiting expanded new local investment on the island; and a fourth set that involves competition with the other Asian NIEs as well as the pull of the ASEAN, with their attractive investment incentives and lower-cost labour. This situation could either contribute to the possible "hollowing out" of the Taiwan economy or accelerate the development of possible future competitors to Taiwan companies.

CHALLENGES AHEAD FOR TAIWAN

Some scholars have suggested that one of the most significant phenomena affecting existing patterns of trade and technology intercourse in the international economy has been the "globalization of technology." As a result of the expanded and extended diffusion of technology throughout the world, new, alternative centres of technological capability are springing up outside the traditional areas in the United States, Western Europe and Japan. The emergence of increasingly strong, indigenous manufacturing systems in places such as Taiwan has prompted greater interest in new types of collaboration with these economies. The global integration of capital markets together with the spread of information technologies and the development of global transportation links have further facilitated this collaboration. Within the realm of international business, there is some evidence to suggest that the traditional joint venture with its generally hierarchical character may have become a thing of the past, as it is replaced by new forms of network-oriented co-operation, such as those associated with strategic alliances.

If this is indeed what is happening in the world economy today, then there are important implications for the Taiwan economy. Simply put, Taiwan's technological assets are going to assume an increased importance in the playing out of global competition in the years ahead. This has already occurred to some extent in the new agreement between Acer and Texas Instruments to manufacture sophisticated computer memory chips. It is also reflected in the emerging plan among Taiwan computer manufacturers to set up a computer-industrial zone in one of the EC countries as a way to ensure a piece of the market in the coming years. As one commentator in *The Economist* has suggested, "the multi-layered structure of the new computer industry and the large number of firms it now contains, mean that any single firm, no matter how powerful, must work closely with many others. Often this is to obtain access to technology or manufacturing expertise. A web of a thousand joint ventures, cross-equity holdings, and marketing pacts now entangles every firm in the industry." Firms that are left out of these alliances and linkages will be hard pressed to maintain their viability even over the short term.

The role of Japan in Taiwan's high technology development is likely to become significant in this context as Japanese capital has already begun to provide the cement for a more integrated East Asian regional economy. Japanese firms are recognizing that Taiwan has an important role to play in the regional emerging division of labour, perhaps not along the lines of the now obsolete "flying geese model," but according to some new model of interaction distinguished by technological complementarities rather than differential costs. Of course, Japanese firms will remain cautious in their approach to Taiwan, but there is little doubt that Japan can ill-afford to ignore the potential role that Taiwan firms can play in terms of both regional and global competition. Taiwan will still maintain its close relationship with the United States, but much depends on whether American industry will respond in greater force to the new dynamic situation in the Pacific Rim. Otherwise, concepts such as the "Asianization" of the global semiconductor industry are likely to become a reality.

In the world that is evolving, it is becoming clear that in order to attract technology one already has to possess some technology. With respect to industries such as microelectronics and informatics, this should prove to be a great source of comfort for Taiwan, which is now finding that there are indeed benefits from having made progress after all these years. At the same time, however, there are many challenges to the future success of Taiwan as it faces the rest of the 1990s and the next century. There are growing barriers to entry into many of the high-technology industries that are now the focal point of government officials and business leaders on the island. For example, the cost of building a new state-of-the-art facility for integrated circuit fabrication and production is now over ten times as much as it was a few years ago. Based on current estimates to establish a world-class facility to produce DRAM memory chips, the cost would exceed US$1.0 billion. To offset some of these cost barriers, the government has highlighted eight key technologies and ten high-growth industries in its new six-year economic plan (1990–96). It is clear, however, that despite its huge foreign exchange reserves (US$96 billion), the Taiwan government cannot absorb all the costs associated with these new initiatives; foreign investment as well as private sector contributions are required. Moreover, government initiatives are not always successful, as demonstrated by the failed effort to organize a consortium to develop and produce the first computer notebook on the island. Similar concerns also exist as a result of the failure of the aerospace industry initiative to yield the type of positive collaborative results in technological terms that the government anticipated.

Perhaps this is one reason why the Taiwan government decided in late 1993 to privatize the state-of-the-art semiconductor facility it operates in Hsinchu Park. The plant, which was created as part of the overall programme of high-technology investment orchestrated by the government, remains economically viable, and given the growing demand for memory chips throughout the island, clearly has the potential to be a very profitable venture. Taiwan imports a majority of the DRAMs it needs; unlike Korea which has focused primarily on DRAM production, Taiwan firms had tended to shy away from such projects because of the huge initial investment. This is now changing because of the rapid growth of the information industry. Quite frequently, the government has had to assume a major role to jump-start new high-technology initiatives. Once its mission has been achieved, as in the case of United Microelectronics and several other related projects, it may be appropriate for the government to remove itself from explicit involvement, either through equity ownership or direct managerial control. On Taiwan, there are legitimate concerns about whether private forces can muster the necessary political will and economic commitment to make something substantial happen.[70] This suggests that the government cannot simply abandon what it has accomplished, and must remain in some capacity with the industry, if only to give confidence to outside investors who want to identify the island's "pockets of excellence."[71]

Secondly, the ongoing efforts at technological re-structuring that are occurring on Taiwan are being inhibited to some degree by the general tightening up over access to advanced technology by many who feel threatened by the Asian NIEs.[72] This is especially true for settings such as Taiwan which continue to have a poor reputation as far as IPR protection is concerned. While the forces of globalization are at work, it should not be forgotten that significant forces of technological protectionism are also present. One of the major obstacles to the defunct deal with McDonnell Douglas was the inability of the two parties to agree upon the technology transfer provisions of their proposed collaboration.

Thirdly, there remain major questions in the United States, EC and elsewhere about the viability of a business strategy that relies too heavily on alliance-building in key high technology sectors. Strategic partnering has its advantages, but there are major questions of trust, cross-cultural understanding and politics that must be confronted in working to make these alliances truly mutually beneficial. Fourthly, there are major information and skills barriers in terms of the adoption and application of new technologies such as informatics.[73] This suggests that without an adequate infrastructure or training programmes, many Taiwan firms are going to have similar if not worse problems with assimilating many of the new technologies. It is estimated, for example, that by the latter part of the 1990s, the total number of engineers on Taiwan will be only enough to fill 70 per cent of the projected needs, with the greatest dearth occurring in information engineering and computer science. Whether this shortage can be handled through the use of engineers from the PRC raises a very interesting and provocative question. And finally, it is one thing to desire to get beyond OEM status and enter into both product and process design in advanced industrial sectors on a regular basis, but it is another thing to succeed at doing them well. While there clearly is a strong foundation that suggests a high potential for Taiwan's success, with firms such as Acer, the reality is that the dynamics of global competition in all segments of the world economy call for a degree of responsiveness and flexibility that may or may not be present in view of the existing industrial structure in the local economy.[74] All these factors will weigh heavily on Taiwan as it seeks to establish a new position for itself in the still evolving international division of labour. Moreover, the confluence of these factors suggests that Taiwan companies as well as government officials must be extremely aware of the assorted pushes and pulls on the local economy, especially since they can ill afford to fall behind in those technologies that are providing the foundation for future growth.

NOTES

1 Denis Fred Simon (ed.), *Corporate Strategies Towards the Pacific Rim* (London: Routledge, 1996).
2 Rosabeth Moss Kanter, *World Class* (New York: Simon and Schuster, 1995).
3 See Kenichi Ohmae, *The End of the Nation State: The Rise of Regional Economies* (New York: The Free Press, 1995).
4 Edward Chen and Peter Drysdale (eds.), *Corporate Links and Foreign Direct Investment in Asia and the Pacific* (Pymble, Australia: Harper Collins, 1995).
5 C. Fred Bergsten and Marcus Noland (eds.), *Pacific Dynamism and the International Economic System* (Washington, DC: Institute of International Economics, 1993).
6 Michael Hobday, *Innovation in East Asia* (Brookfield, VT: Edward Elgar, 1995).
7 Denis Fred Simon, "The international technology market: globalization, regionalization and the Pacific Rim," *Business in the Contemporary World*, Spring 1993.
8 Denis Fred Simon (ed.), *The Emerging Technological Trajectory of the Pacific Rim* (Armonk, NY: M.E. Sharpe, 1995).
9 "Technology transfer policy to Taiwan revised," *Sankei shimbun*, 23 July 1991, p. 11.
10 "Survey: Japan needs higher profile in Asia," *Nikkei Weekly*, 25 April 1992, p. 28.
11 Gustav Ranis (ed.), *Taiwan: From Developing to Mature Economy* (Boulder: Westview Press, 1992).
12 Thomas Gold, *State and Society in the Taiwan Miracle* (Armonk, NY: M.E. Sharpe, 1986).
13 Walter Galenson (ed.), *Economic Growth and Structural Change in Taiwan* (Ithaca: Cornell University Press, 1979).
14 Chi Schive, *The Foreign Factor: The Multinational Corporation's Contribution to the Economic Modernization of the Republic of China* (Stanford: Hoover Institution Press, 1990).
15 Robert Wade, *Governing the Market: Economic Theory and the Role of Government in East Asian Industrialization* (Princeton: Princeton University Press, 1990).
16 Denis Fred Simon and Michael Y.M. Kau (eds.), *Taiwan: Beyond the Economic Miracle* (Armonk, NY: M.E. Sharpe, 1992).
17 Maurice Estabrooks, *Electronic Technology, Corporate Strategy, and World Transformation* (Westport, CI: Quorum Books, 1995).
18 N.T. Wang (ed.), *Taiwan's Enterprises in Global Perspective* (Armonk, NY: M.E. Sharpe, 1992).
19 Russell Flannery, "Taiwan companies switch to hi-tech," *Asian Business*, April 1991, pp. 52–54.
20 See the articles by Thomas Gold and Denis Fred Simon in Edwin Winckler and

Susan Greenhalgh (eds.), *Contending Approaches to the Political Economy of Taiwan* (Armonk, NY: M.E. Sharpe, 1988).

21 See the article by Gee San on Taiwan in Richard R. Nelson (ed.), *National Innovation Systems: A Comparative Analysis* (Oxford: Oxford University Press, 1993).

22 Even though he does not specifically address the Taiwan case, the work of Harvard Business School economist Michael Porter is relevant here. See Michael Porter, *The Competitive Advantage of Nations* (New York: Free Press, 1990).

23 Dieter Ernst and David O'Connor, *Technology and Global Competition: The Challenge for Newly Industrializing Economies* (Paris: OECD Development Centre, 1989).

24 David Teece (ed.), *The Competitive Challenge* (Cambridge: Ballinger Publishers, 1989).

25 Denis Fred Simon, "Taiwan, technology transfer and transnationalism," Ph.D. dissertation, Berkeley, 1980 (unpublished).

26 Interviews conducted by author in 1991–92 in Taipei as part of research project under the auspices of the Fujitsu Research Institute in Japan.

27 K.T. Li, *The Evolution of Policy Behind Taiwan's Development Success* (New Haven: Yale University Press, 1989).

28 "Taiwan business highlights – R&D requirement," *China Economic News Service*, 1 June 1996.

29 According to government statistics, R&D spending on Taiwan was up over 400% between 1985 and 1995. See "Taiwan: R&D spending up 400% in decade," *China Economic News Service*, 22 December 1995.

30 See several of the articles in Hellmut Schutte (ed.), *The Global Competitiveness of the Asian Firm* (New York: St. Martin's Press, 1994).

31 Philip Liu, "ITRI at the crossroads," *Business Taiwan*, 4 September 1994.

32 Peter Gwynne, "Directing technology in Asia's dragons," *Research-Technology Management*, 4 March 1993, pp. 12–15.

33 "ITRI celebrates its 20th anniversary with symposium," *Business Taiwan*, 19 July 1993, p. 1.

34 See Simon, "Taiwan, technology transfer and transnationalism."

35 Philip Liu, "Hsinchu science-based industrial park," *Business Taiwan*, 28 October 1991.

36 Danielle Yang, "Industrial parks seen as engines of Taiwan economy," *Central News Agency*, 13 November 1995.

37 K.K. Chadha, "Taiwan science hits record year," *South China Morning Post*, 13 December 1994, p. 8.

38 "Taiwan: science park achieves record performance," *Business Taiwan*, 14 November 1994.

39 "Science park to be built in Taiwan," *China Economic News Service*, 22 March 1996.

40 "Authorities predict Taiwan to be science-island in a decade," *China Economic News Service*, 5 May 1995.

41 "Taiwan: government plan to boost R&D spending," *Business Taiwan*, 6 March 1995.

42 "On Asian competitiveness," *AsiaWeek*, 3 November 1995, p. 30.

43 "Taiwan wafer fabs are booming," *Electronic Buyers News*, 12 January 1996, p. 8.

44 "Taiwan's hi-tech race," *Business Week* (International Edition), 6 May 1996.

45 "Yin and Yang of flat panels," *Electronic Buyers News*, 29 May 1995, p. 2.

46 At the same time, some Japanese firms are arriving on the island to move into the higher end segment of the monitor industry. See "NEC ties up with Taiwan firm for CRT production," *Asian Economic News*, 15 April 1996, p. 1.

47 "A new view to the future: Taiwan special supplement," *Asia Money*, September 1995, pp. 14–29.

48 "What? You haven't heard of MITAC," *Business Week* (International Edition), 10 April 1995.
49 Brian Levy and Wen-jeng Kuo, "The strategic orientations of firms and the performance of Korea and Taiwan in frontier industries: lessons from comparative studies of the keyboard and personal computer assembly," *World Development*, Vol. 19, No. 4 (1991), pp. 363–374.
50 See the various articles in Harvard Business Review (ed.), *Global Strategies* (Boston: Harvard Business Review Press, 1994).
51 See Denis Fred Simon (ed.), *Techno-Security in an Age of Globalization* (Armonk, NY: M.E. Sharpe, 1996).
52 Kenichi Ohmae, "The global logic of strategic alliances," Harvard Business Review, March/April 1989, pp. 143–154.
53 Keith D. Brouthers *et al.*, "Strategic alliances: choose your partners," *Long Range Planning*, Vol. 28, No. 3 (June 1995), pp. 18–25.
54 Peter Pekar and Robert Allio, "Making alliances work – guidelines for success," *Long Range Planning*, Vol. 27, No. 4 (August 1994), pp. 54–65.
55 B. Bowonder, "Creating and sustaining competitiveness: an analysis of the world civil aircraft industry," *World Competition*, June 1993, pp. 5–47.
56 Ohmae, "The global logic of strategic alliances."
57 David Mowery (ed.), *International Collaborative Ventures in U.S. Manufacturing* (Cambridge: Ballinger Publishers, 1988).
58 For an interesting discussion of the attractiveness of Taiwan from a competitive perspective, see the forthcoming manuscript edited by George Yip, *Asian Advantage* (forthcoming, 1996).
59 Alan Lonelson, "The perils of techno-globalism," *Issues in Science and Technology*, Summer 1995, pp. 31–38.
60 Fred Warshotsky, *The Patent Wars* (New York: John Wiley & Sons, 1994).
61 Kuo-shu Liang, "International strategic alliances and technology transfers," *Business Taiwan*, 22 March 1993, p. 1.
62 See the article by Denis Fred Simon and Yongwook Jun on Japanese foreign investment in Chen and Drysdale, *Corporate Links and Foreign Direct Investment*.
63 See United Nations Center for Transnational Corporations (ed.), *World Investment Report 1991* and *1993* (New York: United Nations, 1991, 1993).
64 See Poh Kam Wong, *Technological Development Through Subcontracting Linkages: A Case Study* (Tokyo: Asian Productivity Organization, 1991).
65 For a discussion of the global behavior of multinational firms and their subcontracting behaviour see John H. Dunning, *Multinational Enterprises and the Global Economy* (Reading, MA: Addison-Wesley, 1993).
66 "Who's NICst?" *The Economist*, 13 August 1994, p. 31.
67 This new thinking is part of the larger changing attitude of Japanese firms towards Asia. See "Survey: Japan needs higher profile in Asia," *Nikkei Weekly*, 25 April 1992, p. 28.
68 "Taiwan government opens doors to technology transfers to/from China," *Nikkei Weekly*, 6 June 1992, p. 27.
69 "Mainland and Taiwan hold first joint metrology seminar," Xinhua News Agency, 30 October 1995.
70 Julian Baum, "Mid-course correction," *Far Eastern Economic Review*, 15 July 1993, pp. 60–61.
71 Joel D. Auerbauch *et al.* (eds.), *The Role of the State in Taiwan's Development* (Armonk, NY: M.E. Sharpe, 1994).
72 See Simon, *Techno-Security in an Age of Globalization*.

73 See S.P. Bradley, J.A. Hausman and R.L. Nolan, *Globalization, Technology and Competition* (Boston: Harvard Business School Press, 1993).
74 Richard Schonberger, *World Class Manufacturing: The Next Decade* (New York: Free Press 1996).

17

TECHNOLOGICAL LEARNING IN SINGAPORE

A Test Case of Leapfrogging

Michael Hobday

INTRODUCTION

The diffusion of the information technology paradigm and the rapid growth of the electronics industry have led some observers to believe that some developing countries (DCs) may be able to 'leapfrog' older vintages of technology and begin to catch up with advanced economies.[1] According to this view, some DCs are less hampered by investment commitments to previous generations of technology. DCs with adequate levels of skills and infrastructure (absorptive capacity) may benefit from the 'windows of opportunity' provided by the new paradigm, especially at the early stages of diffusion when barriers to entry are relatively low and markets are in a state of upheaval. Leapfrogging is consistent with Schumpeter's notion of 'gales of creative destruction', where radical new innovations give rise to the destruction of industries based upon older technologies [Schumpeter, 1950].

In the area of telecommunications infrastructure, research shows that many DCs have adopted digital, electronics-based systems more rapidly than advanced countries.[2] Less committed to older vintages of technology, they 'jumped' directly to advanced electronics systems. However, the position with respect to industrial development is less clear. There has been little empirical study of whether or not firms in DCs can leapfrog – or indeed what the term actually means in practice. As Archambault [1992] argues, the leapfrogging argument is based on theory rather than empirical research.[3] Furthermore, many studies show that firms acquire technology through 'learning'. Learning is usually a costly, difficult and incremental process [Malerba, 1992]. On the face of it, the notion of learning contradicts the idea of leapfrogging.

This article looks at the case of Singapore, a DC which has had industrial success in electronics. Its purpose is to examine the character and determinants of technological accumulation at the firm level to see whether or not

Source: *Journal of Development Studies*, Vol. 30(4), July 1994, pp. 831–58.

Singapore's experience is consistent with the leapfrogging hypothesis. It also hopes to shed some light on how firms in DCs accumulate technology in electronics.

In several respects Singapore is a special case among DCs. It has a small population (just over three million). The government has promoted education and a skilled workforce and developed a modern telecommunications and electronics infrastructure.[4] The country appears to have quickly developed the absorptive capacity required for leapfrogging to take place. Indeed, electronics has grown rapidly to become the largest industrial sector. Singapore is therefore an interesting, if partial, test case of leapfrogging.[5]

Section 17.I briefly reviews government policies for electronics and the contribution of electronics to the manufacturing sector. Section 17.II introduces the concept of learning. It then presents a sample of qualitative case studies of firms operating in each of the four leading electronics sub-sectors: semiconductors, disk drives, consumer electronics and computing. An effort is made to identify the changing patterns and mechanisms of learning within the large transnational corporations (TNCs) which dominate the sector. Two major local firms are also included. The case studies try to show how firms adjusted to changing technology and markets and to the improving infrastructure within the economy.

The article argues that the case of electronics in Singapore is inconsistent with the leapfrogging hypothesis. Technological accumulation was gradual and cumulative. The TNC subsidiaries and local firms engaged in a long-term, incremental path of learning, responding to changing market and infrastructural conditions – a process of 'hard slog', rather than 'leapfrog'.[6] Much of their technological advance was in 'pre-electronic' fields such as machine tooling, plastic moulding, and mechanical and precision engineering, suggesting a close and complex relationship between old and new technological paradigms. The case of Singapore warns that there are no 'easy options' for DCs in electronics.

17.I THE ROLE OF GOVERNMENT

After achieving self-government status in 1959 the Singapore government played a very active role in the development of the economy. According to Vogel [1991: p. 77] Singapore developed an 'administrative state', with government agencies taking a leading role in business through both direct and indirect means.[7] State-owned or controlled enterprises were set up in oil exploration, petroleum refining, petrochemicals, defence, shipbuilding and airline travel. In other sectors, such as electronics, the government left most decisions to private firms, providing incentives, manpower training and infrastructure to attract TNCs to the economy. By 1990 more than 3,000 TNCs (including 600 large firms) from the US, Japan and Europe had established operations in Singapore. Cumulative foreign manufacturing investment in

Singapore increased from around S$7bn in 1980 to S$13bn in 1985 to nearly S$24bn in 1990.[8]

Foreign firms were attracted to Singapore partly by the efficiency of the transportation and communications infrastructure. The freedom granted to foreign firms, administrative support from government and macroeconomic stability made Singapore an attractive regional investment centre for TNCs. Some firms were initially attracted by the low costs of labour and overheads. Philips of the Netherlands located in Singapore in 1951 and gradually expanded its consumer appliance production. In semiconductors, Texas Instruments of the US and SGS of Italy both set up assembly and testing facilities in 1969. In the early 1960s the government suppressed the militant trade unions, reducing industrial unrest. Several investment incentives schemes also operated, although few firms in the electronics sector cited government incentives as their main reason for locating in Singapore.[9]

In order to promote the manufacturing sector the government established policies for education, training and skills development. Basic technical education was provided by vocational institutes set up in the 1960s. During the 1970s the Economic Development Board (EDB) organised apprenticeship schemes and set up government-industry training centres with Japan, France and Germany. As of 1991 the EDB operated five training institutes with an enrolment of 2,500 students: the French–Singapore Institute, the German–Singapore Institute, the Japanese–Singapore Institute, the Precision Engineering Institute and the Philips–Government Training Centre. Their main focus was engineering, technology and craft education for manufacturing industry. Today, the institutes provide two and three-year training courses in tool and die and precision machining, plastics technology, factory automation, mechatronics and industrial electronics. Many other programmes of re-training and continuous education operate.

By 1991, the National University of Singapore, Nanyang Technological University, the polytechnics and the training institutes together supplied around 22,000 engineers and craftsmen per annum. This represents an annual output of roughly 38 per 100,000 population, one of the highest levels world-wide on a per capita basis.[10] The availability of low-cost engineers, technicians and skilled workers was often cited by TNCs as a primary reason for locating in Singapore.

Another instrument of training policy was the Skills Development Fund (SDF), set up to provide training grants of between 30 per cent to 70 per cent of total costs. During the early 1980s the SDF was financed by a levy on employers of around four per cent of workers' wages, matched by government contributions. As of 1992, the SDF was funded by a levy of around one per cent on wages less than S$750 per month. Many firms received funds to finance training programmes.[11]

Recently the government has set up institutes for software training, electronics engineering, advanced mechanical engineering and research. This is part of the government's policy to encourage manufacturing to move into higher value-added activities such as design and research and development (R&D). Technology support institutes for electronics and information technology in 1991 included: the Institute of Manufacturing Technology; the Information Technology Institute; the Institute of Systems Science; the Institute of Microelectronics; the Magnetic Technology Institute (EDB 1992). So far, the institutes have had little impact on industry. Their aim is to supply high-level skilled manpower and to provide engineering and research back-up for industry. The advisory boards of the institutes include managers of TNCs who advise on specific projects and overall direction.

The new institutes are targeted at high technology sectors. The Magnetics Technology Centre, for example, carries out engineering and research work for the disk drive industry. Its work includes the design and control of actuators and motors, magnetic data coding and electromagnetic field computational techniques. The Institute of Microelectronics was set up in 1992 to support the semiconductor industry with silicon processing technology, component reliability and failure analysis, computer-aided circuit design and systems applications. One of its long-term aims is to enable the large semiconductor producers to carry out complex developmental work locally.[12]

In contrast with its strong supply of technicians and production engineers Singapore lags behind other countries in the supply of research engineers and scientists. In 1990, Singapore had around 28 research engineers and scientists per 10,000 workers (a total of 4,300), compared with 87 for Japan, 77 for the US, 44 for Switzerland, 43 for Taiwan and 33 for the Republic of Korea).[13] Similarly, government spending on R&D as a percentage of GDP lags behind many developed countries as well as Taiwan and the Republic of Korea.[14] Singapore's lack of research engineers and scientists in part reflects the past priorities of industry. During the 1970s and 1980s, industry did not require a large supply of high technology researchers and scientists. As shown in section 17.III, the main demand was for semi-skilled and skilled workers and production engineers.

The government plans to encourage the growth of high technology manufacturing (especially electronics). A large effort is being made to build up the science and technology infrastructure of the economy. Under a 'National Technology Plan' laid out in 1991, the National Science and Technology Board aims to spend S$2bn over a five-year period to increase the number of researchers from 28 to 40 per 10,000 workers. By making this investment the government hopes to lift the economy on to a higher plane of research-intensive, high value-added activities during the 1990s.

The government has also set up a so-called 'Growth Triangle' to shift labour-intensive production out to Malaysia and Indonesia, while retaining higher wage activities in Singapore. The Growth Triangle consists of two adjoining low-cost regions within neighbouring Malaysia (Johor) and Indonesia (the Riau Islands). In 1990 agreement was reached between the parties to develop and manage a 500-hectare industrial estate (the Batam Industrial Park in Indonesia, 20 kilometres south of Singapore). By 1992, 29 tenants had set up operations including AT&T (see section 17.III), Sumitomo, Philips, Thomson and Bowater Packaging. A further 22 were to begin operations in 1992. The government-owned firm, the Singapore Technologies Industrial Corporation, was reported to have allocated S$5bn for infrastructural development in the Triangle.[15]

17.II CONTRIBUTION OF ELECTRONICS TO MANUFACTURING

Singapore's economic achievements are well documented. GDP per capita rose from US$435 in 1960 to US$13,236 in 1991[16] The structure of the economy changed significantly as a result of economic progress. Manufacturing grew from around 18 per cent of GDP in 1960 to 27 per cent in 1991. By 1991 manufacturing accounted for more than 50 per cent of Singapore's foreign exchange earnings. Within manufacturing, electronics production was the largest sector in 1991, accounting for 34 per cent of gross manufacturing value-added.[17] The second largest sector was chemicals and chemical products which accounted for 11 per cent of gross value-added. Total electronics output amounted to S$24.5bn in 1989 and S$28.8bn in 1991. The bulk of production was carried out by large TNCs for export. Exports increased from S$21.2bn in 1989 to S$26.0bn in 1991, while employment increased from 116,000 in 1989 to around 124,000 in 1991 (Table 17.1).

Table 17.1 Electronics exports and employment by major product categories (S$bn)

	Exports			Employment
Selected Product Lines	*1989*	*1990*	*1991*	*1991*
Disk drives	5.5	7.2	7.0	25,000
Integrated circuits	3.7	3.8	4.5	16,000
Printed circuit boards	2.6	3.0	3.1	13,870
Computer systems	1.0	1.2	2.4	2,577
Audio equipment	2.1	2.0	2.0	n.a.
Colour TVs	1.3	1.4	1.4	n.a.
TV and audio subassemblies	1.5	1.5	1.4	n.a.
Telecommunications	0.7	0.8	0.7	8,000
Sub totals				
Industrial electronics	11.0	13.6	14.7	n.a.
Consumer electronics	5.4	5.6	5.7	26,000
Components	4.8	4.9	5.7	n.a.
Total	21.2	24.1	26.1	123,516

Source: Compiled from EDB [*1992b*].

Total value-added for the industry was estimated at S$7.0bn in 1989, S$7.7bn in 1990, and S$7.8bn in 1991 (roughly US$4.5bn).[18]

Table 17.1 shows Singapore's main product specialisation for 1991. The largest product group was disk drives. Disk drive exports amounted to S$7bn in 1991 (around 27 per cent of total electronics exports). Singapore was the world's largest producer of hard (that is, Winchester) disk drives in 1991 accounting for some 50 per cent of global output.[19] During the 1980s, Singapore attracted a large 'cluster' of international producers, including Seagate and Conner of the US.[20] Semiconductors (or integrated circuits), the second largest electronics sub-sector, accounted for S$4.5bn of exports in 1991 (17 per cent of the total). The case studies below show that leading firms have begun wafer fabrication and product design by transferring advanced technology from parent to Singapore plants. Industrial electronics (including disk drives, integrated circuits, computers and printed circuit boards) grew during the 1980s and by 1991 represented 56 per cent of total electronics exports. Singapore has evolved from assembly based on cheap labour to advanced, automated manufacturing. One of the reasons the TNCs increased production of complex industrial electronics was Singapore's improving infrastructure and technical training (discussed in section 17.III).

The contribution of local firms to total electronics investment and output is very small. In 1991 Singaporean-owned firms accounted for around 16 per cent (approximately S$472.9m) of total manufacturing investment, much less for electronics investment. Some local firms supply the TNCs, but most of the materials, components and capital goods needed by the TNCs are imported. Other domestic firms (for example, in computers) provide additional capacity for TNCs through original equipment manufacture (OEM) and sub-contracting arrangements.[21] A few provide plant and engineering support for large firms.

Several local firms have grown to become medium-sized TNCs in their own right. As of 1991 the two largest local firms were Singapore Technologies Industrial Corporation and Wearnes Technology. Other major firms were PCI Inc., Eltech Electronics and Goh Electronics Singapore. Combined electronics sales of these top five firms were around US$0.7bn in 1989, a tiny proportion of total output.[22] Local firms produced personal computers, Winchester disk drives, printed circuit boards and data communications equipment. Local computer manufacturing tends to be carried out under OEM arrangements with TNCs. A few local firms have begun to develop their own brand names (for example, Wearnes and Creative Technology) and to establish their own distribution networks and R&D centres abroad. Despite these developments, in comparison with Hong Kong, Taiwan and the Republic of Korea, the contribution of local firms to electronics output is very small.

17.III CORPORATE LEARNING IN SINGAPORE

Objectives, method and sample

Studies of learning attempt to show *how* technological know-how is acquired within firms and related institutions. Learning refers to the mechanisms by which technological progress proceeds. Malerba [1992] demonstrates the importance of learning to incremental technical change, productivity growth, and to different types of product and process improvement. Learning normally involves substantial and deliberate effort and investment on the part of the firm. Dodgson [1991: 23] defines learning as: 'the ways firms build and supplement their knowledge bases about technologies, products and processes, and develop and improve the use of the broad skills of their work-forces'. Learning has proved important to technological and institutional progress and industrialisation in DCs [Fransman and King, 1984].

Learning is difficult to observe or accurately measure or indeed to distinguish from other activities. The present study is therefore limited to generating a broad, qualitative understanding of the nature, extent and determinants of learning among firms, over time. The intention is to identify the mechanisms by which firms accumulated technology in electronics, not only to assess the leapfrogging hypothesis but also to illustrate how firms, in practice, accumulated technology in electronics.

The study was carried out in 1991 to 1992. Thirty-two interviews were conducted in Singapore with TNCs, local firms, industry associations and academic and government organisations connected with economic development, science, technology and engineering. For each company, managing directors, senior engineers and/or production directors were interviewed with an open-ended questionnaire covering organisational history, methods of gaining technology (learning), training schemes and so on. The questionnaire attempted to identify the key categories of learning and to describe how these changed through time. The main findings of the field research are presented for each of the four major sectors in turn and summarised in the conclusion.

The firm sample was structured to include: (a) leading firms; (b) foreign, local and joint venture firms; (c) large, medium and small companies; (d) early and late entrants; (e) firms in each of the four major sectors; (f) firms from Europe, the US and Japan. Total sales of the sample of firms amounted to around S$11.6bn. Estimating additional sales of roughly S$2.0bn for AT&T, this represents just over one-third of Singapore's electronics output. Total employment was 32,680, roughly one-quarter of total electronics employment.[23]

Semiconductors

Sector overview

With exports of around S$4.5bn in 1991, the semiconductor (or 'chip') industry was the second largest electronics sub-sector in Singapore. The major producers in Singapore were Texas Instruments (TI), National, AMD, NEC, AT&T Microelectronics, Siemens, SGS-Thomson, Fujitsu, Matsushita, TECH Semiconductor, Chartered Semiconductor, Unitrode and Linear Technology. The sample included three TNC subsidiaries, one joint venture and a local company (Table 17.2). Semiconductor activities began with assembly and testing, a large volume of which is still carried out in Singapore (around 5 per cent of the world's total in 1992). During the 1980s, integrated circuit design (for semi-customised chips) and wafer fabrication were introduced selectively. Companies also introduced regional management, marketing and distribution for the Asia-Pacific region.

In 1969 TI became the first chip maker to begin production in Singapore. In the same year TI was followed by SGS (now SGS-Thomson). NEC Singapore was incorporated in 1976.[24] The three TNCs chose Singapore because of its air and sea ports, low-cost skilled labour, efficient economic infrastructure and government co-operation and incentives. In each case,

Table 17.2 Electronic study sample – employment, sales and origin of companies

Sector	*Firm*	*Start Date*	*Origin**	*Employment*	*Sales 1990 (S$m)* **
Semi-conductors	Texas Instruments	1969	US	2,000	1,123
	SGS-Thomson	1969	I/F	1,000	1,194**
	NEC	1976	J	700	330
	TECH	1990	JV	420	71
	Chartered	1987	S	400	450**
Disk Drives	Seagate	1982	US	12,000	4,833
	Conner	1987	US	4,300	2,000
Consumer Electronics	Philip s	1951	N	6,100	2,000**
	AT&T/ACP	1986	US	4,000	n.a.
Computers/ professional	Wearnes***	1983	S	510	128

Notes:
* Codes: US = United States; I/F = Italy/France; J = Japan: N = Netherlands; S = Singapore; JV = Joint venture between Singapore's EDP (26%) and US and Japanese firms.
** Denotes 1991 data (exchange rate for 1990 US$1 = US$1.81; for 1991 US$1 = US$1.73.
*** Includes Wearnes Hollingworth and Wearnes Automation.

Sources: Interviews, company annual reports and *Singapore Electonics Manufacturers Directories* (various issues).

operations began with labour-intensive production, primarily the assembly and testing of (now) mature products such as discrete semiconductors, linear and bipolar integrated circuits.

In each case the choice of location was determined by three sets of factors: corporate strategies regarding internationalisation and capacity expansion; the division of tasks in semiconductors, allowing firms to relocate parts of the production process overseas; and host country attractions (for example, the infrastructural advantages of Singapore over competing locations such as Taiwan and the Republic of Korea).

Technological upgrading of TNC subsidiaries

Over time, the three TNCs introduced more complex products requiring greater engineering support, more complex processes, personnel training, progressive automation and more intensive quality control. NEC, for instance, went through a series of product transitions, beginning with transistors in 1977 and linear integrated circuits in 1979. By 1986 the factory was assembling 256k DRAMs, and by 1991 one and four megabit DRAMs. TI followed a similar path. Initially, wafer fabrication took place outside Singapore in the TNC parent plants overseas.

With each product transition, testing and assembly evolved from a simple, labour-intensive line task to a substantially automated activity. In 1980 the ratio of test operators to machines was roughly 1:1. By 1991 the ratio was roughly 1:4. Several tasks remained labour-intensive (for example, loading and unloading), requiring large numbers of employees.[25] Recent product innovations (for example) the four megabit DRAM, required continuous engineering development work (for example, for failure analysis and advanced packaging). This led firms into cooperation with local university engineering departments and, more recently, the government's Institute for Microelectronics.

Introduction of wafer fabrication by the TNCs

Wafer fabrication is the core manufacturing technology activity in semiconductors. As such, it requires investments in skills (especially engineering), plant, machinery, technology and management. It is a jump from testing and assembly. In 1984 SGS-Thomson became the first chip maker to set up wafer fabrication in Singapore (also the first in the Asia-Pacific region outside of Japan). Since 1984 the company set up three wafer 'modules', expanding the wafer capacity of its Singapore plant. Following SGS-Thomson, in 1990, TI became a partner in a sub-micron (that is, leading edge) joint venture (called TECH Singapore) to fabricate 4 and 16 megabit semiconductors in Singapore. TECH was a shared US$330m venture between TI (26 per cent), the Singapore Economic Development Board (26 per cent), Canon (24 per cent) and Hewlett-Packard (24 per cent).

TI and SGS-Thomson illustrate the technological upgrading of chip firms within Singapore. The TECH facility was scheduled to begin production in March 1993. Its aim was to supply local users of DRAMs (including Hewlett-Packard and Canon) as well as other companies in East Asia. NEC had no plans to introduce fabrication facilities to Singapore. It had, however, set up a design centre staffed with engineers.

Firms cited several reasons for fabricating wafers in Singapore. First, the growing importance of the Asia-Pacific market justified investments closer to customers (TI's sales to the region were around US$1.5bn in 1992, roughly 30 per cent of its non-military turnover).[26] Second, firms were able to achieve high levels of capacity utilisation, due to Singapore's efficient infrastructure and the willingness of management and workers to work long overtime hours. Third, firms benefited from policies organised through the EDB. Fourth, the relatively low cost of production engineers in Singapore, compared with Europe, the US and Japan proved important. One source estimated that the entry level salary for an electronics engineer in Singapore was roughly 50 per cent of the cost of an American equivalent.

TNC plant expansion

By 1991, each of the three TNCs had expanded their production considerably and set up regional and marketing headquarters. TI, for example, employed around 2,000 people, of which 1000 were line workers with basic training, with the balance made up of engineers, technicians, marketing and other administrative staff. By 1991, SGS-Thomson's sales reached US$690m, making the Singapore plant one of SGS-Thomson's largest operations. Sales were expected to increase to $1.25bn by 1995.[27] Each company had introduced design support facilities for local customers (for example, ASIC design offices). SGS-Thomson began product design in 1979 and by 1992 employed around 30 full-time design engineers.

Most senior engineers and managers were trained and promoted from within the Singapore operations. Two of the three TNCs carried out extensive computer-based training, developed by engineers within the local plants. According to the firms, graduates from local universities and polytechnics were adequate for most engineering and management tasks. The need for additional supplies of engineers and technical back-up had led all three firms into arrangements with university engineering departments as well as the government's new Institute for Microelectronics (IME). SGS-Thomson, for instance, conducted some product development work with the local universities and polytechnics and had donated equipment for use by the IME.

Plants were able to expand as a result of Singapore's continuous improvements in educational quality, the increased supply of technicians and engineers, and the capacity and efficiency of the transportation and telecommunications infrastructure which consistently improved during the 1970s and 1980s. Government incentives were introduced to encourage TNCs to locate headquarters and higher value-added activities in Singapore. In the TI case, direct involvement by the government through its risk-sharing investment encouraged the firm to expand.

Technological catching up by the TNC subsidiaries

As new products were introduced to the Singapore plants, more mature products (for example, bipolar TTL, ceramic and linear integrated circuits) were transferred to Malaysia and other low-cost labour sites. In terms of the product life-cycle, Singapore progressed towards the newer (early stage) products, requiring a larger number of more complex production activities than before. *Absolute* technological progress occurred as the Singapore subsidiaries graduated to more complex products and processes.

TI's joint venture (TECH) and SGS-Thomson's wafer fabrication facilities (and other investments such as Hewlett-Packard's gallium arsenide fabrication facility and Chartered's fabrication facilities), suggest a *relative* catch up with TNC parent firms in the developed economies. The gap between parents and subsidiaries narrowed in response to regional market growth, increasing labour costs, and improved absorptive capacity in Singapore. However, the catch-up process was by no means complete. As of 1992, little mainstream product design or R&D was carried out in Singapore. Highly advanced manufacturing processes tended to be introduced first to headquarter locations and only afterwards to Singapore. Product output in Singapore was advanced and mainstream, but not at the leading-edge of experimental technology (for example, 4 and 16 megabit DRAMs, rather than 64 megabit). In TI, for instance, most product design and R&D was conducted at the Dallas headquarters, although the Singapore plant worked continuously with Dallas, learning more about failure analysis, packaging design and other 'near market' technology activities.

As the TNC subsidiaries progressed technologically, they increasingly integrated their activities within the South-East Asian region. This is indicated by the growing number of forward and backward linkages among firms. SGS-Thomson, for instance, forged backward linkages with local suppliers of capital goods (for example, Varian and Ultratech), substrates, gases, chemicals and other materials, some of which were based in Singapore, others nearby in the region. TI formed close forward links with customers such as Canon and Hewlett-Packard. Sales to clients within Singapore increased. For instance, Seagate, the disk drive producer, became a major customer of SGS-Thomson. All three chip subsidiaries established design centres and marketing headquarters to work more closely with regional clients. They also formed educational links with local universities. Integration of production and technology occurred partly due to market growth within the Asia-Pacific region and partly as a natural consequence of the upgrading of the plants.

A local entrant: learning to overcome entry barriers

Turning to the local chip firm, Chartered Semiconductor Manufacturing Pte. Ltd. was the first Singaporean company to begin wafer fabrication. Chartered began in 1989 as a joint venture between the Singapore Technology Industrial Corporation (STIC), Sierra Semiconductor and National of the US. STIC was a part of Singapore Technology Holdings, a large state-owned subcontractor to the Singapore military, with employment of roughly 12,000 in 1991.[28] Chartered produced sophisticated chips (mainly mixed signal, analog and digital devices). It began with start up capital of roughly US$40m, supplied by the Singapore government.[29] Total investment increased to around US123m in 1991 by which time the company employed around 400 staff, of which 70 were engineers.[30]

Chartered 'jumped in' at more or less world best practice technology (1.0 and 1.2 micron process) with 20 or so domestic R&D staff. The company suffered various teething problems. National pulled out of the operation in 1989 and Sierra departed in 1991. In 1991, the firm hired a new President, formerly the head of a successful chip start-up company in Taiwan (the Taiwan Semiconductor Manufacturing Corporation). Under a revised strategy, the firm re-modelled itself on the Taiwanese company, producing semiconductors designed by small US chip firms.

The case of Chartered shows that entry into the semiconductor industry is a risky business. Its initial strategy was to learn by hiring, by licensing and by forming alliances with proven technology suppliers. The company was able to reshape its strategy due to financial backing from the government-owned STIC. A less well-financed company could well have failed.

Implications for learning and leapfrogging

The case of the recent local entrant (Chartered) shows how high-technology entry may take place once market and infrastructural conditions are suitable. As a latecomer, entry was facilitated by international technology suppliers and overseas experts. Rather than leapfrogging, Chartered provides a fairly conventional example of a large, well-financed, high technology firm diversifying into a new business with government support. Whether it succeeds or not remains to be seen.

Among the TNC subsidiaries various forms of learning occurred over time. These ranged from production to innovation learning, from elementary to advanced learning, and from technological to non-technological learning.[31] The subsidiaries began simple learning by assembly and testing. As these tasks became more complex, learning involved more in-house, formalised training. Learning from foreign engineers and managers was widespread and is still in progress. Senior foreigners continue to oversee specific operations, assist in the installation of new capital equipment and so on. NEC, for instance, employed 29 senior Japanese staff in its plant of around 700 employees.

Leapfrogging is not a term which captures the cumulative nature of technological progress among the TNCs. Within firms, learning by experience and promotion occurred gradually. All firms recruited, trained and promoted local employees to senior positions in engineering, management and marketing, building up their technological and organisational capabilities. By 1992, the companies had acquired capabilities in product design, process adaptation, continuous engineering and selective R&D back-up. Learning extended beyond technology to management and marketing. Firms learned to market directly to customers nearby as the Asia-Pacific market grew. Customers demanded further services, requiring further learning on the part of the TNCs: learning to design applications specific integrated circuits (ASICs), learning to market and learning to provide after sales services.

In contrast to the leapfrogging hypothesis, firms progressed incrementally in response to market growth, local labour costs, the supply of engineers, and the improving infrastructure. Learning by imitation took place when firms followed others into the region, clustering in Singapore. Once one company had 'taken the plunge' and proved successful in assembly, test and wafer fabrication, others followed. The local firm learned by hiring and by imitation. Recent evidence hints at the start of learning between local input suppliers and the chip makers (producer-user learning). This began to occur as the subsidiaries required greater support from local material and component suppliers.

Also in contrast with leapfrogging, the TNCs began in 'pre-electronic' production activities, mainly assembly and testing based on low-cost labour and basic assembly skills. Gradually, firms progressed to more complex engineering tasks. This suggests that the stark contrast between the new (electronics) and old (mechanical) technology paradigms implied by industrial leapfrogging is misleading. Paradigms appear to overlap and may well be linked together in various ways.[32] Furthermore, firms began at the standardised, mature end of the product cycle, rather than the early stage. They then progressed stage-by-stage to more complex, advanced products.

As firms developed, the government improved the infrastructure, education and the supply of engineers and technicians. Incentives were recently changed to encourage firms to extend their value-added activities (for example, the special tax status for headquarter activities). The EDB responded to human resource needs by improving the engineering and R&D facilities in universities and polytechnics and by setting up special R&D institutes such as the IME. It is unlikely that the TNCs would have upgraded their activities to the extent witnessed without learning and competence accumulation on the part of the government.

The hard disk drive (HDD) industry

Sector overview

During the 1980s Singapore's Winchester or HDD industry grew from humble beginnings to become a multi-billion dollar industry. The HDD industry is dominated by US manufacturers which account for around 80 per cent of the world's output. Japanese firms such as JVC, Toshiba, Fujitsu, Matsushita and Sony also compete. Singapore was the world's largest producer of HDDs in 1991. Most production was in 2.5 inch, 3.5 inch and 5.25 inch drives. Also produced were tape drives ($\frac{1}{2}$ inch and $\frac{1}{4}$ inch cartridge) and back up systems. Major US HDD producers in Singapore included Seagate, Conner Peripherals, Maxtor, Micropolis, Western Digital and Archive. Employment in the industry stood at 25,000 in 1991. Firms began with simple assembly tasks but quickly moved to manufacturing and product development as well as marketing.

Modern HDD production is a large volume, high precision, automated engineering activity. It requires investments in computerisation, continuous engineering and R&D back-up for new product design. The production process involves clean rooms and sophisticated testing equipment. The TNCs in Singapore assimilated a range of technological capabilities in HDDs, reflected in locally designed spindle motors, servo mechanisms and CD-ROM drives. Some firms have introduced computer-integrated manufacturing. Within Singapore, the general market slow-down in the late 1980s led to fierce price competition and two industry casualties (Prairietek and Rodime).

History and choice of location

The two largest HDD firms are included in the study sample. Seagate began business in the US in 1979 making HDDs and other inputs for microcomputers. Sales grew to just under US$1.0bn by 1987 and reached US$2.7bn in 1991. Today Seagate is among the 200 largest corporations in the US, employing 40,000 people in 17 countries. In 1982 Seagate became the first HDD maker to set up operations in Singapore. It began manufacturing printed circuit boards and other computer-related products. In 1983 the first HDDs were produced. By 1991 the Singapore subsidiary employed more than 12,000 people. Conner Peripherals began in the US in 1986 and started operations in Singapore in 1987. By 1991 Conner's three Singapore factories employed more than 4,300 workers. Sales were around S$2.0bn.

The companies chose to locate in Singapore for a variety of reasons. Among them were tax and other incentives, low labour and engineering costs (compared with the US), effective local technical training schemes and efficient air and sea freight systems. Most HDD sales were to the US (around 60 per cent, compared with 25 per cent to the EC and 10 per cent to Asia Pacific).

Expansion was mainly the result of cost advantages relative to the US. Conner, for instance, found that within three months of plant start-up, Singapore unit costs were already far lower than those of its US parent.

Seagate's Singapore subsidiary grew rapidly through internal expansion and outside acquisition. In 1984 it acquired Grenex (now Seagate Magnetics). Afterwards, it set up a product design and development team for thin-film magnetic media at the Singapore Science Park. In 1985 it expanded its printed circuit board facilities. In 1987 it purchased Aeon Corporation (now Seagate Substrates) and Integrated Power Systems (now Seagate Microelectronics), a maker of custom power integrated circuits. In 1989 Seagate made two further acquisitions: Imprimis Technology (for storage devices for workstations and mainframes) and Peripheral Components International (for advanced magnetic storage heads). Both Seagate and Conner integrated vertically in order to grow, to control input quality and to ensure adequate supplies of motors, discs, substrates, heads, media, printed circuit boards and custom semiconductors.

Backward linkages and technological upgrading

At the time of start-up, there was little HDD supporting industry in Singapore. However, as the TNCs expanded, foreign materials and component suppliers followed them into Singapore. By 1991, most of Seagates's materials were purchased locally. Some inputs were manufactured locally. Seagate's early success attracted other US HDD producers to the island, bringing with them more material and component suppliers. Most of Seagate's US production was shifted to Singapore, leaving the US parent responsible for pilot production, design and R&D. During the 1980s, a significant upgrading of the local support industry took place. Supply firms grew up in components, sub-assemblies such as precision machined and stamped parts, die-casting and surface-mount printed circuit board assembly.

During the 1980s, Singapore's production of HDDs became highly automated and sophisticated as a result of the increasing complexity of new products. Computerised control systems were installed to ensure capacity utilisation, high yields and to control inventories. Automated surface-mount technology was in widespread use by the late 1980s. By 1992 production required continuous process engineering and some product development work. In the case of Seagate, new product design was carried out largely in the US. However, Seagate's Singapore plant worked closely with the US parent to facilitate the manufacture of new product designs. Two or three Singapore engineers were constantly in the US plant.

Conner's main Singapore plant evolved to become its world centre for corporate manufacturing. The local Managing Director was in charge of manufacturing operations overseas. Most of Conner's product design was still carried out at an R&D centre in Colorado, although much product engineering work had been transferred to Singapore, encouraged by the presence of qualified, low-cost engineers. Conner's production automation systems were designed in-house by staff in Singapore. The Singapore facility was also responsible for transferring new processes to Conner's plants in Scotland, Italy and Malaysia.

Implications for learning and leapfrogging

HDD is a case of rapid technological learning among firms in Singapore. Initially, firms located in Singapore for cost and infrastructural reasons. The first entrants were followed by others, creating a cluster of large companies. Most engineers graduated from Singapore and neighbouring countries of the region. The companies formed links with the local universities, polytechnics and the recently established Government-funded Magnetics Technology Centre (see section 17.II). The plants rapidly graduated from simple production learning to advanced investment-led, innovative learning. This was partly due to the fast developing nature of the industry. It was also due to Singapore's host country advantages.

In contrast with leapfrogging, HDD is an example of entry into a precision engineering industry, largely pre-electronic in character. The types of skills needed were those associated with small precision motors, circuit board assembly, electromagnetic computation, fine machinery and electromechanical interfacing. Rather than software engineering (the core skill for microelectronics) the source of Singapore's technology advantage was its supply of precision engineers.

Firms were able to quickly exploit the infrastructure generated during the 1960s and 1970s by other high technology assembly industries. Firms learned to set up production systems, to develop new processes and to transfer these processes abroad. Firms grew by acquisition and diversification. Learning-by-imitation occurred, once the leaders were producing successfully in Singapore. The HDD case shows how leading firms were able to stimulate the growth of a new industry, once the country's infrastructure was adequate.

Consumer electronics

Origin and expansion

Consumer goods firms were the first to become established in Singapore. In 1991 consumer electronics employed around 26,000 people, with sales of S$5.7bn. The two cases below, Philips Singapore and AT&T, compare learning within an early and late entrant to the economy. Philips Singapore (a subsidiary of NV Philips of the Netherlands) began its commercial activities in Singapore in 1951 with a trading office of four staff. It began producing radios and private automatic branch exchanges in the late 1960s. In the

1970s the firm diversified into domestic appliances (mostly flat irons), cassette recorders, TVs and components. By 1980 Philips was producing test automation machines, precision moulds and domestic appliances. During the 1980s, the firm added audio equipment, colour TVs, compact disk players and tuners to its product range. It continued to manufacture precision tools and dies for other Philips factories. In 1991 Philips Singapore employed 6,100 people in five separate factories. With sales of around S$1.5bn, Philips was one of the largest TNC subsidiaries in Singapore.

AT&T Consumer Products Pte. Ltd. (ACP) is an example of a recent entrant. ACP is one of the largest AT&T factories outside the US. It employs nearly 4,000 staff and supplies a wide range of products and services. ACP was AT&T's first offshore manufacturing facility. It started with an investment of around S$100m in 1986 making corded (standard) residential telephones. Most production was for the US market.

Technological advance and automation

Production lines at Philips became progressively more complex and automated over the decades. By 1992, operations generally required sophisticated engineering support. Graduate engineers and technicians were mostly from Singapore (at M.Sc. Level). In 1992, the tuner factory was the largest Philips' plant of its type world-wide.[33] It made four major product families, each with a wide variety of designs. Computer integrated manufacturing systems were in operation. Quality control and testing were computerised. As in the cases of semiconductors and HDD, many line workers were still required for tasks not yet automated, such as loading and checking. Philips' video factory was also modern and highly automated. Production was able to switch from one TV model to another in around ten minutes. Local designers used computer aided design/manufacture (CAD/CAM) to assist in the design, development and manufacture of audio products.

As labour costs increased, firms had relocated more mature products to other parts of the region. ACP for instance made an initial investment of about US$5.6m in a satellite factory in Batam in Indonesia (part of the Growth Triangle, 20 km South of Singapore) because of labour shortages in Singapore. New products were introduced to the main plant, while labour-intensive operations were relocated to Batam.

By 1990 ACP had become AT&T's corporate production centre for top-of-the-range cordless telephones. Company engineers had developed sophisticated digital products in-house. The plant was advanced by world standards, using automated production processes and computerisation. As with Philips, production required continuous engineering support to ensure the quality of output. The types of processes generally in use at ACP were surface mounting (as compared with hand placed) technology, reflow soldering and automatic testing. The lines were able to switch from one type of product to another fairly quickly. Computers were used to schedule production, measure performance and to carry out planning, purchasing and shipping tasks.

As in the other case studies, automation had not led to a reduction in staff at either company. Employment had risen due to output expansion and the continuation of non-automated tasks. ACP's local R&D laboratory was organised as a division of AT&T Bell Laboratories. It provided design support to ACP and to OEM suppliers in the region. The local laboratory was responsible for introducing new products, including a recently designed top-of-the-range cordless telephone.

ACP was linked to several local OEMs and sub-contractors.[34] OEM arrangements enabled ACP to increase capacity rapidly in response to market changes. Under OEM arrangements, ACP imposed strict quality and delivery controls upon its suppliers, including computerised 'just-in-time' systems. OEM arrangements required a close business and technological relationship between the partner firms. Suppliers were linked to ACP by computer so that purchasing and other business information could be relayed quickly. ACP provided ongoing engineering support to its OEMs. In this case OEM agreements acted as a training ground for local firms to learn advanced manufacturing techniques and modern business practices.

Both firms carried out in-house training programmes and had formed educational links within the country. As of 1992, ACP ran around 70 in-house programmes for basic training, the upgrading of skills and quality control. The company contributed towards scholarships at the National University of Singapore, Nanyang Technological University and other organisations. Like Philips, it was involved in the government's Local Industry Upgrading Programme, working to assist local suppliers improve their production systems, product quality and management efficiency. Philips' first educational links began in 1971 with a four year craft apprenticeship programme organised in conjunction with the Ministry of Education. Its purpose was to increase the supply of craftsmen and technicians for Philips. In 1975 the EDB-Philips Government Training Centre was established for precision engineering training.

Implications for learning and leapfrogging

In contrast with the idea of leapfrogging, the case of Philips shows how skill requirements began with craft and engineering. As a late entrant ACP began production at a more advanced engineering level. Both examples point to the importance of precision engineering to production and product design in modern consumer electronics.

As an early entrant, Philips learned by upgrading its activities over 30 years or so. The firm incrementally accumulated technology, beginning with craft and technical skills and, later, process engineering, precision engineering and product design. As it expanded, Philips subsidiaries learned to provide increased technical back-up, engineering support, design services and computerisation of production. Although Philips lagged behind the research frontier set by its parent, it had narrowed the manufacturing and design gap.

The case of ACP (like the HDD examples) shows how a late entrant was quickly able to exploit Singapore's infrastructure, producing high value-added goods, requiring sophisticated product design and process engineering capabilities. The ACP plants were among AT&T's most advanced world-wide. While early investors like Philips took three decades to reach this stage, ACP took less than five years. This reflected the advanced capacity of the physical and human resource infrastructure built up over the past decades.

Professional electronics: an example of a local entrant

Origin and expansion

In 1992, the Wearnes Hollingsworth (WH) Group was the largest locally owned manufacturer of personal computers, peripherals and components. WH was originally an Australian owned distributor of British cars. In the 1930s a majority share (33 per cent) of the company was purchased by the Overseas Chinese Banking Corporation. The company began making connectors for electronics systems some 30 years ago. High precision stamping, plastic injection moulding and plating began in the mid-1970s. WH's entry into the personal computer market began in 1983. Computer sales expanded rapidly during the 1980s within a subsidiary company Wearnes Automation, established in 1983. The Group also entered Winchester disk drives, floppy disk drives, add-on cards and a range of electromechanical components such as connectors.

The Group expanded and gained technological know-how by acquiring several small companies in the US, including a 40 per cent share of Advanced Logic Research and two other chip design firms. It acquired United Circuits (Hong Kong) in 1989 (a maker of printed circuit boards) and a chip packaging firm OMEDATA (in Indonesia) in 1986. Previously, OMEDATA carried out chip packaging for National Semiconductor of the US. Some of the acquisitions proved difficult and costly. Most firms were purchased with a view to acquiring US technology to further expand WH's computer business.

To organise and advise on the move into electronics, a director was hired from a relatively small Singaporean electronics venture, previously engaged in printed circuit board manufacture. This individual advised on the expansion into the PC business and by 1992 had become a senior member of the Board.

The firm built up its range of personal computers and related products, largely based on its competences in high precision electromechanical technologies. As of 1992, WH's main technological strengths were in connector manufacture, stamping, chip packaging, plastic moulding and electroplating. The company acquired chip design capabilities through its US acquisitions. Around 6 per cent of its semiconductor sales was invested in R&D. Most R&D was applied work, oriented towards production. Engineers up to MSc level were recruited for most divisions. In general, MBA's were not recruited unless they also held engineering degrees.

Up until the early 1990s the firm operated as a follower in the market, moving into areas with established channels of distribution, acquiring technology as and when necessary. In the past two years a new division (Wearnes Computer Systems) set up more than 50 service centres in Pacific-Asia and Europe to stock Wearnes computers and provide after-sales support. A total of 200 such centres were planned in Europe, the US and elsewhere. This event marked a new phase of internationalisation and confidence.

Learning through OEM

Company sales grew rapidly during the 1980s, especially personal computer sales. The computer subsidiary built up a reputation as a high quality, fast delivery OEM manufacturer of computer systems, printed circuit boards and components. Senior managers were hired in from TNC subsidiaries in Singapore as and when necessary. Engineers and technicians were recruited from local universities and polytechnics.

Under OEM deals, the TNCs provided WH with technical specifications for given products. Once manufactured, the TNC buyers sold the products under their own brand names. From the point of view of WH, the arrangement yielded several advantages including increased output, economies of scale in production and in the purchase of materials and key inputs (for example, microprocessors), and provided a justification for investments in automation technology. The latter led to improved productivity and output quality. Under OEM the firm learned the rigours of high quality, fast turn-around production.

Gradually, the firm developed its own in-house designs and brand name, progressing beyond OEM. Nevertheless the firm continued with OEM, despite its in-house competences. For instance, in 1992, the firm agreed to a large OEM arrangement with IBM, the US computer maker. According to WH, the arrangement offered market prestige and advantages of scale. This indicates that learning of advanced competences does not necessarily displace ones learned earlier. In this case, in-house design skills tended to augment OEM competences, rather than displace them. Capabilities were not accumulated in a linear fashion. Rather, the firm acquired a set of competences which could be deployed as and when necessary to maximise competitive advantage, according to the company strategy.

Implications for learning and leapfrogging

As with other examples, WH's accumulation of technology was a gradual process, rather than a radical jump. Also in contrast with leapfrogging, the company built its strength upon its precision and mechanical engineering skills, rather than information technology skills. WH progressed from low-cost, subcontract assembly to OEM and then to in-house product design. During the company's progress, capabilities were learned with respect to technology, organisation, management and marketing. Recent US acquisitions enabled the company to obtain advanced semiconductor technology needed for the design of personal computers. On the marketing side, the company had began to establish its own brand name, setting up international sales offices for distribution and computer services.

CONCLUSION

Analysis of Singapore's electronics industry indicates that firms engaged in a painstaking and cumulative process of technological learning, rather than a leapfrog from one vintage of technology to another. Contrary to the leapfrogging hypothesis, much of the learning occurred in 'pre-electronic' areas such as mechanical, electromechanical and precision engineering. Competences tended to build upon each other incrementally. Indeed, the historical evidence testifies to the importance of gradual technological accumulation to the growth of Singapore's electronics industry. Also in contrast with the idea of leapfrogging, firms generally entered the electronics industry at the mature, well-established phase of the product life-cycle, rather than at the early stage.

As far as industrial development is concerned the evidence from Singapore suggests that technology paradigms are closely connected. Singapore's progress in electronics required the development of capabilities in plastics, mouldings, machinery, assembly and electromechanical interfacing. Such capabilities are common to earlier vintages of technology. Furthermore, the products themselves embodied a combination of inputs, many of which were pre-electronic. Some of the products (for example, disk drives) were based largely on electromagnetic, precision engineering inputs. As a DC, Singapore's route towards information technology was by systematically building up competences in basic industrial technologies, rather than by leapfrogging.[35]

For other DCs, the evidence from Singapore suggests a complex evolutionary process of cumulative learning, rather than a simplistic leap from one technological paradigm to another. Even at today's advanced stage, Singapore's progress is centred upon low-cost, high-quality production engineering, rather than information-based software skills or R&D. Although the latter are increasingly a target of Singapore's technology policy, they are not yet the basis of the industry's success. Indeed, Singapore's capacity in science and advanced technology remains conspicuously weak in relation to leading OECD countries (and other Asian newly industrialising countries).

The case studies suggest that, given the appropriate conditions, TNCs can be persuaded to transfer substantial amounts of technology to their subsidiaries. In the Singapore case the TNCs trained local employees and formed educational links within the country. This occurred partly due to the improving infrastructure put in place by the government. It also occurred in response to an expanding Pacific-Asian market and changing factor costs. For Singapore, the TNCs provided a direct channel into overseas markets as well as a 'training school' for technological learning on the part of local engineers and managers, and some domestic firms.

Corporate learning is difficult to accurately measure. However, a variety of learning mechanisms were evident in Singapore. The early entrants learned by assembling and testing. Local technicians learned from foreign engineers and managers, and from in-house training and promotion. Firms learned by upgrading production processes and eventually by designing new products. Early entrants (for example, Philips in consumer goods) tended to graduate from simple to advanced learning over a period of decades. Late entrants (for example, Seagate in disk drives) very quickly advanced to innovative learning in areas such as precision engineering and electro-mechanical interfacing. Late entrants benefited from the modernised infrastructure, the experience of others and government education policies. Learning extended beyond product and process technology to management, organisation and marketing. Leading firms learned to market directly to their Pacific-Asian customers as the regional market for electronics grew. The TNC subsidiaries became more technologically advanced as time progressed. Gradually, they narrowed the technology gap between themselves and their parent plants abroad.

Learning by imitation took place once leading firms (for example, Philips in consumer goods, TI in semiconductors and Seagate in disk drives) had demonstrated the advantages of local production. Competitors quickly followed, as did overseas input suppliers. A few local firms learned under OEM arrangements, becoming medium-sized producers of electronics under their own brand names. Learning by OEM was a 'training school' by which some firms entered the industry, secured a market channel and acquired technology.[36]

Government learning also progressed through time. The government attracted the TNCs to Singapore and encouraged them to expand their electronics activities. The supply of human resources, and the transportation and telecommunications infrastructures were improved over time. Infrastructural provision was not a 'once-and-for-all' activity. On the contrary, it evolved according to the needs of the economy.

Although it is not possible to generalise from a single case study, at least three broad considerations follow for DCs wishing to develop an electronics industry. First, the Singapore case suggests that electronics development requires firms to engage in a hard slog of cumulative competence building across a range of engineering and basic industrial skills. Software and computer-based skills alone are unlikely to prove sufficient in many sub-sectors of the electronics industry. Second, governments should adapt educational policies to meet the changing needs of industry. In particular, policies should seek to ensure a sufficient supply of technicians and graduate engineers in craft, mechanical and electro-mechanical disciplines as well as electronics. Third, continuous improvements to the infrastructure are probably essential to sustained technological progress in the corporate sector. In contrast with leapfrogging, the route to electronics in DCs is likely to be a gradual, painstaking path of technological learning.

ACKNOWLEDGMENTS

Mike Hobday, Science Policy Research Unit, University of Sussex, UK. This article is based on research funded by the Economic and Social Research Council (ESRC) of the UK, grant reference R000 23 3116. The author is grateful to Martin Bell and an anonymous referee for detailed comments on a first draft. Any remaining mistakes are the author's.

NOTES

1 Soete [1985] first put forward the leapfrogging view. Since then it has become common parlance in policy making circles, despite the lack of empirical evidence for the claim. Perez and Soete [1988] argue that 'windows of opportunity' arise at the early stages of the diffusion of a new paradigm. See Perez [1985] for the pioneering institutional work on 'techno-economic paradigms'. The latter study explores the complex relationship between the techno-economic sphere and the socio-institutional framework within which new paradigms diffuse. Dosi [1982] provides an introduction to the semiconductor technology paradigm. Pavitt [1984] was the first to criticise the leapfrogging view, arguing that the diffusion of semiconductor technology was a complex, gradual process with the new technology building on the old: a process of 'creative accumulation'. Unlike the present article, Pavitt's data were based on an industrialised country (the UK). The terms information technology, semiconductor, microelectronics or electronics paradigm tend to be used interchangeably in the literature. The new paradigm consists of industries based primarily on semiconductor and software technologies (including the computer, telecommunication, semiconductor, software and consumer electronic industries). It also includes the application of information technology to 'conventional' industries such as automobiles and aerospace.

2 See Hobday [1990] for the case of Brazil. Antonelli [1991] provides international evidence on the relatively fast diffusion of advanced telecommunications in DCs. Given the transition in technology and the advantages of modern systems, DCs have little choice but to leapfrog earlier generations of electro-mechanical telecommunications.

3 Archambault looks at the case of the semiconductor industry in the Republic of Korea. He argues that, contrary to the view of Perez and Soete [1988], Korean

firms entered into the industry at the mature, not the early stage of the product life cycle.

4 See, for example. Sisodia [1992], National Computer Board [1992], Gilbert [1990] and Davies [1988]. The role of information technology in banking and insurance is discussed by Onn [1991].

5 Of course, one cannot generalise from a single case study. The results of the study are therefore indicative rather than conclusive. However, Singapore is one DC where leapfrogging might be expected to occur. It lacked an extensive industrial base in the 1960s. It rapidly developed an absorptive capacity for electronics through educational and infrastructural investments. It was also able to access technology through foreign firms. If leapfrogging did not occur in Singapore, it is unlikely to occur in less well-endowed DCs.

6 I thank an anonymous referee for coining the term 'hard slog', which accurately describes the process of technology accumulation in electronics in Singapore.

7 Similarly, other writers refer to an 'entrepreneurial' or 'corporate' state [Sisoda, 1992; Yuan and Low, 1990 respectively].

8 EDB [1992: 10]. Figures are in current prices (the Singapore-dollar exchange rate in 1991 was US$1 = S$1.73.

9 See section 17.III below. For an historical discussion of incentives and their effect, see Yue [1985].

10 Singapore Investment News [1991: 10].

11 EDB [1992a: 15].

12 Normally, TNCs would carry out such work in their domestic headquarters. The Institute's other main aim is to supply skilled researchers for semiconductor firms (Interview with Institute for Microelectronics, 1992).

13 NSTB [1991: 13]. Research scientists and engineers are defined as those with a bachelor's degree or above.

14 NSTB [1991: 17].

15 Information from the British High Commission. Singapore.

16 EDB [1992a: 2].

17 EDB [1992a: 21].

18 EDB [1992b: 2].

19 EDB [1992b: 1].

20 The importance of industrial clustering to economic development is discussed by Porter [1990: 149].

21 Under sub-contracting a product, sub-assembly or component is supplied to the TNC by a local firm. Under OEM the local firm manufactures a complete product to the buyer's specification. The product is then sold bearing the buyer's brand name. With most TNCs, OEM necessitates close technological cooperation with the local supplier, stringent quality control and some technology transfer (see the AT&T and Wearnes case studies below). In practice, the two categories often overlap. Some local firms have moved on from OEM to own design and manufacture (ODM), where most or all of the design task is carried out by the local manufacturer in-house but the product is sold under the brand name of the purchaser.

22 IEEE [1991: 27]. The progress of two of the largest local firms (Wearnes and Chartered) is discussed below.

23 The study sample cannot be said to be fully representative. Some companies not in the sample declined to participate. Some who took part were willing to furnish more details than others.

24 TECH and Chartered were very recently established, both with close government involvement (see below).

25 This partly explains the observed increase in employment as automation proceeded. The continuing expansion of plant output also contributed to employment expansion.
26 *Far Eastern Economic Review*, 17 Sept. 1992, p.62.
27 *Electronics Times*, 27 Feb. 1992, p.40.
28 *Electronic Business Asia*, Feb. 1991, pp.36–7.
29 *Electronics Times*, 19 Nov. 1987, p.48.
30 *Electronic Business Asia*, Feb. 1991, p.36.
31 Dahlman *et al.* [1985] explain the distinctions between production, investment and innovation capabilities. Lall [1982] discusses the passage from elementary to intermediate to advanced learning. He also shows how non-technological learning is important to organisational development (for example, marketing and managerial skills). Lundvall (ed.) [1992] contains a collection of studies which show how learning is intimately linked to the institutional framework within which it occurs.
32 Of course, this evidence is not conclusive. Others firms in other DCs may follow different routes. Other electronics sub-sectors may exhibit less 'paradigm overlap'.
33 *Singapore Electronics Manufacturers Directory 1992*, p.76.
34 See note 21 for a definition of OEM.
35 This is consistent with Pavitt's [1984] findings for the UK. There may be significant differences between DCs and advanced economies regarding the accumulation of electronics technology. DCs may differ from developed in terms of factor costs, domestic demand, R&D capacity, advanced local users, sources of innovation and other factors. Such differences, however, are unlikely to be explained by the notion of leapfrogging.
36 Learning by OEM is more important for firms in Taiwan, Hong Kong and the Republic of Korea, as electronics development in these countries is largely based on locally-owned companies. For these countries, OEM provides access to export markets as well as a supply of technology [IEEE. 1991].

REFERENCES

Antonelli. C., 1991, *The Diffusion of Advanced Telecommunications in Developing Countries.* Paris: OECD.

Archambault. E., 1992, 'Incremental or Radical Change in Semiconductors? Some Evidence from South Korea', unpublished mimeo, Science Policy Research Unit, University of Sussex, England.

Dahlman. C.J., Ross-Larson, B. and L.E. Westphal, 1985, *Managing Technological Development: Lessons from the Newly Industrialising Countries*, Washington, DC: World Bank.

Davies, J., 1988, 'The Singapore Vision: An Information-Based Economy', *Journal of Information Science Principles and Practice* (Netherlands) Vol.14, No.4, pp.237–42.

Dodgson, M., 1991, 'Technological Collaboration and Organisational Learning', DRC Discussion Paper, First Draft, SPRU, University of Sussex, England.

Dosi, G., 1992, 'Technological Paradigms and Technological Trajectories: A Suggested Interpretation of the Determinants of Technical Change', *Research Policy*, Vol.11, No.3, June, pp.147–62.

EDB, 1991, *Economic Development Board Year-book 1990/91*, Economic Development Board, Singapore.

——, 1992a, *The Economic Development of Singapore, 1960 to 1990*, Economic Development Board, Singapore.
——, 1992b, *The Electronics Industry in Singapore*, Economic Development Board, Singapore.
——, 1992c, *The Disk Drive Industry in Singapore*, Special Report, Economic Development Board, Singapore.
Electronic Business Asia, various issues.
Electronics Times, various issues.
Far Eastern Economic Review, 17 Sept. 1992.
Fransman, M. and K. King, (eds.), 1984, *Technological Capability in the Third World*, London: Macmillan.
Gilbert, A.L., 1990, 'Information Technology Transfer: the Singapore Strategy'. in M. Chatterji (ed.), *Technology Transfer in the Developing Countries*, London: Macmillan.
Hobday, M.G., 1990, *Telecommunications in Developing Countries: the Challenge from Brazil*, London: Routledge.
IEEE, 1991, *IEEE Spectrum*, 'Special Report: AsiaPower', June, pp.24–66.
Koh, A.T., 1987, 'Saving, Investment and Entrepreneurship', in L.B. Krause, A.T. Koh and T.Y. Lee, *The Singapore Economy Reconsidered*, Singapore: Institute for Southeast Asian Studies.
Lall, S., 1982, *Developing Countries as Exporters of Technology*, London: Macmillan Press.
Lundvall, B.A. (ed.), 1992, *National Systems of Innovation: Towards a Theory of Innovation and Interactive Learning*, London: Pinter Publishers.
Malerba, F., 1992, 'Learning by Firms and Incremental Technical Change', *The Economic Journal*, Vol.102, July, pp.845–59.
National Computer Board,. 1992, *A Vision of an Intelligent Island*, Singapore: National Computer Board.
NSTB, 1991, *Science and Technology: Windows of Opportunity*, Singapore: National Technology Plan, National Science and Technology Board.
Onn, F.C., 1991, 'Impact of New Information Technology in the Banking and Insurance Industries in Malaysia and Singapore', World Employment Programme, Working Paper, International Labour Office, Geneva.
Pavitt, K., 1984, 'Chips and Trajectories: How Does the Semiconductor Influence the Sources and Directions of Technical Change?' mimeo, Science Policy Research Unit, University of Sussex.
Perez, C., 1985, 'Microelectronics, Long Waves and World Structural Change: New Perspectives for Developing Countries', *World Development*, Vol.13, No.3, pp.441–63.
—— and L. Soete, 1988, 'Catching up in Technology: Entry Barriers and Windows of Opportunity', in G. Dosi *et al.* (eds.), *Technical Change and Economic Theory*, London: Pinter.
Porter, M., 1990, *The Competitive Advantage of Nations*, London: Macmillan.
Schumpeter, J.A., 1950, *Capitalism, Socialism, and Democracy*, 3rd edn., New York: Harper & Row.
Singapore Electronics Manufacturers Directory 1992.
Singapore Investment News, 1991, Precision Engineering Supplement, Economic Development Board, Singapore.
Singapore Investment News, 1992, Economic Development Board, Singapore, February Issue.
Singapore Times, 7 Oct. 1991.
Sisodia, R.S., 1992, 'Singapore Invests in the Nation Corporation', *Harvard Business Review*, May–June, pp.40–50.

Soete, L., 1985, 'International Diffusion of Technology, Industrial Development and Technological Leapfrogging', *World Development*, Special Issue on Microelectronics, Vol.13, No.3, pp.409–23.

Vogel, E.F., 1991, *The Four Little Dragons: the Spread of Industrialisation in East Asia*, Cambridge, MA: Harvard University Press.

Yuan, L.T. and L. Low, 1990, *Local Entrepreneurship in Singapore, Private and State*, Singapore: Times Academic Press for Institute of Policy Studies.

Yue, C.S., 1985, 'The Role of Foreign Trade and Investment in the Development of Singapore', in W. Galenson, (ed.), *Foreign Trade and Investment: Economic Development in the Newly Industrialising Asian Countries*, WI: University of Wisconsin Press.

Part V

HUMAN RESOURCE DEVELOPMENT AND CHANGING LABOUR MARKETS

18

EDUCATION AND ECONOMIC GROWTH IN TAIWAN

A Case of Successful Planning

Jenni Hay Woo

18.1 INTRODUCTION

Much has been written extolling investment in education as the key to successful economic growth. "Human resources . . . constitute the ultimate basis for the wealth of nations."[1] From this derived the science (or art) of educational planning wherein the limited resources of a country are marshalled to develop most effectively its human resources. Educational planning is now under siege. Education literature is filled with critical reevaluations and dissections of planning disasters.[2] There is a general consensus that much educational planning has been tried in many countries but little has been successful. There are many analyses of why various models and methods have failed and why economies have performed dismally. Much rarer have been analyses of instances where an economy has flourished and what role education and educational planning may have played. Could labor forecasting have led to useful allocations of resources in some cases?

This paper will examine the case of Taiwan. By all the usual economic measures, Taiwan has had extraordinarily successful economic growth in the past 35 years. Moreover, the wealth which was created has been distributed fairly equally. This economic success has been attributed to Taiwan's emphasis on labor-intensive export industries, its attention to land reform and agricultural productivity, the spread of decentralized rural industry, and the small average firm size. While these factors are of great significance, it is argued here that education has also been instrumental in Taiwan's successful economic growth. Taiwan's economic success was based upon a literate work force. It is worth examining what made education in Taiwan different from education in similar developing countries, how educational development contributed to Taiwan's economic success, and what role educational planning might have played.

Taiwan's labor resources had some unique preconditions which gave

Source: *World Development*, Vol. 19 (8), 1991, pp. 1029–44.

Taiwan advantages over other resource-poor countries at the same stage of development. The Japanese left a good educational infrastructure and in 1949 there was an influx of skilled managers, technicians and entrepreneurs from the Mainland. Most important, Taiwan had a development plan which carefully channeled labor through education and training programs to meet the country's changing personnel needs. This planning was crucial in allowing Taiwan to both develop its human resources in an appropriate and timely fashion and to industrialize quickly and successfully.

Section 18.2 of this paper outlines the initial conditions that gave Taiwan an educational advantage over similar Asian countries. Section 18.3 is an analysis of Taiwan's educational planning from 1950 onwards. It describes the school system, gives a history of its growth and analyzes the efforts made to link the growth of education to the needs of the economy. Section 18.4 examines education's contribution to macroeconomic growth in Taiwan and Section 18.5 gives conclusions.

18.2 THE PRECONDITIONS

(a) Infrastructure left by the Japanese

The Japanese colonists established an education system that was limited in size, but comprehensive and modern. The Japanese wanted to replace traditional, rote-method Chinese schools with a progressive, scientific education that would supply literate clerks and officials for their colonial administration. They left Taiwan in 1945 with one of the most literate populations in Asia. The literacy rate among Taiwanese, measured by the ability to read or write Japanese, went from 1% in 1905 to 12% in 1930, to 27% in 1940. The Japanese built a network of common schools beginning in 1898 that eventually encompassed most Taiwanese children. The primary enrollment rate for ages 6–14 was 37% in 1930–31 and by 1943–44 it was 71%.[3] By 1950, Taiwan had 1,231 elementary schools, 77 vocational schools, six colleges or junior colleges and one university.[4] It had over one million students attending school at elementary level or above, making a student to population ratio of 140.

The Japanese, however, severely limited the supply of postelementary education. In the beginning, it was available only for the Taiwanese elite. The number of places expanded slowly, particularly at the senior secondary or higher levels. In 1915 the first Taiwanese middle school was founded and by 1939 there were only nine middle schools that enrolled significant numbers of Taiwanese. Until 1915, the only opportunities for higher education for Taiwanese were in a normal school (teachers' college) or a medical school. Together, these two institutions enrolled only a few hundred students. The Japanese adamantly opposed encouraging the expansion of higher education for the Taiwanese because they feared the creation of an educated unemployed population and of political opposition.

One innovative goal of Japanese education was to popularize education for Taiwanese girls. This was in part to extend the reach of Japanization, but it did have the effect of extending opportunities to Taiwanese women. In 1920 less than 10% of the female Taiwanese elementary school-aged population attended school, as compared to 39% for males. By 1944, 60.7% of girls were attending school and 80.7% of boys.[5]

The gross enrollment ratio (the ratio of school enrollment to the population of school age) in 1950 was 80% for the first level, a very high figure for a country just emerging from wartime destruction. This put Taiwan far ahead of Mainland China and most of Asia in the proportion of its population receiving some education. In 1950, Malaysia's enrollment ratio was 39% and Indonesia's was 45%. Hong Kong had a ratio of 61% in 1955. Taiwan also already had a major university, founded in 1928 for the Japanese colonists. Taihoku National University became National Taiwan University in 1947 when the Nationalist Chinese government regained sovereignty over Taiwan.

(b) Influx of Mainlanders

The Japanese held all the management and entrepreneurial posts in colonial Taiwan. The Japanese abruptly left Taiwan in 1945 with the end of the war. In the late 1940s, when it became apparent that the Nationalists would not hold the Mainland, a large number of refugees escaped to Taiwan. During 1946–50, Taiwan received more than 1.5 million refugees from Mainland China, increasing the population by 25%.[6] Among the refugees were administrators, technicians, and doctors—many of China's elite educated class. They were able to fill the places which the Japanese had left. Unlike the Japanese, however, they were part of the same broader culture as the local Taiwanese and would rebuild the economy as an integral unit, rather than as an appendage to the Japanese economic system. Consequently, during the initial stages of industrialization Taiwan did not lack administrative personnel, as is often the case in developing countries.

18.3 EDUCATION PLANNING

(a) Brief description of the school system

Taiwan's education system has three levels—primary, secondary and higher. The primary level is for children 6–12 years old. The secondary level is made up of three years of junior high school and three years of senior high school or senior vocational school. The first nine years of school, six years of primary school and three years of junior high, are tuition-free and compulsory. All students who wish to continue schooling must sit for an exam after junior high school. This exam determines whether they enter a senior high school (which tends to be university track), a senior vocational school or a five-year junior college (both usually vocational track). After senior high school or senior vocational school there is a unified university entrance exam and a two- or three-year junior college entrance exam.

The vocational track is very large in Taiwan. Currently, about 45% of Taiwan's higher education students attend a university (all degree levels) and 55% are in junior colleges. The proportion of students who reach higher education is fairly large. In 1986, about 75% of junior high graduates went on to senior high, senior vocational or five-year junior colleges. About 82% of senior high graduates (including previous years) went on to a university, college or junior college. There are, however, some major quality distinctions.

At the senior high and senior vocational school level and above there are many private schools, about half of the total. In higher education, especially junior college, more students are enrolled in private than public schools. In 1986–87 there were 53,536 public junior college students and 190,946 private students. Private schools are managed independently but they are strictly regulated by the government. The government dictates not only enrollments, curricula, and degree requirements, but also the fees private schools are allowed to charge. Private schools, in turn, receive government funds but not as much per capita as public schools. They must charge higher fees to make up the difference. Private universities and colleges, which enroll 60% of students in higher education, get only 26.4% of the higher education budget.[7] (See Table 18.1.)

(b) Brief history

The principal change in Taiwan's education system since 1950 has been its phenomenal growth. Taiwan achieved universal primary enrollment (98%) in

Table 18.1 Total educational budget for public and private schools by level FY1985–86 and percentage private enrollment (unit: NT$1,000)

	Total	*Public*	*Private*	*Private budget as a percentage of total for that level*	*Private students as percentage of total for that level*
Elementary schools	31,004,799	30,616,558	388,241	1.3%	1.1%
Junior high schools	21,695,522	21,529,198	166,324	0.8%	4.2%
Senior high schools	9,468,731	5,695,499	3,773,232	39.8%	24.3%
Senior vocational schools	12,073,361	7,132,949	4,940,412	40.9%	60.5%
Junior colleges	10,932,201	4,662,550	6,269,651	57.4%	76.5%
Universities and colleges	18,727,605	13,786,686	4,940,919	26.4%	59.8%
Total	103,902,219	83,423,440	20,478,779	19.7%	15.1%

Source: Ministry of Education (1987), p. 43.

about 1970. Secondary level enrollment reached 80% in 1980. Tertiary level enrollment rates increased steadily to 14% for men and 12% for women in 1985, with the gap between male and female rates gradually diminishing. In 1968, junior high school became free and compulsory schooling was extended through junior high to make nine years of formal education. Thus enrollment in junior high schools jumped in the 1968–69 academic year and continued to climb rapidly. The average annual increase for the decade 1960–69 was 12.7%. (See Table 18.2.) In 1965, the five-year junior college was introduced. That level began to expand very rapidly, especially after 1968, when it absorbed many of the new junior high graduates. The junior college rate of average annual increase for 1960–69 was almost 34%.

In general, the percentage increases were quite high in the early years, since the base was so low, and high in absolute numbers in the 1960–69 decade. In 1972 there was a peak in primary school student enrollment, after which the numbers began to decline. This occurred because universal enrollment had been reached and the birth rate was declining. The birth rate rose in 1976 and caused another rise in the 5–9 year old population and in primary enrollments around 1982.

From 1966 onward, educational expansion in Taiwan has been guided very explicitly by a Manpower Development Plan (MDP). The first plan was developed by a team from the Council for International Economic Cooperation and Development (CIECD), now the CEPD (Council for Economic Planning and Development). They were assisted by experts from the International Labor Office and the US Department of Labor. They developed the plan from economic projections of growth by industrial sector and then derived projections of occupational requirements for various education levels. They had specific targets for employment levels (usually keeping unemployment at 3% or 4%) and for reducing the share of employment in agriculture and increasing it in industry and services. To do this, the plans set enrollment distributions between senior high schools, senior vocational schools, and junior colleges, and between various departments in universities and colleges. Eventually the plans set enrollment quotas. They also established an index for total expenditure on education as a proportion of GNP. From this, the Department of Education would set fees and enrollment levels for the specific schools, both public and private, at all levels.

The first MDP was promulgated in October 1966 and the subsequent plans were formulated roughly every three or four years after that.[8] An important feature of these plans was that they were actually implemented. The planning process mobilized the various sectors of the government into discussion and negotiation about key issues. But unlike many government plans, once they were agreed upon these plans were then implemented according to a strict timetable with deadlines. Specific agencies were made responsible and other agencies were required to oversee them.[9] In fact, as explained below, the enrollment and budget statistics indicate that most plan targets were met.

Table 18.2 Enrollments and average annual increase in enrollment, 1950–86 (number of students)

Academic year	*Total*	*Primary*	*Junior high (& jr voc & normal before 1973)*	*Senior high*	*Senior voc (and normal 1973 and after)*	*Jr college*	*College & univ and above*	
1950	1,033,651	906,950	89,944	18,866	11,226	1,286	5,379	
1955	1,475,624	1,244,029	162,235	30,169	21,186	4,545	13,460	
1960	2,279,117	1,888,783	253,145	57,152	44,617	7,888	27,172	
1965	3,006,828	2,257,720	473,442	116,197	74,114	29,543	55,812	
1968	3,465,707	2,383,204	652,083	152,877	116,206	79,456	81,881	
1969	3,641,008	2,428,041	729,651	161,459	137,642	95,988	88,227	
1970	3,803,467	2,445,405	800,402	178,537	175,650	108,328	95,145	
1972	4,034,054	2,459,743	909,197	197,151	216,905	138,310	112,748	
1975	4,160,389	2,364,961	1,036,357	185,181	284,455	150,226	139,209	
1980	4,181,801	2,233,706	1,075,532	180,665	349,370	183,134	159,394	
1982	4,266,038	2,226,699	1,082,358	187,015	394,270	203,722	171,971	
1985	4,429,043	2,321,700	1,062,226	194,757	421,784	236,824	191,752	
1986	4,498,602	2,364,438	1,052,993	200,599	437,924	244,482	198,166	
Average annual increase								*5–9 year old population*
1953–59	9.1%	8.5%	11.5%	14.7%	16.2%	9.2%	20.4%	8.5%
1960–69	5.5%	3.2%	12.7%	11.6%	13.1%	33.9%	13.9%	1.8%
1970–79	1.4%	–0.7%	4.1%	1.3%	9.3%	6.3%	5.8%	1.0%
1980–86	1.1%	0.7%	–0.4%	1.5%	4.2%	4.9%	3.6%	1.4%
1953–86	4.1%	2.6%	7.2%	7.1%	10.8%	14.7%	10.7%	2.3%

Source: Ministry of Education (1987), p. 18 and Council for Economic Planning and Development (1987), pp. 9–29.

(c) The shift to vocational education

The most important result of the first MDP was the shift in emphasis from general to vocational education (see Table 18.3). In 1963, 40% of high school students were in vocational schools (more than half of those were business schools) and 60% were in senior high schools, studying a more general curriculum. The first MDP set a target of 60% vocational and 40% senior high enrollment. This emphasis was continued in subsequent MDPs. In 1972 the actual ratio was 52 : 48 (vocational to senior high) and by 1980 it was 66 : 34, close to the fifth MDP's target of 70 : 30. This policy was designed specifically to meet the greater economic demand for semiskilled labor. It was a deliberate and carefully planned effort to match educational output with economic need.

The design and management of vocational education in Taiwan appears to have been very successful.[10] As in other aspects of the Taiwanese economy, there was close cooperation between the government and the business sector. In general, the government confined its role to fostering an environment conducive to the supply of training by firms, and let industry choose or influence the form and type of this training. There was little government-mandated training. In 1972, a National Vocational Training Fund was set up, based on a 1.5% payroll tax of employers with over 40 staff members. Almost half the money went to private enterprises for approved training programs in cooperation with vocational schools. But the fund was suspended in 1974 because of an economic downturn, and not reinstituted until 1983 by the new Employment and Vocational Training Administration.[11] Instead, the government focuses on more basic vocational training within the formal school system. Employers worked closely with the government on planning the vocational schools. Vocational education was emphasized in preparation for

Table 18.3 Enrollment ratios between academic and vocational stream at senior high level 1950–86

Year	*Senior high total enrollment*	*Academic enrollment*	*Vocational enrollment*	*Vocational enrollment as a % of total senior high enrollment*
1950	30,092	18,866	11,226	37.3%
1955	51,355	30,169	21,186	41.3%
1960	102,129	57,512	44,617	43.7%
1963	137,314	82,893	54,421	39.6%
1965	190,311	116,197	74,114	38.9%
1970	354,187	178,537	175,650	49.6%
1972	414,056	197,151	216,905	52.4%
1975	469,636	185,181	284,455	60.6%
1980	530,035	180,665	349,370	65.9%
1986	638,523	200,599	437,924	68.6%

Source: Ministry of Education (1987), p. 18.

the implementation of 10 major construction projects in 1973 and their anticipated large demand for labor.

There are no specific studies of the jobs which vocational school graduates eventually took but the indications are that they were successfully trained. In 1985 they comprised 17% of the total labor force. In that year, 48% of all senior vocational school graduates in the labor force were employed in business and commerce, 38% in engineering, 8% in agriculture and the remaining 6% in various other fields such as health science, the armed forces, or the police. The unemployment rate for senior vocational school graduates was extremely low, averaging 4.0% during 1967–80.[12]

The success of the vocational schools can also be seen in the rate-of-return studies which were conducted for the period. In 1972, Gannicott calculated private rates of return for males in senior high over junior high and senior vocational over junior high and found them to be comparable, 12.7 and 13.2 percentage points respectively.[13] Rates for women, in the same report, are similar—14.5 and 13.5. Other rates calculated by the Ministry of Education and collected by Chang, show the private rates of return for vocational school over junior high to be the same or higher than for senior high school for 1974 and 1976.[14] This evidence shows that vocational education is good enough that its graduates find jobs with significant earnings. It means that the government's emphasis on vocational training has paid off. The success is all the more impressive because this effort ran counter to social demands for university education.[15]

(d) Countering the demand for higher education

Since the founding of the Republic of China, the demand for higher education has been very strong. This demand is reflected not only in the sacrifices children and their families will make for schooling, but also in the expense they are willing to incur to continue. Many students will spend several years in self-study, attempting to pass the high school or university exams, despite income foregone and the expense of tutors and books. Some of this drive can be attributed to cultural factors—the traditional Chinese respect for learning and scholarship. Much, however, can be attributed to economic reasons. Rate-of-return calculations for university over senior high have ranged from 11 to 16 percentage points. For any individual, it is rational to desire more education. While Gannicott found little difference in the rates of return between senior high school and senior vocational, the demand for senior high school would obviously have been much greater because it was the only route to university. Partly to relieve the pressure for more higher education opportunities, the government set up the National Institute of Technology in 1974. It recruited graduates from vocational high schools and junior colleges with two or more years of working experience and awarded its graduates with an advanced degree.

At the higher education level, the effect of this shift was to keep the number of students who entered university below what would have occurred if demand for higher education had been fully met. Since only senior high graduates had a realistic hope of passing the university exam (anyone was eligible to sit for it), the number of candidates was limited. In fact, from the fourth MDP (1972) the rate of increase of student enrollments in colleges and universities was stipulated not to exceed 5% a year. In the fifth MDP (1977) this rate was lowered to 3%. Table 18.2 shows that the college and university level increases were indeed kept at those levels. For 1970–79 the average annual increase was 5.8% and for 1980–86 it was 3.6%. Enrollment ratios in higher education have steadily increased (3.2–14.1% for men during 1956–85), but they probably have not come close to meeting demand. Although there is not a direct measure of demand for higher education, there are some fairly good proxies as shown in Table 18.4.

The crude entrance ratio is the number of students who enter all kinds of higher education (universities, colleges and three-year junior colleges) compared to the number of senior high graduates. It can be assumed that most senior high school graduates would want to continue to some form of higher education since the curriculum is oriented toward university and college entrance and the vocational students have been selected out. This ratio was 82% in 1986. Although the ratio is high, it has hardly changed since 1954 when it was 75%. But it masks several factors. First, many of those first-year students sat for the exam many times before succeeding. The ratio of applications to sit for entrance exams to the number of current high school graduates has remained about 1.68 to one for many years. There is thus a large group of "over-age" students in each year's entering class.[16] If these repeaters are removed, the net entrance ratio for 1986 falls to 48%. Only 48% of current-year graduates can expect to enter higher education the next year.

University entrance exams also have a lower pass rate than colleges or junior colleges. The entrance exam pass rate for the universities was 30% in 1986. This rate is lower than that of the expansionary 1960s when it was as high as 40%, and is thus far below student demand for university places, as measured by the number of applicants.

Besides limiting the number of entrants to the universities and shifting the focus to terminal vocational degrees, the MDPs called for a shift in the focus of university and college curricula. To meet economic growth requirements, emphasis was placed on engineering and natural sciences rather than on the humanities. The results, however, were rather modest. The percentage of students in engineering went from 30% in 1975 to 33% in 1986 and in natural sciences from 4.8% to 6.5% in those same years. The percentage in humanities was reduced from 10% in 1975 to 7% in 1986 and in fine arts from 3.5% to 2%.

This trend probably coincides with a change in market demand for graduates, since the average salaries for engineers and scientists were usually higher

Table 18.4 Acceptance ratio for higher education, 1954–86 (%)

Year	*Crude entrance ratio* *	*Net entrance ratio* †	*University exam-passing ratio* ‡
1954	75.17	—	20.27
1956	76.17	—	30.83
1958	66.22	—	35.09
1960	76.37	—	35.38
1962	72.74	—	38.48
1964	77.51	—	40.29
1966	68.11	—	38.54
1968	71.19	—	35.96
1970	71.93	41.92	34.60
1972	83.43	42.62	26.95
1974	73.41	39.68	26.83
1976	77.05	42.39	27.63
1978	74.27	40.42	28.30
1980	79.90	44.64	29.25
1982	81.00	44.03	31.22
1984	82.15	44.36	32.10
1986	82.26	48.19	30.66

Note:

* Crude entrance ratio =

$$\frac{\text{Number of 1st grade students in universities, colleges, \& 3-year junior colleges}}{\text{Number of senior high school graduates}} \times 100\%$$

† Net entrance ratio =

$$\frac{\text{Number of current-year graduates entering the 1st grade of universities, colleges, \& 3-year junior colleges}}{\text{Number of senior high chool graduates}} \times 100\%$$

‡ Exam-passing ratio =

$$\frac{\text{Number of students who passed entrance exams}}{\text{Number of applications to take exams}} \times 100\%$$

Source: Ministry of Education (1987), pp. 32, 34.

than for other graduates. A survey of 1,977 university graduates done in 1981 by the National Youth Commission found that there were differences in the average salaries of graduates when differentiated by field.[17] Thus medicine, engineering and oceanography graduates earned significantly more than arts or literature graduates. Engineering graduates earned on average NT$16,225 per month in 1981, while arts graduates earned on average NT$13,286 per month. Medicine, with the highest average earnings of NT$17,790 per month, has also seen a slight proportionate increase in enrollments, which the government has encouraged.

(c) The role of private schools in higher education expansion

Another policy development which resulted from labor planning was the decision to expand the role of private schools. This decision was perhaps the most crucial step in the expansion of the Taiwanese education system. As Table 18.5 shows, for the compulsory stage of education 95–98% of students were enrolled in public schools. There was a fairly large private sector of up to 18% of enrollment for junior high and junior vocational schools until 1968, when tuition-free and compulsory schooling was extended through junior high. Then the number of public junior high schools expanded greatly and the private sector dwindled to 4% of enrollment.

At senior high and senior vocational levels and above, the private sector has always been much larger than it is at lower levels. It has also grown through the years. In 1950 10% of students at the senior high level and above attended private schools. In 1986 that figure was almost 60%. For junior colleges, the private sector reached almost 80% of students. This private sector expansion has serious implications for the entire school system, particularly for financing.

Private schools, in general, receive fewer government funds than public schools and must make up the difference by charging higher tuition and fees. Table 18.6 summarizes all the funds that are spent on education, both public and private, from all sources, in the academic year 1985–86. Most students at the lower levels are in public schools, but for senior vocational and higher education more students are in private schools. The public expenditure per student is generally much greater for public schools. Adding public expenditure per student to private expenditure per student (consisting of average tuition and fees), gives the total expenditure per student for that year. This is an estimate of the unit costs for education.

At the junior college and university levels there is a dramatic difference in the unit costs between public and private schools. In 1981 the total annual unit cost—including tuition, fees and government subsidies—for public higher education was $83,200. For private higher education it was only $31,800.[18] This cost difference is reflected in sharp quality differences between public and private colleges and universities. Private schools have much higher student–teacher ratios. For example, the public university student–teacher ratio is 12:1. For private universities it is 29:1 (see Table 18.1). The quality gap is particularly apparent in the disciplines with higher unit costs such as the natural sciences and engineering which require labs and equipment. One indication of the lower quality of private schools is their graduates' poorer performance in the labor market. According to graduate surveys conducted by the National Youth Commission, private university and college graduates were twice as likely as public graduates to be unemployed and took longer to find employment.[19]

Aside from a difference in total resources available for private versus public

Table 18.5 Private enrollment in education by level, 1950–86

Academic year		*Total*	*Primary*	*Junior high (and jr voc and normal before 1973)*	*Senior high*	*Senior voc. (and normal 1973 and after)*	*Jr college*	*College & univ. and above*
1950	Total	1,033,651	906,950	89,944	18,866	11,226	1,286	5,379
	Private	11,560	0	7,823	2,502	861	374	0
	Percentage private	1.1%	0.0%	8.7%	13.3%	7.7%	29.1%	0.0%
1955	Total	1,475,624	1,244,029	162,235	30,169	21,186	4,545	13,460
	Private	23,886	0	14,050	4,624	2,765	992	1,455
	Percentage private	1.6%	0.0%	8.7%	15.3%	13.1%	21.8%	10.8%
1960	Total	2,279,117	1,888,783	235,145	57,512	44,617	7,888	27,172
	Private	97,750	36,386	31,050	10,289	10,564	2,854	6,607
	Percentage private	4.3%	1.9%	12.3%	17.9%	23.7%	36.2%	24.3%
1965	Total	3,006,828	2,257,720	473,442	116,197	74,114	29,543	55,812
	Private	216,455	40,558	86,228	23,442	23,208	18,022	24,997
	Percentage private	7.2%	1.8%	18.2%	20.2%	31.3%	61.0%	44.8%
1970	Total	3,803,467	2,445,405	800,402	178,537	175,650	108,328	95,145
	Private	320,514	22,955	35,590	43,876	89,154	79,882	49,057
	Percentage private	8.4%	0.9%	4.4%	24.6%	50.8%	73.7%	51.6%

1975	Total	4,160,389	2,364,961	1,036,357	185,181	284,455	150,226	139,209
	Private	462,701	27,425	42,957	38,507	163,372	110,527	79,913
	Percentage private	11.1%	1.2%	4.1%	20.8%	57.4%	73.6%	57.4%
1980	Total	4,181,801	2,233,706	1,075,532	180,665	349,370	183,134	159,394
	Private	550,461	25,523	47,063	39,008	205,634	140,292	92,941
	Percentage private	13.2%	1.1%	4.4%	21.6%	58.9%	76.6%	58.3%
1985	Total	4,429,043	2,321,700	1,062,226	194,757	421,784	236,824	191,752
	Private	667,826	24,781	44,527	47,340	255,298	181,178	114,702
	Percentage private	15.1%	1.1%	4.2%	24.3%	60.5%	76.5%	59.8%
1986	Total	4,498,602	2,364,438	1,052,993	200,599	437,924	244,482	198,166
	Private	698,493	24,969	45,333	50,176	268,179	190,946	118,890
	Percentage private	15.5%	1.1%	4.3%	25.0%	61.2%	78.1%	60.0%

Source: Ministry of Education (1987), p. 18.

Table 18.6 Expenditure per student by public and private education, 1985–86 (unit – NI$1,000 or persons)

	Primary	*Junior high*	*Senior high*	*Senior vocational*	*Junior college*	*University and college*
Total public expenditure*						
Public	30,616,558	21,529,198	5,695,499	7,132,949	4,662,550	13,786,686
Private	388,241	166,324	3,773,232	4,940,412	6,269,651	4,940,919
Enrollment						
Public	2,296,919	1,017,699	147,417	166,486	55,646	77,050
Private	24,781	44,527	47,340	255,298	181,178	114,702
Total public expenditure per student						
Public	13.33	21.15	38.64	42.84	83.79	178.93
Private	15.67	3.74	79.70	19.35	34.60	43.08
Total private expenditure per student						
Public	0.00	1.50	3.63	3.41	11.41	14.63
Private	10.80	13.11	16.95	17.15	30.73	42.95

Total expenditure per student						
Public	13.33	22.65	42.27	46.25	95.20	193.56
Private	26.47	16.85	96.95	36.50	65.34	86.02
Percent total expenditure from private sources						
Public	0.0%	6.6%	8.6%	7.4%	12.0%	7.6%
Private	40.8%	77.8%	17.5%	47.0%	47.0%	49.9%

Notes:
* Includes central, provincial, municipal, country, city, village, and town expenditures.
† Average tuition and fees they vary by school and subject matter).
‡ Public expenditure per student plus tuition and fees.

Source: Ministry of Education (1987), pp. 18, 38.

students in higher education, there is also a difference in who bears the cost. Students in public schools pay only about 7% of the total expenditure themselves. In private schools, this figure is close to one-half (see Table 18.6). This has not always been the case.

Table 18.7 shows the percentage of public funds spent on private students compared to the percentage of students enrolled in private schools from 1958 onward. It reveals that the large discrepancy between the percentage of state funds given to private schools and the percentage of students attending private schools first appeared after 1965, when the government began to expand public junior college and college education. The total figures in Table 18.7 show the percentage of private expenditure to total expenditure nearly always exceeded the percentage of private students to total students. But this ratio masks the fact that most of the private enrollment was at the higher and more expensive levels. From 1976 onward, the more detailed breakdown by level shows that while 50–60% of junior college expenditure was for private schools, they enrolled 76% of all junior college students. At the university level, the gap was even greater. Private universities received only 27–37% of the total university budget while they enrolled almost 60% of university students.

Since private schools were under government control, this change did not reflect a decision to allow schooling to respond more to private or local pressures. It was, in effect, a shift in the burden of the costs of education from the public to the individual. With the expansion of the national education system in 1968, the government was overburdened by the increased costs. Expanding enrollment in private education at the higher levels would allow more student places at a cheaper per student cost for the government than expanding public education.

One point to be made about this policy of allowing the growth of high-tuition, private schools is that it fosters inequality. Since there is a dramatic difference in quality between the public and private sectors, those who get into public schools benefit twice—from a better quality education and a cheaper one. Those who attend universities with high entrance standards are more likely to come from wealthier families that can afford the extra tutors, fees and income foregone which help in passing exams.[20] They are more able to pass entrance exams regardless of their innate abilities. Private university students pay about 50% of their total educational costs, whereas public university students pay 7% of their total costs. There is thus a transfer of the benefits of tax revenues from the whole population to the elite few who make it into public university. Further, for political reasons the tuition policy of higher education is not likely to change in the near future.[21] The policy is based on an important social myth that anyone can make it to the prestigious public universities if he or she is smart enough, and that fees will not be a barrier.

This policy is, however, efficient. The use of private financing for expansion

Academy	*Total*		*Elementary*		*High*		*Junior college*		*Higher education*		*College and University*	
year	*Expenditure*	*Students*	*Expenditure*	*Students*	*Expenditure*	*Students*	*Expenditure*	*Students*	*Expenditure*	*Students*	*Expenditure*	*Students*
1958	8.4%	2.1%	0.0%	0.0%	13.8%	12.2%	—	—	19.4%	22.4%	—	—
1959	9.2%	4.1%	0.0%	2.0%	15.8%	14.0%	—	—	21.0%	23.4%	—	—
1960	13.2%	4.3%	2.7%	1.9%	19.5%	14.6%	—	—	28.6%	27.0%	—	—
1961	12.2%	4.6%	2.1%	1.9%	19.0%	15.4%	—	—	24.3%	27.9%	—	—
1962	13.8%	5.0%	2.0%	1.9%	21.0%	16.4%	—	—	32.3%	30.4%	—	—
1963	14.9%	5.6%	2.0%	1.9%	22.8%	17.8%	—	—	32.4%	35.2%	—	—
1964	19.7%	6.4%	2.1%	1.9%	24.7%	19.1%	—	—	45.6%	42.0%	—	—
1965	19.5%	7.2%	2.4%	1.8%	20.9%	20.0%	—	—	45.5%	50.4%	—	—
1966	19.6%	7.9%	2.0%	1.5%	22.0%	20.6%	—	—	44.5%	57.2%	—	—
1967	20.4%	8.4%	1.3%	1.0%	22.2%	21.4%	—	—	44.6%	59.6%	—	—
1968	18.1%	8.0%	2.2%	0.8%	15.3%	17.3%	—	—	41.9%	61.4%	—	—
1969	16.9%	8.1%	0.9%	0.8%	13.8%	15.5%	—	—	39.3%	62.6%	—	—
1970	19.9%	8.4%	4.3%	0.9%	18.0%	14.6%	—	—	36.9%	63.4%	—	—
1971	23.5%	9.0%	3.2%	1.0%	22.7%	15.2%	—	—	50.5%	63.2%	—	—
1972	22.2%	9.6%	3.1%	1.1%	20.7%	15.4%	—	—	49.6%	62.2%	—	—
1973	18.5%	10.1%	2.1%	1.1%	14.7%	15.5%	—	—	49.2%	63.7%	—	—
1974	21.6%	10.6%	1.9%	1.1%	20.7%	15.8%	—	—	51.9%	64.8%	—	—
1975	18.4%	11.1%	1.9%	1.2%	18.8%	16.3%	—	—	40.3%	65.8%	—	—
1976	16.9%	11.5%	1.4%	1.1%	19.8%	16.3%	73.8%	75.2%	—	—	31.9%	59.6%
1977	18.7%	11.7%	1.3%	1.1%	23.2%	16.4%	63.4%	75.9%	—	—	35.9%	57.7%
1978	17.3%	12.0%	1.3%	1.1%	21.6%	16.6%	58.7%	76.3%	—	—	33.4%	57.8%
1979	16.7%	12.6%	1.3%	1.1%	21.0%	17.4%	62.1%	76.9%	—	—	25.7%	58.2%
1980	18.6%	13.2%	1.4%	1.1%	22.1%	18.2%	57.2%	76.6%	—	—	31.2%	58.3%
1981	18.5%	13.8%	1.4%	1.1%	21.0%	19.0%	56.5%	76.4%	—	—	27.1%	58.8%
1982	17.4%	14.2%	1.3%	1.1%	20.0%	19.4%	54.9%	76.4%	—	—	28.1%	59.3%
1983	18.2%	14.4%	1.3%	1.1%	20.2%	19.5%	57.9%	76.4%	—	—	37.8%	59.5%
1984	18.2%	14.7%	1.1%	1.1%	21.0%	19.9%	57.8%	76.1%	—	—	36.6%	60.0%
1985	18.2%	15.1%	1.3%	1.1%	20.5%	20.7%	57.4%	76.5%	—	—	26.4%	59.8%

Notes:
* Figures for preschool or special education not included. Figures for high school include junior high.

Source: Ministry of Education (1987), pp. 18, 20, 38, & 42.

of higher education levels reveals three efficiencies that Taiwan was able to use in its educational planning. The first was the combination of state planning and private finance. Control of private education curricula was primarily in the hands of the national government, so individual enrollment in private education was strictly an economic decision, not a desire for a different educational experience. This makes the system highly externally efficient on economic grounds because presumably those who invest in the higher fees would only do so if they felt commensurate returns were likely in the market. There may be inefficiencies, however, in keeping strict central control of all forms of education. Administrators are accountable only to central authorities and have little discretion or incentive to respond to local conditions or the needs of the students and parents.

The second efficiency of this arrangement was a means of rationing quality education to the most competent. The best quality education was fully subsidized and rationed by entrance exams. Lower quality private education was available for the marginal students to invest in themselves. Where the perceived private returns were high enough, students (and their families) were willing to pay more for an inferior good. Over time, as the supply of university and secondary school graduates increases, the market demand for graduates will lessen. This trend should result in a decline in demand for higher education, and therefore lower enrollment in the more expensive, lower quality private sector.

The final efficiency which Taiwan captured was that of allocative efficiency. By initially building a strong state-supported education system at the lower levels. Taiwan used the bulk of its public funds at the primary level which had the highest marginal returns. When primary school development was complete and further expansion was required at the middle and higher levels, where returns were lower, Taiwan increased user fees through the private system to replace government expenditures. Available evidence shows that labor development for economic growth is more efficient if the greatest education investments are put where the highest social returns are gained. For developing countries, highest returns come first from the primary and lower middle school levels.[22] Thus Taiwan was able to keep its social educational investments at the levels with the highest returns.

(f) Education expenditure

The labor development plans also forged another direct link between the education system and the economy with the educational expenditure policy. It specifically indexed total expenditure for education to a proportion of the GNP. This meant that as the country's wealth grew its commitment of resources to education kept pace. Thus, in 1970 educational expenditure was 4.6% of GNP; in 1980 it was 4.7% and in 1985 it was 5.5% (see Table 18.8).

Education's share of total government expenditure has also increased. Table

Table 18.8 Educational expenditure as a percentage of GNP and of total government expenditure, 1955–87

Fiscal year	*Total government expenditure* (*NT$*)	*Total education expenditure* (*NT$*)	*Education expenditure as a % of total govt. expenditure*	*Education expenditure as a % of GNP*
1955–56	5,808,999	673,263	11.6	2.1
1960–61	11,037,305	1,671,962	15.1	2.5
1965–66	22,187,853	3,959,628	17.8	3.3
1970–71	54,906,850	11,236,766	20.5	4.6
1975–76	139,130,086	25,377,015	18.2	4.2
1980–81	409,667,961	74,112,578	18.1	4.7
1985–86	686,662,474	138,667,203	20.2	5.5

Source: Ministry of Education (1987), p. 40.

18.8 shows an increase from 11% in 1955 to 20% in 1970, where it has remained roughly ever since. Compared to similar countries, Taiwan's educational expenditure is high and represents an especially large share of total government expenditure. At 5.8% of GNP, Taiwan's educational expenditure is comparable to countries such as South Korea at 4.3%, Singapore at 4.4%, and Japan at 5.7%.[23] Taiwan also ranks relatively high in its expenditure on education as a proportion of total government expenditure. Taiwan spends 19.9% of government expenditures on education. South Korea spends 21.5%, and Singapore spends 9.6%. Like comparable newly industrialized countries, Taiwan devotes a large proportion of both its wealth and its public funds to education.

18.4 EDUCATION'S CONTRIBUTION TO ECONOMIC GROWTH

The strong commitment to educational development and the resulting high enrollments have allowed Taiwan to achieve a rising educational level for its labor force. Illiteracy in the labor force has virtually disappeared. Those who have graduated from junior college and above increased from 4% of the labor force in 1966 to 13% in 1986. Those with senior vocational degrees were 5% of the labor force in 1966 and are now 18%.

The contribution of education to economic growth can be measured directly through growth accounting. The basic framework comes from the aggregate production function:

$$Y = f(K,E,L,D) \tag{1}$$

where Y is GDP, K the national physical capital stock, E the human capital stock, L the labor force, and D the amount of land. Equation (1) can be rewritten as:

$$g_v = s_k g_k + (l_e/Y)r_e + s_1 g_1 + s_d g_d \tag{2}$$

where g_i is the growth rate of i, s_i is the share of GDP paid to factor i, l_e is the amount of human capital investment undertaken and r_e is the social rate of return on human capital. So $(l_e/Y)r_e$ is the *ceteris paribus* contribution of education to the growth rate. Solow and Denison have shown that equation (2) does not hold empirically because the sum of the terms on the right-hand side is generally less than g_y.[24] This residual was labeled *technical changes*. Calling technical changes x, noting that g_d equals zero for Taiwan, and multiplying education's contribution with p, the labor participation ratio,[25] we get:

$$g_y = s_k g_k + s_1 g_1 + p(l_e/Y)r_e + x \tag{3}$$

Since all growth accounting exercises concerning Taiwan have lumped the contributions of the last two terms together, this sum will be termed *gross residual factors*.

Samuel Ho found that 18% of total output growth in the 1953–72 period could be attributed to labor, 28% to capital formation and 55% to gross residual factors.[26] Ho's estimate of the contribution of gross residual factors was confirmed by Chi-ming Hou and Yu-chu Hsu who used a different estimation method for 1953–70 data.[27] They found that 18% of output growth was due to capital growth, 35% to labor growth, and 47% to gross residual factors. Thus these studies found factors other than capital and labor to account for half the growth in output for this period.[28]

Chien-sheng Shih measured the contribution of formal education directly.[29] He found it to average 0.65% annually in the 1963–72 period when g_y averaged 10.39%. The low contribution of education is primarily due to a low l_e/Y. Taiwan's l_e/Y was 6.6% in 1968 compared with 22.1% in South Korea, 13.5% in Malaysia and 9.8% in India. What is most significant in Shih's calculations is that the contribution of education to growth has been rising secularly throughout his sample period. The value of education went from 0.50 percentage point in 1963 to 0.74 percentage point in 1972, accounting for 5.2% and 6.5% of the growth rate in 1963 and 1972 respectively.

Taking Ho's estimate of gross residual factors to be 44.4% of g_y during 1963–73, a value of 3.96% was obtained for technical changes. The contribution of education could have been under-estimated because it is likely to have prompted technical changes. The World Bank's 1987 *World Development Report* reported a positive correlation between the openness of the trade regime and the growth rate,[30] so it appears that part of Taiwan's technical changes could be due to the competitive conditions ensured by its almost free trade policies. This trade regime connection is of course speculative. Lucas recently noted that the removal of trade barriers is "a level effect, analogous to the one-time shifting upward in production possibilities, and not a growth effect".[31] (A level effect raises or lowers the balanced growth path without changing its slope, and a growth effect changes the growth rate of the balanced growth path.)

Finally, it may be useful to refer to some analysis of South Korea, where the growth pattern has been quite similar to that of Taiwan. Dornbusch and Park have argued that the basis of South Korean growth was a highly trained and productive labor force with low wages. They maintain that South Korea's labor force was a precondition for the high rates of investment and capacity expansion that made the export expansion possible.[32] A similar argument could be made for Taiwan. It was probably not just investment in education alone, but the interaction between education, wage moderation, and the Taiwanese industrial investment strategy that led to such spectacular growth.

An important reason for the successful planning of labor development in Taiwan was the highly competitive labor market. Throughout most of its postwar history, Taiwan had few severe labor imbalances and a low and steadily declining unemployment rate. (The highest recorded level was 2.9%

in 1952 and the lowest was 0.7% in both 1979 and 1980. The average rate during 1952–86 was 1.7%.[33] Most studies indicate that wages are competitively determined (there are few labor unions), there is a high degree of labor mobility, and little market distortion by either the government or foreign firms.[34] Wages are therefore a good index of labor productivity and thus labor supply and demand can be estimated fairly accurately. The labor requirements approach has major weaknesses because it cannot capture shifts in supply, demand or the resultant wage changes. But a competitive labor market will at least ensure a more accurate measure of these variables.

18.5 CONCLUSION

Taiwan's successful development of human resources coincided with careful and efficient planning of its education system. While it cannot be proved that the plans caused this success, nonetheless the plans were almost fully implemented and they certainly did not hinder economic growth. The MDPs linked the type and amount of growth in the education system to the needs of the economy. The plans have no doubt been the decisive influence in both the slower rate of increase in higher education enrollments and the shift to more vocational areas of enrollment at all levels. These links are summarized in Table 18.9.

The first panel shows that the plan targets for shifting senior high level students from general to vocational education were met by 1986. The second panel shows that the rate of increase in student enrollment in higher education was reduced almost as much as planned during 1970–80. The last panel indicates that the actual educational expenditure as a proportion of GNP came very close to plan targets. These figures indicate there was a definite correlation between the plan targets and actual changes in the education system. This correlation is good evidence that the education plans were actually implemented.

By limiting the number of students who enter university and by shifting many of them into vocational streams, Taiwan was probably able to keep a close match between students' skills and labor market demands. This effort may also explain why Taiwan did not have a large educated unemployment problem.[35] By making elementary education universal, the education system could meet the needs of the economy for a more literate basic work force. Since the expansion of higher education was supported largely by private resources, there was little oversupply of educated labor, albeit some inequalities. Overall, the education system appears to have been remarkably successful in meeting the needs of Taiwan's economy.

In summary, Taiwan's education system had several initial features which differentiated it from the systems of similar developing countries. By 1950, it already had an infrastructure for broad-based, basic education. Moreover, a supply of highly educated labor arrived in 1949–50 from the Mainland to

Table 18.9 Summary of MDP plan targets and results

1. Shift from general to vocational education at sr. high level

Year	*Plan*	*Targeted ratio (voc:gen)*	*Year*	*Actual ratio (voc:gen)*
			1963	45:55
1966	1st MDP	60:40		
			1972	52:48
1977	5th MDP	70:30		
			1980	66:34
1981	7th MDP	70:30		
			1986	72:28

2. Rate of increase of student enrollment in colleges and universities

Year	*Plan*	*Targeted rate*	*Year*	*Actual rate*
			1970–71	9%
1972	4th MDP	5% (max.)		
			1975–76	3%
1977	5th MDP	3% (max.)		
			1980–81	4.4%

3. Educational expenditure indexed as a proportion of GNP

Year	*Plan*	*Targeted expenditure*	*Year*	*Actual expenditure*
			1970	4.6%
1971	3rd MDP	6% by 1980		
1972	4th MDP	5.4% by 1976		
			1976	4.5%
			1980	4.4%
			1986	5.5%
1980	6th MDP	5–5.5% by 1989		

Sources: Chang (1980); Hou (1978); Hou and Chang (1981).

replace the Japanese and to begin the process of building the local economy.

Most important, the education system grew steadily but in a manner that closely matched the changing requirements of the growing economy. Particularly after 1966 the supply of educated labor was geared to meet the economy's needs by national plans. The compulsory basic education was raised from six to nine years, the secondary level curriculum was shifted more toward vocational fields, the supply of university graduates was strictly limited, and the university curriculum was changed to emphasize science and engineering subjects. The levels above basic junior high were expanded, but disproportionately shifted into the private sector so they were not as costly.

ACKNOWLEDGMENTS

This paper is part of the Employment and Enterprise Project at the Harvard Institute for International Development. I am grateful to the Chung Hua Institution for Economic Research for its kind hospitality during the summer of 1987. The views expressed here are mine and should not be attributed to the Chung Hua Institution for Economic Research. I am grateful to Liu Liang-Yng, Chang Ching-Hsi, and Douglas Windham for their valuable comments.

NOTES

1 Harbison (1973), p. 3.
2 See the symposium and comments in *Comparative Education Review*, Vol. 30, No. 4 (November 1986), p. 3.
3 Ho (1978), p. 33.
4 Ministry of Education (1987).
5 Tsurumi (1977), p. 62 and p. 113.
6 Ho (1978), p. 105; Galenson (1979a), p. 454.
7 Senior high schools are a notable exception. Private schools enroll 24.3% of senior high school students, but receive almost 40% of the budget. This is because there are some heavily state-subsidized private senior high schools which cater to the elite. They use their private status to avoid some government-mandated curricula and give more emphasis to cramming for the university exams.
8 For an analysis of the plans until 1976, see Hou (1978).
9 See Council for Economic Planning and Development (1986).
10 See Djang (1977), chapter 9.
11 Salome and Charmes (1988).
12 Hou and Chang (1981).
13 Gannicott (1973).
14 Chang, C.H. (1981).
15 Chang, C.H. (1981).
16 Hou and Chang (1981), p. 481.
17 See Kao, Lu and Kai (1983), p. 148.
18 Gai (1980), p. 6.
19 Kao, Lu and Kai (1983), p. 81 and p. 88.
20 Kao cites a study of the family income of college students in 1979 which shows that the percentage of students from the highest income bracket attending public universities was five times greater than that bracket's representation in the entire population (Kao, 1984, p. 6).
21 Interview with CEPD official.
22 Psacharopoulos (1973), p. 62.
23 Educational expenditures for Taiwan are from the Ministry of Education. Other countries' figures are from UNESCO (1985).
24 Solow (1960); Denison (1962).
25 This adjustment is based on Psacharopoulos's observation that not everyone who receives education participates in the labor force (see Psacharopoulos, 1973, p. 62).
26 Ho (1978), p. 126.
27 Hou and Hsu (1972).
28 External observers were in agreement with these estimates. See Galenson (1979), p. 395 and Little (1979), p. 462.

29 Shih (1976).
30 World Bank (1987).
31 Lucas (1988), p. 12.
32 Dornbusch and Park (1987).
33 Council for Economic Planning and Development (1987).
34 Hou and Wu (1985).
35 Taiwan's unemployment rate for those with a senior high education never exceeded 6.4% during 1967–80 and was on average 4.0%. Senior vocational graduates also had an average rate of 4.0% for those years. All other levels were much lower (Hou and Chang, 1981, p. 505).

REFERENCES

Chang, Ching-Hsi, "Supply of education in Taiwan," Mimeo (Taipei: National Taiwan University, 1981).

Chang, Pei-Chi, "Higher education and manpower planning in Taiwan, the Republic of China," *Industry of Free China* (July 1980).

Council for Economic Planning and Development, *Taiwan Statistical Data Book 1987* (Taipei: Council for Economic Planning and Development, Republic of China, 1987).

—— *Plan Displaying Division of Labor for Mid-Term Plans and Policies* (in Chinese) Mimeo (Taipei: Republic of China, 1986).

Denison, E. F., *The Sources of Economic Growth in the United States and the Alternatives Before Us* (New York: Committee for Economic Development, 1962).

Djang, T. K., "Industry and labor in Taiwan," Monograph Series No. 10 (Taipei: Institute of Economics, Academia Sinica, March 1977).

Dornbusch, Rudiger, and Yung Chul Park, "Korean growth policy," *Brookings Papers on Economic Activity*, Vol. 2 (1987).

Gai, Kenneth, C. S., *A Survey of Educational Costs* (Taipei: Ministry of Education, Republic of China, 1980).

Galenson, Walter (Ed.), *Economic Growth and Structural Change in Taiwan* (Ithaca, NY: Cornell University Press, 1979a).

—— "The labor force, wages, and living standards," in Walter Galenson (Ed.), *Economic Growth and Structural Change in Taiwan* (Ithaca, NY: Cornell University Press, 1979b).

Gannicott, K., *Rates of Return to Education in Taiwan, Republic of China* (Taipei: Executive Yuan, Council for International Economic Cooperation and Development, and Manpower Development Work-group, 1973).

Harbison, Frederick H., *Human Resources as the Wealth of Nations* (Oxford: Oxford University Press, 1973).

Ho, Samuel P. S., *Economic Growth and Structural Change in Taiwan, 1869–1970* (New Haven, CN: Yale University Press, 1978).

Hou, Chi-ming, "Manpower planning and development in Taiwan," *Industry of Free China* (August and September 1978).

—— and Ching-hsi Chang, "Education and economic growth in Taiwan: The mechanism of adjustment," in *Conference on Experiences and Lessons of Economic Development in Taiwan* (Taipei: Institute of Economics, Academia Sinica, 1981).

—— and Hui-lin Wu, "Wages and labor productivity in Taiwan," *Industry of Free China* (May and June 1985).

—— and Yu-chu Hsu, "Nonagricultural employment, factor intensity and growth. The case of Taiwan," Paper presented to the Sino-American Conference on Manpower in Taiwan (Taipei, 1972).

Kao, Charles H., "An evaluation of ROC's policy on tuition for public higher education," *Industry of Free China* (May 1984).
—— C., Kuang Lu, and Che Sheng Kai, *Current Problems and Policies of College and University Graduate Manpower* (in Chinese) (Taipei: National Youth Commission, 1983).
Little, Ian M. D., "An economic reconnaissance," in Walter Galenson (Ed.), *Economic Growth and Structural Change in Taiwan* (Ithaca, NY: Cornell University Press, 1979).
Lucas, Robert, "On the mechanics of development," *Journal of Monetary Economics* (July 1988).
Ministry of Education, *Education Statistics of the Republic of China* (Taipei: Republic of China, 1987).
Psacharopoulos, George, *Returns to Education: An International Comparison* (Amsterdam: Elsevier-Jossey Bass, 1973).
Salome, Bernard and Jacques Charmes, *In-Service Training: Five Asian Experiences* (Paris: Development Center, Organization for Economic Cooperation and Development, 1988).
Shih, Chien-sheng, "The contribution of education to economic development in Taiwan," Paper prepared for the Conference on Population and Economic Development in Taiwan (Taipei, 1976).
Solow, Robert, "Investment and technical progress," in K. J. Arrow, F. Karlin, and P. Suppes (Eds.), *Mathematical Methods in Social Sciences* (Stanford, CA: Stanford University Press, 1960).
Tsurumi, F. Patricia, *Japanese Colonial Education in Taiwan 1895–1945* (Cambridge, MA: Harvard University Press, 1977).
UNESCO, *Statistical Yearbook 1985* (Paris: UNESCO, 1985).
World Bank, *World Development Report* (New York: Oxford University Press, 1987).

19

RESPONSES TO LABOUR SCARCITY AND AGEING IN SINGAPORE

John Bauer

19.1 INTRODUCTION

Singapore has progressed rapidly through its demographic transition from high to low birth and death rates. This rapid transition suggests two important future trends: slowing labour force growth and ageing of the work force. Singapore's labour force grew relatively rapidly during the 1980s with an average annual growth rate of 3.4% according to population census data. This rapid growth, however, did not prevent wages from rising sharply. Labour demand increased even more strongly than supply, and labour became increasingly scarce. Projections imply that labour force growth will slow dramatically throughout the 1990s and beyond. This slower growth, assuming continued strong economic performance, suggests that labour scarcity will become even more severe.

Shantakumar's labour force projections are summarized in Table 19.1. Labour force projections rest on assumptions regarding both underlying demographic trends and future labour force participation behaviour. The projections in this table are based on his median variant population projection.[1] Two sets of assumptions regarding labour force participation rates were adopted. The first projection assumes that the age-sex specific participation rates observed in 1990 will persist throughout the projection period. Labour force growth declines rapidly in this scenario. The average annual growth rate drops from 3.4% in the 1980s to roughly 0.7% in the 1990s and 0.3% during the first decade of the next century. Singapore's labour force grew by an average of 45,000 workers per year during the 1980s. These projections suggest it will grow by only 10,600 per year during the 1990s.

Of course, it is unlikely that the current labour force participation rates will persist. Participation among prime age women and the elderly, for example, is expected to increase. The second projection in Table 19.1 assumes

Source: *Economic Policy Management in Singapore*, Lim Chong Yah (Editor), Singapore: Addison-Wesley Publishing Company, (1996), pp. 119–46.

Table 19.1 Projected growth of Singapore's labour force

	Constant labour force participation rates		*Extropolated labour force participation rates*	
	Growth rate (%)	*Absolute increase*	*Growth rate (%)*	*Absolute increase*
1990–1995	0.94	13,046	1.35	18,898
1995–2000	0.57	8165	1.12	16,629
2000–2005	0.38	5517	0.82	12,799
2005–2010	0.24	3650	0.57	9265
2010–2015	−0.06	−860	0.01	114

Source: Shantakumar (1996), Scenarios 4 and 3.

that observed rates of change in participation rates will persist. For example, rates among prime-age women are assumed to increase as they have in the recent past. This projection suggests a slightly more robust labour force growth in the future. The projected average annual growth rate throughout the 1990s, for example, is 1.2%. However, even this rate is relatively low and whichever projection variant one adopts the general inference is the same: Singapore's labour force growth will become increasingly modest over the next two decades. Labour scarcity should worsen, and labour costs will continue to grow in the long run.

Singapore is certainly not alone in this regard. Substantial declines in labour force growth are projected for the other Asian Newly Industrialised Economies (NIEs) and Japan (Table 19.2). Japan, the most demographically advanced country in Asia, already has extremely low labour force growth rates. The projected growth rates for Korea and Taiwan, though greater than those for Singapore, represent substantial declines from the 1980s.

Moreover, the growth rates for Singapore, the other NIEs, and Japan are already much lower than that of the labour-abundant countries of Asia. In Southeast Asia, demographic and economic trends suggest that labour will continue to be relatively abundant in Indonesia, the Philippines, and Vietnam for the foreseeable future. In China, large labour surpluses imply that labour will continue to be abundant despite slower labour force growth in the future. For example, several studies suggest that roughly a third of China's agricultural labour is 'surplus' (Bauer, 1990). In South Asia, very rapid labour force growth is projected to persist, with larger and larger cohorts of youth entering the labour market each year.

These very distinct labour supply trends across Asian countries imply that Singapore and the other NIEs will find it increasingly difficult to compete in industries where low labour costs are critical. The well-recognized shift in comparative advantage away from labour-intensive manufacturing in the NIEs will continue.

Table 19.2 Projected labour force growth rates (%), selected Asian countries

	1990–2000	*2000–2010*
Japan and the NIEs		
Singapore	0.76	0.31
Japan	0.36	−0.35
Korea (Rep. of)	1.81	1.08
Taiwan	1.66	0.71
China	1.22	0.87
Southeast Asia	2.35	1.68
Indonesia	2.93	2.58
Malaysia	2.82	2.64
Philippines	1.77	1.00
Thailand		
South Asia		
Bangladesh	3.60	3.27
India	2.09	2.03
Pakistan	3.66	4.29

Note: Bauer's (1990) projections for Singapore are much the same as those presented above.

Source: Singapore's rates are taken from Shantakumar (1996), Scenario 4. Rates for all other countries are taken from Bauer (1990).

19.2 POPULATION AND LABOUR FORCE AGEING

19.2.1 Ageing trends

Population ageing has been an area of interest in Singapore for at least a decade. However, concerns over both the growing burden of supporting the elderly and the potentially adverse impacts of labour force ageing have grown recently. The elderly dependency burden is projected to rise very rapidly in the early part of the next century. For example, Shantakumar projects that the population aged 60 and older will approximately double between 1990 and 2010. In 1990, there were roughly 13 persons over the age of 60 for every 100 persons aged 15 to 59 in Singapore. In 2020, it is expected that there will be 39 for every 100.

Again, Singapore is not unique in this regard. Table 19.3 presents recent World Bank projections for the increases in proportions of populations aged 60 and older in selected Asian countries. Japan has by far the oldest population, but the NIEs are rapidly catching up. Among the NIEs, Singapore is expected to age especially rapidly. Ageing will be much less dramatic throughout the rest of Southeast Asia.

Singapore's labour force, like the general population, will age rapidly. Projections by Shantakumar suggest that the median age of male workers will

Table 19.3 Percent of population age 65 and older, selected Asian countries

	1990	*2000*	*2010*	*2020*	*2030*
Singapore	5.57	7.31	9.64	15.30	21.38
Korea (Rep. of)	4.97	6.90	9.64	13.04	18.80
Taiwan	6.03	8.14	9.12	12.69	17.52
Japan	11.54	15.36	18.68	21.91	26.13
China	5.87	7.07	8.18	11.39	15.30
Indonesia	3.91	4.78	5.81	7.31	9.91
Malaysia	3.79	4.31	5.61	7.89	11.19
Philippines	3.38	3.75	4.66	6.45	9.09
Thailand	3.80	4.75	6.01	8.34	12.34

Source: World Bank, 1991.

rise from approximately 35 in 1990 to 42 by 2010. The median age of female workers is projected to increase from 31 to 36. Table 19.4 summarizes expected changes in the age composition of the labour force between 1990 and 2020. The percentage of workers under age 35 drops rapidly from 55% in 1990 to about 41% by 2000. The proportion of workers in prime ages (35 to 44) first rises from 1990 to 2000 and then declines. The proportion of workers over age 45 increases steadily.

19.2.2 Potential consequences of an ageing work force

Labour force ageing could affect a country's ability to respond to structural change, its productivity growth, and labour costs. Clark and Spengler (1980), for example, have argued that ageing can constrain the ability of economies to adjust to structural and technological change. Younger workers tend to be more mobile, and it is easier to adjust to change in an economy with large cohorts of youth entering the job market. Also, the rate of investment in job skills is lower for older workers, and they may find it more difficult to respond to changing production techniques or new technologies (Clark, 1988). In the

Table 19.4 Projected age composition of Singapore's labour force

	1990	*2000*	*2020*
15–24	19.3	15.5	15.8
25–34	35.7	25.8	25.6
35–44	25.9	30.0	20.6
45–54	12.1	20.4	19.6
55–59	3.4	3.8	8.1
60+	3.6	4.5	10.3

Source: Shantakumar (1996), Scenario 4.

case of Singapore, Lim *et al* (1988) have noted that an older work force is more likely to resist restructuring which requires retraining or job switching.

It is also likely that ageing will affect labour productivity growth, average wage levels, and, therefore, labour costs. A standard gauge of competitiveness is unit labour costs, which are determined by the ratio of wage rates to labour productivity. If wage rates rise by more than productivity, then unit labour costs increase and competitiveness may decline. Ageing should affect both wages and productivity. Wages are likely to rise as average levels of seniority increase. The important question is the extent to which productivity also rises and offsets the increases in average wage bills.

Unfortunately, there is little direct evidence, in Singapore or elsewhere, on the relationship between productivity and age. It is generally believed, however, that productivity first increases with age and then declines. This is the pattern predicted by standard human capital investment theory. Productivity is believed to increase because of post-schooling investments in human capital, such as on-the-job training. The rate of investment tends to be higher among younger workers and declines as workers near the end of their careers. Eventually, productivity declines because of lower rates of post-schooling investment in human capital, depreciation of skills and declines in physical prowess. The age at which productivity peaks and the extent to which it declines thereafter should vary by occupation.

Whereas the relationship between age and productivity is usually not observed, the relationship between age and earnings is. Wages tend to rise with experience and, therefore, age. Why they do so, however, is not entirely clear. There are two competing economic theories explaining this relationship, and each has very different implications concerning the impact of ageing on labour costs.

Human capital theory argues that earnings rise because productivity increases with experience and specific training (Becker, 1962).[2] Training increases productivity, and increased productivity is rewarded with higher wages. Note that ageing of the work force in this case need not increase unit labour costs, since the higher wages of more senior workers are offset by their higher productivity. In fact, in the case of specific training, older workers are paid a spot wage which is lower than their productivity.

Many economists believe that human capital theory alone, however, does not provide a satisfactory explanation of why earnings rise with age. One puzzle is the existence of mandatory retirement practices. Human capital theory does not explain why such practices are adopted. The other major explanation of the earnings profile is provided by agency theory (Lazear, 1979). Firms and workers may enter into implicit contracts under which wages increase with age even if productivity does not.

Agency theory maintains that seniority-based pay schemes have been established to minimize labour turnover and shirking. Workers are paid less than their productivity early in their career and are 'overpaid' later in their career in order to provide a strong incentive for workers to stay with the firm and to provide the expected work effort. If workers shirk, the firm would become aware of it over time and dismiss them. Note that this theory does provide an explanation of why mandatory retirement practices are adopted. If older workers are paid more than their productivity, the firm has to limit the number of years they are employed.

Deferred payment schemes help to reduce labour turnover, encourage loyalty to a firm, and provide strong work incentives. A negative aspect of such schemes is that if older workers are paid more than their marginal product, ageing would increase unit labour costs. Japan's labour market provides an example where ageing has put pressure on labour costs, and its seniority-wage system appears to have been moderated as a result.

19.2.3 An illustration from Japan

Japan has perhaps the strongest seniority-wage system in the world. Earnings rise dramatically with tenure, especially for male workers in large firms. Scholars have resorted to both human capital and agency theory to explain the strong returns to tenure in Japan. One argument in favour of the agency theory explanation is the widespread adoption of mandatory retirement policies in Japan. Also, the Lazear contracting model predicts that an increase in the age of mandatory retirement will result in a flattening of the tenure-earnings profile. The specific human capital model predicts the opposite. Clark and Ogawa (1992) have found that increases in ages of mandatory retirement have been associated with flatter earnings profiles, supporting the contracting model of Lazear.

The seniority-wage system in Japan has had desirable effects. Japanese workers have been loyal to their firms and worker turnover is relatively low, especially in large firms. However, labour force ageing does appear to have put pressure on the seniority system. Bauer and Ogawa (1994) estimate age-earnings profiles for Japan and simulate the impact of labour force ageing on the wage bill. They find that ageing did put considerable pressure on wages between 1976 and 1991, especially in larger firms.

The seniority-wage system in Japan appears to have been moderated in response to the pressures imposed by ageing. Clark and Ogawa (1992b), for example, found that the returns to tenure in Japan did decline during the 1980s. Hashimoto and Raisian (1992) note that this decline has been largely confined to the larger firms, where the seniority wage system is especially strong. Recent government surveys have found that the importance of seniority-oriented remuneration has been reduced in many companies (Ogawa and Clark, 1993).

Another matter of concern in Japan is the impact of ageing on pension costs. Japan's post-war baby boom generation will begin to retire in the early part of the next century, placing an increasing burden on the country's public pension system. In a controversial move aimed at reducing this burden, the ruling coalition parties agreed in December 1993 to increase the age at which people can begin receiving their full employee welfare pension from age 60 to 65. The new system will be implemented over a period of 13 years starting in 2001.

19.2.4 The wage system in Singapore

I expect the future impact of ageing on labour costs in Singapore, though substantial, to be more moderate than in the case of Japan for two reasons. First, the seniority-wage system appears to be less strong in Singapore, and recent reforms have been trying to nudge the labour market away from seniority-based pay schemes. Secondly, the old-age support system is very different from Japan's. Relatively few workers have an employer-funded pension scheme. Most workers are covered by the Central Provident Fund (CPF) which is essentially a compulsory saving scheme rather than a defined benefit pension scheme.

Two different wage systems exist in Singapore (Chew and Chew, 1992). Workers are generally rewarded under a seniority-based wage system where wages increase with length of service. Some workers, however, are paid according to a flexible-wage system. Wages consist of two components under the flexible system: a basic-wage component and a variable annual bonus, which depends on the firm's profitability and the worker's performance.

Historically, the wage structure was typically seniority-based, with long salary scales and pre-determined wage increases. Salary scales became very steep and resulted in wide wage differentials by age. It is believed that the salary at the maximum of the scale exceeded the 'value' of the job (Ministry of Labour, 1992). This system came under pressure during the 1985–86 recession. Many companies became less competitive and in order to reduce labour costs resorted to retrenching workers. The worst hit, according to the Ministry of Labour, were the older workers whose higher wages undermined labour cost competitiveness.

After the recession of 1985–86 the National Wage Council (NWC) established the Subcommittee on Wage Reform which recommended the adoption of a flexible-wage system.[3] One of the aims of the flexible-wage system is to reduce the importance of seniority in determining wages. It was recommended that wages should reflect the value of the job and that salary ranges should not be too wide. The NWC, for example, stated that a reasonable ratio between starting and maximum salaries would be 1.5 times. The move to the flexible wage system, according to the Ministry of Labour, was fairly strong. By 1991, 82% of unionised and 69% of non-unionised companies had formal flexible-wage systems in place (Ministry of Labour, 1992). Moreover, progress has been made in narrowing the gap between minimum and maximum salary points based on seniority (Ministry of Labour, 1993). Earnings data presented below, however, suggest that the overall impact of seniority on earnings remains substantial.

There are several potential benefits from adopting a flexible wage system (Chew and Chew, 1992). Moreover, a seniority-based system can be problematic in an ageing society. Under seniority-based systems, where the wages of older workers exceed their productivity, ageing of the work force would increase labour costs and reduce competitiveness. The adoption of a flexible system, however, is not without cost. Firms and workers lose the benefits accruing from a seniority system, such as lower turnover and greater amounts of specific training. High labour turnover is considered to be a serious problem in Singapore's labour market, and the government is concerned that it may discourage foreign investment (Chew and Chew, 1992). Turnover in Singapore is high for many reasons. The tightness of the labour market tends to promote job-hopping. The structure of the CPF scheme encourages this also. In many countries, pension schemes act to reduce turnover, since pension benefits are at least partially contingent on length of service to the firm. This is not true under the CPF scheme. Unfortunately, data availability does not permit me to rigorously assess the extent to which earnings do rise with tenure in Singapore. The simple relationship between age and earnings, however, is presented in Figure 19.1. This figure was constructed using income from work data presented in the 1990 Census on Population.[4] Earnings do rise dramatically with age for men, more than doubling between the age groups 20–24 and 40–44. Growth in earnings with age is much more

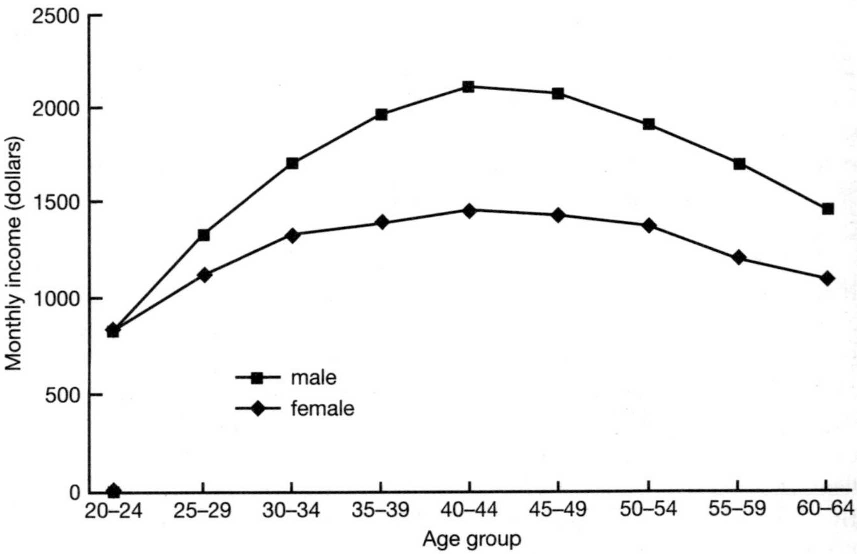

Figure 19.1 Income from work by age, 1990
Source: 1990 Census on Population.

modest among women. Earnings decline strongly, especially for men, after age 50.

Given this relationship between age and earnings, what impact will expected future changes in the age composition of the labour force have on the wage bill? One would expect that as the proportion of workers in the peak-earnings ages increases, average wage bills will increase. If we make the rather unrealistic assumption that the age-earnings profiles in Figure 19.1 will persist, we can roughly gauge the extent to which this will occur in Singapore.

Consider the following simple exercise. First I project the age composition of the labour force from 1990 to 2010. I do this by assuming that the age-sex specific labour force participation rates observed today will persist and apply these rates to the population projections provided by Shantakumar (1996).[5] The resulting projected changes in the age composition of the male labour force are presented in Figure 19.2. Whereas the proportion of male workers under age 35 drops substantially during the 1990s, the proportion in peak-earning ages (40–54) increases. The proportion of workers aged 54 and older increases strongly between 2000 and 2010. Projected movements in the age composition of the female labour force follow the same general trend, though the changes are less dramatic.

I then examine the impact of projected changes in age composition on the wage bill. This is done by calculating weighted averages of wages for male and female workers in 1990, 2000, and 2010, using the projected age

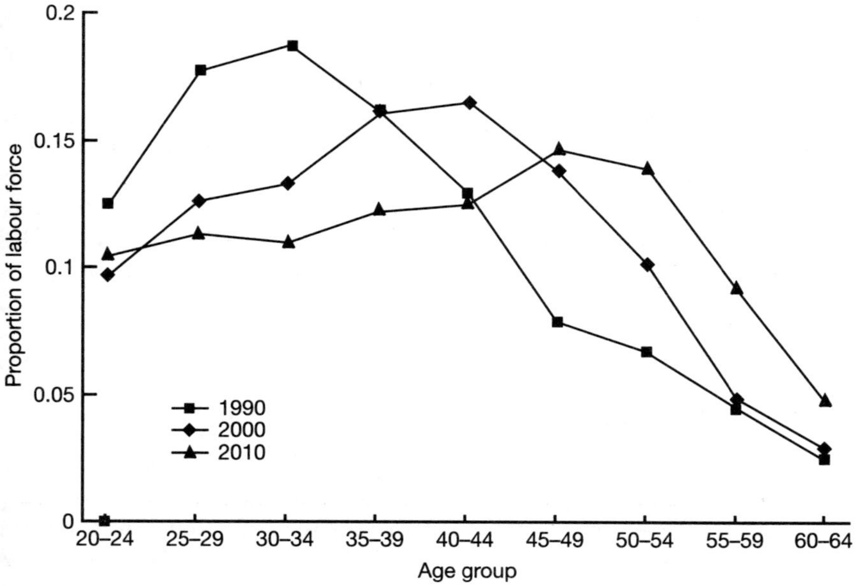

Figure 19.2 Projected age composition of the male labour force

compositions as the weights and the age-sex specific wage rates presented in Figure 19.1. Changes in the calculated average wages reflect only the impact of changing age composition.

The exercise suggests that ageing of the labour force will, as expected, put pressure on wages during the 1990s. Wage bills should increase as greater proportions of workers enter the 40 to 54 age groups. The increase, however, is less than one might expect. This simple simulation implies that ageing will increase average real wages between 1990 and 2000 by a total of 5% for men and 3.5% for women.

Moreover, the pressure on wages will be short lived, if the earnings of workers over age 50 actually decline with age as reflected in Figure 19.1. After the year 2000 the proportion of workers over age 50 is expected to increase strongly, and this will tend to reduce average wages. The simulation suggests that ageing will actually tend to reduce average wage levels between 2000 and 2010.

Unfortunately, we should not put too much faith in this simulation. Figure 19.1 does not represent an estimated earnings function. One problem is that education is not controlled for. Older workers today tend to be much less educated than their juniors, and this is one reason that earnings appear to decline with age in Figure 19.1. The situation will change as younger cohorts of more educated workers age.

Another important point is that the relationship between earnings and age varies substantially across different types of labour. Consider the data on monthly gross wages for different occupations presented in Figure 19.3.[6] The slope of the earnings profile, and, therefore, the impact of ageing on average wage levels varies dramatically across occupations. Wages rise substantially with age for managers and professionals. This group, however, currently comprises only about 15% of the labour force. Wages rise moderately with seniority among technicians, who make up about 18% of the labour force. However, for the majority of workers (clerical, sales, production and service workers, craftsmen, cleaners, labourers and operators), the earnings profile is relatively flat. If this relation persists, ageing should have little impact on the wage bill for these types of workers.

19.3 RESPONSES TO LABOUR SCARCITY AND AGEING

19.3.1 Accommodating responses affecting labour demand

Singapore and the other NIEs have, to varying degrees, responded to rising labour costs by restructuring their economies, automating production, and transferring labour-intensive production overseas via foreign direct investment (FDI). Labour scarcity and higher costs have worsened the competitive position of the NIEs in labour-intensive production. As a result, there has been substantial industrial restructuring of these economies.

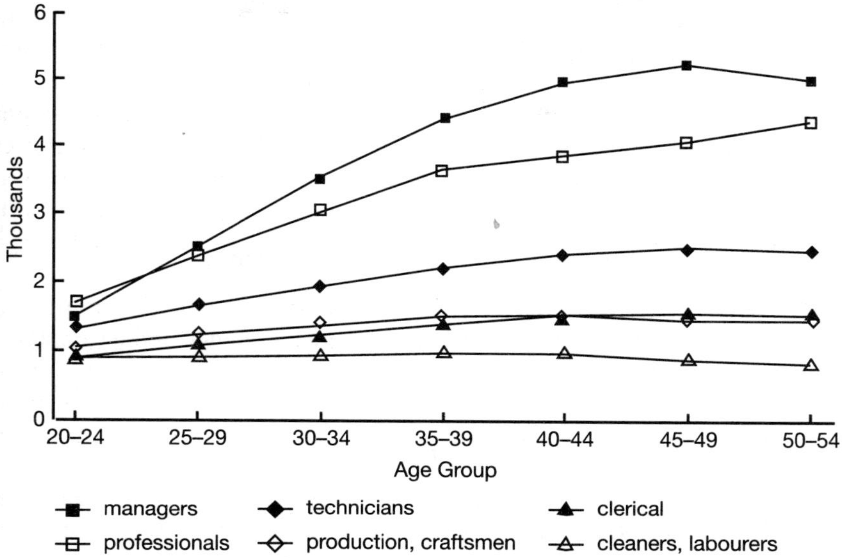

Figure 19.3 Monthly gross wages by occupation.
Note: Profiles for service/sales workers and operators are similar to that for clerical workers.
Source: Ministry of Labour, Report on Wages in Singapore 1992.

Within the manufacturing sectors of Singapore, Taiwan, Korea and Hong Kong, employment has shifted out of labour-intensive manufacturing and into higher value-added, more skill-intensive production. In some of the NIEs, there has also been a shift out of manufacturing altogether and into finance and business services. In Singapore, the share of employment in manufacturing has been robust. However, employment in finance and business services has been growing most rapidly (Bauer, 1992).

This restructuring process has been going on for well over a decade, at least in Singapore, where the government has been actively supporting restructuring efforts. The National Wage Council in Singapore, as early as 1979, adopted the goal of accelerating the shift to skill-intensive, higher value-added activities (Lim, 1980 and 1984). One of the early actions which discouraged labour-intensive manufacturing was the government's high wage policy from 1979 to 1981.

Singapore's government has encouraged industrial upgrading by promoting R&D activities, investment in high value-added and high-tech manufacturing, and the growth of the financial and business service sectors. For example, generous tax concessions have been granted to companies establishing R&D reserves and for the establishment of 'Pioneer Industries' and 'New Technology Companies.' The government has also invested heavily in the human capital required by restructuring. Enrolments at the national universities and polytechnics have been increased substantially.

In addition to restructuring domestic production, the NIEs have been exploiting their managerial and technical expertise by transferring labour-intensive production overseas via massive foreign direct investment flows into China and lower-wage countries in Southeast Asia. Singapore has invested heavily in Malaysia and Indonesia. More recently, the government has been spearheading investment drives into China, Vietnam and India.

19.3.2 Responses aimed at increasing labour supply

The NIEs have also been responding to rising labour scarcity by importing labour, increasing labour force participation among women and encouraging later retirement.

Importation of labour

The importation of labour into Japan and the NIEs has been growing substantially (Bauer, 1990). Labour immigration, however, is a socially divisive issue and these countries restrict it. Despite this, severe labour shortages and pressures from business groups have forced governments to rethink their labour importation policies.

Singapore has made extensive use of foreign labour at all skill levels. However, there has been concern over the influx of foreign workers into the country. There are fears that labour importation incurs substantial political and social costs, depresses wages of low income domestic workers and limits restructuring efforts. In April 1987, the government instituted the foreign worker levy scheme which made foreign labour more expensive. The scheme was adopted to encourage employers to use more capital and skill-intensive methods of production (Lim *et al*, 1988).

Increased female labour force participation

It is widely recognized in Singapore that given the general labour scarcity, there is a need to make better use of the economically inactive, especially housewives and older men and women. In fact, increases in participation among women and the older population could have substantial impacts on labour supply. Whereas labour force participation rates among younger women in Singapore are high, the rates for older women are relatively low (Figure 19.4). For example, the participation rates for women aged 35 and older are substantially lower in Singapore than in Japan, Korea and the United States. Many older women in Singapore have relatively low educational attainments and little work experience, and therefore command low wages in the labour market.

Female labour force participation rates in Singapore, however, have been increasing dramatically (Table 19.5). This trend will continue. Rising wages

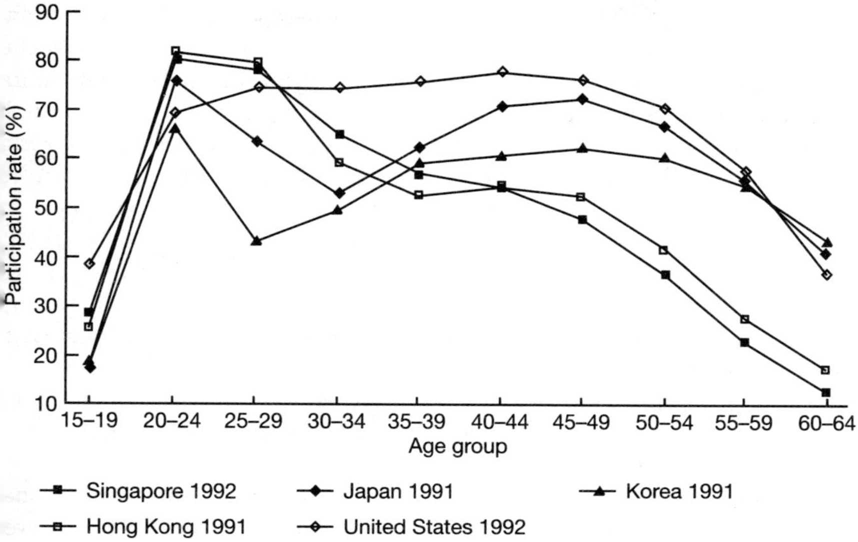

Figure 19.4 Female labour force participation rates, selected countries
Source: International Labour Organisation, Yearbook of Labour Statistics 1992 and Dept. of Statistics, Singapore, Yearbook of Statistics Singapore 1992.

will draw more and more women into the labour market. Moreover, rising levels of education among women, continued low rates of fertility and, possibly, the establishment of more flexible work arrangements will encourage women to work.

The trend toward higher and more continuous participation among women can be easily seen through an analysis of birth cohorts. Figure 19.5

Table 19.5 Female labour force participation rates, Singapore, 1970–1990

	1970	*1975*	*1980*	*1985*	*1990*
Age					
15–19	43.0	39.2	50.7	33.8	27.8
20–24	53.6	64.5	78.4	78.9	79.6
25–29	30.8	43.3	58.7	66.5	76.3
30–34	22.7	32.9	44.2	48.8	63.0
35–39	19.3	28.1	37.1	44.7	54.9
40–44	17.8	25.4	33.2	39.6	51.9
45–49	17.5	20.1	26.5	36.3	45.0
50–54	17.5	18.3	20.4	25.9	34.1
55–59	16.2	14.2	14.5	18.4	21.4
60–64	13.4	14.0	11.3	11.9	12.8

Source: Census of Population (1970, 1980, 1990) and Ministry of Labour, Singapore Yearbook of Labour Statistics (1976, 1986).

summarizes the participation behaviour of different cohorts. It examines how the participation of women in a given five-year birth cohort changes as the cohort ages. The figure clearly shows that the participation among more recent birth cohorts has increased at all ages.

Figure 19.5 also indicates that much of the decline in female participation rates with age, observed in cross-sectional data, is due to the fact that older cohorts of women had consistently lower participation. It does not appear to be primarily caused by the exit of older women from the labour market.[7] Participation rates at the older ages will rise as the younger cohorts, which are more committed to the labour market, age.

Singaporean women will become increasingly attached to the labour market in the future, and this will happen regardless of government interventions. The government should consider, however, various policies that could accommodate this trend and minimize any adverse impacts on children and the women themselves.

Part-time employment has permitted women in the United States and Europe to better balance labour market and household responsibilities. The 1990 National Wage Council report notes that part-time employment in Singapore is low compared with many of the developed countries. Yet surveys indicate that many Singaporean women would like to work part-time.

Fixed costs of employment can affect the extent to which women accept

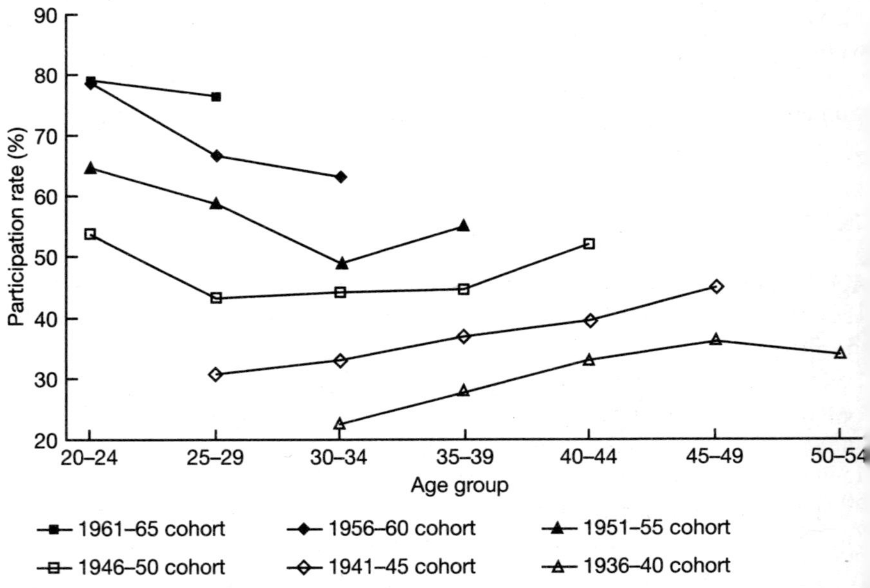

Figure 19.5 Female labour force participation rates, selected birth cohorts
Source: Constructed from data given in Table 19.5.

part-time jobs. These are costs that are incurred if a woman works, such as transportation and child-care costs, but which do not vary directly with the number of hours she works. An increase in fixed costs has two effects. The more obvious is that it induces some women to stay at home, since the net returns to employment are reduced. Another effect is that women who decide to participate in the labour market will tend to work longer hours. The intuition is that these women would work longer in order to cover the higher fixed costs of employment.

This suggests that if the government wanted to encourage women to accept part-time employment, it should try to lower the fixed costs of employment. One of the most important of these costs is child care. Subsidizing child-care facilities not only encourages female participation, but it also makes part-time work more feasible. Reducing the levy on foreign maids could have a similar effect.

Whereas increasing female participation will not reverse the trend of slower labour force growth, it could moderate the decline significantly. Consider the following simple simulation. I project labour growth between 1990 and 2010, making two different assumptions. The first scenario assumes that female labour force participation rates will remain fixed at their 1992 levels. The second assumption is that the rates among women aged 30 to 54, for whom rates are now relatively low, will by 2010 approach the rates currently observed in the U.S.[8] The participation rates are then applied to Shantakumar's (1996) population projections.

The female labour force would be roughly 25% larger in 2010 if participation rates increased as specified, rather than remaining at their 1992 levels. The total labour force, male and female, would be 9% larger. Under the higher female participation scenario, the average annual growth rate of the total labour force between 1990 and 2010 would be about 1%, as opposed to 0.5% in the constant participation scenario.

Increased participation among the elderly

Older Singaporeans are another labour pool which will be tapped as labour scarcity worsens. Participation rates among older men and women are low by international standards (Table 19.6). This is largely due to mandatory retirement practices which were established when labour was in surplus and life expectancy lower. These practices are now being changed, and participation among older men and women should increase.

Higher participation among the elderly could also have a significant impact on labour supply. Consider the following exercise. I project the labour force up to 2010 by assuming that participation rates among older Singaporeans remain at their 1992 levels. I also project by assuming that these rates increase. The participation rates for men aged 50 to 64 and women aged 50 to 64 are assumed to approach the levels currently observed in Japan by 2010.[9]

Table 19.6 Labour force participation rates among the elderly, selected countries (1992)

	Males		*Females*	
	55–59	*60–64*	*55–59*	*60–64*
Singapore	71.3	49.2	22.7	12.6
Hong Kong	80.4	54.6	25.6	16.3
Japan	93.6	75.0	55.7	40.7
Korea (Rep. of)	84.9	71.0	54.1	44.9
U.S.	79.8	55.1	57.4	36.6

Source: International Labour Organisation, Yearbook of Labour Statistics 1993.

In both projections, I also assume that participation rates among prime-aged women will increase as specified in the simulations given in the previous section. The simulations suggest that the total labour force in 2010 would be roughly 7.4% larger if the participation rates of older Singaporeans increased as specified.

We should also keep in mind that the characteristics of Singapore's older population will be quite different in 2010. One of the problems associated with the employment of older workers today is that many of them have relatively little education. This situation will change dramatically as the younger, more educated cohorts of workers age. For example, among workers currently aged 50 to 59, about 44% have only a lower primary or no schooling at all (Table 19.7). However, only 22% of workers aged 40 to 49 and 10% of those aged 30 to 39 have such little schooling.

There are long-standing schemes, such as the Skills Development Fund, which promote worker training in Singapore. More recently, there have been calls to target older workers for training. Increasing educational attainments among older workers will facilitate these efforts. Increases in the retirement age will also do this by extending the age beyond which training is no longer a profitable investment. For example, firms and workers may not find it worthwhile to invest in the training of a 50 year old worker who will retire at age 55. However, both the worker and the firm may find it a good investment if retirement does not occur until age 67.

19.4 SINGAPORE'S ELDERLY AND THE LABOUR MARKET

Dramatic declines in labour force growth and rising life expectancies suggest that older workers will have to play a greater role in Singapore's labour market. Mandatory retirement practices limited the extent to which older workers could contribute to the economy, and recent legislation has attempted to relax this constraint.

Table 19.7 Educational attainment of older workers (1992)

	Composition (%) Age Group		
	50–59	*40–49*	*30–39*
Never attended/lower primary	44.6	22.0	10.0
Primary/lower secondary	26.5	32,8	31.1
Secondary	13.5	24.9	34.4
Post-secondary	7.8	9.8	9.8
Diploma	1.1	2.3	5.1
Tertiary	6.5	8.3	9.6

Source: Ministry of Labour, Report on the Labour Force Survey of Singapore 1992.

19.4.1 Mandatory age of retirement

The experience of Japan can provide a useful background for examining retirement practices in Singapore.

Retirement practices in Japan

Low mandatory ages of retirement in Japan have forced workers out of firms. Because of growing labour scarcity and increasing pension costs, the mandatory age of retirement has been increased over time in Japan, but only by an average of four years since 1965. In 1974, about one half of firms with mandatory retirement had a retirement age of 55 or younger. By 1991, roughly 71% had retirement ages of 60 or older. The strong seniority-based wage system acted to limit the increase in retirement ages. However, there have been recent calls for increasing the retirement age further. In December of 1993, the Employment Council, a government advisory panel, suggested that companies should retain employees until the age of 65 as a way of coping with ageing.

Firms have been reluctant to retain older workers because of their relatively high wages. The government has therefore offered subsidies to encourage firms to retain older workers (Clark and Ogawa, 1993). In 1986, for example, the government implemented the comprehensive 'Law Concerning Stabilisation of Employment for Older Persons' and subsequently revised this law in 1990. The law established several subsidy schemes to promote employment of older workers. The strength of the incentives vary with firm size and numbers of older workers hired.[10] The Ministry of Labour also enacted a program in January 1994 which subsidizes companies that hire workers age 45 and older from firms other than their affiliates. The government also subsidizes 'Silver Human Resource Centres' which provide supplementary or short-term employment opportunities for the elderly.

Retirement practices in Singapore

Prior to recent legislation adopted in 1993, the mandatory age of retirement in Singapore was only 55. This age was widely perceived as being too low given increases in life expectancy and growing labour scarcity in Singapore. As early as 1984 a Ministry of Health committee report, popularly known as the Howe report, recommended increasing the retirement age, first to 60 and later to 65.[11] The National Wage Council had, since 1988, exhorted companies to raise the retirement age norm from 55 to 60 or above. Employers were reluctant to do so, largely because of the seniority wage system. Because employers were generally unwilling to change retirement practices, the government passed the Retirement Age Act in April 1993. This act prohibits employers from dismissing workers below age 60 on the basis of age. The mandatory retirement age will be raised to 67 by the year 2003.

The new law gives workers the opportunity to postpone retirement. The extent to which they will do so remains to be seen. My expectation is that participation rates among older workers will rise substantially. Firstly, the old retirement age of 55 was very low. Secondly, survey data suggest that older workers wish to remain employed. For example, the Ministry of Labour's National Survey of Senior Citizens in 1989 found that 68% of economically active men age 50 and older would like to continue working for as long as possible. Finally, the mandatory age of retirement should establish a social norm affecting retirement behaviour. Whereas increasing the mandatory age of retirement should permit, and even induce, greater labour force participation among the older population, the choice of retirement age will be increasingly influenced by the factors discussed below.

19.4.2 Modelling the retirement decision

Three broad economic factors influence the decision to retire: preferences for work and leisure, lifetime nonwork income at the earliest feasible age of retirement, and gains in lifetime income from postponing retirement for another year. (See Ehrenberg and Smith, 1991, for a brief exposition.) Economists have relatively little to say about preferences, and I will focus on the two remaining factors.

Assume that age 55 is the earliest feasible age of retirement in Singapore. Actually, retirement may not be feasible at age 55 for some workers, however, this has been the norm until recently. It is the age at which workers can withdraw their Central Provident Fund (CPF) balances. Lifetime nonwork income at age 55 would determine the standard of living a worker could sustain if he or she retired at this age. Nonwork income reflects a worker's level of savings, wealth, and pension benefits.

The general prediction of economic theory is that an increase in lifetime nonwork income would induce earlier retirement. In the jargon of economics, a pure income effect would induce individuals to consume more leisure. The greater the level of savings or wealth an individual has amassed by age 55, the greater are the chances he or she will retire earlier.

In Singapore, perhaps the most important factor determining the level of lifetime nonwork income is the CPF. Roughly three quarters of the labour force currently contribute to the fund. The CPF is not specifically a retirement scheme. Workers, for example, can withdraw their balances from the fund upon reaching age 55, even if they do not retire at age 55. However, the level of a worker's CPF balances could have an important impact on his or her decision to retire. Larger balances should, other things being equal, induce earlier retirement.

Two other aspects of the CPF scheme could also influence retirement behaviour: the age of withdrawal and the minimum sum. An increase in the withdrawal age above 55 should tend to induce later retirement. An increase in the minimum sum should have, qualitatively, the same effect. Unfortunately, the extent of empirical work on Singapore's labour market does not permit me to gauge the potential magnitudes of these effects. I will, however, speculate on this below. Pensions can also affect the level of lifetime nonwork income, but their importance in Singapore is limited. Pension schemes are largely limited to older, top civil servants.

The second major economic factor affecting retirement decisions is the gain in lifetime income from postponing retirement. This gain is largely determined by the wage rates received by older workers. In some countries the impact of postponing retirement on pension benefits can also be important. Again, this is not an important factor in Singapore. However, employers' contribution rates to the CPF would affect these gains. Increasing the gains from working should induce later retirement. These economic factors are discussed in greater detail below.

Nonwork lifetime income at the earliest possible age of retirement

I have argued above that CPF balances are the most important determinant of nonwork lifetime income at the earliest feasible age of retirement in Singapore. It should be noted, however, that at present the CPF is not the major source of old-age support for many. Chew and Chew (1992), analyzing a subsample of 131 retired respondents in the 1987 NUS Census Survey, found that about 50% relied primarily on relatives for old-age support. Roughly 27% relied on their CPF balances or pensions, 19% on savings, and the remaining 4% on social welfare or investment income.

Children do currently provide a major source of support for retired workers. In the future, however, reliance on children for old-age support will most likely decline, and the importance of the CPF will grow. Firstly, rising educational levels among workers will encourage this trend. Chew and Chew (1992) found that reliance on children for old age support declines dramatically with the educational attainment of the retiree. Secondly, increasingly large proportions of retirees will have had a history of contribution to the CPF. Finally, lower fertility rates imply that the elderly will have fewer children to rely upon for support.

Three aspects of the CPF could have potentially important impacts on retirement behaviour: the size of CPF balances at age 55, the CPF withdrawal age and the minimum sum. Larger balances would, other things being equal, induce earlier retirement. In the future, CPF balances among potential retirees should grow substantially given rising wages and longer CPF contribution histories. However, the general view seems to be that, at present, balances for most older workers are relatively low, and this is likely to be the case for quite some time. This suggests that CPF balances will not induce large proportions of older workers to retire before the new mandatory age of retirement. Lim *et al* (1986), for example, conclude that 'for all Singaporean workers, it is necessary to work beyond the age of 55 to provide for a comfortable life after retirement.'

It is useful to consider two types of older workers: those with low balances and those with high ones. I expect that relatively few workers in either group will opt to retire before the mandatory age. The former cannot afford to do so, and the latter will not choose to do so, because their relatively high wages imply high gains from postponing retirement.

The low balance group is currently large. Lower wages and lower contribution rates in the past imply that many older workers have relatively low balances. Asher (1991) notes that about half of the CPF contributors in the 45–54 age group have balances below $60,000. He concludes that financing old age from their own CPF sources will be a problem for a significant proportion of older workers.

Some workers do have large balances, and their numbers should increase. The accumulation of large balances could affect retirement decisions and labour supply. It is not clear, however, that the effect will be large, even among the high balance contributors. The reason is that this group includes high-wage workers. High wage rates, which imply high gains from working, should moderate the move toward early retirement. For example, studies in the US have found that individuals with higher social security wealth are less likely to retire early. Lazear (1986) concludes that these individuals are likely to have been high-income, high-hours-of-work individuals earlier in their lives, and it is not unreasonable to expect this behaviour to persist in old age.

A second important element of the CPF scheme is the age of withdrawal. At present, workers are allowed to withdraw their CPF savings at age 55.[12] There have been calls to increase the age of withdrawal. It was first proposed during 1984 in the Howe report, which argued that the age of withdrawal should be deferred first to 60 and later to 65. The report stated that keeping the present age of withdrawal would militate against efforts to encourage workers to continue working beyond 55, because the lump sum of CPF money gives them an illusion of financial security. The proposal proved to be very controversial and politically unacceptable at the time.

Recently, government officials have again begun to propose raising the age of withdrawal in order to bring it in line with increases in the age of retirement and life expectancy. Since this measure was first proposed during the mid-1980s, a number of changes have occurred. Perhaps the most significant is the increase in the mandatory age of retirement discussed above. Life expectancy has also continued to increase, and there is growing concern over the financial security of retirees. Moreover, several schemes have been adopted which permit substantial CPF withdrawals before the age of 55 for the purchase of property, stock shares and other investments.

I would like to focus on the potential labour supply effects of the withdrawal age. Theoretically, assuming capital market imperfections which make it difficult for workers to borrow on CPF wealth, raising the withdrawal age would radically alter workers' budget constraints and would tend to promote later retirement. The overall impact on retirement behaviour, however, depends upon worker preferences. It depends upon how many workers would have chosen to retire early if the age of withdrawal was kept at 55. If substantial numbers of workers do decide to exit the labour market before the mandatory age of retirement, raising the age of withdrawal could be a powerful lever for keeping older workers in the market. However, it is not clear that many would choose to do so.

The experiences of Japan and the United States suggest that altering budget constraints in such a manner can have a strong impact on retirement behaviour. Ogawa and Clark (1993) claim that the relatively high labour force participation among Japan's elderly is accounted for by the fact that the age for pension eligibility is quite high. Basic pension benefits, which are the core component of Japan's pension system, are suspended until the worker reaches the age of 65.[13] In the US, decreasing the age of social security eligibility from 65 to 62 made earlier retirement attractive for many (Levine and Mitchell, 1991).

Whereas the government has not changed the age of withdrawal, it did adopt the minimum sum policy in 1986. This policy, which requires CPF contributors to leave a certain sum in their accounts until age 60, should have an effect on retirement decisions which is similar, qualitatively at least, to changing the age of withdrawal. In 1994, the government decided to raise the minimum sum from $34,600 to $80,000 over ten years. CPF members can use their property to pledge half to this amount. The minimum sum withdrawal age is pegged to the age of retirement. It is now 60 but will be gradually raised to 67 as the retirement age is increased.

Increases in lifetime income from postponing retirement

The economic returns from postponing retirement should also affect labour force participation rates. In Singapore, there are two main factors which determine the increase in lifetime income associated with later retirement: wage rates among older workers and employer CPF contributions. Whereas economic theory does not unambiguously predict the impact of a change in these returns, it is generally believed that a decrease in the returns would induce earlier retirement. For example, reductions in wages and employer CPF contributions for older workers should induce some to exit the labour market. Raising wage levels would coax them into postponing retirement. Empirical studies for Singapore do not yet provide an indication as to the magnitude of this effect. I suspect that the labour supply of older workers, especially men, is fairly inelastic and, therefore, the impact of such changes should be modest. However, reducing total compensation could have a substantial adverse impact on the morale and work effort of older workers.

There is a general presumption, in Singapore and elsewhere, that wage rates for older workers should decline after some critical age. In fact, wage reduction among older workers has been one of the responses to ageing in Japan. In Singapore, compensation schemes based purely on seniority have been criticised for some time. The Howe report, for example, stated that '. . . workers must accept that, in most occupations, they become less productive as they grow older and are less dexterous, flexible and adaptable. . . Hence, to ensure cost-effectiveness, older workers must be prepared to accept lower wages on account of their lower productivity' (Ministry of Health, 1984, p. 22). The belief that productivity declines after a certain age and that older workers are 'over-paid' under strong seniority-based pay schemes has led to government intervention. In Japan, as noted above, the government provides subsidies to encourage firms to employ older workers. In Singapore, in order to encourage the employment of older workers, the government has lowered the rate at which employers must contribute to the CPF for employees over age 55. As of July 1993, the employer CPF contribution rate was 18.5% of the gross salary for workers below age 55. The rate is only 7.5% for workers aged 55 to 65 and 5% for those over age 65.

Older workers have gained in that they can now work beyond age 55 if they so choose. The 11 percentage point decline in the employer CPF contribution rate, however, represents a substantial decrease in their total compensation. If the decline in compensation does cause many older workers to exit the labour market or has an adverse impact on their work effort, the labour market will respond, and wage rates for older workers will rise. It will do so, however, selectively by occupation and skill level in response to productivity and other demand considerations.

Other factors

There are two additional factors that should be noted: the impact of health on retirement and the need to provide part-time work for older workers. The health status of older workers can be an important determinant of retirement behaviour. It does not, however, appear to be the major factor. In the US, for example, Fields and Mitchell (1984) found that economic factors such as wages and retirement benefits accounted for three quarters of the variance in retirement ages across individuals, while poor health accounted for only one quarter. In Singapore, Chew and Chew (1992) found that roughly 19% of retirees cited poor health as a reason for retirement. It is also interesting to note that Chew and Chew (1992) view the cost of health care as a factor that may induce older Singaporeans to keep working. If the worker remains in the labour market, the cost of his health care is assumed largely by the employer.

It is generally believed that the provision of more part-time work opportunities would encourage participation among the elderly. Whereas this is likely to be true, we should be aware that it is often difficult for employers to provide it. Hurd (1993) notes that most older workers in the US retire completely from full-time work with no intervening spell of part-time work. Normal business practices resulting from fixed costs of employment and team production tend to prohibit part-time employment. He concludes that workers face a limited choice between either relatively high-paying full-time and low-paying part-time work.

19.5 SUMMARY

Demographic factors, though often ignored by scholars, can have substantial long run implications for an economy. Singapore, where fertility declines have been strong and swift, is an excellent example. The legacy of these fertility declines is apparent: slower labour force growth and an ageing work-force. Firms, workers and the government have already begun to respond to these trends.

Singapore's labour force grew at an average annual rate of 3.4% during the 1980s. Labour force growth could be as low as only 0.7% per year during the 1990s and 0.3% during the first decade of the next century. Whereas roughly 45,000 workers were added to the labour force each year during the 1980s, it could increase by as little as 10,600 annually during this decade. Changes in labour supply behaviour, such as greater participation among women and the elderly, could significantly moderate the projected decline in labour force growth. It will not, however, reverse the trend. Growth in Singapore's labour force will become increasingly modest, and, assuming strong economic performance continues, labour will become increasing scarce.

Labour costs will continue to rise, and comparative advantage will shift even further away from labour-intensive manufacturing. The challenges these trends pose, of course, are not unique to Singapore. Japan has faced them, and the other NIEs, to varying degrees, are also experiencing problems associated with labour scarcity. In contrast to Singapore and the other NIEs, however, labour surpluses will persist for the foreseeable future in Indonesia, the Philippines, Vietnam, China and virtually all of South Asia.

Singapore's population and labour force will age rapidly, and support for the elderly will consume an expanding share of the country's resources. There were only 13 persons aged 60 and older for every 100 persons aged 15 to 59 in 1990. This number will more than triple by 2020. Ageing of the workforce could also have a potentially strong impact on the economy. Some fear that this ageing will constrain the ability to respond to technological and structural changes. There is also a concern that ageing, given seniority-based pay systems, puts pressure on wages and labour costs. The promotion of flexible-wage systems, which place less emphasis on seniority, should help to moderate the impact of ageing on labour costs in Singapore.

Labour scarcity is caused by the interaction of demand and supply factors, and responses to labour scarcity have been directed at both. There have been three important responses on the demand side. First, substantial industrial restructuring has occurred, with a strong drive into higher-value-added manufacturing, finance and other business services. The government has actively supported this drive with investment, R&D, tax and educational policies. Second, automation and capital intensity in production has increased. Third, labour-intensive manufacturing has been transferred overseas via foreign direct investment. That these responses must continue is a demographic imperative.

Labour scarcity has induced three important labour supply responses: the importation of labour, rising female participation, and postponement of retirement among older workers. Foreign workers have long been an important component of Singapore's labour force. The use of foreign labour is restricted, however, and many believe that the economy should not increase its reliance on foreign workers. Female labour force participation in Singapore has been rising rapidly. Participation among women over age 30 is relatively low at present. This will change quickly, however, as younger cohorts of women age. The labour market attachment of these younger cohorts is substantially stronger than that of earlier cohorts. Rising wages, increasing educational levels among women and continued low fertility will bring women into the labour market in greater and greater numbers.

The contribution of older Singaporeans to the labour market has been severely constrained until recently by mandatory retirement practices formulated in a period when labour was abundant and life expectancies much lower. The Retirement Age Act of 1993, which has raised the mandatory age of retirement, should substantially relax this constraint, and participation rates among the elderly will rise. Moreover, as the mandatory age of retirement is increased, other factors which affect retirement decisions, such as the structure of the CPF scheme, will become increasingly important. Changes in the size and distribution of CPF balances, the age of withdrawal, the minimum sum, and employer contribution rates can radically alter the budget constraints of older Singaporean workers. These alterations could affect their labour supply behaviour, though I speculate that these effects will be modest.

NOTES

1 See Shantakumar (1996) for specific assumptions regarding fertility, mortality, migration and age-sex specific labour force participation rates.

2 Specific training increases the productivity of the worker only in the firm which offers the training. General training, on the other hand, provides skills which would be beneficial to several potential employers.

3 The National Wage Council was established by the government in 1972 to help bring about orderly wage increases. The NWC includes high level representatives from employers, unions and the government. The Council assists in the formulation of guidelines on wage policy and recommends necessary adjustments in wage structure.

4 Income from work for employees includes gross monthly wages or salaries (including commissions, overtime payments, NWC supplements and other allowances) and 1/12 of annual bonuses. Income for the self-employed includes profits from business, trade, or professions.

5 I use five-year age-specific rates.

6 Monthly gross wages refer to all remuneration received by an employee before deductions of employee's CPF contributions and personal income tax. It excludes employer's CPF contributions and bonuses. Unfortunately, these data were not presented separately for male and female workers.

7 Note that the participation rates for the oldest age groups reported for each cohort trace out the declining age profile of participation for 1992 observed in Figure 19.4.

8 The hypothetical age-specific rates in this simulation are as follows: 0.778 for those aged 25–29, 0.700 for 30–34, 0.725 for 35–39, 0.750 for 40–44, 0.778 for 45–49, 0.750 for 50–54.

9 I assume that the rates for men aged 15 to 49 remain at their 1992 levels. The rates are assumed to increase from 0.89 to 0.95 for men aged 50 to 54, from 0.71 to 0.94 for men aged 55 to 59, and from 0.49 to 0.75 for those aged 60 to 64. The rates for women aged 15 to 54 are the same as those adopted in the earlier exercise. In other words, I keep the assumption that rates among prime-age women will increase. Here, however, I also assume that participation rates among older women will also increase from 0.23 to 0.56 for women aged 55 to 59 and from 0.13 to 0.41 for women aged 60 to 64.

10 For example, if a medium or small sized firm hires an older worker, so that older workers exceeded 4% of the workforce, the company would receive a subsidy of 30,000 yen per person month. If a large company hired an older worker so that older workers exceeded 6% of the workforce, the company would receive a subsidy of 40,000 yen per person month.

11 Howe Yoon Chong was the committee's chairman. The reports full title is the *Report of the Committee on the Problems of the Aged.*

12 Actually, the scheme permits substantial withdrawals before age 55 for the purchase of property, stock shares, other investments and insurance.

13 This is a major problem in Japan since mandatory ages of retirement are usually

below age 65. Workers receive large lump sum payments upon retirement. However, many choose or are forced to continue working after formal 'retirement.'

REFERENCES

Asher, M.G. (1991). Social Adequacy and Equity of the Social Security Arrangements in Singapore (Singapore: Centre for Advanced Studies Occasional Paper, National University of Singapore).

Bauer, J. (1992). Industrial Restructuring in the NIEs: Prospects and Challenges, *Asian Survey* XXXII(11), pp. 1012–1025.

Bauer, J. (1990). Demographic Change and Asian Labor Markets in the 1990s, *Population and Development Review* 16(4), pp. 615–645.

Bauer, J. and Ogawa N. (1994). Population Ageing and Japan's Seniority-Wage System, unpublished working paper, Nanyang Technological University, Singapore.

Becker, G. (1962). Investment in Human Capital: A Theoretical Analysis, *Journal of Political Economy* 70 (Supplement), pp. 9–49.

Carmichael, H.L. (1989). Self-Enforcing Contracts, Shirking, and Live Cycle Incentives, *Journal of Economic Perspectives* 3(4), pp. 65–83.

Chew, S.B. and Chew R. (1992). The Singapore Worker: A Profile (Singapore: Oxford University Press).

Clark, R. (1990). Japanese Retirement Systems (Homewood, Ill: Dow Jones-Irwin).

—— (1988). Ageing Urban Populations and the Economic Vitality of the Cities of the World, paper presented at the Ageing and Urban Economic Development Conference, sponsored by the United Nations, Sendai, Japan, September.

—— and Ogawa N. (1992). The Effects of Mandatory Retirement on Earnings Profiles in Japan, *Industrial and Labor Relations Review* 45(2), pp. 258–266.

—— and Ogawa N. (1992b). Employment Tenure and Earning Profiles in Japan and the United States: Comment, *American Economic Review* 82(1), pp. 336–345.

—— and Spengler J. (1980). *The Economics of Individual* and *Population Ageing* (Cambridge, Mass: Cambridge University Press).

Department of Statistics, Singapore (1992). *Yearbook of Statistics Singapore* 1992.

Ehrenberg, R. and Smith R. (1991). *Modern Labor Economics*, Fourth Edition (New York: Harper Collins).

Fields, G.S. and Mitchell O.S. (1984). *Retirement, Pensions, and Social Security* (Cambridge, Mass: MIT Press).

Hashimoto, M. and Raisian J. (1992). Employment Tenure and Earnings Profiles in Japan and the United States: Reply, *American Economic Review* 82(1), pp. 346–354.

Hurd, M. (1993). The Effect of Labor Market Rigidities on the Labor Force Behaviour of Older Workers, NBER Working Paper No. 4462 (Cambridge, Mass: National Bureau of Economic Research).

Hutchens, R. (1989). Seniority, Wages and Productivity: A Turbulent Decade, *Journal of Economic Perspectives* 3(4), pp. 49–64.

Lazear, E. (1979). Why is There Mandatory Retirement? *Journal of Political Economy* 87, pp. 1261–84.

—— (1986). Retirement From the Labour Force in Ashenfelter, O. and Layard, R., eds., *Handbook of Labour Economics*, Volume 1, (London: Elsevier Science Publishers).

Lim, C.Y. (1980). *Economic Development in Singapore* (Singapore: Federal Publications).

—— (1984). *Economic Restructuring in Singapore* (Singapore: Federal Publications).

—— *et al* (1986). Report of the Central Provident Fund Study Group, *Singapore Economic Review* 31(1).
—— *et al* (1988). *Policy Options for the Singapore Economy* (Singapore: McGraw Hill).
Ministry of Health, Singapore (1984). *Report of the Committee on the Problems of the Aged.*
Ministry of Labour, Singapore (1992). 21 *Years of the National Wage Council* (Singapore: SNP Publishers Pte. Ltd.)
—— (1993). *Report of the Flexible Wage System Review Committee* (Singapore: SNP Publishers Pte. Ltd.)
Ogawa, N. and Clark R. (1993). Ageing Labor Force and Labor Market Responses in Japan, unpublished paper, Nihon University.
Shantakumar, G. (1996). Population and Labour Supply in Singapore, in Lim C.Y., ed., *Economic Policy Management in Singapore* (Singapore: Addison-Wesley).
Tyabji, A. (1993). Social Security in the Asian-Pacific Region, *Asian-Pacific Economic Literature* 7(1), pp. 53–72.

20

INCOME DISTRIBUTION AND GROWTH IN EAST ASIA

Jong-Il You

Europe was so organised socially and economically as to secure the maximum accumulation of capital. While there was some continuous improvement in the daily condition of the mass of the population, society was so framed as to throw a great part of the increased income into the control of the class least likely to consume it . . . Herein lay in fact the main justification of the capitalist system. If the rich had spent their new wealth on their own enjoyment, the world would long ago have found such a regime intolerable [Keynes, 1919: 18].

INTRODUCTION

Faster growth and more egalitarian income distribution have been the main objectives of development. There is a wide-ranging consensus among economists that East Asia holds a special place in the developing world as a case in which both these objectives have been successfully attained. *The East Asian Miracle* report by the World Bank [1993] (to be referred to henceforth as *The Miracle* report) mirrors this consensus in its analysis of the economic success of what it calls the High Performing Asian Economies (HPAEs) – Japan, the Republic of Korea (simply Korea hereafter), Taiwan, Hong Kong, Singapore, Malaysia, Thailand and Indonesia. It says that the essence of the miracle is the rapid growth combined with 'unusually low and declining income inequality, underscoring the exceptional nature of this achievement'.

If this is correct, the contrast with the historical experience of the European development as analysed by Kuznets or described in the above quote from Keynes could not be stronger. The first contrast is about whether growth tends to increase or decrease inequality. Another difference is whether greater or less inequality is conducive to growth. Yet another difference concerns the political economy of distribution and growth: does growth lead people to accept inequality or does a good distribution lead people to accept growth-oriented policies? Is the East Asian experience truly exceptional? Do we now

Source: Journal of Development Studies, Vol. 34 (6), August 1998, pp. 37–65.

have to discard the classical/Keynesian understanding of the accumulation process based on profits?

The interaction between policies, income distribution and growth is complex. This study tries to sort out some of the issues and answer the questions raised by the claims of exceptionality of income distribution in East Asia. The central findings are (i) that the exceptionality claim has a limited validity with respect to Japan, Korea and Taiwan only, where low inequality prevails as a consequence of the exceptionally equal initial distribution of wealth resulting from post-war reforms and the rapid employment expansion in the subsequent growth process; (ii) that the classical/Keynesian view of the accumulation process, in which high profits play a crucial role as a source of savings and an incentive for investment, is very much relevant in understanding the East Asian experience; (iii) that a relatively high inequality in the functional distribution of income went hand in hand with a relatively low inequality in the size distribution, primarily owing to the unusually even distribution of wealth, resulting from the initial conditions as well as the rather high savings propensity of the low-income households.

The rest of the study is devoted to substantiating the above claims and organised as follows. We begin by an examination of the records and explanation of income distribution in East Asia (Section 20.I). In the next section, we analyse the relationship between income distribution and the accumulation process in East Asia from the classical/Keynesian perspective (Section 20.II). Then, we go on to discuss the reasons why East Asian countries managed to have low inequality despite relatively high shares of profits in income (Section 20.III). The following section presents an analytical framework on the relationship between growth and income distribution within which the East Asian experience can be understood (Section 20.IV). The concluding Section 20.V provides a brief summary.

20.I IS EAST ASIAN INCOME DISTRIBUTION TRULY EXCEPTIONAL?

(1) Level of inequality: not all in the same league

Here we examine the evidence on income inequality in East Asia to see if they are truly exceptional. An appropriate place to start the discussion is *The Miracle* report. The World Bank economists classify only seven economies as 'high growth-low inequality' in a sample of 40, all of which are HPAEs, with Malaysia as the only HPAE that does not qualify [World Bank, 1993: Fig. 1.3: 31]. Putting aside the question of reliability of the data, this impressive evidence of 'growth with equity' in East Asia becomes suspect once we ask what the rationale for sample selection is. *The Miracle* report gives absolutely no explanation whatsoever. We do not know why France, Switzerland and Spain are included in the sample, but Germany, Sweden and Portugal are not;

nor do we have a clue as to why India, Colombia and Mauritius are, but China, Costa Rica and Morocco are not. It seems therefore worthwhile to see if the conclusion of *The Miracle* report stands when we change the reference samples.

For obvious reasons, we shall use the World Bank's own data [World Bank, 1994: Table 30] and the inequality measure it uses (the ratio of the income shares of the richest 20 per cent and the poorest 20 per cent of the population).[1] As a way of excluding arbitrariness from the sample choice, we may consider a sample that includes all countries for which the data are available from the above World Bank table. To this, we add Taiwan to get a more complete picture on the HPAEs, using the official government data for 1990 taken from CEPD [1995]. This gives us a sample of 66 economies, and Table 20.1 ranks them from the lowest inequality to the highest. It shows that Japan, Indonesia, Taiwan and Korea may indeed be characterised as having low income inequalities as they rank in the top third of the sample. The other four HPAEs, however, rank in the bottom half, with Malaysia ranking in the bottom third. Given this, it seems unreasonable to say that the HPAEs as a group stand out for their low inequalities. Excluding from the sample the

Table 20.1 Ranking of income inequality in 66 countries

Country	*IR*	*Rank*	*Country*	*IR*	*Rank*	*Country*	*IR*	*Rank*
Hungary	3.2	1	Finland	6.0	23	Australia	9.6	45
Bulgaria	3.5	2	Italy	6.0	24	UK	9.6	46
Poland	3.9	3	Ghana	6.3	25	Venezuela	10.3	47
Rwanda	4.0	4	China	6.5	26	Peru	10.5	48
Bangladesh	4.1	5	Israel	6.6	27	*Malaysia*	11.7	49
Japan	4.3	6	Algeria	6.7	28	Costa Rica	12.7	50
Nepal	4.3	7	Morocco	7.0	29	Mauritania	13.2	51
Spain	4.4	8	Canada	7.1	30	Dominican R.	13.2	52
Sri Lanka	4.4	9	Denmark	7.1	31	Mexico	13.6	53
Netherlands	4.5	10	Jordan	7.3	32	Colombia	15.5	54
Belgium	4.6	11	Philippines	7.4	33	Zimbabwe	15.6	55
Sweden	4.6	12	France	7.5	34	Botswana	16.4	56
India	4.7	13	Tunisia	7.8	35	Senegal	16.7	57
Pakistan	4.7	14	Jamaica	8.1	36	Chile	17.0	58
Ethiopia	4.8	15	*Thailand*	8.3	37	Kenya	18.2	59
Indonesia	4.9	16	Switzerland	8.6	38	Lesotho	20.7	60
Uganda	4.9	17	Bolivia	8.6	39	Honduras	23.5	61
Taiwan	5.2	18	*Hong Kong*	8.7	40	Tanzania	26.1	62
Korea	5.7	19	New Zealand	8.8	41	Guinea-Bissau	28.0	63
Germany	5.8	20	Zambia	8.9	42	Panama	29.9	64
Côte d'Ivoire	5.8	21	USA	8.9	43	Guatemala	30.0	65
Norway	5.9	22	*Singapore*	9.6	44	Brazil	32.1	66

Note: IR (inequality ratio) = income share of the top quantile/income share of the bottom quantile.

Source: Calculated from *World Development Report, 1994*, Table 30.

outliers – the three former socialist countries at the top of the ranking and the seven poor countries with the inequality ratio over 20 – hardly changes the overall picture.

Next, we consider dividing the sample into groups according to the growth performance. From the reduced sample of 56 economies that excludes the outliers, we construct a high-growth group (12 economies), a medium-growth group (22 economies) and a low-growth group (22 economies).[2] Figure 20.1 depicts the median and the average inequality ratios of each of the three groups as well as the inequality ratios of all the HPAEs. An interesting feature of this figure is the negative relationship between growth and median inequality, which suggests a possibility that countries with lower inequality have better chances of high economic growth. As for the HPAEs, all of them except Japan belong to the high-growth group. Among them, only three (Indonesia, Taiwan, Korea) have lower inequality than the group median, and the other four have higher inequality than both the group average and the group median. Neither the most equal countries (Nepal, India, Pakistan) nor the most unequal country (Botswana) in this group are HPAEs. This finding flies in the face of *The Miracle* report's claim that all the high growth-low inequality countries are HPAEs.

Finally, we consider the inequality rankings within groups of economies classified on the basis of the level of income. This is probably the most significant exercise, given that the level of income is thought to be one of the

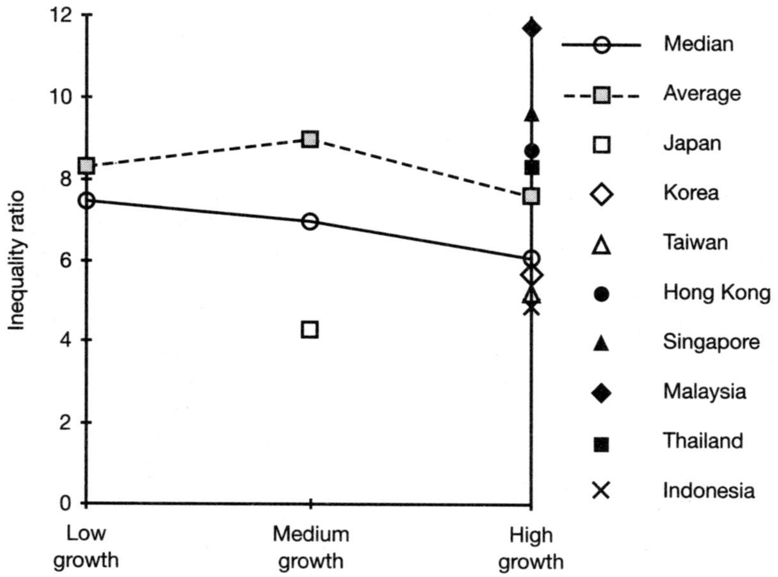

Figure 20.1 Inequality across growth groups and in HPAEs.
Source: Calculated from Table 20.1 above and World Bank [1994: Table 2].

basic determinants of inequality. We follow the World Bank classification of countries into four levels of income and obtain a low income group (15 economies), a lower-middle income group (15 economies), an upper-middle income group (six economies), and a high income group (20 economies). Figure 20.2, which depicts the median and the average inequality ratios of each of these four groups, clearly supports the Kuznets hypothesis of an inverted U-shaped relationship between inequality and the level of income. Both the median and the average inequality rise as the level of income rises up to the upper-middle income, before falling at the high income level.

From Figure 2 we can also compare the inequality ratios of the HPAEs with the average and the median of the income groups to which they belong. Among the three HPAEs that belong to the high income group, only Japan has low inequality. Inequality in Hong Kong and Singapore is at the higher end of this group. In the upper-middle income group Taiwan and Korea have low inequality, but Malaysia's inequality is very high. Among the lower-middle income economies, Thailand is the only HPAE and its inequality is the same as the group median (though lower than the group average). As the only HPAE that belongs to the low income group, Indonesia's inequality is also the same as the median of this group.

It is clearly an overstatement to say that the HPAEs all have 'unusually low inequality'. Instead, in terms of inequality, we have three sub-groups within the HPAEs: Japan, Korea and Taiwan – let us call them 'the super three' –

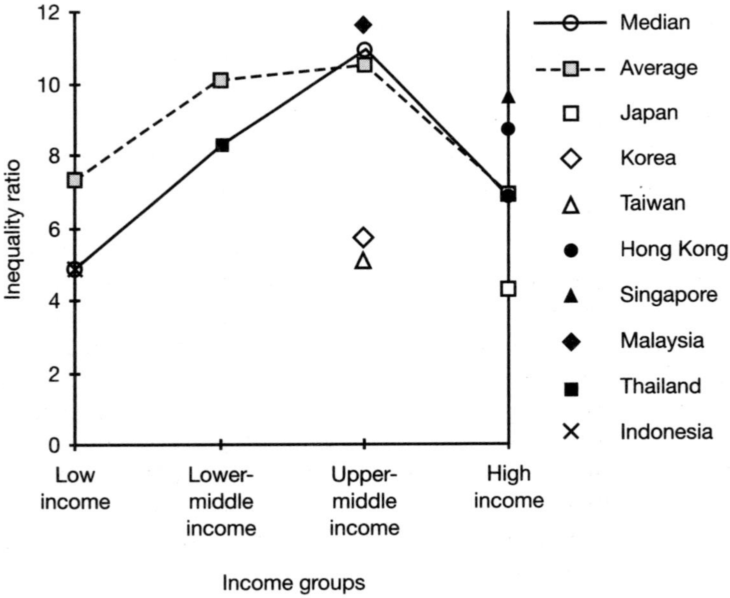

Figure 20.2 Inequality across income groups and in HPAEs.
Source: Calculated from Table 20.1 above.

indeed deserve to be thus described. Thailand and Indonesia have the median inequality in their respective income groups; while Malaysia, Hong Kong and Singapore have one of the highest inequality in their respective income groups.[3] The diversity of HPAEs in terms of income inequality in comparison to other countries in their income group is not surprising, once we recognise that the model of development itself is diverse within the HPAEs [Perkins, 1994].

(2) Declining income inequality: more than meets the eye

Based on a comparison of the average growth rates and the changes in the Gini coefficient from the 1960s to the 1980s in 15 developing countries [World Bank, 1993: Fig. 1.1: 4], *The Miracle* report claims that in the HPAEs, except for Korea and Taiwan, income distribution improved by as much as, or more than, in other developing economies. Furthermore, it notes the uniqueness of the HPAEs in combining high growth and declining inequality. Both these claims seem stretched.

First, there is a question about the sample choice. In particular, it is nonsensical to say that the HPAEs are unique in combining high growth and declining inequality in a sample that does not contain any other high-growth countries. If the implicit reference group were the advanced Western countries that followed the inverted-U curve of Kuznets, it would not be a valid comparison, since their historical growth rates were not as high as those of today's high-growth developing countries.

Second, even in the given sample, declining inequality is nothing unique to East Asia, nor is the East Asian performance in this regard particularly distinguished. *The seven developing HPAEs rank second, third, fifth, seventh, eighth, eleventh and twelfth out of the 15 samples*. To say that Korea and Taiwan are exceptions because they began with highly equal income distribution is rather deceptive, unless some reason is given why it becomes more difficult to reduce inequality if initial inequality is low. In fact, as we see below, these countries had large reductions in inequality from their low initial level at the early stages of high growth, and it is because of the recent rise in inequality that the reductions during the three decades 1960s–80s turn out to be small.

If we look at the more detailed picture on the change in inequality in the HPAEs, the rosy picture put out by the World Bank is substantially undermined. Figure 20.3 shows the time path of inequality as measured by the Gini coefficient in the HPAEs minus Indonesia from late 1950s to mid-1980s. The performance of the HPAEs in reducing inequality as seen in Figure 20.3 is not unequivocally good. Both Malaysia and Thailand show higher levels of inequality at the end of the period than at the beginning. Furthermore, with Korea, Malaysia and Thailand showing something like the inverted-U curve pattern and Taiwan, Hong Kong and Singapore showing the opposite trend of U-shaped curves, while Japan's Gini coefficient remains

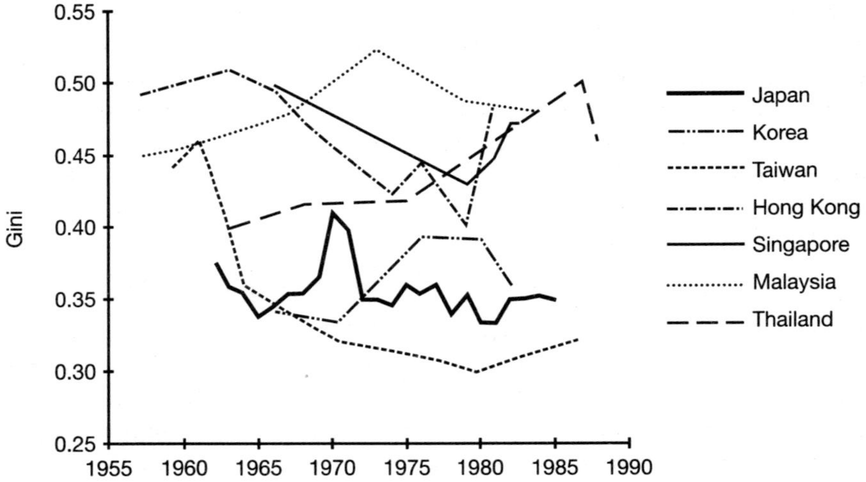

Note: Original data sources are:

Japan: T. Mizoguchi, 'Economic, sociological and institutional factors related to changes in the size distribution of household income: Japan's experience in a century' (mimeo).

Taiwan: S.W.Y. Kuo, 'Income distribution in Taiwan'. For data in 1986–1987, *Survey of Personal Income Distribution in Taiwan {1986, 1987}*.

Hong Kong; L.C. Chau, 'Economic growth and income distribution of Hong Kong since early 1950s'. For data for 1963–64, 1973–74 and 1979–80, Tzon-biau Lim, March 1985, 'Growth, equity and income distribution policies in Hong Kong' (mimeo).

Korea: Hakchung Choo, 1985, 'Estimation of size distribution of income and its sources of changes in Korea, 1982', *Korean Social Science Journal*, Vol.12, p.95

Singapore: Gini ratios from V.V.B. Rao (Dept. of Economics, National University of Singapore), 1968, 'Income distribution in East Asian developing countries', *Asian-Pacific Economic Literature*, Vol.1, No.1, March p. 28. Gini ratio for 1973 from V.V.B. Rao and M.K. Ramakrishnan, 1976, 'Income distribution in Singapore, 1966–1973', *Malayan Economic Review*.

Thailand: S. Hutaserani and S. Jitsuchon, 1988, 'Thailand's income distribution and poverty profile and other current situations', December, paper for TDRI Year-End Conference on income Distribution and Long-Term Development, 1988.

Malaysia: Gini ratio from V.V.B. Rao (Dept. of Economics, National University of Singapore), 1988, 'Income distribution in East Asian developing countries', *Asian-Pacific Economic Literature*, Vol.2, No.1, March. Data for 1984 from *Fifth Malaysian Plan 1986–1900*, p.100.

Figure 20.3 Trend of inequality in HPAEs, 1957–88
Source: Reproduced from Oshima [1991: Fig. 1, 120 and Fig. 2, 122]

essentially constant, no sweeping statement about inequality trend in HPAEs seems warranted. In particular, Taiwan, Hong Kong and Singapore, with their U-shaped curves, are exhibiting a worsening distribution of income since the late 1970s or the early 1980s.

Even Korea and Japan, which show either declining or constant inequality during the 1980s according to Figure 20.3, may have actually undergone a worsening of income distribution in the same period. In Japan, the Gini coefficient estimated from the Survey of Income Redistribution rose from 0.35 in 1980 to 0.43 in 1989, and that estimated from the Household Survey rose from 0.26 in 1979 to 0.28 in 1991 [Ishikawa, 1994]. In the case of Korea, some recent studies have found inequality rising throughout the 1980s right up to the early 1990s [Ahn, 1992; Adelman, 1995]. The rise in inequality in Taiwan that began in the 1980s continued into the 1990s, surpassing the late 1960s level, according to the official estimates [CEPD, 1995].

Admittedly, there are a variety of estimates of the Gini coefficients, and it is beyond the scope of this paper to try to find the most reliable or comparable estimates. The point here is simply that the World Bank's conclusion should not be accepted without further inquiries. The picture on the change in inequality can be very sensitive to the choice of data and the time period.[4]

(3) Explaining low inequality in the super three

The Miracle report argues that the HPAEs attained low inequality because of the 'principle of shared growth' [World Bank, 1993, Ch. 4]. The governments of the HPAEs, it is argued, recognised the importance of including non-elites in sharing the benefits of growth and engaged in activist policies – policies to address ethnic inequalities, government provision of universal primary education, housing and health services, support for small- and medium-sized industries, etc. – to redress the inadequacies of the market system in distribution. This sounds nicer than the cold-blooded 'trickle-down' thesis, but is it true?

The presence of seemingly distribution-oriented policies does not explain much. It would be very difficult to come up with examples of governments that do not have any kind of distribution-improving, cosmetic or substantive, policies. What matters is the overall thrust of government policy rather than the existence of some programmes.[5] In looking at the big picture of the governments' proclivity to sharing the fruits of growth and protecting the poor, the share of government social expenditure is probably as good a measure as any. And by this standard the East Asian governments have invariably shown little such proclivity. In 1980, for instance, the share of central government expenditure on social security, housing and welfare was 21.1 per cent in Japan and 7.6 per cent in Singapore. This compares poorly with the other high-income economies' levels that range from 30 to 50 per cent; 7.5 per cent in Korea, 11.1 per cent in Taiwan, and 7.0 per cent in Malaysia; while the typical figures for the upper-middle income economies range from 20 to 30 per cent; 5.1 per cent in Thailand and 1.8 per cent in Indonesia, which are on the low side even by the standard of the poor countries [data from: World Bank, 1995, Table 11; Ministry of Finance, 1995; CEPD, 1995].

In fact, having debunked the myth of low inequality in the HPAEs except in the super three, we should no longer search for an explanation of low inequality that covers the entire HPAEs as a group. Instead, we must look for the distinguishing features of the super three that set them apart from the rest of the HPAEs. The land reform and the rapid expansion of employment in the modern sector seem to offer the most powerful explanations of the low inequality in the super three.

It is well known that Japan, Korea and Taiwan had thorough land reforms in the aftermath of the Second World War, and as a result have unusually egalitarian distribution of farmland. Post-war reforms in Japan also included the dissolution of the *zaibatsu* and the imposition of almost punitive wealth tax, with the highest marginal tax rate reaching 90 per cent [Minami, 1996]. In Korea, much real wealth was redistributed in the immediate post-war period through confiscation and selling-off of the former Japanese assets, inflation fighting measures that hit those who possessed financial wealth, and the extensive destruction of properties during the Korean War [Adelman, 1995]. Thus, the super three had one of the most egalitarian distributions of real and financial assets at the beginning of the high growth period.

The above historical condition is no doubt a crucial reason for the relatively egalitarian distribution of income in the super three, but it is far from being the end of the story for a number of reasons. First, it is possible to have relatively even distribution of land and yet still have high income inequality, if for example rural-urban income difference or some other unequalising factor is strong. Thailand is an example. It has considerably higher income inequality than Japan or Taiwan, although its distribution of land is more egalitarian than in the latter economies.[6] Second, because of the declining importance of agriculture in the super three – the agricultural shares of employment in these countries decreased to between two and 12 per cent in 1994 – land distribution is no longer such an important factor accounting for income equality. Third, a fundamental characteristic of capitalist development is its unevenness, as it tends to build on the best. Even if the initial distribution of assets is equal, capitalist development tends to produce highly concentrated asset distributions [You, 1996].[7] It is therefore necessary to explain how the initially low level of inequality was preserved through the prolonged period of rapid growth that brought about revolutionary changes in the structure of the economy.

This is precisely why the rapid expansion of employment in the modern sector is another crucial explanation of the low inequality in the super three. Employment expansion in labour-intensive export industries and consequent rises in real wages increased the incomes of the poor sections of the population, which had few assets other than labour [Ranis and Fei, 1975; World Bank, 1987]. This was a particularly powerful mechanism to hold inequality down at the earlier stage of rapid growth when there was substantial amount of open and disguised unemployment. While this was common to all the HPAEs, the super three attained the highest growth rates and therefore the most rapid job creation and wage increases. In doing so, they did not simply rely on a free trade strategy of emphasising labour-intensive exports based on comparative advantage.

The super three are in fact distinct from the rest of the HPAEs in that their governments vigorously pursued activist industrial policies with a mix of import substitution and export promotion. When we look at the pattern of employment expansion in the super three, we find that employment in the capital-intensive sector expanded as fast as that in the labour-intensive one in what has been called a 'dual-industrial growth' [Ohno and Imaoka, 1987]. In a recent paper analysing Korean wage inequality, Kim and Topel [1995: 229] find that 'sectors that employ relatively unskilled workers did not expand more rapidly than others. Instead, the data point to improvements in human capital as the major force that narrowed wage differences'. While sustained employment expansion and productivity growth have been important in maintaining 'growth with equity' in the super three, it is a process involving much more than free trade.

To the extent that the activist industrial policies were successful in promoting growth and creating jobs, they may have contributed to keeping the inequality levels low in the super three East Asian countries. Another aspect of the industrial policy may also be relevant here. The super three had a highly restrictive policy against foreign direct investment (FDI) as a part and parcel of their industrial policy. Many empirical studies have come to the conclusion that reliance on FDI has an adverse effect on income distribution [Bornschier and Chase-Dunn, 1985; Tsai, 1995]. This conclusion is also born out by the East Asian data; those HPAEs that have higher inequality than their income group median (Singapore, Hong Kong, Malaysia) all show very high FDI reliance, while those HPAEs that have lower inequality than their income group median (the super three) all have FDI reliance below the world average (see UNCTAD [1993: Annex Table 3] for data on FDI).

20.II DISTRIBUTION OF INCOME AND CAPITAL ACCUMULATION IN EAST ASIA

To provide an account of the dynamic interaction between income distribution and growth in East Asia, the classical/Keynesian view that accords central importance to the role of profits as the source of, and the incentive for, accumulation seems to be an indispensable perspective. In the classical/Keynesian tradition income distribution is at least to some extent an institutionally determined exogenous variable, and capital accumulation and growth are influenced by the given distribution of income. The central aspect of income distribution here is that between wages and profits, because profits are saved to a much greater extent than wages and thus become the main source of accumulation.[8] In this perspective the rapid growth in East Asia is attributable primarily to the extraordinary rates of capital accumulation rather than efficient allocation of given resources.[9]

High share of profits may not be necessary for rapid accumulation, but most existing capitalist economies are so structured institutionally that it is. East Asian countries did manage to have high shares of profits, partly with the help of active government policies. They also distinguished themselves in successfully translating high profits into high savings and high business investment by a variety of policy measures and institutional structures, something many developing countries with high profit shares have failed to do. Furthermore, the relatively egalitarian distribution of household income in the super three was conducive to rapid accumulation of human capital.

(1) Income distribution and savings

In order to maintain rapid capital accumulation without running into inflation and balance of payment problems, it is essential to raise the domestic saving rate to a level close in the long run to the investment rate. The increase in the saving rates in East Asia, from the rather unremarkable levels of below 20 per cent in the 1960s to the extraordinary levels of 35 per cent or more in the 1990s, is therefore no doubt an important part of the success story. However, there has not been a satisfactory account of this [Singh, 1995].

According to the life-cycle hypothesis, the main determinants of the household saving rate are the interest rate, the demographic variables, the social security system and the growth rate.[10] In most time-series or cross-section studies, however, the only variable that performs consistently well is the growth rate (see, for example, Edwards [1995]). This suggests that the habit consumption hypothesis proposed by Marglin [1984] or the buffer stock saving behaviour put forward by Deaton [1992] may be more relevant than the life-cycle hypothesis in understanding household saving behaviour. At any rate, saying that the growth rate must be raised in order to increase the saving rate would not be a useful policy advice for a country trying to raise the saving rate in order to increase the growth rate. But it does mean – as Nam [1990] says in interpreting his conclusion that growth is the overwhelmingly important determinant of Korean savings – that deflationary adjustment policies, like high interest rate policy, may be self-defeating as deteriorating growth could sharply reduce national savings.

The Miracle report can only point to macroeconomic stability as the main reason for the high saving rates in East Asia. While it is hard to dispute that macroeconomic stability is generally conducive to savings and growth, two problems exist. First, it is very difficult to define precisely what macroeconomic stability is. At what level does inflation threaten stability, five per cent, 20 per cent or 50 per cent? How do we judge if the budget deficit is sustainable? This problem is confounded by the fact that, as Fischer [1993: 21] notes after reviewing the evidence, 'low inflation and small deficits are not necessary for high growth, over even quite long periods'. Second, there is also a reverse causality: macroeconomic stability is to a great extent a result of high savings.

It seems that the neoclassical emphasis on household savings is one of the reasons why the high saving rates in East Asia have not been properly understood. In a strictly neo-classical world, any increases in government savings and business retained earnings are exactly offset by an equivalent reduction in household savings on account of the Miller-Modigliani theorem and the Ricardian equivalence theorem. However, the econometric evidence as well as the reasoning based on the assumption of imperfect information suggest that they are not [Malinvaud, 1986]. Once we recognise the independent role of these institutional savings, in particular the connection between profits and business savings, there is no more mystery about high saving rates in East Asia.

Sectoral savings data in developing countries are hard to come by. Table 20.2 reports the available data, constructed from Honohan and Atiyas [1989] and supplemented by Taiwanese data calculated from national income accounts. It gives the five-year averages for sectoral savings, investment and surpluses in the early 1980s (three-year averages for some countries, late 1970s for others). It can be seen that the East Asian countries have unusually high business saving rates, but that their household and government saving rates are not particularly high. These economies, including China, have business saving rates higher than 8.3 per cent of GNP, while all the other advanced and developing countries, except the United Kingdom and Cameroon, have business saving rates lower than 6.2 per cent of GNP. Table 20.2 also shows that, between the East Asian averages and the non-East Asian averages, the figures are practically identical except for the significantly higher business saving rates and business investment rates in East Asia.

A high business saving rate may be due to a high share of business profits in the distribution of income and/or a high profit retention ratio. Can we say then that the high rates of business savings in East Asia derive from the income distribution that is unusually favourable to profits? The answer is a qualified yes. All the East Asian countries have relatively high profit shares (equivalently, low wage shares), but almost a half the developing countries have profit shares similar to or higher than the East Asian level.

Table 20.3 gives summary information on the distribution of the wage share across countries. The wage share is measured by total employee earnings as a percentage of the manufacturing value added. This of course is not a proper measure of the wage share, since the employee earnings do not include the labour income of the self-employed, which can be quite large in developing countries. We could in principle estimate the imputed wage of the self-employed, but the required information to carry out the calculations

Table 20.2 Sectoral savings and investment in selected countries

		Household		*Business*		*Government*		*National economy*		
	Country	*Sh*	*Ih*	*Sb*	*Ib*	*Sg*	*Ig*	*Sd*	*Id*	*Sf*
EA	China	12.54	5.53	14.05	22.13	5.95	5.69	32.54	33.35	0.81
	Korea	10.27	5.33	8.30	19.98	4.11	3.05	22.69	28.36	5.69
	Malaysia	19.69	2.90	9.13	16.28	−1.16	11.07	27.66	30.25	2.59
	Taiwan	13.7	...	12.0	...	6.2	4.1	31.9	26.9	−5.0
	Thailand	10.40	3.62	8.67	15.19	0.16	4.46	19.23	23.27	4.04
	Japan	16.92	7.76	10.83	15.56	6.43	8.34	34.18	31.66	−2.52
East Asian average		13.92	5.03	10.50	17.83	3.61	6.12	28.03	28.97	0.94
Adv.	France	11.72	7.61	6.17	10.94	2.66	4.09	20.54	22.64	2.10
	Italy	21.34	7.42	4.13	6.95	−7.64	4.51	17.83	18.88	1.05
	UK	9.35	5.51	9.96	9.07	−0.64	2.74	18.67	17.32	−1.35
Dev.	Cameroon	4.43	0.41	9.23	18.66	9.36	6.72	23.02	25.79	2.77
	Columbia	8.58	5.07	5.46	10.43	2.06	4.62	16.10	20.12	4.02
	Côte d'Ivoire	4.09	2.99	3.36	12.33	14.40	11.62	21.85	26.94	5.09
	Ecuador	9.55	4.97	3.64	11.08	4.55	7.85	17.74	23.90	6.16
	India	16.59	10.0	1.91	3.13	4.64	11.24	23.14	24.36	1.23
	Philippines	10.04	0.97	3.28	10.24	4.44	8.08	17.76	19.28	1.52
	Portugal	24.12	10.28	0.05	16.93	−2.55	4.75	21.62	31.95	10.33
	Turkey	12.13	4.46	3.92	16.13	5.16	6.38	21.20	26.96	5.76
	Tunisia	6.66	4.34	5.88	20.42	9.55	5.07	22.09	29.83	7.74
Non-East Asian average		11.58	5.34	4.75	12.17	3.83	6.48	20.13	24.00	3.87

Notes:
Sh = household savings/GNP; 1h = household investment/GNP, etc.
Sd = Sh + Sb + Sg, Id = Ih + Ib + Ig, Sf = Id – Sd.
Figures are five-year averages for 1980–84, where available, or the closest period.

Source: Calculated from Honohan and Atiyas [*1989*] and *Taiwan Statistical Data Book, 1995.*

Table 20.3 Share of earnings in manufacturing value added in HPAES and the world

Income group	*1970*	*1989–91*
Low income economies:		
Number of countries	20	14
Range	16–54	18–44
Median, average	30,32	31,31
Indonesia	26	19
Lower-middle income economies:		
Number of countries	22	20
Range	19–45	15–51
Median, average	31,32	28,30
Thailand	24	28
Upper-middle income economies:		
Number of countries	11	16
Range	22–46	2–77
Median, average	31,32	27,31
Malaysia	28	27
Korea	25	29
High income economies:		
Number of countries	19	21
Range	32–56	27–60
Media, average	49,48	42,44
Hong Kong	...	55
Singapore	36	32
Japan	32	33

Note: The above table gives figures for 1970, 1989, 1990 and 1991.

Source: Calculated from *World Development Report, 1994*, Table 7.

is lacking in many developing countries. We would have exactly the same problem if we were to use the share of the gross operating surplus in the value added from the national income accounts. Although for some countries direct survey data on the wage share are available, we chose the above measure for reasons of comparability and availability for a large number of countries. In order to minimise the problem of the self-employed sector, we made comparisons within the four income groups. However, except for the fact that the high-income economies have on the whole substantially higher wage shares, there is no systematic relationship between the earnings share and the level of income in the rest.

From Table 20.3 we find that Japan and Singapore among the high-income economies and Indonesia among the low-income economies have one of the lowest wage shares; the other HPAEs in the middle-income group have wage shares which are close to the group median values; and Hong Kong has one of the highest wage shares. On the other hand, the wage shares in all the HPAEs, with the exception of Hong Kong, are all below the group averages.

The observation of the relatively high profit shares and business saving rates in East Asia does not by itself establish the causality. We may explore the correlation between the two variables across countries, but the paucity of the sectoral savings data prevents this. On the other hand, since a substantial part of household savings is either business savings of small establishments or personal savings from profit-related income [Akyüz and Gore, 1995], we may look at the correlation between the aggregate savings and the profit share. Among the advanced countries, there is indeed a close correlation between these variables [OECD, 1990]. However, we should not expect such a close correlation for developing countries, given the fact that there are too many countries where high profits fail to find their way into savings. For example, Kaldor [1964] found that the chief problem in Chile was precisely that high profits were not generating much savings because of the conspicuous consumption of the rich. Countries such as Colombia, Ecuador and the Philippines also have low saving rates (see Table 20.2) but their wage shares are also comparatively low.

The high saving rates in East Asia must be attributed not only to profit-oriented income distribution but to the fact that somehow an unusually large proportion of profits was saved.[11] The most fundamental factor in this is investment demand, since the business saving rate is closely related to the need for investment funds. Having noted the fundamental importance of buoyant animal spirits, we must also recognise that, at least in part, the corporate saving rate is influenced by institutional settings and policies. Both Japan and Korea have a corporate financing system with heavy reliance on bank loans and the relatively insignificant role of the stock market, with the controlling shares in the hands of other firms within the group or with close business relations. This has allowed the firms to retain high portions of profits instead of paying dividends. At the same time preferential tax treatment of capital gains over distributed income has acted as an incentive to retain profits.

East Asian governments also utilised various policies to promote household savings – whether the household income out of which savings are made is profit-related or not. They restricted consumption in various ways, including restrictions on importation of consumer goods and suppressing consumer financing (for example, requiring a large down-payment for housing loans) [UNCTAD, 1997]. This was especially vigorous in Korea, where the government periodically mounted campaigns for belt-tightening and demonised what it deemed luxury consumption and conspicuous consumption. Furthermore, East Asian countries complemented the consumption restriction policy by tight foreign exchange controls to prevent capital flight before they were relieved of the balance-of-payment problems. Finally, the East Asian governments created financial institutions and schemes such as postal savings, forced saving schemes for school children, incentive measures for workers' savings, etc., to maximise mobilisation of savings.

(2) Profits and investment

It goes without saying that it is more important to maintain high rates of investment than to generate high rates of saving. While investment can create savings to some extent, savings do not create investment. On the contrary, if the high saving rate is not matched by vigorous investment demand, the result will be declining output and stagnation and, consequently, a shrinking volume of savings. If a high profit share gives rise to a high saving rate, therefore, it can be bliss or a disaster, depending on whether the high profit share also induces a high rate of investment. This point relates to the controversy on the relationship between income distribution and growth, between the classical and Keynesian approaches.

The classical position is that a higher saving rate stemming from a higher share of profits naturally leads to a higher rate of investment and growth. However, the Keynesian 'paradox of thrift' says that a higher saving rate means lower effective demand and hence lower output, and the latter, via the accelerator principle, will cause investment demand to fall. Describing what they call the 'profit-investment nexus' in East Asia, Akyüz and Gore [1995] argue that high profits were the key to the rapid growth in East Asia, thus taking a position close to the classical one. On the other hand, taking the stagnationist position, Dutt [1984] points to the high share of profits as a cause of low growth in India.

Why would high profits lead to rapid accumulation in some countries and stagnation in others? Is it because some economies are supply-constrained (classical) and others demand-constrained (Keynesian)? It is not necessary to make such an arbitrary assumption. As Bhaduri and Marglin [1990] have shown, the classical position that a higher profit share leads to a higher rate of accumulation does not require the classical assumption that the economy is supply-constrained. Even in a demand-constrained economy, the classical result may obtain provided that investment demand is sufficiently responsive to profitability (a case that Bhaduri and Marglin call 'exhilarationist' as opposed to 'stagnationist').[12] Apart from the responsiveness of investment demand to profitability, the presence of an intercept, that is, other determinants than profitability, in the investment function may explain the diversity of the relationship between distribution and accumulation. Investment in East Asia may be greater because of the entrepreneurs' higher animal spirits or for some institutional reasons.

A high profit share in the distribution of income is not a sufficient condition for rapid accumulation of capital. For the latter it is necessary to have strong investment demand – very responsive to profitability in the case of an exhilarationist regime or with a large intercept in the case of a stagnationist one. As with savings, therefore, a satisfactory account of the high rates of investment in East Asia must explain the ways in which the high profits motivated vigorous investment activities instead of complacence in the *status quo* or indulgence in speculation.

It is here that the role of the government becomes pivotal. Historically speaking, modern economic growth came along with the emergence of the 'progressive' bourgeois class, with a strong investment drive, and the problem of underdevelopment was precisely the lack of such a class [Baran, 1957]. The government must therefore step in. In an extensive survey of developing country growth experience, Reynolds [1986] finds that the single most important moment for the 'take-off' is the emergence of a development-oriented state. The government can jump-start the investment process not only by public investment but also through establishment of the appropriate financial system to mobilise and channel the savings into investment and providing incentives for private investment. As the World Bank [1993] observes, the more successful countries like the HPAEs are the ones that succeeded in generating buoyancy of private investment demand (see Table 20.2). Private investment of course responds to profit expectations, for which both profitability and risks of investment matter. And these were not left by the East Asian governments for the market forces to determine.

First, a number of policies were aimed at improving the profitability of investment, particularly in the strategic industries chosen by the government. The most important in this regard was the policies to reduce the cost of investment by such means as low interest rate policy loans, low import duties for investment goods, allowing accelerated depreciation for tax purposes, provision of industrial infrastructure, etc. Another element was the suppression of independent unionism to maintain competitive wage rates (that is, keeping real wages from rising above the productivity growth rates) and foster a good investment climate.

Second, policies to reduce investment risks take on a particular significance when the economy is diversifying into unknown areas of activities in a process of catching-up and industrial upgrading [Chang, 1994]. This is in the area of industrial policy. East Asian governments reduced risks by coordinating private sector investment according to their carefully planned development strategy. This coordination went beyond simply indicating which areas to invest in to regulating the overall amount of investment to prevent excessive investment and organising recession cartels to protect profits. All of this reduces risks considerably, although it does not eliminate risks altogether, as instances of failure demonstrate. Combined with various financial and other supports, risk-reducing coordination policies produce powerful incentives for investment.[13]

(3) Household distribution of income and human capital accumulation

In the above we explored the connection between the functional distribution of income and physical capital accumulation. There is also some recent literature concerning the effect of exogenous income distribution on human capital accumulation. The relevant distribution here is the household distribution.

Given the imperfections in the capital market and the lumpiness of the educational investment, it is argued that the distribution of income decides how many in the population can invest in human capital [Galor and Zeira, 1993]. High inequality may be conducive to growth at low levels of income, but once a certain level of income is reached lower inequality allows more people to invest in human capital, and thus produces higher output growth [Perotti, 1993]. *The Miracle* report, which makes much of human capital accumulation as an explanatory variable for the high growth in East Asia, also makes the point that egalitarian income distribution was an important reason for the rapid increase in the level of education.

It is hard to dispute the plausibility of the virtuous circle linking egalitarian income distribution and human capital accumulation. However, such a virtuous circle cannot operate unless demand for educated workers rises at a pace similar to the rise in education [Singh, 1994]. To the extent that the virtuous circle argument is correct, it is correct in East Asia only because East Asia was successful in generating rapid growth in output and rapid accumulation of physical capital, embodying ever more sophisticated technologies that demand more educated workers.

20.III HIGH PROFIT SHARE AND LOW INEQUALITY: A CONUNDRUM?

Income distribution in the East Asian super three is characterised by high profit shares in the functional distribution of income and low inequality in the size distribution of income, which has had favourable consequences for physical capital accumulation and human capital formation, respectively. Since a high profit share and low inequality normally do not go together, a question arises as to how it was possible for the super three East Asian countries to have both at the same time [Akyüz and Gore, 1995]. This is the question we now turn to. In searching for the answers, we first examine the evidence on the distribution of income-generating wealth and the distribution of wages, and then consider some other factors.[14]

(1) Distribution of wealth

It seems quite clear that part of the answer lies in the unusually low inequality in the distribution of assets. Table 20.4 presents some of the available evidence on wealth distribution. Although there may be data comparability problems between Japan and Korea on the one hand and France and the United States on the other, the difference in the Gini coefficients of wealth distribution in these two groups of countries is sufficiently large to suggest that the East Asian wealth distribution is more egalitarian. The Gini coefficient for the distribution of gross assets is 0.71 for France and 0.77 for the United States, while it is only 0.58 for Korea. For the distribution of net worth, the Gini is 0.69 for France and 0.75 for the United States, but in Japan only 0.52 in 1984 and, even after a serious deterioration during the bubble economy, 0.64 in 1989. Another revealing piece of information is that the top five per cent owns 43 per cent of wealth in the United States [Kessler and Wolff, 1991], while in Korea the top ten per cent owns as much [Kwon *et al.*, 1992].[15]

What are the reasons, then, for the unusually even distribution of wealth in the East Asian economies? For one thing, the evenness of the initial distribution of land and other real and financial assets may be exerting a long-lasting

Table 20.4 Gini coefficient for wealth distribution in four countries

	France 1980	*US 1983*		*Japan 1984*	*Japan 1989*	*Korea 1988*
I. Assets	0.71	0.77	I. Assets			0.579
1. Owner-occupied housing	0.32	0.43	1. Land	0.553	0.721	
2. Other real estate	0.56	0.75	2. Housing	0.620	0.602	
3. Unincorporated business	0.49	0.79	3. Consumer durables	0.268	0.371	
4. Currency and demand deposits	0.65	0.74	4. Real assets (=1+2+3)	0.529	0.677	0.596
5. Time deposits and savings accounts	0.70	0.77	5. Financial assets	0.535	0.564	0.770
II. Liabilities	0.61	0.68	II. Liabilities	0.775	0.794	
III. Net worth	0.69	0.75	III. Net worth	0.519	0.639	

Note: For France and the United States, other items of financial assets that are not reported here include securities, shares, insurance and pension reserves, and the Gini coefficients are calculated for owners of the assets concerned.

Source: Kessler and Wolff [*1991*] for France and the United States, Takayama and Arita [*1994*] for Japan, and Kwon *et al.* [*1992*] for Korea.

effect (although, according to the information given in Table 20.4, land distribution in Japan no longer retains a particularly egalitarian character). Another reason for the low inequality of wealth distribution may be found in the saving behaviour of different income classes. As noted by Kwon *et al.* [1992], the saving rates of low income households in the East Asian countries are surprisingly high, especially in Japan and Taiwan. The relatively low Gini coefficient for the distribution of financial assets in Japan is a consequence of such behaviour. The Japanese may have a point when they boast that theirs is capitalism without capitalists.

Clearly, the two reasons given above are not unrelated. The less the difference between the savings propensities of high and low income households, the longer the effects of the initially egalitarian distribution of assets will last. It is also obvious that an egalitarian distribution of wages will have similar influences in terms of prolonging the initially favourable distribution of wealth as well as improving the size distribution at a given point in time.

(2) Distribution of wages

The evidence on wage inequality is not so clear. Davis [1992] presents an analysis of the wage differential among men in five countries – Korea, France, the United States, the United Kingdom and Canada. He shows that the overall wage inequality among men in Korea was initially quite high compared to the advanced countries, but that it has decreased over time. In the 1980s it became lower than in the United States and France, although higher than in the United Kingdom and Canada, in the upper half of the distribution, and lower than in the United States and Canada, although higher than in the United Kingdom and France, in the bottom half of the distribution. Another piece of available evidence on cross national comparison of wage inequality is in Katz *et al.* [1995], where wage inequality among men and among women are separately analysed for Japan, the United States, the United Kingdom and France. It shows that Japan had the lowest wage inequality for both sexes among the four countries, although the United Kingdom also had low inequality in the 1970s. However, the overall wage inequality for all – both male and female – workers in Japan may not be as favourable as that, since the wage difference between male and female workers in Japan is by far the highest among the advanced countries. It is no surprise that Rowthorn [1991] finds the interindustry wage dispersion, when calculated by taking the male and female wages in the same industry as separate observations, to be the highest in Japan among 17 advanced countries. A similar tendency must exist for Korea, which also has an extremely high gender wage differential.

From the above discussion we can only conclude that wage distributions in Japan and Korea are not particularly equal in comparison to advanced Western countries. Comparison with other developing countries is difficult owing to the paucity of relevant data. Davis [1992] compares educational wage differences in eight countries – the United States, Canada, the United Kingdom, Japan, Korea, Brazil, Colombia and Venezuela. It is shown that the educational wage differences in Japan declined steeply until the mid-1970s and continued the downward trend in the 1980s, unlike in the United States or the United Kingdom and, as a result, is significantly lower than in both these countries as well as Canada. They also declined sharply in the late 1980s in Korea, reaching levels comparable to the Anglo-Saxon countries. These developments owe probably to the increase in the relative supply of educated labour [Kim and Topel, 1995] as well as to the rapid tightening up of the labour market, which has a tendency to narrow wage differences between skilled and unskilled workers [Blank and Blinder, 1986]. Latin American countries – Brazil, Colombia and Venezuela – also had declining wage differences across educational groups, with roughly similar levels to those of Korea.

In conclusion, we do not find strong evidence of more equal wage distribution in East Asia, either in Japan against other advanced countries or in Korea against Latin American countries. This finding may be taken as strengthening the earlier assertion that it is the unusually egalitarian distribution of wealth in the East Asian countries that explains the low income inequality, in spite of high profit shares in those countries. There is another possibility, however, which relates to wage-earning opportunities. The same degree of wage inequality across individuals may be associated with different wage inequalities across households, depending on how widespread employment opportunities are. The rapid expansion of employment, accompanied by a substantial rise in the participation rate, and the near-full employment conditions in the super three strongly suggest that employment opportunities are more widely available there. Therefore, it seems likely that if, for example, the distribution of wage income across households is compared between East Asian and Latin American countries, East Asian distribution would be less unequal than Latin American distribution, despite the fact that wage inequality is similar in the two regions.

(3) Other considerations

There may well be some other factors that explain the puzzle. First, as the World Bank [1993] argues, the urban-rural income differential may be lower and human capital distribution more equal in East Asia. However, there is simply no good evidence that these factors make a substantial difference.[16]

Second, another point the World Bank makes, that the presence of relatively large and vibrant small-scale businesses reduces overall income inequality, may be of some relevance, especially in Taiwan, and may be related to the savings behaviour and assets distribution in East Asia.

Finally and most importantly, the fact that corporate profits are retained to a greater extent in East Asia may be partly the reason for the coexistence of high profit shares and low inequality. Since retained corporate profits are not reflected in the household income, the effect of a higher profit share on the size distribution of income will be mitigated as the retention rate rises. Indeed, some recent studies of income distribution in Japan and Korea show that inequality increases dramatically when capital gains are included in the household income.[17]

20.IV GROWTH WITH EQUITY: MAKING SENSE OF THE EAST ASIAN EXPERIENCE

This section attempts to wrap up our discussion on the East Asian experience with income distribution and growth and draw some lessons, both theoretical and practical.

It is convenient to start from the age-old debate about the trade-off between growth and equity. One argument in favour of the existence of such a trade-off relates to our discussion in Section 20.II: a higher rate of growth goes with a higher share of profits, which implies, other things being equal, a more unequal distribution of income. This logic is depicted in Figure 20.4, where a downward-sloping growth-equity (g-e) curve in the first quadrant is generated from the supposed positive relationship between growth and the profit share (g-π curve) in the second quadrant and the negative relationship between the profit share and equity (π-e curve) in the fourth quadrant.

However, there are serious flaws in the above argument. In the short run, it is quite possible for an economy to be stagnationist; that is, a negative relationship may prevail between the profit share and the growth rate. In such a case, there would be no trade-off between growth and equity. To the contrary, a higher growth rate would be associated with an improving income distribution. It might therefore be tempting to interpret the East Asian experience with growth with equity as an instance of wage-led growth in a stagnationist regime, as opposed to profit-led growth. However, given the limits to capacity utilisation, it is unlikely that such a wage-led growth can be sustained in the long run [Skott, 1989]. Moreover, as we discussed earlier, high profits did play a crucial role in enabling rapid capital accumulation and growth in East Asia.

Another objection to the simplistic growth-equity trade-off based on profit-led growth is that, in the long run, it is absurd to suppose that other things will remain unchanged. With the passage of time, a number of institutional and market factors that determine the position of the g-π curve and the π-e curve are likely to change. In particular, the diversity of institutional and structural factors makes it extremely unlikely that the trade-off will be found in cross-section data. We now relate the latter point to the main arguments of the previous sections.

First, in Section 20.II we have argued that the East Asian countries

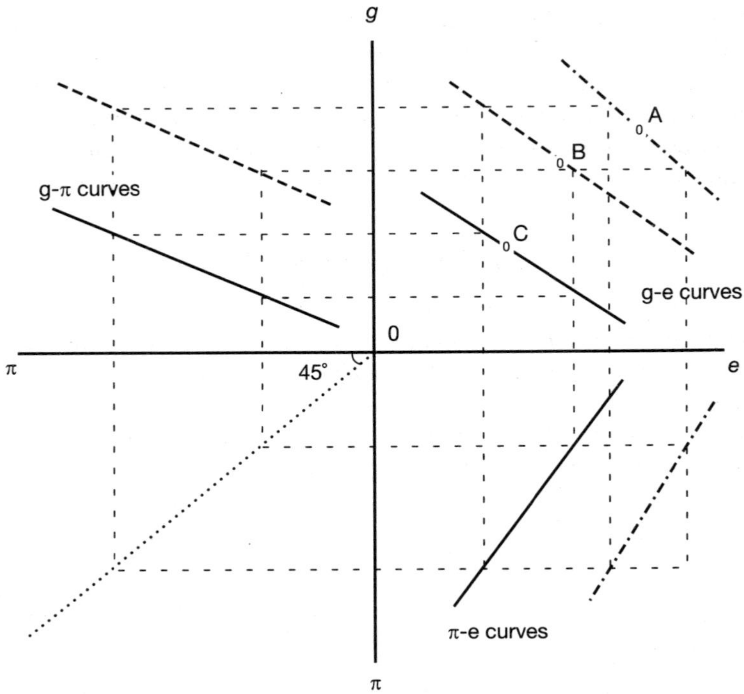

Figure 20.4 Growth-equity trade-offs

distinguished themselves not so much by high profit shares as by the effective institutions and policies with which they succeeded in translating high profits into high savings and investment. In other words, the location of the g-π: curve in East Asia was above that in most other countries. As the dotted lines in Figure 20.4 show, the growth-equity trade-off, while still there, becomes less agonising: compared to the countries on the original trade-off curve, it is possible to have both a higher rate of growth and a more equitable distribution of income.

Second, as we discussed in Section 20.III, there are a variety of factors that may associate different levels of inequality for a given profit share. In the case of the East Asian super three the distribution of wealth, among other things, may have caused inequality to be relatively low, even at quite high levels of the profit share. The broken lines in Figure 20.4 indicate that this would further shift the g-e curve away from the origin.

The moral of the above analysis is threefold. First, it is neither appealing nor necessary to discard the classical/Keynesian view of the relationship between income distribution and growth in trying to understand the unusual achievement of East Asia in combining rapid growth with a relatively equitable distribution of income. In terms of Figure 20.4, it may be understood as being on a point like A instead of B or C. Second, it follows that it is important to analyse the institutional and policy factors which put the g-π curve and the π-e curve in a more outward position than usual when we try to understand the East Asian achievement. Third, as a practical policy lesson, the East Asian experience suggests that the growth-equity trade-off may be alleviated by either a one-shot wealth redistribution, such as land reform, or measures to ensure that the bulk of profits are saved and reinvested.

20.V CONCLUSION

This study began with an examination of the empirical evidence on income inequality in the HPAEs and found that only the super three – Japan, Korea and Taiwan – may be characterised as having unusually low inequality. In the subsequent sections we have tried to understand how it was possible for these countries to combine low inequality with rapid growth. The picture that emerges may be summarised as follows:

1 The super three started the rapid growth phase with an exceptionally egalitarian distribution of real and financial assets as a result of postwar reforms.
2 The rapid growth of income was based on rapid accumulation of capital as well as rapid expansion of employment.
3 High profit shares played a crucial role in the accumulation process, both by generating high saving rates and by inducing high rates of investment. Even though high profits are not a sufficient condition for rapid growth, the East Asian super three achieved rapid accumulation because they complemented high profits with effective institutions and policies which translated them into savings and investment.
4 High profit shares were compatible with relatively low inequality in the size distribution of income, primarily because the wealth distribution was relatively even as a result of the highly egalitarian initial distribution and, especially in Japan and Taiwan, because of the unusual savings behaviour of the low-income households.
5 Although the wage distribution in the super three is not particularly even, the rapid employment expansion and the attainment of near-full employment probably mean that the wage-earning opportunities are more widely distributed across households.

One uneasy implication of the above picture is that the future prospects of income distribution in East Asia are not so sanguine. The favourable influence of the initial wealth distribution will only diminish over time, and it will become harder and harder to expand employment from the already high levels. Indeed, there is evidence of a rising concentration of wealth, markedly so during the bubble period of the late 1980s, in all of the super three countries. This trend is also consistent with the observation that income inequality rose during the 1980s in Japan and Taiwan, and also in Korea by some accounts. These governments, therefore, need to pay more attention to improving income distribution in the future.

ACKNOWLEDGMENTS

Jong-Il You, KDI School of International Policy and Management. The initial version of this study was prepared as a background paper for the UNCTAD *Trade and Development Report 1997*. The author wishes to thank Ha-Joon Chang, Lance Taylor, Yilmaz Akyüz and the editors of *The Journal of Development Studies* for their useful comments.

NOTES

1 As reported in an earlier version, using the ratio of the income shares of the richest ten per cent and the poorest 40 per cent of the population as the inequality measure does not change our findings in any significant way.

2 High growth is defined as a growth rate of five per cent or above in terms of the average annual GDP growth rate during 1980–92, the period in which most of the income distribution data are taken. A growth rate of 2.5 per cent or above but below 5 per cent is defined as medium growth, and a growth rate below 2.5 per cent low growth.

3 This is an important critique of World Bank [1993] since it advises other developing countries to follow the South-East Asian model rather than the super three. This recommendation is based on two arguments: first, the economic performance in terms of growth and equity is roughly the same in both areas; second, the institutional requirement of the interventionist East Asian model is too much for other developing countries. However, it turns out that the performance of the South-East Asian members of the HPAEs is inferior to East Asia both in terms of growth and, especially, in terms of income distribution.

4 Another example of this sensitivity is found in Sundrum [1990: 121]. Looking at an earlier period, he finds only Taiwan to be an exemplary case of low inequality combined with declining inequality. Other HPAEs are found to have either increasing inequality or mixed results.

5 A case in point is the Korean industrial policy. As is well known, the Korean government supported the giant business groups, *chaebol*, with huge amounts of subsidies. This policy was highly detrimental to the small- and medium-sized firms. In particular, the policy loans that went to *chaebol* firms swallowed up much of the bank loans, forcing the small- and medium-sized firms to rely on the much more expensive curb market loans. However, the Korean government also ran programmes to help the small- and medium-sized firms at the same time. Needless to say, the latter were quantitatively rather insignificant when compared to the support given to *chaebol*. See You [1995] for the overall thrust of the Korean government's policy toward growth and income distribution.

6 See the data given in Sundrum [1990: 185]. Jomo has suggested that it might be because there are large differences in the quality of land in Thailand. The poor farmers in the North-East region may own land, but the productivity of land there is much below that in other regions.

7 Adelman [1995: 10] asserts that 'by 1973 the distribution of real and financial assets [in Korea] was no longer even. . . [It] had become more like that of a

typical developing country'. However, she does not give any quantitative evidence. In section 20.III of this study, we examine some evidence suggesting that the distribution of wealth in the super three tended to be relatively equal, even as late as in the 1980s.

8 However, note that the life-cycle hypothesis or its growth theoretic incarnation – the overlapping generations model – implies exactly the opposite.

9 Young [1995] makes the same argument based on growth accounting.

10 However, the implication of the life-cycle hypothesis on the effect of growth on savings is not unambiguous. In a growing economy, on the one hand, workers' savings will increase relative to retirees' dissavings, and thereby raise the aggregate savings. On the other hand, workers may anticipate rising future incomes and increased consumption, as noted by Bosworth [1993].

11 While high profits are not sufficient to generate high savings, they are not necessary either. As Marglin [1975] observes, individuals may not be trusted to save much of their income, so large organisations such as business firms and pension systems or the state must play a substantial role here. Which organisations are to be utilised is a political decision. For example, the Nordic countries have relied on government savings rather uniquely among the advanced countries [Kosonen, 1992]. It might be recalled that the Swedish trade union economists, Meidner and Rehn, argued that 'democratically' enforced government savings must replace the 'undemocratic' profit-based (forced) savings.

12 See You [1994] for the exact conditions for this to happen. It also discusses the possibility of non-linearity in the relationship between the accumulation rate and the profit share, which can arise, for example, if investment is highly responsive to profitability when profitability is low, but is relatively unresponsive when it is already high. In this case, a stagnationist economy may well have a higher accumulation rate than an exhilarationist one.

13 This assessment of risk-reducing policies is not incompatible with the view that the underlying cause of the exchange crisis of 1997 is overinvestment. These policies led to the government's assumption of investment risks, which reduced individual firms' risks radically but not the systemic risks. When the government plan is conceived or ineffectively enforced, the systemic risks are actually amplified.

14 Note that the socialist economies used to have a highly egalitarian income distribution combined with high investment rates financed by the socialist equivalent of profits, the planned surplus, because they had a highly egalitarian distribution of wealth and wages.

15 Similar Gini's for Korea, France and the United States in Table 4 do not imply that distribution in Korea is as unequal as in France and the United States. First, the French and the US Gini's for other financial assets that are not repotted in the table, such as financial securities and corporate stock shares are much higher than those reported. Second, as their Gini's are calculated only for those who own the respective assets, they substantially underestimate the overall in equality.

16 For instance, Table 4.12 of Sundrum [1990] shows that in terms of the ratio of agricultural income to non-agricultural income Korea was worse than Malaysia, Colombia, Turkey and even Mexico in 1970, when its share of agricultural labour force was, at 50 per cent, comparable to the comparator countries. Also, the above comparison between Korea and Latin American countries in terms of educational wage differentials casts doubts on the claim that more equal distribution of education was the decisive factor in bringing down inequality in Korea.

17 See UNCTAD [1997]. See also Kwon *et al.*. [1992] for Korea, and Tachibanaki and Yagi [1994] for Japan.

REFERENCES

Adelman, I., 1995, 'Social Development in Korea, 1953–1993', paper presented at the KDI Conference on 'The Korean Economy, 1945–95: Performance and Vision for the 21st Century', Seoul.

Ahn, K., 1992, 'Trends in the Size Distribution of Income in Korea', *Korean Social Science Journal*, Vol.18.

Akyüz, Y. and C. Gore, 1995, 'The Investment-Profits Nexus in East Asian Industrialization', *World Development*, Vol.24, No.3.

Baran, P., 1957, *The Political Economy of Growth*, Harmondsworth: Penguin.

Bhaduri, A. and S. Marglin, 1990, 'Unemployment and the Real Wage: Economic Basis for Contesting Political Ideologies', *Cambridge Journal of Economics*, Vol.14, No.4.

Blank, R. and A. Blinder, 1986, 'Macroeconomics, Income Distribution, and Poverty', in S. Danziger (ed.), *Antipoverty Policies: What Works and What Does Not*, Cambridge, MA: Harvard University Press.

Bornschier, V. and C. Chase-Dunn, 1985, *Transnational Corporations and Underdevelopment*, New York: Praeger Press.

Bosworth, B., 1993, *Savings and Investment in the Open Economy*, Washington, DC: The Brookings Institution.

CEPD, 1995, *Taiwan Statistical Data Book, 1995*, Republic of China: Council for Economic Planning and Development.

Chang, H-J., 1994, *The Political Economy of Industrial Policy*, London: Macmillan.

Davis, S.J., 1992, 'Cross-country Patterns of Change in Relative Wages', in O. Blanchard and S. Fischer (eds)., *NBER Macroeconomics Annual 1992*, Cambridge, MA: The MIT Press.

Deaton, A.S., 1992, *Understanding Consumption*, Oxford: Clarendon Press.

Dutt, A., 1984, 'Stagnation, Income Distribution and Monopoly Power', *Cambridge Journal of Economics*, Vol.8, No.1.

Edwards, S., 1995, 'Why are Saving Rates so Different Across Countries? An International Comparative Analysis', *NBER Working Paper*, No.5097, Cambridge, MA: The MIT Press.

Fischer, S., 1993, 'The Role of Macroeconomic Factors in Growth', *NBER Working Paper*, No.4565, Cambridge, MA: The MIT Press.

Galor, O. and Joseph Zeira, 1993, 'Income Distribution and Macroeconomics', *Review of Economic Studies*, Vol.60, pp.35–52.

Honohan, P. and I. Atiyas, 1989, 'Intersectoral Financial Flows in Developing Countries', *World Bank PPR Working Paper*, No.164, Washington, DC: World Bank.

Ishikawa, T., 1994, 'Distribution of Income and Wealth in Japan', in T. Ishikawa (ed.), *Nihonno Shotokuto Funo Bunpai*, (Distribution of Wealth and Income in Japan), Tokyo: University of Tokyo Press.

Kaldor, N., 1964, 'Economic Problems of Chile', in *Essays on Economic Policy II*, London: Duckworth.

Katz, L.F. *et al.*, 1995, 'A Comparison of Changes in the Structure of Wages in Four OECD Countries', in R.B. Freeman and L.F. Katz (eds.), *Differences and Changes in Wage Structure*, Chicago, IL: University of Chicago Press.

Kessler, D. and E.N. Wolff, 1991, 'A Comparative Analysis of Household Wealth Patterns in France and the United States', *Review of lncome and Wealth*, Series 37, No.3.

Keynes, J.M., 1919, *The Economic Consequences of peace*, London: Macmillan.

Kim, D-I. and R.H. Topel, 1995, 'Labor Markets and Economic Growth: Lessons from Korea's Industrialization, 1970–1990', in R.B. Freeman and L.F. Katz (eds.),

Differences and Changes in Wage Structure, Chicago, IL: University of Chicago Press.
Kosonen, K., 1992, 'Saving and Economic Growth from a Nordic Perspective', in J. Pekkarinen *et al.*, (eds.), *Social Corporatism: A Superior Economic System?*, Oxford: Clarendon Press.
Kwon, S. *et al.*, 1992, *Realities of Distributional Inequality and Main Policy Agenda* (Punbae Pulgyundengui Siltaewa Chuyo Chongchaek Kwaje), Seoul: KDI Press.
Malinvaud, E., 1986, 'Pure Profits as Forced Saving', *Scandinavian Journal of Economics*, Vol.88, No.1.
Marglin, S., 1975, 'What do Bosses do? The Origins and Functions of Hierarchy in Capitalist Production, Part 2', *Review of Radical Political Economics*, Vol.7
Marglin, S., 1984, *Growth, Distribution and Prices*, Cambridge, MA: Harvard University Press.
Minami, R., 1996, 'Income Inequality in the Economic Development of Japan: An Evaluation of the Kuznets Hypothesis', mimeo, Kunitachi, Japan: Hitotsubashi University.
Ministry of Finance, 1995, *Zaisei Tokei* (Public Finance Statistics), Statistics Division, Japan.
Mizoguchi, T. (ed.), 1991, *Making Economies More Efficient and More Equitable: Factors Determining Income Distribution*, Tokyo: Kinokuniya/Oxford: Oxford University Press.
Nam, S-W., 1990, 'A Sectoral Accounting Approach to National Savings Applied to Korea', *Journal of Development Economics*, Vol.33, No.1.
OECD, 1990, *Historical Statistics, 1960–88*, Paris.
Ohno, K. and H. Imaoka, 1987, 'The Experience of Dual-Industrial Growth: Korea and Taiwan', *The Developing Economies*, Vol.25, No.4.
Oshima, H.T., 1991, 'Kuznets' Curve and Asian Income Distribution', in Mizoguchi [1991].
Perkins, D.H., 1994, 'There are at least Three Models of East Asian Development', *World Development*, Vol.22, No.4.
Perotti, R., 1993, 'Political Equilibrium, Income Distribution and Growth', *Review of Economic Studies*, Vol.60, pp.755–76.
Ranis, G. and J. Fei, 1975, 'A Model of Growth and Employment in the Open Dualistic Economy: The Cases of Korea and Taiwan', in F. Stewart (ed.), *Employment, Income Distribution and Development*, London: Frank Cass.
Reynolds, L., 1986, *Economic Growth in the Third World*, New Haven, CT: Yale University Press.
Rowthorn, R., 1991, 'Wage Dispersion and Employment in OECD Countries', in Mizoguchi [1991].
Singh, A., 1994, '"Openness" and the "Market-friendly" Approach to Development: Learning the Right Lessons from Development Experience', *World Development*, Vol.22, No.4.
—— 1995, 'How did East Asia Grow so Fast?', *UNCTAD Discussion Papers*, No.97, Geneva: UNCTAD.
Skott, P., 1989, *Conflict and Effective Demand in Economic Growth*, Cambridge: Cambridge University Press.
Sundrum, R.M., 1990, *Income Distribution in Less Developed Countries*, London: Routledge.
Tachibanaki, T. and T. Yagi, 1994, 'Recent Trends in Income Distribution', in T. Ishikawa (ed.), *Nihonno Shotokuto Funo Bunpai* (Distribution of Wealth and Income in Japan), Tokyo: University of Tokyo Press.
Takayama, K. and F. Arita, 1994, 'Distribution of Household Assets and its

Changes', in T. Ishikawa (ed.), *Nihonno Shotokuto Funo Bunpai* (Distribution of Wealth and Income in Japan), Tokyo: University of Tokyo Press.

Tsai, P-L., 1995, 'Foreign Direct Investment and Income Inequality: Further Evidence', *World Development*, Vol.23, No.3.

UNCTAD, 1993, *World Investment Report, 1993*, New York and Geneva: UNCTAD.

——, 1997, *Trade and Development Report 1997*, New York and Geneva: UNCTAD.

World Bank, 1987, *World Development Report, 1987*, New York: Oxford University Press.

—— 1993, *The East Asian Miracle: Economic Growth and Public Policy*, New York: Oxford University Press.

—— 1994, *World Development Report, 1994*, New York: Oxford University Press.

—— 1995, *World Development Report, 1995*, New York: Oxford University Press.

You, J-I., 1994, 'Macroeconomic Structure Endogenous Technical Change and Growth', *Cambridge Journal of Economics*, Vol.18, No.2.

You, J-I., 1995, 'A Reflection on the Korean Miracle: Toward a New Concept of Development', *Ritsumeikan Journal of International Relations and Area Studies*, Vol.8.

You, J-I., 1996, 'Capitalism and Inequality: A Complete Model of Endogenous Distribution of Income', mimeo, Kyoto, Japan: Ritsumeikan University.

Young, A., 1995, 'The Tyranny of Numbers: Confronting the Statistical Realities of the East Asian Growth Experience', *Quarterly Journal of Economics*, Vol.110, No.3, pp.641–80.

21

INCOME INEQUALITY IN SINGAPORE

Facts and Policies

V. V. Bhanoji Rao

21.1 INTRODUCTION

In this chapter, first, an attempt is made to review the available evidence on the trends in income inequality in Singapore since 1966, a period characterized by rapid economic growth, structural transformation and physical modernization. Next, the chapter looks into the government policies and initiatives that have a bearing on managing income inequality.

21.2 PERCEPTIONS AND QUESTIONS

In January 1994, the Government announced relatively hefty pay increases for ministers and senior civil servants. Following this, a journalist wrote an article entitled 'Look into poor morale of lower-income groups' (*The Sunday Times*, 9 January 1994). Subsequently, the Public Relations Officer in the Ministry of Finance wrote a letter to the Editor reacting to the article, and among others, made the following points:

> The Government is concerned about income distribution at the national level. Up to now, our income distribution has become more equal, not more unequal. We achieved this by providing full opportunities to Singaporeans, and educating more people to become skilled technicians, graduates and professionals. However, we cannot escape the world-wide trend towards higher incomes for professionals and skilled workers, caused by a global shortage of such workers, and lower incomes for unskilled workers, because of competition from large numbers of such workers from countries like China, India and Vietnam.

Source: *Economic Policy Management in Singapore*, Lim Chong Yah (Editor), Singapore: Addison-Wesley Publishing Company, (1996), pp. 119–46.

Key questions

Based on the above, at least two questions can be posed. First, 'up to now', has the income distribution become more equal in spite of the prevalence of higher incomes among professionals and lower incomes among unskilled workers? Second, is it true that inequality becomes less if more people receive education? If in fact income distribution has not become less unequal, then one must also ask another question: what has the Government been doing about it?

What data to look at?

Income accrues mostly to individuals. However, some income may accrue directly to families. It is therefore useful to look at income disparities among individuals as well as families. The first is closely linked to capabilities, investments, labour market conditions and allied factors influencing individual incomes. (For a review on the determinants of personal income distribution, see Sahota, 1978). The additional factors that determine family income are the number of economically active persons within the family, family assets and the returns on them.

21.3 FACTS: TRENDS IN HOUSEHOLD INCOME INEQUALITY

21.3.1 Income inequality based on census data

A publication of the 1990 Census, commenting on the household income distribution trends based on data from the 1980 and 1990 censuses, drew attention to a 10.4% decline in the degree of income inequality among resident private households. The Gini ratio in 1980 was 0.48 compared to 0.43 in 1990. The various limitations of the database behind this observation have been noted elsewhere (Rao, 1995). Two important limitations are worth repeating here. First, while the 1990 data have been collected for 1989, the published data refer to 1990. Published Census reports have not yet clarified on how the 1989 data have been extrapolated to 1990. The second limitation refers to the extent of income coverage of the two Censuses relative to GNP estimates for the respective years. Income from work of the resident households was 30.1% of GNP in 1980 and 41.1% in 1990. These ratios are not expected to be equal, but the divergence is far too much to assume away the comparability of the data from the two Censuses.

21.3.2 Income inequality based on data from household expenditure surveys

The Censuses of 1980 and 1990 are not single-purpose income inquiries.

Their main purpose is counting the people and obtaining their demographic, social and economic characteristics. In contrast, the quinquennial household expenditure surveys are relatively more focussed, and obtain detailed expenditure data as well as income data. The surveys provide an opportunity to check declared incomes against declared expenditures. The income data from the household expenditure surveys are unlikely to be inferior to the income data from the censuses. However, income data from the Singapore expenditure surveys has one limitation: single person households are not covered. In spite of this limitation, the surveys are an important source for ascertaining trends in household income inequality. The estimated Gini ratios from the four household surveys are given below:

1972/73	*1977/78*	*1982/83*	*1987/88*
0.41	0.42	0.37	0.41

The evidence does not point to any significant change in overall income inequality among the households.

While there is no decline in the overall level of inequality, the data in Table 21.1 do indicate an across-the-board decline in the Gini ratios by household size in 1987/88 compared to 1972/73. It is thus the changing pattern of households by size that is at the root of the invariant overall inequality. The level of inequality tends to be higher at lower household sizes and lower at higher sizes. As the household size distribution moves towards relatively smaller sizes, other things remaining the same, the overall household Gini tends to move up. This, however, is a purely demographic impact on the income distribution. How important then is the issue of overall household income inequality?

Table 21.1 Gini ratios for household income and percent of households by household size, 1972/73 and 1987/88

	Gini ratios		*Percent of households*	
Household size	*1972/73*	*1987/88*	*1972/73*	*1987/88*
2	0.48	0.42	4.8	10.7
3	0.42	0.40	9.8	17.9
4	0.45	0.41	13.2	27.8
5	0.41	0.39	16.4	22.8
6	0.39	0.38	14.1	11.8
7	0.40	0.39	12.7	5.3
8	0.36	0.33	9.6	2.1
9	0.33	0.26	7.6	0.9
10+	0.33	0.25	11.8	0.7
All sizes	0.41	0.41	100.0	100.0

21.3.3 Is overall household income inequality important?

It is notable that at larger household sizes the Gini is rather low. For instance, it is only 0.26 at household size 9 and 0.25 at household size 10 + in 1987/88. The ratio is rather low (0.33) at household size 8 also. However, households of size 8, 9 and 10 + comprised less than 4% of the total households (size 2 and above) in 1987/88, and thus from an overall view, the low Gini ratios at larger household sizes have little consequence in the aggregate. Moreover, since the average household income per household member is negatively related to the household size, the larger households end up having lower per capita incomes and the lower Gini at the larger sizes is an indication of all households being equally poor.

The overall Gini ratio among households is of considerable importance, if households at different income levels compare their relative rankings on the income scale. How often do families compare their relative rank? Inter-family comparisons are perhaps more common in small rural societies. In large cities, individuals rather than families are most likely to indulge in relatively more serious comparisons. In the Singapore context, with nearly 90% of the labour force being employees, and with the human resource being the principal resource of the country, of far greater significance is income inequality in the work force. If the income inequality prevailing in the labour force in general and the employees in particular is considered fair and justified it is good for the maintenance of harmony, peace and stability both on the shop floor and in society at large.

21.4 FACTS: INCOME INEQUALITY IN THE LABOUR FORCE

21.4.1 Gini ratios, 1966–93

The labour force Gini ratios in Table 21.2 indicate an approximate U-shaped trend for the 1966–93 period. Income distribution in the labour force had mostly a Gini of 0.46–0.47 except for relatively low ratios (0.42 to 0.43) obtained during 1978–1981. Table 21.2 has the Gini ratios for CPF contributors and taxpayers also. The CPF Gini has a tendency to stay around 0.43–0.44 with the exception of 1982, 1983 and 1987. The Ginis for tax payers follows a generally rising trend.

CPF contributors make up for more than 90% of the total employees. The Gini ratios for CPF contributors in Table 21.2 thus indicate the trend in the wage gap. In general, the expanded employment opportunities in the 1970s and 1980s and the guidelines on wage increase issued by the National Wages Council since its founding in 1972 have contributed to the remarkable stability in wage gaps. The exception was during 1982, 1983 and 1987, when the wage gap widened slightly. Part of the reason for the rise in 1982 and 1983

Table 21.2 Gini ratios for personal income, 1966–1993

	Income distribution within the			
Year	*Labour force*	*CPF contributors*	*Resident tax payers*	*All tax payers*
1966	0.50	*	0.37	0.38
1970	n.a.	*	0.40	0.41
1971	n.a.	0.43	0.41	0.42
1972	n.a.	0.43	0.41	0.42
1973	0.46	0.42	0.41	0.42
1974	0.44	0.43	0.43	0.44
1975	0.45	0.43	0.42	0.43
1976	0.45	0.44	0.43	0.43
1977	0.46	0.44	0.42	0.43
1978	0.42	0.43	0.41	0.42
1979	0.43	0.43	0.41	0.42
1980	0.43	0.43	0.44	0.44
1981	0.43	0.44	0.43	0.43
1982	0.46	0.46	0.44	0.45
1083	0.47	0.46	0.45	0.46
1984	0.47	0.44	0.45	0.46
1985	0.46	0.44	0.45	0.45
1986	0.46	0.44	0.45	0.45
1987	0.46	0.46	0.45	0.46
1988	0.46	0.43	0.46	0.47
1989	0.47	0.43	0.47	0.48
1990	n.a.	0.43	n.a.	n.a.
1991	0.47	0.43	0.47	0.47
1992	0.47	0.43	0.47	0.48
1993	0.47	0.43	n.a.	n.a.

Note: The estimates of Gini ratios for labour force and CPF conributors have been revised and updated, and hence differ from those in earlier publications (Rao, 1990, for instance).

* CPF contributors comprised 68% of all employees in 1966 and 75% in 1970, as against 90% or more since 1973. The Gini ratios of 0.45 in 1966 and 0.47 in 1970 are thus not comparable with the rest of the 1970s and 1980s.

must be found in the post-1979 efforts towards a policy shift from labour intensive industries, as explained below.

> Rising domestic labour cost – primarily reflecting real wage growth – and keen competition from other low wage economies have eroded the comparative advantage that Singapore initially enjoyed in low cost, labour intensive exports. Given such developments, the government formally launched a programme in 1979 to restructure the economy away from labour intensive and low value-added economic activities towards skill and technology intensive and higher value-added economic sectors (Lim *et al*, 1988, p. 194).

The restructuring also meant an effort to attract and adequately reward the high fliers and talented employees at all levels, and more so, at the top end of the talent/income scale. Thus, the Gini ratios among the CPF contributors rose in 1982 and 1983 to 0.46. In 1983, the 'restructuring' resulted in a 1% decline in the number of CPF contributors, after a continuous increase since 1966. What is more, there were some 70,300 contributors less in 1983 in the monthly wage level groups up to $500 (as against a 'normal' decline of some 30,000–40,000). The situation changed in 1984, the decline in contributors in the low income groups became moderate, and the total number of contributors rose by 2.7%. The Gini ratio declined in 1984 to 0.44 and remained at that level during the recession years 1985 and 1986. After a temporary rise to 0.46 in 1987, the Gini stabilized at 0.43.

In sum, the CPF contributors have an income distribution characterized by a stable Gini ratio of 0.43 to 0.44. Since the 'wage' in the CPF data does not include bonuses and other payments, the stable Gini may at best be interpreted to mean invariant 'formal' wage relativities, and not necessarily an invariance in the income inequality among employees.

The trends in income distribution in the total labour force and among tax payers diverge historically but show a clear convergence in recent years. The overall expansion of employment opportunities during the 1970s has resulted in a drop in the labour force Gini to levels of 0.42–0.43 during the late 1970s and early 1980s. Since then the Gini has stabilized at around 0.47.

21.4.2 Education and income inequality

Major changes have taken place in the educational composition of the labour force. For instance, while half the labour force in 1966 comprised people with no education (or less than primary level), that proportion dropped to 19% in 1989 and 15% in 1993. In about a decade there will be practically none in the Singapore labour force with less than primary education. Those with a post-secondary education made up only less than 5% of the labour force in 1966. In 1989 the proportion was 20.2% and in 1993 it was 25.7%. This is because of the sizeable investments Singapore has made since the late 1960s in the development of its human resources.

Table 21.3 shows the Gini ratios among the workforce by level of education. At secondary and post-secondary levels the Gini turns out to be the highest. It is quite low at the tertiary level. It is most plausible that the future labour force will have three levels of educational qualifications: secondary, post-secondary (but not tertiary) and tertiary with the former two in the large majority. Structurally too, the economy tends to absorb more and more people in the service sector where income inequality tends to be relatively higher. Educational expansion, therefore, may not guarantee an eventual reduction in income inequality, even though it greatly assists in raising the living standards and in improving the quality of life.

Table 21.3 Gini ratios by level of education, 1993

Educational level	*Gini*
Never attended school	0.35
No qualification	0.32
Primary/Post-primary	0.35
Secondary	0.41
Post-secondary (excluding diploma and degree)	0.47
Tertiary	0.27

21.5 POLICIES: MANAGING INEQUALITY

21.5.1 The need to manage inequality

The problem

The available evidence shows that the Gini ratio of personal income in Singapore is generally invariant and close to 0.47, except for transitory and purely temporary changes. Overall, therefore, income distribution has not become more unequal, but also not more equal. In spite of this, there are reasons why the situation needs attention. First, the low income groups can hardly be consoled by the invariant Gini ratio, when they 'perceive' that others are moving faster and that their own situation is worse off. Second, the level of the Gini is not too low to permit a complacent attitude. Third and more importantly, there may be pressures on income distribution towards widening. For instance, effective 1 January 1994, the Government announced a 20–30% pay increase to top civil servants and ministers and a 7% rise at the lowest levels. Other things being equal, this increases the level of the Gini for 1994, although the raises for the top civil servants and ministers are well justified on the basis of comparator earnings in the private sector and the need to attract the best talent to govern the nation.

Can anything be done at all?

In a recent book, Paul Krugman (1990a) pays particular attention to the growing income inequality in the United States. (Excerpts from the book are given in Krugman, 1990b.) According to Krugman, (1990b, p. 5), '. . . the income distribution colors the whole tone of society: a society with few extremes of wealth or poverty is a different, and surely more attractive, place than one with a yawning gulf between rich and poor'. In spite of this, it is not easy to remedy the US income inequality because the underlying causes are complex and can hardly be tackled by generally accepted public policy initiatives. For instance, two factors behind the inequality noted by Krugman were the increasing riches of the executives in the financial sector and the widening of the earnings gap between the relatively less and better educated.

Krugman (1990b, p. 6) asks: 'Whatever the reasons for roaring inequality in the 1980s, what can policy do about it?' He notes that on the one hand not many believe that the poor can be really uplifted by Government policy, while on the other hand, although the rich can be taxed relatively more heavily, this may discourage effort and productivity growth. 'So income distribution. . . . is a policy issue with no real policy debate.' (Krugman, 1990, p. 6).

Managing income inequality: the concept and approaches

When a problem cannot be completely eradicated, it has to be carefully managed. It is by no means easy to significantly reduce the degree of inequality; indeed, even a marginal reduction may turn out to have negative consequences. Inequality, therefore, has to be carefully managed. 'Managing income inequality' may be defined as not necessarily reducing income inequality but making transparent attempts to reduce the real and imagined frustrations arising out of growing or high inequality. Managing may take various forms: rational public discussion so as to assess the situation and agree on courses of action, ensuring equality in educational and other opportunities, use of targeted and general subsidies and various forms of asset redistribution, the extent of redistribution being a function of political will, economic imperatives and stage of development. The policy instruments and specific programmes a country uses to manage income inequality depend on the political and economic philosophy the leadership nurtures.

Philosophy of spreading the benefits of growth

Speaking at the 23rd anniversary dinner of the Housing Board Staff Union on 29 December 1990, Prime Minister Goh said that his Government's twin objectives are securing steady growth and spreading its benefits around. He noted that the business-minded, able, skilled and more hard-working workers ended up better off than their less able colleagues: 'Otherwise, they will lose the incentives to contribute their utmost to the economy. Then everybody will be poorer off. Do not grudge them their higher earnings, or metaphorically speaking, for getting the big prizes in the free market'. (*The Straits Times*, 30 December 1990). The Prime Minister stressed, however, that everyone who contributed to the nation's growth will get part of the benefits. One example is Edusave which benefits all students between ages 6 and 16 years. Another example is the HDB's upgrading exercise, costing the Government $11 billion over 15–20 years and benefiting more than 370,000 families or over 1.5 million people. (Those living in the older HDB estates get an average benefit of $30,000 per family.) These examples of sharing the benefits of growth, however, are not to encourage hand-outs: 'Handouts will destroy our society. We can have participation prizes only when Singaporeans themselves have contributed to economic growth and national prosperity,' observed Mr Goh.

Singapore Government's policy instruments

The Government, almost until 1990, relied on traditional instruments such as progressive income taxes and public expenditures on education (including scholarships and bursaries), health and welfare. Since 1990, however, Government paid particular attention to 'participation prizes' and other instruments targeted towards the low income groups. The more recent initiatives are briefly summarized in the following sections.

21.5.2 Education

Equality of opportunities: education, the key

Speaking to the Citizens' Consultative Committees on 17 December 1990, Prime Minister Goh Chok Tong unveiled the Edusave scheme and commented on the wider issue of equality of opportunities as follows (*The Straits Times*, 18 December 1990):

> Tonight, I want to elaborate on one of the central pillars in my approach to building a better Singapore. Essentially, I want to maximise and equalise opportunities for Singaporeans to improve themselves. I do not want anyone in our society to miss out on a chance to better his life because he cannot afford the opportunities. I want to give everyone the same chance for a good start in life. I shall do this primarily through education.

Edusave scheme

The Government has set up an Education Foundation, with an initial capital sum of $1 billion and a target sum of S$5 billion to be achieved over a few years. Income from the capital fund is used to credit the Edusave accounts with a certain sum of money every year. The holders of the accounts are students from Primary 1 to Secondary 4. The amount in the account can be used for defraying approved educational expenses. The Edusave Scheme benefits eligible pupils in three ways.

(i) The top 25% of Secondary 1 students in independent schools receive Edusave scholarships for four years of education. In Government and Government-aided schools, the top 10% of students get annual scholarships.
(ii) Each of the 130 Government and Government-aided secondary schools

receive, on average, an annual grant of $100,000 to be spent on school-organized programmes.

(iii) Eligible students get an Edusave account and receive a yearly contribution from the Government. The money can be used to pay for enrichment programmes, second-tier miscellaneous fees or other approved fees. Over a ten year period, a family of three children could get up to $15,000 in all in their Edusave accounts.

21.5.3 Targeted instruments

Medifund scheme

Medifund, which became operational on 1 April 1993, is an endowment fund set up by the Government of Singapore to help poor Singaporeans pay for their medical bills. The fund has an initial capital of $200 million, rising by $100 million a year. Income earned on the capital sum will be used for providing benefits. Singapore citizens who are unable to pay for medical treatment at approved hospitals and medical institutions can apply for help. Such help is available only for those who use class C or B2 wards (since B1 and A class wards are normally used by people with relatively higher purchasing power). Outpatients can also seek assistance from the fund.

Small families improvement scheme

On 15 August 1993, the Prime Minister announced a scheme to encourage the poor to limit their family size by committing to have no more than 2 children, by taking part in a regular family planning programme. To qualify, families have to meet the following criteria: husband and wife should be earning less than $750 a month each, both have low education (no N-level passes), wife is aged 35 years or below and at least one spouse is a Singaporean. Such families, in return for their adherence to a small family norm, will receive from the Government up to $26,400 in housing grants and education bursaries. Children get bursaries for education from primary one to pre-university or polytechnic level. For two children, the estimated cost of the bursaries (at $200 to $800 a year) is $10,400. The housing grant is worth $16,000 and is paid into the CPF account of the wife, at $800 for 20 years or until her age 45 whichever is sooner. The housing grant can be used to buy a three-or four-room HDB flat. The grants stop if the couple separates, or has a third child. Then the housing grant has to be paid back to the Government with interest. If a flat has been bought, the money can be returned after the flat is sold.

The Small Families Improvement Scheme became operational on 1 January 1994, and is administered by the Ministry of Community Development

(MCD). An estimated 8000 families may qualify for support (*The Straits Times*, 27 December 1993).

Public assistance

Public assistance benefits are provided by the government to those that can pass the stringent means tests. The rates of assistance are low and close to absolute poverty thresholds. The overall philosophy here seems to follow the 'poor law tradition' where the assistance received is a matter of society's generosity, and is not an entitlement as, for instance, is the case with state welfarism (Fernandez, 1994).

As of March 1994, there were about 2000 recipients of public assistance. The prevailing rates of public assistance were $150 a month for an individual and $430 for a household with one adult and three children. These were raised to $153 and $445 respectively effective 1 April 1994 to take account of the Goods and Services Tax of 3% effective that date. Those on public assistance receive free medical treatment at Government hospitals and clinics.

Relief on account of GST to the low income group

The Goods and Services Tax (GST) was implemented on 1 April 1994. Being a regressive tax, the low income groups will be relatively more adversely affected. The Government announced a number of measures to offset the impact on low income households (*The Straits Times*, 22 March 1994):

1 Those in one-, two- and three-room (rental and purchase) flats enjoy rebates on rent and service and conservancy (S&C) charges for five years. The benefit ranges from $8 to $33 a month.
2 They also enjoy one-off rebates in 1994. The Government pays three months net S&C charges for one- and two-room tenants, and two months net S&C charges for three-room tenants.
3 Grants worth $3 million a year are given to poor households which do not benefit from HDB-related offsets. About 28,000 households with a monthly income of $1,500 or less could benefit from this scheme, obtaining grants up to $200 per household.
4 The Rent and Utilities Assistance Scheme (RUAS) administered by the National Council of Social Service is reviewed to take into account the impact of GST on families under the scheme.
5 Additional grants are also available to be given to voluntary welfare groups providing direct services. The grants are to offset the GST that will be incurred by such groups over the next five years.

Sale of flats at subsidized price to the poor

In May 1994 the Government announced that the Housing and Development Board (HDB) would buy three-room HDB flats on the open market and sell them at subsidized rates to low income families. The market prices for the flats were ranging from $70,000 to $100,000. HDB would sell them at $33,000 to $70,000. Potential buyers are about 2000 families with monthly household income below $1,000. To help the poor families buy the flats, in addition to the subsidy, financing is also provided, with loans repayable over 20–25 years. The overall cost of subsidies is an estimated $60 million.

Sale of rental flats at discount

Starting June 1994, the Government began a programme of selling three-room and two-room rental flats to the existing tenants. Each three-room flat is worth about $100,000 on the open market and most tenants belong to the relatively low income groups. The HDB sale price will be between $35,000 and $59,000. When the offer to sell was made to 263 tenants in June, 90% opted to buy the flats, as against 60% expected by HDB (*The Straits Times*, 18 July 1994).

Sale of HDB shops

Several of the low and lower middle income families earn their livelihood by renting HDB shops and running small scale individual/family businesses. In 1993, the Government decided to allow them to purchase the shops at a price discount of $75,000 per shop.

21.5.4 Other initiatives: asset enhancement, share ownership and wage guidelines

Home upgrading

Government expenditure of the order of $12–15 billion spread over 15–20 years has been planned for upgrading older HDB estates. An additional $600 million has been allocated for upgrading common facilities in the older estates (for example by providing faster lifts, better lift lobbies, covered walkways, games courts, jogging tracks and landscaped gardens).

Grant to couples to stay close to parents

The Government provides a grant of $30,000 to couples who wish to buy their first HDB flat from the resale market in the estate where their parents live.

CPF top-up schemes

In 1993, government allotted $200 for each CPF account holder, as long as he/she has a minimum of $500 in it. Those with less have received less. The estimated cost of the scheme was $200 million. In August 1995, each of the CPF members with a minimum of $750 will get $300. The estimated cost is $300 million.

Preferential share allotments

Singaporeans became a share-owning population when, in 1993, Government allowed each citizen to buy up to 1000 Telecom shares at a discount price. The total cost of the discount to the Government was $3 billion.

Most recent NWC recommendations

The National Wages Council is not unaware of the need to keep the equity dimension in its recommendations. Thus, in its 1994 recommendations, the Council said: 'To benefit the lower income employees, companies may wish to consider in the payment of their wage increase the inclusion of a dollar quantum instead of purely on a percentage basis'. This recommendation is especially significant since overall wage increases in each organization depend on its performance, and the tendency will be to pay individuals within organizations also according to measured or perceived performance levels, ignoring the equity dimension. The NWC recommendation is aimed at rectifying such a practice.

21.5 CONCLUDING NOTE

Singapore has achieved substantial and visible (even enviable) economic and social progress. In the matter of income inequality, the leadership's stand is not to tinker with market forces. The following statement in Parliament (14 January 1994) by the Senior Minister and former Prime Minister Mr Lee Kuan Yew could be considered as the most authoritative stand on income inequality by the leader who has shaped Singapore's economic and social progress since 1965.

> Once upon a time as a young undergraduate, I believed that vast pay differences between the incomes of professionals, bankers and the average worker were unjust and unnecessary, that was why I became a socialist. . . Then I began to understand the law of supply and demand. And over time, I concluded that prices and wages and differences in pay are necessary if you want people to put in their best. I realised that fairness is a question of relativity. And in the end, I concluded that moral values on pay are good only for textbooks on socialism and political tracts on social justice. . .

Despite the above assertion, the Government of Prime Minister Goh Chok Tong appears to be fully aware of the need to manage income inequality and has indeed used several targeted and general purpose instruments to reduce the severity of the social burden of inequality. The Government has to continue to constantly monitor income inequality and, alongside that, be aware of people's perceptions.

REFERENCES

Fernandez, W. (1994). State Welfarism, Singapore Style, *The Sunday Times*, September 18.

Krugman, P. (1990a). *The Age of Diminishing Expectations: US Economic Policy in the 1990s*, Washington: The Washington Post Company.

Krugman, P. (1990b). The Income Distribution Disparity, *Challenge*, July–August, pp. 4–6.

Lim C.Y. and Associates (1988). *Policy Options for the Singapore Economy*, Singapore: McGraw-Hill Book Company.

Rao, V.V. Bhanoji (1990). Income Distribution in Singapore: Trends and Issues, *Singapore Economic Review*, 35(1), April, pp. 143–160.

Rao, V.V. Bhanoji (1995). Singapore Household Income Distribution Data from the 1990 Census: Analysis, Results and Implications, in Basant K. Kapur *et al* (ed.), Volume in Honour of Professor Lim Chong Yah (forthcoming).

Sahota, G. (1978). Theories of Personal Income Distribution: A Survey, *Journal of Economic Literature*, 16(1), March, pp. 1–55.